1985

University of St. Francis
GEN 001.6424 T260
Teglovic Steve

W9-ADR-875
3 0301 00053173 7

STRUCTURED BASIC

A Modular Approach for
the PDP-11 and VAX-11

The Irwin Series in Information and Decision Sciences

Consulting Editors:

Robert B. Fetter
Yale University

Claude McMillan
University of Colorado

LIBRARY

STRUCTURED BASIC

A Modular Approach for the PDP-11 and VAX-11

Steve Teglovic, Jr.
University of Northern Colorado

&

Kenneth D. Douglas
Southwest Missouri State University

 1983

RICHARD D. IRWIN, INC.
Homewood, Illinois 60430

LIBRARY
College of St. Francis
JOLIET, ILL.

© RICHARD D. IRWIN, INC., 1983

All rights reserved. No part of this publication may be
reproduced, stored in a retrieval system, or transmitted,
in any form or by any means, electronic, mechanical,
photocopying, recording, or otherwise, without the prior
written permission of the publisher.

ISBN 0-256-02930-X

Library of Congress Catalog Card No. 82-83834

Printed in the United States of America

3 4 5 6 7 8 9 0 ML 0 9 8 7 6 5 4

001.6424
T260

Preface

With the expansion of minicomputers and personal computers, more individuals and organizations are acquiring systems where BASIC is the predominant language. In fact, industry reports show that BASIC is the most used language for mini and microcomputers today and one of the most popular languages for medium and large computers.

Because of BASIC's high use, this textbook was written to serve three major objectives for the potential BASIC programmer: (1) The material is presented using a modular approach, starting with the very basic concepts and skills needed, and progresses into intermediate and then advanced concepts. The programmer can quickly learn to write meaningful programs, to develop techniques, and to gain confidence in the use of the language. (2) Although BASIC was not designed as a structured language, the authors have used structured programming techniques as an approach to program development. This should result in better program design and programs that are easier to test and maintain. It is the state of the art approach used in many data processing applications today. (3) Since BASIC is not a standardized language and many different versions of it exist in the world of computers, the authors have decided against using a generic BASIC that does not satisfy any one computer's need and have used a machine specific version for DEC computers. The advantage of this approach is that every example, program, and exercise has been actually run on a computer and the reader can study the results to gain a better knowledge of how the language really works. With but a few changes in the version of BASIC used in this text (such as the PRINT USING and IF/THEN/ELSE statements), the reader can use this text for programming any computer that has a BASIC language.

In addition to using a modular and structured approach to BASIC, some other special features of the text are: (1) The examples show applications in mathematics, science, administration, and business. (2) There is extensive use of flowcharts, pseudocode, and BASIC coding. Each of the chapters contain fully developed

117,459

problems to solve with the logic shown in flowchart or pseudocode immediately paired with the actual solution in program form. (3) A section in each programming chapter shows common errors that the student can expect to encounter. (4) The use of Text Editors allows programmers to enter code into a system more efficiently.

The text can be used in a variety of ways. The first 12 chapters can be used as a supplement to an introduction to information processing text in a first data processing or computer literacy course. The first 16 chapters can be used as a stand-alone text for teaching a traditional BASIC programming course. The entire text can be used for those courses covering advanced topics such as file processing and file maintenance. In addition, there is the option of covering the chapters in a different order than presented in the text. Chapter 8 on Structured Programming could be covered before Chapter 4, and Chapter 16 on the use of a Text Editor could be covered at any point in a course.

An Instructor's Manual is available with the text. It has actual programmed solutions for all of the exercises at the end of each chapter. The manual will save many hours of programming and preparation time.

The authors' thanks go to the many reviewers of the text and to the Digital Equipment Corporation for their help and advice on the technical matters during the writing and production of the text.

Finally, we would like to express our sincere appreciation to our wives, Mary and Cecil, for their patience, thoughtfulness, and timely words of encouragement.

Steve Teglovic, Jr.
Kenneth D. Douglas

Contents

Section
1

Introduction to the BASIC Programming Language

1

Chapter One

Introduction to Computers and the BASIC Language

Functions of Computers

Computers are powerful tools that are used by many different types of people in many different types of organizations for many different reasons. They are used by scientists to launch and control space vehicles, by pollsters to predict outcomes of elections, by teachers to educate students, by businesses to determine net profit, and by homemakers to balance the family budget.

Computers also come in various sizes, from a large, multimillion-dollar system used by NASA that may have been manufactured by IBM or Control Data Corporation to a small personal computer used by an individual and manufactured by Apple or Radio Shack.

Regardless of the size or use of a particular computer, they all have the same essential functions, which are performed by the same types of functional units or components.

In almost any computer application, three essential functions are performed: input, processing, and output. The purpose of the input function is to provide a means of entering data into the computer, and the purpose of the processing function is to manipulate the data. The output function provides a means to display the results of the task performed. This relationship is shown in Figure 1.1.

3

4

Figure 1.1
The data processing cycle

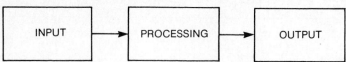

In order for the computer to accomplish these three functions, it must have both hardware and software. Hardware is the physical equipment that makes up the computer system, and software comprises the computer programs that direct the activities of the computer. Software is divided into two types: control and applications software. Control software is written to direct the activities of the computer, such as the actual movement of data from one device to another, while application software is written to solve a particular problem, such as the writing of payroll checks. Control software, normally called the operating system, is usually written by the computer manufacturer. Applications software is written in a computer language such as BASIC. Software is necessary to tell the computer hardware what to do and in what sequence to perform operations. The main purpose of this text is to teach the reader how to direct the computer to perform the solving of problems in BASIC.

Processing Tasks

Software is written and entered into the computer to perform specific tasks. The tasks, regardless of the application, may include calculating, storing, reproducing, summarizing, classifying, and sorting data. These tasks are depicted in Figure 1.2.

Figure 1.2
The data processing tasks

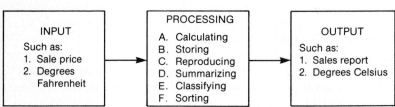

While the input and output functions are performed by devices such as a card reader, a printer, or a terminal, the processing is performed by the central processing unit (CPU) and one or more external devices, such as a magnetic disk. The CPU is comprised of three parts: the control section, the arithmetic/logic unit, and temporary or main storage. The external devices are used for permanent or auxiliary storage. The relationship among these components is illustrated in Figure 1.3.

Figure 1.3
Data processing hardware

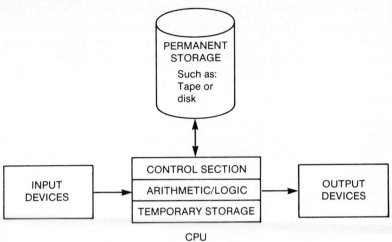

Central Processing Unit (CPU)

The control section of the CPU directs the activities of the entire computer system. Examples of activities controlled are the movement of data and/or programs from an input device into temporary storage and movement of data and/or programs from temporary to permanent storage.

The arithmetic/logic unit performs mathematical functions, such as multiplication and rounding, and gives the computer its logic capabilities, such as comparing two values or changing the sequence of computer operations.

Temporary storage, also called main or primary storage, allows the storage of data and/or programs that are immediately available to the computer system. Main storage is considered to be temporary because of its limited capacity relative to auxiliary storage and because most main storage is volatile in nature. Volatile storage is subject to data loss when a power outage occurs.

Input, Output, and Storage Devices

A brief discussion of some of the different devices that may be used with a computer system is in order. While this discussion is not intended to be an exhaustive list or description, it will show the types of devices that are available on systems like Digital Equipment Corporation's (DEC) PDP-11 or VAX-11 systems. The PDP-11 and VAX-11 systems are widely used minicomputers which are representative of several manufacturers' systems.

Terminals

Terminals are one of the major devices used to enter programs and/or data into a computer system and accept output from the system. They allow for input into a computer via a typewriterlike keyboard; they will accept output from a computer either by means of a cathode ray tube (CRT) or a teleprinter. A CRT looks like a television screen and will display output on the screen. The teleprinter accepts output by printing onto computer paper. Either of these types of terminals are connected to the central processing unit (CPU) by means of some form of communications link, such as a telephone hookup or a direct cable.

Line Printers

Line printers are available to output large amounts of data at high speed. They are available in different sizes, prices, and technologies. Their advantage over the terminal is that larger volumes of reports can be produced at high speeds.

Punched-Card Devices

Punched-card devices can be used to input data and programs in machine-readable form to a computer system. Essentially, a punched-card device electronically senses the presence or absence of a hole punched in the card to enter data into the system. Cards are punched either by a keypunch machine controlled by clerical personnel or by a card-punch machine controlled by the computer system.

Magnetic Tape

Magnetic tape is a medium for permanent storage that provides large capacity and high speed of operation. It is also referred to as auxiliary or secondary storage. Data are stored electronically on the surface of the tape by magnetizing spots on the tape. Because of its high capacity and speed, magnetic tape has become a popular device for low-cost, sequential storage of data. Its major disadvantage is that access to the data is sequential; that is, one cannot locate a single item of information without running the whole tape. Sequential processing requires that the data be in some sequence, either alphabetical or numerical. For instance, if accounts-receivable data were in alphabetical order and the programmers wanted data on someone whose name started with an S, each and every person's data before the one desired would have to read first.

Magnetic Disk

The magnetic disk is a permanent storage device that allows direct access to any location on the disk. This process is called direct or random processing. Direct access to the data makes it unnecessary to search an entire disk, as is true with magnetic tape.

There are two types of disk media; a hard disk and a flexible or floppy disk. Hard disks generally have a greater capacity and are faster than floppy disks, but floppy disks are an important medium because of their widespread use with minicomputers and personal computers.

Batch versus Interactive Processing

Batch processing is one means for a computer system to process large amounts of data in a short amount of time. Essentially, programs and data are accumulated in a batch and then processed all at once. The processing of payroll checks is an example of a task for which batch processing would be useful.

Sometimes, however, immediate feedback for the user of the computer and immediate access to data files are more important than processing large volumes of data. Interactive processing allows this to occur. In an interactive mode, a user interacts directly with the computer system, usually by means of a terminal. This mode also has the advantages of allowing several users access to the computer at the same time, in what is called time sharing. The advent of interactive processing and time sharing has allowed the development of such systems as the airlines' reservations systems, automated banking, and computer-assisted instruction. BASIC is primarily an interactive language.

The BASIC Language

BASIC was developed originally at Dartmouth College by John Kemeny so that students could interact directly with a computer by using a powerful yet simple language. BASIC stands for Beginner's All-purpose Symbolic Instruction Code and is an excellent first language because it is relatively simple. Even though BASIC originated in an educational setting, it has gained widespread usage in business and scientific applications as well. It has also gained special prominence with minicomputer and personal-computer manufacturers because it can be used even when CPU temporary storage is not very large. The major disadvantage of BASIC is that it is not standardized. Each computer manufacturer has its own version of the language, and some have more than one version.

This text illustrates the use of BASIC as applied to computer systems manufactured by Digital Equipment Corporation (DEC), the leading manufacturer of minicomputers. The versions of BASIC used in this text are BASIC-PLUS for the PDP-11, and VAX-11 BASIC. The reader can assume that all instructions presented will work on the VAX-11 except where VAX differences are noted. This text may also be adapted for other computer systems' versions of BASIC.

Levels of Languages

The three levels of computer languages are machine language, assembler language, and high-level language.

Machine language uses codes developed by the manufacturer that specify a computer operation. Programming in machine language is difficult because the programmer must have specific knowledge of the particular computer system in use, and programs written in machine language cannot be used on another computer system. Each computer manufacturer has its own language.

Assembler languages were developed so that mnemonic names could be given to operation codes, such as A to represent an addition. Assembler languages are also unique to particular computer systems. To use an assembler language, a computer program is needed to translate the assembler program written by the programmer (called a source program) into machine language (called an object program). This translator (called an assembler) is usually written by the computer manufacturer.

High-level languages also utilize a translator, called a compiler or interpreter. The program developed in the high-level language (source program) is translated into machine language (object program). The difference between an assembler and a high-level language are: (1) high-level languages are more like English, (2) high-level languages are more standardized and are therefore relatively independent of the computer in use, and (3) a single high-level program instruction can be translated into several machine-language instructions.

How BASIC Works

BASIC is a high-level language. The general concept of how a programmer uses the BASIC language with a computer system is shown in Figure 1.4. The detailed steps necessary to connect to a computer system are outlined in Chapter 2 on system commands.

Program Development

The first step in developing a useful program is to precisely define the problem to be solved. This is an especially critical step involving both the user of the program and the programmer or systems analyst. Cooperation is paramount in order to ensure that the resultant program solves the actual problem.

After the problem has been defined, a solution must be developed. This means determining exact computer operations necessary to solve the problem. Tools that are available to assist the programmer in mapping out the logic of a program include program flowcharts and pseudocode. Standard program-flowcharting symbols are depicted in Figure 1.5, and Figure 1.6 shows a sample flowchart for the calculation and printing of gross pay. Pseudocode will be introduced in Chapter 8. Additional flowcharting examples and techniques will be presented throughout the text.

The next step is to code the program, which means to put the computer operations outlined in a flowchart or pseudocode into the computer language that is to be used; e.g., BASIC.

After the program has been coded, the programmer will enter it into the computer to test and debug the program. Testing and debugging involves the elimination of clerical and logic errors to ensure that the program solution properly solves the problem at hand.

Figure 1.4
Steps to using a BASIC program

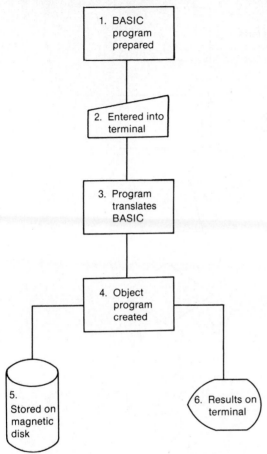

1. The programmer prepares a program in BASIC (source program),
2. enters the program by connecting a terminal to a computer, and
3. a program translates the BASIC program into
4. machine language (object program). The machine language program has been stored in main storage at this point.
5. The system can be directed to store the program on a permanent storage device or
6. can be directed to display the results on a terminal.

Figure 1.5
Program flowcharting symbols

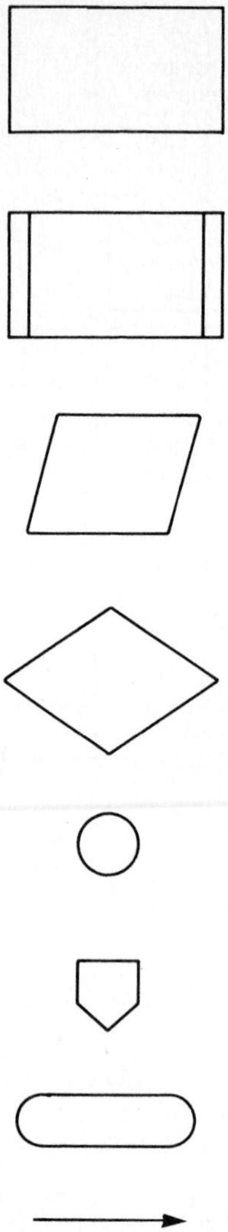

Process. Any operation, such as a calculation, which may change the form, values, or location of the data.

Predefined process. Any previously defined process such as a subroutine.

Input/Output. Any operation that inputs or outputs data from or to a device.

Decision. A method of determining alternative paths through a program.

Connector. Entry to or exit from a particular part of a program.

Off-page connector. Used when the flowchart cannot be completed on one page.

Terminal or interrupt. Shows where a program begins or ends or delays.

Flowline. Used to show direction or flow through the flowchart.

Documentation of the program is the last step in program development and essentially involves communication to future program users of how the program works. Documentation may include program listings, test runs, flowcharts, forms used, and written narratives. A useful program usually is modified several times over its years in use, and adequate documentation is necessary to facilitate such modifications. This is true even though the original programmer completes the modifications.

Figure 1.6
Flowcharting a problem

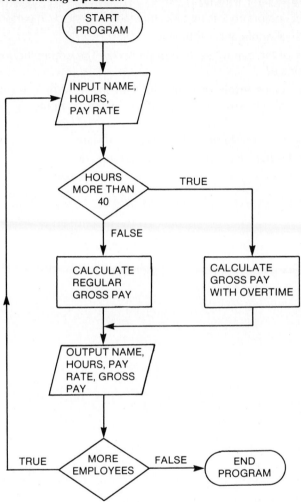

Exercises

1. What are the four major functional components of a computer system? What is the purpose of each component?
2. Discuss the relative merits of each of the input, output, and storage devices discussed in this chapter.
3. What is the difference between batch and interactive processing?
4. Discuss the use of BASIC as an educational language; as a business-applications language; as a mathematical or scientific language.

5. What are the purposes of a program flowchart? Is it better just to write the program and not waste time with flowcharts?

6. What are some of the major processing tasks that the computer can perform?

7. What is the purpose of application software?

8. What is the purpose of the control section of the CPU? The arithmetic/logic unit? Temporary storage?

9. What are the three major levels of computer languages? Which level is easiest to program? Which level is independent of the computer system being used?

10. What is the purpose of a translator? What does it translate?

11. Identify and define the five steps to program development.

Chapter Two

System Commands

In addition to writing and entering BASIC programs, there are several types of instructions necessary to tell the computer system what to do with the program. These are called system commands and are the programmer's means of communicating with an operating system. The operating system is a series of programs written by the manufacturer to control computer operations. It may be desired to have a listing of the program on the terminal; have the program stored for future reference on permanent storage; change a program and re-store it, and so forth. The programmer must inform the operating system when these procedures should be completed. All procedures discussed in this chapter relate to procedures for PDP-11 and VAX-11 systems. Other systems may require different commands, and the system manual or computer-center director should be consulted.

Logging on the System

To become a user on a DEC system, it is necessary to have access to a terminal and be assigned a project-programmer number and a password. After these have been attained, access can be granted to the operating system. A particular version of the operating system may be in operation at a given location, and the system manual in effect should be consulted.

After connecting the terminal to the computer system, type the command HELLO on the terminal and press the return key. Every instruction is entered by pressing the return key. The system will identify itself by printing a system message, which depends on the system being used. An example of a system message can be seen in Example 2.1 later in the chapter. After the system identifies itself, the system asks the programmer to do the same by printing a pound sign #. Programmer inputs are shaded in the following examples.

HELLO

System message
#

The programmer would then respond to the pound sign # by typing in an appropriate project-programmer number separated by a comma and pressing the return key, as is shown below.

HELLO

System message

46,148

The system then prints the word PASSWORD as a signal that the programmer is now allowed to type in the assigned password without the password showing. The programmer then types the password and presses the return key. The pressing of the return key in all cases causes the terminal to perform a carriage return and transmits the response to the computer system over the communication link between the terminal and the computer.

HELLO

System message

46,148

PASSWORD XXXXXX

If the project-programmer number and the password correspond correctly, entry to the operating system will be confirmed by the computer by printing a daily message and the word READY. Any time the computer system prints READY, it means that the system is waiting for a response from the programmer. If the project-programmer number and the password do not correspond, the system will inform the programmer by printing the pound sign # again. The programmer would then repeat the sequence of project-programmer number and password.

HELLO

System message

46,148

PASSWORD
INVALID ENTRY—TRY AGAIN

After several unsuccessful attempts, the system will print the following:

ACCESS DENIED
BYE

It would then be necessary to type HELLO and start the whole process over again.

The programmer can suppress the sometimes lengthy daily message by entering the project-programmer number separated by a slash instead of a comma as shown below:

HELLO

System message

46/148

PASSWORD XXXXXX

READY

Logging off the System

After a programmer has completed work on the system, logging off is required. This is accomplished by typing in the word BYE and pressing the return key. *Note:* Failure to properly log off the system will result in the line to the computer being left open. A programmer should always log off properly:

BYE

Confirm:

The programmer has several options at the point of confirmation, which are described below:

Y   Log me out
N   Don't log me out
I   Individual file deletion
        K to delete
        (CR) to save
F   Fast logout

Typing in Y will cause the system to log off the terminal. In doing so, it will print various messages, as shown below:

BYE

Confirm: Y

Saved all disk files; 48 blocks in use, 2 free
JOB 6 User 46,148 logged off KB20 at 15-Nov-XX 04:22 PM
System RSTS V7.0-07 ABC TIMESHARING
Run time was 8.2 seconds
Elapsed time was 24 minutes
Good afternoon

Typing in N will cause the system to keep the terminal logged in. In that case, the system responds with READY:

BYE

Confirm: N

READY

Typing in I allows a programmer to delete or keep any program that was previously saved in permanent storage. To delete a program, type K. To save the program, simply press the return key (CR).

Typing in F suppresses the ending messages but does log the terminal off the system. Positive confirmation of a log-off, by means of either a Y or an F, causes the destruction of the program being worked on in temporary storage. Further discussion of the ability to save a program is explained in a later section in this chapter. After logging off, the programmer may wish to gain access to the system under a different project-programmer number. This can be accomplished by typing in HELLO and repeating the logging-on procedure. If the programmer does not wish to continue, the terminal should be physically disconnected after the system is logged off.

Logging on and off: VAX Differences

A programmer on the VAX system obtains a user name and a password to gain entry to the system. Instead of typing in HELLO as was done on the PDP system, the programmer simply presses the return key, and the system responds by asking for a user name. The programmer types in the assigned user name, and the system will then ask for the password.

Username: ADM507

Password:

When the programmer enters the password, it will not echo or print on the terminal. This is the method used on the VAX to protect the password. When the user name and password correspond correctly, the system will respond with a system message followed by a dollar sign. The dollar sign signifies that the programmer must enter a system command. An example of a system message is shown in Example 2.2 later in this chapter.

After the programmer has gained entry to the VAX operating system, the word BASIC is typed to enter the BASIC environment. The system responds by printing the VAX BASIC version number.

Username: ADM507

Password:
           System message

$ BASIC

VAX-11 BASIC V1.4

Logging off from the VAX requires leaving the BASIC environment and then issuing either the LOGOUT or the LOGOUT/FULL command. The LOGOUT command logs off the terminal and informs the programmer of the log-off time, while the LOGOUT/FULL command will print additional system information.

EXIT

$ LOGOUT

       ADM 507   logged out at 29-JUL-19XX 08:37:27

Entering a Program

After entry to the operating system has been gained, the programmer is assigned both a temporary and a permanent storage area under the project-programmer number. This enables the programmer to enter, list, and run new programs, to store new programs in permanent storage, or to transfer old programs from permanent storage into temporary storage to run, list, or modify. This concept is shown in Figure 2.1.

The NEW Command

The NEW command allows a programmer to name a new program and enter it in temporary storage. To issue this command, type in the word NEW and press the return key. The system will respond by printing a request for a name as follows:

Figure 2.1
Using temporary and permanent storage

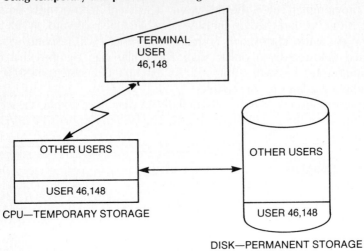

NEW

NEW FILE NAME—

A name of six characters or less on the PDP-11 system or up to nine characters on the VAX-11 system may then be typed in by the programmer; the system will respond with READY.

NEW

NEW FILE NAME— SAMPLE

READY

   A new program can now be entered in temporary storage, and the system will remember the program's name. A word of caution—when the NEW command is issued, any program currently in temporary storage is destroyed.
   A programmer may also issue the following command bypassing the system response:

NEW SAMPLE

READY

   Suppose the programmer then entered the following program in temporary storage under the name SAMPLE by entering each statement one line at a time and pressing the return key after each line.

```
10 REM SAMPLE PROGRAM

20 PRINT "THIS SHOWS THE PRINTING OF WORDS"

30 END
```

The program now exists under the name SAMPLE *only* in temporary storage.

Listing a Program

If the programmer wishes to see a complete listing of the program as it now exists in temporary storage, the LIST command is entered and the return key is pressed.

```
LIST
```

```
SAMPLE 12:54 PM 15-NOV-XX
10 REM SAMPLE PROGRAM
20 PRINT "THIS SHOWS THE PRINTING OF WORDS"
30 END
```

READY

A programmer may also obtain a complete listing of the program without the heading being printed by issuing the LISTNH command. LISTNH is used simply to suppress the printing of the heading by the computer. When a program is entirely correct, a final, current listing *should* be made using the LIST command. This would give the programmer adequate documentation of *when* the list was made (note this difference between LIST and LISTNH).

```
LISTNH
```

```
10 REM SAMPLE PROGRAM
20 PRINT "THIS SHOWS THE PRINTING OF WORDS"
30 END
```

A programmer may also wish to select only certain statements to be listed rather than obtain a complete listing. This is helpful when the program is long or when the program is being listed on a cathode ray tube (CRT). The following list command would print a heading and then list statements 5, 20, and all statements between and including 200 through 250 in a BASIC program.

```
LIST 5,20,200-250
```

To suppress the printing of the heading, use the following command:

```
LISTNH 5,20,200-250
```

Running a Program

To test the results of the program that is currently in temporary storage, issue the RUN command.

> RUN

> SAMPLE 12:56 PM 15-NOV-XX
> THIS SHOWS THE PRINTING OF WORDS
>
> READY

RUNNH may also be used like LISTNH to suppress the printing of the headings.

RUN should always be used to document the most current running of the program.

> RUNNH

> THIS SHOWS THE PRINTING OF WORDS
>
> READY

Storing a Program

After the program has been created in temporary storage, it can be stored on permanent storage by issuing the SAVE command. The system then responds with READY.

> SAVE

> READY

The program now exists in both temporary storage and permanent storage, as shown in Figure 2.2.

Figure 2.2
Temporary and permanent storage of a program

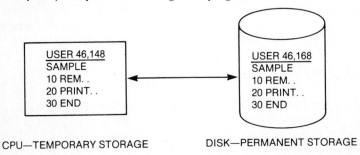

```
USER 46,148
SAMPLE
10 REM. .
20 PRINT. .
30 END
```

```
USER 46,168
SAMPLE
10 REM. .
20 PRINT. .
30 END
```

CPU—TEMPORARY STORAGE   DISK—PERMANENT STORAGE

The issuance of the NEW command at this point would destroy the program named SAMPLE in temporary storage, but the program named SAMPLE is still available in permanent storage.

Accessing a Stored Program

To transfer a previously saved program from permanent storage into temporary storage, the OLD command is issued. The system will respond just as it did when the NEW command was issued. This procedure also destroys any program currently in temporary storage.

OLD

OLD FILE NAME—   SAMPLE

READY

The programmer may also suppress the system response simply by typing in OLD and the file name in one entry and then pressing the return key.

OLD SAMPLE

READY

The program at this point can be listed, run, or modified. To transfer a program into temporary storage and have the system run it immediately, the programmer should issue the command RUN and the file name in one entry.

RUN SAMPLE

THIS SHOWS THE PRINTING OF WORDS

READY

Deleting a Stored Program

To erase a program that is in permanent storage only, issue the UNSAVE command with the file name.

UNSAVE SAMPLE

READY

To erase a program that is in permanent storage and also is currently in temporary storage, issue the UNSAVE command without any file name.

22

UNSAVE

READY

In either case, the program has only been deleted from permanent storage, not temporary storage. Whatever program was in temporary storage prior to the UNSAVE command is still in temporary storage. Only the issuance of the NEW, OLD, or BYE commands will erase a program that is in temporary storage.

Storing a Modified Program

A complete discussion of how to modify programs is presented in Chapter 4. However, one of the types of modifications is to add program statements to a program. This is done by typing in a statement number and the statement that is to be added. Consider the following sequence on the terminal:

OLD SAMPLE

READY

LIST

SAMPLE 01:20 PM 16-NOV-XX
10 REM SAMPLE PROGRAM
20 PRINT "THIS SHOWS THE PRINTING OF WORDS"
30 END

READY

25 PRINT "AND SHOWS HOW A STATEMENT CAN BE ADDED."

LISTNH

10 REM SAMPLE PROGRAM
20 PRINT "THIS SHOWS THE PRINTING OF WORDS"
25 PRINT "AND SHOWS HOW A STATEMENT CAN BE ADDED."
30 END

READY

The program now exists in two forms: one with four statements exists in temporary storage, and one with three statements exists in permanent storage. This concept is illustrated in Figure 2.3.

If the SAVE command is issued, the system will notice that the program in temporary storage and the program in permanent storage have the same name.

Figure 2.3
Modified program stored in temporary storage

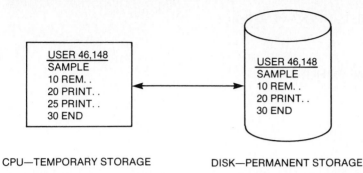

CPU—TEMPORARY STORAGE   DISK—PERMANENT STORAGE

SAVE

?FILE EXISTS—RENAME/REPLACE

READY

One option for the programmer is to REPLACE the program that exists in permanent storage by the program that exists in temporary storage. This is accomplished by issuing the REPLACE command.

REPLACE

READY

After the issuance of the REPLACE command, temporary and permanent storage would have the same program, as shown in Figure 2.4.

The other option is to RENAME the program that exists in temporary and then SAVE the program under its new name. The use of either option depends upon whether the programmer wishes to keep both versions of the program.

Figure 2.4
Storing modified program in permanent storage

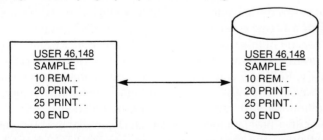

CPU—TEMPORARY STORAGE   DISK—PERMANENT STORAGE

SAVE

?FILE EXISTS—RENAME/REPLACE

READY

RENAME OTHER

READY

SAVE

The above would have the results shown in Figure 2.5, where two versions of the program are saved.

Figure 2.5
Storing two versions of a program

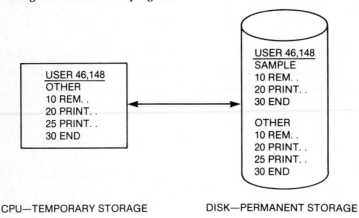

CPU—TEMPORARY STORAGE   DISK—PERMANENT STORAGE

Storing a Modified Program: VAX-11 Differences

When a program is saved using either the PDP or VAX system, the file name is cataloged along with a file-type extension, .BAS for a BASIC program. On the VAX-11 system, a version number is also used. For instance, if a BASIC program named TEST were saved, a catalog listing would reveal TEST.BAS;1. If TEST were to be modified and the REPLACE command issued, the modified program would automatically be saved and given the next-higher version number, i.e. TEST.BAS;2. In addition, the first version would also be retained.

To gain access to either program thereafter the OLD command would need to include both the extension and the version number, i.e. OLD TEST.BAS; 2. The RENAME command can also be used in VAX-11 BASIC.

Getting a Catalog

Should a programmer using the PDP system need to know the names of the programs or files on permanent storage, the CATALOG or CAT command should be issued. On the VAX system the corresponding command is the DIR command, which means directory. On the VAX, the programmer must, however, first issue the EXIT command to leave the BASIC environment.

Example 2.1
A first session using the terminal on the PDP-11

```
HELLO

RSTS V7.0-07 UNC TIMESHARING  Job 9  KB20  01-Jul- 85  09:23 PM
#46/37
Password:██████



Ready

NEW SAMPLE

Ready

10 REM SAMPLE PROGRAM
20 PRINT 'THIS SHOWS THE PRINTING OF WORDS'
30 END
LIST
SAMPLE   09:24 PM          01-Jul-85
10 REM SAMPLE PROGRAM
20 PRINT 'THIS SHOWS THE PRINTING OF WORDS'
30 END

Ready

RUN
SAMPLE   09:24 PM          01-Jul-85
THIS SHOWS THE PRINTING OF WORDS

Ready

CAT
TEMP09.TMP       0          60       01-Jul- 85 01-Jul- 85 09:23 PM

Ready

SAVE

Ready

CAT
TEMP09.TMP       0          60       01-Jul- 85 01-Jul- 85 09:23 PM
SAMPLE.BAS       1          60       01-Jul- 85 01-Jul- 85 09:24 PM

Ready

BYE
Confirm: Y
Saved all disk files; 4 blocks in use, 46 free
Job 9 User 46,37 logged off KB20 at 01-Jul- 85 09:24 PM
System RSTS V7.0-07 UNC TIMESHARING
Run time was 1.8 seconds
Elapsed time was 1 minute
Good evening
```

117,459

LIBRARY
College of St. Francis
JOLIET, ILL.

Example 2.2
A first session using the terminal on the VAX-11

```
Username: STU101
Password:
          Welcome to VAX/VMS Version V2.5


If any problems occur please contact:
          Karen          945-8691 (8:30am to 5:00pm)
          Ross           945-1129 (6:00pm to 10:00pm)


          notenotenotenotenotenotenotenotenoten
          o                                    o
          t          NEXT SCHEDULED DOWNTIME   t
          e                                    e
          n                                    n
          o              26-JULY-1985          o
          t             10:30AM-2:00PM         t
          e                                    e
          notenotenotenotenotenotenotenotenoten


$ BASIC

VAX-11 BASIC V1.4

Ready

NEW SAMPLE
Ready

10 REM SAMPLE PROGRAM
20 PRINT 'THIS SHOWS THE PRINTING OF WORDS'
30 END
LISTNH

10 REM SAMPLE PROGRAM
20 PRINT 'THIS SHOWS THE PRINTING OF WORDS'
30 END

Ready

RUNNH

THIS SHOWS THE PRINTING OF WORDS
Ready

SAVE
Ready

EXIT
$ DIR

Directory _DRA1:[STU101]

SAMPLE.BAS;2        SAMPLE.BAS;1

Total of 2 files.
$ LOGOUT
    STU101        logged out at 29-JUL-1985  08:37:27.79
```

Improper Log-Off

Failure to properly log off the system will result in the connection to the computer being left open. The next programmer on the system will be automatically assigned to the area left open. This can be serious if the area contains confidential programs or data. A user who does become logged into another user's area should immediately log off properly and then use the appropriate logging-on procedure to gain access to another user area.

A Typical Session on the Terminal

A typical session on the terminal, especially for the new programmer, would be to log on, enter a new program, list and run the program, store the program, get a catalog listing, and log off. Examples 2.1 and 2.2 show a typical session on the PDP or VAX system. A new programmer would be well advised to duplicate this session on an available computer system.

Exercises

1. What is the purpose of an operating system? Is the operating system hardware or software?
2. Discuss what occurs when a programmer logs onto a system via a terminal.
3. What are the options available during logging off, and what occurs during each option?
4. What is the difference between temporary and permanent storage? What system commands affect each type of storage?
5. What is the purpose of each of the following system commands?
   a. HELLO
   b. BYE
   c. NEW
   d. OLD
   e. LIST and LISTNH
   f. RUN and RUNNH
   g. RUN TEST 1
   h. SAVE
   I. UNSAVE TEST 4
   j. RENAME
   k. REPLACE
   l. CAT
6. What would occur if a user physically disconnected a terminal without logging off properly?
7. Complete the following steps to gain experience on a terminal:
   a. Obtain a project-programmer number and password from the instructor or system manager.
   b. Log onto a terminal using instructions given in this chapter.
   c. Build the following program, named TEST 1, by entering each BASIC instruction one line at a time and pressing the return key.

   ```
   10   REM THIS IS A PROGRAM NAMED TEST1
   20   LET A = 10
   30   LET B = A * 5
   40   PRINT A, B
   50   END
   ```

d. Use both the LIST and the LISTNH commands after the above program has been entered. What is the difference between the two commands?

e. Test the above program using both the RUN and the RUNNH commands. Note the difference. (If mistakes are made, retype the correct statement.)

f. Save the above program and obtain a catalog or directory.

g. Modify the above program in temporary storage by typing in the following statement:

40   PRINT "A IS"; A, "B IS"; B

h. List and run the program as modified.

i. Try to save the program. What does the computer do when you try to save a program that is already in permanent storage?

j. Issue the RENAME command as described in the chapter and then save the renamed program. Obtain a catalog or directory.

k. Delete any stored programs, and obtain another catalog or directory.

l. Experiment with other commands as time allows.

m. Make sure that the system is properly logged off before leaving the terminal.

Chapter Three

Components of BASIC

To direct the computer to perform operations, it is necessary to prepare a computer program using the components of a particular computer language. The construction of program instructions is called the *syntax* of the language; it involves sometimes strict rules that must be adhered to properly. BASIC uses such components as constants, variables, symbols, statement numbers, and reserved words.

Constants

A constant is a programmer-supplied value in a program that does not change. It may be either a numeric or a nonnumeric value.

Numeric Constants

Numeric constants may be used in three different formats: real or floating-point, exponential, and integer formats. Also, they may be either a single-precision or a double-precision number. A single-precision number can have as many as 6 significant digits, and a double-precision number can have as many as 16 significant digits on the VAX-11 and as many as 15 on the PDP-11. Whether a particular system uses single- or double-precision values depends on a decision made by the systems manager at a particular location. Example of numeric constants are given below.

Real (floating point)	Exponential	Integer
−1.6	1234 E4	235%
4537.92	−45.76 E5	−12%
45		45%

A real number can range from approximately 10^{-38} to 10^{37}. The range of the possible integer numbers is from −32,768 through 32,767. An integer number is used in situations when counting is performed; it results in significant savings of storage space in the computer compared to the use of a real number. Any number followed by a percent symbol will be stored as an integer number. The number 157.8% would be stored as 157. Notice that rounding does not occur; rather, all fractions are truncated.

Further flexibility can be gained by using the E format, where the number after the E signifies the power of 10. For example, the number 4.7932 E4 would be interpreted as 4.7932 times 10 to the fourth power, or 47,932.

Nonnumeric Constants

A nonnumeric constant is a value given to the computer that cannot be used in a calculation. These values, also called strings, provide headings for reports, provide a means for interactive communication with the computer, and also have other uses. Nonnumeric constants are specified to the BASIC language enclosed between a pair of apostrophes or quotation marks. The following are examples of valid string constants:

"YES"
"600"
'WHAT IS YOUR NAME'
'$500.75'

Notice that the string constant is each and every character between the outer quotes, including blank characters. Quotes may also appear within quotes. For example, JOHN'S HOUSE would be given to the computer as a string as "JOHN'S HOUSE".

Variables

A variable is a programmer-supplied, symbolic name given to a temporary storage location that can be assigned different values, either numeric or nonnumeric. A variable name in BASIC can have two characters, the first of which must be one of the letters A through Z and the second, if used, must be one of the numbers 0 through 9. An integer variable is followed by a percent symbol, and a string variable is followed by a dollar sign. Some systems allow more than two characters in a variable name. For example, the PDP-11 system allows up to 30 characters in a variable name in the EXTEND mode, and the VAX-11 always allows up to 30 characters. The following are valid variable names.

Real (floating-point)	Integer	String
A	D%	N$
A3	F1%	P2$
B6	T0%	C$
AMOUNT.SOLD	TOTAL%	NAME$

Modes of Computer Operations

There are several modes that the programmer will find useful when working with a computer: the language mode, the EXTEND mode, the NOEXTEND mode, the immediate mode, and the editing mode.

Language Mode

The programmer can select from various computer languages that are available on a given computer. The VAX system requires that the programmer specify which language is desired; however, the PDP system automatically assumes the use of BASIC unless the programmer specifies otherwise.

Interpreter mode. In this mode, the PDP system translates each BASIC instruction and executes that instruction before going to the next instruction. The VAX system may also be used in the interpreter mode when it is in the BASIC environment. This text assumes the use of the interpreter mode, and all programs have been run on a PDP system. The reader is assured that all programs will also run on a VAX system if necessary statement differences are considered.

Compiler mode. The VAX system also allows the programmer to have the system completely translate the entire BASIC program into machine language before execution or storage of the program. The procedures necessary for the VAX in the compiler mode are not presented in this text.

Compatibility mode. The VAX system allows the user the opportunity to execute programs that are written in BASIC-PLUS for the PDP-11 without any conversion necessary, using the compatibility mode. This is useful when a user has changed from a PDP system to a VAX system. VAX BASIC, however, is more powerful than BASIC-PLUS and should be used for the development of any new programs to be run on the VAX system.

EXTEND Mode

The extend mode allows the user of BASIC-PLUS on the PDP-11 to be more descriptive in the assigning of symbolic names to variables. By using the extend mode, the programmer may use up to 30 characters in a variable name. The name must begin with a letter and may use digits, letters, and periods as the remaining 29 characters. No embedded blanks are permitted. If an integer or string variable is defined, the % or $ symbol must be counted as one of the remaining 29 characters. To have a BASIC-PLUS program be in the extend mode, simply place the EXTEND command as a BASIC statement at the beginning of the program, i.e., 10 EXTEND. VAX BASIC automatically is in the EXTEND mode and assumes the use of up to 30 characters in a variable name and also allows the use of underscores as valid characters after the first alphabetic character.

NOEXTEND Mode

PDP-11 BASIC is automatically in the NOEXTEND mode and is restricted in the construction of symbolic names. These names may have two characters, the first of which must be one of the letters A through Z and the second, if used, must be one of the numbers 0 through 9. A third character may be used to indicate a string ($) or an integer (%) variable. Also, statement continuation does not make use of the ampersand. Unless described otherwise, all programs in this text are in the NOEXTEND mode.

Immediate Mode

The immediate mode allows the user to execute some BASIC instructions without the instructions being a part of a program. The statement is simply issued without a statement number, and the computer will execute the instruction immediately. For example, the following instruction would determine and print immediately the square root of 25, thus allowing an immediate use of the calculating ability of the computer without writing a program.

PRINT 25 ** .5

Editing Mode

A program and/or data can be developed and/or modified in the editing mode rather than the language mode. This is accomplished with the use of an available text editor. This concept is explained in detail in Chapter 16.

Basic Symbols

In addition to the alphabet, BASIC uses several other types of symbols in constructing statements. These include arithmetic symbols, logic symbols, delimiters, and special characters.

Arithmetic Symbols

To specify arithmetic operations, the symbols shown below are used.

Arithmetic symbol		Example
−	(subtraction)	A − 2
+	(addition)	B2 + D9
*	(multiplication)	A1 * B7
/	(division)	B / D
**	(exponentiation)	X ** 2

Logic Symbols

The logic symbols give BASIC its decision-making capabilities and are shown below.

Logic symbol	English meaning
=	Equal to
<	Less than
>	Greater than
<=	Less than or equal to
>=	Greater than or equal to
<>	Not equal to

Note: All of the above can be used on both the VAX and PDP systems. In addition, the following are valid only on the VAX:

=<
=>
><

Delimiters

Delimiters are used to separate fields such as variable names and constants, and in certain program statements have additional meanings. The delimiters used are the coma, semicolon, colon, backslash, and blank. The specific use of each of these delimiters will be shown when necessary. Examples of statements with delimiters are shown below.

    10 PRINT 5, 10, A; B2
    20 READ A,B,C,D

Special Characters

There are also many other special characters used in BASIC, such as the $ and % symbols that were previously discussed. Additional characters will be illustrated when they are needed.

Statement Numbers

An important component of a BASIC program statement is the statement number. Every BASIC instruction, unless used in the immediate mode, must have a statement number, as it is used to determine the sequence in which instructions are executed. Statement numbers are positive numbers from 1 through 32,767.

Reserved Words

BASIC has a lengthy list of reserved words that are used to specify operations to the computer. These words are translated by the compiler or interpreter into a machine-language instruction. Misspelling of any reserved word will cause a syntax error to be generated. None of the reserved words may be used when constructing variable names. Each reserved word will be introduced as necessary; all of them are listed in Appendix A.

The BASIC Statement

The general format of a BASIC statement is:

> n Reserved Word list

where *n* is a mandatory statement number, the *reserved word* is chosen from the available words, and the *list* is some other required or optional entry. Spaces between entries in a statement are optional in the NOEXTEND mode on the PDP-11. However, in the EXTEND mode or on the VAX-11 system, a blank between entries is mandatory. All BASIC statements have a statement number unless used in the immediate mode. All statements hereafter are assumed to have a statement number. This format will be used to describe the format of BASIC statements, where the format of the statement will appear above the boxed explanation.

Remark Statements

The REM statement has the following general format:

> n REM remarks

where *REM* is a reserved word indicating that everything following REM is a remark and not to be interpreted as an instruction, and *remarks* are whatever the programmer wishes to type on the statement.

To provide comments on a particular instruction without using the REM as a separate statement, the ! symbol is used. The ! is usually used after the complete instruction has been given; then everything typed after the ! is ignored and not interpreted as an instruction.

The program in Example 3.1 will illustrate several concepts that will be useful throughout the study of BASIC.

Example 3.1
An illustrative program in BASIC

```
10 REM A COMPUTER PROGRAM
20 READ B                    ! READ 100 INTO B
25 DATA 100
30 LET C = B * 7             ! MULTIPLY B TIMES 7
40 LET D = C ** 2            ! SQUARE C
50 PRINT B, C, D             ! DISPLAY THE RESULTS
60 END                       ! END THE PROGRAM
```

1. Each instruction is entered one line at a time; the return key is pressed after each line.
2. Note that additional statements numbers could be added between statements 10 and 20, 30 and 40, and so forth. It is always a good idea to leave unused statement numbers so that additional statements can be added later.
3. The sequence of statement numbers specifies the order in which the statements are executed by the computer, from low number to high number. If a change in sequence is desired, change the statement number.
4. Internal remarks and comments can be useful to explain what the program is doing. Remarks and comments are only useful to the programmer as a reminder—they are not interpreted by the computer as instructions. Statement 10 illustrates a remark statement, and comments are shown on statements 20, 30, 40, 50, and 60.

Statement Continuation

Normally an instruction can easily be completed on one line. Should it become necessary, a statement can be continued in the NOEXTEND mode on more than one line by pressing the LINE FEED key instead of the RETURN key. This will cause a carriage return but does not enter the statement into the computer until the return key is pressed. Line continuation can only occur between entries in a statement.

In the EXTEND mode, a statement can be continued using the line feed key, or statement continuation can be accomplished by ending the line with an ampersand and pressing the return key instead of the line feed key. The last line of the statement is then terminated by pressing the return key without typing an ampersand.

VAX BASIC uses the latter option only: statements may be continued only by terminating a line with an ampersand and pressing the return key. Also, a REM statement cannot be continued in VAX BASIC. The user who may convert to the VAX system is advised to use the ampersand option in the EXTEND mode on the PDP system.

Example 3.2 illustrates statement continuation using the ampersand option that would work in the EXTEND mode on the PDP and on the VAX. Each physical line is terminated by typing an ampersand and pressing the return key. The last line does not have an ampersand.

Example 3.2
Statement continuation

```
200 PRINT A; B; C; D;              &
         A; F; G; H                &
         ! READING IN VALUES
```

Exercises

1. Identify the type of variable name each of the following represents—integer, real, or string—and if is valid or invalid for NOEXTEND PDP, EXTEND PDP, or VAX BASIC. Also, if any are invalid for mode or system, indicate why.

		Type	Noextend-PDP	Extend-PDP	VAX BASIC
a.	P2$				
b.	X				
c.	3X%				
d.	AB				
e.	R2%				
f.	Z$				
g.	CUSTOMER.NAME				
h.	D9				
i.	SALES_AMOUNT				

2. What is the purpose of delimiters? Statement numbers? Reserved words? Remarks? Comments?

3. When is the ability to continue a statement on more than one physical line important? What two ways can line continuation be done on a PDP system? How is it done on a VAX system?

4. What is the difference between a constant and a variable?

5. How large a number can be stored as an integer? Single-precision real number? Double-precision real number on a PDP-11? Double-precision real number on a VAX-11?

6. When would the E format be used?

7. What is the difference between numeric and string values in a computer?

8. Why cannot implied multiplication be used in BASIC as it is in algebra?

9. Duplicate the procedures outlined in Exercise 7 in Chapter 2 for the program in Example 3.1

Section
2

Beginning
BASIC
Programming

Chapter Four

Simple Assignment and Output

In Chapter 3, we discussed the essential components of the BASIC language, including constants, variables, symbols, reserved words, and the BASIC statement. These components are necessary to construct and use simple assignment and output statements.

Arithmetic Expressions

One of the major purposes of any computer language is to make calculations. BASIC is no exception, and it is necessary, therefore, to know how calculations are performed. In the previous chapter, various symbols were introduced that are used in arithmetic. BASIC uses these symbols along with variables and constants to perform calculations. BASIC also uses the standard algebraic hierarchy to determine the sequence of operations to be performed. The arithmetic symbols (often referred to as arithmetic operators) and their order of execution are listed in Figure 4.1.

If a pair of parentheses is found in an expression, the operations specified within the parentheses will be evaluated first. Parentheses can be used to change the normal order of evaluation. The next operations performed deal with any value raised to a power. If multiplication and/or division are used, those operations are evaluated next, and any addition and/or subtraction are evaluated last. When operations are of equal priority, processing proceeds from left to right. An example will help illustrate this concept.

Figure 4.1
Hierarchy of arithmetic operations

Symbol	Operation	Algebra	BASIC
( )	Parenthesis-used to change order	$\dfrac{a+5}{b}$	(A+5)/B
**	Exponent-raise to a power	a^3	A ** 3
*	Multiplication	ab	A * B
/	Division	$\dfrac{a}{b}$	A / B
+	Addition	a + b	A + B
−	Subtraction	a − b	A − B

Given the following algebraic statement:

$$a + b/c - 5d^2$$

This expression would be written in BASIC as: A + B/C − 5*D**2 and the order of operations would be:

Step 1: D ** 2
Step 2: B/C
Step 3: 5 * Step 1
Step 4: A + Step 2
Step 5: Step 4 − Step 3

Assuming that A = 15, B = 12, C = 2, and D = 2, then A + B/C − 5*D**2 would be evaluated as:

Step 1: 2 ** 2 = 4
Step 2: 12 / 2 = 6
Step 3: 5 * 4 = 20
Step 4: 15 + 6 = 21
Step 5: 21 − 20 = 1

Evaluate the following when A = 4, B = 2, C = 1 and D = 3:

Algebraic	BASIC expression	Answer
$c + \dfrac{a}{b}$	C + A/B	3
$C + b^2 + a$	C + B**2 + A	9
$\dfrac{(ac)^d}{b}$	((A * C)**D) / B	32

The following restrictions about arithmetic operators should be observed:

1. Two operator symbols may not be placed next to each other.

A * − B	invalid	A * (−B)	valid
C—D	invalid	C − (−D)	valid

2. Parenthesis are always used in pairs.

(A + B	invalid	(A + B)	valid
((A*B)/D−C))	invalid	((A*B/D−C))	valid

The LET Statement

The LET statement is an assignment statement, the purpose of which is to store data in a temporary storage location represented by a programmer-supplied variable name. The data assigned to this variable may then be used or accessed by other statements during the execution of the program.

The general format of the LET statement is:

$$n \text{ LET } v = \text{expression}$$

where *LET* is a reserved word, *v* is a programmer-supplied variable name, = means assign (or move) the value of the expression to the temporary storage location represented by v, and *expression* is a constant or variable or any combination of constants and/or variables.

Although arithmetic calculations may be performed in other statements, most of the calculations are performed by the LET statement. Examples of the LET statement are:

10 LET A = 5	! ASSIGNS THE VALUE OF 5 TO A
15 LET B = 10 + 7	! ASSIGNS THE VALUE OF 17 TO B
20 LET C = A + B	! ASSIGNS THE VALUE OF 22 TO C
25 LET D = C/11 + A**2	! ASSIGNS THE VALUE OF 2 + 25 = 27 TO D
30 LET E = D	! ASSIGNS THE VALUE OF 27 TO E
40 LET A = A + 1	! ASSIGNS THE VALUE OF 6 TO A

The above sequence of statements is executed in the order of the statement numbers. Statement 10 would be executed first, followed by statement 15, etc. Assume that, before these statements are evaluated, the contents of all storage locations represented by A, B, C, D, and E are zero. The following table illustrates the changes in each location as these statements are executed.

	Storage locations				
Operation	A	B	C	D	E
1. Before statement 10	0	0	0	0	0
2. Execute statement 10	5	0	0	0	0
3. Execute statement 15	5	17	0	0	0
4. Execute statement 20	5	17	22	0	0
5. Execute statement 25	5	17	22	27	0
6. Execute statement 30	5	17	22	27	27
7. Execute statement 40	6	17	22	27	27

String data (also called nonnumeric data) can also be used in LET statements. For example:

```
10 LET A$ = "THE ANSWER IS"
20 LET B$ = "DIVISION"
30 LET T$ = "123.45"
```

In these statements every character included in the quote marks, even the blanks, will be placed into the string variables. Note in statement 30 that T$ cannot be used in a calculation since it has been defined as string data, even though a number has been placed in this location.

The END Statement

The END statement is a program-termination statement, the purpose of which is to tell the computer that there are no more statements in the program and to terminate the program.

The general format of the END statement is:

n END

where *END* is a reserved word. Important considerations to consider when using the END statement are:

1. It must be the last physical statement in the program.
2. Every program must have an END statement.

The PRINT Statement

The PRINT statement is an output statement, the purposes of which are (1) to display the value of a variable, constant, string, and/or expression, (2) to control the horizontal spacing of variables, constants, strings, and/or expressions, and (3) to control the vertical spacing of data lines.

The general format of the PRINT statement is:

n PRINT list

where *PRINT* is a reserved word and *list* is a sequence of variables, constants, strings, and/or expressions separated by delimiters.

The statement 100 PRINT will cause the terminal to single space. Two PRINT statements together will cause the device to double space. Other examples of the PRINT statement are:

100 PRINT A	! WILL DISPLAY THE CURRENT VALUE OF A
110 PRINT B, 6	! WILL DISPLAY THE CURRENT VALUE OF B AND THE CONSTANT 6
120 PRINT "AMOUNT IS", C	! WILL DISPLAY THE MESSAGE "AMOUNT IS" FOLLOWED BY THE CURRENT VALUE OF C
130 PRINT "TOTAL", A + B	! WILL DISPLAY THE MESSAGE "TOTAL" FOLLOWED BY THE VALUE OF THE EXPRESSION A + B (NOTE: ARITHMETIC CAN BE AC-COMPLISHED WITH THE PRINT STATEMENT, CALLED COMPUTA-TIONAL PRINTING)

Horizontal spacing of the data line is controlled by delimiters, the TAB option, or the PRINT USING option. The PRINT USING option is discussed in Chapter 7.

Use of Comma

When using the comma as a delimiter in a PRINT statement, the data to be displayed are placed in print zones or fields that are 14 spaces wide. Normally there are five of these print zones or fields per line; however, the number varies from four to nine depending on the particular terminal in use. In the examples in this text, it will be assumed that there are five such fields. The comma causes the following to occur:

1. For numeric values; the first location in the field is saved for the sign, and the values are displayed starting with the first digit from left to right.
2. String values start printing in the first location in the field, and the values are displayed starting with the first character from left to right.
3. When more than five data fields are to be displayed on the same line (or there

are more fields than are allowed on the terminal in use), the comma causes a new line to be used for the remaining fields.

The statement:

    100 PRINT 5, B, N$! B = −10, N$ = DENVER

will display the value of 5 in print position 2, the value of B in print positions 15–17, and the value of N$ in print positions 29–34. The statement:

    100 PRINT "A", "BB", "CCC", "DDD", "EEE", 6,−8,8,−100,6.17

will display the data on two lines as follows:

A	BB	CCC	DDD	EEE
6	−8	8	−100	6.17

Use of Semicolon

To display data closer together, the semicolon is used as a delimiter in the PRINT statement. The semicolon causes the following to occur:

1. For numeric values, the first location in the field is saved for the sign. The values are displayed starting with the first digit from left to right. The number displayed is then followed by a blank position.

2. String values start in the first location in the field, and the values are displayed starting with the first character from left to right.

3. Since the length of a display field is determined by the number of characters in each field, the number of fields to be displayed per line is determined by the programmer.

The statement:

    100 PRINT 7; C; X$; Y$! C = 20, X$ = "AB", Y$ = "CD"

will display the value of 7 in print position 2, the value of C in print positions 4–5, the value of X$ in print positions 6–7, and the value of Y$ in print positions 8–9. Since semicolons change the length of each display field, they are best used when displaying a single line of data. Otherwise, when attempting to display data in a table format, the following will occur:

    100 PRINT "HEAD1"; "HEAD2"; "HEAD3"
    105 PRINT X; Y; Z   ! X = 100
    110 PRINT Y; Z; X   ! Y = 5
    115 PRINT Z; X; Y   ! Z = −10

    HEAD1 HEAD2HEAD3
     100   5 −10
      5   −10 100
    −10   100 5

Use of the TAB Option

When several lines of data are to be displayed in table format, the programmer may prefer to use the comma with its spacing limitation, or to use the TAB option. The purpose of the TAB option is to control horizontal spacing of a display line. The general format of the TAB option is:

TAB(c);

where *TAB* is a reserved word and *c* is the number of the print position (plus 1) where the field is to start printing. When using the TAB(c), the semicolon is the required delimiter. Otherwise, the same spacing for numbers and strings occurs with the TAB as for the comma.

The statement:

100 PRINT TAB(1); N$; TAB(9); A   ! N$ = "TOTAL", A = −17

will display the value of N$ in print positions 2–6 (*Note:* c, which is 1 (plus 1) = print position 2 for the first displayed character), and the value of A would be displayed in print positions 10–12. The statements:

```
100 PRINT "STATE"; TAB(9); "AMOUNT"
105 PRINT
110 PRINT X$; TAB(9); A          ! X$ = "COLORADO", A = 100
120 PRINT Y$; TAB(9); B          ! Y$ = "OHIO", B = 50
```

will display the data as follows:

```
STATE          AMOUNT

COLORADO       100
OHIO           50
```

Suppressing Vertical Spacing

When either a comma or a semicolon is placed after the last item in a PRINT statement, it suppresses the vertical spacing of the line. For example, the statements:

```
100 PRINT 10; 20;
105 PRINT 15; 25
```

will display all of the data from the two PRINT statements on one line as:

10   20   15   25

The statements:

```
100 PRINT "ABC",
105 PRINT "DEF",
110 PRINT "GHI"
```

will also display all of the data from the three PRINT statements on one line. Note the difference in usage of the comma and the semicolon.

ABC   DEF   GHI

Skipping Data Fields

When two commas are placed together, the computer will skip a display field. The statement:

```
100 PRINT 10, 15,, 20
```

will display the data as:

10   15   20

Example 4.1 shows a program using several PRINT statements in a program.

Example 4.1
Examples of output from PRINT statements

```
100 PRINT "            P R I N T   P O S I T I O N S"
110 PRINT "       1         2         3         4         5         6"
120 PRINT "12345678901234567890123456789012345678901234567890123456789012"
130 PRINT 25, 7.5, -10, 79, 1000
135 REM
140 PRINT "ONE", "TWO", "THREE", "FOUR", "FIVE"
145 REM
150 PRINT 25; 7.5; -10; 79; 1000
155 REM
160 PRINT "ONE"; "TWO"; "THREE"; "FOUR"; "FIVE"
170 PRINT
180 PRINT TAB(7);25;TAB(12);7.5;TAB(28);-10;TAB(35);79;TAB(41);1000
185 REM
190 PRINT TAB(7);"ONE";TAB(12);"TWO";TAB(28);"THREE";TAB(35);"FOUR";
TAB(41);"FIVE"
195 REM
200 PRINT "       1         2         3         4         5         6"
210 PRINT "12345678901234567890123456789012345678901234567890123456789012"
900 END

READY

RUNNH
         P R I N T   P O S I T I O N S
       1         2         3         4         5         6
12345678901234567890123456789012345678901234567890123456789012
25        7.5       -10       79        1000
ONE       TWO       THREE     FOUR      FIVE
 25  7.5 -10  79  1000
ONETWOTHREEFOURFIVE

      25  7.5        -10   79   1000
      ONE  TWO        THREE FOUR FIVE
       1         2         3         4         5         6
12345678901234567890123456789012345678901234567890123456789012

READY
```

Making Corrections

In writing program statements or entering data into a program, errors in the statements and/or data may occur. Corrections may be made as follows.

1. If a statement is written and *has already been entered* into the system by pressing the return key:
    a. Re-enter the entire statement using the same statement number. This will erase the original statement. For example,

    100 MET A = 10

    has been entered incorrectly. To correct this statement, re-enter the statement as

    100 LET A = 10

    and press the return key. The statement is now entered into temporary storage correctly. In all cases of corrections, the REPLACE or RENAME/SAVE commands would need to be used if the program was already saved to correct the version in permanent storage.
    b. To erase an entire statement from a program, simply enter the statement number and press the return key. For example,

    100 MET A = 10
    110 LET A = 10

    Statement 100 is incorrect, but statement 110 is correct. To erase statement 100 from the program, type 100 and press the return key.

2. If program statements or data are being entered and an error is detected *before* it is entered into temporary storage:
    a. The simplest method is to press the CONTROL (CTRL) key and hold it down and then press the letter U key. This will erase everything that has been typed since the return key was last pressed. Then the correct program statement or data can be typed.
    b. Another method is to press the DELETE key (RUBOUT key on some systems) once for each character that needs to be erased—in effect, backspacing. Each time the DELETE key is pressed, the character erased will be printed by the system. For example, suppose the entry "DENBER" has been typed, and it is misspelled. Press the DELETE key four times, once each for " R E and B. Then retype the correction—in this example, VER." Pressing the CONTROL (CTRL) key and holding it down and then pressing the R key will cause the computer to print out the statement as corrected. Then press the return key or make further corrections, as necessary.

3. If a statement needs to be added to a program that has already been entered into temporary storage, simply enter the omitted statement with an appropriate statement number. For example:

```
100 LET A = 10
110 LET B = 15
120 LET S = A + B
999 END
```

In the above program there is no PRINT statement to print out the results calculated in statement 120. Simply add the following statement:

```
200 PRINT S
```

4. To halt execution of a program, press and hold the CONTROL (CTRL) key and then press the C key. This will stop the program from executing and return the system to the language mode for additional commands or statement entries.

The following examples that were run on a system will illustrate how to make corrections when entering a program. Programmer inputs are shaded.

1. This is a listing of a program that already exists in temporary storage. Note the results in running the program.

Example 4.2
Listing a program

```
LISTNH
10 LET A = 10
20 LET B = A**2
30 PRINT A; 'SQUARED IS'; B
90 END

READY

RUNNH
 10 SQUARED IS 100

READY
```

2. *Changing statements.* If it is desired to change a statement that already exists in temporary storage, simply type in the statement number and the correct statement. Note statement 10 has changed in the listing and has changed the results of the program.

Example 4.3
Changing statements in temporary storage

```
10 LET A = 5
LISTNH
10 LET A = 5
20 LET B = A**2
30 PRINT A; 'SQUARED IS'; B
90 END

READY

RUNNH
 5 SQUARED IS 25

READY
```

3. *Adding statements.* To add a statement, type in an appropriate statement number and the statement. Note line 35 has been added in proper sequence.

Example 4.4

Adding statements in temporary storage

```
35 PRINT "A PLUS B IS";A+B
LISTNH
10 LET A = 5
20 LET B = A**2
30 PRINT A; "SQUARED IS"; B
35 PRINT "A PLUS B IS";A+B
90 END

READY

RUNNH
  5 SQUARED IS 25
A PLUS B IS 30

READY
```

4. *Deleting statements.* To delete a statement that already exists in temporary storage, type in the statement number and press the return key. Note statement 35 has been removed from the listing. If a programmer wishes to delete several statements, this can be accomplished by the use of the system command DELETE. For instance, the command DELETE 100-200 would delete all the statements between and including 100 and 200.

Example 4.5

Deleting statements from temporary storage

```
35
LISTNH
10 LET A = 5
20 LET B = A**2
30 PRINT A; "SQUARED IS"; B
90 END

READY
```

5. *Correcting statements—CTRL U.* If a program statement has been typed incorrectly but has not yet been entered, press and hold the CTRL key and then press the U key. Then type the statement correctly. Note statement 35 was typed incorrectly, CTRL and U keys were pressed (which echoes on the terminal as U), and then statement 35 was entered correctly.

Example 4.6

Deleting statements before entering

```
35 PRINT "A MINUS B IS";A+B¬U
35 PRINT "A MINUS B IS";A-B
LISTNH
10 LET A = 5
20 LET B = A**2
30 PRINT A; "SQUARED IS"; B
35 PRINT "A MINUS B IS";A-B
90 END

READY

RUNNH
  5 SQUARED IS 25
A MINUS B IS-20

READY
```

6. *Correcting statements—deleting characters.* Sometimes when an error has been made it makes more sense just to correct a few characters rather than to erase the whole statement and start over. In statement 40, A-B should be A*B. Pressing the delete key twice will delete the B and -, then * and B are typed correctly. Pressing and holding the CTRL key and then pressing the R key will cause a printing of the statement as corrected. Then press the return key.

Example 4.7

Correcting characters before entering

```
40 PRINT "A TIMES B IS";A-B\B-*\B¬R
40 PRINT "A TIMES B IS";A*B
LISTNH
10 LET A = 5
20 LET B = A**2
30 PRINT A; "SQUARED IS"; B
35 PRINT "A MINUS B IS";A-B
40 PRINT "A TIMES B IS";A*B
90 END

READY

RUNNH
  5 SQUARED IS 25
A MINUS B IS-20
A TIMES B IS 125

READY
```

7. *Correcting Statements—VAX differences.* The VAX system allows the programmer to change program statements in a different manner in addition to the procedures described previously. The following command is used:

EDIT n / error/correction,

where *EDIT* is a system command, *n* is the statement that is to be corrected, the slashes are required delimiters (one can also use apostrophes), *error* is the character or characters to be replaced, and *correction* is the character or characters to put in place of the error. In the example, TIMES is replaced by DIVIDED BY, and the asterisk is replaced by a slash.

Example 4.8
Correcting statements on the VAX

```
10 LET A = 5
20 LET B = A**2
30 PRINT A;"SQUARED IS";B
35 PRINT "A MINUS B IS";A-B
40 PRINT "A TIMES B IS";A*B
90 END

Ready

EDIT 40 /TIMES/DIVIDED BY

40 PRINT "A DIVIDED BY B IS";A*B

Ready

EDIT 40 /*//

40 PRINT "A DIVIDED BY B IS";A/B

Ready

RUNNH

 5 SQUARED IS 25
A MINUS B IS-20
A DIVIDED BY B IS .2
Ready
```

Common Errors

Statement	Explanation
100 LETS S = 10	Reserved word LET is misspelled. Quotation marks are omitted.
100 LET A + B = S	Expression should be to the right of the equal sign: LET S = A + B.
PRINT	Statement number omitted. This would single space in the immediate mode.
100 LET T = X/D$	Arithmetic not allowed with string variables. D$ in error.
100 PRINT AB	Delimiter needed between A and B. Otherwise it is an invalid variable name, unless in the EXTEND mode or on a VAX system.
9A9 END	Invalid statement number.
100 PRINT TAB(5);A;TAB(5);B	A and B cannot be printed in the same position. TAB(5) does not skip 5 columns between A and B.
100 PRINT TAB(5),A,TAB(8),B	The comma should not be used after the TAB. Though this will work, the comma skips to a subsequent print zone rather than printing in print positions 6 and 9.

Sample Programs

Problem Description 4.1

1. Statement of the problem: Compute the average and print out the answer for three test scores.

2. Input: Assign the three values 90, 80, and 100 with a LET statement.
3. Output: Display the message AVERAGE IS and the answer.

Flowchart 4.1

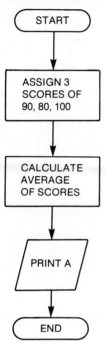

```
1 REM AVERAGE PROGRAM USING LET
100 LET S1 = 90
110 LET S2 = 80
120 LET S3 = 100
130 LET A  = (S1 + S2 + S3) / 3
140 PRINT
150 PRINT "AVERAGE IS"; A
999 END

READY

RUNNH

AVERAGE IS 90

READY
```

Problem Description 4.2

1. Statement of the problem: Convert a temperature of 32 degrees Fahrenheit to its equivalent degrees in Celsius. The arithmetic model is: (F − 32) * 5/9.

2. Input: Create the value 32 with a LET statement.

3. Output: Display headings for Fahrenheit and Celsius and the values of the degrees under the appropriate headings.

Flowchart 4.2

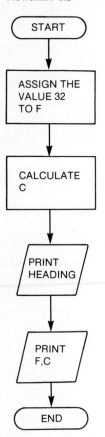

```
1 REM FAHRENHEIT CONVERSION USING LET
100 LET F = 32
110 LET C = (F - 32) * 5 / 9
120 PRINT
130 PRINT "FAHRENHEIT", "CELSIUS"
140 PRINT F, C
999 END

READY

RUNNH

FAHRENHEIT    CELSIUS
 32              0

READY
```

Problem Description 4.3

1. Statement of the problem: Display the heading of a report for the ABC Company.

2. Input: Create the heading within the program.

3. Output: Display a line of heading for the name of the company and a second line with the column names: NAME, ADDRESS, and BLOOD TYPE, centered and underscored. Double space between the headings.

Flowchart 4.3

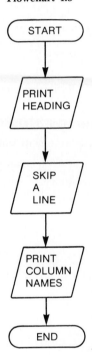

```
1 REM HEADING PROGRAM USING PRINT
100 PRINT TAB(25); "XYZ COMPANY"
110 PRINT
120 PRINT TAB(14); "NAME"; TAB(27); "ADDRESS";
130 PRINT TAB(40); "BLOOD TYPE"
140 PRINT TAB(14); "----"; TAB(27); "-------";
150 PRINT TAB(40); "----------"
999 END

READY

RUNNH
                         XYZ COMPANY

            NAME          ADDRESS      BLOOD TYPE
            ----          -------      ----------

READY
```

Exercises

1. For the following algebraic formulas, construct the equivalent expression in BASIC.
   a. ½bh
   b. $a^2 + b^2$
   c. $\dfrac{(x - y)^3}{a + b^2}$
   d. $a^2 + b^3 - cd^4$

2. What is the purpose of the LET statement? Construct LET statements for the expressions constructed in Exercise 1 above.

3. What is the purpose of the following two LET statements?

   ```
   10 LET N = N + 1
   20 LET T = T + A
   ```

4. In the PRINT statement, the comma, the semicolon, or the TAB may be used. What is the purpose of each, and how do they work?

5. How are the printing of a string and the printing of a numeric value different?

6. How can the computer be made to suppress vertical spacing? skip data fields?

7. What is the purpose of each of the following?
   a. CTRL U.
   b. CTRL C.
   c. CTRL R.
   d. Delete or rubout key.

8. Here are each of the following corrections made?
   a. Modifying a program statement that already exists in temporary storage.
   b. Stopping a program while it is executing.
   c. Adding statements to an existing program.
   d. Deleting statements from an existing program.

9. Modify Sample Program 4.1 by changing the values of S1, S2, and S3 to 75, 80, and 87, respectively.

10. Modify Sample Program 4.2 so that the Celsius equivalent to 96 degrees Fahrenheit can be determined.

11. Modify Sample Program 4.3 allowing for a person's actual name, address, and blood type to be printed below the headings.

12. Write a program that will print the following statement of account. Use LET statements to calculate the total merchandise price and total amount owed to XYZ Company.

    ACME MANUFACTURING
    1223 MAIN STREET
    CENTRAL, NEW JERSEY 01872

PURCHASES FOR THE MONTH OF MMMMMMM 198X

QUANTITY	DESCRIPTION	UNIT COST	TOTAL
2	BARRELS	$10.00	$20.00
10	BUCKETS	5.75	57.50
	TOTAL		$77.50
	SALES TAX AT 6%		4.65
	TOTAL AMOUNT DUE		$82.15

MAKE CHECK PAYABLE TO XYZ COMPANY

13. The most economical order quantity can be determined for a business which purchases merchandise for resale. The formula for the economic order quantity (EOQ) is:

$$Q = \sqrt{\frac{2DC_o}{C_h}}$$

where Q is the quantity of merchandise to order to minimize inventory costs, D is the number of units needed for a year (demand), C_o is the cost of placing an order and C_o is the cost of holding inventory. Write a program that will determine Q when D is 10,000, C_o is $25, and C_h is $0.75. Use appropriate headings for the output.

14. Two financial ratios that are often used as measures of financial liquidity are the current ratio and the quick ratio (also called the acid test). The current ratio is the ratio of current assets to current liabilities. The quick ratio is the ratio of quick assets to current liabilities. Quick assets exclude inventory and prepaid expenses from current assets. Write a program that will calculate and print out the current and the quick ratios if current liabilities total $35,000, current assets total $79,000, and quick assets total $62,000. Use appropriate headings.

Chapter Five

Simple Data Entry

Although the LET statement creates data for a program, it is not a convenient data-entry statement for most programs. The two most-used statements for data entry are READ and INPUT.

The READ/DATA Statements

The READ statement is a data-entry statement. The purpose of the READ statement is to accept data from DATA statements and store them in temporary storage locations represented by programmer-supplied variable names. The data accepted by READ statements may be used by other statements during the execution of the program.

The general format of the READ statement is:

> n READ list

where *READ* is a reserved word and *list* is a sequence of one or more variables separated by a comma or commas.

The DATA statement is a data-storage statement. The purpose of the DATA statement is to store in the program values to be used in a program by a READ statement.

The general format of the DATA statement is:

n DATA list

where *DATA* is a reserved word, and *list* is a sequence of one or more values separated by commas.

It is optional for any string data to be enclosed in quotes. However, the programmer must beware of what happens if a space or comma is intended to be part of the string data. Spaces are ignored by the computer and will not be displayed, and commas are treated as delimiters. Whenever these characters are needed as part of the string, always enclose the string in quotes. Each time a READ statement is executed in a program, its variables are assigned values sequentially from the DATA statement(s).

The following rules about the READ/DATA statements should be observed.

1. There must be at least one DATA statement if a READ statement is used in a program.
2. There may be many DATA statements in a program for the same READ statement.
3. There may be many READ statements in a program for the same DATA statement.
4. The DATA statements may be placed anywhere in the program before the END statement, since all other statements except the READ and RESTORE (which will be discussed in a later chapter) ignore the DATA statement.
5. The values in a DATA statement are assigned in sequence to the programmer-supplied names in the READ statement.
6. The types of data assigned to the variable names in the READ statement must be in agreement (i.e., numeric data must be used for numeric variables and string data for string variables).
7. If the DATA statements contains more values than all the READ statements contain programmer-supplied names, these values are not used.
8. If the DATA statement contains fewer values than all the READ statements contain programmer-supplied names, an out-of-data error occurs. (This problem will be discussed further under transfer statements in a later chapter.)
9. Comments using the ! symbol are not permitted at the end of a DATA statement.
10. A comma should not be used after the last field of data in a DATA statement.

Examples of READ/DATA statements are:

100 READ A   ! 15 IS ASSIGNED TO A FROM
                              STATEMENT 200

```
200 DATA 15
300 PRINT A                    ! DISPLAY THE VALUE 15
400 END

100 DATA NAME
200 READ N$                    ! NAME IS ASSIGNED TO N$ FROM
                                 STATEMENT 100
300 PRINT N$                   ! AND IT IS DISPLAYED WITH
                                 STATEMENT 300

999 END

100 DATA 11
200 READ A, B, C               ! 11 IS ASSIGNED TO A FROM
                                 STATEMENT 100, 12 IS ASSIGNED
                                 TO B FROM STATEMENT 300 AND
                                 13 IS ASSIGNED TO C FROM
                                 STATEMENT 700

300 DATA 12
400 LETS S = A + B + C         ! SUM THE VALUES
500 PRINT A, B, C              ! DISPLAY THE VALUES 11, 12, 13
600 PRINT S                    ! DISPLAY THE SUM OF THE
                                 VALUES 36

700 DATA 13
999 END

100 DATA 15, "AMOUNT IS"
200 READ N, N$                 ! 15 IS ASSIGNED TO N AMOUNT IS
300 PRINT N$, N                ! IS ASSIGNED TO N$ AND
                                 DISPLAYED BY
999 END                        ! STATEMENT 300

100 READ A                     ! 33 IS ASSIGNED TO A
110 READ B                     ! 11 IS ASSIGNED TO B
120 READ N$                    ! KEN IS ASSIGNED TO N$
130 PRINT N$, B, A             ! DISPLAYS KEN, 11, AND 33
900 DATA 33, 11, KEN
999 END

100 READ A, B, N$              ! SAME RESULTS AS THE PREVIOUS
                                 EXAMPLE
300 PRINT N$, A, B
500 DATA 33, 11, "KEN"
700 END
```

It is the responsibility of the programmer to select the appropriate number and/or combination of READ/DATA statements to satisfy the logic of the program.

The INPUT Statement

The INPUT statement is a data-entry statement. The purpose of the INPUT statement is to accept and store data in temporary storage locations, represented by programmer-supplied variable names, from an external device. The data accepted by the INPUT statement may be used by other statements during the execution of the program.

The general format of the INPUT statement is:

n INPUT list

where *INPUT* is a reserved word and *list* is a sequence of one or more variables separated by commas.

The major difference between the READ and INPUT statements is that the READ accepts data from an internal source in the program (the DATA statement) and the INPUT accepts data from an external source: either from the user on an interactive basis or from a permanent device (such as tape or disk, which will be discussed in a later chapter). Whenever the INPUT statement is executed in a program on an interactive basis, the program will display a question mark (?) on a terminal and stop executing until a user interacts by entering a value or values and pressing the return key to inform the program to continue executing. Each time an INPUT statement is executed in this manner, its variables are assigned values sequentially from the external device.

The following rules concerning the INPUT statement should be observed.

1. The values in an INPUT statement are assigned in sequence to the programmer-supplied variable names.
2. The types of data assigned to the variable names in the INPUT statement must be in agreement with them (i.e., numeric data for numeric variables and string data for string variables).
3. If the user attempts to enter more fields of data than there are programmer-supplied names in the list of the INPUT statement, the excess fields are ignored.
4. If the user attempts to enter fewer fields of data than there are programmer-supplied names in the list of the INPUT statement, the computer will print another question mark and wait for the user to enter more data.
5. Although this procedure is not mandatory, an INPUT statement should be preceded by a PRINT statement displaying a message to give the user instructions about the data to be input.

Examples of the INPUT statement are:

100 INPUT A	! TYPE IN A NUMERIC VALUE
200 PRINT A	! DISPLAYS THE VALUE OF A
999 END	
100 PRINT "ENTER THE VALUE OF A"	! WILL INSTRUCT THE USER WHAT TO ENTER
200 INPUT A	! TYPE IN A NUMERIC VALUE
300 PRINT A	! DISPLAYS THE VALUE OF A
999 END	
100 PRINT "ENTER 3 VALUES"	! WILL INSTRUCT THE USER WHAT TO ENTER
200 INPUT A, B, C	! TYPE IN NUMERIC DATA
300 LET S = A + B + C	! FIND THE SUM
400 PRINT S	! DISPLAY THE SUM
999 END	
100 PRINT "ENTER NAME AND AMOUNT"	! WILL INSTRUCT THE USER WHAT TO ENTER
200 INPUT N$, A	! TYPE IN A STRING AND A NUMERIC VALUE
300 PRINT N$, A	! DISPLAY THE VALUE OF N$ AND A
999 END	
100 PRINT "ENTER NAME AND AMOUNT"	! SAME RESULTS AS PREVIOUS EXAMPLE
200 INPUT N$	
300 INPUT A	
400 PRINT N$, A	
999 END	

Common Errors

Statements	Explanation
100 READ A 200 DATA "NAME"	Data types do not match. Should be A$.
100 READ A, B, C 200 DATA 15	Out-of-data error occurs. Must have three fields of data for A, B, C.
100 READ N$, A 200 DATA 10, NAME	Data in the DATA statement should be reversed.
100 READ A 200 END 300 DATA 50	END must be the last physical statement in the program. Change to 400 END.
100 READ A: B: C 200 DATA 1,2, 3	: is an invalid delimiter; use commas.
100 READ A, B 200 DATA 10, 300 DATA 20	Placing a comma at the end of a DATA statement causes unpredictable results or an error to occur.
100 READ 200 DATA 1, 2, 3	Forgot to include variable names with READ.
100 READ A, B	Missing a DATA statement.
100 INPUT	Missing the variable name(s).
100 INPUT A, B 200 DATA 10, 20	DATA statement is used with the READ, not the INPUT.
100 INPUT X, Y ? 10, 5/10	5/10 would be invalid data to input.
100 INPUT N$, A, B, C ? 10, 20, NAME	The order of the values after the ? is not in agreement with the INPUT statement.
100 INPUT C$, A, B ? PORTLAND, MAINE, 10, 20	Too many commas in data being entered; use "PORTLAND, MAINE", 10, 20.

Sample Programs

Problem Description 5.1

1. Statement of the problem: Calculate the average and print out the answer of three test scores. Use two different programs to solve the problem. In Chapter 4 this problem was solved using the LET statement.

2. Input: One program is to enter the three values 90, 80, and 100 with a READ statement. The other program is to enter these values from a terminal using an INPUT statement.

3. Output: Display the message AVERAGE IS and the answer for both programs.

62

Flowchart 5.1a

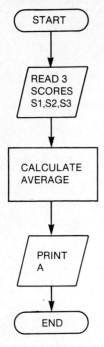

```
1 REM AVERAGE PROGRAM USING READ
100 READ S1, S2, S3
110 DATA 90, 80, 100
130 LET A = (S1 + S2 + S3) / 3
140 PRINT
150 PRINT 'AVERAGE IS'; A
999 END

READY

RUNNH

AVERAGE IS 90

READY
```

Flowchart 5.1.b

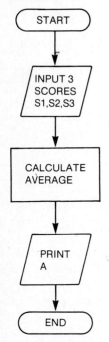

```
1 REM AVERAGE PROGRAM USING INPUT
100 PRINT 'ENTER 3 TEST SCORES'
110 INPUT S1, S2, S3
130 LET A = (S1 + S2 + S3) / 3
140 PRINT
150 PRINT 'AVERAGE IS'; A
999 END

READY

RUNNH
ENTER 3 TEST SCORES
? 90,80,100

AVERAGE IS 90

READY
```

Problem Description 5.2

1.   Statement of the problem: Convert a temperature of 32 degrees Fahrenheit to its equivalent degrees in Celsius. The arithmetic model is: $(F - 32) * 5/9$. Use two different programs to solve the problem. In Chapter 4 this problem was solved using the LET statement.

2.   Input: One program is to enter the value 32 with a READ statement. The other program is to enter the value from a terminal using an INPUT statement.

3.   Output: For both programs, display columns for Fahrenheit and Celsius and the values of the degrees under the appropriate column names.

Flowchart 5.2.a

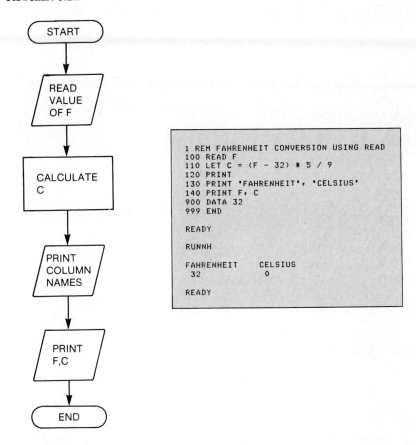

```
1 REM FAHRENHEIT CONVERSION USING READ
100 READ F
110 LET C = (F - 32) * 5 / 9
120 PRINT
130 PRINT "FAHRENHEIT", "CELSIUS"
140 PRINT F, C
900 DATA 32
999 END

READY

RUNNH

FAHRENHEIT     CELSIUS
  32              0

READY
```

64

Flowchart 5.2.b

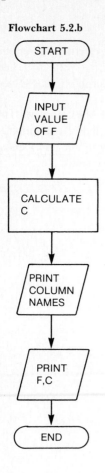

```
1 REM FAHRENHEIT CONVERSION USING INPUT
100 PRINT "ENTER FAHRENHEIT DEGREES"
110 INPUT F
115 LET C = (F - 32) * 5 / 9
120 PRINT
130 PRINT "FAHRENHEIT", "CELSIUS"
140 PRINT F, C
999 END

READY

RUNNH
ENTER FAHRENHEIT DEGREES
? 32

FAHRENHEIT      CELSIUS
   32              0

READY
```

Problem Description 5.3

1. Statement of the problem: Write a program to list the name, address, and blood type of employees of the ABC Company. Use two different programs to solve the problem.

2. Input: One program is to enter the data with a READ statement, and the other program is to enter data from a terminal using the INPUT statement.

3. Output: For both programs, use two lines of heading, with the first heading to display the name of the company and the second heading to display the column names: NAME, ADDRESS, and BLOOD TYPE, centered and underscored. Double space between the headings. List the employee data, one line for each employee, under the appropriate column names.

Flowchart 5.3.a

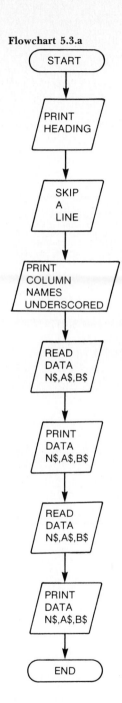

```
1 REM BLOOD TYPE LISTING USING READ STATEMENTS
50 ! N$ = NAME
     A$ = ADDRESS
     B$ = BLOOD TYPE
100 PRINT TAB(25); "XYZ COMPANY"
110 PRINT
120 PRINT TAB(14); "NAME"; TAB(27); "ADDRESS";
130 PRINT TAB(40); "BLOOD TYPE"
140 PRINT TAB(14); "----"; TAB(27); "-------";
150 PRINT TAB(40); "----------"
160 READ N$, A$, B$
170 PRINT TAB(10); N$; TAB(24); A$; TAB(44); B$
180 READ N$, A$, B$
190 PRINT TAB(10); N$; TAB(24); A$; TAB(44); B$
900 DATA "HINKLE, DAVID", "355 MAIN STREET", "AB"
902 DATA "JAMES, MILTON", "123 ELM DRIVE",  " O"
999 END

READY

RUNNH
                    XYZ COMPANY

          NAME         ADDRESS      BLOOD TYPE
          ----         -------      ----------
       HINKLE, DAVID 355 MAIN STREET    AB
       JAMES, MILTON 123 ELM DRIVE       O

READY
```

66

Flowchart 5.3.b

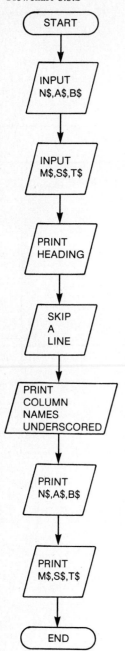

```
1 REM BLOOD TYPE LISTING USING INPUT STATEMENTS
50 ! N$ = FIRST NAME          M$ = SECOND NAME
     A$ = FIRST ADDRESS         S$ = SECOND ADDRESS
     B$ = FIRST BLOOD TYPE     T$ = SECOND BLOOD TYPE
100 PRINT "ENTER 3 FIELDS OF DATA"
110 INPUT N$, A$, B$
120 PRINT "ENTER 3 FIELDS OF DATA"
130 INPUT M$, S$, T$
140 PRINT TAB(25); "XYZ COMPANY"
150 PRINT
160 PRINT TAB(14); "NAME"; TAB(27); "ADDRESS";
170 PRINT TAB(40); "BLOOD TYPE"
180 PRINT TAB(14); "----"; TAB(27); "-------";
190 PRINT TAB(40); "----------"
200 PRINT TAB(10); N$; TAB(24); A$; TAB(44); B$
210 PRINT TAB(10); M$; TAB(24); S$; TAB(44); T$
999 END

READY


RUNNH
ENTER 3 FIELDS OF DATA
? "HINKLE, DAVID","355 MAIN STREET","AB"
ENTER 3 FIELDS OF DATA
? "JAMES, MILTON","123 ELM DRIVE"," O"
                        XYZ COMPANY

            NAME            ADDRESS        BLOOD TYPE
            ----            -------        ----------
         HINKLE, DAVID 355 MAIN STREET        AB
         JAMES, MILTON 123 ELM DRIVE          O

READY
```

Exercises

1. Explain the difference between the ways the READ and INPUT statements are used.
2. What delimiters can be used in the READ, DATA, and INPUT statements to separate items in the list?
3. For the following statements or sets of statements, indicate whether they are correctly or incorrectly used. If they are incorrect, write the correct statements.

    a. 100 READ A, B,
    b. 100 READ A, B, C
          110 DATA 10, 50
    c. 100 INPUT C$
          ?SPRINGFIELD, MISSOURI
    d. 100 READ C$, A
          110 DATA 25.7, "LUBBOCK, TEXAS"
    e. 100 READ A, B
          110 DATA 40, 75, 92.7

4. Given the following program:

    ```
    100 READ A
    110 LET X = (5 * A + 10 * A) / 2
    120 READ B, C
    130 LET Y = B * C ** 2
    140 READ D
    150 LET S = (X + Y) * D
    160 PRINT S
    900 DATA 8, 6, 5, 2
    999 END
    ```

    What is the value of S that is to be printed?

5. Modify the program written in Exercise 12 in Chapter 4 so that the detail information for quantity, description, and unit cost is entered into the computer via READ/DATA statements instead of LET statements.

6. Modify the program written in Exercise 13 in Chapter 4 so that the demand, the cost of an order, and the cost of holding inventory are entered via an INPUT statement. Include a PRINT statement to explain to the user what to enter.

7. Rewrite the program written in Exercise 14, Chapter 4, so that the current liabilities, current assets, and quick assets are entered via INPUT statements. Run the program using the data listed in Chapter 4. Run the program again using current liabilities of $150,000, current assets of $200,000, and quick assets of $10,000.

8. A manufacturer of color TV sets has collected the following data for last year: fixed cost = $500,000, variable cost = $20 per TV set, capacity of company

= 25,000 sets per year, selling price = $70 per set. Write a program that will calculate the following:

a. Breakeven point in units = fixed cost / (selling price − variable cost).
b. Breakeven point in dollars = fixed cost / (1 − variable cost / selling price).
c. Breakeven point by percent of capacity = (fixed cost / ((selling price − variable price)*(capacity of company))*(100 percent)

Use a READ statement and print the above calculations with appropriate headings.

9. The numbers of employees in each of the departments for a local firm are:

Department	Number of Employees
A	150
B	125
C	50
D	75

Enter the data with a READ statement. Calculate the number of employees in the firm, then calculate the percentage of employees in each department. Print the results in the following format:

DEPT	NUMBER	PERCENT
A	150	.5
etc.	etc.	etc.

Chapter Six

Simple Transfer

Usually the statements in a program are executed in sequential order. That is, processing passes from one statement to the next by the order in which statements are numbered. Many times the logic of a program requires that statements not be executed in this manner. Transfer statements provide for this deviation. They cause the computer to switch from one point in a program to another point, thus changing the normal sequence in which statements are executed. When a transfer is made regardless of existing conditions, it is referred to as an unconditional transfer. When the execution of a transfer statement is determined by certain conditions being met, it is referred to as a conditional transfer.

The GO TO Statement

The GO TO statement is an unconditional transfer statement. The purpose of the GO TO statement is to cause control of the program to be transferred to some other statement.

The general format of the GO TO statement is:

n GO TO n

where *GO* and *TO* are reserved words and *n* is a statement number. Whenever this statement is executed, transfer of control in the program is made to the statement number following the reserved words GO TO.

The GO TO statement is often used to skip to another part of a program or to create a loop where a sequence of instructions is to be repeated. In most cases, a GO TO statement should be used in conjunction with a conditional transfer statement.

The IF Statement

The IF statement is a conditional transfer statement. The purpose of the IF statement is to determine if a certain condition exists in the program, and if it does, to take an appropriate action. There are several forms of the IF statement. At this point in the text, only the simple IF statement is discussed.

The general format of the simple IF statement is:

n IF condition THEN n

or

n IF condition GO TO n

where *IF* is a reserved word, *condition* is the comparison of numeric or string values, *THEN, GO* and *TO* are reserved words, and *n* is a statement number.

The following conditions can be tested for on a PDP-11: $=$ (equal to), $<$ (less than), $>$ (greater than), $<=$ (less than or equal to), $>=$ (greater than or equal to), and $<>$ (not equal to). Additional conditions that can be tested for on a VAX-11 are: $=<$ (equal to or less than), $=>$ (equal to or greater than), and $><$ (not equal to).

Whenever the condition tested is true, transfer is made to the statement number which follows the word THEN or the words GO TO. Either form may be used with identical results. When the condition tested is false, the next statement following the IF statement is executed.

Examples of transfer statements are:

```
100 GO TO 999            ! AN UNCONDITIONAL TRANSFER
                           IS MADE TO STATEMENT NUMBER
                           999
100 IF A = B THEN 500     ! IF THE VALUE OF A IS EQUAL TO
                           B
110 LET X = 0             ! TRANSFER TO 500 ELSE EXECUTE
                           STATEMENT 110
```

```
100 IF A*B > 100 THEN 500          ! IF THE VALUE OF A*B IS GREATER
                                     THAN 100 TRANSFER TO
                                     STATEMENT 500

100 IF 5.5 < = A THEN 500          ! IF 5.5 IS LESS THAN OR EQUAL
                                     TO A TRANSFER TO STATEMENT
                                     500

100 IF A <> (B/C) GO TO 600        ! IF THE VALUE OF A IS NOT
                                     EQUAL TO B/C
110 GO TO 400                      ! TRANSFER TO 600 ELSE TRANSFER
                                     TO 400

100 READ X                         ! READ IN A VALUE, IF IT IS−9
110 IF X = (−9) GO TO 999          ! TRANSFER TO 999, ELSE SQUARE
                                     THE
120 LET S = X**2                   ! VALUE
130 PRINT S, X                     ! DISPLAY S AND X AND
140 GO TO 100                      ! TRANSFER TO 100 AND READ IN
                                     ANOTHER VALUE

900 DATA 2,4,6,8,−9
999 END
100 INPUT N                        ! INPUT A VALUE
110 IF N > 0 THEN 140              ! IF IT IS GREATER THAN ZERO
                                     TRANSFER TO 140
120 PRINT "N LESS THAN ZERO"       ! ELSE DISPLAY THE MESSAGE IN
                                     120
130 GO TO 999
140 PRINT "N GREATER THAN
      ZERO"
999 END
100 READ A, B                      ! READ TWO VALUES
110 LET S = A + B                  ! FIND THE SUM
120 PRINT S                        ! DISPLAY THE SUM
130 LET N = N + 1                  ! ADD 1 TO A COUNTER
140 IF N = 3 THEN 999              ! IF THE VALUE OF THE COUNTER
                                     IS 3
150 GO TO 100                      ! TRANSFER TO 999 ELSE
                                     CONTINUE IN THE LOOP

900 DATA 1,1,2,2,3,3
999 END
100 READ A, B                      ! READ TWO VALUES
110 IF B = (−9) THEN 999           ! IF B IS −9 TRANSFER TO 999
120 LET S = A + B                  ! ELSE SUM THE VALUES AND
130 PRINT S                        ! DISPLAY THE SUM
140 GO TO 100                      ! CONTINUE LOOP
900 DATA 1,1,2,2,3,3,−9,−9
999 END
```

```
100 PRINT "ENTER 2 TEST SCORES"    ! TELL OPERATOR TO ENTER DATA
110 INPUT A, B                     ! NOW ENTER TWO VALUES
120 LET S = A + B                  ! SUM THE VALUES
130 PRINT S                        ! DISPLAY THE SUM
140 PRINT "ENTER YES TO            ! ASK OPERATOR WHAT TO DO
         CONTINUE NO TO
         STOP"
150 INPUT N$                       ! ENTER THE ANSWER
160 IF N$ = "YES" THEN 100         ! IF YES CONTINUE THE LOOP
170 IF N$ = "NO" THEN 999          ! IF NO TERMINATE THE PROGRAM
180 GO TO 140                      ! TRY AGAIN IF ERROR MADE IN
                                     ANSWER

999 END
```

ON—GO TO Statement

The ON—GO TO statement is a conditional transfer statement. The purpose of the ON—GO TO statement is to allow for the transfer of control to different segments of a program.

The general format of the ON—GO TO statement is:

ON expression GO TO list

where *ON* is a reserved word, *expression* is a value that directs the transfer to one of the statement numbers, *GO* and *TO* are reserved words, and *list* is a group of statement numbers to be transferred to, depending on the value of the expression.

The statement 100 ON N GO TO 200,300,250 would be evaluated as follows: The integer portion of N is evaluated. If the value is 1, transfer will be made to the first statement in the list (200); if the value is 2, transfer will be made to the second statement in the list (300); if the value is 3, transfer will be made to the third statement in the list (250). If the integer portion of the value of N is not between 1 and the number of statement numbers in the list, in this example 3, an error occurs, and a message will be displayed on the terminal.

Examples of the ON—GO TO statement are:

```
100 ON 3 GO TO 320,310,330         ! TRANSFER IS MADE TO
                                     STATEMENT 330

100 ON J GO TO 300,290,280,600     ! INTEGER PORTION OF J MUST BE
                                     1,2,3, OR 4
```

100 ON N*X/2 GO TO 50,60,70   ! EXPRESSION IS EVALUATED AND
                                   TRANSFER IS MADE TO 50, 60, OR
                                   70, OTHERWISE AN ERROR IS
                                   DISPLAYED

100 ON X GO TO 10,20,10,20,10,20   ! TRANSFER TO 10 ON ODD VALUE
                                   AND TO 20 ON EVEN VALUE

Common Errors

Statement	Explanation
100 GO TO 100	Infinite loop, will always GO TO 100.
100 IF A = B THEN 100	Infinite loop when A = B.
100 IF N$ = 10 THEN 999	Cannot mix modes; N$ = 10 invalid.
100 IF A = > B THEN 700	Invalid condition for PDP-11, valid for VAX-11.
100 INPUT N 110 IF N > 0 THEN 130 120 PRINT "N LESS THAN ZERO" 130 PRINT "N GREATER THAN ZERO" 999 END	A logic error. Statement 130 will always be displayed. Insert 125 GO TO 999.
100 READ A, B 110 IF A = (−9) THEN 999 120 LET S = A + B 130 PRINT S 140 GO TO 100 900 DATA 1,1,2,2,3,3,−9 999 END	An out-of-data condition at statement 100 will result on the fourth time the program attempts to execute statement 100. The DATA statement must have a value for both A and B in the READ. Place another value in statement 900 after the −9.
100 LET N = 0 110 READ A, B 120 PRINT A, B 130 LET N = N + 1 140 IF N > 5 THEN 999 150 GO TO 100 999 END	A logic error. Statement 100 will cause N to be equal to zero. Statement 140 will never be true. Change statement 150 to GO TO 110.
100 IF N$ = YES GO TO 999	YES must in quotes.
100 ON N$ GO TO 30,40,50	N$ is invalid; must be a numeric value.
100 ON X GO TO 10,50,80	If X is less than 1 or greater than 3, it is out of range, and an error occurs.

Sample Programs

Problem Description 6.1

1. Statement of the problem: Three tests are to be given in a course. The number of students who will be given these tests is not known until the tests are actually taken. Calculate the average score for each student and display the student's average. In addition, calculate the overall class average.

2. Input: The program is to enter three test scores for a student from a terminal after the message ENTER 3 TEST SCORES appears. Since the number of students who will take the test is unknown, the message ENTER YES TO CONTINUE, NO TO STOP must appear on the terminal after a set of test scores has been entered. Input from the terminal and value YES or NO depending on whether more test scores are to be processed.

3. Output: Display the message AVERAGE IS and the answer for each student. After the final set of test scores has been processed and displayed, display the message OVERALL AVERAGE IS and the answer.

Flowchart 6.1

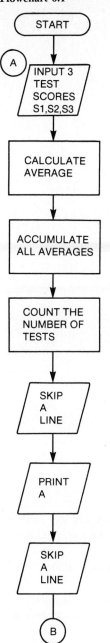

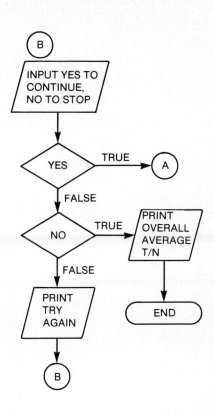

```
1 REM COMPUTES INDIVIDUAL TEST AND CLASS AVERAGE
50 ! S1, S2, S3 = TEST SCORES
       A = AVERAGE SCORE
       T = ACCUMULATION OF AVERAGE SCORE
       N = NUMBER OF STUDENTS
       R$ = RESPONSE TO CONTINUE RUNNING PROGRAM
100 PRINT "ENTER 3 TEST SCORES"
110 INPUT S1, S2, S3
120 LET A  = (S1 + S2 + S3) / 3
130 LET T = T + A
140 LET N = N + 1
150 PRINT "AVERAGE IS"; A
160 PRINT
170 PRINT "ENTER YES TO CONTINUE, NO TO END"
180 INPUT R$
190 IF R$ = "YES" THEN 100
200 IF R$ = "NO" THEN 230
210 PRINT "TRY AGAIN"
220 GOTO 160
230 PRINT "OVERALL AVERAGE IS"; T/N
999 END

READY

RUNNH
ENTER 3 TEST SCORES
? 90,80,100
AVERAGE IS 90

ENTER YES TO CONTINUE, NO TO END
? YES
ENTER 3 TEST SCORES
? 75,85,95
AVERAGE IS 85

ENTER YES TO CONTINUE, NO TO END
? NO
OVERALL AVERAGE IS 87.5

READY
```

Problem Description 6.2

1. Statement of the problem: Create a table that will display the Fahrenheit degrees from 32 through 40 and the corresponding Celsius degrees. The arithmetic model is: $(F - 32) * 5/9$.

2. Input: Assign the value 32 with a LET statement. Keep adding 1 to this initial value until the value is equal to 40.

3. Output: Display column names for Fahrenheit and Celsius, skip a line, and list in table form the values of the degrees under the appropriate column names.

Flowchart 6.2

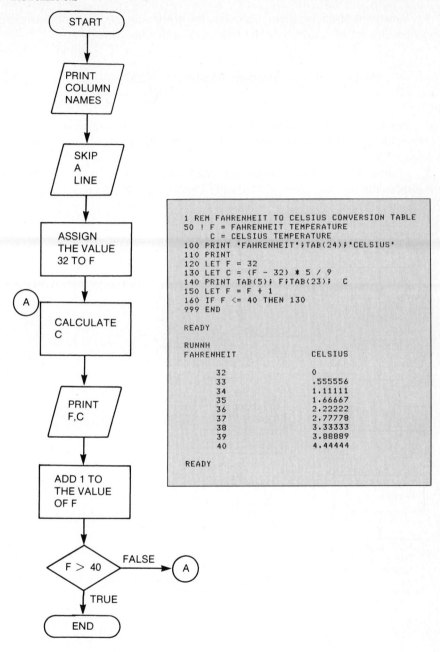

```
1 REM FAHRENHEIT TO CELSIUS CONVERSION TABLE
50 ! F = FAHRENHEIT TEMPERATURE
     C = CELSIUS TEMPERATURE
100 PRINT "FAHRENHEIT";TAB(24);"CELSIUS"
110 PRINT
120 LET F = 32
130 LET C = (F - 32) * 5 / 9
140 PRINT TAB(5); F;TAB(23);  C
150 LET F = F + 1
160 IF F <= 40 THEN 130
999 END

READY

RUNNH
FAHRENHEIT                 CELSIUS

      32                 0
      33                 .555556
      34                 1.11111
      35                 1.66667
      36                 2.22222
      37                 2.77778
      38                 3.33333
      39                 3.88889
      40                 4.44444

READY
```

Problem Description 6.3

1. Statement of the problem. Calculate the arithmetic mean and the standard deviation of a set of values. Use the following arithmetic models:

$$\text{Mean} = \frac{\Sigma X}{N} \qquad \text{Standard deviation} = \sqrt{\frac{\Sigma X^2 - \frac{(\Sigma X)^2}{N}}{N}}$$

2. Input: Enter the number of values to be used with a READ statement; in this problem, there are five. Use another READ statement to enter the data values, one at a time. Use the values 1,3,5,7,9.
3. Output: Display the message THE MEAN IS and the answer. On the next line display the message THE STANDARD DEVIATION IS and the answer.

Flowchart 6.3

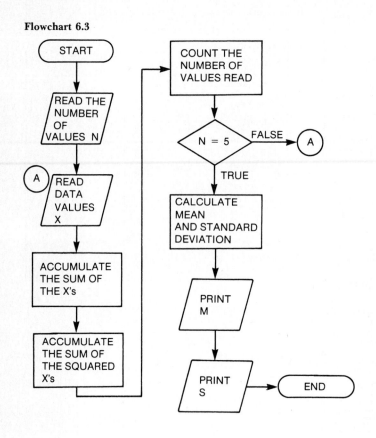

```
  1 REM COMPUTES MEAN AND STANDARD DEVIATION FOR
       A SET OF VALUES
 50 ! N = NUMBER OF VALUES TO BE READ
      X = INDIVIDUAL VALUE
     S1 = SUM OF INDIVIDUAL VALUES
     S2 = SUM OF INDIVIDUAL SQUARED VALUES
      C = COUNTER THAT COUNTS THE NUMBER OF TIMES
          STATEMENT 140 IS EXECUTED
      M = CALCULATED MEAN
      S = CALCULATED STANDARD DEVIATION
130 READ N
140 READ X
150 LET S1 = S1 + X
160 LET S2 = S2 + X ** 2
170 LET C  = C + 1
180 IF C < N THEN 140
190 LET M  = S1 / N
200 LET S  = ((S2 - S1 ** 2 / N) / N) ** .5
210 PRINT "THE MEAN IS            "; M
220 PRINT "THE STANDARD DEVIATION IS"; S
900 DATA 5
910 DATA 1,3,5,7,9
999 END

READY

RUNNH
THE MEAN IS                  5
THE STANDARD DEVIATION IS 2.82843

READY
```

Problem Description 6.4

1. Statement of the problem: Write a program to list the name, address, and blood type of employees of General Hospital. In addition, keep a total of the number of persons having the following blood types: A, B, AB, O, and other.

2. Input: Enter with a READ statement the name, address, and blood type.

3. Output: Display two lines of heading. The first heading should give the name of the hospital, centered and underscored; the second heading should include the column names—name, address, and blood type—centered and underscored. Skip a line and then list the data for each employee on a separate line, single spaced and under the appropriate column name. After the last employee line, skip a line and then print column headings underscored for all of the blood types. Skip another line and display the totals by blood type under the appropriate column names.

Flowchart 6.4

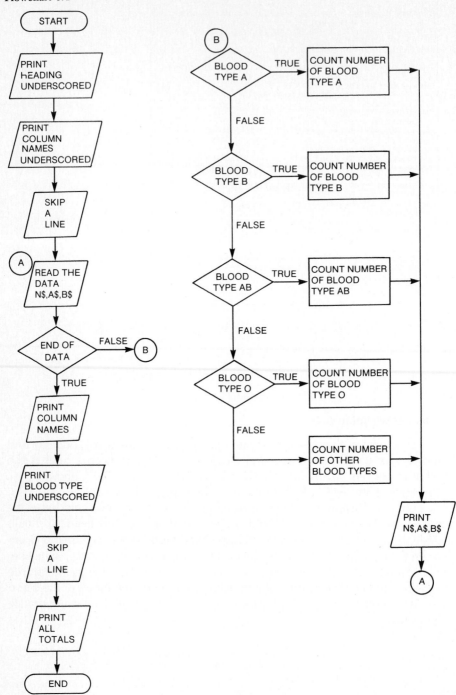

```
1 REM BLOOD TYPE LISTING WITH TOTALS OF EACH TYPE
50 ! N$ = NAME
     A$ = ADDRESS
     B$ = BLOOD TYPE
     COUNTERS FOR BLOOD TYPES:
         COUNTERS       BLOOD TYPE
         --------       ----------
           A                A
           B                B
           A1               AB
           0                0
           01               OTHER
100 PRINT "   G E N E R A L   H O S P I T A L"
110 PRINT "   --------------------------------"
120 PRINT "NAME", "ADDRESS", "BLOOD TYPE"
125 PRINT "----", "-------", "----------"
140 READ N$, A$, B$
150 IF B$ = "END" THEN 990
160 IF B$ = "A"   THEN 200
170 IF B$ = "B"   THEN 300
180 IF B$ = "AB"  THEN 400
190 IF B$ = "O"   THEN 500
195 LET 01 = 01 + 1
197 GOTO 600
200 LET A  = A  + 1
210 GOTO 600
300 LET B  = B  + 1
310 GOTO 600
400 LET A1 = A1 + 1
410 GOTO 600
500 LET 0  = 0  + 1
600 PRINT N$, A$, B$
700 GOTO 140
990 PRINT
999 PRINT "TOTAL", "TOTAL", "TOTAL", "TOTAL", "TOTAL"
1000 PRINT "TYPE A", "TYPE B", "TYPE AB", "TYPE O", "OTHER"
1002 PRINT "------", "------", "--------", "------", "-----"
1005 PRINT A, B, A1, O, 01
9000 DATA "HINKLE, DAVID", "355 MAIN",      AB
9001 DATA "HAMES, MILTON", "123 ELM DRIVE", O
9002 DATA "JAMES, BRIAN ", "555 FIRST AVE", O
9003 DATA "WHITE, RALPH ", "410 TENTH",     OTHER
9004 DATA 0,0,END
9999 END

READY

RUNNH
     G E N E R A L   H O S P I T A L
     --------------------------------
NAME            ADDRESS         BLOOD TYPE
----            -------         ----------
HINKLE, DAVID 355 MAIN      AB
HAMES, MILTON 123 ELM DRIVE O
JAMES, BRIAN  555 FIRST AVE O
WHITE, RALPH  410 TENTH     OTHER

TOTAL         TOTAL         TOTAL         TOTAL         TOTAL
TYPE A        TYPE B        TYPE AB       TYPE O        OTHER
------        ------        --------      ------        -----
  0             0             1             2             1

READY
```

Problem Description 6.5

1. Statement of the problem: Discounts are given on dollar amounts depending on the class of customer. Calculate the net amount of a sales order for the following: class 1 = 20% discount, class 2 = 10% discount, class 3 = 5% discount, class 4 = no discount. Accumulate totals for net and gross amounts for the customer data and list.

2. Input: Enter with a READ statement the class code, number of items, dollar amount, and customer number.

3. Output: Display with a heading the column names: customer number, net amount, and gross amount. Display all values under the appropriate column names. After all customers have been listed, display a line for the total net and gross amounts.

Flowchart 6.5

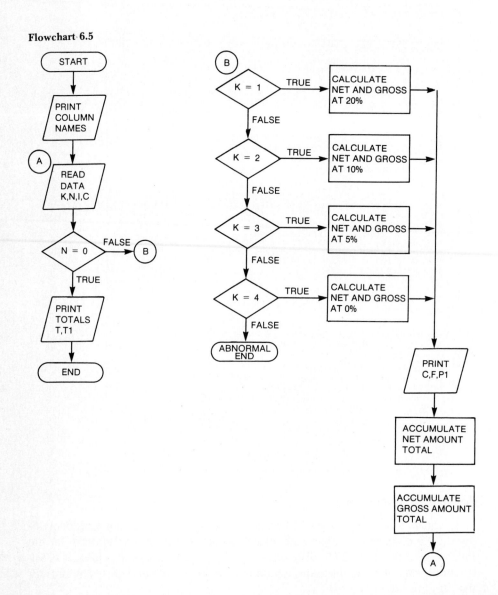

```
1 REM DISCOUNTED SALES REPORT
50 ! K = CLASS CODE          N = NUMBER OF ITEMS
   I = DOLLAR AMOUNT         C = CUSTOMER NUMBER
   P = NET AMOUNT           P1 = GROSS AMOUNT
   T = TOTAL NET AMOUNT     T1 = TOTAL GROSS AMOUNT
100 PRINT 'CUSTOMER NUMBER'; TAB(20);
'NET AMOUNT'; TAB(35); 'GROSS AMOUNT'
130 READ K, N, I, C
140 IF N = 0 THEN 800        ! END OF JOB WHEN NO ITEMS
                               ARE PURCHASED
150 ON K GO TO 200, 300, 400, 500
200 LET P  = (N * I) * .80
210 LET P1 = N * I
220 GO TO 600
300 LET P = (N * I) * .90
310 LET P1 = N * I
320 GO TO 600
400 LET P = (N * I) * .95
410 LET P1 = N * I
420 GO TO 600
500 LET P  = (N * I)
510 LET P1 = P
600 PRINT C; TAB(20); P; TAB(35); P1
610 LET T = T + P
620 LET T1 = T1 + P1
630 GO TO 130
800 PRINT 'TOTAL'; TAB(20); T; TAB(35); T1
900 DATA 3,5,100,1234
901 DATA 2,4,200,1345
902 DATA 4,2,100,1456
903 DATA 1,3,200,1567
904 DATA 0,0,0,0
999 END

READY

RUNNH
CUSTOMER NUMBER      NET AMOUNT       GROSS AMOUNT
  1234                 475               500
  1345                 720               800
  1456                 200               200
  1567                 480               600
TOTAL                 1875              2100

READY
```

Exercises

1. Why should an IF statement normally be used in conjunction with a GO TO statement?

2. What are the valid conditions that can be tested on the PDP-11? on the VAX-11?

3. When would an ON—GO TO statement be useful?

4. The following statements have been incorrectly constructed. In each case, correct the statement.

    a. 100 IF A$ = "YES" 999
    b. 200 IF N$ = 10 THEN 400
    c. 100 ON B$ GO TO 70, 50, 270
    d. 300 IF (A+B) = 14.75 THEN 300
    e. 500 IF A = <B THEN 900
    f. 700 GO TO 700
    g. 100 LET A = 4
        200 ON A 175, 250, 400

5. Rewrite the program written in Exercise 5 in Chapter 5 so that the detail information below is entered into the computer via one READ statement:

Quantity	Description	Unit Cost
2	Barrels	10.00
10	Buckets	5.75
30	Washers	0.60
35	Brackets	1.75

6. Rewrite Exercise 6 in Chapter 5 so that the detail information below is entered via an interactive program using an INPUT statement. Use a YES or NO response to continue inputting.

Demand	Cost to Order	Cost to Hold
10,000	$25	$0.75
5,000	$50	$1.50
4,500	$10	$2.75
3,800	$75	$3.50

7. Professor MIS has given three exams and would like to have a list of all students whose average on the tests is less than 65. Using the following data, write a program to produce the list of names and the average for each student. Include a count of how many students are in the class and how many students have an average less than 65. Have the program discontinue reading when the student's name is "END".

Student	Exam 1	Exam 2	Exam 3
Mary	56	42	86
Sam	47	81	86
Bob	60	49	84
Jane	86	50	55
Betty	76	55	86

8. Modify Sample Program 6.2 to produce a Fahrenheit-to-Celsius temperature conversion table for Fahrenheit degree from −30 to +95 in increments of 5 degrees Fahrenheit.

9. Modify Exercise 8 above so that a user of the program could interactively define the beginning and ending Fahrenheit degrees and the increment used in the table.

10. Write an interactive program using an INPUT statement to calculate the mean and standard deviation of a set of values. Inform the user what to enter and have the user enter a zero when no more values are to be entered. Test the program with the following two sets of values.

    Set 1: 75, 85, 62, 97, 150, 87
    Set 2: 500, 420, 475, 600, 720, 975, 210, 495

11. Using a single READ statement, write a program to determine the amount of pay each employee is to receive and the total pay of all employees in Department A of the U. S. Bank. Pay is determined by the following calculations:
    a. Multiply hours worked times rate.
    b. If hours worked are over 40, add a bonus of 15% to a above. Otherwise, pay is the result of a above.
    c. Disregard employees not working in Department A.
    d. Construct program so as to allow for an unknown number of employees.
    e. Display appropriate headings centered. Display all calculations, employee names, and departments worked in.
    Run the program twice. The first time use the following data:

Employee name	Hours worked	Rate	Department
Brown	40	7.35	B
Smith	40	6.83	A
Zeller	40	7.10	A
Knapp	48	5.95	A
Snell	44	8.05	B

    The second time add the following data to the list above:

Archer	49	8.00	A
Mann	40	7.70	B

12. Write an interactive program to enter three values and determine which of the three has the lowest value. Print out this low value. Allow the program to accept an unknown number of sets of values. Use the following as test data: 50, 110, 85, 90, 65, 100, 118, 119, 117.

13. Write a program to calculate the exact interest for loans with a code of 1 or 3 and ordinary interest with a code of 4. Skip the loan if the code is 2. All other codes are invalid. The program must allow for an unknown number of loans. Use the following test data:

Loan number	Principle	Rate (%)	Time (years)	Code
1,122	$1,000	15	2	1
6,544	$10,000	16	5	4
3,111	$7,000	17	6	3
4,633	$15,000	20	3	2

a. Exact interest = principle * rate * time / 365.
b. Ordinary interest = principle * rate * time / 360.
c. Amount of loan = principle + interest.
Print the results in the following format:

LOAN NUMBER	PRINCIPLE	AMOUNT
XXXX	$XX,XXX.XX	$XX,XXX.XX
etc.	etc.	etc.

14. Write an interactive program to determine the average markup for merchandise on cost and on selling price. Allow for an unknown number of entries.
a. Gross margin = sales − cost.
b. Average markup on cost = gross margin / cost.
c. Average markup on selling price = gross margin / selling price.
Use the following test data:

Item	Sales	Cost
Lamps	$ 5,000	$ 2,000
Chairs	$30,000	$19,500
Tables	$25,000	$17,000

Print appropriate headings and the above calculations.

Section
3

Intermediate BASIC Programming

Chapter Seven

Intermediate Assignment, Output, and Data Entry

The LET Statement

The reserved word LET is optional in a statement and may be omitted. The format 100 X = A + 5 is usually more convenient than 100 LET X = A + 5. Another format of the LET statement is:

$$n \ v1, v2, \text{ etc. } = \text{expression}$$

where *v1, v2, etc.* are variables that are given the value of the *expression*. For example: 100 X,Y,Z = 10, will assign the value 10 to all three variables. Note that the variables must be separated by commas.

Internal Function Subprograms

Often it is desired to use relatively common mathematical operations in an expression. One can write all the necessary instructions every time they are needed in a program, or write general programs to do these operations, and store them for future use. These stored programs are referred to as subprograms. There are several such mathematical subprograms built into the language. To make use of these it is necessary to call them into a particular program and provide a value for them to operate on. This is done by writing an expression that contains the name of the subprogram followed by parentheses that enclose an argument.

The general format is:

function-subprogram (arg)

where the name of the *function-subprogram* is a reserved word selected from the options available and the argument (*arg*) is an expression which is evaluated and supplied to the called program.

Figure 7.1 lists some of the subprograms provided by the language.

Figure 7.1
Internal function subprograms

Name of function	Explanation
COS(arg)	Finds the cosine of arg where arg is in radians.
SIN(arg)	Finds the sine of arg where arg is in radians.
TAN(arg)	Finds the tangent of arg where arg is in radians.
ATN(arg)	Finds the arctangent of arg where arg is in radians.
EXP(arg)	Finds the value of e^{arg} where e = 2.171828. . . .
LOG(arg)	Finds the natural logarithm of arg where arg cannot be negative or zero.
LOG10(arg)	Finds the common logarithms of arg where arg cannot be negative or zero.
ABS(arg)	Finds the absolute value of arg.
SGN(arg)	Finds the sign of arg. $+1$, 0 or -1 is returned.
INT(arg)	Finds the greatest integer value of arg which is not greater than arg.
FIX(arg)	Finds the integer value of arg.
SQR(arg)	Finds the square root of arg where arg cannot be negative.
PI	Has a constant value of 3.1415927.
RND or RND(arg)	Finds a random number between 0.000000 and 1. Since arg is ignored, its use is optional on the PDP-11 and can be omitted. It must be omitted on VAX-11.

Trigonometry Functions

The trigonometric functions are self-explanatory. Example 7.1 shows the results of their use in a program. The arguments can be any expression as long as the value of the expression does not violate any of the conditions stated in the explanation of these functions.

Example 7.1
Using trigonometry functions

```
100 I = 1
110 IF I > 5 THEN 999
120 PRINT COS(I); SIN(2*I); TAN(I*3); ATN(3+I);
                EXP(I/2); LOG(2+I); LOG10(I+3)
130 I = I + 2
140 GO TO 110
999 END

READY

RUNNH
 .540302   .909297 -.142547  1.32582  1.64872  1.09861  .60206
-.989992 -.279415 -.452316  1.40565  4.48169  1.60944  .778151
 .283662 -.544021 -.855993  1.44644  12.1825  1.94591  .90309

READY
```

Integer Function

This function finds the value of the greatest integer not greater than the argument. For example: INT(16.67) = 16. Rounding may occur to the nearest integer by INT(16.67 + .5) = 17. For negative numbers the largest integer is a negative number with the same or larger absolute value. For example: INT(−16) = −16 and INT(−16.33 = −17. Observe the results of Example 7.2.

Example 7.2
Using the INT function

```
100 I = -5
110 IF I > 5 THEN 999
120 PRINT INT(I), INT(I+.5), INT(I/1.5)
130 I = I + 1.5
140 GO TO 110
999 END

READY

RUNNH
-5          -5          -4
-4          -3          -3
-2          -2          -2
-1           0          -1
 1           1           0
 2           3           1
 4           4           2

READY
```

Random Number Function

This function finds a random number between .000000 and 1. Since the first time RND is called in a program it always returns the same value, it may be used for validation of program results. Example 7.3 illustrates its use.

When using the PDP-11 the argument can be any value since it is ignored, but this option cannot be used on the VAX-11. Example 7.4 illustrates using an

Example 7.3
Using the random number generator without an argument

```
100 I = 1
120 IF I > 5 THEN 999
130 PRINT RND,
140 I = I + 1
150 GO TO 120
999 END

READY

RUNNH
 .204935       .229581       .533074       .132211       .995602
READY

RUNNH
 .204935       .229581       .533074       .132211       .995602
READY

RUNNH
 .204935       .229581       .533074       .132211       .995602
READY
```

Example 7.4
Using the random number generator with an argument

```
100 I = 1
115 X = 15
120 IF I > 5 THEN 999
130 PRINT RND(X),
140 I = I + 1
150 GO TO 120
999 END

READY

RUNNH
 .204935       .229581       .533074       .132211       .995602
READY

RUNNH
 .204935       .229581       .533074       .132211       .995602
READY
```

argument with RND. If a program is to obtain different random numbers each time a program is run, the RANDOMIZE statement is used. This will cause RND to choose a random starting value. Example 7.5 shows the use of the RANDOMIZE statement. Notice the difference in values from Example 7.4.

Example 7.5
Using the RANDOMIZE statement

```
100 RANDOMIZE
110 I = 1
120 IF I > 5 THEN 999
130 PRINT RND,
140 I = I + 1
150 GO TO 120
999 END

READY

RUNNH
 .58073        .484165       .678416       .713013       .172334
READY

RUNNH
 .719363       .316078       .422202       .688511       .33125
READY
```

To convert the random value to a one- , two- , or three-digit random number, simply multiply the RND value by 10, 100, or 1,000. Notice statement 135 in Example 7.6. This technique could be expanded to find random numbers more than three digits long.

Example 7.6
Converting random numbers to integers of various length

```
110 I = 1
120 IF I > 5 THEN 999
130 X = RND
135 PRINT X, INT(10*X), INT(100*X), INT(1000*X)
140 I = I + 1
150 GO TO 120
999 END

READY

RUNNH
 .204935        2             20            204
 .229581        2             22            229
 .533074        5             53            533
 .132211        1             13            132
 .995602        9             99            995

READY
```

The Sign Function

This function returns a +1, 0, or −1, depending on the value of the argument. For example: SGN(16.67) = +1, SGN(−16.67) = −1, and SGN(16 − 16) = 0. Observe Example 7.7.

Example 7.7
Using the SGN function

```
100 I = -3
110 IF I > 3 THEN 999
120 PRINT SGN(I), SGN(I*2), SGN(3+I)
130 I = I + 1
140 GO TO 110
999 END

READY

RUNNH
-1             -1              0
-1             -1              1
-1             -1              1
 0              0              1
 1              1              1
 1              1              1
 1              1              1

READY
```

Miscellaneous Functions

The function ABS(−10) will always return a positive value. In this example, it would be 10. The PI will always return the constant 3.1415159. The function FIX(arg) will only return the integer portion of a value (note, it is a little different than INT). The function SQR(25) will return the value 5. Statement 120 in Example 7.8 illustrates the use of these functions.

94

Example 7.8
Using the ABS, SQR, FIX, INT, and PI functions

```
100 I = 1
110 IF I > 5 THEN 999
120 PRINT ABS(I-5), SQR(I), FIX(I-1.7), INT(I-1.7), PI
130 I = I + 1
140 GO TO 110
999 END

READY

RUNNH
4         1           0        -1        3.14159
3         1.41421     0         0        3.14159
2         1.73205     1         1        3.14159
1         2           2         2        3.14159
0         2.23607     3         3        3.14159

READY
```

The PRINT USING Statement

One of the advantages of the BASIC language is its number of options for editing of printed reports. In order to edit output, a special form of the PRINT statement is used.

The general format of the PRINT USING statement is:

> n PRINT USING "string", list

where *PRINT and USING* are reserved words, *"string"* is a format field or fields, the *comma* is a required delimiter, and *list* is a list of values to be displayed in the format(s) specified by the format field(s). All characters in the string are displayed except for the editing symbols. The string, or portions of it, are repeated until the list is completed.

Numeric Fields

The # character is the edit character for a numeric digit. Any decimal arrangement can be made. The format field will round decimal values when necessary and suppress leading zeros. When a value is too large for a format to be displayed, the % character is printed to indicate that the value is too large. Example 7.9 has one numeric format field. Leading zeros are suppressed, and all values are edited one at a time until there are no more values in the list. The value 4444 is too large for the edit format, so the % is displayed before the value to alert the programmer to the error.

Example 7.10 has a numeric format field with two-decimal-place accuracy. Leading zeros are suppressed except for one zero to the left of a decimal point. The values are edited one at a time and displayed with all decimal points lined up. Since the value 1234 is too large for the edit format, the % is displayed.

Example 7.9
Suppressing leading zeros in a numeric field

```
100 PRINT USING '###', 0, 1, 22, -22, 333, 4444
999 END

READY

RUNNH
   0
   1
  22
 -22
 333
% 4444

READY
```

Example 7.10
Suppressing leading zeros and alignment of decimal points

```
100 PRINT USING '###.##', .1267, 1.267, -12.67, 126.7, 1267
999 END

READY

RUNNH
   0.13
   1.27
 -12.67
 126.70
% 1267

READY
```

Comma and Minus Sign

To print a minus sign after a value rather than before it, the format has a trailing minus sign. A sign in the format in any other position will be treated as a character to be displayed. If commas are to be displayed by the format, insert one or more in the proper location to the left of the decimal point; however, only one comma is necessary. If commas are inserted incorrectly in the format, the computer may shorten or lengthen the number of digits to be displayed.

Example 7.11 illustrates the use of the comma. Notice the zero suppression, the alignment of decimal points, the placement of commas, and the error for the value 12345678.

Example 7.11
Using commas in a numeric format field

```
100 PRINT USING '#,###,###.##',0, 2.345, -1111, 1234567, 12345678
999 END

READY

RUNNH
        0.00
        2.35
   -1,111.00
1,234,567.00
% .123457E 8

READY
```

Example 7.12 uses a trailing minus sign in the format field. All values that are negative have a minus sign displayed as the last character in the field.

Example 7.12
Using the minus sign in a numeric format field

```
100 PRINT USING '#,###.##-', 2.345, -234, 7654, -8765, 12345
999 END

READY

RUNNH
     2.35
   234.00-
 7,654.00
 8,765.00-
% 12345

READY
```

Example 7.13 has two numeric format fields. The data will be displayed two values per line with the editing called for by the edit characters. The values −1234 and 12345 are too large for the format #, ### and are treated as errors.

Example 7.13
Using more than one numeric format field in the same statement

```
100 PRINT USING '##,###- #,###', 123, 123, -1234, -1234,
               12345, 12345
999 END

READY

RUNNH
   123     123
 1,234- %-1234
12,345  % 12345

READY
```

Example 7.14 uses a single $ as an edit character in the format field. This will cause the $ to be printed in the same position for every value. There will also be normal editing, such as zero suppression, insertion of commas, alignment of decimals, and detection of data fields in error.

Example 7.14
Using the $ as the first character in a numeric format field

```
100 PRINT USING '$#,###.##', .1, 10, 100, 1000, 10000, -10
999 END

READY

RUNNH
$     0.10
$    10.00
$   100.00
$1,000.00
$% 10000
$   -10.00

READY
```

Example 7.15 is similar to Example 7.14. The differences are: the $ will float to the closest significant digit to the left of the decimal point because $$ (called the floating dollar sign) was used as the edit character, and minus values are not allowed unless a trailing minus sign is used in the format. The value 100000 is too large, and − 10 is invalid.

Example 7.15
Using a floating dollar sign in a numeric format field

```
100 PRINT USING '$$###.##', .1, 10, 100, 1000, 10000, -10
999 END

READY

RUNNH
    $0.10
   $10.00
  $100.00
 $1000.00
% 10000
?BAD NUMBER IN PRINT-USING AT LINE 100

READY
```

Example 7.16 has several numeric format fields. The $$$# and $$$$ will cause data to be edited, but usually not in the way the programmer intended. Do not create these types of formats. Notice the format field − ##. It should be ##−; otherwise the − will always be displayed for a value (not as an edit character), and if the value is negative two minus signs will be displayed.

Example 7.16
Using numeric format fields in the wrong way

```
100 PRINT USING '-## $### $### $$## $$$$', -1, 2, 3, 4, 5, 6, 7
999 END

READY

RUNNH
--1  $   2    $3  $4$5  $6$7

READY
```

Example 7.17 is an asterisk fill format field. Instead of suppressing zeros with spaces, the position is filled with an *. There must only be two asterisks in this type

Example 7.17
Using an asterisk fill in a numeric format field

```
100 PRINT USING '**##.##', 0, .167, 123, 1234.5,
                          12345, 123E4, -13
999 END

READY

RUNNH
***0.00
***0.17
*123.00
1234.50
% 12345
% .123E 7
?BAD NUMBER IN PRINT-USING AT LINE 100

READY
```

of format field. The value 12345 is too large for the format field, and when using an asterisk fill, exponential data cannot be used. Therefore the value 123E4 is considered invalid data. To edit a minus value, an asterisk fill format must use a trailing minus sign (just like the floating dollar sign).

Example 7.18 shows examples of incorrect asterisk fill fields. The field *### is a valid edit, but not an asterisk fill. It will always print an * as the first character and then edit the data accordingly.

Example 7.18
Using asterisk fill format fields in the wrong way

```
100 PRINT USING '*###  *###  *###  *###', 1, 2, 3, 4, 5, 6, -7
999 END

READY

RUNNH
*  1   ***2  *3*4  *5*6
*  -7

READY
```

Exponential

When the exponential form of a value is needed, the format of the string is: ##^^^^. Actually, any number of pound signs may be used, but there must be four carat characters. The significant digits are left justified, and the exponent is adjusted. The exponential format cannot be used with asterisk fill, floating dollar sign, or trailing minus sign format fields.

Example 7.19 illustrates the use of one exponential format field, and Example 7.20 illustrates the use of two exponential format fields and a numeric format

Example 7.19
Using the exponential numeric format field

```
100 PRINT USING '##^^^^', .1111, 22.22, 3333, 4444.4444
999 END

READY

RUNNH
11E-02
22E 00
33E 02
44E 02

READY
```

Example 7.20
Using more than one exponential numeric format field

```
100 PRINT USING '#####^^^^  ##^^^^  #####',
    11, 11, 11, 2222, 2222, 2222
999 END

READY

RUNNH
11000E-03  11E 00     11
22220E-01  22E 02   2222

READY
```

field. The number of spaces left between format fields will also be left between the
fields displayed after the execution of the statement.

Nonnumeric Fields

Messages, labels, headings, string variables, etc. may be displayed with the
PRINT USING. Example 7.21 uses the message TOTAL and a numeric format. The
message will display on each line with a numeric value.

Example 7.21
Using nonnumeric constants with a numeric format field

```
100 PRINT USING 'TOTAL   #,###', 10, 20, 30, -40
999 END

READY

RUNNH
TOTAL      10
TOTAL      20
TOTAL      30
TOTAL     -40

READY
```

Example 7.22 illustrates that a format may be placed in a literal, given a string
variable name, and then used in the PRINT USING statement. Notice F$ in
statement 100. When used in statement 110, the F$ is just like the format
"X= #, ### Y= #,###". X= and Y= will be displayed on each line. This
method of using a format will simplify some programming problems with editing.

Example 7.22
Using a string variable for a format

```
100 LET F$ = 'X= #,###   Y= #,###'
110 PRINT USING F$, 10, 5, 20, 15, 30, 20, -40, -35
999 END

READY

RUNNH
X=      10   Y=       5
X=      20   Y=      15
X=      30   Y=      20
X=     -40   Y=     -35

READY
```

Example 7.23 uses only string data for headings in statements 100 and 110.
These data, along with all blanks in the string, are displayed when these statements are executed. Statement 140 has many spaces between two numeric format
fields to center the data under the proper column headings.

Example 7.24 illustrates that string variables may be used with a PRINT USING
statement. Insert a pair of backslashes in the positions where the data are to be
displayed. The backslashes reserve n + 2 character positions where n is the
number of spaces between the two backslashes. Notice the spacing between the

Example 7.23
Using nonnumeric constants as a heading

```
100 PRINT USING '     STATE UNIVERSITY'
110 PRINT USING 'GPA               STUDENT NUMBER'
120 READ G, N
130 IF N = 0 THEN 999
140 PRINT USING '#.##              #########', G, N
150 GO TO 120
900 DATA 2.61, 145247357, 3.43, 475823614, 2.87, 773283758
902 DATA 3.06, 323857238, 0, 0
999 END

READY

RUNNH
      STATE UNIVERSITY
GPA               STUDENT NUMBER
2.61              145247357
3.43              475823614
2.87              773283758
3.06              323857238

READY
```

Example 7.24
Using format fields for nonnumeric data

```
100 PRINT USING '     STATE UNIVERSITY'
110 PRINT USING 'GPA     NAME          STUDENT NUMBER'
120 READ G, N, N$
130 IF N = 0 THEN 999
140 PRINT USING '#.##  \      \  #########', G, N$, N
150 GO TO 120
900 DATA 2.61, 145247357, BARBER
901 DATA 3.43, 475823614, JAMES
902 DATA 2.87, 773283758, WINSLOW
903 DATA 3.06, 323857238, WAYNE
904 DATA 0,0,0
999 END

READY

RUNNH
      STATE UNIVERSITY
GPA   NAME      STUDENT NUMBER
2.61  BARBER    145247357
3.43  JAMES     475823614
2.87  WINSLOW   773283758
3.06  WAYNE     323857238

READY
```

format fields and within the string format field in statement 140. G and N provide the numeric variable data and N$ provides the string variable data where the string data are always left justified in the format field.

The Digital Equipment Corporation recommends that backslashes not be used for string variable fields on a VAX-11 (although they are valid and will work). The VAX-11 has several additional edit characters for string data. They are:

1. ' (single quotation mark), which starts every string field.
2. L, which left-justifies fields and reserves a place for one character. Strings too long to fit the format field are truncated starting with the rightmost character.
3. R, which right-justifies fields and reserves a place for one character. Strings too long to fit the format field are truncated starting with the rightmost character.

4. C centers the string and reserves a place for one character. If the string cannot be exactly centered, the string is displayed one character off center to the left. Strings too long to fit the format field are left-justified and truncated starting with the rightmost character.
5. E expands the field as necessary to display the entire string and reserves a place for one character. If the string is smaller than the format field, the data are left justified.

Some examples are:

100 PRINT USING " 'LLLLL", "DEC"   ! WILL DISPLAY DEC LEFT
                                     JUSTIFIED
100 PRINT USING " 'RRRRR",
    "DEC"   ! WILL DISPLAY DEC RIGHT
                                     JUSTIFIED
100 PRINT USING " 'CCCCC",
    "DEC"   ! WILL CENTER DEC WITHIN
                                     THE 5 POSITIONS
100 PRINT USING " 'E", "DEC"   ! WILL EXPAND THE FIELD TO
                                     3 POSITIONS

Exceeding Allowable Number of Digits

Six significant digits may be used with single-precision data fields, and 15 (PDP-11) and 16 (VAX-11) significant digits may be used with double-precision fields. (Check with the computer center to determine significant digits for the computer being used.) If an attempt is made to display a value larger than single or double precision allows, zeros are substituted for all digits following the last significant digit. Example 7.25 allows for 15 significant digits; however, the value contains 19 digits. Notice that the last four digit spaces have been filled with zeros.

Example 7.25
Exceeding the allowable number of significant digits

```
100 PRINT USING '$$$,$$$,$$$,$$$,$$$,$$$,$$$,$$$',
    1234567890123456789
999 END

READY

RUNNH
    $1,234,567,890,123,460,000

READY
```

Quotes

There are two types of quote symbols available in the language. The " symbol has been used to identify string data in most examples in the text. The ' may also be used. Both may be used in the same statement. Examples are:

100 PRINT "GENERAL HOSPITAL"	! WILL DISPLAY GENERAL HOSPITAL
100 PRINT 'GENERAL HOSPITAL'	! WILL ALSO DISPLAY GENERAL HOSPITAL
100 PRINT "ST. MARY'S HOSPITAL"	! WILL DISPLAY ST. MARY'S HOSPITAL
100 PRINT 'WHO SAID, "TO BE OR NOT TO BE"?'	! WILL DISPLAY WHO SAID, "TO BE OR NOT TO BE"?

The RESTORE Statement

The purpose of the RESTORE statement is to allow a program to reuse the same DATA statements in a program as many times as needed.

The general format of the RESTORE statement is;

n RESTORE

where RESTORE is a reserved word.

Example 7.26 uses the RESTORE statement. At statement 100, $X = 4$ and $Y = 1$. After T1 is calculated, its value is 25. At statement 130, the data value pointer is reset to the first value in the DATA statement. The values for statement 140 are $A = 4$ and $B = 1$, and after T2 is calculated its value is 6.

Example 7.26
Using the RESTORE statement

```
100 READ X, Y
110 LET T1 = (X+Y)**2
120 PRINT T1
130 RESTORE
140 READ A,B
150 LET T2 = (A-B)*2
160 PRINT T2
900 DATA 4,1,20,10
999 END

READY

RUNNH
 25
 6

READY
```

When large amounts of data in the DATA statements may exceed internal storage capacity, or certain problems require the use of the same data more than once, the RESTORE statement can be used.

The INPUT Statement

The INPUT statement allows data to be entered into a program from an external device. If this device is a terminal, then good programming dictates that a PRINT statement be used with an INPUT statement to inform the user of the terminal what data to enter. Another form of the INPUT statement allows the insertion of string data before variables are input.

Either a comma, a semicolon, or a blank can be used after the string data if only one string is in the INPUT statement. The comma and the semicolon delimiters have the same function here as they did in the PRINT statement. The blank causes the ? to be printed on the next line. Example 7.27 shows the use of the PRINT and the INPUT separately. Notice where the ? appears when each of the INPUT statements are executed.

Example 7.27
Using the PRINT and INPUT for data entry from a terminal

```
100 PRINT "ENTER NAME AND AMOUNT";
110 INPUT N$, A
120 PRINT "ENTER NAME AND AMOUNT",
130 INPUT N$, A
140 PRINT "ENTER NAME AND AMOUNT"
150 INPUT N$, A
999 END

READY

RUNNH
ENTER NAME AND AMOUNT? STEVE,400
ENTER NAME AND AMOUNT       ? STEVE,400
ENTER NAME AND AMOUNT
? STEVE,400

READY
```

Example 7.28 replaces the PRINT statement with string data in the INPUT statement. Notice that the results are the same as for Example 7.27.

Example 7.28
Using a string as part of the INPUT statement

```
100 INPUT "ENTER NAME AND AMOUNT"; N$, A
110 INPUT "ENTER NAME AND AMOUNT", N$, A
120 INPUT "ENTER NAME AND AMOUNT"  N$, A
999 END

READY

RUNNH
ENTER NAME AND AMOUNT? STEVE,400
ENTER NAME AND AMOUNT       ? STEVE,400
ENTER NAME AND AMOUNT
? STEVE,400

READY
```

If string data are placed between variables in an INPUT statement, Example 7.29 shows what will always be the result.

Example 7.29
Using multiple strings of data as part of the INPUT statement

```
100 INPUT "ENTER NAME"; N$; "ENTER AMOUNT"; A; "THANK YOU"
105 PRINT   !NOTE: AFTER A TRAILING STRING, YOU MUST
               INSERT A PRINT STATEMENT
110 INPUT "ENTER NAME", N$, "ENTER AMOUNT", A, "THANK YOU"
115 PRINT
120 INPUT "ENTER NAME"  N$  "ENTER AMOUNT"  A  "THANK YOU"
999 END

READY

RUNNH
ENTER NAME? STEVE
ENTER AMOUNT? 400
THANK YOU
ENTER NAME     ? STEVE
ENTER AMOUNT   ? 400
THANK YOU
ENTER NAME
? STEVE
ENTER AMOUNT
? 400
THANK YOU
READY
```

Common Errors

Statement	Explanation
100 X = SIN	Missing an argument for SIN.
100 Y = PI + SQR(ABS(I)	Missing a right parenthesis.
100 Z = B**A + LOG(SQR(I,J))	SQR can have only one argument.
100 PRINT USING ###, A	Must be "###" or '###'.
100 PRINT USING "##-##-##",X	Treats the string as 3 formats.
100 PRINT USING "##,##",Y	Place comma properly; otherwise, results may be in error.
100 PRINT USING "-$$#,###.##",X	Cannot have a sign in front of $$.
100 PRINT 'UCLA'S TEAM'	Use "UCLA'S TEAM".
100 INPUT "ENTER X , X	Missing ", should be X".
100 PRINT USING "\ \",N	Should be N$.
100 PRINT USING " 'LRR",N$	Cannot mix edit characters L and R.

Sample Programs

Problem Description 7.1

1. Statement of the problem: Calculate a table of common and natural logarithms for the values 10 through 15 in increments of .5.

2. Input: Assign the value 10 with a LET statement. Increment this value by .5 after the logarithms are determined and displayed until the value is equal to 15.

3. Output: Display the appropriate column headings and table of values.

Flowchart 7.1

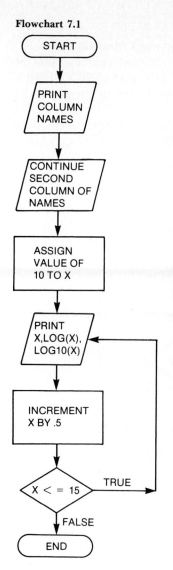

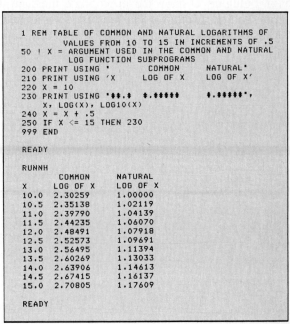

Problem Description 7.2

1. Statement of the problem: Use Euclid's algorithm to determine the greatest common divisor between two integers for an unknown number of sets of integers. Use the following arithmetic models:

$$A = INT(X/Y)$$

where X and Y are the two integers and INT determines the integer value of the division.

$$B = X - A*Y \qquad X = Y \qquad Y = B$$

where the final value of Y at the time B = 0 is the greatest common divisor.

2. Input: Enter two integers with an INPUT statement from a terminal after the message ENTER TWO INTEGERS. After the message ENTER YES TO CONTINUE OR NO TO STOP, enter the appropriate response. Use the sets of integers 24, 56 and 125, 275 for test data.

3. Output: Display the appropriate message, the two integers entered for input, and the value for the greatest common divisor for each set of integers processed by the program.

Flowchart 7.2

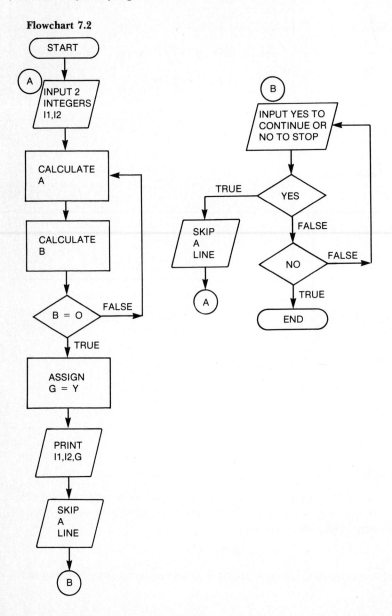

```
1 REM DETERMINES THE COMMON DIVISOR BETWEEN 2 INTEGERS
50 ! I1, I2 = INTEGERS        X, Y = TEMPORARY STORAGE OF I1,I2
   A, B = USED TO DETERMINE GREATEST COMMON DIVISOR
   G = GREATES COMMON DIVISOR
   F$ = STRING VARIABLE USED TO DEFINE PRINTING FORMAT
   R$ = RESPONSE TO CONTINUE RUNNING PROGRAM
190 PRINT
200 INPUT "ENTER 2 INTEGERS"; I1, I2
210 X = I1
220 Y = I2
230 A = INT(X/Y)
240 B = X - A*Y
250 IF B = 0 THEN 290
260 X = Y
270 Y = B
280 GO TO 230
290 G = Y
300 F$ = "INTEGER-1 = ####   INTEGER-2 = ####   GCD = ####"
310 PRINT USING F$, I1, I2, G
320 PRINT
330 INPUT "ENTER YES TO CONTINUE OR NO TO STOP", R$
340 IF R$ = "YES" THEN 190
350 IF R$ = "NO" THEN 999
360 GO TO 330
999 END

READY

RUNNH

ENTER 2 INTEGERS? 24,56
INTEGER-1 =    24  INTEGER-2 =    56  GCD =     8

ENTER YES TO CONTINUE OR NO TO STOP        ? YES

ENTER 2 INTEGERS? 125,275
INTEGER-1 =   125  INTEGER-2 =   275  GCD =    25

ENTER YES TO CONTINUE OR NO TO STOP        ? NO

READY
```

Problem Description 7.3

1.   Statement of the problem: Write a program to simulate the rolling of two dice to play the game of "craps." The program is to display if and how the game was won or lost.

2.   Input: Use a random-number generator to simulate the value of a die. The arithmetic model INT(6*RND + 1) will determine a value between 1 through 6.

3.   Output: Display appropriate messages to tell the players how they won or how they lost, what their point is, and the value of each roll of the dice until the point is made.

Flowchart 7.3

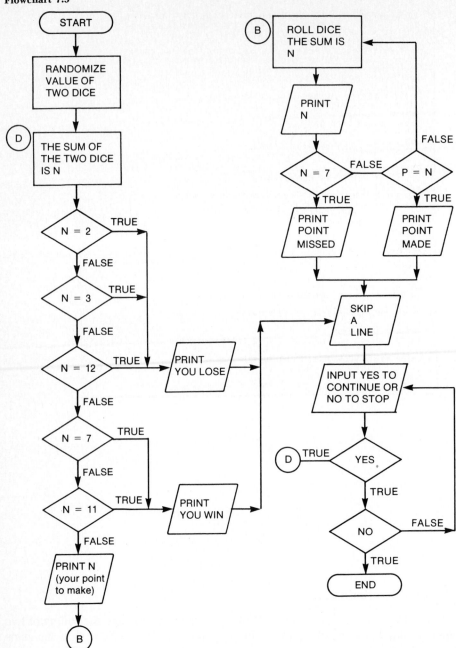

```
1 REM SIMULATING A GAME OF CRAPS
50 ! N1 = VALUE OF 1ST DIE ROLLED
     N2 = VALUE OF 2ND DIE ROLLED
      N = TOTAL OF TWO DICE
      P = TEMPORARY STORAGE OF N
100 RANDOMIZE
110 N1 = INT(6*RND+1)             ! FIND RND VALUE
120 N2 = INT(6*RND+1)             !  BETWEEN 1 AND 6
130 N = N1 + N2                   ! SUM THE DICE
140 IF N = 2 THEN 400             ! YOU LOSE
150 IF N = 3 THEN 400             !  ON THE
160 IF N =12 THEN 400             !     FIRST ROLL
170 IF N = 7 THEN 500             ! YOU WIN ON
180 IF N =11 THEN 500             !   THE FIRST ROLL
190 P = N
200 PRINT 'YOUR POINT IS'; P,
220 N1 = INT(6*RND+1)             ! ROLL
230 N2 = INT(6*RND+1)             !  THE DICE
240 N = N1 + N2                   !    AGAIN
245 PRINT N;
250 IF N = 7 THEN 600
260 IF P = N THEN 700             ! YOU WIN BY MAKING YOUR POINT
270 GO TO 220
400 PRINT 'YOU LOSE, YOU THREW A'; N; 'ON THE FIRST ROLL'
410 GO TO 800
500 PRINT 'YOU WIN, A'; N; 'ON YOUR FIRST ROLL'
510 GO TO 800
600 PRINT
610 PRINT 'YOU LOSE, MISSED YOUR POINT'
620 GO TO 800
700 PRINT
710 PRINT 'YOU WIN, MADE YOUR POINT'
800 PRINT
805 INPUT 'ENTER Y TO CONTINUE OR N TO STOP'; R$
807 PRINT
810 IF R$ = 'Y' THEN 110
820 IF R$ = 'N' THEN 999
830 GO TO 800
999 END

Ready

RUNNH
YOUR POINT IS 10                5  10
YOU WIN, MADE YOUR POINT

ENTER Y TO CONTINUE OR N TO STOP? Y

YOUR POINT IS 6                9  2  5  9  6
YOU WIN, MADE YOUR POINT

ENTER Y TO CONTINUE OR N TO STOP? Y

YOUR POINT IS 8                6  7
YOU LOSE, MISSED YOUR POINT

ENTER Y TO CONTINUE OR N TO STOP? N

Ready
```

Problem Description 7.4

1.   Statement of the problem: Two ranger stations located 10 miles apart in Tall Mountain National Park are on the constant lookout for fires. Electronic equipment allows them to determine that a fire is a certain angle from each of the stations. Station A can dispatch a firefighting unit that can travel toward the fire at 10 miles per hour. Given the angles of the fire from the stations, how far away in miles is the fire and how long will it take to arrive at the fire in minutes

(The law of sines is: given two angles and the length of one side, the length of the other two sides can be determined.)

Given:

$$C = 10 \, SIN(C)/SIN(B)$$

where

B = 180 − (A+B)
1 degree = PI/180 in radians

2.   Input: Enter two angles with a READ statement.
3.   Output: For each pair of angles entered, display the two answers with appropriate messages.

Flowchart 7.4

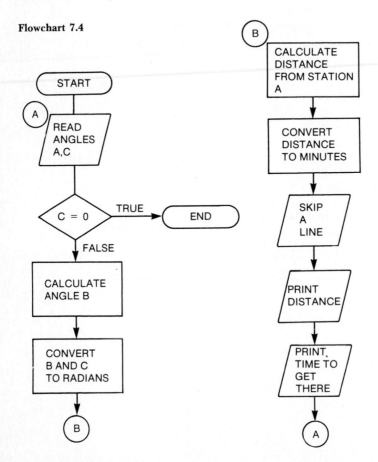

```
1 REM USING LAW OF SINES TO DETERMINE THE DISTANCE
     FROM ONE POINT TO ANOTHER
50 ! A, C = GIVEN ANGLES
     B = DETERMINED ANGLE
   R1 = ANGLE A IN RADIANS
   R2 = ANGLE C IN RADIANS
    D = DISTANCE BETWEEN 2 POINTS
    T = TIME TO TRAVEL DISTANCE IN MINUTES
100 READ A,C                          ! ENTER THE ANGLES A AND C
110 IF C = 0 THEN 999                 ! CHECK FOR END OF DATA
120 B = 180 - (A+C)                   ! FIND ANGLE B
130 R1 = B*(PI/180)                   ! CONVERT ANGLE B TO RADIANS
140 R2 = C*(PI/180)                   ! CONVERT ANGLE C TO RADIANS
150 D = 10*SIN(R2)/SIN(R1)            ! FIND THE DISTANCE FROM
                                        STATION A
160 T = (D/10)*60                     ! CONVERT TO MINUTES
170 PRINT
180 PRINT USING "DISTANCE IS ###.## MILES", D
190 PRINT USING "IT WILL TAKE ###.## MINUTES", T
200 GO TO 100
900 DATA 34,120,120,34
901 DATA 50,50,60,40
902 DATA 0,0
999 END

READY

RUNNH

DISTANCE IS  19.76 MILES
IT WILL TAKE 118.53 MINUTES

DISTANCE IS  12.76 MILES
IT WILL TAKE  76.54 MINUTES

DISTANCE IS   7.78 MILES
IT WILL TAKE  46.67 MINUTES

DISTANCE IS   6.53 MILES
IT WILL TAKE  39.16 MINUTES

READY
```

112

Exercises

1. What is the purpose of an argument in an internal function subprogram?
2. What are the following PRINT USING edit characters used for?
   - *a.* #
   - *b.* \
   - *c.* *
   - *d.* $
   - *e.* ^
3. Write PRINT USING statements that would print according to the following:
   - *a.* Three numeric variables, A, B, and C, are rounded to two decimal places with four digits to the left of the decimal point. Have each number printed on a separate line. Edit the numbers with a floating dollar sign and a comma.
   - *b.* Perform the same operations as in a above, except print all numbers on one line with each number separated by appropriated heading identifiers, such as A IS.
   - *c.* Print four nonnumeric variables, A$, B$, C$, and D$, five positions in length on four separate lines.
4. Write a program to produce a table of numbers from 100 to 500 in increments of 25. For each number include on the same line the square root of the number, the square of the number, and the common logarithm of the number. Include appropriate headings using Sample Program 7.1 as a model. Edit the numbers with the PRINT USING statement to obtain three-decimal accuracy for the square root and common logs, and edit with commas for the square of the number.
5. Rewrite Exercise 5 in Chapter 6 using a PRINT USING statement.
6. Rewrite Exercise 8 in Chapter 6 using a PRINT USING statement. Have the Celsius temperature printed out with two-decimal-place accuracy.
7. Write a program with one READ statement to solve the following inventory control problem.
   - *a.* If the number of items on hand listed on any data record is greater than or equal to the reorder point, do not process the data record; enter the next data record instead.
   - *b.* If the number on hand is less than the reorder point, subtract the number on hand from the stock maximum.
   - *c.* Subtract the amount on order from the results of b above. The result is the number of units to order. If this number (of units to order) is zero or negative, the processing of the record is finished. Enter the next data record.
   - *d.* Multiply the number of units to order by the unit price. The result is the total cost for that type of unit.
   - *e.* Accumulate the total reorder cost of all type of units.
   - *f.* The output should have the exact headings, vertical spacing, and horizontal spacing as shown under OUTPUT below.

g. Use the data records listed under DATA; however, your program must allow for an unknown number of data records.

DATA:

Item number	Cost per unit	Amount on order	Number on hand	Reorder point	Stock maximum
12345	6.00	135	120	125	150
12456	3.25	150	110	100	260
34567	0.20	600	300	800	950
45678	5.00	0	400	450	500
56789	7.70	100	200	200	300
67890	4.50	150	300	500	700

OUTPUT:

(YOUR NAME)
INVENTORY REPORT

ITEM NUMBER	UNITS TO ORDER	UNIT COST	TOTAL COST
XXXXX	XXX	$XXX.XX	$X,XXX.XX
	TOTAL INVENTORY ORDERED		$XX,XXX.XX

Chapter Eight

Structured Programming

Over the last several chapters, major attention has been given to the syntax of the BASIC language—that is, the rules of constructing individual program instructions. Little attention has been given to program development except that standard flowcharts have been used to represent the logic of a program. Structured programming is an additional approach to program development that usually results in more efficient code, less time spent on development, program logic that is easier to follow, and a resultant program that is easier to debug and modify.

Structure Charts

Structured programming's major emphasis is to divide a program into manageable segments or modules that can be developed and tested separately. Structure charts portray the purpose of each module and how they are related to each other and also show the level of detail represented in each module. The programmer first defines the program in general terms and then proceeds to define it in more detail. The emphasis is on *what* must be done, not on *how*. Consider a simple application represented by the structure chart shown in Figure 8.1.

From Figure 8.1, several concepts of structured programming can be illustrated.

1. The purpose of the main module, or driver module, is to direct each module below it to be executed in sequence from left to right.
2. If any module is further subdivided, the module's purpose is to direct each module below it to be executed in sequence from left to right. As an example, the module labeled "Determine taxes" is further defined in detail by three modules: *(a)* "Determine FICA taxes", *(b)* "Determine federal taxes", and *(c)*

Figure 8.1
Structure chart of a payroll program

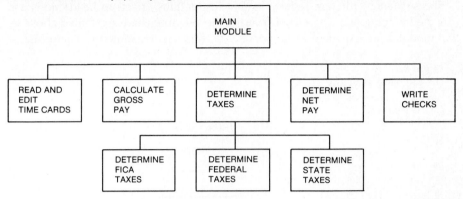

"Determine state taxes". The "Determine taxes" module would direct the three modules below it to be executed in sequence.

3. Each module has one entry point and one exit point. The program would be executed in the following manner:

    a. The main module would first transfer control of the program to the first module, "Read and edit time cards".

    b. The first module would complete all of its instructions, then transfer control back to the main module.

    c. The main module would transfer control to the second module, "Calculate gross pay"; that module would complete its instructions and then transfer control back to the main module.

    d. The main module would transfer control to the "Determine taxes" module, which in turn would transfer control to the three modules below it in sequence. Then, when FICA taxes, federal taxes, and state taxes had been determined, control would be transferred back to the main module. Then the pattern would be repeated for subsequent modules.

4. Each module represents several program instructions and may actually be a subroutine, as will be shown in Chapter 11. The emphasis in structure charts is on what must be done and in what sequence rather than on how it is done. For example, program instructions to determine federal income taxes would require several instructions to fully define the amount of the federal income tax. During the initial development of a program, the programmer is concerned with defining in general terms what must be done; the specific instructions are then defined in detail.

Program Structures

One premise of structured programming is that any set of instructions can be represented by one of three simple program structures: (1) the sequence, (2) the dowhile and (3) the if-then-else structure.

Sequence Structure

The sequence structure represents that instructions or sets of instructions are executed in sequence. This closely follows the structure charts explained above in that modules are executed in sequence. The flowchart is shown in Figure 8.2.

Figure 8.2
The sequence structure

Read name, hours worked, pay rate.
Calculate gross pay.
Write name, gross pay.

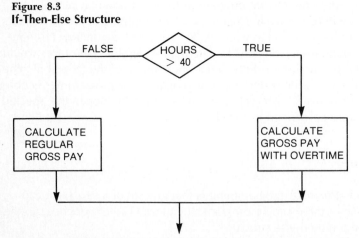

If-then-else Structure

The if-then-else structure allows for alternative paths through a program depending on a condition being tested. Consider the flowchart illustrated in Figure 8.3, which tests the number of hours a person works and calculates gross pay with

Figure 8.3
If-Then-Else Structure

If hours greater than 40 calculate gross with overtime else calculate regular gross pay endif.

overtime if hours are greater than 40 and otherwise calculates regular gross pay. In either case, the program continues in sequence.

Dowhile Structure

In the dowhile structure, instructions or sets of instructions will be executed so long as some tested condition exists. This is an iteration or looping technique. In the flowchart in Figure 8.4, the set of instructions for reading, calculating, and writing will be executed while there are more data.

Figure 8.4
The dowhile structure

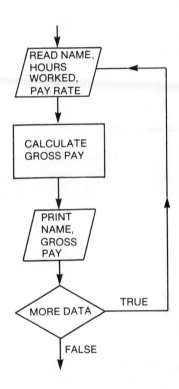

Dowhile there are more data
    Read name, hours worked, pay rate
    Calculate gross pay
    Print name, gross pay
Enddo

Structure Combinations

The flowchart in Figure 8.5 illustrates how a program would use these three structures in combination.

Pseudo Code

Next to each of the previous flowcharts, an English-like interpretation of each operation, called pseudocode, is illustrated in table form. Pseudocode is essentially a way that a programmer can write out in English the steps necessary to solve a problem: what operations must be performed and in what sequence. The programmer may use either flowcharts or pseudocode to map out the logic and

118

Figure 8.5
Structure Combinations

Dowhile there are more data
 Read name, hours, pay rate
 If hours greater than 40 calculate gross with overtime
 else calculate regular gross pay
 Endif
 Print name, gross pay
Enddo

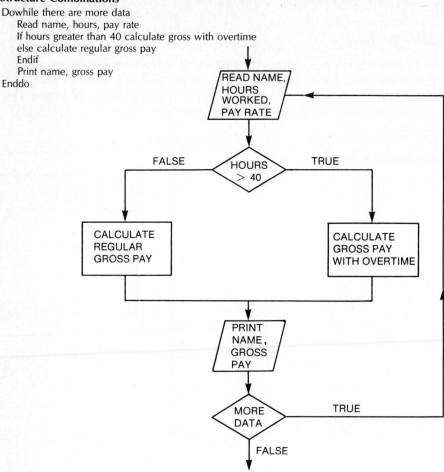

then write the actual program instructions on that basis. Note the use of the words *endif* and *enddo*. These pseudowords are simply a means to show when an operation has ended. After the endif, the logic continues with the next statement or operation. An enddo signifies that everything before the enddo is repeated; when the repetitions are completed, the program will continue with the next operation specified.

Standards

It is very important that programs be well documented. Programs must often be changed or updated, and many times the person who wrote the program is not the one who is available to do the job. Many computer installations have coding standards for their programmers. A few of the typical standards are:

1.   Program identification: The first thing to be documented about a program is what problem it solves. This is best done by using remarks or comments as the beginning statements. In addition, any subroutines or subprograms should be documented. A liberal use of comments throughout the program allows the programmer to set off ideas or techniques and emphasize them for easier debugging and for more clarity if the program is reviewed at a later date.

2.   Data dictionary: All programmer-supplied names should be defined. This is typically done with comments following the definition of the problem.

3.   Indenting: Whenever nested IF statements are used, indenting the IF or the ELSE words usually will allow a reader to better follow the logic of the program. The same is true for FOR/NEXT statements.

Exercises

1.   What are the advantages of structured programming?

2.   What BASIC statements would be used to effect the dowhile structure? the if-then-else structure?

3.   Write pseudocode and a flowchart that could be used to solve a payroll program in the determination of net pay. Gross pay is calculated by multiplying the hours worked by the pay rate. Federal income tax is determined by multiplying $20 times the number of exemptions and subtracting this amount from gross pay to obtain taxable income. The taxable income thus determined is taxes at the rate of 25%. Net pay is determined by subtracting taxes from gross pay. If a person works more than 40 hours in a week, overtime pay is calculated at 1.5 times the normal pay rate. Have the program determine and print out gross pay, taxes, net pay, the person's name, and the totals for each field for all employees. Have the program work for any number of employees.

4.   Write pseudocode and a flowchart for an interactive program that would ask for a person's name, height, and weight. Determine the ratio between the person's weight in pounds and the person's height in inches. If the determined ratio is more than 2.5, have the program print a message informing the person that he or she is overweight; otherwise print a message that the person's ratio is satisfactory. Have the pseudocode indicate that a yes/no response is necessary to continue the program for another person.

Chapter Nine

Intermediate Looping

Most programs require looping—that is, performing a sequence of instructions over and over again. Example 9.1 is a simple example of looping using the transfer instruction discussed in Chapter 6.

Example 9.1
Looping using a simple IF statement

```
100 X = 1
110 IF X > 5 THEN 999
120 PRINT X,
130 X = X + 1
140 GO TO 110
999 END

Ready

RUNNH
 1              2              3              4              5
Ready
```

This technique requires counting the number of times a set of statements is to be executed and then counting the operations of the program to determine if it has completed the required number of loops. This method is not always the most convenient way of looping in a program. There are other statements to use in situations that require loops.

The FOR/NEXT Statements

The FOR/NEXT statements are controlled transfer statements. The purpose of these statements is to provide the operations necessary for looping (iterating) a set of statements for a specific number of times.

The general format of the FOR/NEXT statements is:

n FOR variable = expression-1 TO expression-2 STEP expression-3

n NEXT variable

where *FOR* is a reserved word which initializes the conditions which must exist for the first execution of the loop, *variable* is a programmer-supplied name that contains values that are used during the execution of the loop, = means to move the value of expression-1 to the variable, *expression-1* is the initial value to be used in the loop, *TO* is a reserved word, *expression-2* is the value that determines when the loop is to be terminated, *STEP* is an optional reserved word that increments the variable each time the loop is executed, and *expression-3* is the amount of the increment. *NEXT* is a reserved word which indicates this is the last statement within the range of the loop, and *variable* is the same programmer-supplied variable name as specified in the FOR statement.

Example 9.2 illustrates how a FOR/NEXT works.

Example 9.2
Looping using a FOR/NEXT set of statements

```
100 FOR N = 1 TO 5 STEP 1
110 PRINT N,
120 NEXT N
130 PRINT
140 PRINT "THE PRESENT VALUE OF N IS"; N
999 END

Ready

RUNNH
 1              2              3              4              5
THE PRESENT VALUE OF N IS 5

Ready
```

The range of the loop is from statement 100 through statement 120. When statement 100 is executed, it compares the value 1 to the value 5. As long as expression-1 (1) is not greater than expression-2 (5), it will continue to execute the loop. Whenever expression-1 is greater than expression-2, the next statement to be executed is the statement following the NEXT (statement 130). Since in this example expression-1 does not present a condition to "get out of the loop" the first time it is executed, N takes on the value 1, and the next statement within the loop is executed. At the NEXT statement, statement 120, the computer asks the question to itself, "if expression-3 is added to expression-1, would the value be greater than expression-2"? If not, then an internal transfer is made to the STEP where expression-3 is in fact added to expression-1, and that result is placed in the variable N. This sequence is then followed until, at the NEXT statement, expression-1 would be greater in value than expression-2. Then the next statement following NEXT in the program is executed.

In the above example, the loop is executed five times, starting with N having the value 1 and incrementing it by 1 each time through the loop. When the loop is terminated, the present value of N is 5.

The STEP reserved word may be omitted along with expression-3. When it is omitted, the expression-3 is always assumed to be +1. The STEP may be a positive value, a negative value, an integer, a fraction, an algorithm, and so forth.

Given the following statements:

```
100 FOR N = 1 TO 10 STEP 2
110 NEXT N
```

the values of N would be 1, 3, 5, 7, 9. The loop would be executed five times. The value of N would be 9 when the loop was terminated.

In the next set of statements:

```
100 FOR N = 10 TO 0 STEP −2
110 NEXT N
```

the values of N would be 10, 8, 6, 4, 2, 0. The loop would be executed six times. The value of N would be 0 when the loop was terminated. Note that for negative STEP values, the loop continues until incrementing the expression-1 would cause it to be less than its final value.

Both negative and positive values can be used to control the loop. The statements:

```
100 FOR N = −3 TO 3
110 NEXT N
```

would cause N to have the values −3, −2, −1, 0, 1, 2, 3. The loop would be executed seven times, and the value of N would be 3 when the loop was terminated.

The STEP value does not have to be an integer. The statements:

```
100 FOR N = 0 TO 5 STEP 1.5
110 NEXT N
```

give N the values 0, 1.5, 3, 4.5. The loop would be executed four times, and the final value of N when the loop was terminated would be 4.5.

Be careful of using the following logic in your statements:

```
100 FOR N = 10 TO 5 STEP 1
110 NEXT N
```

Here, the value of N would be 10; however, since 10 is greater than 5 on the first conditional test, the loop would not be executed at all. The value of N would be 10 at the next statement after the NEXT statement. No statements within the range of the loop would be executed.

A similar problem would be caused with the statements:

```
100 FOR N = -5 TO -10
110 NEXT N
```

The value of N would be -5; however, since the assumed STEP is $+1$ and since -5 is greater than -10 in the first conditional test, the loop would not be executed at all. The value of N would be -5 at statement 120.

The following conditions should be observed when using FOR/NEXT statements:

1. Control can be transferred out of a loop with a PDP-11, but transfer into the range of the loop may cause unpredictable results. The VAX-11 will not allow either of these transfers. Good structured programming practices dictates that such transfers not be made.
2. If control is transferred to the statement number of the FOR, the loop will start completely over again.
3. The variable (index) can appear in a statement inside the range of the loop; however, if its value is changed it will affect the number of times the loop is executed.
4. There is no limit to the number of statements contained within the range of the loop.
5. Each FOR variable must have a NEXT variable with the same programmer-supplied name.

Programs frequently require a loop to appear with another loop (called nested loops). Figure 9.1 illustrates valid nested loops, and Figure 9.2 illustrates invalid nested loops.

Figure 9.1
Valid loops within loops

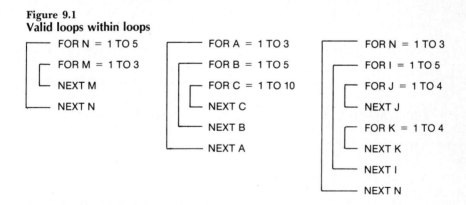

The following rules must be observed for nested loops:

1. The same rules apply for nested loops as for single loops.
2. There are limits as to how many nested loops may be used; these limits vary depending on the computer being used. For example, on a VAX-11 the limit is usually 12.

Figure 9.2
Invalid loops within loops

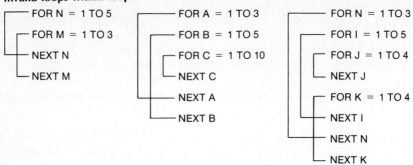

3. Each loop must be completely within the range of another loop.
4. Each loop must have different programmer-supplied variable names.
5. Inner loops are completely executed before outer loops are completed.

Examples of FOR/NEXT statements are:

```
100 FOR N = 1 TO 10          ! WILL SKIP 10 LINES ON THE
110 PRINT                    ! DISPLAY DEVICE
120 NEXT N
```
```
100 FOR I = 1 TO 100 STEP 2  ! WILL SUM ALL THE ODD
                               INTEGERS
110 S = S + I                ! FROM 1 to 100 AND SAVE
                               THE VALUE

120 NEXT I                   ! IN THE VARIABLE S
```
```
100 DATA 2,4,6,3,5           ! WILL READ 5 VALUES 1 AT A
                               TIME
110 FOR J = 1 TO 5           ! SUM THEM AND PRINT OUT
                               THE
120 READ N                   ! ANSWER 20 WHEN THE
                               LOOP IS
130 A = A + N                ! TERMINATED
140 NEXT J
150 PRINT A
```
```
100 N = 5                    ! WILL USE VARIABLES IN THE
110 M = 10                   ! EXPRESSIONS TO CONTROL
                               THE
120 P = .5                   ! EXECUTION OF THE LOOP
                               AND C
130 C = 0                    ! COUNTS THE NUMBER OF
                               TIMES
```

```
140 FOR A = N TO M STEP P        ! THE LOOP IS EXECUTED
150 C = C + 1
160 NEXT A

100 FOR A = 1 TO 5               ! A NEST OF 3 LOOPS WHERE
                                   THE
110 FOR B = 1 TO 4               ! A-LOOP IS EXECUTED 5
                                   TIMES THE
120 FOR C = 1 TO 3               ! B-LOOP IS EXECUTED (4*5)
                                   20 TIMES
130 N = N + 1                    ! AND THE C-LOOP IS
                                   EXECUTED (3*4*5)
140 NEXT C                       ! 60 TIMES
150 NEXT B                       ! N COUNTS THE NUMBER OF
                                   TIMES STATEMENT 140
160 NEXT A                       ! IS EXECUTED WHICH IS 60

100 FOR I = 1 TO 10              ! TWO NESTS OF TWO LOOPS
                                   WHERE N COUNTS
110 FOR J = 1 TO 5               ! THE NUMBER OF TIMES THE
                                   J-LOOP IS
120 N = N + 1                    ! EXECUTED (50) AND M
                                   COUNTS THE
130 NEXT J                       ! NUMBER OF TIMES THE K-
                                   LOOP IS
140 FOR K = 1 TO 3               ! EXECUTED (30)
150 M = M + 1
160 NEXT K
170 NEXT I

100 INPUT N                      ! ANY EXPRESSION CAN BE
                                   USED WITH
110 FOR X = −5 TO 5/N            ! THE FOR AND THE
                                   VARIABLES X AND Y
120 FOR Y = N to N*5             ! MAY BE USED IN AN
                                   EXPRESSION
130 PRINT X*Y                    ! WITHIN THE RANGE—BE
                                   CAREFUL—
140 NEXT Y                       ! DO NOT CHANGE THE X
                                   AND Y VALUES IN
150 NEXT X                       ! A STATEMENT WITHIN THE
                                   LOOP
```

The WHILE/NEXT Statements

The WHILE/NEXT statements are also used for looping. They differ from FOR/NEXT statements because they have no explicit control variable.

126

The general format for the WHILE/NEXT statements is:

n WHILE condition

n NEXT

where *WHILE* is a reserved word and *condition* is what controls the loop. *NEXT* is a reserved word which indicates that this is the last statement within the range of the loop. Notice it does not have a variable like the NEXT statement used with a FOR/NEXT.

Example 9.3 illustrates the use of a WHILE/NEXT loop that is executed five times.

Example 9.3
Looping using a WHILE/NEXT set of statements
```
100 WHILE X < 5
110 X = X + 1 \ PRINT X
120 NEXT
999 END

READY

RUNNH
1
2
3
4
5

READY
```

At statement 100 the condition X < 5 controls the loop. Statement 110 increments the variable X in the conditional expression, and the NEXT allows the loop to continue while the condition has not been satisfied. When X = 5 at statement 100, the remaining statements in the loop are executed, and the next time an attempt is made to execute the loop, the condition X < 5 is true, so the loop is terminated. Control is transferred to the statement following the NEXT statement.

When using a WHILE/NEXT loop, remember that the program must control the variable that is used in the conditional expression of the WHILE. If it does not, the loop executes indefinitely. When a program leaves a loop, the value of the variable controlling the loop is the last value it had during execution of the loop. In the above example, the value of X is 5 when the loop terminates.

The UNTIL/NEXT Statements

The UNTIL/NEXT statements are similar to the WHILE/NEXT statements. The general format for the UNTIL/NEXT statements is:

n UNTIL condition

n NEXT

> where *UNTIL* is a reserved word and *condition* is what controls the loop. *NEXT* is a reserved word with the same function it has when used with a WHILE statement.

Example 9.4 illustrates the use of an UNTIL/NEXT loop that is executed five times.

Example 9.4
Looping using an UNTIL/NEXT set of statements

```
100 UNTIL X = 5
110 X = X + 1 \ PRINT X
120 NEXT
999 END

READY

RUNNH
 1
 2
 3
 4
 5

READY
```

At statement 100 the condition X = 5 controls the loop. Statement 110 increments the variable X in the conditional expression, and the NEXT allows the loop to continue while the condition has not been satisfied. When X = 5 at statement 100, the loop is terminated, and control is transferred to the statement following the NEXT statement.

The following rules should be observed when using either the WHILE/NEXT or the UNTIL/NEXT statement.

1. Unless the initial conditional expression is false, the loop must increment or decrement a variable in the conditional expression.
2. Control can be transferred out of a loop, but transfer into the range of a loop may cause unpredictable results. Good structured programming practice dictates that such transfers not be made.
3. If control is transferred to the statement number of the WHILE or UNTIL, the loop will start over again, and the control variable in the conditional expression may or may not be logically correct for the program.
4. There is no limit to the number of statements within the range of the loop.
5. Each WHILE and UNTIL must have a NEXT as the last statement in the range.

Examples of WHILE/NEXT and UNTIL/NEXT statements are:

```
100 A,B = 5              ! WILL PRINT THE VALUES OF Z: 0, 3,
                           6, 9
110 WHILE Z < A + B      ! AND TERMINATE THE LOOP
120 PRINT Z              ! Z HAS A FINAL VALUE OF 12
130 Z = Z + 3
140 NEXT

100 N = 5                ! WILL PRINT THE VALUES OF N: 5, 7, 9
110 UNTIL N > 10         ! AND TERMINATE THE LOOP
120 PRINT N              ! N HAS A FINAL VALUE OF 11
130 N = N + 2
140 NEXT
```

Common Errors

Statement	Explanation
100 FOR N$ = 1 TO 5	N$ invalid, must be numeric variable.
100 FOR N = 1 TO 5 200 NEXT M	Either N or M invalid. Variable names must be the same for both FOR and NEXT.
100 FOR I = 1 TO 5 STEP .5 110 PRINT I 120 S = A * Z	Missing the NEXT statement.
100 FOR X = 3 TO 1 110 PRINT X 120 NEXT X	Would skip to statement 130 because 3 is larger than 1.
110 FOR A = −10 TO 0 120 INPUT X 130 IF X = 0 THEN 110 140 PRINT X 150 NEXT A	Might be a logic error. Statement 130 transfers out of loop when X = 0, to statement 110. This would set A = to −10 again.
110 FOR B = 1 TO 5 120 PRINT B 130 NEXT B . . . . 400 GO TO 120	Unpredictable results if transfer is made into the range of a FOR/NEXT loop. Poor programming practice.
100 FOR A = 1 TO 5 110 FOR B = 1 TO 3 120 PRINT A, B 130 NEXT A 140 NEXT B	Must complete inner loop first. Statements 130 and 140 should be reversed.
100 FOR X = 1 TO 5 110 READ X 120 NEXT X	READ X causes a conflict with the X in the FOR/NEXT.
100 WHILE A < 10 110 PRINT A 120 NEXT	Must increment the value of A or there is an infinite loop.
100 UNTIL B = 10 110 B = B + 3 120 NEXT	B will be 3, 6, 9, 12, etc. Infinite loop because B will never equal 10.

Sample Programs

Problem Description 9.1

1. Statement of the problem: Create a table of factorials (N!) from 1 to 10. The factorial of a number is found by multiplying the number by all positive integers less than the number. That is, N! for N = 5 is: 5*4*3*2*1 = 120. By definition the value of 0! is 1.

2. Input: Generate the values 1 through 10 within the program.

3. Output: Display the appropriate column names and in table form the values of N and N!. Suppress leading zeros.

Flowchart 9.1

Pseudocode 9.1

Print column names
Assign the value 1 to factorial
FOR N = 1 to 10
    Calculate new factorial
    Print number and factorial
Endfor
Endprogram

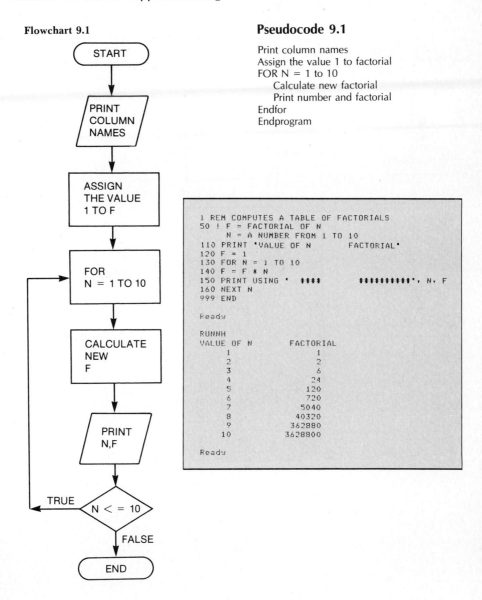

```
1 REM COMPUTES A TABLE OF FACTORIALS
50 ! F = FACTORIAL OF N
      N = A NUMBER FROM 1 TO 10
110 PRINT "VALUE OF N        FACTORIAL"
120 F = 1
130 FOR N = 1 TO 10
140 F = F * N
150 PRINT USING "   ####          ##########", N, F
160 NEXT N
999 END

Ready

RUNNH
VALUE OF N         FACTORIAL
    1                  1
    2                  2
    3                  6
    4                 24
    5                120
    6                720
    7               5040
    8              40320
    9             362880
   10            3628800

Ready
```

Problem Description 9.2

1.   Statement of the problem: Calculate a table that shows the conversion of miles per hour to kilometers per hour in increments of 5 miles per hour from 5 through 60. The arithmetic model is: (miles per hour) divided by (1/1.6093).

2.   Input: Generate the values 5 through 60 within the program.

3.   Output: Display a two-line heading for: CONVERSION TABLE PER HOUR. Also display the column names MILES and KILOMETERS and their values in table form. Suppress leading zeros, and allow for one-decimal-place accuracy for kilometers.

Flowchart 9.2

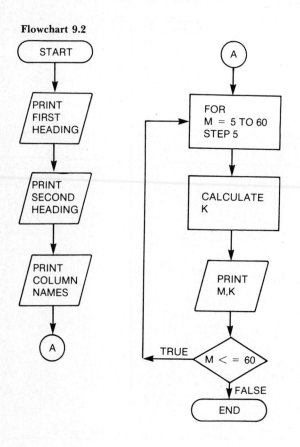

Pseudocode 9.2

Print headings
FOR miles = 5 to 60 step 5
    Calculate kilometers
    Print miles, kilometers
Endfor
Endprogram

```
1 REM CONVERTS MILES PER HOUR TO KILOMETERS PER HOUR
50 ! M = MILES PER HOUR
     K = KILOMETERS PER HOUR
100 PRINT USING "  CONVERSION TABLE"
101 PRINT USING "      PER HOUR"
102 PRINT USING "MILES     KILOMETERS"
110 FOR M = 5 TO 60 STEP 5
120 K = M / (1 / 1.6093)
130 PRINT USING "####      ####.#", M, K
140 NEXT M
999 END

Ready

RUNNH
   CONVERSION TABLE
      PER HOUR
MILES    KILOMETERS
  5         8.0
 10        16.1
 15        24.1
 20        32.2
 25        40.2
 30        48.3
 35        56.3
 40        64.4
 45        72.4
 50        80.5
 55        88.5
 60        96.6

Ready
```

Problem Description 9.3

1. Statement of the problem: It is not always known how many individuals will be taking a test on a given day or how many different tests will be given for several classes. Write a program that will accept an unknown number of scores for a particular test and provide for an unknown number of different tests. Find the lowest, highest, and average scores for each test.

2. Input: Use a READ statement to enter the number of scores for a particular test. If this number is zero, there are no more tests to process. Use a READ statement to enter the individual scores, one at a time, for each test.

3. Output: Display the appropriate messages for the lowest, highest, and average scores for each test.

Flowchart 9.3

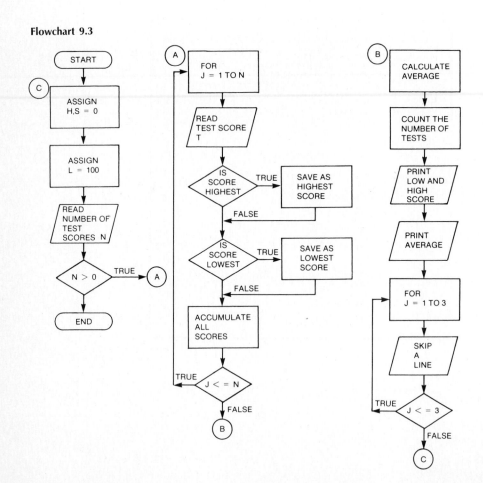

Pseudocode 9.3

Assign 0 to H and S
Assign 100 to L
Read number of test scores
Dowhile there are more tests to read
    For J = 1 to number of tests
        Read test score
        IF score is highest so far, save it as highest
        IF score is lowest so far, save it as lowest
        Add score to total
    Endfor
    Calculate average
    Count the number of tests
    Print low, high, and average
    FOR J = 1 to 3
        Skip a line
    Endfor
Enddo
Endprogram

```
1 REM DETERMINES LOWEST, HIGHEST AND AVERAGE
        SCORE FOR A PARTICULAR TEST
50 ! H = HIGHEST SCORE
     L = LOWEST SCORE
     S = SUM OF ALL SCORES
     N = NUMBER OF STUDENTS TAKING ONE TEST
     T = INDIVIDUAL TEST SCORE
     A = AVERAGE TEST SCORE
     C = NUMBER OF TESTS
100 H,S = 0
102 L = 100
110 READ N
120 IF N = 0 THEN 999            ! QUIT WHEN NO MORE SCORES
130 FOR J = 1 TO N               ! SET RANGE OF LOOP
140 READ T                       ! READ IN ONE SCORE AT A TIME
150 IF T <= H THEN 170           ! IF HIGH SCORE
160 H = T                        !    SAVE IT
170 IF T >= L THEN 190           ! IF LOW SCORE
180 L = T                        !    SAVE IT
190 S = S + T                    ! SUM THE SCORES
200 NEXT J                       ! END OF LOOP?
210 A = S / N                    ! AT END OF LOOP FIND AVERAGE
215 C = C + 1                    ! COUNT THE NUMBER OF TESTS
220 PRINT USING "LOW SCORE IS ### HIGH SCORE IS ###", L, H
230 PRINT USING "AVERAGE FOR TEST ## IS ###.##", C, A
260 FOR J = 1 TO 3               ! SET RANGE OF 2ND LOOP
270 PRINT                        ! SPACE A LINE
280 NEXT J                       ! END OF LOOP?
290 GO TO 100                    ! IS THERE ANOTHER TEST?
901 DATA 5
902 DATA 60, 70, 80, 90, 100
903 DATA 6
904 DATA 85, 75, 95, 95, 75, 85
905 DATA 0
999 END

Ready

RUNNH
LOW SCORE IS  60 HIGH SCORE IS 100
AVERAGE FOR TEST  1 IS  80.00


LOW SCORE IS  75 HIGH SCORE IS  95
AVERAGE FOR TEST  2 IS  85.00


Ready
```

134

Problem Description 9.4

1. Statement of the problem: Write a program to calculate a table showing the present value of $1 and $1,000 for percentages of from 10 through 15 in increments of 1%, for two years. The arithmetic model for present value is: $V = A/(1+P)^N$ where V is the present value, A is the dollar amount, P is the interest percentage, and N is the number of years.

2. Input: Generate all necessary values within the program.

3. Output: Display a message to indicate the dollar amount. Then, in table form, using appropriate column names, list the year, percent, and present value. Use appropriate edit fields with two-decimal-place accuracy for percent and present value fields.

Flowchart 9.4

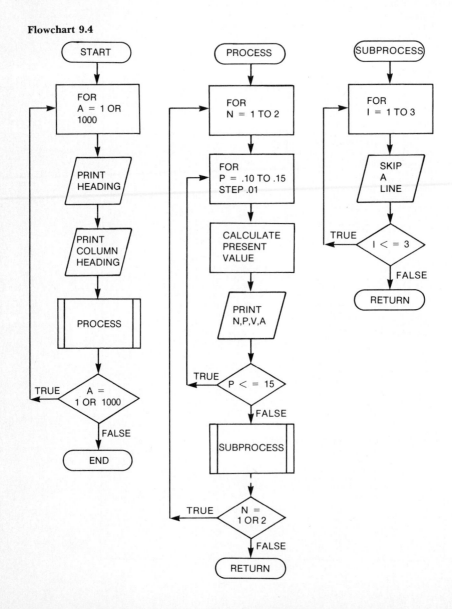

Pseudocode 9.4

Dowhile the dollar is $1 or $1,000
    Print headings
    FOR number of years = 1 to 2
        FOR percentages from .10 to .15 in increments of .01
            Calculate present value
            Print results
        Endfor
        FOR I = 1 to 3
            Skip a line
        Endfor
    Endfor
Enddo
Endprogram

```
1 REM PRESENT VALUE TABLE
50 ! A = CURRENT VALUE
     N = NUMBER OF YEARS
     P = PERCENTAGE VALUE
     V = PRESENT VALUE
100 FOR A = 1 TO 1000 STEP (1000 - A)
110 PRINT USING "    DOLLAR AMOUNT IS $$,$$$", A
120 PRINT USING "YEAR  PERCENT  PRESENT VALUE"
130 FOR N = 1 TO 2
140 FOR P = .10 TO .15 STEP .01
150 V = A / ((1 + P) ** N)
160 PRINT USING "$$$    $$.$$      $$$$.$$ ", N, P*100,V
170 NEXT P
180 FOR I = 1 TO 3
190 PRINT
200 NEXT I
210 NEXT N
220 NEXT A
999 END

Ready

RUNNH
     DOLLAR AMOUNT IS $     1
YEAR   PERCENT   PRESENT VALUE
  1     10.00         0.91
  1     11.00         0.90
  1     12.00         0.89
  1     13.00         0.88
  1     14.00         0.88
  1     15.00         0.87


  2     10.00         0.83
  2     11.00         0.81
  2     12.00         0.80
  2     13.00         0.78
  2     14.00         0.77
  2     15.00         0.76


     DOLLAR AMOUNT IS $1,000
YEAR   PERCENT   PRESENT VALUE
  1     10.00       909.09
  1     11.00       900.90
  1     12.00       892.86
  1     13.00       884.96
  1     14.00       877.19
  1     15.00       869.57


  2     10.00       826.45
  2     11.00       811.62
  2     12.00       797.19
  2     13.00       783.15
  2     14.00       769.47
  2     15.00       756.14
```

Exercises

1. What would be the results of the following program?

```
10 N = 1
20 PRINT N, N**2
30 N = N + 2
40 IF N = 99 THEN 99
50 GO TO 20
99 END
```

2. Rewrite the program in Exercise 1 by using FOR/NEXT statements.

3. What is wrong with the following statements?

   a. 10 FOR I = 1 TO −10

   b. 40 NEXT A, B

   c. 50 N = 100
      60 FOR I = 1 TO N STEP −2

   d. 70 FOR A$ = 3 TO 71

   e. 85 FOR A = 1 TO 5
      90 FOR B = 1 TO 4
      100 PRINT A, B
      110 NEXT A
      120 NEXT B

   f. 100 FOR X = 1 TO 10
      100 READ X
      120 PRINT X
      130 NEXT X

   g. 100 UNTIL N = 10 −A
      100 READ A
      120 LET X = A**2
      130 PRINT X
      140 NEXT
      900 DATA 1,3,9,12,15

   h. 100 WHILE M < 10
      110 PRINT M+1
      120 NEXT

   i. 100 UNTIL N$ = "END"
      110 READ A,B,C,N$
      120 PRINT N$, A+B +C
      130 NEXT
      900 DATA 1,2,3,JOE,
             4,5,6,END
      999 END

4. Rewrite Sample Program 7.1 using a FOR/NEXT loop.

5. Write a program to add the numbers from 1 to 100 and print the result.

6. For the following data, use a loop to read rental car information and produce a report. The report should list those customers who rented for more than

two days and drove more than 300 miles. Calculate for each customer a rental charge if the daily rate is $20 and the mileage rate is 30 cents per mile. Include calculations that would display the average days rented, average miles driven, and total rental charges for those customers who meet the above criteria. Use appropriate headings for the report and use the PRINT USING statement to format the details of the report.

Customer	Days rented	Miles driven
Barclay	10	300
Brown	5	400
Custer	3	200
Drake	1	1,000
Lister	7	800
Poe	2	50
Sandoval	4	900
Tucker	12	1,200

7. Write a program using looping statements that will produce a table with an appropriate format and the following headings:

Miles per hour

Kilometers per hour (1.6 * miles)

Feet per second

Meters per second

Seconds per mile

Seconds per kilometer

The detail beneath the headings will display the data for miles per hour from 10 to 200 in increments of 10 miles per hour. Write a standard flowchart and appropriate pseudocode before writing the program.

8. Write a program to compute a listing of electric bills as might be done by a public utility company. The billing rate is 10 cents per kilowatt hour, and there is a combined city and state tax of 6%. A base bill of $10 is charged if less than 10 kilowatts have been used. The program is to use the PRINT USING and READ statements. Allow for only five customer bills in this problem. Output is to be as follows:

BILLING LISTING

CUSTOMER NUMBER	METER READING PAST	PRESENT	SALES TAX	TOTAL AMOUNT
12345	58121	60000	$XX.XX	$X,XXX.XX
34523	01687	09999	$XX.XX	$X,XXX.XX
52231	33333	34444	$XX.XX	$X,XXX.XX
69423	99896	00511	$XX.XX	$X,XXX.XX
83838	78555	79555	$XX.XX	$X,XXX.XX

Use as input the customer numbers and past and present meter readings in kilowatts above.

9. Write a program that will create a table of Celsius-to-Fahrenheit conversion for Celsius degrees from 100 down to 0 in decrements of 10. The formula for Celsius-to-Fahrenheit conversion is: Fahrenheit = (Celsius * 9/5) + 32

10. A soft-drink manufacturer is studying sales patterns for three flavors of soft drinks in five different states. The manufacturer would like to know:
  a. Total number of bottles sold in each state.
  b. Total number of bottles sold by soft-drink type.
  c. Total number of bottles sold.
  Write pseudocode and a program to answer these questions using the following data:

State	Cola	Orange	Root beer
Colorado	1,150	375	1,105
Arizona	2,005	1,225	2,095
New Mexico	1,744	1,237	1,485
Wyoming	2,075	1,154	1,488
Nebraska	1,371	1,000	993

The output should look like this:

STATE	COLA	ORANGE	ROOT BEER	TOTALS
COLORADO	1,150	375	1,105	2,630
..				
..				
	___	___	___	___
TOTALS	8,345			

11. Interest calculations involve arithmetic progressions. If P is the principal placed at interest rate I (expressed as a decimal) for a period of N years, the amount at the end of N years is: Amount = P(1 + NI), which is often referred to as add-on interest. Write a program for the bank that will do the following:
  a. Use an input statement to enter the value of P (the dollars to be borrowed) and I (the rate of interest on an annual basis).
  b. Calculate the amount at the end of each period (years) for five years in table form. Also calculate the payments for each period on a monthly and weekly basis.
  c. Use the test data listed under data for P and I; however, the program must allow for an unknown number of values for P and I. Use an INPUT statement to determine when the processing of the program is to be terminated.
  d. The output from the program must have the headings, spacing, and editing as shown under output.

DATA:

P	I
1000	.10
25000	.175

OUTPUT:

PRINCIPAL = $XX,XXX.XX   INTEREST RATE = .XXX

PERIOD	AMOUNT	MONTHLY PAYMENT	WEEKLY PAYMENT
1	$XX,XXX.XX	$XX,XXX.XX	$X,XXX.XX
2	$XX,XXX.XX	$XX,XXX.XX	$X,XXX.XX
3	$XX,XXX.XX	$XX,XXX.XX	$X,XXX.XX
4	$XX,XXX.XX	$XX,XXX.XX	$X,XXX.XX
5	$XX,XXX.XX	$XX,XXX.XX	$X,XXX.XX

Chapter Ten

Intermediate Transfer

Comparisons

When the computer executes an IF statement, it is really comparing two fields of data. There are two types of comparisons, numeric and nonnumeric. A numeric field cannot be compared to a nonnumeric field or vice versa.

The PDP-11 and VAX-11 systems use the ASCII character set. Nonnumeric comparisons are made a character at a time from left to right. Numeric comparisons are made one character at a time starting at the decimal point. Integers are compared from right to left, and the decimal portions are compared from left to right. The order of comparison proceeds from the lowest-valued character to the highest, as shown in Figure 10.1. This is called the collating sequence.

Figure 10.1
The ASCII collating sequence

1. Blank (lowest value)

2. ! " # $ % & ( ) * + ' − . ?

3. 0 1 2 3 4 5 6 7 8 9

4. : ; = ? @

5. A B C through Z

6. [\ ] ↑ ←

7. a b c through z (highest value)

The IF Statement

In Chapter 6 simple IF statements were discussed. The general format of a more useful IF statement is:

> n IF condition THEN statement(s)

where *IF* is a reserved word, *condition* is the comparison of numeric values or the comparison of string values, *THEN* is a reserved word, and *statement(s)* is any executable statement(s).

Single Conditions

There are times when, after a condition has been tested and found to be true, certain statements are to be executed and control is to be returned to the next statement in the program. Given the following statements:

    100 IF A = B THEN N = N + 1
    200 PRINT "EXIT"

Figure 10.2 illustrates that a single statement is to be executed under a true condition.

Figure 10.2
A single statement after a true condition

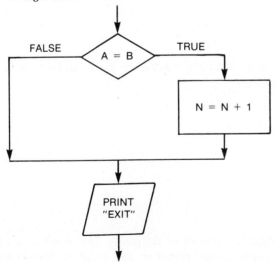

Multiple Statements on a Single Line

More than one statement can be written on a single line. To do so, use the backslash (\) to separate the statements. Given the following statements:

```
100 IF X > Y THEN C = C + 1 \ B = B + 1
200 PRINT "EXIT"
```

the logic is illustrated by Figure 10.3.

Figure 10.3
A multiple statement after a true condition

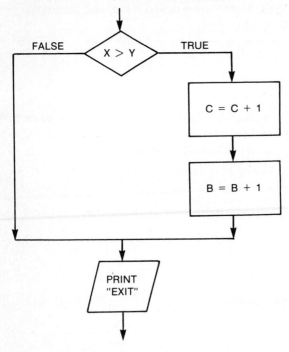

Multiple statements are not restricted to IF statements. They can be used with most executable statements such as:

```
100 PRINT \ X = 5 \ Y = A * B
```

which would be equivalent to:

```
100 PRINT
200 X = 5
300 Y = A * B
```

Nested IF Statements

At times programs will contain a network of decisions. The result of a true condition requires testing for another true condition, and so on. In these situations, the programming is simplified by the use of nested IF statements. The statements:

```
100 IF N > 0 THEN
            IF A = B THEN
                    IF N$ = M$ THEN PRINT N$
     200 PRINT "EXIT"
```

are illustrated in Figure 10.4. All false conditions go immediately to statement 200. If all of the conditions are true, PRINT N$ is executed and then statement 200 is encountered.

Figure 10.4
Nested IF statements

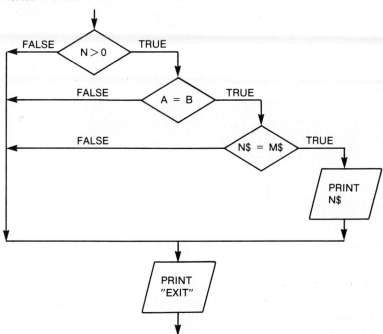

Notice the above example is not considered as multiple statements on the same line. Each THEN may be followed by another statement. If the statement is an IF statement, THEN may be followed by another statement, and so on. The following statements combine nested IFs and multiple statements:

```
100 IF A = B THEN
            IF Y = X THEN A = A + 1 \ Y = Y + 1
     200 PRINT "EXIT"
```

Figure 10.5 illustrates the logic.

Figure 10.5
Multiple statements after all true conditions using nested IFs

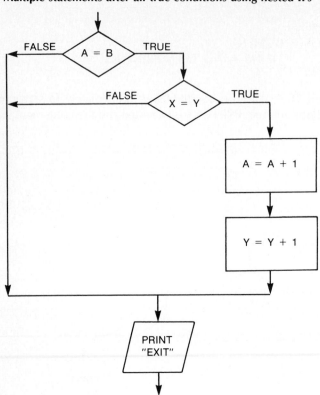

Compound Conditions

More than one condition may be tested in a single IF statement. The logical operators AND and OR are used to make such tests. AND means all conditions for that compound test must be true for the statement to be true. OR means that if any of the conditions for that compound test is true the statement is true. Both AND and OR can be used in the same IF statement. A hierarchy of execution takes place when more than one AND or OR appear in the same statement. ANDs are tested first, in the order in which they appear (unless enclosed in parentheses). Then ORs are evaluated in the same manner. If AND and OR are both used in the same statement, the programmer may be confused. Enclosing conditions to be tested in parentheses may help in these cases.

Given the statements:

```
100 IF A > 18 AND A < 21 THEN N = N + 1
200 PRINT "EXIT"
```

Both conditions A > 18 and A < 21 must be true before N = N + 1 is executed. If either is false, N = N + 1 is ignored, and statement 200 is executed. The logic is shown in Figure 10.6

Figure 10.6
Using the logical operator AND in an IF statement

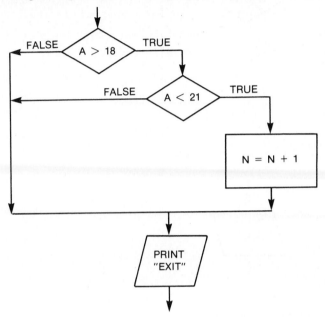

Replacing the AND with an OR in the above statements gives the following statements:

    100 IF A < 18 OR A > 21 THEN N = N + 1
    200 PRINT "EXIT"

If either one of the conditions is true, N = N·+ 1 is executed. If both are false, N = N + 1 is ignored, and statement 200 is executed. Observe this logic in Figure 10.7.

    The following statements combine AND and OR in the same conditional test. Observe the logic of Figure 10.8.

    100 IF (S$ = "F" OR A > = 21) AND C$ = "SENIOR"
        THEN PRINT "STUDENT A SENIOR"
    200 PRINT "EXIT"

    Notice that conditions within the parentheses are evaluated first. If any one of the conditions is true, C$ = "SENIOR" is evaluated. If that condition is true, the PRINT "STUDENT A SENIOR" statement is executed. Do not make a practice of mixing AND and OR in a statement. The results may be illogical.

146

Figure 10.7
Using the logical operator OR in an IF statement

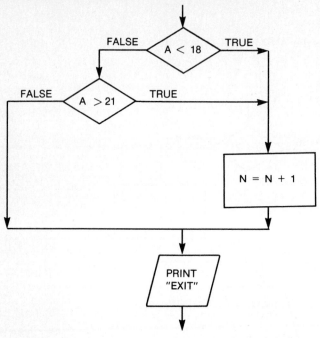

Figure 10.8
Using both the AND and OR in an IF statement

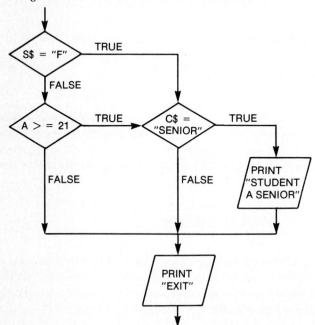

ELSE Option

In programming certain problems, a true condition may require one set of calculations, and a different set of calculations may be required if the condition is false. To accomplish this, the ELSE reserved word may be used in an IF statement. The general format of the IF-THEN-ELSE statement is:

> n IF condition THEN statement-1 ELSE statement-2

where *IF* is a reserved word, *condition* is the comparison of numeric values or the comparison of string values, *THEN* is a reserved word, *statement-1* is any statement to be executed under a true condition, *ELSE* is a reserved word, and *statement-2* is any statement to be executed under a false condition.

Given the statements:

```
100 IF A = B THEN N = 0 ELSE N = N + 1
200 PRINT "EXIT"
```

after statement 100 is executed, control will always be given to statement 200, as Figure 10.9 illustrates.

Figure 10.9
Using an ELSE clause in an IF statement

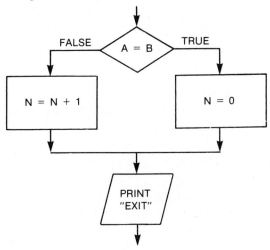

Given the statements:

```
100 IF X > Y THEN PRINT "X IS GREATER THAN Y"
        ELSE Y = Y + 1 \ PRINT "X IS LESS THAN OR EQUAL TO Y"
200 PRINT "EXIT"
```

The statement PRINT "X IS GREATER THAN Y" is executed under a true condition, and the multiple statements Y = Y + 1 and PRINT "X IS LESS THAN OR EQUAL TO Y" are executed under a false condition. Figure 10.10 illustrates the logic.

Figure 10.10
Using multiple statements after an ELSE clause

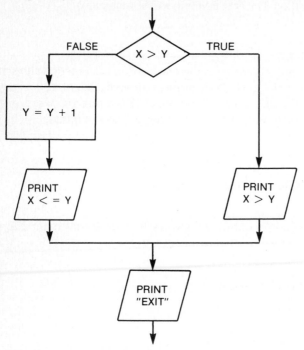

IF statements can follow either the THEN or the ELSE reserved words allowing for nested IF statements. Observe the following statements and the logic of Figure 10.11.

```
100 IF A > B THEN
            IF A > C THEN PRINT "FIRST TRUE CONDITION"
                ELSE PRINT "FIRST FALSE CONDITION"
          ELSE IF B > C THEN PRINT "SECOND TRUE CONDITION"
                ELSE PRINT "SECOND FALSE CONDITION"
   200 PRINT "EXIT"
```

Give special notice to the following example:

```
100 IF A > B THEN IF A > C THEN IF A > B
                         THEN PRINT "TRUE"
                         ELSE PRINT "FALSE"
```

Figure 10.11
Using the nested IF with ELSE clauses

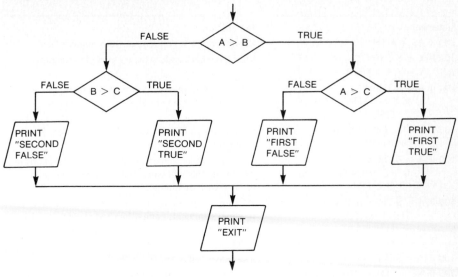

There are more IF statements than ELSE clauses. When this is the case, the last (innermost) IF is paired with the first ELSE encountered. All other false conditions default to the next statement in the program.

When using nested IF statements with the ELSE option, indenting parts of the statement on subsequent physical lines makes it easier to follow the logic.

Note!!! On a PDP-11, multiple statements cannot be used after the THEN if an ELSE is contained in the statement. Also, in statements having more than one ELSE, multiple statements may be used only after the last ELSE. The following statements are *invalid* for PDP-11s:

```
100 IF X > Y THEN X = X + 1 \
              PRINT "X IS GREATER THAN Y"
          ELSE Y = Y + 1 \
              PRINT "X IS LESS THAN OR EQUAL TO Y"
```

ELSE Option: VAX-11 Differences

The above example would be *valid* on a VAX-11. Multiple statements can be used at any time following the THEN and ELSE. Also, the PDP-11 allows the use of both the backslash (\ ) and the semicolon (:) for multiple statements, whereas the VAX-11 allows only the use of the backslash (\ ).

150

Common Errors

Statement	Explanation
100 IF A$ = A THEN PRINT A	Cannot compare nonnumeric with numeric fields.
100 IF X = Y THEN Z = 0 Y = Y + 1 X = X + 1	Must have backslash between multiple statements.

100 IF A > B THEN
        IF X > Y THEN PRINT N
        ELSE PRINT M
	May be OK. Will default to next statement if A = B because there is no corresponding ELSE clause.

100 IF A = 10 OR 5 OR 20 THEN PRINT N	Cannot use an implied subject and operation. Missing a variable for 5 and 20.

100 IF A > B OR A > C AND
        B > C THEN GO TO 200
        ELSE PRINT N
	Check the logic. Remember it evaluates conditions of AND first. This will work, but the logic may be in error. Poor programming.

100 IF A = B THEN IF B = C
        THEN GO TO 200
            ELSE PRINT X \ B = B+1
            ELSE PRINT Y \ B = B+1
	When more than one ELSE in a PDP-11 statement multiple statements cannot be used except after the *last* ELSE clause. However, this is valid for a VAX-11 statement.

100 IF A = B IF B = C K = K+1	Must have THEN after each IF.
100 IF N$ = "END" THEN STOP 101 GO TO 500	Will cause a permanent termination if programmer does not type in CONT.

Sample Programs

Problem Description 10.1

1. Statement of the problem: Write a program to simulate the "flipping" of a coin. Have the program allow the player to stop the simulation at any time. When the simulation is completed, display the number of times a "correct" guess was made of the outcome of each flip and the number of times an "incorrect" guess was made.

2. Input: Using INPUT statements, display the message DO YOU WANT TO PLAY, YES OR NO, so that a player can stop at any time. Also display the message ENTER T FOR TAILS, H FOR HEADS so that a player can enter a guess of the outcome of a flip.

3. Output: Display the message YOU WIN or the message YOU LOSE, depending upon the outcome of the simulation. At the completion of the simulation, display the total of wins and the total of losses.

Flowchart 10.1

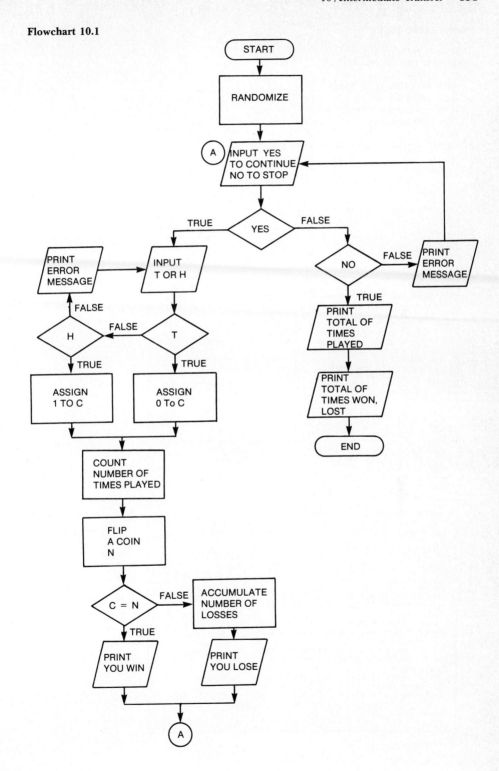

Pseudocode 10.1

Randomize
Input yes to continue, no to stop
IF person wants to play
    Input T for tails, H for heads
    Flip coin randomly
    IF the coin matches the guess, print 'you win'
    ELSE print 'you lose'
    Endif
ELSE print number of times played, won, and lost
Endif
Endprogram

```
1 REM COIN TOSSING GAME
50 ! L = COUNTER FOR LOSSES
    T = COUNTER FOR TOSSES
   R$ = RESPONSE TO CONTINUE RUNNING PROGRAM
   I$ = RESPONSE FOR HEAD OR TAILS
   N = RANDOM DETERMINATION OF HEAD OR TAIL
   C = CODE FOR HEAD OR TAIL
100 RANDOMIZE                    ! GET A FAIR COIN
120 INPUT "DO YOU WANT TO PLAY, YES OR NO"; R$
130 IF R$ = "YES" THEN GO TO 140
             ELSE IF R$ = "NO" GO TO 200
                  ELSE PRINT "RESPONSE IN ERROR"
                       \ GO TO 120
140 INPUT "ENTER T FOR TAILS, H FOR HEADS"; I$
150 IF I$ = "T" THEN C = 0
             ELSE IF I$ = "H" THEN C = 1
                  ELSE PRINT "ANSWER CAN ONLY";
                            "BE T OR. H"
                       \ GO TO 190
160 T = T + 1
170 N = INT (2*RND)
180 IF C = N THEN PRINT "YOU WIN"
             ELSE PRINT "YOU LOSE"
                  \ L = L + 1
190 GO TO 120
200 PRINT "YOU HAVE TOSSED THE COIN";T;"TIMES"
210 PRINT "YOU HAVE WON";T-L;"TIMES AND LOST";
          L; "TIMES"
999 END

Ready

RUNNH
DO YOU WANT TO PLAY, YES OR NO? YES
ENTER T FOR TAILS, H FOR HEADS? T
YOU WIN
DO YOU WANT TO PLAY, YES OR NO? YES
ENTER T FOR TAILS, H FOR HEADS? H
YOU WIN
DO YOU WANT TO PLAY, YES OR NO? YES
ENTER T FOR TAILS, H FOR HEADS? H
YOU LOSE
DO YOU WANT TO PLAY, YES OR NO? NO
YOU HAVE TOSSED THE COIN 3 TIMES
YOU HAVE WON 2 TIMES AND LOST 1 TIMES

Ready
```

Problem Description 10.2

1. Statement of the problem: For an unknown number of customers, write a program to prepare loan schedules for loans with different interest rates and different amounts of time to pay back the loan. The annual interest rate is always to be converted to a "periodic rate". The number of payments to be made is found by multiplying the number of years of the loan and the payments per year. The number of payments then determines the amount of the payment. The following models are to be used:

a. Number of payments = Years of loan * Payments per year
b. Periodic rate = Annual interest rate / (Number of payments per year * 100)
c. Periodic payment = Amount of loan * Periodic rate / (1 − (1 / (1 + periodic rate))) ** Number of payments
d. Interest per payment = Periodic rate * Amount of loan balance
e. Principal per payment = Periodic payment − Interest per payment
f. Balance of loan = Old balance of loan − Principal per payment

2. Input: Use an INPUT statement displaying appropriate messages on what to enter and enter the data for the name of the customer, the amount of the loan, the number of payments to make per year, the number of years of the loan, and the annual interest rate.

3. Output: Display an appropriate two-line heading that includes the name of the customer, the amount of the loan, and the annual interest rate. Skip two lines and display appropriate column names. List, in table form, edited data for the payment number, amount of the payment, current interest paid, current principal paid, total interest paid, and balance after each payment. *Note:* The balance must be zero at the end of the loan period. This may mean making proper adjustments in the final payment for the loan. Skip three lines between customer loan schedules.

Pseudocode 10.2

```
Dowhile there are more customers
    Assign counters a value of zero
    Input name, principal, interest rate, number of payments, years of loan
    Save original amount of loan
    Determine the number of payments for the loan
    Determine periodic rate
    Determine periodic payment rounded
    Print headings
    Dowhile X less than or equal to years of loan
        Determine interest component
        Determine principal component
        Determine total interest paid
        Determine total principal paid
        Determine new principal balance
        Print results
    Enddo
Enddo
Endprogram
```

154

Flowchart 10.2

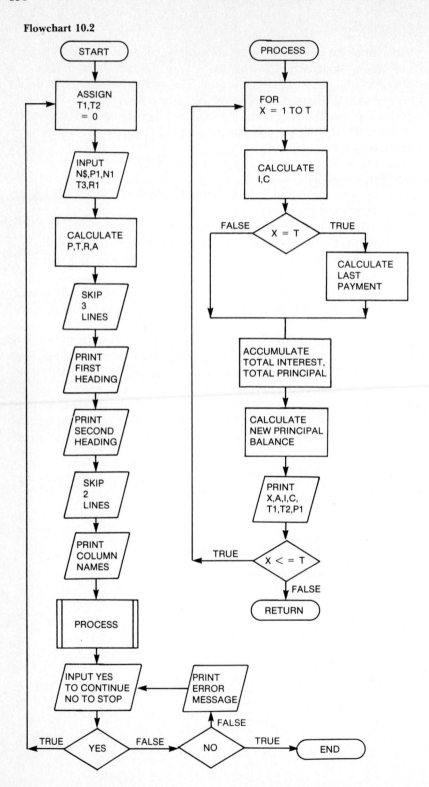

```
1 REM AMORTIZATION SCHEDULE
50 ! N$ = NAME OF CUSTOMER                     P1 = BALANCE OF THE LOAN
     N1 = NUMBER OF PAYMENTS PER YEAR           R1 = ANNUAL INTEREST RATE
     T3 = YEARS OF LOAN                         P = ORIGINAL AMOUNT OF LOAN
     T = NUMBER OF PAYMENTS FOR LOAN
     R = PERIODIC RATE                          A = PERIODIC PAYMENT
     I = INTEREST COMPONENT PER PAYMENT         C = PRINCIPAL COMPONENT
     T1 = CURRENT TOTAL INTEREST PAID           T2 = CURRENT TOTAL PRINCIPAL
     X = NUMBER OF PAYMENTS TO BE MADE
110 T1,T2 = 0                        ! SET UP COUNTERS
120 INPUT "NAME OF CUSTOMER";N$;"PRINCIPAL BALANCE";P1;
          "NUMBER OF PAYMENTS PER YEAR";N1;
          "YEARS OF LOAN";T3;"ANNUAL INTEREST RATE";R1
130 P = P1                           ! SAVE ORIGINAL AMOUNT OF THE LOAN
140 T = T3 * N1                      ! FIND THE NUMBER OF PAYMENTS FOR THE LOAN
145 R = R1 / (N1 * 100)              ! R = PERIODIC RATE
150 A = P1*(R/(1-1/(1+R)**T))        ! A = PERIODIC PAYMENT WHICH IS CONSTANT
155 A = (INT((A+.005)*100))/100      ! ROUND A TO NEAREST CENT
156 PRINT\PRINT\PRINT
160 PRINT TAB(13); "REPAYMENT SCHEDULE FOR ";N$
170 PRINT TAB(8); "THE LOAN IS FOR  $"; P1; "AT"; R1; "PERCENT INTEREST"
180 PRINT
185 PRINT USING
"                     CURRENT     CURRENT     TOTAL       TOTAL"
186 PRINT USING
"                     INTEREST    PRINCIPAL   INTEREST    PRINCIPAL"
190 PRINT USING
"PAYMENT    AMOUNT    PAID        PAID        PAID        PAID      BALANCE"
200 FOR X = 1 TO T
210 I = R * P1                        ! INTEREST COMPONENT
220 C = A - I
230 IF X = T THEN C = P1\
                 A = I + C
240 T1 = T1 + I                       ! T1 = TOTAL INTEREST
250 T2 = T2 + C                       ! T2 = TOTAL PRINCIPAL
260 P1 = P1 - C                       ! P1 = NEW PRINCIPAL BALANCE
270 PRINT USING
"  ###  ##,###.##   ##,###.##  ##,###.##   ##,###.##  ##,###.##  ##,###.##",
X, A, I, C, T1, T2, P1
280 NEXT X
285 PRINT
290 INPUT "ANOTHER CUSTOMER, YES OR NO"; A$
300 IF A$ = "YES" THEN 110
              ELSE IF A$ = "NO" THEN 999
                   ELSE PRINT "WRONG ENTRY"\GO TO 290
999 END

Ready
```

```
RUNNH
NAME OF CUSTOMER? DAVID KELLY
PRINCIPAL BALANCE? 15000
NUMBER OF PAYMENTS PER YEAR? 1
YEARS OF LOAN? 1
ANNUAL INTEREST RATE? 6


            REPAYMENT SCHEDULE FOR DAVID KELLY
         THE LOAN IS FOR  $ 15000 AT 6 PERCENT INTEREST

                    CURRENT    CURRENT    TOTAL      TOTAL
                    INTEREST   PRINCIPAL  INTEREST   PRINCIPAL
PAYMENT    AMOUNT    PAID       PAID       PAID       PAID       BALANCE
   1    15,900.00    900.00   15,000.00    900.00   15,000.00      0.00

ANOTHER CUSTOMER, YES OR NO? YES
NAME OF CUSTOMER? BRENT DEWEY
PRINCIPAL BALANCE? 25000
NUMBER OF PAYMENTS PER YEAR? 12
YEARS OF LOAN? 1
ANNUAL INTEREST RATE? 15


            REPAYMENT SCHEDULE FOR BRENT DEWEY
         THE LOAN IS FOR  $ 25000 AT 15 PERCENT INTEREST

                    CURRENT    CURRENT    TOTAL      TOTAL
                    INTEREST   PRINCIPAL  INTEREST   PRINCIPAL
PAYMENT    AMOUNT    PAID       PAID       PAID       PAID       BALANCE
   1     2,256.46    312.50    1,943.96    312.50    1,943.96  23,056.04
   2     2,256.46    288.20    1,968.26    600.70    3,912.22  21,087.78
   3     2,256.46    263.60    1,992.86    864.30    5,905.08  19,094.92
   4     2,256.46    238.69    2,017.77  1,102.98    7,922.86  17,077.14
   5     2,256.46    213.46    2,043.00  1,316.45    9,965.85  15,034.15
   6     2,256.46    187.93    2,068.53  1,504.38   12,034.38  12,965.62
   7     2,256.46    162.07    2,094.39  1,666.45   14,128.77  10,871.23
   8     2,256.46    135.89    2,120.57  1,802.34   16,249.34   8,750.66
   9     2,256.46    109.38    2,147.08  1,911.72   18,396.42   6,603.58
  10     2,256.46     82.54    2,173.92  1,994.26   20,570.34   4,429.66
  11     2,256.46     55.37    2,201.09  2,049.63   22,771.43   2,228.57
  12     2,256.43     27.86    2,228.57  2,077.49   25,000.00      0.00

ANOTHER CUSTOMER, YES OR NO? NO

Ready
```

Exercises

1. It is easy to understand why a 9 is larger than a 2 in the collating sequence. What purpose is served in having an H larger than a D?

2. What do the following statements accomplish?
   a. 100 FOR I = 1 TO 100 \ PRINT I \ N = N + I \ NEXT I \ PRINT N
   b. 100 IF A > B THEN 400
   　　　　　ELSE IF A = B THEN 500
   　　　　　　　　ELSE X = A+B \ PRINT X, A, B
   c. 200 IF A = 20 OR A = 30 OR A = 40 AND
   　　　　B = 200 THEN PRINT A, B \ GO TO 300

3. What is wrong with the following statements?
   a. IF A < A$ THEN PRINT A$
   b. IF B = 20 OR 30 OR 40 THEN 900
   c. IF R$ = "YES" N = N + 1 \ B = B + N \ PRINT N, B
   d. IF X$ = "PURPLE" PRINT X$
   e. IF X = Y IF B = D IF X = B PRINT X

4. Data for a group of employees are provided below. Write a program that will produce a listing of those employees who meet all of the following conditions:
   a. Employed more than six months.
   b. Department number 2, 4, or 6.
   c. Work code number 1, 7, or 9.
   d. Piece quota above 500.
   e. Pieces produced more than 600.
   Also state the total number of employees who meet all of the conditions. Then use the RESTORE statement to produce a listing of all employees who meet *any* of the above conditions. Use appropriate headings for the two reports.

Name	Months employed	Department number	Work code	Piece quota	Pieces produced
James	5	1	7	600	1,000
Brown	7	2	9	700	620
Kincade	6	8	2	500	800
Sutton	8	2	1	400	900
Brokaw	10	7	1	700	400
Hoffman	8	6	7	600	700
Duff	7	4	8	600	800
Roy	12	9	4	550	1,200
Fenton	24	2	3	400	400
Burnett	30	5	2	400	400

5. Write a program to find the average of three test scores and assign a letter grade. The assignment is as follows: 0–59 = F, 60–69 = D, 70–79 = C, 80–89 = B, 90–100 = A. Count the number of scores for each grade, and determine the percentage of students with each grade. Also, determine the

arithmetic average of all scores and the highest average score for a student in the class. Edit all output. The format for the output is:

RANGE   GRADE   PERCENT
90–100   A   XX.X
80–89   B   XX.X
70–79   C   XX.X
60–69   D   XX.X
 0–59   F   XX.X
HIGHEST AVERAGE SCORE: XXX.X
AVERAGE SCORE FOR CLASS: XXX.X

Use as test data:

Name	Test scores	Name	Test scores
Able	95, 76, 81	Duss	91, 89, 76
Bull	76, 76, 76	Eien	45, 76, 41
Cain	41, 63, 55	Fenn	90, 93, 98

Chapter Eleven

Subroutines

Whenever it is necessary to execute instructions that perform some function several times in a program, they may be inserted as a separate part of the program, usually near the end, and called upon as often as they are needed. This reduces the number of times those instructions need to be written. Also, using a module in an appropriate place in the program for instructions that may be only executed once allows the programmer to use structured programming techniques, which generally simplifies the program logic. These statements or sets of statements are referred to as subroutines. There are two different types of subroutines to be discussed. One type is also referred to as multiple-line functions. That type of subroutine will be discussed in a later chapter. The other type of subroutine uses the GO SUB/RETURN statements.

GO SUB/RETURN

The general format of the GO SUB statement is:

n GO SUB n

where *GO and SUB* are reserved words that transfer control of the program and *n* is the statement to which control is transferred. A *GO SUB* statement must have at least one corresponding RETURN statement.

The general format of the RETURN statement is:

n RETURN

where *RETURN* is a reserved word that transfers control of the program to the statement following the corresponding GO SUB statement. There may be more than one RETURN to the same GO SUB statement.

The following is an example of how the GO SUB/RETURN works.

```
100 READ A, B, C, N$
110 IF N$ = "END" THEN 999
120 GO SUB 700
130 PRINT S
140 IF S > 100 THEN GO SUB 800
              ELSE GO SUB 810
150 GO TO 100
. . . . . . . . .
. . . . . . . . .
700 FOR I = 0 TO A              ! START OF SUBROUTINE
710 S = S + I
720 NEXT I
730 RETURN                      !!! END OF SUBROUTINE
. . . . . . . . .
. . . . . . . . .
800 IF B = 0 THEN 840           ! FIRST ENTRY POINT OF SUB
                                  ROUTINE
810 IF B < 5 THEN X = 0         ! SECOND ENTRY POINT OF SUB
                                  ROUTINE
820 PRINT A+B
830 RETURN                      !!! ONE END OF SUBROUTINE
840 PRINT A−B
850 RETURN                      !!! ANOTHER END OF SUBROUTINE
. . . . . . . . .
. . . . . . . . .
999 END
```

There are two subroutines in the example. At statement 120 the first subroutine is entered at statement 700. This subroutine sums the values of 1 through A and stores them in S. Statement 730 returns control to statement 130. At statement 140, if a true condition exists, the second subroutine is entered at statement 800. If B = 0, it exits the subroutine from statement 830; otherwise, it exits from statement 850. In both cases, it returns to statement 150. If at statement 140 a false condition exists, the second subroutine is entered at statement 810. It exits the subroutine from statement 830 and also returns to statement 150. Notice that statement 150 prevents entering the first subroutine except with a GO SUB statement. The second subroutine is placed immediately following the first. The RETURN at statement 730 prevents entry to following statements except with a

GO SUB statement. Also, if statement 110 is false, the same subroutines are executed again until statement 110 is true.

GO SUB/WHILE

Another form of the GO SUB is the GO SUB/WHILE, which allows the programmer to more fully implement structured programming concepts in BASIC. The general format of the GO SUB/WHILE statement is:

n GO SUB n WHILE condition

where *GO SUB* are reserved words, the second *n* is the statement number to which control is transferred, and *WHILE* is a reserved word and a modifier, which can be used on many different statements. The modifier concept is explained more fully in Chapter 13. *Condition* is a condition that is tested. The subroutine named will be executed so long as the condition tested is true. If the condition tested is not true, the next sequential instruction will be executed.

This form of the GO SUB allows full implementation of modular program design concepts of structured programming. One major stumbling block in BASIC-PLUS on the PDP-11 is the restrictions placed on the IF/THEN/ELSE statement. Multiple instructions are allowed only after the last ELSE clause; previous ELSE or THEN clauses can be followed only by a single instruction. If the programmer wishes to have more than one instruction, the GO SUB and the GO SUB/WHILE may be used. A full implementation of this concept is shown in Sample Program 11.3.

It is also possible to nest subroutines. An example of a nested subroutine follows.

```
. . . . . . . . . .
. . . . . . . . . .
. . . . . . . . . .
500 GO SUB 700
510 PRINT S
600 STOP
700 N = X+Z \ M = Y+4 \ S = 0
710 GO SUB 800                          ! NESTED SUBROUTINE AT
                                          STATEMENT 800

720 PRINT S+X
730 RETURN
800 FOR I = N TO M
810 S = S + I
820 NEXT I
830 PRINT S
840 RETURN
999 END
```

At statement 500, control is transferred to the first subroutine at statement 700. Notice this is a multiple statement. At statement 710, control is transferred outside this subroutine to another subroutine at statement 800. When the second subroutine is completed at statement 840, control is returned to the first subroutine at statement 720. At statement 730, control is transferred back to the main program at statement 550. The STOP at statement 600 prevents an unwanted entry into the subroutine and terminates the program. Notice the program must still have an END statement as the last physical statement in the program.

The ON—GO SUB Statement

The purpose of the ON—GO SUB statement is to conditionally transfer control to one of several subroutines. It functions very similarly to the ON—GO TO discussed in a previous chapter.

The general format of the ON—GO SUB statement is:

> n ON expression GO SUB list

where *ON* is a reserved word, *expression* is a value that directs the transfer to one of several subroutines, *GO and SUB* are reserved words, and *list* is a group of statement numbers that are subroutines to be transferred to depending on the value of the expression.

The statement: 100 ON N GO SUB 600,700,800 would be evaluated as follows: The integer portion of N is evaluated. If the value of N is 1, transfer will be made to the subroutine starting at statement 600. If the value of N is 2, transfer will be made to the subroutine starting at statement 700, and if the value of N is 3, transfer will be made to the subroutine starting at 800. If the integer portion of the value of N is not between 1 and the number of statement numbers that are in the list, in this example 3, an error occurs.

Examples of the ON—GO SUB statement are:

100 ON 2 GO SUB 600,700,800	! TRANSFER TO STATEMENT 700 AND
110 PRINT	! RETURN TO STATEMENT 110
100 ON X GO SUB 710,720,730	! INTEGER PORTION OF X BETWEEN 1 AND 3
100 ON N*M GO SUB 800,850,800,850	! TRANSFER TO 800 ON ODD TO 850 ON EVEN VALUES

The following rules should be observed when using GO SUB/RETURN and ON—GO SUB/RETURN statements.

1. Subprograms should be placed at the end of the program.
2. The RETURN always transfers control, after completing the subroutine, to the statement following the corresponding GO SUB.
3. Exit from a subroutine with a GO TO or an IF/THEN will cause problems on some systems. Good structured programming practice dictates that such transfers not be made.
4. There may be several RETURNs in one subroutine to the same corresponding GO SUB.
5. A GO SUB subroutine may be entered as many times as necessary.
6. There may be several GO SUB subroutines in the same program. When this is the case, place one after the other at the end of the program.
7. Subroutines may be nested. A subroutine may call another subroutine, which may call another subroutine, etc.
8. The number of allowable nested GO SUBs is only limited by the amount of internal memory available.
9. A subroutine may call itself as a subroutine, but be careful of the logic.
10. A particular subroutine may have multiple entry points.
11. A subroutine should only be entered by a GO SUB statement.
12. The statement immediately preceeding the entry to a subroutine must block an unauthorized entry to the subroutine. Typical blocking statements are the GO TO and the STOP.
13. The same rules apply for the GO SUB as for the ON—GO SUB statement.

Common Errors

Statement	Explanation
100 X = 10	Statement 120 does not prevent entrance into the subroutine
110 GO SUB 130	at statement 130. Subroutine will be executed a second
120 PRINT X**Z	time. After the second time, an error message will appear
130 IF Y = 100 THEN N = N + 1	because it is looking for the RETURN.
140 X = X + 5	
150 RETURN	
999 END	
100 GO SUB 200	Two problems. Statement 400 follows a subroutine and will
110 PRINT X	never be executed. A transfer is made out of the subroutine
120 STOP	to statement 100 instead of the RETURN transferring control
200 FOR I = 1 TO 5	to statement 100.
210 S = S + 1	
220 NEXT I	
230 GO TO 100	
240 RETURN	
400 PRINT S	
999 END	

Statement	Explanation
200 GO SUB 500	Statement 510 cannot call the subroutine at statement 200. Program no longer remembers where control is. The message IN SUBROUTINE is infinitely displayed.
210 GO TO 999	
500 PRINT "IN SUBROUTINE"	
510 GO SUB 200	
520 RETURN	
100 GO SUB 700	Missing the return statement. It will display the values 1, 3, 6, 10, 15 and then quit. Statement 110 will never be executed.
110 PRINT "END"	
120 STOP	
700 FOR J = 1 TO 5	
710 S = S + J	
720 PRINT S	
730 NEXT J	
999 END	
100 ON Y GO SUB 600,700,800	If Y is less than 1 or greater than 3, it is out of range and an error will occur.
100 ON A$ GO SUB 810,820	A$ is invalid, must be numeric.

Sample Programs

Problem Description 11.1

1.   Statement of the problem: Write a program to list the employee payroll by department for the ABC Company. Display a total for each department and the grand total for the company. Assume employee records are in department-number sequence. Use structured programming with subroutines.

2.   Input: Use a READ statement to enter the number of the department, the employee number, the number of hours worked, and the rate of pay per hour. Whenever the employee number is zero, all data have been entered.

3.   Output: Display all appropriate headings. Edit the dollar amounts with a dollar sign, commas, and zero suppression. Center all output.

Pseudocode 11.1

Main routine
   Do headings subroutine
   Process data subroutine while there are more employees
   Do store total subroutine
   Endprogram
Heading subroutine
   Print heading
   Print column names
   Return to main routine
Process subroutine
   Read department number, employee number, hours worked, pay rate
   IF end of data, return to main routine
   IF new department, do department total subroutine
   Calculate gross pay
   Accumulate department total
   Print department number, employee number, and gross pay

Department total subroutine
    Save new department number
    IF first employee, reset switch and return to process subroutine
    Print department total
    Skip a line
    Accumulate final total
    Zero out department total
    Return to process subroutine or final total subroutine

Store total subroutine
    Do department total subroutine for last department
    Print store total
    Return to main routine

Flowchart 11.1

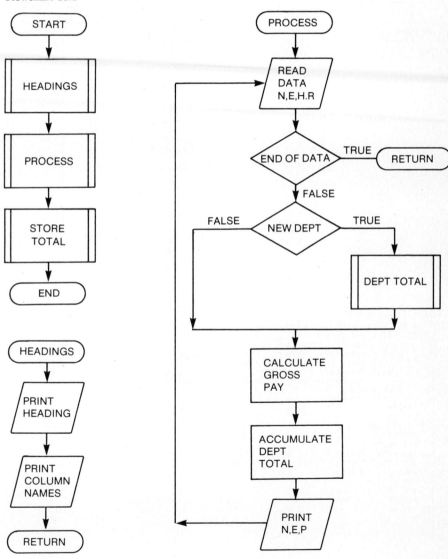

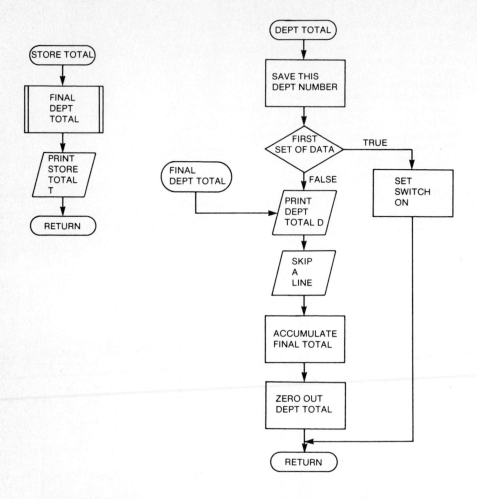

```
1 REM PAYROLL REPORT WITH TOTALS
50 ! S$ = SWITCH USED TO DETERMINE IF THE
           FIRST RECORD IS BEING READ
   N = DEPARTMENT NUMBER    E = EMPLOYEE NUMBER
   H = HOURS WORKED         R = PAY RATE
   N1 = TEMPORARY STORAGE OF DEPARTMENT NUMBER,
        INDICATING WHICH NUMBER IS BEING PROCESSED
   P = GROSS PAY
   D = DEPARTMENT TOTAL GROSS PAY
100 S$ = 'OFF'
120 GO SUB 200                ! HEADING ROUTINE
130 GO SUB 400                ! PROCESS ROUTINE
140 GO SUB 800                ! FINAL TOTAL ROUTINE
150 GO TO 999
200 PRINT TAB(11); "ABC COMPANY"
210 PRINT "DEPT"; TAB(12); "EMPLOYEE";
TAB(25); "GROSS PAY"
220 RETURN
400 READ N, E, H, R
410 IF E = 0 THEN 470          ! TERMINATE PROGRAM WHEN
                                 SOCIAL SECURITY NUMBER
                                 IS ZERO
```

```
420 IF N <> N1 THEN GO SUB 600 ! IF NEW DEPARTMENT, GO TO
                                  DEPARTMENT TOTAL ROUTINE
430 P = H*R                     ! FINAL GROSS PAY
440 D = D + P                   ! ACCUMULATE TOTAL FOR
                                  DEPARTMENT

450 PRINT USING
'###        #########    $#,###.##',N, E, P
460 GO TO 400
470 RETURN
600 N1 = N                      ! SAVE NEW DEPARTMENT NUMBER
610 IF S$ = 'OFF' THEN S$ = 'ON'
     \GO TO 660                  ! IF FIRST RECORD TURN SWITCH
                                   TO 'ON'

620 PRINT USING
.         DEPT TOTAL $#,###.##', D

630 PRINT
640 T = T + D                   ! ACCUMULATE FINAL TOTAL
650 D = 0                       ! CLEAR OUT OLD DEPARTMENT
                                  TOTAL

660 RETURN
800 GO SUB 620
810 PRINT USING
.          STORE TOTAL $#,###.##', T

820 RETURN
900 DATA 1, 123456789, 40.0, 10.00
901 DATA 1, 234567890, 40.0,  5.00
902 DATA 1, 345678912, 38.0, 10.00
903 DATA 2, 245678901, 40.0, 10.00
904 DATA 2, 256789012, 40.0,  5.00
905 DATA 3, 456789012, 37.0,  7.00
906 DATA 4, 124680357, 40.0, 10.00
907 DATA 4, 111111111, 40.0, 10.00
908 DATA 0,0,0,0
999 END

Ready

RUNNH
           ABC COMPANY
DEPT       EMPLOYEE        GROSS PAY
  1        123456789      $   400.00
  1        234567890      $   200.00
  1        345678912      $   380.00
                DEPT TOTAL $   980.00

  2        245678901      $   400.00
  2        256789012      $   200.00
                DEPT TOTAL $   600.00

  3        456789012      $   259.00
                DEPT TOTAL $   259.00

  4        124680357      $   400.00
  4        111111111      $   400.00
                DEPT TOTAL $   800.00

            STORE TOTAL $2,639.00

Ready
```

Problem Description 11.2

1. Statement of the problem: Write a program to use one or all of the following methods of computing the annual depreciation for a depreciable item: sum of the year's digits, straight line, and double declining balance. Use any appropriate arithmetic model from a standard accounting book. Use structured programming with subroutines. Allow the program to calculate the depreciation for an infinite number of items.

2. Input: Use an INPUT statement to enter for each item (a) a code for the method of depreciation, (b) the life of the item in years, and (c) the value of the item.

3. Output: Display all appropriate headings. Suppress leading zeros in all numeric fields, and place dollar signs, commas, and two decimal places in dollar-amount fields. Center all output.

Pseudocode 11.2

Main routine
    Dowhile there are more data
        Input method, life of item, value of items
        IF an incorrect method code is input, print error message
        IF method code is 0 or 1, do sum-of-the-year's-digits subroutine
        IF method code is 0 or 2, do straight-line subroutine
        IF method code is 0 or 3, do double-declining-balance subroutine
    Enddo
    Endprogram

Sum of the year's digits subroutine
    Do headings subroutine
    Save depreciable value
    FOR I = 1 to number of years
        Calculate varying rate
        Calculate varying amount
        Calculate current value
        Do detail subroutine
    Endfor
    Return to main routine

Straight-line subroutine
    Do headings subroutine
    Calculate depreciation
    FOR I = 1 to number of years
        Calculate current value
        Do detail subroutine
    Endfor
    Return to main routine

Double-declining-balance subroutine
    Do heading subroutine
    FOR I = 1 to number of years
        Calculate rate of depreciation
        Calculate current value
        Do detail subroutine
    Endfor
    Return to main routine

Detail subroutine
   Print detail line
   Return to calling statement
Heading subroutine
   Print heading
   Print column names
   Return to calling subroutine

Flowchart 11.2

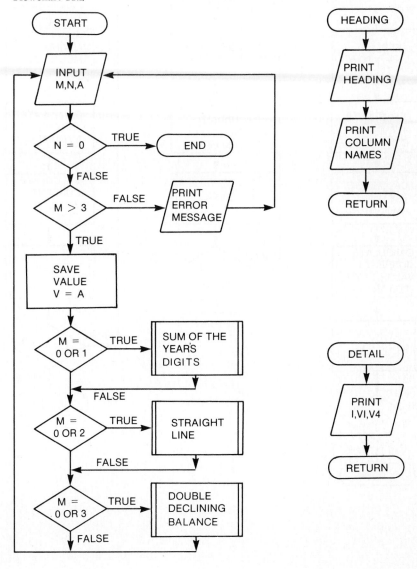

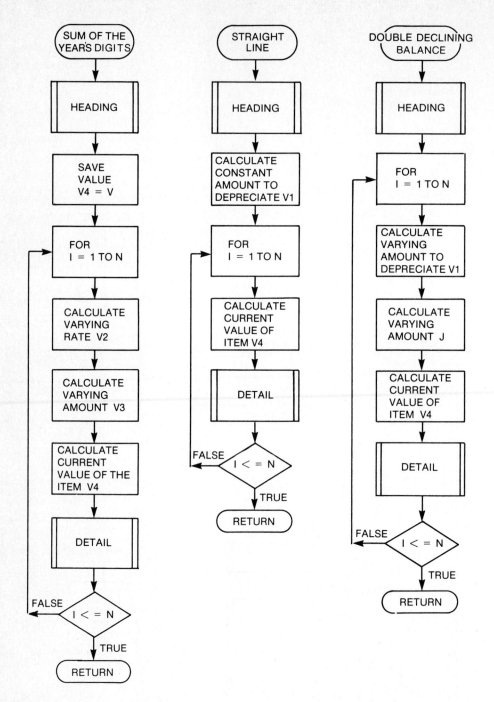

```
1 REM DEPRECIATION SCHEDULES
50 ! M = DEPRECIATION METHOD
   N = LIFE OF ITEM IN YEARS
   A = VALUE OF ITEM
   V = CHANGING VALUE OF THE ITEM
   V1 = YEARLY DEPRECIATION   V2 SUM OF THE YEARS
   V3 = AMOUNT DEPRECIATED GIVEN THE METHOD
   V4 = CURRENT VALUE
   F$ = STRING VARIABLE USED TO DEFINE FORMAT
100 INPUT "ENTER M, N, A";M,N,A
110 IF N = 0 THEN 999              ! TERMINATE WHEN LIFE OF
                                     ITEM IS ZERO
115 IF M <> 0 AND M <> 1 AND M <> 2
       AND M <> 3
       THEN PRINT "ERROR IN METHOD CODE"\ GO TO 100
120 IF M = 1 OR M = 0 THEN V = A\ GO SUB 300
130 IF M = 2 OR M = 0 THEN V = A\ GO SUB 400
140 IF M = 3 OR M = 0 THEN V = A\ GO SUB 500
150 GO TO 100
300 F$ = "    SUM OF THE YEARS FOR"
305 GO SUB 700
310 V4 = V
315 FOR I = 1 TO N
320 V2 = N-I+1
325 V3 = V/((N*(N+1))/2)*V2
330 V4 = V4-V3
335 V1=V3
340 GO SUB 800
345 NEXT I
350 RETURN
400 F$ = "        STRAIGHT LINE FOR"
410 GO SUB 700
420 V1 = V/N
430 FOR I = 1 TO N
440 V = V-V1
459 V4 = V
460 GO SUB 800
470 NEXT I
480 RETURN
500 F$ = "   DOUBLE DECLINING BALANCE"
505 GO SUB 700
510 FOR I = 1 TO N
520 V1 = (2/N)*V
530 V = V - V1
540 V4 = V
550 GO SUB 800
560 NEXT I
570 RETURN
700 PRINT\PRINT F$,A
710 PRINT "YEAR   DEPRECIATION  CURRENT VALUE"
720 RETURN
800 PRINT USING
"###       ###,###.##  ###,###.##", I, V1, V4
810 RETURN
999 END

Ready
RUNNH
ENTER M, N, A? 0,6,15000

    SUM OF THE YEARS FOR      15000
YEAR   DEPRECIATION  CURRENT VALUE
  1     $ 4,285.71   $10,714.29
  2     $ 3,571.43   $ 7,142.86
  3     $ 2,857.14   $ 4,285.71
  4     $ 2,142.86   $ 2,142.86
  5     $ 1,428.57   $   714.29
  6     $   714.29   $    -0.00

        STRAIGHT LINE FOR      15000
YEAR   DEPRECIATION  CURRENT VALUE
  1     $ 2,500.00   $12,500.00
  2     $ 2,500.00   $10,000.00
  3     $ 2,500.00   $ 7,500.00
  4     $ 2,500.00   $ 5,000.00
  5     $ 2,500.00   $ 2,500.00
  6     $ 2,500.00   $     0.00
```

172

```
     DOUBLE DECLINING BALANCE   15000
  YEAR    DEPRECIATION   CURRENT VALUE
    1      $ 5,000.00   $10,000.00
    2      $ 3,333.33   $ 6,666.67
    3      $ 2,222.22   $ 4,444.44
    4      $ 1,481.48   $ 2,962.96
    5      $   987.65   $ 1,975.31
    6      $   658.44   $ 1,316.87
 ENTER M, N, A? 0,0,0

 Ready
```

Problem Description 11.3

1. Statement of the problem: For a car-rental company, determine the dollar amount owed for each rental customer. The amount owed depends on the miles driven, the days rented, and the type of car used. Volkswagons are rented at the rate of $22 per day and 15 cents per mile. Oldsmobiles rent at $30 per day and 20 cents per mile. Cadillacs rent for $37 per day and 25 cents per mile. All cars rented are allowed the first 50 miles per day free. Use structured programming techniques with GO SUB/WHILE and IF/THEN/ELSE statements.

2. Input: Read from data statements the customer's name, type of car, miles driven, and days rented.

3. Output: Print a single line of detail for each customer after appropriate headings have been printed. Include a total of the amounts owed, days driven, miles driven, and free miles.

Pseudocode 11.3

Main routine
   Print headings
   Assign 'no' to end of file switch
   Read first customer's name, type of car, miles driven, and days rented
   Do process subroutine while end of file switch is 'no'
   Print totals
   Endprogram

Process subroutine
   IF car is a Volkswagon, do Volkswagon subroutine
   ELSE IF car is an Oldsmobile, do Oldsmobile subroutine
      ELSE IF car is a Cadillac, do Cadillac subroutine
         ELSE print error message and read next customer
   Endif
   Do amount owed subroutine
   Read next customer information
   IF name is 'end' assign 'yes' to end of file switch
   Return to main routine

Volkswagon subroutine
   Assign $22 to daily rate
   Assign 15 cents to mileage rate
   Return to process subroutine

Oldsmobile subroutine
   Assign $30 to daily rate
   Assign 20 cents to mileage rate
   Return to process subroutine

Cadillac subroutine
>   Assign $37 to daily rate
>   Assign 25 cents to mileage rate
>   Return to process subroutine

Amount owed subroutine
>   Calculate free miles by multiplying 50 times the days rented
>   IF free miles are greater than or equal to miles driven, mileage charge is zero
>   ELSE mileage charge is the mileage rate times (miles driven − free miles)
>   Endif
>   Calculate amount owed by multiplying the daily rate times the number of days and
>   adding the mileage charge calculated
>   Add amount owed, days driven, miles driven, and free miles to totals
>   Print detail line
>   Return to process subroutine

Flowchart 11.3

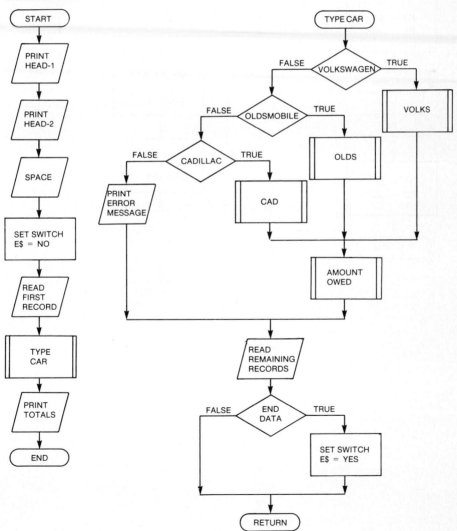

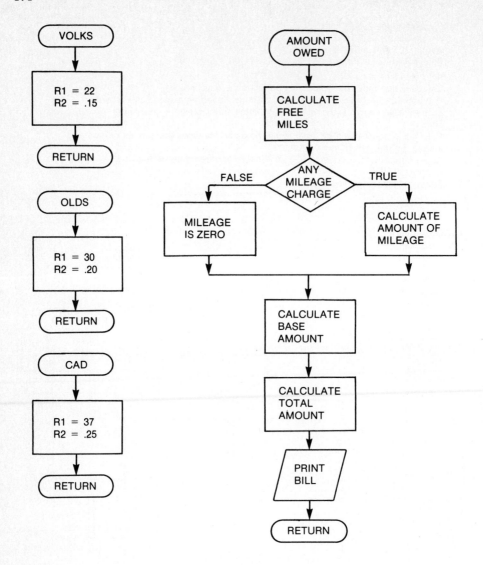

```
1 REM CAR RENTAL REPORT
50 ! E$ = END OF FILE SWITCH
   N$ = CUSTOMER NAME
   T$ = TYPE OF CAR
    M = MILES DRIVEN
    D = DAYS RENTED
  F1$ = PRINTING FORMAT FOR TOTAL LINE
  F2$ = PRINTING FORMAT FOR DETAIL LINE
   T1 = TOTAL OF MILES DRIVEN
   T2 = TOTAL OF DAYS RENTED
   T3 = TOTAL OF FREE MILES
   T4 = TOTAL OF AMOUNT OWED
   R1 = DAILY RATE
   R2 = MILEAGE RATE
    C = MILEAGE CHARGE
    A = AMOUNT OWED BY CUSTOMER
100 REM MAIN ROUTINE
110 PRINT 'CUSTOMER  TYPE OF     MILES      DAYS       FREE       AMOUNT'
120 PRINT ' NAME      CAR       DRIVEN     RENTED      MILES       OWED'
125 PRINT
130 E$ = 'NO'
140 READ N$, T$, M, D              ! END OF FILE SWITCH
150 GOSUB 200 WHILE E$ = 'NO'      ! PROCESS DATA
160 F1$ = '          TOTALS       ####         ##          ###    $###,###.##'
170 PRINT USING F1$, T1, T2, T3, T4 ! PRINT TOTALS
180 GO TO 999                      ! END PROGRAM
200 REM PROCESS SUBROUTINE
210 IF T$ = 'VOLKSWAGON' THEN GOSUB 300
    ELSE IF T$ = 'OLDSMOBILE' THEN GO SUB 400
        ELSE IF T$ = 'CADILLAC' THEN GO SUB 500
             ELSE PRINT '=====CAR TYPE INVALID FOR '; N$;'====='\
                  GO TO 230
220 GO SUB 600                     ! AMOUNT OWED SUBROUTINE
230 READ N$, T$, M, D              ! READ NEXT CUSTOMER
240 IF N$ = 'END' THEN E$ = 'YES'
250 RETURN
300 REM VOLKSWAGON SUBROUTINE
310 R1 = 22
320 R2 = .15
330 RETURN
400 REM OLDSMOBILE SUBROUTINE
410 R1 = 30
420 R2 = .20
430 RETURN
500 REM CADILLAC SUBROUTINE
510 R1 = 37
520 R2 = .25
530 RETURN
600 REM AMOUNT OWED SUBROUTINE
610 F = 50 * D                     ! CALCULATE FREE MILES
620 IF F >= M THEN C = 0
    ELSE C = R2 * (M-F)            ! CALCULATE MILEAGE CHARGE
630 A = R1 * D + C                 ! CALCULATE AMOUNT OWED
640 T1 = T1 + M                    ! TOTAL OF MILES DRIVEN
650 T2 = T2 + D                    ! TOTAL OF DAYS RENTED
660 T3 = T3 + F                    ! TOTAL OF FREE MILES
670 T4 = T4 + A                    ! TOTAL OF AMOUNT OWED
680 F2$ = '\        \\           \ ####         ##          ###    $###,###.##'
690 PRINT USING F2$, N$, T$, M, D, F, A
700 RETURN

Ready
900 DATA JONES, CADILLAC, 400, 5
901 DATA KELLY, VOLKSWAGON, 575, 2
902 DATA BROWN, OLDSMOBILE, 200, 6
903 DATA MARIANA, VOLKSWAGON, 1000, 7
904 DATA STARK, CADILLAC, 500, 2
905 DATA END, 0, 0, 0
999 END

Ready

RUNNH
CUSTOMER   TYPE OF     MILES      DAYS       FREE       AMOUNT
  NAME      CAR       DRIVEN     RENTED      MILES       OWED

JONES     CADILLAC     400         5          250    $    222.50
KELLY     VOLKSWAGON   575         2          100    $    115.25
BROWN     OLDSMOBILE   200         6          300    $    180.00
=====CAR TYPE INVALID FOR MARIANA=====
STARK     CADILLAC     500         2          100    $    174.00
           TOTALS     1675        15          750    $    691.75

Ready
```

Exercises

1. How does the use of subroutines fit into the concept of structured programming?
2. What is the purpose of the RETURN statement?
3. Can a subroutine have more than one entry point or exit point? Should it?
4. How does the GO SUB/WHILE allow a fuller implementation of structured programming?
5. When would the use of the ON—GO SUB statement be advised?
6. Acme Distributors wants a weekly listing of sales for those products whose price is $50 or over and that were sold in departments 2 or 4. Write a program that will do the following:

   a. Assign discounts as follows:

Unit price	Discount percentage
$50 through $99.99	10%
$100 through $149.99	15
$150 and over	20

   b. Accumulate the amount of total net sales (Sales price − Discount) and the amount of total discounts for each of the three discount categories, and display the results in table form as shown under output below.
   c. Use the data listed below to test the program, but allow for an unknown number of items sold.
   d. Use structured programming by developing at least three modules (subroutines) that are accessed by GO SUB statements. For instance, the writing of the headings, the processing of the data, and the printing of the table could be the three modules. More than three subroutines may be used if desired.
   e. Completely document the program with REM statements and/or with the use of the exclamation point !.

   Data:

Item	Price	Department number
Bedding	49.95	2
Carpet	134.50	4
Clothing	72.50	1
Fans	5.00	2
Fams	365.50	4
Grills	150.00	5
Lamps	99.99	3
Radios	151.25	2
Tires	79.25	2

Output:

SALES REPORT
ACME DISTRIBUTORS

ITEM	NET SALES
-----	----------
(list all that apply)	
TOTAL NET SALES	$XX,XXX.XX
TOTAL DISCOUNT AT 10%	$XX,XXX.XX
TOTAL DISCOUNT AT 15%	$XX,XXX.XX
TOTAL DISCOUNT AT 20%	$XX,XXX.XX

7. One of the advantages of structured programming is the ability to modify an existing program with relatively ease. What would need to be done to modify Sample Program 11.3 to allow for the rental of a Chevrolet if the daily rate is $25 and the mileage rate is 17 cents?

8. Write a program that will list the products sold by department and by store. The data to be used are listed under data below and are to be appropriately edited on output to correspond with the output format shown. Use structured programming techniques with subroutines. Document your program with remarks and comments.

Data:

Product number	Department number	Store number	Quantity sold	Price
757	10	1	100	5.75
863	10	1	150	.75
972	20	1	20	1.15
743	20	1	75	20.05
897	20	1	95	19.75
732	15	2	100	10.57
757	15	2	42	20.00
863	15	2	175	19.95
921	25	2	100	17.50
871	25	2	200	4.02

Output:

PRODUCT NUMBER	DEPARTMENT NUMBER	STORE NUMBER	QUANTITY SOLD	PRICE	TOTAL SALES
XXX	XX	X	XXX	$XX.XX	$X,XXX.XX
XXX	XX	X	XX	$X.XX	$ XXX.XX
	TOTALS FOR DEPT X		X,XXX		$XX,XXX.XX
XXX	XX	X	XX	$.XX	$ XXX.XX
	TOTALS FOR DEPT X		X,XXX		$ X,XXX.XX
	TOTALS FOR STORE X		X,XXX		$XX,XXX.XX
	GRAND TOTALS		X,XXX		$XXX,XXX.XX

9. The local gas company bills customers according to the following rate schedule:

   a. First 1,000 cubic feet: $10 base fee.
   b. Next 3,000 cubic feet: $0.20 per hundred.
   c. Next 21,000 cubic feet: $0.19 per hundred.
   d. Next 100,000 cubic feet: $0.17 per hundred.
   e. Next 200,000 cubic feet: $0.16 per hundred.
   f. Next 325,000 cubic feet: $0.15 per hundred.
   g. Remaining cubic feet: $0.10 per hundred.

   In addition to the rate fees, there is a 3% sales tax on the above amount and a franchise fee depending on user classification as follows: code 1 = $2, code 2 = $8, and code 3 = $15. For example, a code 1 customer using 26,000 cubic feet would have a bill of: 1,000 cubic feet = $10 plus 3,000 cubic feet = $6 plus 21,000 cubic feet = $39.90 plus 26,000 − 25,000 cubic feet = $1.70. Three percent of this total of $57.60 = $1.73. Total bill is $57.60 + $1.73 + $2 = $61.33. Write a program for an unknown number of customers to make the above calculations. Print these calculations in a list with appropriate headings. Use structured programming techniques with subroutines. Document your program with remarks and comments. Write pseudcode or draw a flowchart. Use the following as test data:

Customer number	Cubic feet	Code
6,121	23,123	1
1,265	2,003	1
4,822	125,015	2
3,121	326,000	3
5,411	910	1
6,126	205,500	3

10. A baking company wants to determine its best inventory policy in terms of maximum profit. Its "Good" brand bread is baked in units of 40 and the following data have been compiled:

Daily demand:	1,100, 1,140, 1,180, 1,220, 1,260, 1,300, 1,340
Probability of selling:	0.100, 0.155, 0.200, 0.175, 0.150, 0.125, 0.095

The bread sells for $1.05 a loaf and costs 65 cents a loaf delivered to a store. Bread left over at the end of three days is sent to the "day-old" store and sold for 55 cents a loaf. Calculate and display a payoff matrix and expected value matrix. Also, display the maximum expected profits under uncertainty.

   a. Find the conditional profits for each cell in the payoff matrix where conditional profits equal sales minus cost plus salvage value.
   b. Find the expected values for each cell in the expected values matrix where expected values equal probability times conditional profit.
   c. Total expected values equal the sum of all expected values per column. Largest value is the maximum expected profits under uncertainty.

The output format is:

PAYOFF MATRIX

INVENTORY

DEMAND	1100	1140	1180	1220	1260	1300	1340

****

1100
1140
1180
1220
1260
1300
1340

****

EXPECTED VALUES MATRIX

INVENTORY

DEMAND	1100	1140	1180	1220	1260	1300	1340

****

1100
1140
1180
1220
1260
1300
1340

****

MAXIMUM EXPECTED PROFITS UNDER UNCERTAINTY: $$XX,XXX.XX

Chapter Twelve

Table Handling and Subscripted Variables

The variables that have been discussed so far in this text can hold one value at a time. There are many situations where all the values for some application need to be stored in temporary memory at the same time. This group of values could then be referred to as tables or arrays. Examples are income-tax tables for different levels of income and numbers of dependents; airline fares between various cities; a set of values to determine standard deviation, correlations, and other statistics; areas under a normal curve; a list of 50 states; and numerous other examples.

Such data are normally short enough to be placed in temporary storage in tables (thereafter referred to as arrays). An array comprises a set of values stored in consecutive storage locations and assigned one variable name. Arrays are described as one dimensional or two dimensional and as numeric or string.

One-Dimensional Arrays

A one-dimensional array is simply a column of values or a row of values in a list. The values 21, 54, 16, 35 make up a row array that is a one-dimension numeric value array. The values:

COLORADO
MISSOURI
PENNSYLVANIA
WASHINGTON

make up a column array that is a one-dimension string value array.

Reference to a specific value in an array is made by the use of a variable name along with a subscript which identifies the location of the specific value. Given an array named A with the following list of values—21, 54, 16, 35—reference would be made to each value as follows: A_1 would be 21, since it is the first value in the array; A_2 would be 54; A_3 would be 16; and A_4 would be 35. The number written to the right of the array name is called a subscript. The values in the array then are referred to as: A sub one, A sub two, etc.

Array named A

A_1	A_2	A_3	A_4
21	54	16	35

The rules for using variable names for arrays are the same as for simple variables, with one exception. Since it is not possible to write A_1 in a computer language, all array names are written with the subscript in parentheses following the variable name. Thus, the example above would be:

One-dimensional array named A

A(1)	A(2)	A(3)	A(4)
21	54	16	35

Two-Dimensional Arrays

A two-dimensional array lists values by rows and columns. The subscripts in the variable name indicate in which row and in which column a specific value is located.

Two-dimensional array named B

	Column 1	Column 2	Column 3
Row 1	142	532	17
Row 2	97	279	634

To reference a value in a two-dimensional array, both the particular row and the column where the value is located are used. The value 634 is located in row 2 and column 3. It is referred as B sub two, three; or using the syntax of the language, the reference is B(2,3). Notice that there are two subscripts within the parentheses. B(2,1) is the location of value 97; B(1,3) is the location of value 17;

and so on. Usually the first subscript indicates the row and the second subscript indicates the column.

Subscripted Variables

The same variable name can be used as both a simple variable (unsubscripted) and a subscripted variable name. For example, X and X(4) are both valid variable names in the same program, but they are interpreted by the computer as different names in that X does not refer to an array. In a program, 100 PRINT A cannot be used to refer to an array called A. It must be 100 PRINT A(1), etc. It is important to note that a variable name *cannot* be used to represent both a one-dimensional array and a two-dimensional array in the same program. There are two cases in the language where a simple variable name does refer to an entire array and not just one storage location. That is in the use of the CHANGE and MAT statements, which are discussed in a later chapter.

Subscripts must be positive values and may be constants, variables, or expressions. Subscripts are always evaluated first and then the location of the value in the array is determined. For example, assume that $N = 8$ and $M = 4$ in the following subscripted variables.

$X(N)$	$= X(8)$	$=$ The 8th numeric value in the array
$X(M+N)$	$= X(12)$	$=$ The 12th numeric value in the array
$X(N/M)$	$= X(2)$	$=$ The 2nd numeric value in the array
$X\$(6)$	$= X\$(6)$	$=$ The 6th string value in the array
$X\$(M*2)$	$= X\$(8)$	$=$ The 8th string value in the array
$X(3,2)$	$= X(3,2)$	$=$ The numeric value in the 3rd row, 2nd column in the array
$X(N,M)$	$= X(8,4)$	$=$ The numeric value in the 8th row, 4th column in the array
$X\$(N-1,M*2)$	$= X\$(7,8)$	$=$ The string value in the 7th row, 8th column in the array

Subscripts should be integer values because they represent discrete locations in an array. If, in fact, they are real or floating point numbers, the decimal portions are truncated, and only the integer values are used as the subscript. $X(4.6)$ would be treated as $X(4)$.

The location in an array in the language always starts at zero (0) and continues for whatever length is desired so long as it does not exceed the amount of internal storage available. A one-dimensional array might be:

A$(0)	A$(1)	A$(2)

and a two dimensional array might be:

	Column 0	Column 1	Column 2
Row 0			
Row 1			
Row 2			

It is common practice with the PDP-11 or VAX-11 to ignore the 0 locations and always start with 1 as the first location in a row and column. The remainder of this text will use that practice.

The DIM Statement

The language will automatically reserve 11 positions for a single-dimension array if the variable name uses subscripts. If more locations are needed in an array, the programmer must tell the computer to reserve them. It is a good practice to always tell the computer to save storage locations for an array, regardless of its size. That is the approach that will be used throughout this text.

The DIM statement is a nonexecutable specification statement. The purpose of the DIM statement is to define the number of storage locations to be saved for use in an array.

The general format of the DIM statement is:

n DIM v1(k), v2(k), etc.

where *DIM* is a reserved word, the *comma* is a delimiter and *v1, v2,* etc. are the names of variables that are arrays. The *k* is an unsigned integer constant that is the maximum value a subscript for the dimension may obtain.

One DIM statement may be used to dimension any number and type of arrays. Examples are:

100 DIM A(10)   ! A 1 DIMENSION NUMERIC ARRAY WITH
                             A MAXIMUM OF 10 LOCATIONS

100 DIM X(5), X$(10)   ! X IS A 1 DIMENSION NUMERIC ARRAY
                             FOR 5 LOCATIONS AND X$ IS A 1
                             DIMENSION ARRAY FOR 10 LOCATIONS
                             OF STRING DATA

```
100 DIM N$(5), M(5,5)    ! N$ IS A 1 DIMENSION STRING ARRAY
                           FOR 5 LOCATIONS AND M IS A 2
                           DIMENSION NUMERIC ARRAY FOR 5
                           ROWS AND 5 COLUMNS (25 LOCATIONS)
100 DIM D(2,3), D$(2,3)   ! D IS A 2 DIMENSION NUMERIC ARRAY
                           FOR 2 ROWS AND 3 COLUMNS (6
                           LOCATIONS) AND D$ IS A 2 DIMENSION
                           ARRAY FOR STRING DATA FOR 2 ROWS
                           AND 3 COLUMNS (6 LOCATIONS)
```

The following rules should be observed when using DIM statements.

1. DIM statements must be placed in the program prior to any statement that will use those storage locations. It is typically best to place all DIM statements at the beginning of the program.
2. The data placed in a numeric array must not contain any string data.
3. The data placed in a string array may contain numeric values but are always treated as string data. In other words, arithmetic can no longer be done with those data.
4. Only unsigned integers may be used to dimension an array.
5. Not all of the locations that have been dimensioned need to be used.
6. If a program attempts to store a larger number of values in an array than it has been dimensioned for, an error will occur.
7. If only one subscript is given to an array, it cannot be referenced later in the program by using two subscripts in the array.

The program in Example 12.1 will compute the average of three numeric values, then find the difference of each value from the average and display the results.

Statement 100 will reserve a maximum of three numeric entries in an array named T. Statements 110 through 120 are a loop to input three values into T, one value at a time. The value of the subscript changes each time through the loop in order to store the values in different locations. Statement 140 sets the initial value of X to 0. Statements 150 through 170 are a loop to accumulate the sum of the three values stored in T. Statement 180 computes the average of the three values of T summed in A. Statements 190 through 200 will subtract the first value of T from the average, store this difference in D, and then print D and the first value of T. It will loop again and do the same thing for the second and the third value of T. Notice that if the values of T had not been saved in an array, the values of D could not have been computed without again inputting the three values of T into the program.

The program in Example 12.2 is commonly referred to as a "bubble sort." That is, the program will sort values in an array and place them in sequence—in this case, from low to high values. Notice that it was not necessary to use all locations in the B array.

Example 12.1
A Simple Example Using an Array and Subscripts

```
100 DIM T(3)
110 FOR I = 1 TO 3
115 PRINT "ENTER A NUMBER"
120 INPUT T(I)
130 NEXT I
140 X = 0
150 FOR J = 1 TO 3
160 X = X + T(J)
170 NEXT J
180 A = X / 3
190 FOR K = 1 TO 3
200 D = A - T(K)
210 PRINT D, T(K)
220 NEXT K
999 END

Ready

RUNNH
ENTER A NUMBER
? 10
ENTER A NUMBER
? 5
ENTER A NUMBER
? 15
  0            10
  5            5
 -5            15

Ready
```

Example 12.2
Using an Array and Subscripts to Sort Data

```
100 DIM B(10)
110 READ N
120 FOR I = 1 TO N
130 READ B(I)
135 PRINT B(I),
140 NEXT I
145 PRINT
150 FOR I = 1 TO N-1
160    FOR J = 1 TO N-I
170        X = B(J)
180        Y = B(J+1)
190        IF X<= Y THEN 200
                 ELSE B(J) = Y\
                      B(J+1) = X
200    NEXT J
210 NEXT I
220 FOR I = 1 TO N\ PRINT B(I),\ NEXT I
900 DATA 4
901 DATA 70,60,50,40
999 END

Ready

RUNNH
  70           60          50          40
  40           50          60          70
Ready
```

Statement 110 reads in the number of values to be processed, in this case four. Statements 120 through 140 will store these values in array B. Statement 150 will decrease the number of times to execute the outer loop by one each time through the loop. Statement 160 will decrease the number of times to execute the inner loop by the index I each time through the loop. Statement 170 will temporarily save the current value of B. Statement 180 will temporarily save the current value following the current value of B. Statement 190 compares the first value of B (called X for now) and the second value of B (called Y for now). If the condition tested is true—that is, X< = Y—then the remaining instructions are bypassed and control is transferred to statement 200, which increments J to find the next value of B. What happens during this process is that the largest value in the array is "pushed" down to the last position used in the array.

Following completion of the inner loop, control is passed back to the outer loop, and I becomes 2. The inner loop is processed again except that, since the largest value is now located in B(4), that position will be ignored. This happens because statement 160 is now FOR J = 1 TO 2 (because N − I = 4 − 2). This entire process continues until both the outer and inner loops have been completed. Figure 12.1 illustrates what happens as this program is processed.

Figure 12.1
Numeric Illustration of a Sort Procedure

		When I = 1 J = 1	When I = 1 J = 2	When I = 1 J = 3	When I = 2 J = 1	When I = 2 J = 2	When I = 2 J = 1
B array before loop is entered for above subscripts	=	70,60 50,40	60,70 50,40	60,50 70,40	60,50 40,70	50,60 40,70	50,40 60,70
B(J)	=	70	70	70	60	60	50
X	=	70	70	70	60	60	50
B(J + 1)	=	60	50	40	50	40	40
Y	=	60	50	40	50	40	40
B(J)	=	60	50	40	50	40	40
B(J + 1)	=	70	70	70	60	60	50
B array after loop is completed	=	60,70 50,40	60,50 70,40	60,50 40,70	50,60 40,70	50,40 60,70	40,50 60,70

Example 12.3 illustrates that a program can input or output values one at a time or several values at a time. It can also work with more than one array during any type of processing.

Statement 100 reserves a one-dimensional string array and a two-dimensional numeric array. Statements 110 through 130 will read in three string values, one at

Example 12.3
Using More Than One Array in a Program

```
100 DIM N$(3), A(3,4)
110 FOR I = 1 TO 3
120    READ N$(I)
130 NEXT I
140 FOR I = 1 TO 3
150    FOR J = 1 TO 4
160       READ A(I,J)
170    NEXT J
180 NEXT I
190 FOR I = 1 TO 3
200    PRINT N$(I);A(I,1);A(I,2);A(I,3);A(I,4)
210 NEXT I
900 DATA NAME1,NAME2,NAME3
901 DATA 10,20,30,40
902 DATA 20,30,40,10
903 DATA 30,40,10,20
999 END

Ready

RUNNH
NAME1 10   20   30   40
NAME2 20   30   40   10
NAME3 30   40   10   20

Ready
```

a time. Statements 140 through 180 will read in 12 numeric values, 1 value at a time. Statements 190 through 210 will display the first string value in N$ and the first complete row of numeric values in A. Then the second string value and second complete row of numeric values, then the third string value and the third row of numeric values will be displayed.

Additional examples of arrays are:

```
100 DIM A(5),B(5),C(5)       ! WILL READ 3 NUMERIC VALUES AT A TIME
110 FOR I = 1 TO 5           ! FOR 3 DIFFERENT VALUES
120   READ A(I),B(I),C(I)
130 NEXT I
100 DIM A(3)                 ! WILL READ 3 NUMERIC VALUES AT A TIME
110 READ A(1),A(2),A(3)      ! FOR THE SAME ARRAY
100 DIM X(4,3)               ! WILL INPUT 1 NUMERIC VALUE AT A TIME
110 FOR R = 1 TO 4           ! IN ROW ORDER FOR AN ARRAY
120   FOR C = 1 TO 3
130    INPUT X(R,C)
140   NEXT C
150 NEXT R
100 FOR I = 1 TO 10          ! WILL SUM 1 NUMERIC VALUE AT A TIME
110   S = S + A(I)           ! 10 TIMES FROM A(I) AND ACCUMULATE  THE
120 NEXT I                   ! RESULT IN S
100 FOR I = 1 TO 3           ! WILL SUM 1 NUMERIC VALUE AT A TIME
110   FOR J = 1 TO 4         ! IN COLUMN ORDER 1 ROW AT A TIME FROM
120    C(I) = C(I) + D(J,I)  ! D(J,I) WHERE THE FINAL RESULT WILL BE
130   NEXT J                 ! 3 TOTALS STORED IN C(1), C(2), C(3)
140 NEXT I                   ! OF THE COLUMNS
```

```
100 FOR I = 1 TO 3          ! WILL SUM 1 NUMERIC VALUE AT A TIME
110   FOR J = 1 TO 4        ! IN ROW ORDER 1 COLUMN AT A TIME
120     R(I) = R(I) + D(I,J) ! FROM D(I,J) AND THE FINAL RESULT WILL BE
130   NEXT J                ! FROM TOTALS STORED IN R(1), R(2), R(3), R(4)
140 NEXT I

100 FOR I = 1 TO 5          ! WILL DISPLAY 5 STRING VALUES OF N$(5)
110   PRINT N$(5)           ! 1 AT A TIME ON THE SAME LINE
120 NEXT I

100 FOR I = 1 TO 4          ! WILL DISPLAY 1 STRING VALUE FROM A$(I,J)
110   FOR J = 1 TO 3        ! AND 1 NUMERIC VALUE FROM X(I,J) AT A
120     PRINT A$(I,J),X(I,J) ! TIME ON THE SAME LINE
130   NEXT J
140   NEXT I
```

Common errors

Statement	Explanation
100 DIM A1(12),A1(4,3)	Cannot use the same variable name for two different arrays.
100 DIM B(10),C(N)	Cannot use the variable N to dimension an array. Must be an unsigned integer.
100 PRINT X(I);X(I+1);X(I+2) 110 DIM X(9)	Must place DIM before it is used in the program.
100 DIM A(10),B(10,10),N$(10) 110 FOR I = 1 TO 100 120 B(I) = I 130 NEXT I	There is only room for 10 values per row in B. Also B(I) is 1-dimensional and should be 2-dimensional. An error will occur.
100 DIM X$(100) 110 FOR I = 1 TO 50 120 X$(I) = I 130 NEXT I	Will actually store the numeric values 1 to 50 in X$ but they are now nonnumeric values and cannot be used in arithmetic. May be a logic error.
100 DIM X(2,3) 110 FOR I = 1 TO 2 120 FOR J = 1 TO 3 130 READ X(I,J) 140 NEXT J 150 NEXT I 900 DATA NAME1, 10, 100 901 DATA NAME2, 20, 200	Cannot mix string and numeric data in a numeric array.
100 DIM A(5) 110 FOR I = 1 to 10 \ INPUT A(I) \ NEXT I	Cannot store more values in A(5) than there is room for.
100 DIM Y(3,3) 110 FOR I = 1 TO 3 \ FOR J = 1 TO 3 120 S = S + Y(1,J) 130 NEXT J \ NEXT I	Will never sum all the values in Y because in statement 120, Y(1,J) will sum the same values in row 1 three times.

Sample Problems

Problem Description 12.1

1.   Statement of the problem: A local TV station wants a list of the ski resort areas whose snow depth in inches is above the average for all ski resort areas in the state.

2.   Input: Use a READ statement to enter the name of the ski resort and the snow depth in inches. There are 15 areas in the sample.

3.   Output: Display on a terminal the names of the ski resort areas and their snow depth in inches.

Flowchart 12.1

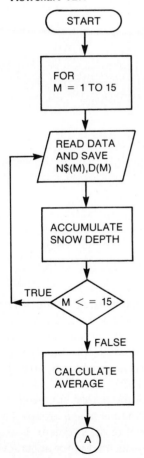

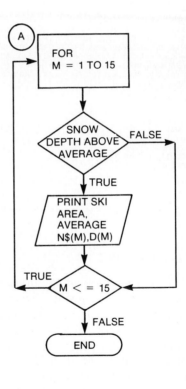

Pseudocode 12.1

```
FOR M = 1 to 15
   Read name and snow depth and place into two arrays
   Accumulate snow depth
Endfor
Calculate average
FOR M = 1 to 15
   IF snow depth above average, print area and snow depth
Endfor
Endprogram
```

```
1 REM SNOW DEPTH REPORT OF AREAS WITH ABOVE
      AVERAGE SNOWFALL
50 ! N$ = SKI AREA NAMES        D = SNOW DEPTHS
       M = COUNTER FOR LOOP CONTROL
       T = TOTAL OF ALL SNOW DEPTHS
       A = AVERAGE DEPTH
100 DIM N$(15), D(15)
110 FOR M = 1 TO 15
120 READ N$(M), D(M)
130 T = T + D(M)
140 NEXT M
150 A = T/15
210 FOR M = 1 TO 15
220 IF D(M) <= A THEN 240
230 PRINT N$(M), D(M)
240 NEXT M
900 DATA ARAPAHOE, 32, ASPEN MTN, 24, BERTHOUD, 32
901 DATA BRECKENRIDGE, 30, ELDORA, 30, KEYSTONE, 40
902 DATA LOVELAND, 32, MARY JANE, 35, MONARCH, 42
903 DATA SNOWMASS, 30, STEAMBOAT, 40, TELLURIDE, 28
904 DATA VAIL,29, WINTER PARK,24, WOLF CREEK, 38
999 END

Ready

RUNNH
KEYSTONE       40
MARYJANE       35
MONARCH        42
STEAMBOAT      40
WOLFCREEK      38

Ready
```

Problem Description 12.2

1. Statement of the problem: A group of Chicago citizens are conducting a drive to expand the size of a hospital. You have contracted to make a survey of the persons in southwest Chicago between the ages of 0 through 70 years of age. The results of the research are to be analyzed so as to determine the number and percentage of persons whose ages belong in the following groups: 0 to 9, 10 to 19, 20 to 29, 30 to 39, 40 to 49, 50 to 59, and 60 through 70.

2. Input: Use a READ statement to enter the age of the person surveyed.

3. Output: Display appropriate headings and descriptions of age groups. For each age group, list what was asked for in the statement of the problem. Use a string variable for edit fields. Show percentages with two-decimal-place accuracy.

Pseudocode 12.2

Main routine
 Print headings
 Dowhile there are data
   Read age
   Do age group subroutine
   Do output subroutine
 Enddo
 Endprogram

Age group subroutine
 Determine appropriate age group
 Add 1 to appropriate age group
 Return to main routine

Output subroutine
 FOR I = 1 to 7 age groups
   Print age group category, number, and percentage in category
 Endfor
 Return to main subroutine

Flowchart 12.2

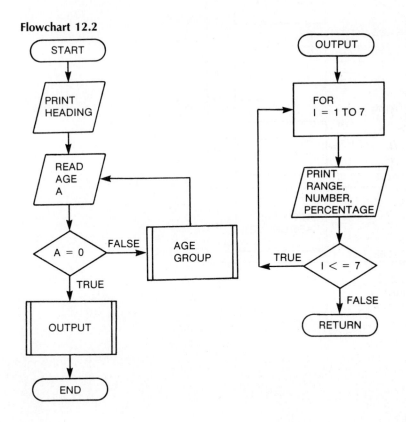

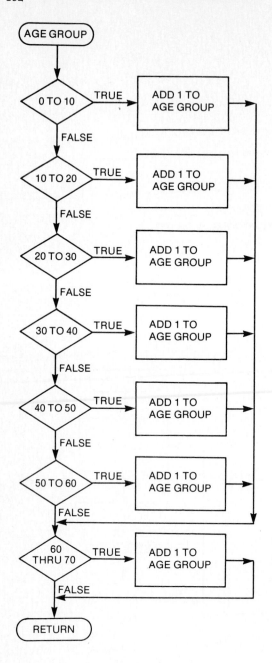

```
1 REM HOSPITAL SURVEY - FREQUENCY TABLE
50 ! T = TOTAL WITHIN EACH CATEGORY
       A = AN INDIVIDUAL'S AGE
       N = TOTAL NUMBER IN SURVEY
       F$ = STRING VARIABLE USED TO DEFINE
            PRINTING FORMAT
       J = LOWER CLASS INTERVAL OF EACH
            CATEGORY
100 DIM T(7)
105 PRINT "       SURVEY RESULTS"
110 PRINT "CATEGORY     TOTAL   PERCENTAGE"
120 READ A
130 IF A <> 0 THEN GO SUB 500\ GO TO 120
140 GO SUB 700
150 GO TO 999
500 IF A >= 0 AND A < 10 THEN T(1) = T(1) + 1
        ELSE IF A < 20 THEN T(2) = T(2) + 1
        ELSE IF A < 30 THEN T(3) = T(3) + 1
        ELSE IF A < 40 THEN T(4) = T(4) + 1
        ELSE IF A < 50 THEN T(5) = T(5) + 1
        ELSE IF A < 60 THEN T(6) = T(6) + 1
        ELSE IF A <=70 THEN T(7) = T(7) + 1
505 IF A < 1 OR A > 70 THEN 510
        ELSE N = N + 1
510 RETURN
700 FOR I = 1 TO 7
705 F$ =  "## TO ##      ##        .##"
710 PRINT USING F$, 10*J,I*10,T(I),T(I)/N
711 J = I
720 NEXT I
730 RETURN
900 DATA 20,31,46,9,7,25,36,41,52,52
901 DATA 65,70,8,19,19,18,25,27,33,40
902 DATA 0
999 END

Ready

RUNNH
      SURVEY RESULTS
CATEGORY     TOTAL   PERCENTAGE
  0 TO 10      3        .15
 10 TO 20      3        .15
 20 TO 30      4        .20
 30 TO 40      3        .15
 40 TO 50      3        .15
 50 TO 60      2        .10
 60 TO 70      2        .10

Ready
```

Problem Description 12.3

1. Statement of the problem: A company sells four different types of soft drinks and distributes these products to six distribution centers in Minnesota. The sales manager wants to know what percentage of the company's sales is accounted for by each product at each distribution center and the total percentage of all products by each center.

2. Input: Use a READ statement to enter in row order, one value at a time, the number of cases of Coke, 7up, orange, and Sprite.

3. Output: Display appropriate headings, column and row names, and the percentages asked for in the statement of the problem.

194

Flowchart 12.3

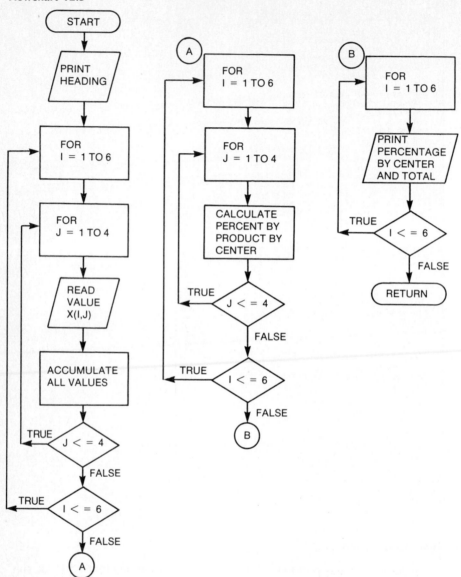

Pseudocode 12.3

Print headings
FOR I = 1 to 6 centers
  FOR J = 1 to 4 products
    Read sales value
    Add sales value to total
  Endfor
Endfor
FOR I = 1 to 6 centers
  FOR J = 1 to 4 products
    Calculate percentages of products by center
  Endfor
Endfor
FOR I = 1 to 6 centers
  Print percentages
Endfor
Endprogram

```
1 REM SALES REPORT BY PERCENTAGES
50 ! X = SALES AMOUNTS BY CENTER AND PRODUCT
     P = PERCTNTAGE AMOUNTS BY CENTER AND PRODUCE
     C = TOTAL PERCENTAGE SALES BY CENTER
     T = TOTAL SALES
100 DIM X(6,4), P(6,4), C(6)
110 PRINT "           SALES REPORT"
120 FOR I = 1 TO 6
130     FOR J = 1 TO 4
140         READ X(I,J)
150         T = T + X(I,J)
160     NEXT J
170 NEXT I
200 FOR I = 1 TO 6
210     FOR J = 1 TO 4
220         P(I,J) = X(I,J)/T
230         C(I)   = C(I) + P(I,J)
240     NEXT J
250 NEXT I
260 PRINT USING "          COKE    7-UP   ORANGE SPRITE   TOTAL"
300 FOR I = 1 TO 6
310 PRINT USING "CENTER # .####  .####   .####   .####   .####",
I, P(I,1), P(I,2), P(I,3), P(I,4), C(I)
320 NEXT I
900 DATA 200,400,600,350
901 DATA 150,600,900,250
902 DATA 250,475,875,455
903 DATA 100,720,550,275
904 DATA 175,420,730,445
905 DATA 250,580,840,220
999 END

Ready

RUNNH
              SALES REPORT
           COKE    7-UP   ORANGE SPRITE  TOTAL
CENTER 1  .0185   .0370   .0555  .0324   .1434
CENTER 2  .0139   .0555   .0833  .0231   .1758
CENTER 3  .0231   .0439   .0809  .0421   .1901
CENTER 4  .0093   .0666   .0509  .0254   .1522
CENTER 5  .0162   .0389   .0675  .0412   .1637
CENTER 6  .0231   .0537   .0777  .0204   .1748

Ready
```

Problem Description 12.4

1. Statement of the problem: Write a program to read in a list of a maximum of 20 names of majors and a list of five class levels for students (freshman through graduate). Then read in data records for the number of students by class level within a major for all the different majors at a university. Output a graphic profile of majors by class. Used structured programming with subroutines.

2. Input: Use a READ statement to enter the names of majors until the name END is entered. Use a READ statement to enter the names of class levels until the name END is entered. Use a READ statement to enter the following data: name of major, class level, and number of students.

3. Output: Display an appropriate heading, row and column names and descriptions, and rows of asterisks indicating the number of students by class level within a major. Space four lines between each major's graphic profile.

Pseudocode 12.4

Main routine
  Do tables subroutine
  Do number of students subroutine
  Do graphing subroutine
  Endprogram
Tables subroutine
  Dowhile name of major is not 'end'
    Read names of majors
    Count number of majors read
  Enddo
  Dowhile class is not 'end'
    Read names of classes
    Count number of classes
  Enddo
  Return to main routine
Number of students subroutine
  Dowhile major name is not 'end'
    Read major name, class level, number of students
    FOR I = 1 to number of majors
      IF an appropriate major name was read
        FOR J = 1 to number of classes
          IF a proper class level was read, add number to total
          ELSE read another record
          Endif
        Endfor
      Endif
    Endfor
  Return to main routine
Graphing subroutine
  Print heading
  FOR I = 1 to number of majors
    Print major name
    FOR J = 1 to number of classes
      Print class name
      FOR M = 1 to number in class in increments of 2
        Print appropriate number of asterisks
      Endfor
    Endfor
    Skip 4 lines
  Endfor
  Return to main routine

Flowchart 12.4

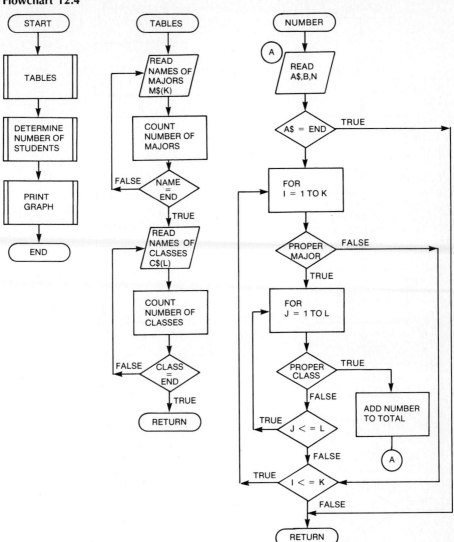

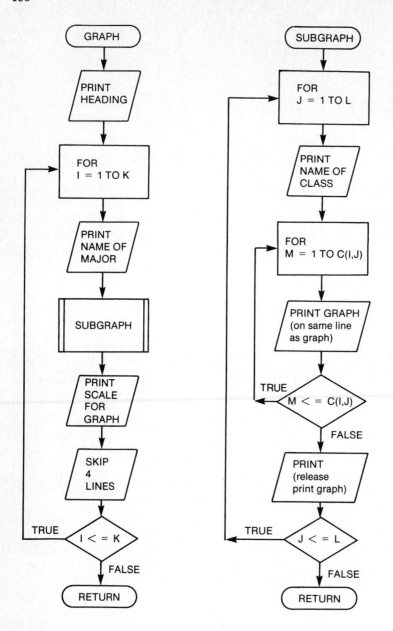

```
1 REM BAR CHART GRAPH OF MAJORS BY CLASS FOR
      UP TO 20 MAJORS
50 ! M$ = NAMES OF MAJORS
     C$ = CLASS NAMES
     A$ = NAME OF MAJOR ON DATA RECORD
     B$ = CODE OF CLASS ON DATA RECORD
           1 = FR, 2 = SO, 3 = JR, 4 = ST, 5 = GRAD
     C = FREQUENCY TABLE OF MAJORS BY CLASS
     K = NUMBER OF DIFFERENT MAJORS
     L = NUMBER OF DIFFERENT CLASSES
     M = NUMBER OF ASTERISKS TO PRINT
100 DIM M$(20), C$(6), C(20,5)
120 GO SUB 300                  ! ENTER ALL MAJOR AND CLASS
                                  NAMES AND COUNT THEM
140 GO SUB 500                  ! DETERMINE NUMBER OF MAJORS BY
                                  CLASS WITHIN MAJOR
160 GO SUB 700   ! PRINT THE NAME OF THE MAJOR, CLASSES WITHIN
                   THE MAJOR, AND A GRAPH FOR THE NUMBER BY
                   CLASS WITHIN THE MAJOR.  REPEAT FOR ALL MAJORS.
200 GO TO 999                   ! END THE PROGRAM
300 K = 1
310 READ M$(K)
320 IF M$(K) <> "END" THEN K = K + 1\ GO TO 310
325 K = K - 1
330 L = 1
340 READ C$(L)
350 IF C$(L) <> "END" THEN L = L + 1\ GO TO 340
355 L = L - 1
360 RETURN
361 !
500 READ A$, B, N
505 IF A$ = "END" THEN 570
510 FOR I = 1 TO K
520     IF A$ <> M$(I) THEN 560
530     FOR J = 1 TO L
540         IF B = J THEN C(I,J) = C(I,J) + N\ GO TO 500
550     NEXT J
560 NEXT I
570 RETURN
571 !
700 PRINT TAB(25); "TABLES BY CLASS WITHIN MAJOR"
710 FOR I = 1 TO K
720     PRINT TAB(34); M$(I)
730     FOR J = 1 TO L
740         PRINT C$(J); TAB(10);
750         FOR M = 1 TO C(I,J) STEP 2
760             PRINT "*";
770         NEXT M
775         PRINT
780     NEXT J
800     PRINT TAB(10); "---10---20---30---40---50";
                       "---60---70---80---90--100"
810     PRINT\PRINT\PRINT\PRINT
820 NEXT I
830 RETURN
900 DATA ACCOUNTING, COMPUTER SCIENCE, MATHEMATICS, ZOOLOGY, END
901 DATA FRESHMAN, SOPHOMORE, JUNIOR, SENIOR, GRADUATE, END
902 !
949 DATA COMPUTER SCIENCE, 5, 10, ZOOLOGY, 5, 8
950 DATA COMPUTER SCIENCE, 4, 30, COMPUTER SCIENCE, 3, 50
951 DATA ZOOLOGY, 1, 16, ZOOLOGY, 2, 26, ZOOLOGY, 3, 30, ZOOLOGY, 4, 20
952 DATA MATHEMATICS, 2, 20, MATHEMATICS, 3, 40, MATHEMATICS, 4, 30
953 DATA ACCOUNTING, 4, 60, ACCOUNTING, 3, 74, ACCOUNTING, 2, 80
954 DATA ACCOUNTING, 1, 90, END, 0, 0
999 END
```

200

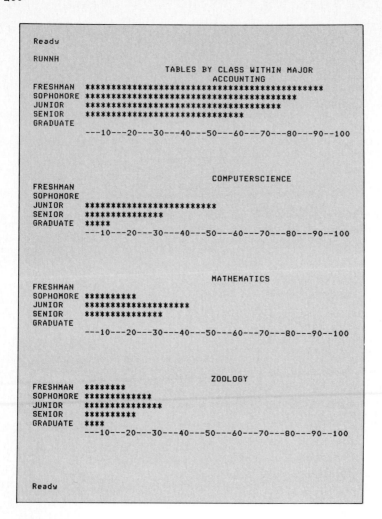

```
Ready

RUNNH
                    TABLES BY CLASS WITHIN MAJOR
                           ACCOUNTING
FRESHMAN   *************************************************
SOPHOMORE  *******************************************
JUNIOR     ***************************************
SENIOR     ******************************
GRADUATE
           ---10---20---30---40---50---60---70---80---90--100



                           COMPUTERSCIENCE
FRESHMAN
SOPHOMORE
JUNIOR     **************************
SENIOR     ***************
GRADUATE   *****
           ---10---20---30---40---50---60---70---80---90--100



                           MATHEMATICS
FRESHMAN
SOPHOMORE  **********
JUNIOR     ********************
SENIOR     ***************
GRADUATE
           ---10---20---30---40---50---60---70---80---90--100



                           ZOOLOGY
FRESHMAN   ********
SOPHOMORE  *************
JUNIOR     ***************
SENIOR     **********
GRADUATE   ****
           ---10---20---30---40---50---60---70---80---90--100



Ready
```

Exercises

1. What can be used as a subscript when manipulating values in an array? Of what value is the use of a variable in a subscript? A constant?
2. Where should the DIM statement be placed? What is the purpose of the DIM statement? When does the DIM statement have to be used?
3. In a two dimensional array, which subscript is used to designate rows in the array? Columns?
4. Correct the errors, if any, in the following statements.
   a. 100 DIM B(10), C(X)

    b.   100 DIM A, B(25)
    c.   100 PRINT X(I)
          200 DIM X(12)
    d.   100 DIM A(10)
          110 FOR I = 1 TO 50
          120   T = T + A(I)
          130 NEXT I
    e.   100 DIM A(10)
          110 FOR J = 1 TO 10
          120   READ A(J)
          130 NEXT J
          140 DATA 15, 75, . .
    f.   100 DIM A(10)
          110 FOR J = 1 TO 10
          120   READ A(J)
          130 NEXT J
          140 DATA NAME1,NAME2, . .

5. What would be the results of each of the following statements?
    a.   100 DIM A(100)
          120 FOR M = 1 TO 100 STEP 2
          130   READ A(M)
          140   A(M+1) = A(M) ** 2
          150 NEXT M
    b.   100 DIM B(50)
          110 FOR I = 1 TO 50
          120   READ B(I)
          130   T = T + B(I)
          140   PRINT B(I)
          150 NEXT I
          160 PRINT T ·
    c.   100 DIM X(5)
          .
          .
          .
          500 FOR I = 1 TO 5
          510   PRINT X(I);
          520 NEXT I
    d.   100 DIM X(10,4), C$(10)
          .
          .
          .
          500 FOR R = 1 TO 10
          510   PRINT C$(R),
          520   FOR C = 1 TO 4
          530   PRINT X(R,C),
          540   T = T + X(R,C)

```
550        NEXT C
560        PRINT T
570        T = 0
580 NEXT R
```

6. Write a program that will read the following names and sales totals into two separate arrays. Then have the program do the following:
   a. List the data in table form for the first, third, and fifth persons.
   b. List the data in table form for the second, fourth, and sixth persons.
   c. Determine the total sales and average sales for all the data.
   d. List the data for all people and print out the message "ABOVE AVERAGE" next to those people who have sales above average.
   e. After the list in d above, print out total and average sales.

Data:

Name	Sales
Jim	$7,500
Brent	6,000
Cecil	2,000
Mary	5,000
John	4,500
Lucile	8,000

7. The following is a tax table for different levels of weekly income and different numbers of employee exemptions. For instance, if an employee had gross pay of $650 and had two exemptions, the tax rate would be 15% of $650, and the tax withheld would be $97.50. A person with $895 gross pay and four exemptions would have 10% withheld, or $89.50.

Income levels	Number of exemptions					
	0	1	2	3	4	5
Up to $399.99	15	10	7	5	3	0
$400 through $599.99	20	15	10	7	5	3
$600 through $799.99	25	20	15	10	7	5
$800 through $999.99	30	25	20	15	10	7
$1,000 and up	35	30	25	20	15	10

Write a program that will do the following:
   a. Read the above tax table into an appropriately defined two-dimensional array.
   b. For the people listed below under data, determine:
      (1) Gross pay (time and a half for hours over 40).
      (2) Withholding tax, given the appropriate entry in the tax table.
      (3) FICA tax, given a 7% FICA tax rate.
      (4) Profit-sharing deduction, given a 10% rate.
      (5) Net pay after deductions.

c. Provide an appropriately formated report including totals of each item calculated in *b* above for each department and for the entire company.

d. Use structured programming techniques.

Data:

Employee name	Hours worked	Pay rate	Number of exemptions	Department number
Bill	40	10.00	2	1
Bob	35	7.50	4	1
Bruce	50	12.00	3	1
Garth	42	8.75	1	2
Jack	40	9.00	2	2
Steve	30	15.00	4	2
Brian	25	8.25	3	2
Kathy	41	11.50	0	3
Harry	40	9.75	2	3
Judy	45	10.50	4	3
Ken	50	22.00	5	4

8. A fast-food restaurant is trying to determine which day of the week and which times of the day are the busiest so that the number of personnel available can be determined. Write a program that will help this restaurant answer these questions:

a. The number of customers by day by time of day.

b. The total number of customers each day of the week.

c. The total number of customers each time period.

d. The total number of customers for the week.

The following codes were used in the data records:

Code	Weekday	Code	Time of day
1	Sunday	1	0800–1200
2	Monday	2	1200–1600
3	Tuesday	3	1600–2000
4	Wednesday	4	2000–2400
5	Thursday		
6	Friday		
7	Saturday		

e. Using the data shown below, use structured programming techniques to test the program and display the results exactly as shown under output. The program must allow for an unknown number of customers to be entered. The names of the weekdays must be displayed from arrays for the output.

Data:

Weekday	2,4,6,5,3,1,2,3,4,2,6,6,1,5,2,4,5,6,6,2
Time of day	3,1,1,2,4,1,2,1,1,2,1,2,4,2,3,1,3,2,1,1

(To be entered a pair at a time, weekday and time of day)

OUTPUT:

YOUR NAME
CURRENT DATE   WEEKLY CUSTOMER REPORT

	0800–1200	1200–1600	1600–2000	2000–2400	TOTAL
SUNDAY	XX	XX	XX	XX	XX
MONDAY	XX	XX	XX	XX	XX
TUESDAY	XX	XX	XX	XX	XX
WEDNESDAY	XX	XX	XX	XX	XX
THURSDAY	XX	XX	XX	XX	XX
FRIDAY	XX	XX	XX	XX	XX
SATURDAY	XX	XX	XX	XX	XX
TOTAL	XXX	XXX	XXX	XXX	XXX

9. Write a program to determine the total vote for all candidates, the total vote for each candidate and the total vote for each district. Also, determine the percentage of registered voters in each district that voted in this election. Use the following data:

Candidate	District				
	1	2	3	4	5
Browning	168	100	22	125	140
McDonnel	791	545	99	310	985
Whiteman	583	392	89	431	919

Total registered voters by district:

1	2	3	4	5
3,120	2,785	806	2,413	4,123

Format for the output is:

DISTRICT

CANDIDATE	1	3	3	4	5	TOTAL
BROWNING						X,XXX
MCDONNEL						X,XXX
WHITEMAN						X,XXX
TOTAL	X,XXX	X,XXX	X,XXX	X,XXX	X,XXX	XX,XXX
PERCENT VOTING	XX.X	XX.X	XX.X	XX.X	XX.X	

Chapter Thirteen

Modifiers

There are many ways to write a collection of statements to create a program. To even further increase the flexibility and ease of expression, the BASIC language has provided statement modifiers. These modifiers can be appended to program statements to specify conditional execution, implied looping, and structured programming techniques. A word of caution: The programmer should avoid too much complexity when using modifiers.

The WHILE Modifier

The general format of the WHILE modifier is:

> statement WHILE c

> where *statement* is a single BASIC statement, *WHILE* is a reserved word, and c is a condition that allows the statement to continue to be executed as long as the condition is "true".

The statement 100 N = N + 1 WHILE N < 100 will allow the statement to be executed until N < 100 is false. From this statement one can see that the WHILE modifier is only useful if the statement is in an iterative loop where the loop structure modifies the value(s) that terminate the loop. The WHILE modifier does not automatically increment a control variable. The above statement could be rewritten as shown in Example 13.1. Statement 100 is executed while N < 100 is

Example 13.1
An iterative process with the WHILE

```
100 N = N + 1   WHILE N< 100
110 PRINT N
999 END

Ready

RUNNH
 100

Ready
```

true, which means when N is 99 N = N + 1 is executed again. Then the statement becomes false, and the execution is terminated.

Example 13.2 demonstrates the use of such a modifier for structured programming techniques. The subroutine will continue to execute as long as the READ statement has data to be entered. Notice, statement 515 is required. Otherwise, 0,0,0,ENDJOB will be considered data, as statement 100 will be executed once more because the condition is still true. The RETURN statement passes control back to statement 100 each time through the subroutine to check the modifier.

Example 13.2
The WHILE with a GO/SUB

```
100 GO SUB 500   WHILE N$ <> "ENDJOB"
110 GO TO 999
500 !!!START SUB
510 READ A,B,C,N$
515 IF N$ = "ENDJOB" THEN 540
520 S = (A + B + C)/3
530 PRINT "AVERAGE FOR "; N$; " IS "; S
540 RETURN
900 DATA 5,10,15,JONES, 6,7,8,SMITH, 0,0,0,ENDJOB
999 END

Ready

RUNNH
AVERAGE FOR JONES IS   10
AVERAGE FOR SMITH IS   7

Ready
```

The WHILE can be used with a FOR/NEXT loop. Example 13.3 uses the WHILE modifier to determine when the loop is to terminate. I prints the values 1, 2, 3, 4.

Example 13.3
The WHILE with a FOR/NEXT

```
100 FOR I = 1 WHILE I < 5
110 PRINT I;
120 NEXT I
999 END

Ready

RUNNH
 1   2   3   4
Ready
```

The UNTIL Modifier

The general format of the UNTIL modifier is:

> statement UNTIL c

where *statement* is a single statement, *UNTIL* is a reserved word, and c is a condition that allows the statement to continue to be executed until the condition becomes true.

The statement 100 N = N + 1 UNTIL N = 100 will allow the statement to be executed until N = 100 is true. The UNTIL has the same limitations as the WHILE, but the logic is different.

Examples 13.1 and 13.2 are rewritten using the UNTIL modifier in Examples 13.4 and 13.5.

Example 13.4
An iterative process with the UNTIL

```
100 N = N + 1  UNTIL N = 100
110 PRINT N
999 END

Ready

RUNNH
 100

Ready
```

Example 13.5
The UNTIL with a GO/SUB

```
100 GO SUB 500  UNTIL N$ = "ENDJOB"
110 GO TO 999
500 !!!START SUB
510 READ A,B,C,N$
515 IF N$ = "ENDJOB" THEN 540
520 S = (A + B + C)/3
530 PRINT "AVERAGE FOR "; N$; " IS "; S
540 RETURN
900 DATA 5,10,15,JONES, 6,7,8,SMITH, 0,0,0,ENDJOB
999 END

Ready

RUNNH
AVERAGE FOR JONES IS   10
AVERAGE FOR SMITH IS   7

Ready
```

In Example 13.4, N has a value of 100 when printed because statement 100 was executed until the condition N = 100 was true. Notice the difference in the logic between the WHILE and UNTIL modifiers. In Example, 13.5, the subroutine was executed as long as the READ statement had data to be entered.

The logic to be used in solving the problem being programmed best determines whether to use the WHILE or the UNTIL modifier. Example 13.6 uses the UNTIL with a FOR/NEXT loop. I prints the values 1, 2, 3, 4, 5.

Example 13.6
The UNTIL with a FOR/NEXT

```
100 FOR I = 1 UNTIL I > 5
110 PRINT I;
120 NEXT I
999 END

Ready

RUNNH
 1  2  3  4  5
Ready
```

The FOR Modifier

The general formats for the FOR modifiers are:

$$\text{statement FOR } v = e_1 \text{ TO } e_2 \text{ STEP } e_3$$

$$\text{statement FOR } v = e_1 \text{ STEP } e_3 \begin{cases} \text{WHILE c} \\ \text{UNTIL c} \end{cases}$$

where *FOR* is a reserved word which initializes the conditions that must exist for the first execution of the loop, *v* is a programmer-supplier variable name that contains values used during the execution of the loop, = means to move the value of e_1 to the variable, where e_1 is the initial value to be used in the loop, *TO* is a reserved word, e_2 is the value that determines when the loop is to be terminated, *STEP* is an optional reserved word that increments the variable each time the loop is executed (if STEP is omitted, e_3 is always 1), and e_3 is the amount of the increment. If needed, either the WHILE or UNTIL modifier can be used along with the FOR modifier or with the FOR/NEXT statement. When FOR is used as a modifier, the NEXT statement is not used.

Example 13.7 uses the FOR modifier to sum five integers. The modifier is often referred to as an implied loop, and the result is the same as if one used a FOR/NEXT loop such as

100 FOR I = 1 TO 5 \N = N + 1 \ NEXT I \ PRINT N

There can only be one statement preceding the FOR modifier. In this example that statement is N = N + 1.

Example 13.7
Implied loop using a FOR modifier

```
100 N = N + 1 FOR I = 1 TO 5
110 PRINT N
999 END

Ready

RUNNH
 5

Ready
```

Example 13.8 uses the FOR modifier for both entering and displaying data.

Example 13.8
Using more than one modifier in a program

```
100 DIM N$(100)
110 READ N$(I)  FOR I = 1 TO 5
120 PRINT N$(I) FOR I = 1 TO 5
900 DATA "MAYS, WILLIE", "WILLIAMS, TED", "RUTH, BABE"
901 DATA "JACKSON, REGGIE", "TEGLOVIC, STEVE"
999 END

Ready

RUNNH
MAYS, WILLIE
WILLIAMS, TED
RUTH, BABE
JACKSON, REGGIE
TEGLOVIC, STEVE

Ready
```

The IF Modifier

The general format of the IF modifier is:

statement IF c

where *statement* is a single BASIC statement, *IF* is a reserved word, and c is a condition that determines if the statement is to be executed.

For example: 100 N = N + 1 IF N < 10 will allow N = N + 1 to be executed as long as the IF statement is true. The statement has the same results as 100 IF N < 10 THEN N = N + 1. An important point to remember about the IF modifier is that you should be careful using the ELSE option. Because of the logic, the ELSE option may not always be tested. In the example 100 IF N = N THEN PRINT "CONTINUE" ELSE PRINT "STOP" IF M = M, since N = N is true CONTINUE is printed. M = M is also true, but it applies to the ELSE clause and is never tested.

The UNLESS Modifier

The general format for the UNLESS modifier is

statement UNLESS c

> where *statement* is a single BASIC statement, *UNLESS* is a reserved word, and *c* is a condition that allows the statement to continue to be executed if the condition is false.

The use of the UNLESS modifier simplifies the negation of a logical condition. The statement 100 N = N + 1 UNLESS N = 0 will only execute if N is not equal to 0. Notice, the statement 100 IF A <> 0 THEN N = N + 1, has the same results. At times the logic is more straightforward when using the UNLESS modifier.

Multiple Modifiers

One can use several modifiers in the same statement if the logic permits. When multiple modifiers are to be used in a statement, they are executed starting with the rightmost modifier and ending with the leftmost. Examples are:

1. 100 READ N(I,J) FOR J = 1 TO 3 FOR I = 1 TO 5
    This statement will enter values into a five-by-three array, one row at a time. The outer loop starts first and then the inner loop is completed before a second return to the outer loop. The above statement is equivalent to the following statements:

    100 FOR I = 1 TO 5
    110 FOR J = 1 TO 3
    120 READ N(I,J)
    130 NEXT J
    140 NEXT I

2. 100 Y(I,J) = X(I,J) FOR J = 1 TO 5 FOR I = 1 TO 5
    This statement will copy the contents of the X array into the Y array. Equivalent statements would be:

    100 FOR I = 1 TO 5 \ FOR J = 1 TO 5
    110 Y(I,J) = X(I,J)
    120 NEXT J \ NEXT I

3. 100 X = Y IF X > 0 IF Y > 0

    This statement will copy Y into X when both Y and X are values greater than 0. An equivalent statement would be:

    100 IF X > 0 AND Y > 0 THEN X = Y

4. 100 GO SUB 500 IF X = 0

    This statement will go to the subroutine 500 if X = 0. Otherwise, it will go to the next statement in the program. An equivalent statement would be:

    100 IF X = 0 THEN GO SUB 500

5. 100 GO SUB 500 FOR J = 1 TO 5 UNLESS A = 10 OR B = 10

    This statement will execute the subroutine 5 times unless either A or B = 10 before statement 200 is executed. Equivalent statements would be:

    100 . . . .
    110 A = ...
    120 . . . .
    130 B = ...
    140 . . . .
    200 FOR J = 1 TO 5
    210 GO SUB 500
    220 NEXT J
    230 GO TO 100
    240 . . . .
    500 . . . .
    510 X = N * M
    520 Y = N / M
    530 . . . .
    540 RETURN

Common Errors

Statement	Explanation
100 IF M − N = N THEN N = 5 ELSE M = 6 IF M = N	Be careful about including an ELSE option with IF modifier. It may not make the decision desired.
100 X = −1 110 PRINT N WHILE X < 0	An infinite loop.
100 M = M + 1 UNTIL Y < 0	An infinite loop unless Y defined as a negative number prior to statement 100.
100 DIM N$(10) 110 READ N$(I) FOR I = 1 UNTIL N$ = "ENDJOB" 900 DATA A,B,C,ENDJOB	Will get error message ?OUT OF DATA AT LINE 110.
100 N = 0 \ IF M = 0 \ PRINT	If statement can not be used as a modifier in a statement by itself, it results in missing the THEN condition part of the statement. The statement 100 N = 0 IF M = 0 PRINT is all right.
100 GO SUB 500 FOR J = 1 UNLESS X	X is an incomplete condition.
100 GO SUB 500 FOR J = 1 TO 5 UNTIL Y=1	If Y = 1 before statement 100, the statement is ignored. Within GO SUB 500, the subroutine will execute five times even if Y = 1 at some point. If Y = 1 never happens in the subroutine, it is an infinite loop.

Sample Programs

Problem Description 13.1

1. Statement of the problem: Create a table to show the equivalent Celsius degree for a Fahrenheit degree between 0 and -35 in increments of 5. The arithmetic model is: $(F - 32) * 5/9$.
2. Input: Create the data within the program.
3. Output: Display appropriate column names and a listing of the Fahrenheit and Celsius degrees.

Pseudocode 13.1

```
Print column heading
Skip a line
FOR F = 0 to -35 STEP -5
      Print degrees Fahrenheit and Celsius
Endfor
Endprogram
```

Flowchart 13.1

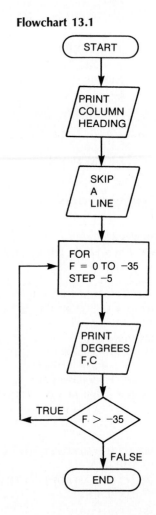

```
1 REM FAHRENHEIT TO CELSIUS CONVERSION TABLE
50 ! F = FAHRENHEIT
200 PRINT "FAHRENHEIT"; TAB(24); "CELSIUS" \ PRINT
210 PRINT TAB(5); F; TAB(23); (F-32)*5/9  FOR F = 0 TO -35 STEP -5
999 END

Ready

RUNNH
FAHRENHEIT                 CELSIUS

        0              -17.7778
       -5              -20.5556
      -10              -23.3333
      -15              -26.1111
      -20              -28.8889
      -25              -31.6667
      -30              -34.4444
      -35              -37.2222

Ready
```

Problem Description 13.2

1. Statement of the problem: The Fibonacci series of numbers has the following properties: (a) Each number in the series is the sum of the two numbers immediately preceeding it. That is, 1,1,2,3,5,8, etc. is the beginning part of the series. (b) The square of any number in the series and the product of the first numbers before and after it always differ by one. (c) Note from the numbers above that the series consists of two odd numbers followed by an even number. This sequence is always repeated. Write a program that computes the first 10 Fibonacci numbers in a series, squares each number, and finds the product of the first numbers before and after a number in the series.

2. Input: Create the data within the program.

3. Output: Display appropriate headings and column names. List the values for the series, square, and product. Suppress leading zeros.

Pseudocode 13.2

Print heading and column names
Assign values of 1 to the series
FOR I = 1 to 9
    Find Fibonacci number and save it
    Find square of Fibonacci number and save it
Endfor
FOR I = 2 to 10
    Calculate product of each number and save
Endfor
For I = 1 to 10
   Print series
Endfor
Endprogram

214

Flowchart 13.2

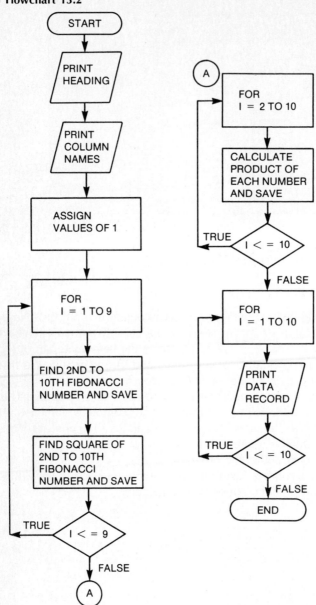

```
1 REM A TABLE OF FIBONACCI NUMBERS
50  ! S1 = FIBONACCI SERIES
       P = PRODUCT
      S2 = SQUARE OF A FIBONACCI NUMBER
200 DIM S1(15), P(15), S2(15)
210 PRINT TAB(7); "FIBONACCI SERIES"
220 PRINT "SERIES"; TAB(8); "SQUARE"; TAB(15); "PRODUCT"
300 S1(1), S1(2), S2(1), S2(2), P(1) = 1
310 S1(I+2) = S1(I+1) + S1(I)     FOR I = 1 TO (10-1)
320 S2(I+2) = S1(I+2) ** 2        FOR I = 1 TO (10-1)
330 P(I)    = S1(I-1) * S1(I+1)   FOR I = 2 TO 10
340 PRINT USING "####    ######    ####", S1(I),S2(I),P(I)   FOR I = 1 TO 10
999 END

Ready

RUNNH
        FIBONACCI SERIES
SERIES  SQUARE PRODUCT
   1       1      1
   1       1      2
   2       4      3
   3       9     10
   5      25     24
   8      64     65
  13     169    168
  21     441    442
  34    1156   1155
  55    3025   3026

Ready
```

Problem Description 13.3

1. Statement of the problem: A current sales commission report is to be prepared for only those employees in departments 2, 4, or 6 who have year-to-date sales of over $10,000 and who also have been employed six months or more. For each record meeting these conditions, determine the amount of the commission by the following rules:

a. If current sales are under $3,000, the commission rate is 3%.
b. If current sales are $3,000 and under $4,000, the commission rate is 5%.
c. If current sales are $4,000 or over, the commission rate is 7%.

Print each data record where a commission is determined, and skip all other records. Keep separate totals of the number of employees receiving a 3%, 5%, or 7% commission.

2. Input: Use a READ statement to enter the department number, employee number, year-to-date sales, current sales, and months employed.

3. Output: Display appropriate headings and column names. List the data as discussed in the statement of the problem. Edit the output.

Pseudocode 13.3

Main routine
    Do headings subroutine
    Do process subroutine until M = −1
    Do final total subroutine
    Endprogram

Heading subroutine
    Print heading
    Print column names
    Skip a line
    Return to main routine

Process subroutine
    Read department number, employee number, year-to-date sales, current sales, and months employed
    IF department number is 2 or 4 or 6
    AND IF months employed is greater than 5
    AND IF year to date sales is greater than 10,000 do commission subroutine
    Endif
    Return to main routine

Commission subroutine
    IF current sales are less than 3,000, assign 3% to commission and add 1 to total
    IF current sales are between 3,000 and 4,000, assign 5% to commission and add 1 to total
    IF current sales are greater than 4,000, assign 7% to commission and add 1 to total
    Print detail line
    Return to process subroutine

Final total subroutine
    Skip 3 lines
    Print total lines 1, 2, and 3
    Return to main routine

Flowchart 13.3

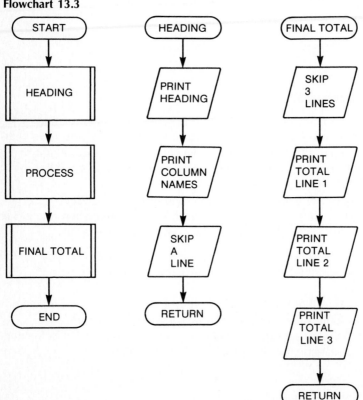

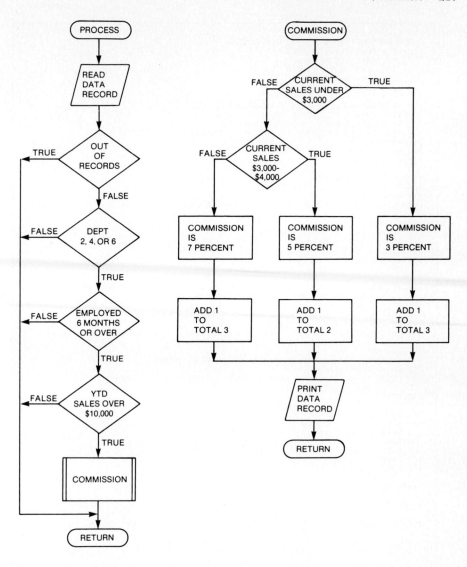

```
1 REM CURRENT SALES COMMISSION REPORT
50 ! D = DEPARTMENT NUMBER
     E = EMPLOYEE NUMBER
     Y = YEAR TO DATE (YTD) SALES
     S = CURRENT SALES
     M = MONTHS  EMPLOYED
     C = COMMISSION EARNED
     T1 = NUMBER RECEIVING 3% COMMISSION
     T2 = NUMBER RECEIVING 5% COMMISSION
     T3 = NUMBER RECEIVING 7% COMMISSION
     F$ = STRING VARIABLE TO DETERMINE FORMAT
200 GO SUB 300                  ! HEADING SUBROUTINE
210 GO SUB 400 UNTIL M = -1     ! PROCESS SUBROUTINE
220 GO SUB 500                  ! TOTALS SUBROUTINE
230 GO TO 999
300 !!!PRINT HEADINGS
305 F$ = SPACE$(27) + "DEC"
310 PRINT USING F$
320 PRINT USING "DEPT  EMPLOYEE    YTD SALES   CURRENT SALES   COMMISSION"
330 PRINT
340 RETURN
400 !!!PROCESS THE DATA RECORDS
410 READ D, E, Y, S, M
420 IF M = -1 THEN 440
430 GO SUB 450  IF D = 2 OR D = 4 OR D = 6
                   IF M >= 6
                      IF Y > 10000
440 RETURN
450 !!!SUB WITHIN SUB 400 TO FIND COMMISSION
460 IF S < 3000 THEN C = S*.03 \ T1 = T1 + 1
470 IF S >= 3000 AND S < 4000 THEN C = S*.05 \ T2 = T2 + 1
480 IF S > 4000 THEN C = S*.07 \ T3 = T3 + 1
490 PRINT USING " ##       ###    ###,###.##     ##,###.##     $###.##",
        D, E, Y, S, C
495 RETURN
500 !!!PRINT TOTALS FOR EACH COMMISSION PERCENTAGE
510 PRINT\PRINT\PRINT
520 PRINT USING "TOTAL OF ### EMPLOYEES RECEIVING #% COMMISION",
        T1, 3, T2, 5, T3, 7
530 RETURN
900 DATA 2, 110, 12000, 1000, 8
901 DATA 3, 120, 09000, 2000, 9
902 DATA 4, 130, 09000, 3000, 7
903 DATA 6, 140, 11000, 2500, 5
904 DATA 6, 150, 12000, 3500, 7
905 DATA 4, 160, 13000, 5000, 9
907 DATA 0,0,0,0,-1
999 END

Ready

RUNNH
                           DEC
DEPT  EMPLOYEE    YTD SALES   CURRENT SALES   COMMISSION

   2      110    $12,000.00    $1,000.00     $ 30.00
   6      150    $12,000.00    $3,500.00     $175.00
   4      160    $13,000.00    $5,000.00     $350.00


TOTAL OF   1 EMPLOYEES RECEIVING 3% COMMISION
TOTAL OF   1 EMPLOYEES RECEIVING 5% COMMISION
TOTAL OF   1 EMPLOYEES RECEIVING 7% COMMISION
```

Exercises

1. What is the purpose of a modifier in a statement?
2. What is the difference between how the WHILE and UNTIL modifiers work?
3. When you have nested modifiers in a single statement, in what order are they executed?
4. Indicate the errors, if any, in the following statements:

   a. 100 FOR N = 5 UNTIL N = 10
   110 M = M + N \ PRINT N, M
   120 NEXT N

   b. 100 PRINT X WHILE Y = 0

   c. 100 UNTIL Y = B AND X = A GO SUB 500

   d. 100 N = N + 1 UNLESS X

   e. 100 PRINT A(I) FOR I = 1 TO 5 FOR J = 1 TO 5

   f. 100 PRINT B IF N < 10 AND IF M < 10

5. Indicate the errors, if any, in the programs below. If there is an error, correct it and for each program determine what are the values printed.

   a. 100 GO SUB 500 FOR J = 1 TO 5 UNTIL Y = 13
   110 GO TO 999
   500 Y = 15 IF J = 3
   520 RETURN
   999 END

   b. 100 N = N + 1 FOR I = 1 TO 10
   FOR J = 1 UNTIL J = 10
   110 PRINT N
   999 END

   c. 100 N = N + 10 IF X AND Y = 0
   110 M = M + 10 IF N = 10 WHILE M < 50
   120 Y = Y + 1
   130 GO TO 100 IF Y < 1
   140 PRINT N, M, Y
   999 END

6. Write the equivalent of each statement or statements without the modifier to accomplish the same logic.

   a. 100 PRINT A IF X = 0

   b. 100 N = N + 1 IF X = 0

   c. 100 READ A(I,J) IF A(I,J) <> 11

   d. 100 PRINT B(I) IF X(I) = 0 FOR I = 1 TO 100

   e. 100 READ X(I,J) FOR J = 1 TO 2 FOR I = 1 TO 3

   f. 100 M = 0 UNLESS N = 0

    g. 100 N = N + 1 WHILE N < SQR(100)

    h. 100 N = N + 1 UNTIL N = 10
           110 PRINT N

    i. 100 READ A$(I) FOR J = 1 TO 5
          110 B$(J) = A$(J) FOR J = 1 TO 5
          120 PRINT B$(K), A$(K) FOR K = 1 TO 5

7. Rewrite Program 7.1 using modifiers.

8. Rewrite Program 7.3 using modifiers and intermediate IF statements.

9. Rewrite Program 9.4 using modifiers, and structured programming.

10. Rewrite Program 12.3 using modifiers and structured programming.

Section
4

Advanced BASIC Programming

Chapter Fourteen

Advanced Assignment and Output

User-Defined Functions

Many common mathematical operations used in a program are provided by such function subprograms as COS, TAN, LOG, INT, and SQR in the BASIC language. When necessary one may write one's own function subprogram. Such statements are referred to as user-defined functions and are incorporated in a program when such a function is to be used in several different places. The function may be defined anywhere in the program, even before its first use. However, usually all such functions are placed together at or near the beginning of a program.

The general format for a user-defined function is:

n DEF FNv(a) = expression

where *DEF* is a reserved word and *FNv* is the function name with FN required as the first two letters followed by an nonsubscripted variable name *v*. The arguments (*a*) may consist of from 0 to 5 (8 on the VAX-11) dummy numeric variable names. If no argument is used, the function name is just FNv or FNv(). The = sign assigns a single value from the expression to FNv, and the expression informs the computer what calculations are to be made and may or may not use the arguments in the calculations.

Examples are:

```
100 DEF FNA(F) = (F − 32) * 5/9
100 DEF FNB (X,Y) = (X + Y)/2
100 DEF FNC(B) = SQR(B)
100 DEF FND(N) = (N**2 + 5)/(N −2)
100 DEF FNE(X) = X * 1.6093
100 DEF FNF(Z) = ABS(Z) + 1.5
100 DEF FNG(A) = A + 3*A
110 DEF FNH$ = "APRIL 24"
100 DEF FNI(A1,A2,A3) = A1 * A2 + 5
```

A user-defined function must be called in the program by writing the function name FNv(a) in an expression. Any arguments are separated by commas. These arguments differ from those used in defining the user-defined function in that they can be constants, subscripted or nonsubscripted variables, expressions, a function subprogram, or a user-defined function. The arguments must correspond with the arguments in the defined user-defined function in order, number, and type. The values of these arguments are passed to the function, and the names of the arguments can be different from those in the function. During execution of the function, the arguments that have been passed are used in the expression. A single value is then passed back to the calling statement, and the execution of the program continues from that point in the program.

Examples are:

200 X = FNA(10)   ! THE FUNCTION NAME IS FNA AND THE ARGUMENT IS THE CONSTANT 10

200 X = A*FNB(N,M)   ! THE FUNCTION NAME IS FNB AND THE ARGUMENTS ARE THE NONSUBSCRIPTED VARIABLES N AND M

200 X = FNC(A(I)) + B   ! THE FUNCTION NAME IS FNC AND THE ARGUMENT IS SUBSCRIPTED VARIABLE A(I)

200 PRINT FNE(A), FNE(50)   ! THE FUNCTION NAME IS FNE AND THE ARGUMENT IS THE VARIABLE A THE FIRST TIME THE FUNCTION IS CALLED AND THE CONSTANT 50 THE SECOND TIME

200 IF FNF(A) + FNF(SQR(B)) = X THEN 300   ! THE FUNCTION NAME IS FNE AND THE ARGUMENT IS THE VARIABLE A THE FIRST TIME THE FUNCTION IS CALLED AND THE FUNCTION SUBPROGRAM SQR(B) THE SECOND TIME

200 PRINT FNG(A), FNH$! THE FIRST FUNCTION NAME IS FNG AND ITS ARGUMENT IS THE VARIABLE A. THE SECOND FUNCTION NAME IS FNH$ AND IT HAS NO ARGUMENT

```
200 X = FNI(FIN(A,B,C))        ! THE FUNCTION NAME IS FNI AND THE
                                 ARGUMENTS ARE THE VARIABLES A,B,
                                 C—NOTE: A FUNCTION IS NESTED
```

An example of a portion of a program with calling statements for a user-defined function is:

```
100 DEF FNA(A,B,C) =           ! USER/DEFINED FUNCTION
    A+5+(C−B)**2
150 DIM K1(9), K2(9), K3(9)
200 READ A,B,C
. . . . . . . . . .
260 N = FNA(C,B,A)             ! CALL FNA AND SEND THE VALUES
                                 OF C,B,A TO A,B,C IN THAT
                                 ORDER, RETURN TO 260

. . . . . . . . . .
300 READ X,Y,Z
340 IF FNA(X,Y,Z) = 0 THEN 999 ! CALL FNA AND SEND THE VALUES
                                 OF X,Y,Z TO A,B,C IN THAT
                                 ORDER, RETURN TO 340

. . . . . . . . . .
400 READ P,Q
430 I = SQR(ABS(FNA(P,17,Q**2)))  ! CALL FNA AND SEND THE VALUES
                                     P,17,Q**2 TO A,B,C IN THAT
                                     ORDER, RETURN TO 430

. . . . . . . . . .
540 FOR J = 1 TO 9
550 PRINT FNA(K1(J), K2(J), K3(J))  ! CALL FNA AND SEND THE VALUES
                                       K1(J), K2(J), K3(J) TO A,B,C IN THAT
                                       ORDER, RETURN TO 550

. . . . . . . . . .
600 NEXT J
. . . . . . . . . .
```

At statements 260, 340, 430, and 450, the function is called. Each time, three values are sent through the statement arguments to the dummy arguments A, B, C. The function is evaluated each time, and one value is sent back to the function variable in the calling statement. The programmer must make sure that the arguments in the calling statement agree with the dummy arguments in the function in order (from left to right), in number (in this example, 3), and in type (in this example, they are all floating point).

A function's expression may contain variables for which the values are not passed as arguments but have been defined in the program, as Example 14.1 illustrates. M has been defined in the program and may be used in the function without passing it through an argument.

Example 14.1
A function without arguments

```
100 DEF FNX = M * 1.6093
200 FOR M = 5 TO 15 STEP 5
300 PRINT USING 'MILES = ## KILOMETERS = ##.##', M, FNX
400 NEXT M
999 END

Ready

RUNNH
MILES =  5 KILOMETERS =  8.05
MILES = 10 KILOMETERS = 16.09
MILES = 15 KILOMETERS = 24.14

Ready
```

Multiple-Line Functions

User-defined functions are convenient for situations that only require a single statement. When a function needs to make a decision or solve a problem through an iterative or recursive process, multiple-line functions can be used. The function may be defined anywhere in the program, even before its first use. A multiple-line function, which is also referred to as a subroutine, allows the programmer to use structured programming techniques and generally simplifies the program logic in the same way the GO SUB/RETURN statements do.

The general format of the multiple-line function is:

```
n DEF FNv(a)
. . . . . . . . . .
. . . FNv = expression
. . . . . . . . . .
n FNEND
```

where *DEF* is a reserved word and *FNv* is the function (subroutine) name with FN required as the first two letters followed by a nonsubscripted variable name v. The arguments (a) may consist of from 0 to 5 (8 on the VAX-11) dummy numeric and/or nonnumeric variable names. If no argument is used, the function name is just *FNv* or *FNv()*. These dummy arguments are meaningful only within the subroutine. Changing dummy argument values during subroutine execution will not change the value of the equivalent argument in the calling statement. However, any variable referenced in the subroutine itself which is not an argument of the function can have its current value used in the rest of the program. The function *FNv* must be assigned a value at least once in the subroutine (if it has an argument). If *FNv* has been assigned values two or more times during the execution of the subroutine, the last value assigned is its current value. *FNEND* is a reserved word and when encountered causes the subroutine to terminate and returns the current value of *FNv* to the calling statement. Control should not be transferred into or out of functions. Such transfers do not enhance structured programming, and on the VAX-11 system they are not allowed.

Examples of a multiple-line function statement are:

```
100 DEF FNA
100 DEF FNB()
100 DEF FNC(A,B,C)
100 DEF FND(Z,X,Y)
100 DEF FNE(A,N$,M$,X)
100 DEF FNF$(X,Y,X$)
```

Examples of assigning values to a function are:

```
200 FNA = 10
200 FNB = B
200 FNC = (A+B+C)/3
200 IF A = B THEN FND = 1 ELSE FND = 2
200 IF S = 0 THEN FNE = X + 1 ELSE FNE = FNE(X**2) + FNF(Y)
```

A multiple-line function must be called in the program by writing the function name FNv(a) in an expression. Any arguments are separated by commas. The same rules apply as for user-defined functions.

Examples of calling statements are:

```
300 PRINT FNA
300 PRINT FNA()
300 X = FNC(A) + B*C
300 IF FND(X,Z,Y) = 0 THEN 500
300 PRINT FNE$, FNF$(C,B,A$)
```

The following are examples of how multiple-line functions work. Example 14.2 determines which is the lower of two values entered into a program.

Example 14.2
Multiple-line function with arguments

```
100 DEF FNA(X,Y)
110 IF X <= Y THEN FNA = X ELSE FNA = Y
120 FNEND
200 INPUT "ENTER 2 VALUES"; A,B
210 PRINT "THE LOWEST VALUE IS"; FNA(A,B)
999 END

Ready

RUNNH
ENTER 2 VALUES? 25,52
THE LOWEST VALUE IS 25

Ready
```

The function starts at statement 100, and at statement 110 it is given a value depending on the existing condition. Statement 120 terminates the function. Statement 200 enters the data into the program, and statement 210 displays the results.

Example 14.3 uses a function to determine the lowest of three values entered into a program. In doing so, the function will have to be nested within itself. The values are input at statement 200. Statement 210 has a nested function: first it

Example 14.3
Nested functions

```
100 DEF FNA(X,Y)
110 FNA = X
120 IF X > Y THEN FNA = Y
130 FNEND
200 INPUT "ENTER 3 VALUES"; A,B,C
210 PRINT "THE LOWEST VALUE IS"; FNA(FNA(A,B), FNA(B,C))
300 INPUT "TO CONTINUE ENTER YES, TO STOP ENTER NO"; N$
400 IF N$ = "YES" THEN 200
        ELSE IF N$ = "NO" THEN 999
            ELSE 300
999 END

Ready

RUNNH
ENTER 3 VALUES? 55,62,17
THE LOWEST VALUE IS 17
TO CONTINUE ENTER YES, TO STOP ENTER NO? YES
ENTER 3 VALUES? 45,2,20
THE LOWEST VALUE IS 2
TO CONTINUE ENTER YES, TO STOP ENTER NO? Y
TO CONTINUE ENTER YES, TO STOP ENTER NO? NO

Ready
```

sends the arguments A, B to the function, so that at statements 120 and 130 the lowest value is determined. Then, second, the arguments B, C are sent, and their lowest value is determined. Finally, the function is called a third time from statement 210. The arguments are the lowest values between A, B and B, C. Statements 300 and 400 allow the user to enter as many sets of three numbers as needed.

Example 14.4 calculates a table of factorials from 0 to 10. It also demonstrates that the function may be placed anywhere in the program.

Example 14.4
Placing a function anywhere in the program

```
100 PRINT USING " N       N FACTORIAL"
105 FOR N = 1 TO 10
110 PRINT USING "##       #########", N, FNA(N)
120 NEXT N
500 DEF FNA(N)
510 IF N = 0 THEN FNA = 1 ELSE FNA = N * FNA(N-1)
530 FNEND
999 END

Ready

RUNNH
  N       N FACTORIAL
  1             1
  2             2
  3             6
  4            24
  5           120
  6           720
  7          5040
  8         40320
  9        362880
 10       3628800

Ready
```

Statement 510 uses a function that uses itself in order to calculate the factorial. Statement 110 displays the results of the function one line at a time.

The purpose of Example 14.5 is to show that arguments are not always necessary, string functions are allowed, and variables used in a function that are not arguments can be used throughout the entire program with their current values.

Example 14.5
A function without arguments using string data

```
100 DEF FNA$
110 IF N < 0 THEN FNA$ = "ENTERED INVALID CODE" \ GO TO 130
120 IF N < 10 THEN FNA$ = "GIVE A 10% DISCOUNT" ELSE
        IF N < 100 THEN FNA$ = "GIVE A 15% DISCOUNT" ELSE
            FNA$ = "GIVE A 20% DISCOUNT"
130 FNEND
200 FOR I = 1 TO 5
300 READ N \ PRINT "ITEM"; N; FNA$
400 NEXT I
900 DATA 12, 5, 150, -8, 55
999 END

Ready

RUNNH
ITEM 12 GIVE A 15% DISCOUNT
ITEM 5 GIVE A 10% DISCOUNT
ITEM 150 GIVE A 20% DISCOUNT
ITEM-8 ENTERED INVALID CODE
ITEM 55 GIVE A 15% DISCOUNT

Ready
```

Statement 300 calls a string function without arguments. Statements 110 and 120 determine the value of the function. Notice at statement 110 the instruction GO TO 130 was used to terminate the function. It would have been invalid to use FNEND because it can only be used once in the function. The variable N is used in the function but was not sent as an argument. The current value of N from statement 300 is used for N in the function, and that value changed five times within the FOR/NEXT loop. Statement 300 also displays five lines of output.

String Functions for Extracting Substrings

So far in this text, numeric data have been manipulated in many ways, but the use of string data has been limited to such applications as testing, displaying, and storing names, messages, and headings. BASIC contains various functions which allows the programmer to search for a substring within a larger string, determine the number of characters in a string, replace or remove part of a string, concatenate two or more strings, perform arithmetic operations with numeric strings, and do many other operations. The next several parts of this chapter will deal with these topics.

BASIC provides three functions to break a string into substrings. The first of these is the LEFT(s,v) function where *LEFT* is a reserved word, s is either a string variable or string constant, and v is an integer variable or string constant that informs the function of the number of characters that are in the substring starting with the first character in s.

Example 14.6 illustrates this function.

Example 14.6
Extracting substrings with the LEFT function

```
100 PRINT LEFT ('ABCDEFGH', 5)
999 END

Ready

RUNNH
ABCDE

Ready
```

The first five characters ABCDE are extracted as a substring and displayed. Example 14.7 is another example of the LEFT function that gives the same results.

Example 14.7
Using the LEFT function in a different way

```
100 V = 5
110 S$ = 'ABCDEFGH'
120 L$ = LEFT(S$, V)
130 PRINT L$
999 END

Ready

RUNNH
ABCDE

Ready
```

The string variables L$ and S$ and the numeric variable V are used instead of constants.

The second function is $\boxed{\text{RIGHT}(s,v)}$ where *RIGHT* is a reserved word, *s* is either a string variable or a string constant, and *v* is an integer variable or integer constant that informs the function where to start the substring counting from the first position in the string.

Example 14.8 illustrates this function.

Example 14.8
Extracting substrings with the RIGHT function

```
100 PRINT RIGHT('PQRSTUVWXYZ', 9)
110 S$ = 'ABCDEFGH'
120 L$ = LEFT(S$,3)
130 PRINT L$
999 END

Ready

RUNNH
XYZ
ABC

Ready
```

Here a substring is extracted from PQRSTUVWXYZ starting with the ninth character, and these characters are displayed as the substring XYZ. Also, a substring is
extracted from S$ and displays the first three characters ABC.

The third function is   MID(s,n_3,n_4)   where *MID* is a reserved word, *s* is either a
string variable or a string constant, and n_3 and n_4 are integer variables or integer
constants. n_3 informs the function where to start the substring counting from the
first position in the string, and n_4 is the number of the characters in the
substring.

Example 14.9 illustrates this function.

Example 14.9
Extracting substrings with the MID function

```
100 PRINT MID('DEFGHIJK', 3, 4)
999 END

Ready

RUNNH
FGHI

Ready
```

Here the substring is extracted from DEFGHIJK starting with the third character
and is displayed as FGHI.

In Example 14.10, the length of the substring is changed several times.

Example 14.10
Using the MID function in a different way

```
100 S$ = 'MISSISSIPPI'
110 FOR L = 1 TO 11
120 PRINT MID(S$, 1, L)
130 NEXT L
999 END

Ready

RUNNH
M
MI
MIS
MISS
MISSI
MISSIS
MISSISS
MISSISSI
MISSISSIP
MISSISSIPP
MISSISSIPPI

Ready
```

Each time through the loop the MID function starts with the first character in the
string, and L is incremented by 1.

The VAX-11 system can utilize the functions MID, RIGHT, and LEFT. However, it is recommended that VAX users use the SEG$ function, which can replace all three.

The SEG$ format is SEG$(s,$v_1$,$v_2$) where *SEG$* is a reserved word, *s* is either a string variable or a string constant, v_1 is the position in the string where the first character is located, and v_2 is the position in the string where the last character to be included in the substring is located.

Whenever it is necessary to know the length of a string, the LEN(s) function can be used. *LEN* is a reserved word and *s* is either a string variable or string constant.

Observe Example 14.11

Example 14.11
Determining the length of a string

```
100 READ N$
110 IF N$ = "END" THEN 999
120 PRINT N$; " IS"; LEN(N$); "CHARACTERS IN LENGTH"
130 GO TO 100
900 DATA "GEORGE WASHINGTON","JOHN ADAMS","END"
999 END

Ready

RUNNH
GEORGE WASHINGTON IS 17 CHARACTERS IN LENGTH
JOHN ADAMS IS 10 CHARACTERS IN LENGTH

Ready
```

At statement 120 the function is set up so that it counts the number of all characters in the string N$ each time through the loop. Although the function does not have a very practical use in this example, problems presented later in the text will demonstrate it is a necessary function for many applications.

String Functions for Searching and Linking

The function INSTR(n,s_1,s_2) searches for the location of a specific character or substring within a string. *INSTR* is a reserved word, *n* is an integer which indicates the first character in the string to be searched, s_1 is either a string variable or a string constant being searched, and s_2 is either a string variable or a string constant that is the character or substring being searched for by the function. If s_2 is found within s_1, its character position in the string is returned to the function. If s_2 is not found, a 0 is returned. If both s_1 and s_2 are null strings (strings that do not contain any characters, such as, S$ = ""), a value of 1 is returned.

The use of the INSTR is illustrated by Example 14.12.

Example 14.12
Searching a string to determine the position of a character

```
100 READ N$
110 IF N$ = "END" THEN 999
120 PRINT "THE 1ST BLANK IN "; N$; " IS IN POSITION"; INSTR(1, N$, " ")
130 GO TO 100
900 DATA "MARTIN KING", "SARAVAUGHN", "JOE LEWIS", "END"
999 END

Ready

RUNNH
THE 1ST BLANK IN MARTIN KING IS IN POSITION 7
THE 1ST BLANK IN SARAVAUGHN IS IN POSITION 0
THE 1ST BLANK IN JOE LEWIS IS IN POSITION 4

Ready
```

The READ statement will enter several names into the program. At statement 120 the function INST(1,N$," ") will determine where the first blank is in the name (if any), starting with the first character in the name.

VAX BASIC can use the INSTR function. However, the use of the POS function for substring searches is recommended.

The format of the POS function is   POS(s$_1$,s$_2$,n)   where *POS* is a reserved word, s$_1$ is the string to be searched, s$_2$ is the substring being searched for, and *n* is the character position where the search begins. If the function finds the substring, it returns the position of the substring's first character. If the substring is not found, it returns the value zero.

The function   SPACE$(n)   indicates how many spaces are to be used within a character string. SPACE$ is a reserved word and *n* is a number greater than zero.

Example 14.13 illustrates a convenient method of inserting spaces for a PRINT USING statement.

Example 14.13
Placing spaces in a line to be printed

```
100 N$ = "##" + SPACE$(25) + "##"
110 PRINT USING N$, 10, 20
999 END

Ready

RUNNH
10                        20

Ready
```

Concatenation takes place when substrings or various characters are linked together to form another string or substring. Example 14.14 is a simple illustration.

Example 14.14
Illustration of concatenation

```
100 L$ = "ABC" \ M$ = "DEF" \ R$ = "GHI"
120 PRINT L$ + M$ + R$
999 END

Ready

RUNNH
ABCDEFGHI

Ready
```

The result is the string ABCDEFGHI. Of course statement 120 could have been written: 120 PRINT "ABCDEFGHI" and statement 100 omitted. But this example is only for an illustration of how concatenation works. Example 14.15 is more meaningful.

Example 14.15
Concatenation using varying spacing

```
100 FOR I = 1 TO 5
110 PRINT SPACE$(5-I) + "*" + SPACE$(I+I+1) + "*"
120 NEXT I
999 END

Ready

RUNNH
    *   *
   *     *
  *       *
 *         *
*           *

Ready
```

The Change Statement

All characters in the BASIC language have an ASCII decimal code. These decimal codes (which are given in Appendix A) can be used in statements to impose special controls on the software or hardware being used and for conversion of one type of character to another. There are statements and special functions to accomplish this. The CHANGE statement is one of them.

The general format of the CHANGE statement is:

> n CHANGE v$ TO a

where *CHANGE* is a reserved word, v$ can be either a string or a string variable, and *a* is a one-dimensional numeric array. When used in the CHANGE statement, a does not use subscripts. The number of characters changed into decimal values is stored in the zero position of the array.

The program shown in Example 14.16 will store all the characters for the string ASCII in the X array.

Example 14.16
Changing characters into ASCII decimal codes

```
100 DIM X(5)
110 V$ = 'ASCII'
120 CHANGE V$ TO X
130 FOR I = 0 TO 5
140 PRINT X(I);
150 NEXT I
999 END

Ready

RUNNH
  5  65  83  67  73  73
Ready
```

The loop displays the converted decimal code of the string from the array. Notice that the first value displayed is the number of characters in the array, and the the remaining five values are decimal codes for each of the characters in the character string ASCII. *Note:* In statement 120, the array X does not have subscripts.

Another form of the CHANGE statement is:

$$n \text{ CHANGE } c \text{ TO } v\$$$

where *CHANGE* is a reserved word, *c* is the ASCII decimal code of the character stored there, and *v*$ is the converted character. The statement 100 CHANGE A TO A$ will convert the ASCII decimal code 65 stored in A to the character A and store it in A$.

String Functions for Conversion

The STRING$(i,c) function will create a string of characters. STRING$ is a reserved word, *i* is a positive integer variable or constant, and *c* is the ASCII decimal code of the character. The statement 100 PRINT STRING$ (10, 49) will display ten 1's.

Observe Example 14.17. Statement 110 will vary the spacing and the number of asterisks to display.

Example 14.17
Creating strings of characters

```
100 FOR I = 1 TO 5
110 PRINT SPACE$(10) + SPACE$(5-I) + STRING$(I,42) + STRING$(I-1,42)
120 NEXT I
130 FOR I = 1 TO 2
140 PRINT SPACE$(13) + STRING$(3,42)
150 NEXT I
999 END

Ready

RUNNH
                *
               ***
              *****
             *******
            *********
              ***
              ***

Ready
```

> The ASCII(s) function generates an integer that is an ASCII decimal code. *ASCII* is a reserved word, and *s* is a string variable or string constant. If s contains more than one character, only the first character is converted into the ASCII decimal code. ASCII("A") and ASCII("ABC") will both return the decimal code 65 for A.

The following was used for statement 140 in Example 14.17: 140 PRINT SPACE$(13) + STRING$(3,42). The statement 140 PRINT SPACE$(13) + STRING$(3, ASCII("*")) also will give the same result.

> The VAL(s) function converts decimal values in strings to numeric values that can be used in arithmetic. *VAL* is a reserved word and *s* is a numeric variable or a numeric constant stored as a string. If s is not a number, an error message occurs.

Example 14.18 illustrates the use of the VAL function.

Example 14.18
Converting string numbers to arithmetic numbers

```
100 PRINT "CONVERT THE STRING VALUE 13 TO THE NUMBER"; VAL("13")
999 END

Ready

RUNNH
CONVERT THE STRING VALUE 13 TO THE NUMBER 13

Ready
```

The numeric string value "13" is converted to the numeric value 13 which now can be used in arithmetic.

The CHR$(c) function will convert an ASCII decimal code for a character into the character itself. *CHR$* is a reserved word, and *c* is the ASCII decimal code to be converted to a character.

The program shown in Example 14.19 will convert the ASCII decimal codes 66, 44, 46 and 89 to the characters B, . Y respectively.

Example 14.19
Converting ASCII decimal codes into characters

```
100 PRINT CHR$(66), CHR$(44), CHR$(46), CHR$(89)
999 END

Ready

RUNNH
B               ,                          Y

Ready
```

The NUM$(n) function indicates a string of numeric characters. *NUM$* is a reserved word, and *n* is the numeric value as it would be displayed by a PRINT statement.

NUM1$ is also a function indicating a string of numeric characters. *NUM1$* is a reserved word, and *n* is the numeric value as it would be displayed by a PRINT statement. It is similar to the NUM$ function except that no spaces or exponential results are returned to the function. It may be used to convert integer and floating point values for use as a string function.

Example 14.20 illustrates the use of both the NUM$ and NUM1$ functions. Notice that for the variable M there is the normal space reserved for the sign using the NUM$, while the space is not reserved with the NUM1$ function. Also, for NUM$, 1234567890 is a regular numeric value, while the NUM1$ uses the expression 15*2+5*PI and displays the results in normal form. The NUM$ is displayed in exponential form.

Example 14.20
The NUM and NUM1$ functions

```
100 N = -12345 \ M = 67890
110 PRINT NUM$(N), NUM$(M), NUM$(1234567890)
120 PRINT NUM1$(N), NUM1$(M), NUM1$(15 * 2 + 5**PI)
999 END

Ready

RUNNH
-12345          67890          .123457E 10
-12345          67890          186.992545308866

Ready
```

String Functions for Time and Date

> The **TIME$(n)** function can be used to find the time of day. *TIME$* is a reserved word. When *n* is 0, the current time of day is returned as a character string. If *n* is greater than 0, a string corresponding to the time at n minutes before midnight is returned. *n* must be less than 1,441 to return a valid string. TIME$ always returns an eight-character string.

Observe Example 14.21.

Example 14.21
Finding the time of day

```
100 PRINT TIME$(0), TIME$(1), TIME$(1440), TIME$(720)
999 END

READY

RUNNH
08:48 PM        11:59 PM        12:00 PM        12:00 M

READY
```

This example illustrates the use of 0 for the current time and examples of time using a number of minutes from midnight. Other values for *n* can be used. Consult your data-processing center for their use.

Example 14.22 is another way to use the time of day in a program.

Example 14.22
A different use of the TIME$ function

```
100 IF RIGHT(TIME$(0), 7) = "AM" THEN
    PRINT "GOOD MORNING THE TIME IS "; TIME$(0)
    ELSE PRINT "GOOD AFTERNOON THE TIME IS "; TIME$(0)
999 END

Ready

RUNNH
GOOD MORNING THE TIME IS 09:36 AM

Ready
```

Depending upon the time of day, various messages can be displayed.

> The **DATE$(n)** function can be used to find the current date. *DATE$* is a reserved word. When *n* is 0, the current date is returned to the function in the form day-month-year.

Example 14.23 is one method of finding the current date. There are several other values for *n* that can be used. Consult the data-processing center for their use.

Example 14.23
Finding the current date

```
100 PRINT SPACE$(15) + DATE$(0)
999 END

Ready

RUNNH
                30-Jun-82

Ready
```

Common Errors

Statement	Explanation
100 DEF ABC = X + Y	First two letters of function must be FN.
100 DEF FNA(A+B) = X	Arguments in DEF statement cannot be expressions.
100 DEF FNA(X) = "NAME"	FNA is numeric and expression is string.
100 DEF FNA$ = JULY 4, 1776	String data should be enclosed in quotes.
200 X = FN	FN must have a name with it.
100 DEF(A,B) = A + B	FNv is missing.
100 DEF FNA(A,B) = A + B 200 Y = FNA(A) + B	FNA has only one argument in the calling statement.
100 DEF FNA(A,B) = A + B 200 Z = FNA(FNA(A,B))	Outer FNA only has one argument.
100 DEF FNA(A,B) = A apl B 200 A = B + FNA(X,Y$)	Y$ is invalid, must be numeric.
200 PRINT FNA (K1(J),K2(J)	Missing a) at end of statement.
100 DEF FNA(X) 110 X = A + B 120 FNEND	Inconsistent use of X at 110; should be FNA(X).
100 DEF FNA(Z) 110 X = A + B 120 FNEND 200 PRINT FNA(Z)	FNA(Z) must be defined at least once in the function because it has an argument.
100 DEF FNA(A,A$,5) 110 FNA = A + 5/B 120 FNEND	5 is an invalid argument in a DEF statement.
100 DEF FNA(A,B) 110 FNA(A,B) = A + B 120 FNEND	The function receiving a value cannot have arguments, should be FNA = A + B.
100 DEF FNA(X,Y) 110 FNA = X + Y 120 FNEND 200 PRINT X,Y,FNA	The FNA in the calling statement 200 must have arguments if the DEF statement does.
100 DEF FNA(X) 110 IF X = 0 THEN FNEND ELSE IF X 0 THEN X = X + 1 120 FNEND	Only one FNEND can be used in a function, and it should be the last statement.

200 PRINT LEFT(I,5)	I must be a string variable or constant.
200 X = LEFT(N$,I)	X must be a string variable name.
200 Y$ = MIS(ABC,1,2)	ABC must be in quotes.
200 Z$ = RIGHT("XYZ",5)	5 cannot be greater than number of characters in "XYZ".
200 X = LEN(5)	5 must be a string constant.
200 X$ = LEN(X$)	X$ must be a numeric variable name.
200 A = INSTR(1,B$,C)	C must be a string value.
200 PRINT X$, INSTR(5,N,N$)	N must be a string value.
200 F$ = "## + SPACE$ + ##" 210 PRINT F$, 1,2	Will treat SPACE$ as data and will display 1 + SPACE$ + 2.
200 N = A$ + B$	N must be a string variable.
200 PRINT N + "5" + A$	Since N is a numeric integer variable, it treats part of it as an expression.
200 DIM V(5) 210 X$ = "ABCDE" 220 CHANGE X$ TO V(5)	V(5) invalid; use only V without subscripts.
200 CHANGE A TO B	Either A or B must be a string variable.
200 V$ = VAL("10")	V$ must be a numeric variable name.
200 PRINT NUM$(A$)	A$ must be numeric.
200 PRINT CHR$(500)	No ASCII decimal code 500.
200 PRINT TIMES$(0)	Should be TIME$(0)/
200 PRINT DATE$(A$)	A$ invalid, must be numeric.

Sample Programs

Problem Description 14.1

1. Statement of the problem: Discounts are given on dollar amounts depending on the class of customer. Calculate the net amount of a sales order for the following: class 1 = 20% discount, class 2 = 10% discount, class 3 = 5% discount, class 4 = no discount. Calculate the individual customer net and gross amounts and the total net and gross amounts.

2. Input: Use a READ statement to enter the discount code, number of items sold, dollar amount of item, and customer number.

3. Output: Display appropriate column names. List the data in table form for customer number, net amount, and gross amount for each customer. List totals for net amount and gross amount. Center and edit the output.

Pseudocode 14.1

Print heading
Skip a line
Read discount code, number of items sold, dollar amount per item, and customer number
IF customer number not equal to zero
  IF discount code is 1, discount calculated at 20%
  ELSE IF discount code is 2, discount calculated at 10%
  ELSE IF discount code is 3, discount calculated at 5%
  ELSE IF discount code is 4, discount calculated at 0%

```
        Endif
        Calculate gross amount
        Print customer number, net, and gross amounts
        Calculate total net price
        Calculate total gross price
ELSE print totals
Endif
Endprogram
```

Flowchart 14.1

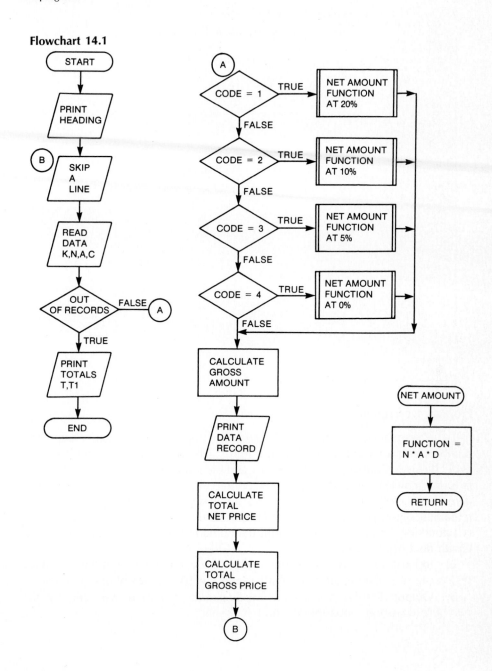

```
1 REM DISCOUNTED SALES REPORT
50 ! K = DISCOUNT CODE
      N = NUMBER OF ITEMS SOLD
      A = DOLLAR AMOUNT PER ITEM
      C = CUSTOMER NUMBER
      D = PERCENT OF GROSS WITH DISCOUNT
      G = GROSS PRICE
      T = TOTAL NET PRICE
     T1 = TOTAL GROSS PRICE
     D1 = NET PRICE
     F$ = STRING VARIABLE TO DETERMINE FORMAT
200 DEF FNA(D) = N * A * D
250 PRINT USING "CUSTOMER NUMBER  NET AMOUNT  GROSS AMOUNT"
260 PRINT
300 READ K, N, A, C
310 GO TO 600 IF C = 0           ! NOTICE USE OF MODIFIER
320 IF K = 1 THEN D1 = FNA(0.80)
      ELSE IF K = 2 THEN D1 = FNA(0.90)
        ELSE IF K = 3 THEN D1 = FNA(0.95)
          ELSE IF K = 4 THEN D1 = FNA(1.00)
330 G = N * A
399 F$ = "      #####        ####.##      ####.##"
400 PRINT USING F$, C, D1, G
410 T = T + D1
420 T1 = T1 + G
430 GO TO 300
600 PRINT
799 F1$= "      TOTAL        ##,###.##    ##,###.##"
800 PRINT USING F1$, T, T1
900 DATA 3,5,100,1234
901 DATA 2,4,200,1345
902 DATA 4,2,100,1456
903 DATA 1,3,200,1567
904 DATA 0,0,0,0
999 END

Ready

RUNNH
CUSTOMER NUMBER  NET AMOUNT  GROSS AMOUNT

      1234        $475.00      $500.00
      1345        $720.00      $800.00
      1456        $200.00      $200.00
      1567        $480.00      $600.00

      TOTAL      $1,875.00    $2,100.00

Ready
```

Program Description 14.2

1. Statement of the problem: A national company always enters telephone numbers into a record by a 10-digit number. The first three digits are the area code, the next three digits are the prefix, and the remaining digits are the number. In a company telephone directory to be printed, the area code is to be enclosed in parentheses, followed by a space, the three digit prefix, a hyphen, and the remaining digits. For example: 3033411890 would be written (303) 351-1890. It is a good idea in programming to edit the numeric data to make sure the proper length field has been entered.

2. Input: Use a READ statement to enter, for each department, the company region number, the department number, and the 10-digit telephone number.

3. Output: Display appropriate heading and column names, and list the numbers for region, department, and telephone.

Pseudocode 14.2

Main routine
 Do heading subroutine
 Do process subroutine until 'end of list'
 Endprogram
Heading subroutine
 Print heading
 Print column names
 Return to main routine
Process subroutine
 Read region, department, unedited telephone number
 IF the telephone number is 10 characters in length, do editing subroutine
 ELSE print error message and read the next record
 Endif
 Do detail print subroutine
 Return to main routine
Editing subroutine
 Create area code, prefix, and number fields
 Create the edited telephone number
 Return to process subroutine
Detail print subroutine
 Print detail line
 Return to process subroutine

Flowchart 14.2

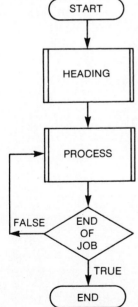

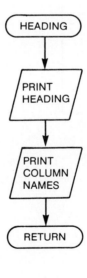

244

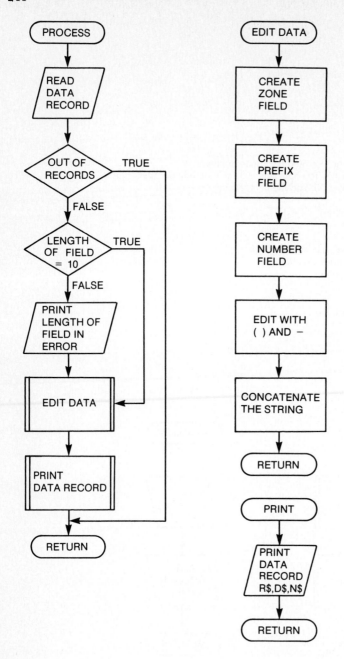

```
1 REM STRING EDITTING OF TELEPHONE NUMBERS
50 ! R$ = REGION
     D$ = DEPARTMENT
     T$ = UNEDITTED TELEPHONE NUMBER
    T1$ = ZONE
    T2$ = PREFIX
    T3$ = NUMBER
    N$ = EDITTED TELEPHONE NUMBER
150 GO SUB 200                        ! PRINT HEADING
160 GO SUB 300 UNTIL R$ = 'END OF LIST'
                                      ! MAIN SUBROUTINE
170 GO TO 999
199 !!!
200 !!!PRINT HEADINGS
210 PRINT USING '          LIFO INSURANCE COMPANY'
220 PRINT USING 'REGION    DEPARTMENT    TELEPHONE NUMBER'
230 RETURN
299 !!!
300 !!!READ DATA AND CHECK LENGTH OF NUMBER
310 READ R$, D$, T$
320 IF R$ = 'END OF LIST' THEN 360
330 IF LEN(T$) = 10 THEN 340
        ELSE PRINT R$; D$; 'TELEPHONE #'; T$; 'IN ERROR'
            \ GO TO 310
340 GO SUB 400                        ! EDIT TELEPHONE NUMER
350 GO SUB 500                        ! PRINT DETAIL LINES
360 RETURN
399 !!!
400 !!!EDIT AND CONCATENATE THE TELEPHONE NUMBER
410 T1$ = LEFT(T$,3)          ! FROM POSITION 1 CREATE THE ZONE
420 T2$ = MID(T$,4,3)         ! FROM POSITION 4 CREATE THE PREFIX
430 T3$ = RIGHT(T$,7)         ! FROM POSITION 7 CREATE THE NUMBER
440 N$ = '(' + T1$ + ')' + ' ' + T2$ + '-' + T3$
450 RETURN
499 !!!
500 !!!DISPLAY DETAIL LINES
510 PRINT TAB(3); R$; TAB(15); D$; TAB(24); N$
520 RETURN
899 !!!
900 DATA 1,1,6506121530,1,2,6506126314
901 DATA 2,1,4632914568,2,2,4634123132
902 DATA 3,1,5734151168,'END OF LIST',0,0
999 END

Ready

RUNNH
          LIFO INSURANCE COMPANY
REGION    DEPARTMENT    TELEPHONE NUMBER
   1          1          (650) 612-1530
   1          2          (650) 612-6314
   2          1          (463) 291-4568
   2          2          (463) 412-3132
   3          1          (573) 415-1168

Ready
```

Program Definition 14.3

1. Statement of the problem: A 10-question true/false test is given in various courses where in any particular course the number of students to take the test is unknown. The key for the test and the individual student tests are all records of two strings of data. The key has the name of the class and the answers are either T or F. The student responses have the name of the student and the answers as either T or F. Each student test record should be checked to make sure that 10 T or F responses have been entered. If not, display an error message and have the test record reentered. Sort the student records in alphabetical order by last name and calculate the individual student test score and the average test score for the class.

2.   Input: Use a READ statement to enter name of course and key to the test. Use an INPUT statement with appropriate message to enter the name of a student or the name END-OF-JOB to terminate the job.

3.   Output: Display appropriate headings to include the current date and time from the computer system. Display another heading for the course name, and use appropriate column names. Skip a line, and list the students in alphabetical order by last name with their test score. Skip a line and display AVERAGE IS and the average for the test.

Pseudocode 14.3

Main routine
   Read answer key as two strings
   FOR I = 1 to 10
     Create answer fields from answer string
   Endfor
   Do process subroutine until 'end-of-job'
   Do sort subroutine
   Do heading subroutine
   Do output subroutine
   Endprogram

Process subroutine
   Input student name or 'end-of-job'
   IF name not 'end-of-job'
     Input 10 true or false responses
     IF length of responses is not 10, print error message
     ELSE IF all responses are not T or F, print error message
     Endif
     Do storing of student responses subroutine
   Endif
   Return to main routine

Storing of student responses subroutine
   FOR I = 1 to 10
     Store answer field
   Endfor
   Count number of students taking test
   Store student name
   FOR I = 1 to 10
     IF correct answer count how many correct
   Endfor
   Accumulate total of all scores
   Store student scores
   Assign score a value of zero for next student
   Return to process subroutine

Sort subroutine
   FOR I−1 to C−1
     FOR J = 1 to C−I
       Save current name and score
       Save next name and score
       IF current name is greater than next name
         Store current name and score temporarily
         Swap next name and score for current name and score
       ELSE
     Endfor
   Endfor
   Return to main routine

Heading subroutine
    Skip 3 lines
    Print lines of asterisks
    Print time and date
    Print line of dashes
    Print name of course
    Print column names
    Return to main routine

Output subroutine
    FOR I = 1 to C
       Print detail of record
    Endfor
    Print average
    Return to main routine

Flowchart 14.3

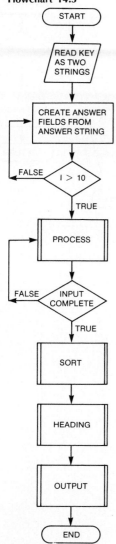

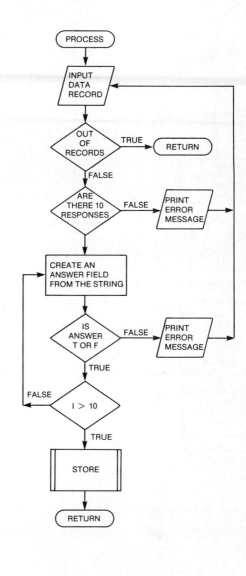

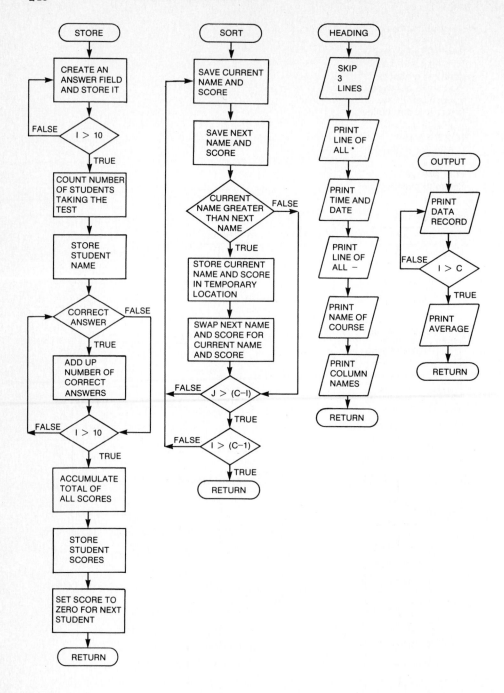

```
1 REM STRING EDITTING AND SCORING OF A TEST
50 ! N$ = CLASS OR STUDENT NAME
      A$ = 25 T OR F RESPONSES
CHR$(7) = FUNCTION TO RING TERMINAL BELL
      X$ = EITHER T OR F RESPONSE
      K$ = KEY
     K1$ = STUDENT RESPONSES
       C = NUMBER OF TESTS
      C$ = NAME OF COURSE
       T = TOTAL SCORES OF TESTS
       S = ARRAY OF STUDENT SCORES
      S1 = STUDENT SCORE PER TEST
      S$ = ARRAY OF STUDENT NAMES
      P, P1, Q, Q1 = TEMPORARY STORAGE WITH SORTING
200 DIM S(100), S$(100), K1$(10), K$(10)
300 READ C$,K$ \ FOR I = 1 UNTIL I > 10 \ K$(I) = MID(K$,I,1) \ NEXT I
310 GO SUB 400 UNTIL
        N$ = "END-OF-JOB"          ! PROCESS STUDENT RECORDS
320 GO SUB 700                     ! SORT STUDENT RECORDS
325 GO SUB 800                     ! PRINT HEADINGS
330 GO SUB 900                     ! PRINT STUDENT SCORES AND CLASS AVERAGE
340 GO TO 999
400 !!!CHECK FOR 10 T OR F ANSWERS
405 INPUT "ENTER STUDENT NAME TO CONTINUE OR END-OF-JOB TO STOP" N$
406 IF N$ = "END-OF-JOB" THEN 660
408 INPUT "ENTER 10 T OR F RESPONSES" A$
410 IF LEN(A$) = 10 THEN 420
        ELSE PRINT CHR$(7); "NUMBER OF T/F IN ERROR"
        \ GO TO 400                ! RING BELL AND MAKE CORRECTION
420 FOR I = 1 UNTIL I > 10
430 X$ = MID(A$,I,1)
440 IF X$ = "T" OR X$ = "F" THEN 450
        ELSE PRINT CHR$(7); "NOT ALL RESPONSES ARE T OR F"
        \ GO TO 400                ! RING BELL AND MAKE CORRECTION
450 NEXT I
460 GO SUB 500
470 RETURN
500 !!!STORE STUDENT RESPONSES
510 FOR I = 1 UNTIL I > 10
520 K1$(I) = MID(A$,I,1)
530 NEXT I
600 !!!SCORE EACH TEST, FIND NUMBER OF STUDENTS TAKING
        TEST AND FIND TOTAL OF ALL TESTS
605 C = C + 1
606 S$(C) = N$
610 FOR I = 1 UNTIL I > 10
620 IF K$(I) = K1$(I) THEN S1 = S1 + 1
630 NEXT I
650 T = T + S1
655 S(C) = S1
656 S1 = 0
660 RETURN

Ready

700 !!!SORT STUDENT NAMES AND SCORES
710 FOR I = 1 TO C-1
720     FOR J = 1 TO C-I
730         P$ = S$(J)
740         Q$ = S$(J+1)
750         P1 = S(J)
760         Q1 = S(J+1)
770         IF P$ <= Q$ THEN 780
                ELSE S$(J) = Q$ \ S$(J+1) = P$
                \ S(J) = Q1 \ S(J+1) = P1
780     NEXT J
790 NEXT I
795 RETURN
800 !!!PRINT HEADINGS
810 PRINT\PRINT\PRINT
820 PRINT STRING$(40,42)
830 PRINT "TEST WAS SCORED ON "; DATE$(0); " AT "; TIME$(0)
840 PRINT STRING$(40,45)
850 PRINT SPACE$(16) + C$
860 PRINT USING "      STUDENT NAME      SCORE"
870 PRINT
880 RETURN
```

```
900 !!!PRINT STUDENT SCORES AND CLASS AVERAGE
910 FOR I = 1 UNTIL I > C
920 PRINT USING "          \              \         ##", S$(I), S(I)
930 NEXT I
940 PRINT
950 PRINT USING "        AVERAGE IS         ##.##", T/C
970 RETURN
990 DATA "MIS-180","TTTTTTTTTT"
999 END

Ready

RUNNH
ENTER STUDENT NAME TO CONTINUE OR END-OF-JOB TO STOP
? BRENDA
ENTER 10 T OR F RESPONSES
? TTTTTFFFFF
ENTER STUDENT NAME TO CONTINUE OR END-OF-JOB TO STOP
? BRANDON
ENTER 10 T OR F RESPONSES
? TTTTTTTTFFF
NUMBER OF T/F IN ERROR
ENTER STUDENT NAME TO CONTINUE OR END-OF-JOB TO STOP
? BRANDON
ENTER 10 T OR F RESPONSES
? TTTTTTTTFF
ENTER STUDENT NAME TO CONTINUE OR END-OF-JOB TO STOP
? BRENT
ENTER 10 T OR F RESPONSES
? FFTTTTTTTT
ENTER STUDENT NAME TO CONTINUE OR END-OF-JOB TO STOP
? END-OF-JOB


****************************************
TEST WAS SCORED ON 30-Jun-82 AT 07:41 AM
----------------------------------------
              MIS-180
    STUDENT NAME     SCORE

    BRANDON            8
    BRENDA             5
    BRENT              8

    AVERAGE IS        7.00

Ready
```

Exercises

1. What is the difference between dummy and actual arguments when using user-defined functions?
2. Give three different examples of how arguments in a calling statement can be expressed.
3. How must arguments in a user-defined function statement be expressed?
4. When are user-defined or multiple-line functions used in a program?
5. How many values are returned from a user-defined function to the calling statement? from a multiple-line function?

6. What is the value of X printed by statements 120, 140, 160 below?

```
100 DEF FNA(A,B,C) = A**2 − 3*C + B
110 READ A,B,C
120 X = FNA(C,B,A)\PRINT X
130 READ X,Y,Z
140 X = FNA(X,Y,Z) − 5 \ PRINT X
150 READ P,T,A
160 X = A*FNA(T,5,P) \ PRINT X
900 DATA 3,1,5,2,2,12,6,3,5
999 END
```

7. Indicate the errors, if any, in the programs below. If there is an error, correct it, and for each program determine what are the values printed.

a.
```
100 DEF FNA = A + B
110 B = 5 \ A = B*2
120 C = FNA \ PRINT C
999 END
```

b.
```
100 DEF FNB(X,Y)
110 FNB(X,Y) = SOR(X)*Y
120 FNEND
200 PRINT FNB(3,2)
999 END
```

c.
```
100 DEF FNC$() =
    "THE ANSWER IS"
110 DEF FND(A)
120 FND(A) = X*A
130 FNEND
200 X = 10\Y = 5
210 Z = FND(Y)
220 PRINT FNC$();FND(Z)
999 END
```

8. Indicate the errors, if any, in each of the following statements.

a. `100 A$ = B$ + C$ + D`

b. `100 B$ = LEFT("XYZ",1)`

c. `100 C$ = RIGHT("XYZ",5)`

d. `100 D$ = MID("ABCD",2,2)`

e. `100 E$ = "CALIFORNIA"\`
     `FOR I = 10 TO 1\`
     `PRINT MID(E$,1,I)\`
     `NEXT I`

f. `100 F$ = LEN(E$)`

g. `100 G$ = INSTR(1,I,J)`

h. `100 H$ = SPACE$(5) + STRING(10,45) + SPACE$(5)`

i. `100 CHANGE I$ TO J$`

j. `100 PRINT CHRD(66)+CHR$(45)+CHR$(49)+CHR$(56)+CHR$(48)`

k. `100 K$ = VAL(LEFT("123",3))`

l. `100 L$ = NUM1$(L)`

m. `100 PRINT TAB(N); DATES$(0)`

9. Write a program that will check the length of a social security number and determine whether it is nine positions long. If not, the program should allow the number to be reentered and checked again. Also, edit the valid numbers with hyphens in proper positions (such as 123-45-6789).

10. Write a program that will enter the names of 10 states and print out these names backwards.

11. Write a program using a multiple-line function to determine the lowest of four values entered into a program. Allow for an unlimited number of these sets of values to be entered in the program. (*Hint:* You might want to consider using two multiple-line functions in the program.)

12. Write a program that enters the names of an unknown number of people, alphabetized by first names, with only one space between first and last names. Do not use middle initials. Print the names with the last name first, followed by a comma, a space and the first name. Use appropriate headings that include the DATE function.

13. Write a program that will print a three-line mailing label for an unknown number of records. The data are to be entered as with the fields separated by commas, as follows: name, street address, city and state, zip. Print two labels per record.

14. Write a program to convert hexademical numbers into decimal numbers. It is suggested you treat hexademical numbers as string data. (*Hint:* The Hexadecimal number $1B9 = 1*16^2 + B*16^1 + 9*16^0$ where $B = 11$.)

15. Many retail organizations use check digits in their customer account codes. Write a program that will use 10 six-digit customer codes with the sixth digit the check digit. Use the modulus 11 arithmetic method as follows: Assign weights to each of the first five digits, multiply the digit by the weight, sum these results, divide this sum by 11, and save the remainder. Subtract the remainder from 11 to determine the check digit. Example:

$$\text{Code} \quad = \quad 43210$$
$$\text{Weight} = \quad 65432$$

The sum of the multiplication: $4*6 + 3*5 + 2*4 + 1*3 + 0*2 = 50$. Divide 50 by 11 and the remainder is 6. Subtract the remainder from 11 ($11 - 6 = 5$) to determine the check digit 5. The account code is then 432105. Now redo the above steps for the new code 432105, using as weights 654321. You should get a remainder of 0, or the check digit is incorrect.

Chapter Fifteen

Matrix Operations

A matrix can be defined as an array of values arranged into rows and/or columns. Chapter 12 dealt with operations on individual values within an array. Often, however, it is useful to deal with an entire row or column or the entire array in an operation. FOR/NEXT statements are used to access individual values within an array. MAT statements are used to access the values of a complete row or column or the entire array. The DIM statement is used to define either one-dimensional or two-dimensional arrays (which will be referred to as matrices in this chapter). A matrix is composed of a single type of data: string, integer, or floating point.

Entering Values in a Matrix

The read, input, and initialization statements are used to enter values in a matrix.

The MAT READ statement

The general format for the MAT READ statement is:

n MAT READ $m_1(k_1)$, $m_2(k_2)$, etc.

where *MAT* and *READ* are reserved words, the *comma* is a delimiter, and m_1, m_2, etc. are the names of variables that are matrices. The k_1, k_2, etc. are unsigned integer constants or variable names that indicate the number and order of values to be entered into the matrix. If the k is omitted the statement will read as many values as indicated by the DIM statement. In no case can k be greater than the dimensional size of the matrix. One MAT READ statement may be used to enter any number and type of matrix.

Examples are:

```
100 DIM X(10)
200 MAT READ X(10)
```
! WILL ENTER 10 VALUES INTO X

```
100 DIM Y(10)
200 MAT READ Y(5)
```
! WILL ENTER 5 VALUES INTO Y. THE REMAIN-
! ING LOCATIONS ARE NOT CHANGED. THE MATRIX IS REDIMENSIONED AND SHOULD NOW BE REFERENCED AS A 5 POSITION MATRIX

```
100 DIM Z(10)
200 MAT READ Z
```
! THE ENTIRE MATRIX Z IS READ, IN THIS
! CASE 10 VALUES

```
100 DIM A(10,10)
200 MAT READ A(10,10)
```
! WILL READ ENTIRE MATRIX A, WHICH IS 10
! BY 10, IN ROW ORDER; THAT IS, THE SEC-OND SUBSCRIPT VARIES MOST RAPIDLY INTO THE MATRIX A

```
100 DIM B(10,10)
200 MAT READ B(5,5)
```
! WILL ENTER 5 BY 5 MATRIX, IN ROW
! ORDER. THAT IS, THE SECOND SUBSCRIPT VARIES MOST RAPIDLY INTO THE MATRIX B. THE REMAINING LOCATIONS ARE NOT CHANGED. THE MATRIX IS REDIMEN-SIONED AND SHOULD NOW BE REF-ERENCED AS A 5 BY 5 MATRIX

```
100 DIM C(10,10)
200 MAT READ C
```
! THE ENTIRE MATRIX IS ENTERED IN ROW
! ORDER, IN THIS CASE 10 VALUES PER ROW FOR 10 ROWS, C IS A 10 BY 10 MATRIX

```
100 DIM N1(10), N2(5,10)
200 MAT READ N1, N2
```
! WILL ENTER THE ENTIRE MATRIX N1 THEN
! WILL ENTER THE ENTIRE MATRIX N2 IN ROW ORDER

```
100 DIM E1(10,10), E2(10,10)
200 MAT READ E1(5,10), E2
```
! WILL ENTER A REDEFINED 5 BY 10 MATRIX
! IN ROW ORDER FOR MATRIX E1 THEN WILL ENTER THE ENTIRE MATRIX E2 IN ROW ORDER

```
100 DIM N$(10), M(10,5)
200 I = 10 \ J = 5
300 MAT READ N$, M(I,J)
```
! WILL ENTER THE ENTIRE STRING MATRIX
! FOR N$ THEN WILL ENTER THE ENTIRE
! MATRIX M IN ROW ORDER (NOTE I AND J ARE USED AS SUBSCRIPTS TO INDICATE THE SIZE OF THE MATRIX)

The MAT INPUT Statement

The general format for the MAT INPUT statement is:

n MAT INPUT $m_1(k_1)$, $m_2(k_2)$, etc.

where *MAT* and *INPUT* are reserved words, the *comma* is a delimiter, and m_1, m_2, etc. are the names of variables that are matrices. The k_1, k_2, etc. are unsigned integer constants or variable names that are the number and order of values to be entered into the matrix. If the k is omitted, the statement will input as many values as indicated by the DIM statement. In no case can k be greater than the dimensional size of the matrix. Input is accepted from a device as with a regular INPUT statement after the ? is displayed. Values may be input one at a time, separating the values with commas. One MAT INPUT statement may be used to enter any number and type of matrices.

Examples are:

```
100 DIM X(10)              ! WILL ENTER 10 VALUES INTO THE MATRIX X
200 MAT INPUT X
100 DIM X(10), Y(10,5)     ! WILL ENTER THE ENTIRE MATRIX X THEN WILL
200 MAT INPUT X, Y         ! ENTER THE ENTIRE MATRIX Y ALL IN ROW
                             ORDER
100 DIM X(10), Y(10,10)    ! WILL ENTER THE ENTIRE MATRIX X THEN WILL
200 I = 5 \ J = 5          ! ENTER A REDEFINED 5 BY 5 MATRIX IN ROW
300 MAT INPUT X, Y(I,J)    ! ORDER FOR MATRIX Y
100 DIM N$(10,10)          ! WILL ENTER THE ENTIRE MATRIX N$ IN ROW
200 MAT INPUT N$           ! ORDER
```

At times a person entering data using the MAT INPUT statement may enter the wrong number of values. Two reserved words are provided to help in these situations. Following the INPUT of a matrix, the reserved word NUM contains the number of rows input (for a one-dimensional matrix this is the number of values entered). The reserved word NUM2 contains the number of values in the last row. The program shown in Example 15.1 illustrates their use.

Displaying Values in a Matrix

The MAT PRINT statement displays each value in a matrix. If the matrix name does not have a subscript, the entire matrix is printed. Otherwise, the subscript indicates that only part of the matrix is to be printed. Only one matrix may be displayed by a single MAT PRINT statement.

The general format for the MAT PRINT statement is:

n MAT PRINT m

Example 15.1
Determining the size of a matrix

```
100 DIM X(5,5)
200 PRINT "ENTER A 5 BY 5 MATRIX"
300 MAT INPUT X            !REMEMBER---ENTER BY ROW ORDER
400 PRINT "YOU HAVE ENTERED"; NUM; "ROWS"
500 PRINT "AND THE NUMBER OF VALUES IN THE LAST ROW IS"; NUM2
999 END

Ready

RUNNH
ENTER A 5 BY 5 MATRIX
? 1,1,1,1,1,2,2,2,2,2,3,3,3,3,3,4,4,4,4,4,5,5,5,5,5
YOU HAVE ENTERED 5 ROWS
AND THE NUMBER OF VALUES IN THE LAST ROW IS 5

Ready
```

> where *MAT* and *PRINT* are reserved words and *m* is the variable name of a matrix.

If a matrix name is followed by a semicolon or a comma, after a semicolon the values are displayed one per print zone. If no character follows the matrix name, each value is printed on a separate line. No other method can be used to display values using the MAT PRINT. Observe the results of Example 15.2

Initialization Statement

In matrix algebra calculations, it is often necessary to create special matrices. The most common are the summation, zero, and identity matrices. These matrices must be defined as two-dimensional in a DIM statement. A summation matrix contains values of 1 in all positions, a zero matrix contains values of 0 in all positions, and an identity matrix contains values of 0 in all positions except along the principle diagonal, where those values are 1. An identity matrix must always have the same number of rows and columns (called a square matrix). Figure 15.1 shows examples of such matrices.

Figure 15.1
Summation, zero, and identity matrices

Summation matrix	Zero matrix	Identity matrix
1 1 1 1	0 0 0	1 0 0
1 1 1 1	0 0 0	0 1 0
(2 by 4)	0 0 0	0 0 1
	0 0 0	(3 by 3)
	(4 by 3)	

The general format for the initialization statement is:

$$n \text{ MAT } m = f$$

Example 15.2
Packing and zone methods of printing a matrix

```
100 DIM X(5,3)
110 MAT READ X                        !ENTER BY ROW 15 VALUES
115 PRINT "MATRIX X PACKED 5 BY 3"
120 MAT PRINT X;
125 PRINT "MATRIX X ZONE 5 BY 3"
130 MAT PRINT X,
135 PRINT "MATRIX X ONE POSTION AT A TIME"
140 MAT PRINT X
145 PRINT "UPPER LEFT PORTION OF MATRIX X BY ZONE"
150 MAT PRINT X(2,2),
900 DATA 1,1,1,2,2,2,3,3,3,4,4,4,5,5,5
999 END

Ready

RUNNH
MATRIX X PACKED 5 BY 3
  1   1   1

  2   2   2

  3   3   3

  4   4   4

  5   5   5


MATRIX X ZONE 5 BY 3
  1              1              1

  2              2              2

  3              3              3

  4              4              4

  5              5              5


MATRIX X ONE POSTION AT A TIME
  1
  1
  1
  2
  2
  2
  3
  3
  3
  4
  4
  4
  5
  5
  5

UPPER LEFT PORTION OF MATRIX X BY ZONE
  1              1

  2              2
```

where *MAT* is a reserved word, *m* is the variable name of a two-dimensional matrix, and *f* is one of the functions CON, ZER, or IDN (which are all reserved words). Function names may redefine the size of a matrix. The VAX-11 system allows the use of the function NUL$, which sets the value of all elements in a string array to a null string.

Example 15.3
The use of CON, ZER, IDN

```
100 DIM X(2,4), Y(4,3), Z(5,5)
200 MAT X = CON                    !MOVE ALL ONES TO X
300 MAT Y = ZER                    !MOVE ALL ZEROS TO Y
400 MAT Z = IDN(3,3)               !REDEFINE Z TO A 3 BY 3 AND
                                    MOVE ONES TO THE PRINCIPLE DIAGONAL
500 PRINT 'MATRIX X' \ MAT PRINT X,
600 PRINT 'MATRIX Y' \ MAT PRINT Y,
700 PRINT 'MATRIX Z' \ MAT PRINT Z,
999 END

Ready

RUNNH
MATRIX X
 1           1           1           1

 1           1           1           1


MATRIX Y
 0           0           0

 0           0           0

 0           0           0

 0           0           0


MATRIX Z
 1           0           0

 0           1           0

 0           0           1


Ready
```

Matrix Calculations

The operations of assigning, addition, subtraction, and multiplication can be performed on matrices. Each matrix involved must be defined with a DIM statement. Only one operation can be performed per statement.

Assignment

One matrix can be copied into another matrix provided the receiving matrix is large enough. Typically both matrices are the same size.

The general format for the matrix assignment statement is:

$$n \text{ MAT } m_3 = m_2$$

where *MAT* is a reserved word, m_3 is the variable name of the matrix being assigned values, and m_2 is the variable name of the sending matrix.

Observe the results of Example 15.4.

Example 15.4
Assigning the values of one matrix to another matrix

```
100 DIM X(2,4), Y(2,4)
110 MAT READ X
120 MAT Y = X              !COPY X INTO Y
130 PRINT "MATRIX X" \ MAT PRINT X,
140 PRINT "MATRIX Y" \ MAT PRINT Y,
900 DATA 1,2,3,4,5,6,7,8
999 END

Ready

RUNNH
MATRIX X
 1              2              3              4

 5              6              7              8


MATRIX Y
 1              2              3              4

 5              6              7              8


Ready
```

Addition and Subtraction

Addition and subtraction can be performed on matrices if the matrices are of the same dimension and size.

The general formats for matrix addition and subtraction are:

$$n \text{ MAT } m_3 = m_1 + m_2$$

$$n \text{ MAT } m_3 = m_1 - m_2$$

where *MAT* is a reserved word, m_3 is the variable name of the matrix where the result will be stored, m_1 and m_2 are the variable names of the matrices to be added or subtracted, and $\pm$ or $=$ are the operations to be performed.

Example 15.5 illustrates their use.

Multiplication

Multiplication can be performed on matrices if the number of columns in the first matrix is equal to the number of rows in the second matrix. The size of the matrix resulting from the multiplication is the number of rows of the first matrix and the number of columns in the second matrix.

The general format for multiplication is:

$$n \text{ MAT } m_3 = m_1 * m_2$$

Example 15.5
Adding and subtracting matrices

```
100 DIM X(2,3), Y(2,3), A1(2,3), A2(2,3)
150 MAT READ X, Y              !ENTER VALUES FOR X AND Y
200 MAT A1 = X + Y             !ADD X AND Y AND STORE RESULT IN A1
250 MAT A2 = X - Y             !SUBTRACT Y FROM X AND STORE RESULT IN A2
300 PRINT "MATRIX X" \ MAT PRINT X,
350 PRINT "MATRIX Y" \ MAT PRINT Y,
400 PRINT "MATRIX A1"\ MAT PRINT A1,
450 PRINT "MATRIX A2"\ MAT PRINT A2,
900 DATA 10,10,10,10,10,10,5,5,5,5,5,5
999 END

Ready

RUNNH
MATRIX X
 10            10            10

 10            10            10


MATRIX Y
 5             5             5

 5             5             5


MATRIX A1
 15            15            15

 15            15            15


MATRIX A2
 5             5             5

 5             5             5


Ready
```

where *MAT* is a reserved word, m_3 is the variable name indicating where the results of the matrix multiplication are stored, m_1 is the variable name of the first matrix, m_2 is the variable name of the second matrix, and * is the operation to be performed.

Observe Example 15.6.

Each value in a matrix can also be multiplied by just a constant or variable or expression (called scalar multiplication).

The general format for scalar multiplication is:

$$n \text{ MAT } m_3 = (s) * m_2$$

where MAT is a reserved word; m_3 is the variable name indicating where the results of the scalar multiplication are stored; s is either a constant, a variable, or an expression that must be enclosed within a set of parentheses; m_2 is the variable name of the matrix being multiplied; and * is the operation to be performed.

Example 15.6
Multiplying matrices

```
100 DIM M3(4,4), A3(10,10), X(4,3), Y(3,4)
110 MAT READ X,Y
120 MAT M3 = X * Y      ! COLUMN OF X AND ROW OF Y = 3, M3 = A 4 BY 4
130 MAT A3 = Y * X      ! COLUMN OF Y AND ROW OF X = 4, A3 = A 3 BY 3
                        ALTHOUGH A3 WAS A 10 BY 10 IT IS NOW A 3 BY 3
140 PRINT "MATRIX X" \ MAT PRINT X,
150 PRINT "MATRIX Y" \ MAT PRINT Y,
160 PRINT "MATRIX M3"\ MAT PRINT M3,
170 PRINT "MATRIX A3"\ MAT PRINT A3,
900 DATA 1,1,1,2,2,2,3,3,3,4,4,4
901 DATA 3,3,3,3,2,2,2,2,1,1,1,1
999 END

Ready

RUNNH
MATRIX X
 1             1             1

 2             2             2

 3             3             3

 4             4             4


MATRIX Y
 3             3             3             3

 2             2             2             2

 1             1             1             1


MATRIX M3
 6             6             6             6

 12            12            12            12

 18            18            18            18

 24            24            24            24


MATRIX A3
 30            30            30

 20            20            20

 10            10            10


Ready
```

Matrix Functions

Inverse of a Matrix

Although division is not a calculation that can be directly accomplished using matrices, a function is permitted that will allow its equivalent. This function is called matrix inversion, and it greatly simplifies the typical matrix algebra operations necessary to accomplish the task. Only a square matrix can be inverted, and the results of the inversion are stored in a different square matrix of the same size. Not all square matrices can be inverted. If an attempt is made to invert a matrix that cannot be inverted, the system will print out an error message.

The general format for the matrix inversion instruction is:

Example 15.7
Three types of scalar multiplication

```
100 DIM A(6,6), B(3,3), C(3,3), D(3,3)
110 MAT READ D
120 X = 2
130 MAT A = (X) * D          ! MULTIPLY EACH VALUE IN D BY X
140 MAT B = (3) * D          ! MULTIPLY EACH VALUE IN D BY 3
150 MAT C = (X + 3) * D      ! MULTIPLY EACH VALUE IN D BY (X + 3)
                             ! NOTICE A, B AND C MUST BE AT LEAST THE
                             ! SIZE OF D, A 3 BY 3
160 PRINT "MATRIX D" \ MAT PRINT D,
170 PRINT "MATRIX C" \ MAT PRINT C,
180 PRINT "MATRIX B" \ MAT PRINT B,
190 PRINT "MATRIX A" \ MAT PRINT A,
                             ! A(6,6) WAS REDEFINED TO A(3,3) AT LINE 130
900 DATA 1,2,3,4,5,6,7,8,9
999 END

Ready

RUNNH
MATRIX D
 1            2            3

 4            5            6

 7            8            9


MATRIX C
 5           10           15

20           25           30

35           40           45


MATRIX B
 3            6            9

12           15           18

21           24           27


MATRIX A
 2            4            6

 8           10           12

14           16           18


Ready
```

$$n\ \text{MAT}\ m_3 = \text{INV}(m_1)$$

where *MAT* and *INV* are reserved words, m_3 is the variable name of the matrix where the results of the inversion are stored, and m_1 (must be enclosed in parentheses) is the variable name of the matrix to be inverted.

Matrix inversion is illustrated in Example 15.8.

Example 15.8
Matrix inversion

```
100 DIM A(5,5), B(5,5), D(5,5), C(3,3)
110 MAT READ A, C
120 MAT B = INV(A)          ! INVERTS A AND STORES RESULTS IN B
130 MAT D = INV(C)          ! INVERTS C AND STORES RESULTS IN D
                              AS A 3 BY 3
140 PRINT 'MATRIX A' \ MAT PRINT A,
150 PRINT 'MATRIX B' \ MAT PRINT B,
160 PRINT 'MATRIX C' \ MAT PRINT C,
170 PRINT 'MATRIX D' \ MAT PRINT D,
900 DATA 3,1,5,3,4,7,0,2,6,7,2,5,7,0,2,1,5,3,9,6,4,3,7,5,2
901 DATA 2,4,6,1,3,5,0,2,3
999 END
```

```
Ready

RUNNH
MATRIX A
  3             1             5             3             4

  7             0             2             6             7

  2             5             7             0             2

  1             5             3             9             6

  4             3             7             5             2


MATRIX B
 -.302128      .195745       .851064E-1   -.093617       .114894

 -.355319      .893617E-1    .212766       .659574E-1   -.012766

  .270686     -.125296      -.496454E-1   -.034279       .496454E-1

 -.212766E-1  -.425532E-1   -.148936       .638298E-1    .148936

  .243026      .193853E-1    .567376E-1    .486998E-1   -.256738


MATRIX C
  2             4             6

  1             3             5

  0             2             3


MATRIX D
  .5            0            -1

  1.5          -3             2

 -1             2            -1


Ready
```

Determinant of a Matrix

The general format for the determinant function is:

n matrix-name = DET

where *matrix-name* is the name of a matrix that has been inverted and DET is a reserved word.

264

When a matrix has been inverted, the VAX-11 system calculates the determinant as a by-product of the inversion process. To retrieve a determinant of the last matrix inverted, the DET function is used. If a program has not previously used the MAT INV function, DET returns a value of zero.

Transposition of a Matrix

At times it is necessary to interchange the values of the rows with the values of the columns in a matrix so that the matrices to be used in calculations have conformed to the rules of the arithmetic being performed. In other words, the transposed version of a matrix is used to store the data in a different form.

The general format for the transposition of a matrix is:

$$\text{n MAT } m_3 = \text{TRN}(m_1)$$

where *MAT* and *TRN* are reserved words, m_3 is the variable name of the matrix where the results of the transposition are stored, and m_1 (must be enclosed in parentheses) is the variable name of the matrix to be transposed.

Example 15.9 shows a program for transposing matrices.

Common Errors

Statement	Explanation
100 MAT READ	Left off the matrix to be read.
100 DIM A(5,5), B(5,5) 200 MAT READ A(10,5), B	Cannot redimension A to a size greater than what is in the DIM A(5,5).
100 DIM A(10,10) 200 INPUT A(I,J)	I and J must be defined.
100 DIM A(15), N$(15) 200 INPUT A$(15)	A$ not defined as a matrix, probably meant to INPUT N$.
100 DIM A(4,2) 200 MAT A = IDN	An identity matrix must always have the same number of rows and columns.
100 MAT PRINT A, B	Only one matrix may be displayed by a single MAT PRINT statement.
100 DIM A(10,5) 200 MAT READ A(5,5) 300 MAT PRINT A(10,5)	A has been redimensioned and is now a 5 by 5 matrix, so the size of PRINT A(10,5) may have some data in error.
100 DIM A(10,5), B(5,5) 200 MAT READ A 300 MAT B = A	A is too large to be copied into B.
100 DIM A(3,2), B(3,2), C(2,2) 200 MAT C = A * B	A and B are not conformable to the rules of multiplication.

Example 15.9
Transposing matrices

```
100 DIM A(2,3), B(2,3), C(3,2), D(3,2), E(5,5)
110 MAT READ A, D
120 MAT C = TRN(A)      ! A 2 BY 3 A BECOMES A 3 BY 2 C
130 MAT B = TRN(D)      ! A 3 BY 2 D BECOMES A 2 BY 3 B
140 MAT E = TRN(D)      ! A 3 BY 2 D BECOMES A 2 BY 3 D
                          WHERE E HAS BEEN REDEFINED TO A 3 BY 2
150 PRINT "MATRIX A" \ MAT PRINT A,
160 PRINT "MATRIX C" \ MAT PRINT C,
170 PRINT "MATRIX D" \ MAT PRINT D,
180 PRINT "MATRIX B" \ MAT PRINT B,
190 PRINT "MATRIX E" \ MAT PRINT D,
900 DATA 1,1,1,2,2,2
901 DATA 3,3,4,4,5,5
999 END

Ready

RUNNH
MATRIX A
 1              1              1

 2              2              2


MATRIX C
 1              2

 1              2

 1              2


MATRIX D
 3              3

 4              4

 5              5


MATRIX B
 3              4              5

 3              4              5


MATRIX E
 3              3

 4              4

 5              5


Ready
```

100 DIM A(3,2), B(3,2), C(2,2) 200 MAT C = B * A	C is not large enough to store the results. B * A is invalid; their dimensions do not conform.
100 DIM A(3,2), B(3,2), C(2,2) 200 MAT A = B − C	B and C must be the same size.
100 DIM A(3,2), B(3,2), C(2,2) 200 MAT C = A − B	C must be at least a 3 by 2 matrix to store the results.
100 DIM A(3,2), B(3,2) 101 DIM C(3,2), D(3,2) 200 MAT D = A + B + C	Cannot do more than one operation per statement.
100 DIM A(10), B(10) 200 MAT A = 1.5 * B	The scalar 1.5 must be enclosed in parentheses.
100 DIM A(5,5) 200 A = INV(A)	The inverse of A cannot be stored in the original matrix.
100 DIM A(10,10), B(10,5) 200 MAT A = INV(B)	B must be a square matrix in order to be inverted.
100 DIM A(3,2), B(3,3) 200 MAT A = TRN(B)	A is not large enough to store the results, it must be at least a 2 by 3 matrix.

Sample Programs

Problem Definition 15.1

1. Statement of the problem: The Ace Construction Company builds two types of standard roofs, shingle and regular, for houses in the city of Westmoor. Each shingle roof requires 25 rolls of shingles at $20 a roll and 10 rolls of tar paper at $15 per roll. Each standard roof requires 20 rolls of asphalt at $15 per roll and 25 rolls of tar paper at $15 per roll. It is estimated that 25 shingle roofs and 15 standard roofs will be built this month. Use matrix algebra to determine the total expected cost of the materials.

Number of Houses			Materials required			Costs	
Shingle	Standard		Shingle	Tar Paper	Asphalt		
25	15	Shingle	25	10	0	Shingles	20
		Standard	0	25	20	Tar paper	15
						Asphalt	15

2. Input: Use a MAT READ statement to enter the data in the statement of the problem.

3. Output: Display an appropriate message and the expected cost of all the material in the project. Edit the answer.

Pseudocode 15.1

```
MAT read number of roofs, cost of materials, and materials used
MAT multiply number of roofs and cost
MAT multiply to determine total cost
Print answer
Endprogram
```

Flowchart 15.1

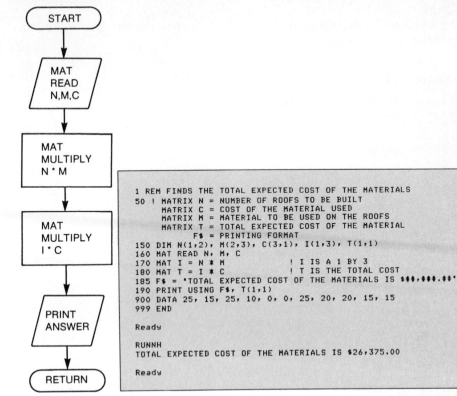

```
START

MAT
READ
N,M,C

MAT
MULTIPLY
N * M

MAT
MULTIPLY
I * C

PRINT
ANSWER

RETURN
```

```
1 REM FINDS THE TOTAL EXPECTED COST OF THE MATERIALS
50 ! MATRIX N = NUMBER OF ROOFS TO BE BUILT
     MATRIX C = COST OF THE MATERIAL USED
     MATRIX M = MATERIAL TO BE USED ON THE ROOFS
     MATRIX T = TOTAL EXPECTED COST OF THE MATERIAL
          F$ = PRINTING FORMAT
150 DIM N(1,2), M(2,3), C(3,1), I(1,3), T(1,1)
160 MAT READ N, M, C
170 MAT I = N * M            ! I IS A 1 BY 3
180 MAT T = I * C            ! T IS THE TOTAL COST
185 F$ = "TOTAL EXPECTED COST OF THE MATERIALS IS $$$,$$$.$$"
190 PRINT USING F$, T(1,1)
900 DATA 25, 15, 25, 10, 0, 0, 25, 20, 20, 15, 15
999 END

Ready

RUNNH
TOTAL EXPECTED COST OF THE MATERIALS IS $26,375.00

Ready
```

Problem Definition 15.2

1. Statement of the problem: Write a program to solve for the unknowns in the following set of equations:

$$5X + 3Y + 2Z = 5$$
$$6X + 2Y + 3Z = 8$$
$$4X + 4Y + 2Z = 4$$

Place the data in the matrix form:

Matrix A				Matrix U		Matrix B
5	3	2		X		5
6	2	3	×	Y	=	8
4	4	2		Z		4

To solve for Matrix U divide Matrix B by Matrix A. This is accomplished by multiplying the inverse of A by B, that is: U = (inverse of A) * B.

2.   Input: Use a MAT READ statement to enter the data in the statement of the problem.

3.   Output: Display the appropriate column names and the answers for the three unknowns: A, B, C.

Pseudocode 15.2

MAT read equation coefficients and equation answers
Determine inverse of coefficients
MAT multiply inverse time equation answers
Print heading
MAT print the unknowns

Flowchart 15.2

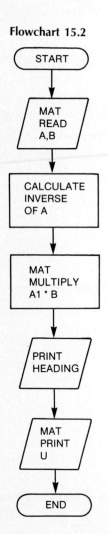

```
1 REM SOLVES FOR 3 UNKNOWNS IN 3 EQUATIONS
50 ! MATRIX A = THE COEFFICIENTS OF THE EQUATION
     MATRIX U = THE UNKNOWNS OF THE EQUATION
     MATRIX B = THE ANSWERS OF THE EQUATION
     MATRIX A1= THE INVERSE OF MATRIX A
150 DIM A(3,3), U(3,1), B(3,1), A1(3,3)
160 MAT READ A, B
170 MAT A1 = INV(A)
180 MAT U  = A1 * B     !COLUMNS IN A1 MATCH ROWS IN B, RESULT IS A 3 BY 1
200 PRINT "X", "Y", "Z" \ MAT PRINT U,
900 DATA 5,3,2,6,2,3,4,4,2
901 DATA 5,8,4
999 END

Ready

RUNNH
X              Y              Z
 .5            -.5            2

Ready
```

Problem Definition 15.3

1. Statement of the problem: A company sells three different types of soft drinks and distributes these products to four distribution centers in Texas. The sales manager wants to know the total dollar amount of sales in Texas and in the four distribution centers for the past three weeks. The table below shows the number of cases sold during the period.

	Week 1				Week 2				Week 3			
	C1	C2	C3	C4	C1	C2	C3	C4	C1	C2	C3	C4
Orange	600	800	900	700	710	720	730	740	560	560	560	560
Cola	950	900	950	900	810	820	830	840	450	500	550	600
Root beer	875	760	890	850	910	810	710	610	600	500	600	500

2. Input: Use a MAT READ to enter the matrices of cases of soft drink sold during weeks 1, 2, and 3 and the price per case by type of soft drink.

3. Output: Display an appropriate heading and column names and the total dollar amount of sales by center. Skip several lines and display the sales for the state.

Pseudocode 15.3

MAT read cases sold of soft drink and price
MAT add the first two weeks
MAT add all three weeks
MAT multiply to find dollar amount by center
Print heading and column names
MAT print dollar sales
Skip a line
Set up a matrix to add by total state
MAT multiply total cases to determine dollar amount for state
Print heading and column names
Print answer
Endprogram

270

Flowchart 15.3

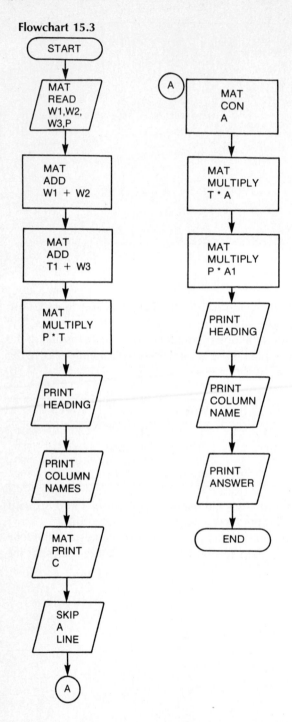

```
1 REM FINDS THE TOTAL DOLLAR SALES BY DISTRIBUTION CENTER AND BY STATE
50 ! MATRICES WS, W2, 23
               = CASES SOLD BY SOFT DRINK AND BY CENTER
       MATRIX P = PRICE PER CASE BY TYPE OF SOFT DRINK
       MATRIX T = TOTAL CASES SOLD BY DRINK AND CENTER FOR 3 WEEKS
       MATRIX T1= TOTAL CASES SOLD BY DRINK AND CENTER FOR 2 WEEKS
       MATRIX C = DOLLAR SALES BY DISTRIBUTION CENTER
       MATRIX A = VALUES ARE ALL ONES
       MATRIX A1= TOTAL CASES BY DRINK
       MATRIX S = DOLLAR SALES FOR THE STATE
200 DIM W1(3,4), W2(3,4), W3(3,4), P(1,3)
210 DIM T(3,4), T1(3,4), C(1,4), S(1,1)
220 MAT READ W1, W2, W3, P
230 MAT T1 = W1 + W2          ! SUM THE FIRST 2 WEEKS
240 MAT T = T1 + W3           ! SUM ALL 3 WEEKS
250 MAT C = P * T             ! FIND DOLLAR AMOUNT BY CENTER
260 PRINT 'DOLLAR SALES BY DISTRIBUTION CENTER'
270 PRINT 'CENTER 1','CENTER 2','CENTER 3','CENTER 4' \ MAT PRINT C,
280 PRINT
290 MAT A = CON(4,1)          ! SET UP MATRIX TO ADD BY TOTAL STATE
300 MAT A1 = T * A
310 MAT S = P * A1            ! FIND DOLLAR AMOUNT BY TOTAL STATE
320 PRINT 'DOLLAR SALES BY STATE'
330 PRINT 'STATE OF TEXAS SALES' \ MAT PRINT S
900 DATA 600,800,900,700,950,900,950,900,870,760,890,850
901 DATA 710,720,730,740,810,820,830,840,910,810,710,610
902 DATA 560,560,560,560,450,500,550,600,600,500,600,500
903 DATA 6.10,7.30,6.90
999 END

Ready

RUNNH
DOLLAR SALES BY DISTRIBUTION CENTER
CENTER 1        CENTER 2        CENTER 3        CENTER 4
 43962           43177           45548           42806



DOLLAR SALES BY STATE
STATE OF TEXAS SALES
 175493


Ready
```

Exercises

1. Correct the errors, if any, in the following statements:

   a. 100 MAT A = B − C + D
   b. 100 MAT A = B(3,4) * C(3,4)
   c. 100 MAT A = INV A
   d. 100 PRINT MAT A
   e. 100 MAT C = B(TRN)
   f. 100 MAT IND = A
   g. 100 MAT PRINT B, A

2. Given:

     100 DIM X(3,3)
     200 DATA 1,2,3,4,5,6,7,8,9

   Write the matrix statement to read in these values.

3. Given:

     100 DIM X(3,3)

   Write the matrix statement to input the redimension matrix X so that it becomes a 2 by 2 matrix.

4. Given the following statements:

     100 DIM X(3,3)
     110 FOR I = 1 TO 3 \ FOR J = 1 TO 3
     120 INPUT X(I,J)
     130 NEXT J \ NEXT I

   Write a matrix statement to replace all but the DIM statement.

5. Write a program that reads data into matrices and performs the following operations. Use matrix algebra and the following data:

	X			Y	
1	1	1	4	4	4
2	2	2	5	5	5
3	3	3	6	6	6

   a. Read in X and Y.
   b. Subtract X from Y and save the results in Z1.
   c. Transpose X and store the results in Z2.
   d. Print X, Y, Z1, Z2 with proper headings.

6. The MAT INV statement finds the inverse of a matrix if one exists. If an inverse exists, when it is multiplied by the original matrix the result is an identity matrix. Write a program to prove this using the following as the original matrix:

	A	
2	3	1
0	1	2
2	2	3

7. Write separate programs to solve for the unknowns in each set of the following equations:

   a. 6X − 2Y = 20
       2X − 3Y = 10

   b. 4A − 4B + 4C − 4D = 12
       3A + 3B − 3C + 3D = 8
       2A + 4B − 3C + 4D = 10
       A − 3B + 2C + 3D = 7

8. Convert to Celsius the Fahrenheit temperatures in increments of 5 from 0 to 100. The model is Celsius = (Fahrenheit − 32) * 5/9. Use matrix statements.

9. A store sells three models each of two brands of radios at different prices. Sales information given below.

	Selling price ($) model			Number sold model			Cost of the radios model		
	A	B	C	A	B	C	A	B	C
X	50	60	55	95	35	70	25	35	35
Y	75	85	70	65	65	30	50	50	45

Write a program to find:

   a. The gross revenue for each model by brand.
   b. The gross revenue for each model.
   c. The gross revenue for each brand.
   d. The difference between the total selling price and the total cost for each model by brand.

10. The bowling team had the following scores last night:

	Game 1	Game 2	Game 3
Jim	170	175	180
Bob	165	180	190
Tim	203	200	210
Ace	195	205	203
Max	230	225	230

Write a program to find the average score for each player and the average score per game.

11. Three companies introduced new brands of toothpaste simultaneously. At

the start each company had approximately one third the market. During a 12-month period the following happened:

Company A retained 75% of its customers but lost 15% to B and 10% to C.

Company B retained 65% of its customers but lost 15% to A and 20% to C.

Company C retained 85% of its customers but lost 5% to A and 10% to B.

Assume the market does not expand and the above percentages remain constant for the next 24 months. What will be the expected market share of each company in 12 months? What will be the expected market share of each company in 24 months?

Chapter Sixteen

EDT Text Editor

This chapter illustrates the usefulness of a text editor on Digital Equipment computer systems, which may include several different text editors. The text editors available on PDP and VAX systems include EDT, EDIT, and TECO. This chapter illustrates the use of EDT. EDIT and TECO are briefly introduced in Appendix E.

Reasons for a Text Editor

The essential reasons for using the text editor EDT with BASIC are to have an efficient means of modifying and/or correcting BASIC programs and to create data files for input into a BASIC program. The use of data files as input to a program will be explained in Chapter 17. Creating a data file for that purpose may be accomplished with a text editor.

Concept of the Text Editor, EDT

When the NEW command is issued, an area of temporary storage is used to create a program. If there are errors in the program or if it needs modifications, individual BASIC statements must be added, deleted, or changed using the procedures described in Chapter 4. These same procedures could be used to modify a previously saved program by issuing the OLD command and then making necessary corrections. While these procedures work, they are sometimes very cumbersome. The text editor EDT can be used more efficiently to modify or correct programs.

The text editor, when used to modify a BASIC program, brings a previously saved program into a temporary storage location that is called a text buffer. The contents of the buffer can then be modified, thereby modifying the program. BASIC statements can be added, deleted, or changed by EDT with considerable ease. The modified program can then be stored on a permanent storage device for access in the normal manner.

Modifying a Saved BASIC Program

The following example deals with a program named AVG that had previously been created and saved in a user area. In any modification of an existing program three steps are necessary:

1. Bring the previously saved program from permanent storage into a text buffer. (This procedure also invokes the text editor.)
2. Make necessary modifications.
3. Store the modified program on permanent storage.

The general format for bringing a saved program into a text buffer may differ from system to system. One format that is used is:

EDT output-program-name = input-program-name

where *EDT* is a system command, *output-program-name* is the name that will be given to the modified program when it is stored on permanent storage in step 3, = is a required operation, and *input-program-name* is the name of the program that was previously saved.

Both the input program name and the output program name may be the same. If they are, the previously saved program version will be destroyed by the new version when the new version is stored on permanent storage. If the names are different, the previously saved program version will be retained, and the new version will be stored on permanent storage under the name given when the text editor EDT was invoked.

The following command would invoke the text editor EDT and, when the modified version is stored on permanent storage, would store the program named AVGMOD along with the previously saved program named AVG.

```
EDT AVGMOD.BAS=AVG.BAS
*
```

The next command would invoke the text editor and store the modified version of AVG by destroying the previous version.

```
EDT AVG.BAS=AVG.BAS
*
```

Note that, in both cases, a three-character extension (BAS) is included in the program name. The BAS extension is created automatically when the NEW command is issued to create a new BASIC program. The extension, however, is required to be used when using the text editor, since other types of program besides BASIC can be modified. Also, programmers commonly use other extensions as a reminder of the contents of the file. They include

DAT   Denotes a data file.
TXT   Denotes a text file.
COB   Denotes a COBOL program.
FOR   Denotes a FORTRAN program.

The extension used is left to the discretion of the programmer and is separated from the program name by a period. The extension must be three characters or less in length, just as the program name must be six characters or less on the PDP-11 and nine characters or less on the VAX-11.

When the text editor is invoked, the system prompts the programmer by printing an asterisk on the line after the command that invoked the text editor. The asterisk denotes that the text editor is waiting for an edit command from the programmer.

Edit Commands

The following are the EDT edit commands necessary to modify a previously saved program.

Type   Prints one or more statements on the terminal.
Substitute   Changes the contents of one or more statements by substitution.
Find   Locates a particular statement
Insert   Allows the programmer to add statements.
Delete   Allows the programmer to delete statements.
EXit   Terminates the edit mode and stores the program under the output program name supplied.
QUIT   Terminates the edit mode but does not store the results of any modifications.
RESequence   Assigns new text line numbers.

In the above commands, the programmer may use the full command word completely spelled out or may simply use the character or characters that are capitalized. For instance, T is equivalent to Type and EX is equivalent to EXit.

To show the use of each of these editorial commands, a program was created and saved under the name AVG. This program will be changed so that it will be better documented by the use of lengthier variable names in the EXTEND mode described in Chapter 3. The second version will be stored using the name

AVGMOD. The old version AVG will remain on the permanent storage device unchanged. In each of the following examples, the statements that the programmer inputs to the system are shaded, while the computer system's responses are not.

The Type command.   There are four forms of the Type command used in Example 16.1.

T %WH
: Displays the entire or whole (WH) contents of the text buffer, including BASIC statement numbers, and assigns an additional number—the *text line number*—to every BASIC statement. When the system has complely displayed the text buffer, it notifies the user by printing [EOB], which indicates the end of the buffer.

T text line number
: Displays the contents of a single text line number.

T range of text line numbers
: Displays the contents of two or more text line numbers (the range is specified by separating the beginning text line number and the ending text line number by a colon).

T
: A Type command by itself will display the contents of a single text line number. The line displayed will depend on the location of a pointer at that particular time. Note when the type command is given by itself, text line number 110 is displayed. The use of the Find command is useful in locating the pointer. This procedure will be explained in a later example.

Example 16.1
The Type command

```
EDT AVGMOD.BAS=AVG.BAS
*TYPE %WH
10        100 PRINT "ENTER 3 TEST SCORES"
20        110 INPUT S1, S2, S3
30        120 LET Z  = (S1 + S2 + S3) / 3
40        130 LET Y = Y + Z
50        140 LET X = X + 1
60        150 PRINT "AVERAGE IS"; Z
70        160 PRINT
80        170 PRINT "ENTER YES TO CONTINUE, NO TO END"
90        180 INPUT N$
100       190 IF N$ = "YES" THEN 100
110       200 IF N$ = "NO" THEN 230
120       210 PRINT "TRY AGAIN"
130       220 GO TO 160
140       230 PRINT "OVERALL AVERAGE IS"; Y/X
150       999 END
[EOB]
*T 50
50        140 LET X = X + 1
*T 100:130
100       190 IF N$ = "YES" THEN 100
110       200 IF N$ = "NO" THEN 230
120       210 PRINT "TRY AGAIN"
130       220 GO TO 160
*T
110       200 IF N$ = "NO" THEN 230
```

The text line numbers created by EDIT may be used with the Find, Type, Substitute, Delete, and RESequence commands. These text line numbers are used by EDT to keep track of each BASIC statement's relative position in the text buffer. Do not confuse the text line number with the BASIC statement number.

The Substitute command.   The purpose of the Type command is to merely display the contents of one or more lines on the terminal. To make changes to existing statements, the Substitute command is used, as illustrated in Examples 16.2.a through 16.2.e.

The Substitute command in Example 16.2.a searches the entire file (%WH) for each occurrence of the variable name X, replaces each occurrence of X with the variable name NUMBER.OF.SCORES, and displays each line in the program that is affected by the command. The parameters in the Substitute command are separated by a slash. After all substitutions have been made, EDT also informs the programmer how many substitutions there were.

Example 16.2.*a*
The Substitute command, entire file searched

```
*S/X/NUMBER.OF.SCORES/%WH
50        140 LET NUMBER.OF.SCORES = NUMBER.OF.SCORES + 1
140       230 PRINT 'OVERALL AVERAGE IS'; Y/NUMBER.OF.SCORES
3 SUBSTITUTIONS MADE IN 2 LINES
```

The Substitute command in Example 16.2.b searches the entire file also and will replace each occurrence of Y with TOTAL.OF.SCORES. However, it uses the Query option to allow the programmer to replace some Y's and not others.

The Query option of the Substitute command works as follows. Whenever the system finds an occurrence of the character or characters to be replaced, it types out the line in question and prints a question mark. The allowable responses are:

Y   Yes, make the substitution.

N   No, do not make the substitution. Search for the next occurrence instead.

Q   Stop substituting.

In Example 16.2.b, the Q to stop substitution was not used because a replacement was necessary in BASIC statement number 230.

Example 16.2*b*
The Substitute command with Query option

```
*S/Y/TOTAL.OF.SCORES/%WH/Q
40        130 LET Y = Y + Z
?Y
          130 LET TOTAL.OF.SCORES = Y + Z
?Y
80        170 PRINT 'ENTER YES TO CONTINUE, NO TO END'
?N
100       190 IF N$ = 'YES' THEN 100
?N
120       210 PRINT 'TRY AGAIN'
?N
140       230 PRINT 'OVERALL AVERAGE IS'; Y/NUMBER.OF.SCORES
?Y
3 SUBSTITUTIONS MADE IN 2 LINES
```

Example 16.2.c illustrates that the programmer may make substitutions in a range of statements or in a single statement.

Example 16.2.*c*
The Substitute command in one or more lines

```
*S/Z/AVERAGE/30:60
30      120 LET AVERAGE   = (S1 + S2 + S3) / 3
40      130 LET TOTAL.OF.SCORES = TOTAL.OF.SCORES + AVERAGE
60      150 PRINT 'AVERAGE IS'; AVERAGE
3 SUBSTITUTIONS MADE IN 3 LINES
*S'S'SCORE'20:30
20      110 INPUT SCORE1, SCORE2, SCORE3
30      120 LET AVERAGE   = (SCORE1 + SCORE2 + SCORE3) / 3
6 SUBSTITUTIONS MADE IN 2 LINES
*FIND 60
*T
60      150 PRINT 'AVERAGE IS'; AVERAGE
*S/'/'THE
60      150 PRINT 'THE AVERAGE IS'; AVERAGE
```

The first Substitute command S/Z/AVERAGE/30:60 replaces all occurrences of Z by AVERAGE in text line numbers 30 through 60. The second Substitute command, S'S'SCORE'20:30, replaces all occurrences of S by SCORE in text line numbers 20 through 30 and illustrates that an apostrophe ' may be used to separate parameters in the Substitute command. This feature is especially useful when the character to be replaced is a slash. The use of next three commands, Find 60, T, and S/'/'THE, shows that the programmer can make substitutions on a single text line. The Find command is necessary to locate the particular text line number in question; the T command displays the line to ensure that the correct statement line has been located; and the S command accomplishes the desired change.

In Example 16.2.*d,* the command S/LET//%WH replaces each occurrence of LET with nothing. Remember that the word LET is optional. Any desired deletion of a character or characters is accomplished by placing two slashes or two apostrophes together without anything in between.

Example 16.2.*d*
The Substitute command, deleting characters

```
*S/LET//%WH
30      120   AVERAGE   = (SCORE1 + SCORE2 + SCORE3) / 3
40      130   TOTAL.OF.SCORES = TOTAL.OF.SCORES + AVERAGE
50      140   NUMBER.OF.SCORES = NUMBER.OF.SCORES + 1
3 SUBSTITUTIONS MADE IN 3 LINES
```

Example 16.2.*e* shows that the programmer may have the text editor make substitutions without displaying the affected text line numbers. This is accomplished by using −T.

Example 16.2.e
The Substitute command, without displaying change

```
*S/N$/RESPONSE$/90:110/-T
 3 SUBSTITUTIONS MADE IN 3 LINES
```

The Find and Insert commands. Example 16.3 shows that a programmer may add statements to a program by using the Find and Insert commands. The Find command locates the text line number *before* which the insertion is to be made.

For instance, F 10 locates text line number 10, and the insertion will be made *before* line 10. The F 80 command will locate text line number 80 and the insertion of new statements will be made *before* line 80. After inserting one or more lines, the programmer presses and holds the CTRL key and then presses the Z key to give EDT additional edit commands. The system types or echoes ^Z when the CTRL and the Z keys are pressed.

Example 16.3
The Find and Insert commands, adding statements

```
*F 10
*INSERT
1 REM MODIFIED PROGRAM USING EDT
50 EXTEND
%^Z
*F 80
*INSERT
165 REM QUERY TO CONTINUE
%^Z
```

The entire contents of the buffer can be displayed at any time using T %WH, as shown in Example 16.4.

Example 16.4
Modified text buffer displayed

```
*T %WH
9          1 REM MODIFIED PROGRAM USING EDT
           50 EXTEND
10         100 PRINT "ENTER 3 TEST SCORES"
20         110 INPUT SCORE1, SCORE2, SCORE3
30         120  AVERAGE  = (SCORE1 + SCORE2 + SCORE3) / 3
40         130  TOTAL.OF.SCORES = TOTAL.OF.SCORES + AVERAGE
50         140  NUMBER.OF.SCORES = NUMBER.OF.SCORES + 1
60         150 PRINT "THE AVERAGE IS"; AVERAGE
70         160 PRINT
71         165 REM QUERY TO CONTINUE
80         170 PRINT "ENTER YES TO CONTINUE, NO TO END"
90         180 INPUT RESPONSE$
100        190 IF RESPONSE$ = "YES" THEN 100
110        200 IF RESPONSE$ = "NO" THEN 230
120        210 PRINT "TRY AGAIN"
130        220 GO TO 160
140        230 PRINT "OVERALL AVERAGE IS"; TOTAL.OF.SCORES/NUMBER.OF.SCORES
150        999 END
[EOB]
```

The RESequence command. In Example 16.4, note the text line numbers that are assigned to the statements that were inserted in Example 16.3. Note particularly BASIC statements 1 and 50. BASIC statement 1 was assigned text line number 9, while BASIC statement 50 was not assigned a text line number. If it is necessary to modify an unnumbered statement that has been inserted, the RESequence command can be used. The program as modified and resequenced is shown in Example 16.5.

The Delete command. Example 16.6 illustrates that the programmer may delete one or more lines from the file using the Delete command. If the programmer desires to delete more than one line at a time, the beginning and ending text

Example 16.5
Buffer contents resequenced and displayed

```
*RES
18 LINES RESEQUENCED
*T %WH
10       1 REM MODIFIED PROGRAM USING EDT
20       50 EXTEND
30       100 PRINT "ENTER 3 TEST SCORES"
40       110 INPUT SCORE1, SCORE2, SCORE3
50       120  AVERAGE  = (SCORE1 + SCORE2 + SCORE3) / 3
60       130  TOTAL.OF.SCORES = TOTAL.OF.SCORES + AVERAGE
70       140  NUMBER.OF.SCORES = NUMBER.OF.SCORES + 1
80       150 PRINT "THE AVERAGE IS"; AVERAGE
90       160 PRINT
100      165 REM QUERY TO CONTINUE
110      170 PRINT "ENTER YES TO CONTINUE, NO TO END"
120      180 INPUT RESPONSE$
130      190 IF RESPONSE$ = "YES" THEN 100
140      200 IF RESPONSE$ = "NO" THEN 230
150      210 PRINT "TRY AGAIN"
160      220 GO TO 160
170      230 PRINT "OVERALL AVERAGE IS"; TOTAL.OF.SCORES/NUMBER.OF.SCORES
180      999 END
[EOB]
```

line numbers of the material to be deleted are entered separated by a colon, just as in the Type command. After the Delete command is issued, the text editor displays the next line that is in the buffer. Resequencing may be accomplished at any time if desired.

Example 16.6
The Delete command

```
*D 100
110      170 PRINT "ENTER YES TO CONTINUE, NO TO END"
```

The EXit command.   To store the modified program on permanent storage and exit the edit mode, use the EXit command as shown in Example 16.7. The system will respond by informing the programmer how many lines were included in the file. When the system displays Ready, the programmer may issue any system command, such as OLD, NEW, or RUN.

Example 16.7
The EXit command, storing the file

```
*EXIT
17 LINES OUTPUT

Ready

RUN AVGMOD
ENTER 3 TEST SCORES
? 70,80,90
THE AVERAGE IS 80

ENTER YES TO CONTINUE, NO TO END
? YES
ENTER 3 TEST SCORES
? 75,85,95
THE AVERAGE IS 85

ENTER YES TO CONTINUE, NO TO END
? NO
OVERALL AVERAGE IS 82.5

Ready
```

Entering New BASIC Programs

If a programmer makes errors in syntax when entering a new program into the system, the system notifies the programmer of the error. Normally the programmer would immediately correct the error by retyping the statement correctly or using the editing option available on the VAX-11. With the text editor available, the programmer may disregard the syntax error message for the time being, continue entering the rest of the program, SAVE the program, and then use the text editor as previously described to correct any errors. This method can be extremely useful when errors are made on lone BASIC statements and statements that are continued on more than one line. In Example 16.8.a, the programmer made syntax

Example 16.8.a
Entering a BASIC program

NEW LOAN

.
.

210 I—R * P1

? ILLEGAL VERB AT LINE 210

READY

220 C = A − I

230 IF X = T THEN C = P1   &

A − I + U

?MODIFIER ERROR AT LINE 230

READY

.
.

SAVE

READY

---

errors in BASIC statements 210 and 230. Statement 210 should be: 210 I = R * P1, and statement 230 should be:

230 IF X = T THEN C = P1 \&
                           A = I + C

Note the use of the ampersand as the terminator of the continued line. Remember, this is one method that can be used in the EXTEND mode on the PDP-11, and it is the only method available on the VAX-11 to continue lines. Also be aware that, while the PDP-11 system notifies the programmer immediately of a syntax error, the VAX-11 system only notifies of an error when the program is run.

Example 16.8.*b* illustrates the correction of the errors made in Example 16.8.*a* using the text editor EDT.

Example 16.8.b
Correcting syntax errors with EDT

EDT LOAN.BAS=LOAN.BAS

*T %WH

.
.
100   210 I − R * P1
110   220 C = A − I
120   230 IF X = T THEN C = P1   &
130   A − I + U
.
.

[EOB]

*S/−/=/%WH/Q

100   210 I − R * P1

?Y

110   220 C = A − I

?N

130   A − I + U

?Y

2 SUBSTITUTIONS MADE IN 2 LINES

*F 120

*S/P1/P1 \

120   230 IF X = T THEN C = P1 \   &

*T %WH

.
.

100   210 I = R * P1
110   220 C = A − I
120   230 IF X = T THEN C = P1 \   &
130   A = I + U

.
.

[EOB]

*EXIT

25 LINES OUTPUT

READY

A programmer may also enter a BASIC program fully with the text editor by invoking EDT only with an output program name, as shown in Example 16.8.c. Remember the use of the CTRL and the Z keys to leave the insertion mode. The created and stored program can then be tested using the OLD or RUN commands. If errors have been made, the text editor can be used again.

A word of caution is appropriate at this point for users of EDT on the PDP-11 system. When EDT is invoked with only an output name, the text editor searches the user area to determine if there is a file already stored under that name. If a file exists, when the EXit command is issued, the previously stored file will retain the same name, but its extension will change to BAK, which denotes a backup file. To guard against making such a change inadvertently, it is best to have the text editor display the entire contents of the file immediately after invoking the editor, as was done in Example 16.8.c.

Example 16.8.c
Entering a BASIC program with EDT

EDT LOAN.BAS

*T %WH

[EOB]

*INSERT

.
.

210 I = R * P1

220 C = A − I

230 IF X = T THEN C = P1 \   &
                 A = I + U

.
.

999 END

^Z

*EXIT

25 LINES OUTPUT

READY

Various Commands

The QUIT command.   In Example 16.9, the QUIT command was used because a file already existed under the name given. The QUIT command exits the edit mode without transferring anything from the text buffer to permanent storage.

Use of other CTRL combinations.   In the text editing mode, the use of the delete or rubout key is valid to erase single characters, as was described in Chapter 4. Also the use of CTRL R and CTRL U may be of benefit. However, do not use CTRL C in the text-editing mode. The pressing of the CTRL and the C keys

Example 16.9
The QUIT command

EDT PGM2.BAS

*T %WH

10   100 REM ACCOUNTS RECEIVABLE PROGRAM
20   110 REM THE PURPOSE OF THIS PROGRAM
.
.
.
[EOB]

*QUIT

READY

---

is used to abort the running of a BASIC program, but when this maneuver used in the text-editing mode, it will have the same effect as the QUIT command and destroy all files currently stored in the buffer in temporary storage.

Text Editor EDT to Enter Data Files

EDT can also be used to enter data files that could then be processed by a BASIC program. However, this topic will be discussed in Chapter 17.

Common Errors

COMMAND	EXPLANATION
EDT PGM1 = PGM2	No extension. If this is a BASIC program, it should be: EDT PGM1.BAS = PGM2.BAS
EDT PGM1.BAS	Only an output file name is specified. Both input and output names are needed unless this is a new program or the programmer wishes to create a backup.
ˆC	Do not use the CTRL and C keys. Doing so will abort the editing session.
*T 120;150	Invalid syntax for a Type command. Use T 120:150
*INSERT 100 REM ADD A STATEMENT T 50:90 RES	Programmer forgot to exit the insertion mode after typing statement 100 with CTRL Z. The lines T 50:90 and RES have been added to the text buffer and will have to be deleted.

Exercises

1. What are the purposes of a text editor when used with programming in BASIC?
2. How does the text editor EDT work? What three steps are necessary to modify a previously stored BASIC program?
3. What does it mean when the system displays an asterisk?
4. What is the purpose of an extension as a part of a file name? What extension is automatically created when entering a BASIC program using the NEW command?
5. What are the purposes of the edit commands T, S, F, I, D, EX, QUIT, and RES?
6. What are the different ways of using the Type command? the Query option?
7. Modify Sample Program 12.3 using the text editor to activate the EXTEND mode. Variables should be changed as indicated below. Enter the program originally using the NEW command. Test the modified program, and correct if necessary.

Current variable name	Changed to
X	SALES.AMOUNT
P	PERCENTAGE
C	CENTER
T	TOTALS
I	ROWS.OF.TABLE
J	COLUMNS.OF.TABLE

8. Use the text editor to enter Sample Program 12.1, then exit the edit mode and test the program. Make corrections as necessary.
9. What are the two ways to enter a BASIC program?
10. What happens if CTRL and C keys are pressed during an editing session?

Chapter Seventeen

Advanced Data Entry and File Processing

Neither the INPUT nor the READ/DATA statements offer acceptable means of entering data with a BASIC program in all cases. The use of the INPUT statement with data from a terminal is very slow and cumbersome when the amounts of data are large. Inputting data from a terminal should mainly be used for small amounts of data and where interactive processing is required.

The use of the READ/DATA statements is also not very efficient in certain cases. This method makes the DATA statements a part of the program, and so, if the data change, the program statements must be modified. Also, since DATA statements are a part of the program, they may not fit in temporary storage. The use of an external device, such as a magnetic disk or tape, to store, retrieve, and process data should be considered when there are large amounts of data relative to temporary storage capacity. There are also many times when the output from one program becomes the input to another program and when more than one programmer uses the same data. Efficient processing of these types of situations would be virtually impossible with the INPUT and the READ/DATA statements.

Types of External Input/Output

Three methods of data storage and retrieval are available on PDP systems:

1. Formated ASCII.

2. Virtual array storage.
3. Block input/output.

Six methods of data storage and retrieval are available on VAX systems:

1. Terminal format (same as formated ASCII on PDP systems).
2. Virtual array storage.
3. Block input/output.
4. Sequential.
5. Relative.
6. Indexed.

The first three methods available on the VAX system are also available on the PDP system. Our discussion of file processing will only cover the three methods common to both systems. The reader is left to consult the system manual for details on Sequential, Relative, and Indexed files.

Terminal format affords the simplest method of data storage because the processing of the resulting files is very similar to the processing of data from a terminal using INPUT and PRINT statements. The data, however, must be in sequential order and must be processed in that order.

Virtual array storage affords the user the ability to randomly gain access to data and process it by using techniques similar to table handling and arrays. This type of access is useful in applications that require immediate feedback, such as an airlines reservation system or a credit check for a credit card purchase.

Block input/output, also referred to as record input/output, is a flexible and efficient means of data storage and retrieval. It is, however, more complex than either terminal format or virtual array storage methods.

Terminal Format

Terminal format is a method of coding data so that a computer can read the data from a device. The system assigns a decimal number to each character and stores that number so that the computer system can understand it. This method of coding is called ASCII (American Standard Code for Information Interchange). When a program was created using the text editor EDT in Chapter 16, the characters in that program were stored in ASCII form. The text editor can also be used to store data onto a device such as magnetic disk in ASCII form. The data are then processed just as if the data were on a terminal; hence the name terminal format. Handling data in this way provides a simple means of storage and retrieval and causes little trouble for most programmers because of its similarity to processing data from a terminal.

Building a Data File in Terminal Format

Suppose that a company wishes to set up a sequential accounts receivable file in terminal format by using the text editor EDT as described in Chapter 16. The data to be included in this file are shown in Figure 17.1.

Figure 17.1
Sequential accounts receivable file

Account	Customer name	Amount owed
13367	ABC Manufacturing	$ 5,076.78
14976	Acme Distributors	456.50
15782	Hinton Music Suppliers	50.23
17975	County Garage	11,575.90

Creation of a data image file.   In Chapter 5, we studied the DATA statement, which makes it possible to process larger amounts of data than could be handled efficiently with the INPUT statement. A terminal format file on magnetic disk can be created with the text editor EDT or some other editor that is essentially in the same format as the DATA statements, using a comma to separate fields of data. For instance, if the data in Figure 17.1 were placed in DATA statements, they would be as shown in Figure 17.2.

Figure 17.2
Accounts receivable data in DATA statements

900 DATA 13367,ABC MANUFACTURING,5076.78
910 DATA 14976,ACME DISTRIBUTORS,456.50
920 DATA 15782,HINTON MUSIC SUPPLIERS,50.23
930 DATA 17975,COUNTY GARAGE,11575.90

These data can be placed in a data image file by using the text editor EDT, as shown in Example 17.1. Note that the file does not include line numbers or the word DATA. Only the data are placed into the file as a data image.

Example 17.1
Creation of a data image file

```
EDT CHG1.DAT
*T %WH
[EOB]
*I
13367,ABC MANUFACTURING,5076.78
14976,ACME DISTRIBUTORS,456.50
15782,HINTON MUSIC SUPPLIERS,50.23
17975,COUNTY GARAGE,11575.90
*^Z
*EX
4 LINES OUTPUT

Ready
```

Listing a data image file.   When a file is created using the text editor EDT, a listing of that file may be obtained by using Type %WH while in the edit mode. The listing can also be obtained using the system command PIP on the PDP-11 system or the system command TYPE on the VAX-11 system, without being in the edit mode.

294

The general format of these system commands to obtain a listing of a terminal format file is:

PIP program-name. extension

and

TYPE program-name.extension

where *PIP* is a system command for the PDP-11, *TYPE* is a system command for the VAX-11, *program-name* is the name of the program or file used to create the file, the period is a required delimiter, and *extension* is an extension of three characters or less, used to remind the programmer of the type of file that is being listed. A program or data file can be listed using these system commands.

A listing of CHG1.DAT that was created in Example 17.1 is shown in Example 17.2.

Example 17.2
Listing of terminal format file using PIP

```
PIP CHG1.DAT
13367,ABC MANUFACTURING,5076.78
14976,ACME DISTRIBUTORS,456.50
15782,HINTON MUSIC SUPPLIERS,50.23
17975,COUNTY GARAGE,11575.90

Ready
```

Creation of a fixed-length record file. While CHG1.DAT was created as a data image file, a second way to create a terminal format file is to set up a file where all the records or lines of data are the same length. This design eliminates the need to have commas inserted as field delimiters. In Example 17.3, CHG2.DAT is created using the text editor EDT by making each record the same length. All customer names are equalized in length by adding blanks; the fields showing amount owed are also made the same length so that the decimal points align.

Example 17.3
Creation of a fixed-length record file

```
EDT CHG2.DAT
*T %WH
[EOB]
*I
13367ABC MANUFACTURING      5076.78
14976ACME DISTRIBUTORS       456.50
15782HINTON MUSIC SUPPLIERS   50.23
17975COUNTY GARAGE         11575.90
%^Z
*EX
4 LINES OUTPUT

Ready
```

Listing a fixed-length record file.   A listing of the file created in Example 17.3 is shown in Example 17.4.

Example 17.4
Listing of fixed-length records using PIP

```
PIP CHG2.DAT
13367ABC MANUFACTURING      5076.78
14976ACME DISTRIBUTORS       456.50
15782HINTON MUSIC SUPPLIERS   50.23
17975COUNTY GARAGE         11575.90

Ready
```

Processing Concepts with Terminal Format Files

In the case of both the record image file and the fixed-length record file, the data are the same. Only the format is different. CHG1.DAT, created as a record image file, will be processed by using an extension of INPUT and PRINT statements already familiar to the reader. CHG2.DAT, created as fixed-length records, will be processed by inputting the entire line of data as a string variable and will require the use of string manipulation functions as described in Chapter 14.

Processing Statements—Terminal Format Files

To use any type of data file, it is necessary to direct the computer to the particular device on which the file is located. In the absence of such direction from the programmer, the computer automatically assumes that the data are to be input from or printed on the terminal.

OPEN statement.   To use an external data file for input or output with a BASIC program, an OPEN statement is required. The general format for the OPEN statement is:

$$n \text{ OPEN 'file-name.extension'} \begin{Bmatrix} \text{FOR INPUT} \\ \text{FOR OUTPUT} \end{Bmatrix} \text{AS FILE channel-number}$$

where *OPEN* is a reserved word, the apostrophes or quote marks are required delimiters, *file-name.extension* is the name under which the file was created for input or the name that will be used for output, *FOR INPUT* and *FOR OUTPUT* are optional reserved words to specify the use of the file, *AS and FILE* are reserved words, and *channel-number* is a logical device number; the programmer substitutes in its place a number from 1 to 12.

For example, if CHG1.DAT was to be used as input to a program, the OPEN statement could be:

OPEN 'CHG1.DAT' FOR INPUT AS FILE 1

The use of the FOR INPUT, the FOR OUTPUT, or neither one depends on the use of a particular file. The forms of the OPEN statement shown in Figure 17.3 are all valid, depending on the use of the file.

Figure 17.3
Valid forms of the OPEN statement

---

100 OPEN "CHG1.DAT" FOR INPUT AS FILE 1
100 OPEN "CHG1.DAT" FOR OUTPUT AS FILE 1
100 OPEN "CHG1.DAT" AS FILE 1

When FOR INPUT is specified, the system searches for an existing file to be used as input. If the file specified does not exist, the system informs the programmer that the file cannot be found.

When FOR OUTPUT is used, the system searches for an existing file, and if a file under the specified name exists, it will be deleted, and a new file with the same name will be created. On the VAX system a new version would be created.

Omitting the use of either FOR INPUT or FOR OUTPUT causes the system to search for an existing file as input. If no file exists under the name specified, a new file will be created.

The channel number is an integer number from 1 to 12 which specifies an identifying number to an external device. A channel number of zero is used to specify the user's terminal. Otherwise, the number is arbitrary, so long as the programmer uses it consistently. For instance, if a program uses two different data files for input and creates a third data file for output, the OPEN statements could be:

```
100 OPEN 'INVEN.DAT' FOR INPUT AS FILE 4
110 OPEN 'TRANS.DAT' FOR INPUT AS FILE 3
120 OPEN 'NEWFLE.DAT' FOR OUTPUT AS FILE 7
```

The programmer should be aware that when a channel number, such as FILE 4, is used, the file to which the program will refer is INVEN.DAT in the above set of statements.

CLOSE statement. Any time a file is opened, it must always be closed somewhere in the program.

The general format of the CLOSE statement is:

n CLOSE channel-number(s)

where *CLOSE* is a reserved word and the *channel-number* is the number used when the file or files were opened. One CLOSE statement can close one file or several.

For example, the following CLOSE statement would close all three of the files opened previously.

500 CLOSE 3, 4, 7

INPUT/PRINT statements. To use INPUT and PRINT for terminal format files, with the addition of the channel number, the procedure is the same as with terminal inputting and printing.

The general formats of the INPUT and PRINT statements using external devices are:

> n INPUT #channel-number, list

> n PRINT #channel-number, list

where *INPUT* and *PRINT* are reserved words, *channel-number* is the same channel number referred to in both the OPEN and the CLOSE statements, and *list* refers to variables, constants, expressions, or literals as used previously with the INPUT and PRINT statements.

Sequential File Processing—Data Image File

Assume that the programmer wishes to use CHG1.DAT, which was created as a data image file, as input to a program that will print a listing of the records in the file along with a total of the amount owed. The program that illustrates these concepts is shown in Example 17.5.

Example 17.5
Processing of a data image file

```
100 PRINT 'ACCOUNT    CUSTOMER                AMOUNT'
110 PRINT 'NUMBER     NAME                     OWED'
120 OPEN 'CHG1.DAT' FOR INPUT AS FILE 1
125 F$ = '\       \     \               \$##,###.##'
126 F2$= '                          TOTAL    $##,###.##'
130 FOR N = 1 TO 4           ! DOWHILE DATA
140     INPUT #1, A$,C$,A    ! INPUT DATA
150     PRINT USING F$,A$,C$,A  ! LIST DATA
155     T = T + A            ! ACCUMULATE TOTAL
160 NEXT N                   ! ENDDO
165 PRINT USING F2$,T        ! PRINT TOTAL
170 CLOSE 1                  ! CLOSE FILE
180 END

Ready

RUNNH
ACCOUNT    CUSTOMER                AMOUNT
NUMBER     NAME                     OWED
13367      ABC MANUFACTURING        $ 5,076.78
14976      ACME DISTRIBUTORS        $   456.50
15782      HINTON MUSIC SUPPLIERS   $    50.23
17975      COUNTY GARAGE            $11,575.90
                              TOTAL  $17,159.41

Ready
```

In Example 17.5, statement 120 opens the data file stored as CHG1.DAT; statement 140 inputs the data, one line at a time, assigning the data to variables A$, C$ and A; statement 150 lists each data line; and statement 170 closes the file when the FOR/NEXT loop is completed.

Sequential File Processing—Fixed-Length Record File

The processing of the data file CHG2.DAT, which was created to store fixed-length records, is illustrated in Example 17.6.*a* for the PDP-11 and Example 17.6.*b* for the VAX system. In both examples, each data line is input as a string variable by statement 140. Statement 141 assigns the leftmost five characters to A$, which is the account number. Statement 142 assigns the customer name to C$. Statement 143 extracts the rightmost characters in the string, starting in position 28, and then converts those characters from the string to a real number. The processing otherwise is the same as in Example 17.5.

Example 17.6.*a*
Processing of a fixed-length record file on the PDP-11

```
100 PRINT "ACCOUNT    CUSTOMER                    AMOUNT"
110 PRINT "NUMBER     NAME                        OWED"
120 OPEN 'CHG2.DAT' FOR INPUT AS FILE 1
125 F$ = '\        \                     \$##,###.##'
126 F2$= '                          TOTAL    $##,###.##'
130 FOR N = 1 TO 4
140    INPUT #1, S$          ! INPUT DATA AS A STRING
141    A$ = LEFT (S$, 5)
142    C$ = MID (S$,6,22)
143    T$ = RIGHT (S$,28) \ A = VAL(T$)
150    PRINT USING F$,A$,C$,A
155    T = T + A
160 NEXT N
165 PRINT USING F2$,T
170 CLOSE 1
180 END

Ready

RUNNH
ACCOUNT    CUSTOMER                    AMOUNT
NUMBER     NAME                        OWED
13367      ABC MANUFACTURING           $ 5,076.78
14976      ACME DISTRIBUTORS           $   456.50
15782      HINTON MUSIC SUPPLIERS      $    50.23
17975      COUNTY GARAGE               $11,575.90
                              TOTAL    $17,159.41

Ready
```

End-of File Conditions—ON ERROR statement

The FOR/NEXT loop was used in the three previous examples because it was known how many data lines were to be input. Normally, however, a programmer does not know how many data lines or records are included in a file; so a FOR/NEXT loop is not feasible. Example 17.7 shows the development of the program in Example 17.5, modified so that the FOR/NEXT loop is not used. This example will also introduce the concept of recoverable-error processing.

Example 17.6._b_
Processing of a fixed-length record file on the VAX-11

```
100 PRINT 'ACCOUNT    CUSTOMER                    AMOUNT'
110 PRINT 'NUMBER     NAME                        OWED'
120 OPEN 'CHG2.DAT' FOR INPUT AS FILE 1
125 F$ ='`LLLLL      `LLLLLLLLLLLLLLLLLLLLLLLL  $$$,$$$.$$'
126 F2$= '                           TOTAL      $$$,$$$.$$'
130 FOR N = 1 TO 4
140     INPUT #1, S$
141     A$ = SEG$(S$,1,5)
142     C$ = SEG$(S$,6,27)
143     T$ = SEG$(S$,28,35) \A = VAL(T$)
150     PRINT USING F$,A$,C$,A
155     T = T + A
160 NEXT N
165 PRINT USING F2$,T
170 CLOSE 1
180 END

Ready

RUNNH

ACCOUNT   CUSTOMER                   AMOUNT
NUMBER    NAME                       OWED
13367     ABC MANUFACTURING          $ 5,076.70
14976     ACME DISTRUBUTORS          $    456.50
15782     HINTON MUSIC SUPPLIERS     $     50.20
17975     COUNTY GARAGE              $11,575.90
                             TOTAL   $17,159.30

Ready
```

Before dealing with statements 90 and 161 in Example 17.7, study the logic of statements 140 through 160. Statement 160 causes an unconditional transfer to statement 140, allowing no way out of the loop. Eventually the data file will run out of data, resulting in an end-of-file error. Statement 90, however, tests to see if a _recoverable_ error occurs during execution of the program.

Example 17.7
ON ERROR statement to detect an end-of-file condition

```
90 ON ERROR GO TO 161
100 PRINT 'ACCOUNT    CUSTOMER                 AMOUNT'
110 PRINT 'NUMBER     NAME                      OWED'
120 OPEN 'CHG1.DAT' FOR INPUT AS FILE 1
125 F$ = '\         \     \           \$$$,$$$.$$'
126 F2$= '                        TOTAL  $$$,$$$.$$'
140     INPUT #1, A$,C$,A    ! INPUT DATA
150     PRINT USING F$,A$,C$,A  ! LIST DATA
155     T = T + A            ! ACCUMULATE TOTAL
160     GO TO 140            ! REPEAT NEXT RECORD
161 IF ERR <> 11 THEN PRINT 'ERROR NOT EOF'
165 PRINT USING F2$,T        ! PRINT TOTAL
170 CLOSE 1                  ! CLOSE FILE
180 END

Ready

RUNNH
ACCOUNT   CUSTOMER                 AMOUNT
NUMBER    NAME                     OWED
13367     ABC MANUFACTURING        $ 5,076.78
14976     ACME DISTRIBUTORS        $    456.50
15782     HINTON MUSIC SUPPLIERS   $     50.23
17975     COUNTY GARAGE            $11,575.90
                           TOTAL   $17,159.41

Ready
```

The general format of the ON ERROR statement is:

> n ON ERROR statement

> where *ON and ERROR* are reserved words and *statement* is any executable statement, normally a GO TO statement.

Statement 90 transfers control of the program to statement 161 whenever a recoverable error occurs during processing. Each recoverable error, meaning a type of error from which a BASIC program can recover, is assigned a number by the manufacturer of the computer system. The number assigned to an end-of-file error for both the PDP and VAX systems is the number 11. Statement 161 then tests the error number and, if the number is not 11, a message will be printed. In either case, the program statements 165 through 180 will then be executed. In this case, use of the ON ERROR statement placed at the beginning of the program allows the programmer a way to test to see if the end of the file has been reached. There are many other uses of the ON ERROR statement in BASIC. For a more complete discussion of error processing, refer to Appendix D.

File Creation Using a BASIC Program

There are cases when it is preferable to create a data file using a program rather than a text editor. Example 17.8 shows how this could be done to create a record image file. In this example, statement 160 prints each line of data on the disk. Notice the use of the semicolon as a delimiter and the literal printing of a comma between fields. A listing of CHG1.DAT is also included in this example to show the result of running this program. Note that there is a space before the field showing amount owed. Remember that when a number is printed by a BASIC program, the first position is reserved for the sign. If these numbers had been negative, a minus sign would have been printed instead of the space.

Example 17.9 illustrates the use of a BASIC program to create CHG2.DAT, which is a fixed-length record file. Statement 155 determines how many trailing blanks to add to each customer-name field by using the LEN and SPACE$ string functions, which make all the name fields the same length. The program has allowed for a maximum of 22 characters in a name field. Remember that concatenation is accomplished with a plus sign. A listing of CHG2.DAT has been included in this example also, to show the results of running this program.

Sequential Updating

In addition to creating files and listing the contents of files, it is also necessary to update files. Essentially, a sequential update merges an old file with transactions and creates a new file that has been updated. All files must be in sequential order, either numerically or alphabetically. To illustrate this concept, assume that

Example 17.8
Record image file created using BASIC

```
100 OPEN 'CHG1.DAT' FOR OUTPUT AS FILE 3
110 PRINT 'ENTER ACCOUNT NUMBER, CUSTOMER NAME AND'
120 PRINT 'AMOUNT OWED SEPARATED BY COMMAS.'
130 PRINT 'TYPE IN 0,0,0 WHEN FINISHED.'
140 INPUT A$, C$, A
150 IF A $ = '0' THEN 180
160 PRINT #3, A$;',';C$;',';A
170 GO TO 140
180 CLOSE 3
190 END

Ready

RUNNH
ENTER ACCOUNT NUMBER, CUSTOMER NAME AND
AMOUNT OWED SEPARATED BY COMMAS.
TYPE IN 0,0,0 WHEN FINISHED.
? 13367,ABC MANUFACTURING,5076.78
? 14976,ACME DISTRIBUTORS,456.50
? 15782,HINTON MUSIC SUPPLIERS,50.23
? 17975,COUNTY GARAGE,11575.90
? 0,0,0

Ready

PIP CHG1.DAT
13367,ABC MANUFACTURING, 5076.78
14976,ACME DISTRIBUTORS, 456.5
15782,HINTON MUSIC SUPPLIERS, 50.23
17975,COUNTY GARAGE, 11575.9

Ready
```

Example 17.9
Fixed-length record file created using BASIC

```
100 OPEN 'CHG2.DAT' FOR OUTPUT AS FILE 3
110 PRINT 'ENTER ACCOUNT NUMBER, CUSTOMER NAME AND'
120 PRINT 'AMOUNT OWED SEPARATED BY COMMAS.'
130 PRINT 'TYPE IN 0,0,0 WHEN FINISHED.'
140 INPUT A$, C$, A
150 IF A$ = '0' THEN 180
155 C$ = C$ + SPACE$(22-LEN(C$))
160 PRINT #3, A$; C$;
161 PRINT #3 USING '######.##' A
170 GO TO 140
180 CLOSE 3
190 END

Ready

RUNNH
ENTER ACCOUNT NUMBER, CUSTOMER NAME AND
AMOUNT OWED SEPARATED BY COMMAS.
TYPE IN 0,0,0 WHEN FINISHED.
? 13367,ABC MANUFACTURING,5076.78
? 14976,ACME DISTRIBUTORS,456.50
? 15782,HINTON MUSIC SUPPLIERS,50.23
? 17975,COUNTY GARAGE,11575.90
? 0,0,0

Ready

PIP CHG2.DAT
13367ABC MANUFACTURING        5076.78
14976ACME DISTRIBUTORS         456.50
15782HINTON MUSIC SUPPLIERS     50.23
17975COUNTY GARAGE           11575.90

Ready
```

300

two of the accounts receivable customers had purchases this month. ABC Manufacturing purchased amounts totaling $1,000, and Hinton Music Suppliers purchased amounts totaling $500. The results of the update program should be as shown in Figure 17.4. The old file, the transactions, and the new file are in sequential order by customer account number.

Figure 17.4
Sequential update

Old file	+	Transactions	=	Updated file
13367 . . 5076.78		13367 . . 1000.00		13367 . . 6076.78
14976 . . 456.50				14976 . . 456.50
15782 . . 50.23		15782 . . 500.00		15782 . . 550.23
17975 . . 11575.90				17975 . . 11575.90

The program that would accomplish the update is shown in Example 17.10. In this example, statements 110 and 120 open the input and output files. Statements 160 and 170 input data lines or records from the terminal and the old disk file. Statement 180 determines whether or not the account numbers are the same from both the transaction and the old file records. If they are the same, the record is updated and moved to the new disk file named NEWCHG.DAT. If they are not the same, the record from CHG1.DAT is move to NEWCHG.DAT without being updated. Statement 240 determines when there are no more transactions.

Statement 270 names the old file called CHG1.DAT as CHG1.OLD, thereby allowing the programmer to keep a backup copy of the old file. Statement 280 renames NEWCHG.DAT as CHG1.DAT, which could then be used as input to the program for subsequent updates. NEWCHG.DAT was used only temporarily during execution of the program. A listing of CHG1.DAT is included to show the results of the running of the program.

The general format of the NAME AS statement is:

n NAME 'file-name-1' AS 'file-name-2'

where *NAME* is a reserved word, *file-name-1* is the name that the programmer wishes to change, and *file-name-2* is the new name assigned to the file.

Should the programmer wish to delete the old file instead of retaining a backup copy, statement 270 could be replaced with the following statement:

270 KILL 'CHG1.DAT'

The general format of the KILL statement is:

n KILL 'file-name'

Example 17.10
Sequential update of a terminal format file

```
100 ON ERROR GO TO 250
110 OPEN 'CHG1.DAT' FOR INPUT AS FILE 1
120 OPEN 'NEWCHG.DAT' FOR OUTPUT AS FILE 2
130 PRINT 'TRANSACTIONS MUST BE IN ACCOUNT # SEQUENCE'
140 PRINT 'ENTER ACCOUNT NUMBER AND'
150 PRINT 'AMOUNT OF SALES (0,0 WHEN FINISHED)'
160 INPUT N$, S                 ! INPUT TRANSACTION
170 INPUT #1, A$, C$, A          ! INPUT MASTER RECORD
180 IF A$ = N$ THEN 210          ! ARE ACCOUNT NUMBERS SAME?
190 PRINT #2, A$;',';C$;',';A    ! MOVE RECORD FROM OLD
                                   FILE TO NEW FILE

200 GO TO 170
210 A = A + S                    ! ADD TRANSACTION AMOUNT
                                   TO OLD RECORD
220 PRINT #2, A$;',';C$;',';A    ! MOVE UPDATED RECORD
                                   TO NEW FILE ON DISK
230 PRINT 'SALES UPDATED FOR '; C$
240 IF N$ = '0' THEN 170 ELSE 140 ! IF THERE ARE NO MORE
                                     TRANSACTIONS, READ
                                     NEXT MASTER RECORD, ELSE
                                     READ NEXT TRANSACTION
250 CLOSE 1,2
260 IF ERR <> 11 THEN PRINT 'NOT EOF ERROR'\
                        GO TO 290
270 NAME 'CHG1.DAT' AS 'CHG1.OLD'
280 NAME 'NEWCHG.DAT' AS 'CHG1.DAT'
290 END

Ready


RUNNH
TRANSACTIONS MUST BE IN ACCOUNT # SEQUENCE
ENTER ACCOUNT NUMBER AND
AMOUNT OF SALES (0,0 WHEN FINISHED)
? 13367,1000.00
SALES UPDATED FOR ABC MANUFACTURING
ENTER ACCOUNT NUMBER AND
AMOUNT OF SALES (0,0 WHEN FINISHED)
? 15782,500.00
SALES UPDATED FOR HINTON MUSIC SUPPLIERS
ENTER ACCOUNT NUMBER AND
AMOUNT OF SALES (0,0 WHEN FINISHED)
? 0,0

Ready


PIP CHG1.DAT
13367,ABC MANUFACTURING, 6076.78
14976,ACME DISTRIBUTORS, 456.5
15782,HINTON MUSIC SUPPLIERS, 550.23
17975,COUNTY GARAGE, 11575.9

Ready
```

> where *KILL* is a reserved word and *file-name* is the name of the file that the programmer wishes to have deleted. The KILL statement has the same effect as UNSAVE file-name.

Virtual Array Storage

There are many applications which require the ability to gain access to records in data files randomly instead of sequentially. Examples of such applications include running a motel reservation system, making a credit check for a credit card purchase, and determining the availability of a particular inventory item. Such applications require an immediate response, which is accomplished by directly reaching a single record in a file rather than searching through the entire file. Virtual array storage allows random access by storing data in an array. The virtual array is on disk, however, not in temporary storage.

Creating a Virtual Array File

Unlike a terminal format file, which can be created using either a text editor or a BASIC program, a virtual array requires a BASIC program. Example 17.11 shows the creation of a virtual array with the same accounts receivable file as previously used, except that each record has one more field, namely a credit limit. In this example, statement 120 opens CREDIT.DAT for output, and statement 130 defines the structure of the virtual array. The OPEN statement is used exactly as with the terminal format files when the file is to be created, except that on a VAX-11 the programmer must add the following clause to the OPEN statement: ORGANIZATION VIRTUAL.

Example 17.11
Creation of a virtual array

```
100 REM ACCOUNTS RECEIVABLE CREATED AS
110 REM A VIRTUAL ARRAY
120 OPEN 'CREDIT.DAT' FOR OUTPUT AS FILE 1
130 DIM #1, A$(4)=8, C$(4)=32, A(4), L(4)
140 FOR I = 1 TO 4
150     A$(I) = '' \ C$(I) = '' \ A(I) = 0 \ L(I) = 0
160 NEXT I
170 PRINT 'ENTER ACCOUNT NUMBER, CUSTOMER NAME,'
180 PRINT 'AMOUNT OWED AND CREDIT LIMIT FOR'
190 FOR I = 1 TO 4
200     PRINT 'CUSTOMER NUMBER';I
210     INPUT A$(I), C$(I), A(I), L(I)
220 NEXT I
230 CLOSE 1
240 END

Ready

RUNNH
ENTER ACCOUNT NUMBER, CUSTOMER NAME,
AMOUNT OWED AND CREDIT LIMIT FOR
CUSTOMER NUMBER 1
? 13367,ABC MANUFACTURING,5076.78,7500.00
CUSTOMER NUMBER 2
? 14976,ACME DISTRIBUTORS,456.50,700.00
CUSTOMER NUMBER 3
? 15782,HINTON MUSIC SUPPLIERS,50.23,500.00
CUSTOMER NUMBER 4
? 17975,COUNTY GARAGE,11575.90,13500.00

Ready
```

The general format to define the structure of a virtual array is:

n DIM # channel-number, array list

where *DIM #* is a reserved word, *channel-number* is the same channel referred to in the OPEN and CLOSE statements, and the *array list* defines the names, types, and sizes of arrays to be stored on disk.

Statement 130 defines two string arrays, A$ and C$, for the account numbers and customer names and defines two numeric arrays, A and L, for the amount owed and the credit limit. All arrays can accept a maximum of four values in this example; together they constitute the file named CREDIT.DAT. The array A$ may contain a maximum of 8 characters and the array C$ can contain a maximum of 32 characters. String arrays are defined with a maximum length in a virtual array. The programmer may choose from nine possible lengths: 2, 4, 8, 16, 32, 64, 128, 256, and 512. Statements 140 through 160 clear the virtual arrays to ensure that the file is empty. This was not necessary when a nonvirtual array was defined, since the computer automatically clears an array in temporary storage. A virtual array, however, is to be stored on disk rather than in temporary storage and is not automatically cleared.

Statements 190 through 210 input values from the terminal to be placed in the virtual array file. Note that a print statement is not necessary to move the data to the virtual array on disk. The system automatically places the data in their proper location in the virtual array with the INPUT statement at statement 210. This arrangement is normally confusing to the beginning programmer because the file to be created has been opened FOR OUTPUT, yet there is no PRINT statement.

Listing a Virtual Array File

A virtual array must be listed with a BASIC program rather than using the system program PIP or TYPE. Example 17.12 illustrates how a virtual file could be listed on the terminal. In this example, statement 130 opens the file for input because the data are to be read from the virtual array file on disk. Note, however, that no INPUT statement is required. This is the same type of confusion noted in Example 17.11, when the file was opened for output yet no PRINT statement was required. Statements 180 through 200 print each element from each of the four

Example 17.12
Listing of a virtual array file

```
100 REM ACCOUNT RECEIVABLE LISTED FROM
110 REM A VIRTUAL ARRAY CREATED IN
120 REM EXAMPLE 17-11
130 OPEN 'CREDIT.DAT' FOR INPUT AS FILE 3
140 DIM #3, A$(4)=8, C$(4)=32, A(4), L(4)
150 PRINT 'CUSTOMER ACCOUNT  CUSTOMER                       AMOUNT      CREDIT'
160 PRINT 'NUMBER    NUMBER   NAME                          OWED        LIMIT'
170 F$ = '  ##        ##       \         \ \              \$##,###.##  $##,###.##'
175 F1$ = '                                    TOTAL       $##,###.##'
180 FOR I = 1 TO 4
190     PRINT USING F$, I, A$(I), C$(I), A(I), L(I)
195     T = T + A(I)
200 NEXT I
205 PRINT USING F1$, T
210 CLOSE #3
230 END
```

Ready

```
RUNNH
CUSTOMER ACCOUNT  CUSTOMER                AMOUNT       CREDIT
NUMBER   NUMBER   NAME                    OWED         LIMIT
   1     13367    ABC MANUFACTURING       $ 5,076.78   $ 7,500.00
   2     14976    ACME DISTRIBUTORS       $   456.50   $   700.00
   3     15782    HINTON MUSIC SUPPLIERS  $    50.23   $   500.00
   4     17975    COUNTY GARAGE           $11,575.90   $13,500.00
                              TOTAL       $17,159.41
```

Ready

arrays and accumulate a total. Notice the similarity between the output in this example and the output in Example 17.5. They are virtually identical.

Random Processing of a Virtual Array

The essential power of virtual array storage is the ability to randomly gain access to the data file and update it selectively. Transactions do not have to be in sequence as they do for updating a terminal format file.

Random access of a virtual array. Example 17.13 illustrates how one can view the contents of single records in the virtual array file without any concern about sequential order. In this example, the user of the program is asked to enter the number of the customer; that number is placed in a variable named N, and N then becomes the subscript used to locate the particular record desired. Note again that the file is opened for input.

Example 17.13
Random access of a virtual array

```
100 REM THIS PROGRAM ANSWERS QUERIES
110 REM ABOUT THE ACCOUNTS RECEIVABLE
120 REM FILE WHICH IS STORED AS A
130 REM VIRTUAL ARRAY
140 OPEN 'CREDIT.DAT' FOR INPUT AS FILE 5
150 DIM #5, A$(4)=8, C$(4)=32, A(4), L(4)
160 INPUT 'WHICH CUSTOMER NUMBER'; N
170 PRINT 'ACCOUNT NUMBER '; A$(N)
180 PRINT 'CUSTOMER NAME  '; C$(N)
190 PRINT 'AMOUNT OWED    '; A(N)
200 PRINT 'CREDIT LIMIT   '; L(N)
210 PRINT \ PRINT
220 INPUT 'ANOTHER CUSTOMER, YES OR NO'; R$
230 PRINT \ PRINT
240 IF R$ = 'YES' THEN 160
250 CLOSE #5
260 END

Ready

RUNNH
WHICH CUSTOMER NUMBER? 4
ACCOUNT NUMBER 17975
CUSTOMER NAME  COUNTY GARAGE
AMOUNT OWED    11575.9
CREDIT LIMIT   13500


ANOTHER CUSTOMER, YES OR NO? YES


WHICH CUSTOMER NUMBER? 2
ACCOUNT NUMBER 14976
CUSTOMER NAME  ACME DISTRIBUTORS
AMOUNT OWED    456.5
CREDIT LIMIT   700


ANOTHER CUSTOMER, YES OR NO? NO


Ready
```

Random updating of a virtual array. Example 17.14.a shows how virtual arrays are used to effect random updating of a file on disk. Statement 140 opens

Example 17.14._a_
Random update of a virtual array

```
100 REM THIS PROGRAM UPDATES THE ACCOUNTS
110 REM RECEIVABLE FILE STORED AS A VIRTUAL
120 REM ARRAY.  BEFORE THE UPDATE OCCURS,
130 REM HOWEVER, A CREDIT CHECK IS MADE.
140 OPEN 'CREDIT.DAT' AS FILE 6
150 DIM #6, A$(4)=8, C$(4)=32, A(4), L(4)
160 INPUT 'CUSTOMER NUMBER'; N
170 INPUT 'SALE AMOUNT      '; S
180 IF L(N) - A(N) >= S THEN GOSUB 300
                         ELSE GOSUB 400
190 PRINT
200 INPUT 'ANOTHER CUSTOMER, YES OR NO'; R$
210 IF R$ = 'YES' THEN 160 ELSE 500
300 A(N) = A(N) + S
310 PRINT C$(N);"'S ACCOUNT UPDATED FOR SALES OF"
320 PRINT S;'AND HAS CREDIT REMAINING OF';L(N)-A(N)
330 RETURN
400 PRINT 'THIS SALE OF';S;'EXCEEDS'
410 PRINT C$(N);"'S CREDIT LIMIT OF";L(N)
420 RETURN
500 CLOSE #6
510 END

Ready

RUNNH
CUSTOMER NUMBER? 1
SALE AMOUNT      ? 1000.00
ABC MANUFACTURING'S ACCOUNT UPDATED FOR SALES OF
 1000 AND HAS CREDIT REMAINING OF 1423.22

ANOTHER CUSTOMER, YES OR NO? YES
CUSTOMER NUMBER? 3
SALE AMOUNT      ? 500.00
THIS SALE OF 500 EXCEEDS
HINTON MUSIC SUPPLIERS'S CREDIT LIMIT OF 500

ANOTHER CUSTOMER, YES OR NO? NO

Ready
```

the file but does not specify input or output. This is done because the file will be updated; both inputting from and writing to the file will occur. Statement 180 checks to see if the remaining credit L(N) − A(N) is sufficiently large to allow the credit purchase. If it is large enough, statement 300 causes the amount owed to be increased by the amount of the sale and informs the user of the program that the update was successful. If the available credit is not sufficient, no updating occurs.

To show that the file has been properly updated, one could run a program listing the contents of the file after the update. For instance, the listing created in Example 17.14._b_ was obtained using the program in Example 17.12.

Example 17.14._b_
Listing of updated virtual array

CUSTOMER NUMBER	ACCOUNT NUMBER	CUSTOMER NAME	AMOUNT OWED	CREDIT LIMIT
1	13367	ABC MANUFACTURING	$ 6,076.78	$ 7,500.00
2	14976	ACME DISTRIBUTORS	$ 456.50	$ 700.00
3	15782	HINTON MUSIC SUPPLIERS	$ 50.23	$ 500.00
4	17975	COUNTY GARAGE	$11,575.90	$13,500.00
		TOTAL	$18,159.41	

```
Ready
```

Block Input/Output

Of the three methods of performing input/output with external data files discussed in this text, block input/output is the most powerful. While terminal format files are relatively simple to use, they do not allow random access. Virtual array storage allows high-speed, random access but can only be used on disk files. Block input/output, also referred as record input/output, gives the programmer complete flexibility in control of input/output operations. It allows either random or sequential access; it allows input/output operations with devices other than disk; and it allows intermixing of numeric and string data.

Creating Files Using Block Input/Output

Example 17.15 illustrates the creation of the accounts receivable file using block I/O concepts. Note the use of the EXTEND mode and the lengthier variable names for internal documentation. In this example, the OPEN statement at statement 130 and the CLOSE statement at statement 270 use the same format as with the terminal format and virtual array methods. The file ACCTS.DAT is opened for output so that it can be created.

Example 17.15
Block I/O file creation

```
100 REM ACCOUNTS RECEIVABLE CREATED AS
110 REM A FILE USING BLOCK I-O
120 EXTEND
130 OPEN 'ACCTS.DAT' FOR OUTPUT AS FILE 1
140 FIELD #1, 5 AS ACCOUNT.NUMBER$,
             22 AS CUST.NAME$,
              8 AS AMOUNT.OWED$,
              8 AS CREDIT.LIMIT$
150 PRINT 'ENTER ACCOUNT NUMBER, CUSTOMER NAME,'
160 PRINT 'AMOUNT OWED AND CREDIT LIMIT FOR'
180 FOR I = 1 TO 4
190    PRINT 'CUSTOMER NUMBER';I
200    INPUT A$, C$, A, L
210    LSET ACCOUNT.NUMBER$ = A$
220    RSET CUST.NAME$      = C$
230    LSET AMOUNT.OWED$    = CVTF$(A)
240    LSET CREDIT.LIMIT$   = CVTF$(L)
250    PUT #1, RECORD I
260 NEXT I
270 CLOSE 1
280 END

Ready

RUNNH
ENTER ACCOUNT NUMBER, CUSTOMER NAME,
AMOUNT OWED AND CREDIT LIMIT FOR
CUSTOMER NUMBER 1
? 13367,ABC MANUFACTURING,5076.78,7500.00
CUSTOMER NUMBER 2
? 14976,ACME DISTRIBUTORS,456.50,700.00
CUSTOMER NUMBER 3
? 15782,HINTON MUSIC SUPPLIERS,50.23,500.00
CUSTOMER NUMBER 4
? 17975,COUNTY GARAGE,11575.90,13500.00

Ready
```

The FIELD statement at statement 140 is required in block I/O on the PDP-11 system to define the records in the file in terms of variable names and field lengths.

VAX-11 BASIC does not use the FIELD statement. This and other differences for the VAX system are explained in a later section in this chapter.

The general format of the FIELD statement is:

n FIELD # channel-number, number AS string-variable-name, etc.

where *FIELD #* is a reserved word; *channel-number* refers to the number between 1 and 12 used to reference an input/output channel in the OPEN, CLOSE, GET, and PUT statements; *number* is a field length in number of characters; *AS* is a reserved word; *string-variable-name* is the string variable name assigned to a particular field; and *etc.* denotes definition of more fields within the block or record.

All fields within the record are specified as string variables, and set commands are necessary to place data in those string variables. It may also be necessary to convert numeric data to a string during the set operation.

The general formats of the set commands are:

n LSET string-variable = variable

n RESET string-variable = variable

where *LSET* and *RSET* are reserved words, *string-variable* is the name defined in the FIELD statement, and *variable* represents a string, a string variable, or converted numeric data.

The selection of LSET or RSET allows the programmer either to left-justify (LSET) or right-justify (RSET) the data in the string. If LSET is used, the data are placed in the string variable from left to right. If the data do not fill the entire length of the defined field, the remaining positions are filled with blanks. Using RSET causes movement from right to left. Any unfilled positions will be filled with blanks. Statement 220 uses the RSET command, and the results will be seen in Example 17.16.

In statements 230 and 240, it is necessary to convert the numeric variables, A and L, to a string. When numeric data are stored in block I/O, they are stored in real form. To do so, either eight characters or four characters must be stored as a string, depending on the particular computer system in use. To determine the storage length of numeric data for the system in use, issue the following command in the immediate mode:

PRINT LEN(CVTF$(0))

The CVTF$ function is required to convert numeric data to real form in block

Example 17.16
Listing of a block I/O file

```
100 REM ACCOUNT RECEIVABLE LISTED FROM
110 REM A FILE CREATED IN
120 REM EXAMPLE 17-15
125 EXTEND
130 OPEN 'ACCTS.DAT' FOR INPUT AS FILE 3
140 FIELD #3, 5 AS ACCOUNT.NUMBER$,
              22 AS CUST.NAME$,
               8 AS AMOUNT.OWED$,
               8 AS CREDIT.LIMIT$
150 PRINT 'CUSTOMER ACCOUNT  CUSTOMER              AMOUNT      CREDIT'
160 PRINT 'NUMBER   NUMBER    NAME                 OWED        LIMIT'
170 F$ = '   ##          \         \ \            \$##,###.##  $##,###.##'
175 F1$ = '                            TOTAL       $##,###.##'
180 FOR I = 1 TO 4
190    GET #3, RECORD I
200    A$ = ACCOUNT.NUMBER$
210    C$ = CUST.NAME$
220    A  = CVT$F(AMOUNT.OWED$)
230    L  = CVT$F(CREDIT.LIMIT$)
240    PRINT USING F$, I, A$, C$, A, L
250    T = T + A
260 NEXT I
270 PRINT USING F1$, T
280 CLOSE #3
290 END

Ready

RUNNH
CUSTOMER ACCOUNT  CUSTOMER              AMOUNT      CREDIT
NUMBER   NUMBER    NAME                 OWED        LIMIT
   1     13367          ABC MANUFACTURING  $ 5,076.78  $ 7,500.00
   2     14976          ACME DISTRIBUTORS  $   456.50  $   700.00
   3     15782     HINTON MUSIC SUPPLIERS  $    50.23  $   500.00
   4     17975             COUNTY GARAGE   $11,575.90  $13,500.00
                              TOTAL        $17,159.41

Ready
```

I/O. This function is literally interpreted as: convert (CVT), a real or floating point number (F), to string ($).

After defining the fields and setting the variables in the fields, it is then necessary to print the block on the external device, which is accomplished with the PUT statement in statement 250.

The general format of the PUT statement is:

> n PUT # channel-number, RECORD expression

> where *PUT #* is a reserved word; *channel-number* is the same number referenced by the OPEN, CLOSE, FIELD and GET statements; RECORD is a reserved word; and *expression* may be any valid expression, such as a variable, constant, or mathematical expression.

Statement 250 writes the defined record onto channel number 1, using I, the index in the FOR/NEXT loop, to number the record.

Listing a File Using Block Input/Output

Example 17.16 shows the use of block I/O concepts to create a listing of the accounts receivable file created in Example 17.15. In this example, the file is opened for input, and the fields are defined in the same format as the previous program. The names used to identify the fields do not have to be the same from program to program; however, the field lengths must be the same. The GET statement in statement 190 inputs the records from the block file ACCTS.DAT.

The general format of the GET statement is:

> n GET # channel-number, RECORD expression

where *GET* and *#* are reserved words; *channel-number* is the same number referenced in the OPEN, CLOSE, FIELD and PUT statements; RECORD is a reserved word; and *expression* may be a constant, variable, or mathematical expression.

After the record has been obtained using the GET statement, statements 200 through 230 are used to assign the fields from the records to other variables. Statements 220 and 230 are required to convert the number fields, which are stored as strings, to numeric variables using the CVT$F function.

The general format for the CVT$F conversion is:

> n numeric-variable = CVT$F(string-variable)

where *numeric-variable* is any valid numeric variable, *CVT$F* is a reserved word, and *string-variable* is the name used to define the number field in the FIELD statement. The CVT$F is literally interpreted as: convert (CVT) a string ($) to a numeric (F) variable.

Notice in the listing that the names in the CUST.NAME$ field are right-justified in the field. This was accomplished in the file-creation program in Example 17.15. using RSET.

Random Processing Using Block Input/Output

In addition to processing data sequentially, block I/O concepts allow the programmer random access to files so as to update them selectively.

Random access. Example 17.17 illustrates the use of block I/O concepts to gain random access to data in the file ACCTS.DAT. Statement 160 asks the user of

Example 17.17
Random access using block I/O

```
100 REM THIS PROGRAM ANSWERS QUERIES
110 REM ABOUT THE ACCOUNTS RECEIVABLE
120 REM FILE WHICH IS STORED USING
130 REM BLOCK I-O CONCEPTS
135 EXTEND
140 OPEN 'ACCTS.DAT' FOR INPUT AS FILE 5
150 FIELD #5, 5 AS ACCOUNT.NUMBER$,
              22 AS CUST.NAME$,
               8 AS AMOUNT.OWED$,
               8 AS CREDIT.LIMIT$
160 INPUT 'WHICH CUSTOMER NUMBER'; N
170 GET #5, RECORD N
180 A$ = ACCOUNT.NUMBER$
190 C$ = CUST.NAME$
200 A  = CVT$F(AMOUNT.OWED$)
210 L  = CVT$F(CREDIT.LIMIT$)
220 PRINT 'ACCOUNT NUMBER '; A$
230 PRINT 'CUSTOMER NAME  '; C$
240 PRINT 'AMOUNT OWED    '; A
250 PRINT 'CREDIT LIMIT   '; L
260 PRINT
270 INPUT 'ANOTHER CUSTOMER, YES OR NO'; R$
280 PRINT
290 IF R$ = 'YES' THEN 160
300 CLOSE #5
310 END

Ready

RUNNH
WHICH CUSTOMER NUMBER? 4
ACCOUNT NUMBER 17975
CUSTOMER NAME            COUNTY GARAGE
AMOUNT OWED     11575.9
CREDIT LIMIT    13500

ANOTHER CUSTOMER, YES OR NO? YES

WHICH CUSTOMER NUMBER? 2
ACCOUNT NUMBER 14976
CUSTOMER NAME        ACME DISTRIBUTORS
AMOUNT OWED      456.5
CREDIT LIMIT     700

ANOTHER CUSTOMER, YES OR NO? NO

Ready
```

the program to input a customer number, which is used as the RECORD identifier in the GET statement in statement 170. Statements 180 through 210 make necessary conversions as shown in Example 17.16. Compare the logic of this program to that shown in Example 17.13.

Random updating. Example 17.18.a illustrates a random update of ACCTS.DAT; it is comparable to the program in Example 17.14. After the sales amount is updated in statement 300, statement 310 converts A to AMOUNT.OWED$ using CVTF$ so that the record can be rewritten onto the disk with the PUT statement in statement 320. After this program has been run, a listing of the data file, as updated, can be obtained. Example 17.18.b shows a listing of the updated files using the program in Example 17.16. Notice that ABC Manufacturing's AMOUNT.OWED$ field has been increased by $1,000.

Example 17.18.*a*
Random update using block I/O

```
100 REM THIS PROGRAM UPDATES THE ACCOUNTS
110 REM RECEIVABLE FILE STORED USING BLOCK I-O
120 EXTEND
130 OPEN 'ACCTS.DAT'AS FILE 6
150 FIELD #6, 5 AS ACCOUNT.NUMBER$,
              22 AS CUST.NAME$,
               8 AS AMOUNT.OWED$,
               8 AS CREDIT.LIMIT$
160 INPUT 'CUSTOMER NUMBER'; N
170 INPUT 'SALE AMOUNT    '; S
190 GET #6, RECORD N
200 A$ = ACCOUNT.NUMBER$
210 C$ = CUST.NAME$
220 A  = CVT$F(AMOUNT.OWED$)
230 L  = CVT$F(CREDIT.LIMIT$)
240 IF L - A >= S THEN GOSUB 300
                      ELSE GOSUB 400
250 PRINT
260 INPUT 'ANOTHER CUSTOMER, YES OR NO'; R$
270 IF R$ = 'YES' THEN 160 ELSE 500
300 A = A + S
310 LSET AMOUNT.OWED$ = CVTF$(A)
320 PUT #6, RECORD N
330 PRINT C$;"'S ACCOUNT UPDATED FOR SALES OF"
340 PRINT S;'AND HAS CREDIT REMAINING OF';L-A
350 RETURN
400 PRINT 'THIS SALE OF';S;'EXCEEDS'
410 PRINT C$;"'S CREDIT LIMIT OF";L
420 RETURN
500 CLOSE 6
510 END

Ready

RUNNH
CUSTOMER NUMBER? 1
SALE AMOUNT     ? 1000.00
     ABC MANUFACTURING'S ACCOUNT UPDATED FOR SALES OF
 1000 AND HAS CREDIT REMAINING OF 1423.22

ANOTHER CUSTOMER, YES OR NO? YES
CUSTOMER NUMBER? 3
SALE AMOUNT     ? 500.00
THIS SALE OF 500 EXCEEDS
HINTON MUSIC SUPPLIERS'S CREDIT LIMIT OF 500

ANOTHER CUSTOMER, YES OR NO? NO

Ready
```

Example 17.18.*b*
Listing of updated file

CUSTOMER NUMBER	ACCOUNT NUMBER	CUSTOMER NAME	AMOUNT OWED	CREDIT LIMIT
1	13367	ABC MANUFACTURING	$ 6,076.78	$ 7,500.00
2	14976	ACME DISTRIBUTORS	$ 456.50	$ 700.00
3	15782	HINTON MUSIC SUPPLIERS	$ 50.23	$ 500.00
4	17975	COUNTY GARAGE	$11,575.90	$13,500.00
		TOTAL	$18,159.41	

```
Ready
```

Block Input/Output VAX Differences

VAX BASIC does not use the FIELD statement. Instead it uses the MAP statement. The general format for the MAP statement is:

312

where *MAP* is a reserved word, *map-name* is a real variable name given to the MAP referred to in the OPEN statement, *variable-name* is the variable name assigned to a particular field, *number* is a field length in number of characters, and *etc.* denotes definition of more fields within the block or record. The MAP statement must appear in a program statement before any reference to a variable in that MAP.

For example, in VAX BASIC the FIELD statement in statement 140 in Example 17.15 would be deleted, and the following statement would be added to the program before the OPEN statement:

```
125 MAP (CUSTOMER.RECORD)  ACCOUNT.NUMBER$(5),    &
                           CUST.NAME$(22),        &
                           AMOUNT.OWED$(8),       &
                           CREDIT.LIMIT$(8)
```

Also, reference must be made to the map in the OPEN statement. The OPEN statement in Example 17.15 would be modified as follows:

```
130 OPEN 'ACCTS.DAT' FOR OUTPUT AS FILE 1,        &
        MAP CUSTOMER.RECORD
```

The GET and PUT statements work the same way as on the PDP-11 except that the RECORD clause is omitted when gaining access to the file sequentially.

Common Errors

Statement	Explanation
100 OPEN 'INVEN.DAT' FOR INPUT AS FILE 1 200 INPUT #2, A$	Channel numbers do not match.
PIP STOCK	Missing extension, cannot use PIP or TYPE without extension.
300 OPEN 'STOCK.OUT' AS FILE 3	Opening a file without specifying FOR INPUT or FOR OUTPUT may lead to unpredictable results, unless the procedure is used to do a random update of a block I/O file.
100 DIM #2, A$(5)=7	Invalid character length 7. Valid options are 2, 4, 8, 16, 32, 64, 128, 256, and 512.
150 OPEN "CREDIT.DAT" FOR INPUT AS FILE 2	Virtual array should be opened FOR OUTPUT when file is to be created.

190 INPUT A$(I), B(I)

250 LSET A$ = A	LSET command used without converting number variable. Should be: 250 LSET A$=CVTF$(A).
390 LSET A$ = CVT$F(L)	Wrong conversion function used. Should be CVTF$(L).
100 FIELD #2, 10 AS AMOUNT.OWED$	If AMOUNT.OWED$ is to be a numeric field, the number of valid characters is four or eight depending on the length of the CVTF$ function.
350 B = CVTF$(A$)	Wrong conversion function used. Should be CVT$F(A$).

Exercises

1. Using a text editor, create the following data as a record image for a terminal format file. Be sure to separate fields with commas. Use the file name INVEN.DAT. Use the system command PIP or TYPE to list the file after creation.

Part number	Inventory part name	Quantity on hand	Cost per unit ($)	Reorder amount
786	Nuts	1,075	0.055	315
796	Bolts	100	0.058	90
815	Screws	275	0.150	40
876	Hammers	90	5.50	85
915	Screwdrivers	46	3.75	30

2. Use the data in Exercise 1 to create a data file called INVEN2.DAT. Use a text editor to create this field as a fixed-length record file. Use PIP or TYPE to list the file after creation.

3. What are the advantages and disadvantages of a terminal format file? Of a virtual array file? Of a block I/O file?

4. What are the valid forms of the OPEN statement? What is the purpose of the channel number?

5. What is peculiar about the use of the OPEN statement when using a virtual array file?

6. Write a program that will list on the terminal the contents of INVEN.DAT created in Exercise 1. Include in the output a column for the total dollar amount of each inventory item on hand. Also include the total dollar amount of a reorder for each inventory item by multiplying the cost per unit times the reorder amount. Also include grand totals for all of the numeric columns except cost per unit. Use the ON ERROR statement.

7. Modify the program developed in Exercise 6 to use the INVEN2.DAT file created in Exercise 2.

8. Write a program to create the data file INVEN.DAT as a record image. Use the program in Exercise 6 to list the file.

9. Write a program to create the data file INVEN2.DAT as a fixed-length record file. Use the program in Exercise 7 to list the contents of the file.

10. Write a program to do a sequential update of either INVEN.DAT or INVEN2.DAT using the following transaction data. The transaction code shown in the transaction indicates whether inventory items were bought or sold. A code of 1 indicates a sale of inventory items, and a code of 2 indicates a purchase.

Part number	Transaction quantity	Transaction code
786	500	1
796	180	2
876	50	1
915	16	1

Include as a part of the program the following:
a. Dollar amount and type of each transaction, including total purchases and total sales for the entire update.
b. Amount that should be reordered if the quantity on hand becomes less than or equal to the reorder amount.
c. Structured programming techniques and documentation.

11. Using the program developed in either Exercise 6 or Exercise 7, list the contents of the updated file after running the update program in Exercise 10.

12. Modify Program 12.1 to create a file called SNOW.DAT as a virtual array. Then write a program to list the contents of SNOW.DAT including the total amount of snowfall.

13. Write a program to do a random update of SNOW.DAT. The snowfalls reported for the different ski areas are shown below:

```
KEYSTONE     10
MONARCH      50
WOLFCREEK    35
```

14. Use the listing program developed in Exercise 12 to list the contents of SNOW.DAT after the random update is accomplished in Exercise 13.

15. Write a program to gain random access to SNOW.DAT either before or after the update program is run. The program should be able to tell the user of the program how many total inches have fallen without concern for sequential order.

16. Using block I/O concepts, write a program to create a salesperson file using the data below. Use SALES.DAT as the file name.

Salesperson number	Salesperson name	Current sales	Current sales returned	Year-to-date sales
1	Barclay	$500	$ 50	$450
2	Cameron	900	25	875
3	Donovan	375	175	200
4	Miles	450	0	450
5	Sanders	595	210	385
6	Turner	200	5	195
7	Zeller	875	175	700

17. Write a program to list sequentially the contents of the file SALES.DAT created in Exercise 16. Include totals of all numeric fields as well as percentage figures showing the ratio of current sales returned to current sales for each salesperson and for all sales.

18. Write a program to randomly print out the data from SALES.DAT that was created in Exercise 16.

19. Write a program to randomly update the file SALES.DAT created in Exercise 16 using the following transaction data. The transaction code indicates whether the transaction amount is a sale or a sale return. Make sure to update the year-to-date field also.

Salesperson number	Transaction amount	Transaction code 1 = sale, 2 = sale return
7	$150	1
5	299	2
2	300	1
4	150	2
2	150	2
1	700	1
3	595	1
7	200	2

20. Modify the program developed in Exercise 17 to list the contents of SALES.DAT after the update accomplished in Exercise 19. The program should also determine who is the most productive salesperson in terms of the lowest sales return percentage and in terms of the highest year-to-date sales. Have the program print out the name of the salesperson who has achieved each of the productivity parameters.

Appendix A

Reserved Words

Many words and abbreviations have been set aside to be used for certain purposes in the BASIC language. Special meanings have been preassigned to these words. The programmer cannot change the meanings of these words, add new words to the list, or use these words as programmer-supplied variable names in a program.

ABORT	BROADCAST	COS	DIF$	FIELD
ABS	BS	COT	DIM	FILE
ABS%	BUCKETSIZE	COUNT	DIMENSION	FILESIZE
ACCESS	BUFFER	CR	DOUBLE	FILL
ACCESS%	BUFFERSIZE	CTRLC	DOUBLEBUF	FILL$
ALIGNED	BUFSIZ	CVT$$	DUPLICATES	FILL%
ALL	BY	CVT$%	ECHO	FIND
ALLOW	CALL	CVT$F	EDIT$	FIX
ALTERNATE	CALLR	CVT%$	ELSE	FIXED
AND	CCPOS	CVTF$	END	FLUSH
ANY	CHAIN	DAT	ENDIF	FNEND
APPEND	CHANGE	DAT%	EQ	FNEXIT
AS	CHANGES	DATA	EQV	FOR
ASC	CHR$	DATE$	ERL	FORCEIN
ASCII	CLK$	DECLARE	ERN$	FORMAT$
ATN	CLOSE	DEF	ERR	FORTRAN
ATN2	CLUSTERSIZE	DEF*	ERROR	FREE
BACK	COM	DEFAULTNAME	ERT$	FROM
BEL	COMMON	DEL	ESC	FSP$
BIN$	COMP%	DELETE	EXP	FSS$
BINARY	CON	DELIMIT	EXTEND	FUNCTION
BIT	CONNECT	DENSITY	EXTENDSIZE	FUNCTIONEND
BLOCK	CONSTANT	DESC	EXTERNAL	FUNCTIONEXIT
BLOCKSIZE	CONTIGUOUS	DET	FF	GE

316

GET	MAR%	POKE	SO	USEAGE%
GO	MARGIN	POS	SP	USEROPEN
GOSUB	MAT	POS%	SPACE$	USING
GOTO	MAX	PPS%	SPAN	USR
GT	MID	PRIMARY	SPEC%	USR$
HANGUP	MID$	PRINT	SQR	VAL
HEX	MIN	PRN	SQRT	VAL%
HEX$	MOD	PROD$	STATUS	VALUE
HT	MOD%	PUT	STEP	VARIABLE
IDN	MODE	QUO$	STOP	VFC
IF	MODIFY	QUOTE	STR$	VIRTUAL
IFEND	MOVE	RAD%	STREAM	VPS%
IFMORE	MXGMAP	RAD$	STRING	VT
IMAGE	NAME	RANDOM	STRING$	WAIT
IMP	NEXT	RANDOMIZE	SUB	WHILE
INDEXED	NOCHANGES	RCTRLC	SUBEND	WINDOWSIZE
INIMAGE	NODATA	RCTRLO	SUBEXIT	WITH
INPUT	DOCUPLICATES	READ	SUBROUTINE	WORD
INSTR	NOECHO	REAL	SUM$	WRITE
INT	NOEXTEND	RECORD	SWAP%	WRKMAP
INTEGER	NOMARGIN	RECORDATTR	SYS	XLATE
INV	NONE	RECORDSIZE	TAB	XOR
INVALID	NOPAGE	RECORDTYPE	TAN	ZER
JSB	NOQUOTE	RECOUNT	TAPE	
KEY	NOREWIND	REF	TASK	
KILL	NOSPAN	RELATIVE	TEMPORARY	
LEFT	NOT	REF	TERMINAL	
LEFT$	NOTAPE	RELATIVE	THEN	
LEN	NUL$	REM	TIM	
LET	NUM	RESET	TIME	
LF	NUM$	RESTORE	TIME$	
LINE	NUM1$	RESUME	TO	
LINO	NUM2	RETURN	TRM$	
LINPUT	OCT$	RIGHT	TRN	
LIST	ON	RIGHT$	TST	
LOC	ONECHR	RND	TSTEND	
LOCK	ONENDFILE	RSET	TYP	
LOF	ONERROR	SCRATCH	TYPE	
LOG	OPEN	SEG$	TYPE$	
LOG10	OR	SEQUENTIAL	UNALIGNED	
LONG	ORGANIZATION	SGN	UNDEFINED	
LSA	OUTPUT	SHIFT	UNLESS	
LSET	PAGE	SI	UNLOCK	
MAGTAPE	PEEK	SIN	UNTIL	
MAP	PI	SINGLE	UPDATE	
MAR	PLACE$	SLEEP	USEAGE	

Appendix B

ASCII Character Codes

Decimal value	ASCII character	Remarks	Decimal value	ASCII character	Remarks
0	NUL	FILL character	22	SYN	CTRL/V
1	SOH	CTRL/A	23	ETB	CTRL/W
2	STX	CTRL/B	24	CAN	CTRL/X
3	ETX	CTRL/C	25	EM	CTRL/Y
4	EOT	CTRL/D	26	SUB	CTRL/Z
5	ENQ	CTRL/E	27	ESC	Escape
6	ACK	CTRL/F,	28	FS	File separator
7	BEL	CTRL/G, Bell	29	GS	Group separator
8	BS	CTRL/H	30	RS	Record separator
9	HT	CTRL/I	31	US	Unit separator
10	LF	CTRL/J	32	SP	Space
11	VT	CTRL/K	33	!	Exclamation mark
12	FF	CTRL/L	34	''	Quotation mark
13	CR	CTRL/M	35	#	Number sign
14	SO	CTRL/N	36	$	Dollar sign
15	SI	CTRL/O	37	%	Percent sign
16	DLE	CTRL/P	38	&	Ampersand
17	DC1	CTRL/Q, XON	39	'	Apostrophe
18	DC2	CTRL/R	40	(	Left parenthesis
19	DC3	CTRL/S, XOFF	41	)	Right parenthesis
20	DC4	CTRL/T	42	*	Asterisk
21	NAK	CTRL/U	43	+	Plus sign

Decimal value	ASCII character	Remarks	Decimal value	ASCII character	Remarks
44	,	Comma	90	Z	
45	–	Hyphen or minus sign	91	[	Left square bracket
46	.	Period or decimal point			
47	/	Slash or divide sign	92	\	Back slash
48	0	Zero	93	]	Right square bracket
49	1				
50	2		94	or	Caret, circumflex
51	3				
52	4		95	or	Underscore or back arrow
53	5				
54	6		96	ò	Grave accent
55	7		97	a	
56	8		98	b	
57	9		99	c	
58	:	Colon	100	d	
59	;	Semicolon	101	e	
60	<	Less than sign	102	f	
61	=	Equal sign	103	g	
62	>	Greater than sign	104	h	
63	?	Question mark	105	i	
64	@	At sign	106	j	
65	A		107	k	
66	B		108	l	
67	C		109	m	
68	D		110	n	
69	E		111	o	
70	F		112	p	
71	G		113	q	
72	H		114	r	
73	I		115	s	
74	J		116	t	
75	K		117	u	
76	L		118	v	
77	M		119	w	
78	N		120	x	
79	O		121	y	
80	P		122	z	
81	Q		123	{	Left brace
82	R		124	|	Vertical line
83	S				
84	T		125	}	Right brace
85	U		126	~	Tilde
86	V				
87	W		127	DEL or RUBOUT	Delete or rubout
88	X				
89	Y				

Appendix C

Error Messages

PDP-11

A PDP-11 program can recover from certain errors but not others. This appendix will show *selected* error messages. (For a complete listing, refer to the DEC manuals for your system.) Recoverable errors will have an error number, and nonrecoverable will not. The first character position of each error indicates the severity of the error as follows:

Character	Severity	Meaning
%	Warning	Execution can continue but may not give expected results.
?	Fatal	Execution cannot continue unless you remove the cause of the error.
	Information	If neither the % nor the ? appears, the message is for information only.

User-Recoverable Errors

ERR	Message	Meaning
2	?Illegal file name	The file name specified is not acceptable. It contains unacceptable characters, or the file name specification format has been violated.
4	?No room for user on device	You have already used the allowed storage space; the device is too full to accept further data.
5	?Can't find file or account	Either the file or account number specified was not found on the device specified.
7	?I/O channel already open	You tried to open 1 of the 12 I/O channels which the program had already opened.
8	?Device not available	The specified device exists on the system, but your attempt to ASSIGN or OPEN it is prohibited.

User-Recoverable Errors

ERR	Message	Meaning
10	?Protection violation	You were prohibited from performing the requested operation because the kind of operation was illegal or because you did not have the privileges necessary.
11	?End of file on device	You tried to perform input beyond the end of a data file, or you called into memory a source file that does not contain an END statement.
13	?User data error on device	One or more characters may have been transmitted incorrectly.
16	?Name or account now exists	Either you tried to rename a file with the name of a file that already exists, or the system manager tried to insert an account number that is already on the system.
24	?Disk pack is private	You do not have access to the specified private disk pack.
37	?Disk error during swap	A hardware error occurs when your job is swapped, and your job area is lost. Report this error to the system manager.
38	?Memory parity failure	A parity error was detected in the memory occupied by this job.
44	?Matrix or array too big	In-memory array size is too large.
45	?Virtual array not yet open	An attempt was made to use a virtual array before opening the corresponding disk file.
47	?Line too long	Buffer overflows because of an attempt to input a line longer than 255 characters.
48	%Floating point error	Attempt to use a computed floating point number outside allowable range of computer.
50	%Data format error	A READ or INPUT statement detected data in an illegal format.
53	%Illegal argument in LOG	Negative or zero argument to LOG function.
55	?Subscript out of range	You have exceeded the range of either a row or column or an array that has been dimensioned.
57	?Out of data	The DATA list was exhausted, and a READ requested additional data.
58	?ON statement out of range	The index value in an ON GO TO or ON GO SUB statement is less than 1 or is greater than the number of line numbers in the list.
59	?Not enough data in record	An INPUT statement did not find enough data in one line to satisfy all the specified variables.

Nonrecoverable errors

Message	Meaning
?Arguments don't match	Arguments in a function call do not match, in number or in type, the arguments defined for the function.
?Bad line number pair	Line numbers specified in a LIST or DELETE command were formated incorrectly.
?Bad number in PRINT-USING	Format specified in the PRINT/USING string cannot be used to print one or more values.
?End of statement not seen	Statement contains too many elements to be processed correctly.
?File exists RENAME/REPLACE	A file of the name specified in a SAVE command already exists. Use REPLACE or use RENAME with SAVE.

Nonrecoverable errors

Message	Meaning
?Illegal expression	Check for missing operators, mismatched parentheses, or other errors in the expression.
?Illegal IF statement	Incorrectly formated IF statement.
?Illegal mode mixing	String and numeric operations cannot be mixed.
%Inconsistent subscript use	A subscripted variable is used with the wrong number of dimensions.
?Number is needed	A character string or variable name was used where a number was necessary.
Please say HELLO	Message printed by the LOGIN. A user who was not logged into the system has typed something other than a legal, logged-out command to the system.
?RETURN without GOSUB	RETURN statement is encountered when a previous GOSUB statement was not executed. Did not block entry to the subroutine.
?Statement not found	Reference is made in the program to a line number which is not within the program.
Stop	STOP statement was executed. You can usually continue program by typing CONT and pressing the RETURN key.
?Syntax error	A statement was incorrectly formated.
?What?	Cannot process entry just made. Most likely an illegal verb or improper format error.

VAX-11

Error messages for the VAX-11 are referred to as compile-time, run-time, command, shared, or compile. This appendix will show *selected* error messages (for a complete listing refer to the DEC manuals for your system). One format of the error message is:

%BAS-x-mnemonic, message

where *x* is a letter indicating the severity of the error as follows: I indicates information, W indicates a warning, E indicates a warning, and F indicates a fatal error. *Mnemonic* is a three-to-nine-character string identifying the error, and *message* is a brief explanation of the error. Another format of the error message is:

-BAS-x-mnemonic, from line n in module m

where instead of a message, the line number where the error occurred (*n*) and the name of the module where the error occurred (*m*) are given.

Although the PDP-11 system notifies the programmer immediately of an error, the VAX-11 only does so when the program is run.

Run-Time

Message	Meaning	Explanation
ARRMUSSAM	Arrays must be same dimension (ERR = 238)	The program attempts to perform matrix addition or subtraction on input arrays with different dimensions. (E)
CANCHAARR	Cannot change array dimensions (ERR = 240)	The program attempts to redimension a one-dimensional array to two dimensions or vice versa. (E)
CANFINFIL	Can't find file or account (ERR = 5)	The specified file or directory is not on the device. (E)
DATFORERR	Data format error (ERR = 50)	The program specifies a data type in an INPUT or READ statement that does not agree with value supplied. (W)
DEVHUNWRI	Device hung or write locked (ERR-14)	The program attempted on operation to a hardware device that is not functioning properly or is protected against writing. (E)
DIVBY_ZER	Division by 0 (ERR = 61)	The program attempts to divide a value by 0. (E)
ENDFILDEV	End of file on device (ERR = 11)	The program attempts to read data beyond the end of the file. (E)
FLOPOIERR	Floating point error (ERR = 48)	A program operation has resulted in a floating point number with absolute value outside the range of the computer. (E)
ILLARGLOG	Illegal argument in LOG (ERR = 53)	The program contains a negative or zero argument to the LOG or LOG10 function. (E)
ILLFILNAM	Illegal file name (ERR = 2)	A file name is too long, is incorrectly formated, or contains embedded blanks or invalid characters. (E)
ILLNUM	Illegal number (ERR = 52)	A value supplied to a numeric variable is invalid. (E)
ILLRECFIL	Illegal record on file (ERR = 142)	A record contains an invalid byte count field. (E)
INVFILOPT	Invalid file options (ERR = 139)	The program has specified invalid file options in the OPEN statement. (E)
IO_CHANOT	I/O channel not open (ERR = 9)	The program attempts to perform an I/O operation before OPENing the channel. (E)
KEYSIZTOO	Key size too large (ERR = 15)	No input is received during the execution of a INPUT, LINPUT, or INPUT LINE statement preceded by a WAIT statement. (E)
MAXMEMEXC	Maximum memory exceeded (ERR = 126)	The program has insufficient string and I/O buffer space because its allowable memory size has been exceeded or the system's maximum memory capacity has been reached. (E)
NAMACCNOW	Name or account now exists (ERR = 16)	The program has attempted to RENAME a file, and a file with that name already exists. (E)
NEGFILSTR	Negative fill or string length (ERR = 166)	A MOVE statement I/O list contains a FILL item or string length with a negative value. (E)

Run-Time

Message	Meaning	Explanation
NOTENODAT	Not enough data in record (ERR=59)	An INPUT statement does not find enough data in one line to satisfy all the specified variables. (E)
NOTIMP	Not implemented (ERR=250)	The program has attempted to use a feature that does not exist in this version of BASIC. (E)
NOTRANACC	Not a random access device (ERR=64)	The program attempts a random access on a device that does not allow such access. (E)
NO_CURREC	No current record (ERR=131)	The program attempts a DELETE or UPDATE when the previous GET or FIND has failed or no previous GET or FIND has been done. (E)
NO_ROOUSE	No room for user on device (ERR=4)	No user storage space exists on the specified device. (E)
ONEOR_TWO	One or two dimensions only (ERR=102)	The program contains a MAT statement that attempts to assign more than two dimensions to an array. (E)
ON_STAOUT	ON statement out of range (ERR=58)	The index value in an ON GO TO or ON GO SUB statement is less than 1 or greater than the number of line numbers in the list. (E)
OUTOF_DAT	Out of data (ERR=57)	A READ statement requests additional data from an exhausted DATA list. (E)
PRIUSIFOR	PRINT-USING format error (ERR=116)	The program contains a PRINT-USING statement with an invalid format string. (E)
PROLOSSOR	Program lost, sorry (ERR=103)	A fatal system error caused your program to be lost. (E)
PROVIO	Protection violation (ERR=10)	The program has attempted to read or write to a file whose protection code did not allow the operation. (E)
RECNOTFOU	Record not found (ERR=155)	A random access GET or FIND has been attempted on a deleted or nonexistent record. (E)
REDARR	Redimensioned array (ERR=105)	The program attempts to redimension an array to have more elements than were originally dimensioned. (E)
RETWITGOS	RETURN without GOSUB (ERR=72)	The program executed a RETURN statement before a GOSUB. (E)
STO	Stop (ERR=123)	The program has executed a STOP statement. Continue execution by typing CONTINUE or terminate execution by typing EXIT. (I)
SUBOUTRAN	Subscript out of range (ERR=55)	The program attempts to reference an array element outside of the array's DIMENSIONed bounds. (E)
TAPNOTANS	Tape not ANSI labelled (ERR=146)	The program attempts to access a file-structured magnetic tape that does not have an ANSI label. (E)

Run-Time

Message	Meaning	Explanation
VIRARRDIS	Virtual array not on disk (ERR=43)	The program attempts to reference a virtual array on a nondisk device. (E)
WHA	What? (ERR=109)	A command or immediate mode statement cannot be processed. (E)

Command

Message	Meaning	Explanation
CHANGES	Unsaved change has been made, CTRL-Z or EXIT to exit.	A source program in memory has been modified, and an EXIT command or CTRL/Z has been typed. If you exit from the compiler, the program modifications will be lost. (W)
MISSINGLN	Noncontinued line has no line number near line n.	A new line in the source file does not follow a line ending with an ampersand (&), does not begin with a line number, or does not start with a space or tab. (E)
NOEDIT	No change made.	The search string in an EDIT command has not been located in the text. (W)
NOFRAME	Compiled procedure is currently not active.	A STOP statement or Contral/C has been encountered, and neither the executing procedure nor any of its callers is the source compiled as a result of the RUN command. (W)
NOLNROOM	No room for line numbers.	The program contains more line-numbered statements than BASIC allows. (E)
UNEXPEOFf	Unexpected end of file.	The compiler has encountered an end-of-file immediately after an ampusand (&) continuation character. (E)
UNKCOMINP	Unknown command input.	An attempt has been made to enter an invalid or unknown command. (E)

Shared

Message	Meaning	Explanation
BADVALUE	Text is an invalid keyword value.	The command has supplied an invalid value for a keyword. (F)
CLOSEIN	Error closing file-name as input.	An error has been detected while closing an input file. (E)
OPENIN	Error opening file-name as input.	An error has been detected in attempting to open a file for input. (E)
READERR	Error reading file-name.	An error has been detected in attempting to read a file. (E)
SYSERROR	System service error.	An error has been detected while executing a system service. (E)

Compile

Message	Meaning	Explanation
ENDSTAWIT	END statement without program	The END statement has no accompanying program. (E)
FOPOIERR	Floating point error	The program contains a numeric expression whose value is outside the valid range for floating point numbers. (W)
FORLOONES	FOR loops nested too deep	The program contains too many levels of nested FOR/NEXT loops. (E)
ILLCHA	Illegal character	The program contains illegal or incorrect characters. (W)
ILLFN_RED	Illegal FN redefinition	The program defines the same function more than once. (E)
ILLMODMIX	Illegal mode mixing	The program contains string and numeric operands in the same operation. (E)
ILLRELOPE	Illegal relative operator	The program specifies an invalid relative operator. (E)
ILLRESWOR	Illegal reserved word	The program uses a reserved word as a variable name. (E)
ILLSTROPE	Illegal string operator	The program specifies an invalid string operation. (E)
MISNEX	Missing NEXT	The program contains a FOR, WHILE, or UNTIL loop which has no accompanying NEXT statement. (E)
NESFORLOO	Nested FOR loops with same index	The program contains nested FOR/NEXT loops that use the same index variable. (E)
PROTOOBIG	Program too big to compile	The program is larger than the compiler allows. (F)
REAWITDAT	READ without DATA	The program contains a READ statement, and there are no DATA statements. (E)

Appendix D

Recoverable Error Processing

In Chapter 17, the use of the ON ERROR statement was introduced to show a means of detecting errors that occur during execution of programs. Execution errors are classified as either recoverable or nonrecoverable. Refer to Appendix C for a list of selected execution errors. When a recoverable error occurs during execution of a program, the ON ERROR can be used to detect that the error has occurred. It is then left to the programmer to determine the type of error so that normal execution of the program can continue.

Program Example 17.8 was used to complete a sequential update of an existing file named CHG1.DAT. Example D.1 shows a modification of that program that illustrates the concepts of recoverable error processing in more detail.

In this example, statement 100 uses the ON ERROR statement to detect execution errors. When an error occurs, control of the program is transferred to statement 250, which begins a series of tests to determine the type of error that has occurred.

Statement 250 tests for an end-of-file condition as was done in Chapter 17. Statement 260 tests for a data format error (ERR = 50) at line 160 (ERL = 160). Error processing allows a test of the type of error and the location where the error has occurred. The use of the ERL function determines that the data format error occurred at line 160, the INPUT statement. Note in the running of the program that the user typed in a dollar sign with the amount, making it an illegal data format.

Statement 270 tests to determine if the user of the program has waited too long (ERR = 15) to input the value at line 160. The WAIT command at statement 155 allows the programmer to set a maximum number of seconds for the program to

Example D.1

Error recovery example

```
100 ON ERROR GO TO 250
110 OPEN 'CHG1.DAT' FOR INPUT AS FILE 1
120 OPEN 'NEWCHG.DAT' FOR OUTPUT AS FILE 2
130 PRINT 'TRANSACTIONS MUST BE IN ACCOUNT # SEQUENCE'
140 PRINT 'ENTER ACCOUNT NUMBER AND'
150 PRINT 'AMOUNT OF SALES (0,0 WHEN FINISHED)'
155 WAIT 30
160 INPUT N$, S                 ! INPUT TRANSACTION
170 INPUT #1, A$, C$, A          ! INPUT MASTER RECORD
180 IF A$ = N$ THEN 210          ! ARE ACCOUNT NUMBERS SAME?
190 PRINT #2, A$;',';C$,',';A    ! MOVE RECORD FROM OLD
                                   FILE TO NEW FILE
200 GO TO 170
210 A = A + S                    ! ADD TRANSACTION AMOUNT
                                   TO OLD RECORD
220 PRINT #2, A$;',';C$,',';A    ! MOVE UPDATED RECORD
                                   TO NEW FILE ON DISK
230 PRINT 'SALES UPDATED FOR '; C$
240 IF N$ = '0' THEN 170 ELSE 140 ! IF THERE ARE NO MORE
                                    TRANSACTIONS, READ
                                    NEXT MASTER RECORD, ELSE
                                    READ NEXT TRANSACTION
250 IF ERR = 11 THEN 280
260 IF ERR = 50 AND ERL = 160 THEN
            PRINT 'ERROR IN DATA FORMAT, RE-TYPE' \
            RESUME 160
270 IF ERR = 15 THEN
            PRINT 'TOO LONG FOR RESPONSE, TRY AGAIN' \
            RESUME 160
280 CLOSE 1,2
290 NAME 'CHG1.DAT' AS 'CHG1.OLD'
300 NAME 'NEWCHG.DAT' AS 'CHG1.DAT'
310 END

Ready

RUNNH
TRANSACTIONS MUST BE IN ACCOUNT # SEQUENCE
ENTER ACCOUNT NUMBER AND
AMOUNT OF SALES (0,0 WHEN FINISHED)
? 13367,$1000
ERROR IN DATA FORMAT, RE-TYPE
? 13367,1000
SALES UPDATED FOR ABC MANUFACTURING
ENTER ACCOUNT NUMBER AND
AMOUNT OF SALES (0,0 WHEN FINISHED)
? TOO LONG FOR RESPONSE, TRY AGAIN
? 15782,500.00
SALES UPDATED FOR HINTON MUSIC SUPPLIERS
ENTER ACCOUNT NUMBER AND
AMOUNT OF SALES (0,0 WHEN FINISHED)
? 0,0

Ready
```

wait for the response. In this case the time was set at 30 seconds. When the user of the program waited too long, an error message was printed.

In both statements 260 and 270, the RESUME command was used to resume normal execution of the program by transferring control back to statement 160. The RESUME statement has the same effect as a GO TO statement.

Appendix E

Text Editors EDIT and TECO

Chapter 16 introduced the concept of a text editor by illustrating one of the available text editors, EDT. While EDT was particularly useful for program modification, EDIT and TECO are more useful for editing data files and for applications of word processing. The following discussion of EDIT and TECO only covers a subset of these text editors and is intended merely as an introduction. Consult the manuals for additional details.

EDIT Text Editor

Examples E.1 and E.2 illustrate the use of EDIT to build the data file CHG!.DAT that was built with EDT in Chapter 17.

Example E.1
Using EDIT to create a file

```
RUN $EDIT
EDIT    V7.0-07 RSTS V7.0-07 UNC TIMESHARING

#CHG1.DAT

*I
13367,ABC MANUFACTURING,5076.78
14976,ACME DISTRIBUTORS,456.50
15782,HINTON MUSSC SUPPLIERS,50.23
17975,COUNTY GARAGE,11575.90


*EX

#%^Z

READY
```

To invoke EDIT, issue the command RUN $EDIT. The text editor will identify itself and prompt the user to name the files used by printing a pound sign #. The programmer then names the files used according to the following format.

output-program-name < input-program-name

This format is the same as for the EDT text editor except for the invoking of the editor as a separate command and the use of the <. In Example E.1 only the output name is used because a file is being created. Example E.2 uses the full format because CHG1.DAT is being corrected. EDIT prompts the user to give further edit commands by printing an asterisk *.

The I (insert) command allows the insertion of lines before the present position. Each line to be inserted is terminated by pressing the return key. When all desired entries have been made, the user presses the line feed key, and the system indicates that further edit commands can be issued by printing the asterisk *.

The EX (exit) command writes the contents of the text edit buffer to the output file named, and editing is terminated on CHG1.DAT. Note that the system responds by printing a pound sign #, indicating that additional files can be named.

During the creation of CHG1.DAT, *Music* was misspelled, necessitating a correction to the file. Example E.2 illustrates this correction.

Example E.2
Using EDIT to correct a file

```
RUN $EDIT
EDIT    V7.0-07 RSTS V7.0-07 UNC TIMESHARING

#CHG1.DAT<CHG1.DAT

*R
*/L
13367,ABC MANUFACTURING,5076.78
14976,ACME DISTRIBUTORS,456.50
15782,HINTON MUSSC SUPPLIERS,50.23
17975,COUNTY GARAGE,11575.90
*1G/MUS/
*2C/IC/
*V
15782,HINTON MUSIC SUPPLIERS,50.23
*EX

#%^Z

READY

PIP CHG1.DAT
13367,ABC MANUFACTURING,5076.78
14976,ACME DISTRIBUTORS,456.50
15782,HINTON MUSIC SUPPLIERS,50.23
17975,COUNTY GARAGE,11575.90

READY
```

The R (read) command reads the file CHG1.DAT into the text buffer for editing. The /L (list) command lists the file from the current pointer position to the end of the buffer. If only a certain number of lines needs to be printed, this number should be specified just before the L. For instance, if the next 10 lines are to be printed, 10L is used. If only the current line is to be printed, the V command is issued.

To move the pointer, the user must explicitly inform EDIT how many lines to move it. For example, 10A would mean advance the pointer 10 lines, and −12A would mean go 12 lines backward. /A means to move the pointer to the end of the buffer, 5J means to jump over the next 5 characters, −25J means jump 25 characters backward, and 0J means move the pointer to the beginning of the current line.

The command 1G/MUS/ in Example E.2 means to search for the first occurrence of the characters string MUS. After finding the string, the pointer is positioned immediately after MUS, so that a correction can be made.

The command 2C/IC/ means to change the following two characters to IC, thereby making the necessary correction. V was used to print the line just corrected.

Simultaneously pressing the CTRL and the Z keys terminates the editing session. A PIP of CHG1.DAT shows that the file was correctly stored using the EX command.

TECO Text Editor

Example E.3 illustrates the use of TECO as a text editor. To invoke TECO, issue the command RUN $TECO. The text editor responds by prompting the user with

Example E.3
Using TECO to create and correct a file

```
RUN $TECO
*EWCHG1.DAT$$
*HKI13367,ABC MANUFACTURING,5076.78
14976,ACME DISTRIBUTORS,456.50
15782,HINTON MUSSC SUPPLIERS,50.23
17975,COUNTY GARAGE,11575.90
$$
*HT$$
13367,ABC MANUFACTURING,5076.78
14976,ACME DISTRIBUTORS,456.50
15782,HINTON MUSSC SUPPLIERS,50.23
17975,COUNTY GARAGE,11575.90
*J$$
*SMUS$$
*1D$$
*II$$
*V$$
15782,HINTON MUSIC SUPPLIERS,50.23
*HT$$
13367,ABC MANUFACTURING,5076.78
14976,ACME DISTRIBUTORS,456.50
15782,HINTON MUSIC SUPPLIERS,50.23
17975,COUNTY GARAGE,11575.90
*EX$$

READY


PIP CHG1.DAT
13367,ABC MANUFACTURING,5076.78
14976,ACME DISTRIBUTORS,456.50
15782,HINTON MUSIC SUPPLIERS,50.23
17975,COUNTY GARAGE,11575.90

READY
```

an asterisk *, which indicates that the user can issue edit commands. All edit commands are terminated by pressing the ESCAPE or ALT MODE key twice, which echoes on the terminal as a dollar sign $. The command EWCHG1.DAT names the output file name to be used. If an input file is to be specified, the ERinput-file-name command is issued.

The HKI command deletes anything that might have been in the text buffer from a previous editing session (HK) and inserts (I) text lines. Each text line is terminated by pressing the return key. When all lines have been inserted, the ESCAPE key is pressed twice.

The HT command prints the entire contents of the text buffer. If the programmer wishes to select lines to be printed, the T command is preceded by the number of lines to be printed.

The J command moves the pointer to the beginning of the text buffer, and the SMUS command searches the buffer for the first occurrence of MUS. The 1D command deletes the following one character, and the II commands inserts one single character, the letter *I*. If the command issued was 1ICT, ICT would have been added.

The V command is used to print the current line, HT is used again to list the entire contents, and the EX command terminates the editing session. EDIT and TECO use very similar commands, one primary difference being the termination of edit commands with the use of the ESCAPE key in TECO. In both, the user is afforded the opportunity to accomplish considerable character correction, making word processing possible. The use of any of the text editors described of course, depends on the availability of the editors at the particular installation.

Index

GRAMÁTICA PARA LA COMUNICACIÓN
◆
REPASO Y CONVERSACIÓN

Jorge Nelson Rojas

University of Nevada–Reno

Richard A. Curry

University of Nevada–Reno

HOUGHTON MIFFLIN COMPANY   BOSTON

Dallas   Geneva, Ill.   Lawrenceville, N.J.   Palo Alto

Acknowledgments

The authors and publisher would like to thank the following persons for their reviews of portions of the manuscript during the development of the text: Rosa Fernández, University of New Mexico, Albuquerque; Juan Fernández Jiménez, Behrend College; G. Ronald Freeman, California State University, Fresno; John Gutiérrez, University of Virginia, Charlottesville; John R. Kelly, North Carolina State University, Raleigh; Donna Reseigh Long, The Ohio State University; Patricia Lunn, Michigan State University; R. Alan Meredith, Brigham Young University; Margery Resnick, Massachusetts Institute of Technology; Fabián Samaniego, University of California, Davis; Geoffrey M. Voght, Eastern Michigan University, Ypsilanti.

Special thanks are due Dr. Jorge Guitart, State University of New York, Buffalo, for his many valuable recommendations and thorough reviews of the manuscript.

Cover Illustration by Anne Sweet
(Photo and illustration credits follow *Index.*)

Copyright © 1987 by Houghton Mifflin Company. All rights reserved.

No part of this work may be reproduced or transmitted in any form or by any means, electronic or mechanical, including photocopying and recording, or by any information storage or retrieval system, except as may be expressly permitted by the 1976 Copyright Act or in writing by the Publisher. Requests for permission should be addressed to Permissions, Houghton Mifflin Company, One Beacon Street, Boston, Massachusetts 02108.

Printed in the U.S.A.
ISBN: 0-395-36411-6
Library of Congress Catalog Card Number: 84-82500

BCDEFGHIJ-VB-8987

Contents

Introduction

Gramática para la comunicación is an intermediate-level review grammar that is also designed to encourage oral communication by offering numerous opportunities for student participation in realistic, functional, and thematically-set communicative exercises. The text provides a thorough review of first-year Spanish grammar and expands upon the topics presented with material suitable for the intermediate level. Grammar is explained clearly, succinctly, and with more richness and detail than is possible in an elementary text.

The text is designed for use in a variety of course situations. It will fit comfortably into any program and work in harmony with diverse teaching materials. It can be used by itself in one-semester grammar review courses or as a supplement in two-semester courses for use with texts such as cultural or literary readers, a composition text, or texts for the professions (see back cover).

Depending on the course objectives, *Gramática para la comunicación* may be used in whole or in part, for in-class or out-of-class study, or for a combination thereof. Instructors may choose to assign the grammar for out-of-class study, reserving class time for discussion of troublesome points only and for oral practice. The chapters are independent of one another for greater flexibility of use. Instructors can use a non-linear approach, if desired, and stress those topics where students need the most practice.

Chapter organization

Gramática para la comunicación is divided into twelve chapters, each of which has a theme, such as life in the city, politics, the world of the future, staying in shape, means of communication, and travel. The theme serves as a lexical focal point for contextual presentation of grammar and for exercises and conversation. Each chapter contains the following parts:

1. *Conversación.* Each chapter begins with six to eight theme-related questions intended as a warm-up to elicit personalized comments from students. The *Conversación* questions can also be used upon completion of a chapter to stimulate class discussion. Used at the end of a chapter, the questions should elicit more complex responses that show student progress in their ability to talk about theme-related topics.

2. *Vocabulario temático.* A list of thematic vocabulary containing words that students are unlikely to know from first year follows the *Conversación* questions. Vocabulary is grouped alphabetically by nouns, verbs, adjectives, and other words and phrases. The list is intended primarily as a reference for use throughout

the chapter, especially in the exercises and *Actividades para la comunicación*. A Spanish-English vocabulary at the end of the text supplies additional intermediate level vocabulary.

3. *Grammar.* Each chapter includes four to five grammar topics. A short theme-related dialogue or narrative (a news item, letter excerpt, ad) introduces each topic in order to illustrate grammar within a context rather than in isolation. These selections also serve as the basis for comprehension questions on grammar and/or as a point of departure for some exercises. Instructors can expand their use by having students vary the dialogues, create similar ones, or add to them.

   Grammar explanations include charts when relevant and abundant theme-related examples in Spanish with English equivalents. Explanations are in English to facilitate individual study outside of class. For selected, important topics, a summary with examples of usage follows the grammar presentation in order to present the main points succinctly and serve as a study reference.

4. *Comprehension questions.* This section, located at the end of each grammar presentation, is designed to assess student understanding of the grammar by asking them to apply what they have learned. The appendices contain an Answer Key to the questions so that students can use the section as a self-check.

5. *Ejercicios.* Each grammar presentation section is followed by a series of three to five exercises ranging from simple and more mechanical to more difficult and open-ended types. Most exercises revolve around a theme-related situation or context and many involve student-paired question-answer types of exchanges to provide grammar practice in meaningful communication settings.

6. *Lexical contrasts.* A lexical section follows the last grammar topic in each chapter and deals with common English words that have several Spanish equivalents and that are often troublesome for English speakers. Brief explanations with examples are followed by exercises that give students practice with the various Spanish words studied.

7. *Actividades para la comunicación.* Each chapter ends with a section containing four to six activities that integrate the various grammar topics of the chapter in contextualized, communicative, and creative exercises. These expand on the *Ejercicios* and give students the opportunity to express themselves in a more personal fashion. Although these activities will usually be done orally, many of them lend themselves to written work.

The appendices consist of a concise review of regular and irregular verb forms, a Spanish-English Vocabulary, an Answer Key to the Comprehension Questions, and an index of grammatical topics.

GRAMÁTICA PARA LA COMUNICACIÓN

CAPÍTULO 1

◆

La vida de la gran ciudad

La Calle Florida, una de las calles más concurridas de Buenos Aires, Argentina, está llena de gente a cualquier hora del día.

Conversación

1. ¿Vive Ud. en una gran ciudad o en un pueblo pequeño? ¿Dónde prefiere vivir?
2. Si Ud. no vive en una ciudad grande, ¿qué impresiones tiene de las ciudades por lo que ve en la televisión o lee en la prensa?
3. ¿Cuáles son los aspectos positivos y los negativos de vivir en una metrópolis? ¿En un pueblo o ciudad pequeña?
4. Mencione las cosas que existen en una gran ciudad y que no existen en el campo. Y vice versa.
5. ¿Qué forma de transporte ofrece problemas a los habitantes de una ciudad? ¿Cuáles son algunos de esos problemas?
6. ¿En qué tipos de viviendas viven la mayoría de los habitantes de una ciudad? ¿Y Ud.?
7. ¿Prefiere Ud. pasar su tiempo libre en la ciudad o en el campo? ¿Por qué?
8. Mire la fotografía de la página anterior. Según Ud., ¿a qué va la gente a la Calle Florida?
9. ¿Por qué cree Ud. que no se ven automóviles en esta calle?

Vocabulario temático

acera, la sidewalk
alcalde(sa), el(la) mayor
almacén, el department store; warehouse
ascensor, el elevator
atasco, el traffic jam
autopista, la freeway
basura, la garbage
bocacalle, la street intersection
bombero(a), el(la) firefighter
ciudadano(a), el(la) citizen
cola, la line
concejo, el council
cuadra, la city block
desempleo, el unemployment
feria, la fair, celebration
gobierno, el government
guía, el(la) guide
guía, la guidebook; telephone book
impuesto, el tax
inquilino(a), el(la) renter
limpieza, la cleanliness
lío, el mess, big problem
mejoramiento, el improvement
peatón(ona), el(la) pedestrian

planta, la plant, factory; floor, story
propietario(a), el(la) landlord, landlady
rascacielos, el skyscraper
ruido, el noise
semáforo, el traffic light
señal, la signal, sign
temporada, la season, time of year
tranvía, el streetcar

alquilar to rent
aparcar to park
atropellar to run over
doblar to turn; to fold
ensuciar to make dirty
multar to impose a fine
recorrer to go over, to go through; to travel, to tour

derecho straight ahead
fastidiado(a) annoyed, upset
horroroso(a) horrible
peligroso(a) dangerous
sano(a) healthy

I. Subject pronouns

Pedro: Hola, Luisa. ¿Qué tal, Paco?
Luisa: Hola, Pedro. ¿Cómo estás?
Pedro: Muy bien. ¿Y **ustedes**?
Paco: **Yo,** bastante bien; pero Luisa está fastidiada con el ruido del tráfico, como siempre.
Luisa: ¡**Tú** y tus exageraciones, Paco! Estoy bien, Pedro. **Nosotros** vamos a tomar el autobús que va al centro. ¿Y **tú**?
Pedro: Pues **yo** también. A ver si esta vez llega antes de la hora de los atascos.

A. *Forms of subject pronouns*

Subject pronouns			
Singular		**Plural**	
yo	*I*	nosotros, nosotras	*we*
tú	*you*	vosotros, vosotras	*you*
usted (Ud., Vd.)	*you*	ustedes (Uds., Vds.)	*you*
él, ella	*he, she*	ellos, ellas	*they*

1. The pronouns **tú, usted, vosotros/as,** and **ustedes** all correspond to the English pronoun *you.*

2. There are no Spanish equivalents for the English subject pronouns *it* and *they* referring to objects.

   ¿El metro? Sí, es más rápido.   *The subway? Yes, it's faster.*
   ¿Esos autobuses? Van al centro.   *Those buses? They're going downtown.*

3. The masculine plural forms **ellos, nosotros,** and **vosotros** refer to an all-male group or to a mixed group of males and females.

B. *Use of subject pronouns*

1. A subject pronoun is used before a verb form for emphasis, clarification, or contrast.

   Las amigas de Pilar van a pie; sólo **ella** toma un taxi.   *Pilar's friends walk (go on foot); only she takes a taxi.*
   José toma el autobús a la universidad, pero **nosotras** tomamos el metro.   *José takes the bus to the university, but we take the subway.*

2. A subject pronoun may be used by itself in response to a question.

—¿Quién toma el autobús?   *Who is taking the bus?*
—**Yo.**   *I am.*

3. The subject pronouns **tú** and **vosotros/as** are used to address children, friends, and persons regarded as social equals.

4. The subject pronouns **usted** and **ustedes** are used to address strangers, persons of higher social standing, or persons to whom one wants to show respect.

5. In Spain, the plural *you* form **vosotros/as** is used for familiar address and **ustedes** for formal address. However, in most of Hispanic America, **ustedes** is used both in formal and familiar address and **vosotros/as** is rarely used.

6. Although **usted** and **ustedes** are second person pronouns, they agree with the third person form of the verb.

Usted toma el autobús de las ocho.   *You take the eight o'clock bus.*
(**Él toma** el autobús de las ocho.)   *(He takes the eight o'clock bus.)*
Ustedes van al centro.   *You're going downtown.*
(Ellas **van** al centro.)   *(They're going downtown.)*

7. The subject pronouns **usted** and **ustedes** are often used for courtesy, even though it is clear who is being addressed.

¿Cómo están **ustedes?**   *How are you?*
Venga **usted** a las tres.   *Come at three.*

C. *Omission of subject pronouns*

The subject pronoun can be omitted when either the verb ending or the context clearly indicates who performs the action. Compare the absence of subject pronouns in the Spanish examples with the use of pronouns in the English examples.

—¿Tomas el autobús?   *Do you take the bus?*
—No, tomo el metro.   *No, I take the subway.*

Comprehension questions

1. Which subject pronoun, **tú** or **usted,** would you use to address the following people? A police officer in the street? A classmate? An elderly gentleman?

2. You are talking to a friend about the following people and things. Which subject pronoun would you use to refer to **Juan**? To **Amanda**? To **Marta y Felipe**? To **los trenes**?

3. Review the dialogue at the beginning of this section. For what expressive purpose does Luisa include the pronoun **nosotros** in utterance 5? Why does she say **nosotros** and not **nosotras**?

4. Which is the more natural answer to the question ¿**Quién toma un taxi?**: **Tomo un taxi** or **Yo**? Explain why.

5. Would Manolo, who lives in Madrid, use **ustedes** or **vosotros** to address a group of his friends? In the same situation, which pronoun would Jairo, a young man from Colombia, use?

Ejercicios

A. Imagínese que Ud. pasea por el centro de su ciudad y que se encuentra con varios conocidos. Diga qué pronombre sujeto (*subject pronoun*) usaría Ud., **tú, usted,** o **ustedes,** para hablar con ellos. Luego, diga en qué casos un español usaría **vosotros.**

MODELO: con el Sr. Gómez   *Ud.*

1. con su médico
2. con Beatriz y Roberto
3. con Pepito

4. con los señores Díaz, unos vecinos
5. con una agente de policía
6. con dos amigos suyos

B. Carmen está en la playa de vacaciones y le escribe a su amiga Pilar en Madrid. Complete la carta con los pronombres sujetos apropiados donde sean necesarios.

Benidorm, 6 de junio
Querida Pilar:

¿Cómo estás? Yo bien. Te escribo desde la playa, donde mi familia pasa los veranos. _____ alquilamos un apartamento aquí para escapar del ruido y los líos de la ciudad. A mi mamá le gusta mucho el Mediterráneo aunque _____ nunca nada en el mar. A Juan, mi hermano pequeño, sí le gusta nadar. _____ nada tres o cuatro horas todos los días, mientras Pedro, mi hermano mayor, toca la guitarra. _____ no toca bien, pero _____ tenemos mucha paciencia con él. Pedro tiene aquí buenos amigos. _____ vamos con ellos a bailar por las tardes. ¿Y qué haces _____ este verano?

Escribe pronto. Un abrazo,

Carmen

II. Present indicative of regular verbs

Ramiro:	¿De qué **hablan** ustedes?
Marta:	**Hablamos** de las noticias de hoy.
Eduardo:	Tú **lees** el periódico, Ramiro, ¿no? Pues, escucha estos titulares.
Marta:	"**Aumenta** el desempleo"; "**empeora** la contaminación".
Eduardo:	"La inflación **llega** ya a un 12%"; "**sube** el número de crímenes". ¡Esto está fatal!
Ramiro:	(*Riéndose*) Para responder a tu pregunta, no, no **leo** el periódico. ¡Y ahora **comprenden** por qué!

A. *Forms of the present indicative*

Present indicative of regular verbs

	-ar verbs	-er verbs	-ir verbs
	trabaj**ar**	com**er**	viv**ir**
yo	trabaj**o**	com**o**	viv**o**
tú	trabaj**as**	com**es**	viv**es**
Ud., él, ella	trabaj**a**	com**e**	viv**e**
nosotros/as	trabaj**amos**	com**emos**	viv**imos**
vosotros/as	trabaj**áis**	com**éis**	viv**ís**
Uds., ellos, ellas	trabaj**an**	com**en**	viv**en**

1. Spanish verbs are grouped into three classes depending upon the ending of the infinitive form: first conjugation verbs end in **-ar (trabajar),** second conjugation verbs end in **-er (comer),** and third conjugation verbs end in **-ir (vivir).**

2. The part of the infinitive that precedes the ending is called the *stem.* **Trabaj-, com-,** and **viv-** are the stems of the infinitives **trabajar, comer,** and **vivir,** respectively.

3. The stem of regular verbs remains constant and the endings vary according to the subject: **(yo) trabajo, (tú) trabajas,** etc. The stem is stressed in all forms except in the **nosotros** and **vosotros** forms.

4. The endings of second and third conjugation verbs are identical except in the **nosotros** and **vosotros** forms.

5. Here is a list of verbs that are regular in the present indicative.

-ar verbs

alquilar *to rent*	comprar *to buy*
aparcar *to park*	empeorar *to get worse*
atropellar *to run over*	llegar *to arrive*
aumentar *to increase*	mejorar *to improve*
ayudar *to help*	mirar *to look at*
buscar *to search, to look for*	necesitar *to need*
caminar *to walk*	trabajar *to work*
cenar *to dine, to have supper*	viajar *to travel*

-er verbs   **-ir verbs**

beber *to drink*	aplaudir *to applaud*
comer *to eat*	decidir *to decide*
creer *to believe*	insistir *to insist*
leer *to read*	permitir *to permit, to allow*
recorrer *to walk through*	recibir *to receive*
temer *to fear*	subir *to climb, to go up*
vender *to sell*	vivir *to live*

B. *Uses of the present indicative*

The present indicative is used more frequently in Spanish than in English. Throughout the following section, observe the similarities and differences in usage by comparing the Spanish examples to their English equivalents.

1. In both Spanish and English, the present indicative is used to state generalizations and universal truths.

Las grandes ciudades **enfrentan** serios problemas.	*Big cities face serious problems.*
El número de accidentes **sube** cada año.	*The number of accidents rises each year.*

2. In both Spanish and English, the present indicative is used to refer to habitual actions or states.

Casi todos los días **veo** accidentes en la autopista.	*Almost every day I see accidents on the freeway.*
Manejo siempre con mucho cuidado.	*I always drive very carefully.*

3. The present indicative is frequently used in Spanish to refer to actions in progress at the moment of speaking. In English, the present progressive is more commonly used to indicate an action in progress. (See *Capítulo 6.2* on the present progressive.)

—¿De qué **hablan** ustedes?   *What are you talking about?*
—**Hablamos** de las noticias de hoy.   *We're talking about today's news.*

4. The present indicative is often used in Spanish to express an action or event that is planned for or that will take place in the future. Although in English the present indicative can be used to express future meaning, the present progressive, *will* + infinitive, or a construction with *going* + infinitive are more likely.

El mes próximo **viajo** a España.   *Next month I'm going to (I will) travel to Spain.*

Celebran en Madrid un congreso sobre los problemas urbanos.   *They're holding a congress on urban problems in Madrid.*

5. The construction present indicative + **desde (hace)** + time expression is used to talk about an action that began in the past and is still going on in the present. Note that in English the present perfect progressive or the present perfect is used. (See *Capítulo 9.4* for more on **hace** with time expressions.)

Vivimos en esta ciudad desde 1984.   *We've been living in this city since 1984.*

No **leo** el periódico desde hace tres días.   *I haven't read the newspaper for three days.*

6. In both Spanish and English, the present indicative is used to make past events seem more vivid and immediate, especially when historical events are being narrated. This use is often referred to as the *historical present.*

Ayer subía a mi oficina en el piso 25 cuando de repente se **para** el ascensor y **escucho** un ruido horroroso. **Toco** la alarma, pero no **funciona.**   *Yesterday I was going up to my office on the 25th floor when suddenly the elevator stops and I hear a horrible noise. I push the alarm, but it doesn't work.*

Bartolomé Colón, hermano de Cristóbal, **funda** la ciudad de Santo Domingo en 1496.   *Bartholomew Columbus, Christopher's brother, founds the city of Santo Domingo in 1496.*

Summary of the uses of the present indicative

Generalizations	La contaminación nos **preocupa** a todos.
Habitual actions	**Leo** el periódico todos los días.
Actions in progress	¿Qué **haces?** ¿**Miras** las noticias en la televisión?
Future actions and events	El próximo mes **alquilamos** un apartamento en el centro.
Ongoing events begun in the past	**Espero** el autobús desde hace quince minutos.
Vivid narration of past events (historical present)	Esperaba la luz verde cuando de repente un camión me **choca** el carro por detrás.

Comprehension questions

1. In Spain, a person might say **¿Tomáis el autobús?** when addressing two or more friends. What verb form would a Spanish speaker from Mexico City use to express the same meaning?

2. In the sentence **La próxima semana el alcalde inaugura un nuevo centro cultural,** is the verb **inaugura** most likely to be translated *(he) inaugurates* or *(he) is going to inaugurate* in English?

3. What is the English equivalent of **tomo** in the sentence **Tomo el metro desde hace un mes**?

4. Review the dialogue at the beginning of this section. Identify a verb that refers to a habitual action or state. Point out several verbs that express an action in progress.

5. To make the following sentence about the past more vivid, what form of **regresar** would you use? **Después de una larga ausencia, Julia _____ a Bogotá.**

Ejercicios

A. Pregúntele a un(a) compañero(a) de clase sobre su vida en la universidad. Luego, otro(a) estudiante informa a los demás compañeros.

MODELO: ¿caminar a la universidad o usar el metro?
E1: *¿Caminas a la universidad o usas el metro?*
E2: *Generalmente yo camino a la universidad.*
E3: *Él (Ella) dice que generalmente camina a la universidad.*

1. ¿vivir en una residencia de estudiantes o en un apartamento?
2. ¿participar en algún club o en algún deporte?
3. ¿asistir a las reuniones del gobierno estudiantil?
4. ¿trabajar durante las horas libres o estudiar la mayor parte del tiempo?
5. ¿sacar buenas notas en todas las clases o solamente en algunas?
6. ¿necesitar usar las computadoras para tus clases?
7. ¿temer las clases avanzadas?
8. ¿mirar las telenovelas con otros estudiantes?

B. Averigüe (*Find out*) Ud. lo que hacen sus amigos en este momento, según el modelo.

MODELO 1: hablar Uds. / de la contaminación del aire
E1: *¿De qué hablan Uds.?*
E2: *Hablamos de la contaminación del aire.*

MODELO 2: buscar (tú) / la guía del año pasado
E1: *¿Qué buscas?*
E2: *Busco la guía del año pasado.*

1. leer tú / un artículo sobre el desempleo
2. escribir Uds. / una carta al director del periódico
3. leer tú / un informe sobre el incendio en la calle Libertad
4. hablar Uds. / de los resultados de las elecciones municipales
5. discutir Uds. / la necesidad de organizar mejor la limpieza de algunos barrios
6. preparar tú / una presentación al Concejo Municipal sobre el aumento de crímenes en esta ciudad
7. organizar Uds. / una reunión para escuchar las opiniones de los vecinos de este barrio
8. temer tú / el desempleo y la inflación

C. Consulte otra vez el diálogo de esta sección. Un(a) estudiante menciona un problema asociado con la vida urbana como los que figuran en el diálogo. Luego otro(a) estudiante expresa su disgusto, sirviéndose de las expresiones que siguen u otras similares.

¡Esto está fatal!	¡No me digas!
¡Qué pena (horror, desastre, lástima)!	¡Vaya qué lío!
¡No faltaba más!	¡Ya no aguanto más!

MODELO: el precio de la comida
E1: *El precio de la comida sube mucho.*
E2: *¡Qué desastre!*

1. el desempleo
2. el número de crímenes
3. la inflación
4. el servicio telefónico

5. la contaminación del aire
6. los atascos
7. los accidentes automovilísticos
8. la limpieza de las calles

D. Imagínese que Ud. vive y trabaja en una ciudad grande. Explíquele a un(a) amigo(a) por lo menos tres cosas de su vida en la ciudad. Use algunas de las siguientes preguntas como punto de partida (*starting point*).

¿Por qué tardas tanto en salir del apartamento por la mañana?
¿Dónde desayunas?
¿A qué hora llegas al trabajo? ¿Qué haces cuando llegas?
¿Qué haces después del trabajo? ¿Y los fines de semana?
¿Dónde viven tus parientes y tus mejores amigos?
¿Visitas a tus amigos con frecuencia?

MODELO: *Yo llego al trabajo un poco antes de las nueve de la mañana, saludo al vendedor de periódicos y luego subo a la tercera planta en ascensor.*

E. Mucha gente sigue la misma rutina todos los días. Diga qué cosa(s) hace Ud. después de hacer lo que se indica a continuación. Puede usar algunos de los verbos que aparecen en la lista u otros de su elección.

abrir	consultar	llevar	tomar
buscar	conversar	saludar	trabajar
comer	escribir	telefonear	ver

MODELO: Después de vestirme,...
Después de vestirme, bajo al comedor y tomo una taza de café.

1. Después de salir de casa por la mañana,...
2. Después de entrar en la sala de clase,...
3. Después de terminar con todas las clases,...
4. Después de llegar al trabajo,...
5. Después de hablar con mi jefe(a),...
6. Después de acabar con mi trabajo y salir a la calle,...
7. Después de entrar en el supermercado,...
8. Después de hacer las compras,...

III. Gender of nouns

Locutor:	La noticia al minuto. Interrumpimos nuestra telenovela para darles las últimas noticias con respecto al accidente de Sabana Grande.
Periodista:	El tráfico está prácticamente paralizado en el sector de Sabana Grande. La policía trata de imponer orden entre la muchedumbre que está en el lugar del accidente. Aquí cerca de nosotros, un policía entrevista a una testigo. Según entendemos, el conductor de una moto está gravemente herido. Afortunadamente, no hay ninguna persona muerta. Es todo por el momento. Dentro de poco, esperamos darles más información.

A. *Noun endings*

All nouns in Spanish are either masculine or feminine. Noun endings often help determine the gender of nouns. Nouns referring to male human beings are masculine, and those referring to females are feminine, regardless of the ending. Masculine nouns may be preceded by the masculine articles **el** or **un**. Feminine nouns may be preceded by the feminine articles **la** or **una**.

B. *Some feminine noun endings*

-a	-dad, -tad, -tud, -d	-ción, -sión -tión, -ión	-umbre	-ez
la autopista	la actitud	la confusión	la costumbre	la honradez
la carretera	la amistad	la congestión	la legumbre	la madurez
la entrevista	la ciudad	la estación	la muchedumbre	la rapidez
la parada	la pared	la religión	la servidumbre	la vejez

1. Although the majority of the nouns ending in **-a** are feminine, there are some common exceptions: **el día, el mapa, el sofá, el tranvía.** Exceptions also include most nouns of Greek origin ending in **-ma: el clima, el drama, el idioma, el problema, el tema.**

2. Some exceptions to feminine nouns ending in **-d** are **el ataúd, el césped.**

3. Common exceptions to feminine nouns ending in **-ión** are **el avión, el camión.**

4. Nouns ending in **-ez** generally express abstract concepts.

C. *Some masculine noun endings*

-o	-al	-or	-ente, -ante
el edificio	el animal	el calor	el accidente
el ruido	el arrabal	el olor	el calmante
el suburbio	el delantal	el temblor	el detergente
el suelo	el hospital	el valor	el diamante

1. Some exceptions to masculine nouns ending in **-o** are **la mano, la foto (foto-grafía),** and **la moto (motocicleta).**

2. Common exceptions to masculine nouns ending in **-al** are **la señal, la central, la catedral.**

3. Exceptions to masculine nouns ending in **-or** are **la flor, la labor.**

D. *Noun endings of either gender*

There is no general rule for determining the gender of nouns with endings other than those previously mentioned in B and C.

el coche	el análisis	el clavel
el pie	el énfasis	el papel
la calle	la crisis	la miel
la torre	la neurosis	la piel

E. *Nouns with two genders and two meanings*

The feminine or masculine article indicates the gender and distinguishes the meaning of some nouns. Compare the meaning and gender of the following pairs of nouns.

el capital *capital (money)*		la capital *capital (city)*
el cura *priest*		la cura *cure*
el guía *guide*		la guía *guidebook; female guide*
el modelo *example; male model*		la modelo *female model*
el orden *order, tidiness*		la orden *order, command*
el Papa *Pope*		la papa *potato*
el policía *policeman*		la policía *police force; policewoman*

F. *Masculine and feminine forms of nouns referring to people*

1. Most nouns referring to people end in **-o** in the masculine and **-a** in the feminine form. The noun **persona** is always feminine and applies to both males and females: **Juan es buena persona, pero Rosa es la mejor persona del grupo.**

el ciudadano	la ciudadana
el inquilino	la inquilina

2. Some nouns referring to people end in a consonant in the masculine and in **-a** in the feminine. Note that the accent is dropped in **ladrona** and **peatona.**

el conductor	la conductora
el ladrón	la ladrona
el locutor	la locutora
el peatón	la peatona

3. Some nouns ending in **-a** that refer to people (often nouns of occupation) are identical in the masculine and feminine forms. Gender is indicated by the form of the article that precedes the noun, by other modifiers, or by context. Most nouns ending in the suffix **-ista** belong in this category.

el/la demócrata	el/la maquinista
el/la dentista	el/la (p)siquiatra
el/la guía	el/la turista

4. Some nouns referring to people have identical masculine and feminine forms. Most nouns ending in **-ente** or **-ante** belong in this category.

el/la agente	el/la habitante
el/la chófer (chofer)	el/la intérprete
el/la estudiante	el/la visitante

5. Some nouns have special masculine and feminine forms, as do their English counterparts.

el actor	*actor*	la actriz	*actress*
el barón	*baron*	la baronesa	*baroness*
el caballero	*gentleman*	la dama	*lady*
el héroe	*hero*	la heroina	*heroine*
el poeta	*poet*	la poetisa	*poetess*
el yerno	*son-in-law*	la nuera	*daughter-in-law*

G. *Gender of nouns referring to animals*

1. Most nouns naming animals use a single form to refer to both the male and the female of the species. To refer to one of the sexes, the word **macho** (*male*) or **hembra** (*female*) is added to the noun: **la llama macho, la llama hembra.**

el camello	la jirafa
el gorila	la llama
el puma	la pantera

2. The names of a few animals have a different form for the male and the female of the species. The feminine is formed according to the rules mentioned for people: an **-a** ending, a special ending **(gall*ina*),** or a word unrelated to the masculine form **(caballo/yegua).**

el perro	la **perra**
el elefante	la **elefanta**
el león	la **leona**
el gallo	la **gall*ina***
el **caballo**	la **yegua**

H. *Gender in other categories of nouns*

1. The names of oceans, rivers, and mountains are masculine. The word **sierra** (*mountain range*) is feminine.

El Pacífico es más profundo que **el Atlántico.**	*The Pacific Ocean is deeper than the Atlantic.*
¿Qué río es más largo, **el Orinoco** o **el Nilo?**	*Which river is longer, the Orinoco or the Nile?*
Quieren escalar **el Aconcagua** y luego **el Everest.**	*They want to climb Mount Aconcagua and then Mount Everest.*
El clima es inestable en **la Sierra Nevada.**	*The climate is unstable in the Sierra Nevada.*

2. Months and days of the week are masculine.

El lunes no es mi día favorito.	*Monday is not my favorite day.*
Enero es lluvioso.	*January is (a) rainy (month).*

3. The letters of the alphabet are feminine.

La **a** es la primera letra del alfabeto y la **i griega** es la penúltima.	*A is the first letter in the alphabet and y is the next-to-the-last.*

Comprehension questions

1. Which of the following nouns are masculine and which are feminine? How do you know? **virtud, información, tráfico, terror, sencillez**

2. Which of the following nouns ending in **-a** are not feminine? **problema, carretera, día, clima, noticia, persona**   Which of the following nouns ending in **-o** are not masculine? **mano, camino, moto, vehículo, foto**   Explain why.

3. Which of the following nouns have different masculine and feminine forms? **pianista, peatón, habitante, camarero, chófer**

4. Which of the following nouns change meaning when used with the masculine article **el** and with the feminine article **la**? **guía, tranvía, tema, costumbre, orden**

5. Which of the following nouns could be used to name a male or a female? **conductora, poeta, ciudadana, artista**

6. Review the news bulletin that appears at the beginning of this section. The newspaper reporter talks about a witness. Explain how information is given about the gender of this person.

Ejercicios

A. Dé el género (*gender*) y el artículo de cada sustantivo (*noun*). Si los dos géneros son posibles, indique los dos artículos.

MODELO 1:   centro   *el centro, masculino*

MODELO 2:   taxista   *el/la taxista, masculino y femenino*

1. autopista	6. acera	11. mapa	16. muchedumbre
2. motocicleta	7. precaución	12. ascensor	17. accidente
3. polvo	8. policía	13. estación	18. crisis
4. camión	9. maquinista	14. trabajador	19. guía
5. solicitud	10. actriz	15. mercancía	20. intérprete

B. ¿Qué palabras de la siguiente lista pueden referirse a Antonio? ¿A Luisa? ¿A los dos?

MODELO 1:   secretaria   *A Luisa, sí; a Antonio, no.*

MODELO 2:   taxista   *A los dos.*

1. turista	3. especialista	5. agente	7. ladrón
2. dueña	4. conductora	6. habitante	8. inspector

C. Rubén y Paula hablan de algunos matrimonios que conocen. Con un(a) compañero(a), cree un diálogo, según el modelo.

MODELO: Guillermo / jefe
              Rubén: *Guillermo es jefe, ¿verdad?*
              Paula: *Sí, y su esposa es jefa también.*

1. Marisa / guía
2. Roberto / camarero
3. Carlos / actor
4. Isabel / pianista
5. Ricardo / modelo
6. Adela / agente de policía
7. Carmen / doctora
8. Marta / condesa
9. Raúl / poeta
10. Ana / demócrata

IV. Plural of nouns

Lucía: Bueno, Carlos, ¿qué opinas ahora de nuestras **ciudades**?
Carlos: Casi todo me parece estupendo: las **calles** llenas de **tiendas** interesantes, los **monumentos** a los **héroes** nacionales, las **catedrales** muy antiguas y aun los **rascacielos** modernos.
Lucía: ¡Qué bueno! Pero dices «casi». ¿Qué pasa?
Carlos: La verdad es que deseo ir al campo un día para ver **árboles** y **flores,** oír el canto de los **pájaros** y sentir el césped bajo mis **pies**...
Lucía: Te comprendo, Carlos. ¿Qué tal si mañana vamos al Parque Campogrande?

1. A noun ending in a vowel generally forms its plural by adding **-s.** The main exceptions are some nouns ending in a stressed vowel: **esquí/esquíes, rubí/ rubíes, tabú/tabúes,** but **menú/menús, papá/papás, sofá/sofás.**

autopista autopistas		espíritu espíritus
café cafés		ruido ruidos
calle calles		taxi taxis

2. A noun ending in a consonant, including final **-y,** generally forms its plural by adding **-es.** However, a noun ending in an unstressed vowel + **-s** remains unchanged in the plural: **lunes/lunes, análisis/análisis, tijeras/tijeras.**

autobús autobuses		interés intereses
capital capitales		ley leyes
ciudad ciudades		motor motores

3. Some nouns undergo a spelling change in the plural: (1) a singular noun ending in **-z** changes **z** to **c** before adding **-es;** (2) a singular noun ending in **-n** that is stressed on the next-to-last syllable adds a written accent in the plural to maintain the stress on that syllable; and (3) a singular noun ending in **-n** or **-s** that is stressed on the final syllable drops the written accent in the plural. The largest group is nouns ending in **-ión.**

z > c	**add accent**	**drop accent**
luz luces	examen exámenes	autobús autobuses
voz voces	joven jóvenes	compás compases
	origen orígenes	ladrón ladrones
	volumen volúmenes	opinión opiniones

Comprehension questions

1. Which one of the following nouns adds **-es** to form the plural? Explain why. **crisis, héroe, tráfico, locutor**

2. Which one of the following nouns has a spelling change when it is made plural? **vía, taxi, lápiz, autopista**

3. Which one of the following nouns does not change in the plural? Explain why. **té, análisis, tranvía, compás**

4. Which one of the following nouns loses the written accent when made plural? **opinión, mamá, número, ángel**

5. Which one of the following nouns has a written accent in the plural? **conductor, volumen, deporte, cantidad**

Ejercicios

A. Lea el diálogo de esta sección y dé la forma singular de cada sustantivo (*noun*) plural. Explique por qué se agrega **-s** o **-es** al sustantivo plural.

B. Imagínese que Ud. acaba de volver a su pueblo en el campo después de hacer una visita a unos primos en la ciudad. Hay varias cosas que no le gustan de la vida urbana. Coméntelas según el modelo. Preste atención a la concordancia (*agreement*) de los adjetivos con los sustantivos.

MODELO: autobús / contaminar el aire
¡Los autobuses contaminan el aire!

1. peatón / no respetar los semáforos
2. policía / no multar a la gente que aparca en doble fila
3. boleto de cine / ser carísimo
4. acera / estar llena de basura
5. tren del metro / pasar siempre lleno de gente
6. taxista / ser descortés
7. trolebús / nunca llegar a tiempo
8. joven / no bajar el volumen de su radio

C. Averigüe lo que opina un(a) amigo(a) que visita su ciudad por primera vez sobre algunos atractivos, lugares y sucesos (*events*). Use cada sustantivo en la forma plural y preste atención a la concordancia de los adjetivos con los sustantivos.

MODELO: rascacielos del centro
          E1:   *¿Qué opinas de los rascacielos del centro?*
          E2:   *Pues, me parecen interesantes.*

1. atractivo turístico
2. estación de autobuses
3. jardín público
4. hotel de la calle Pedro de Valdivia
5. nueva autopista
6. barrio en las afueras
7. flor del parque botánico
8. proyecto de mejoramiento

D. Dé su opinión, siempre en forma negativa, sobre las personas que observa durante un paseo por el centro. Luego, otro(a) estudiante niega que todos sean así, según el modelo.

MODELO: ese taxista / manejar demasiado rápido
          E1:   *Ese taxista maneja demasiado rápido.*
          E2:   *Puede ser, pero no todos los taxistas son así.*

1. ese vendedor de automóviles / tratar de robar a la gente
2. esa guía turística / no comunicar claramente sus ideas
3. esa taquillera / parecer antipática
4. ese obrero / descansar más de lo que trabaja
5. ese motociclista / no parar en los semáforos
6. ese mecánico / cobrar más de lo que debe
7. esa mesera / no cumplir bien sus responsabilidades
8. esa dependienta / interrumpir a sus clientes

V. Definite articles

Queridos papás:

Aunque sólo llevamos dos días en Lima, ya nos encanta el Perú. La arquitectura de la capital es magnífica y los museos muy interesantes. Desgraciadamente, el tráfico y la contaminación nos tienen los nervios de punta. Esta noche vamos a cenar con nuestro amigo, el doctor Quiroga; les envía muchos saludos. El jueves salimos para El Cuzco a respirar un poco de aire puro. Los viajes cansan más que un trabajo de lunes a viernes, pero nos encanta estar fuera de casa. Ya tenemos planes para las próximas vacaciones: visitar las ruinas de la civilización maya.

Víctor y Mariángeles

A. *Forms of the definite article*

1. The definite article agrees in both gender (masculine or feminine) and number (singular or plural) with the noun it precedes.

	Singular	**Plural**
Masculine	**el** bulevar	**los** bulevares
	el municipio	**los** municipios
Feminine	**la** cola	**las** colas
	la población	**las** poblaciones

2. The preposition **a** + the definite article **el** is contracted to **al**. The preposition **de** + the definite article **el** is contracted to **del**. A and de + **la, los, las** are not contracted.

Voy **al** centro por la mañana y **a la** clínica por la tarde.
I'm going downtown in the morning and to the clinic in the afternoon.

El ruido **del** tráfico es horrible.
The noise of the traffic is horrible.

El humo **de las** fábricas contamina la ciudad.
The smoke from the factories pollutes the city.

3. When the definite article immediately precedes a singular feminine noun beginning with a stressed **a-** or **ha-**, the masculine form of the article (**el**) is used. Feminine nouns that begin with an unstressed **a-** or **ha-** require the feminine article **la: la amiga, la hamaca.** Note that the feminine article **las** is used in the plural and that adjectives follow the normal rules of agreement.

El agua del mar es **fría**.
The water of the sea is cold.

Las aguas del mar son **frías**.
The waters of the sea are cold.

El bombero trae **el** hacha.
The fireman brings the ax.

Tenemos **mucha** hambre.
We're very hungry.

B. *General uses of the definite article*

1. In both Spanish and English, the definite article is used to specify a known noun. In the first question that follows, the speaker assumes that the listener knows which bank is referred to. In the second question, the speaker uses the clue **de enfrente** to identify the store.

¿Caminamos **al** banco?	*Shall we walk to the bank?*
¿Por qué no vamos primero a **la** tienda de enfrente?	*Why don't we first go to the store across the street?*

2. In Spanish, the definite article is used to make generalizations about a noun. In English, the article is not used.

En las ciudades grandes **el** tráfico es intenso antes de las ocho de la mañana.	*In big cities traffic is heavy before eight in the morning.*
El transporte público no soluciona todos los problemas.	*Public transportation doesn't solve all the problems.*

3. Contrary to English usage, the definite article is used before each noun in a series.

La contaminación, **el** desempleo y **la** delincuencia son problemas de muchas ciudades.	*Pollution, unemployment, and delinquency are problems in many cities.*

4. The definite article is generally used in Spanish to refer to parts of the body and articles of clothing when the possessor is clearly understood. Possessive forms, such as **mi, tu, su,** are usually avoided when referring to parts of the body. Note that for groups in which each member has one object, the object appears in the singular in Spanish, in the plural in English.

Tengo **las** manos frías.	*My hands are cold.*
Me duele **la** cabeza.	*My head aches.*
Voy a ponerme **los** guantes.	*I'm going to put on my gloves.*
¿Por qué no se quitan ustedes **el** abrigo?	*Why don't you take off your coats?*

5. In Spanish, the definite article is generally used after the prepositions **a, de,** and **en** before a place noun. Exceptions include **a/de/en casa** and **a/de/en clase.** The definite article is generally not used in English.

Van **al** estadio en autobús.	*They're going to the stadium by bus.*
Llevan al ladrón a **la** cárcel.	*They're taking the thief to jail.*
Los niños están en **el** colegio.	*The children are in school.*
Volvemos de **la** iglesia a las doce.	*We'll return from church at twelve.*
Vamos a **la** escuela en autobús.	*We go to school by bus.*
Vamos a **la** iglesia a pie.	*We go to church on foot.*

C. *Use of the definite article with days of the week and units of time*

1. In Spanish, the singular definite article **el** is used with the days of the week to express *on*. The plural definite article **los** is used to express the equivalent of *every*.

Tengo cita en el ministerio **el martes.**   *I have an appointment at the ministry on Tuesday.*

Las oficinas estatales cierran **los sábados.**   *State offices close on Saturdays (every Saturday).*

2. A day of the week is used without the article after the verb **ser** to identify the day of the week. No article is used in the phrase **de... a...** with time expressions.

Hoy es viernes, ¿verdad?   *Today is Friday, isn't it?*
Trabajo **de** lunes **a** viernes.   *I work from Monday to Friday.*

3. The definite article is required in Spanish to express *next* or *last* + a unit of time.

Vamos al Japón **el próximo mes.**   *We're going to Japan next month.*
Las elecciones municipales son **la próxima semana.**   *The city elections are next week.*
Fueron a Madrid **el año pasado.**   *They went to Madrid last year.*

D. *Use of the definite article with languages*

1. In contrast to English, names of languages require the definite article when they are the subject of a sentence in Spanish.

El inglés es una lengua útil en los negocios.   *English is a useful language in business.*

2. In Spanish, the definite article is not used after the verb **hablar** when followed by the name of a language. The article is optional after verbs such as **aprender, enseñar, entender, escribir, estudiar, leer,** and **saber** + the name of a language. Note that no article is used in English.

Hablo español y un poco de francés.   *I speak Spanish and a little French.*
Mi amigo sólo entiende (**el**) inglés, pero su papá entiende y lee (**el**) ruso.   *My friend only understands English, but his father understands and reads Russian.*
¿Sabes (**el**) italiano y también (**el**) español?   *Do you know Italian and also Spanish?*

3. No article is used after the prepositions **en** + the name of a language. The article is usually also omitted after the preposition **de** + a language in phrases that categorize a noun.

Este letrero está escrito **en inglés** y **en español**.	*This sign is written in English and Spanish.*
Mi profesor **de francés** dicta también clases **de italiano**.	*My French teacher also gives Italian classes.*
Espero lograr el dominio total **del español**.	*I hope to achieve total mastery of Spanish.*

E. *Use of the definite article with proper nouns*

1. In Spanish the definite article is used with a courtesy title + a surname when speaking *about* someone; however, no article is used when speaking directly *to* someone and before **don** and **doña**.

El señor González trabaja aquí.	*Mr. González works here.*
Señor González, ¿cómo está Ud.?	*Mr. González, how are you?*
¿Buscas a doña Carlota?	*Are you looking for doña Carlota?*

2. Most names of cities and countries are used without the definite article in both Spanish and English. Note that the definite article is used, however, when it forms part of the name in Spanish: **Los Ángeles, La Habana, El Cairo, Las Antillas, El Salvador, La República Dominicana.** The article is optional with the following countries: **(la) Argentina, (el) Brasil, (el) Canadá, (la) China, (el) Ecuador, (los) Estados Unidos, (la) India, (el) Japón, (el) Perú, (el) Uruguay.**

Nueva York es una ciudad grande.	*New York is a big city.*
España y Alemania son países de Europa.	*Spain and Germany are European countries.*
(La) Argentina, **(el)** Ecuador y **(el)** Perú están en Sudamérica.	*Argentina, Ecuador, and Peru are in South America.*

3. The definite article is used with nouns referring to rivers, mountain ranges, and lakes in Spanish. This is also true in English, except for lakes.

El Orinoco es casi tan largo como **el** Misisipí, ¿verdad?	*The Orinoco is almost as long as the Mississippi, isn't it?*
¿Dónde están **los** Andes?	*Where are the Andes?*
Conoces **el** lago Titicaca, ¿no?	*You are familiar with Lake Titicaca, aren't you?*

4. In Spanish, but not in English, the definite article is required with the names of cities, countries, and people when modified by a descriptive adjective or phrase.

El viejo San Juan es bonito. (But, San Juan es bonito.)
Old San Juan is lovely.

Deseo visitar **la** España antigua.
I want to visit historic (old) Spain.

El pobre Roberto está siempre cansado.
Poor Robert is always tired.

Summary of the main uses of the definite article

Article used

	Example
To talk about a specific noun	¿Vamos **al** banco?
To state a generalization	**El** tráfico es terrible aquí.
To talk about a part of the body or an article of clothing	Tengo **las** manos frías.
With names of languages used as the subject of a sentence	**El** español es fácil.
Before days of the week to express *on* (see omission after **ser**)	El examen es **el** martes.
With courtesy titles and surnames when speaking about someone	**Los** señores Osorio viven en Panamá.
With names of rivers, lakes, and mountains	**El** Amazonas es el río más importante de Sudamérica, ¿verdad?
With modified names of cities and countries	¿Conoce Ud. la Plaza Mayor en **el** viejo Madrid?

No article used

	Example
After **ser** to identify the day of the week	Hoy **es viernes.**
With the phrase **de... a...** to refer to time	El museo está abierto **de viernes a domingo.**
With courtesy titles and surnames in direct address	¿Cómo están Uds., **señores Moreno**?
With unmodified names of most cities	Viajo frecuentemente de **Nueva York** a **Caracas.**
With languages after **hablar,** after **en,** and after **de** in phrases that categorize a noun	**Hablas español** muy bien. Escribimos cartas **en español** y **en inglés.** Es un libro **de español.**

Comprehension questions

1. Is **el** or **la** used before the feminine noun **hambre**? And before the feminine noun **hamaca**? Explain your choice in each case.

2. Is the definite article required in the following sentence? _____ **contaminación es peligrosa.** Explain.

3. Would you use **mi cabeza** or **la cabeza** to tell someone that your head is full of ideas? **¡Tengo _____ llena de ideas!** Explain why.

4. How would you say that Paco works every Saturday? **Paco trabaja _____ .**

5. In which one of the following sentences may the definite article be omitted before **italiano**? **No entiendo el italiano. El italiano es la lengua de la ópera.** Explain.

6. Review the postcard that appears at the beginning of this section. Explain why the article is or is not used in the following instances: **en Lima, el Perú, la arquitectura, el doctor Quiroga, el jueves** and **de lunes a viernes.**

Ejercicios

A. Complete las frases con la forma correcta del artículo definido cuando sea necesario. Preste atención a las contracciones **al** y **del.**

1. Hoy es _____ lunes y _____ transporte público siempre funciona mal _____ lunes; por eso llegué tarde a _____ trabajo. Me quité _____ abrigo y estaba a punto de abrir _____ correo cuando _____ jefe me saludó así: «Buenos días, _____ señora Moreno. ¿Por qué llega Ud. tan tarde? _____ comité ejecutivo la espera en _____ oficina de _____ Presidente».

2. Mi cuñada es intérprete en _____ cortes municipales. Trabaja _____ martes, _____ miércoles y _____ jueves de _____ ocho a _____ dos. Ella habla _____ español y _____ francés y entiende _____ italiano y _____ griego. Naturalmente usa _____ español la mayor parte del tiempo en su trabajo.

B. Con otra persona de la clase, intente llegar a un acuerdo para ir juntos(as) a ver una película al laboratorio de idiomas. Hablen de su horario de lunes a sábado.

MODELO: *E1:*   ¿Qué haces el lunes?
              E2:   *El lunes estoy ocupado/a. (Los lunes tengo mi clase de contabilidad y por la tarde practico tenis.)*

C. Dé direcciones a otro(a) compañero(a) de clase quien le pide ayuda, según el modelo.

MODELO: museo / autobús 15; quinta parada
  E1: *¿Cómo voy al museo?*
  E2: *Puede tomar el autobús 15; el museo está en la quinta parada.*

1. Iglesia de la Concepción / metro; Plaza Argentina
2. Banco Nacional / trolebús; barrio Cuatro Caminos
3. Hotel Estrella / taxi; Avenida Bruselas
4. Calle Menéndez Pidal / autobús 12; cuarta bocacalle de allí
5. Feria del Libro / metro; calle Santa Lucía

D. Se dice que las generalizaciones son muy peligrosas. Viva Ud. "peligrosamente" y haga una generalización para cada uno de los siguientes temas o dé una opinión contraria a la generalización de un(a) compañero(a).

MODELO: coches deportivos
  E1: *Los coches deportivos son muy populares hoy.*
  E2: *De acuerdo, pero los coches más grandes son más seguros.*

1. ciudad
2. precios del cine
3. transporte público
4. discotecas
5. grandes centros comerciales
6. aeropuertos
7. atascos de tráfico
8. películas de hoy en día

VI. **Tomar, llevar(se)**, and other equivalents of *to take*

A variety of verbs in Spanish are used to express the English verb *to take*. Many of these meanings are rendered in Spanish by **tomar** and **llevar(se)**, although numerous other verbs are also used.

A. *Tomar, llevar(se)*

1. **Tomar** is used to express *to take* in the sense of *to take something into one's hand, to take a means of transportation, to eat or drink,* and *to take* in figurative uses.

Toma el mapa; es para ti.	*Take the map; it's for you.*
¿**Tomas** el autobús generalmente?	*Do you generally take the bus?*
¿Qué quieres **tomar**? ¿Un vino?	*What do you want to drink? A glass of wine?*
Siempre lo **toman** por turista.	*They always take him for a tourist.*
¿Van a **tomar** tus quejas en consideración?	*Are they going to take your complaints into consideration?*

2. **Llevar** is used to express *to take* in the sense of *to carry or take someone or something from one place to another.* (Note that **llevar** also means *to wear clothing.*)

¿**Llevaste** el coche al mecánico?	*Did you take the car to the mechanic?*
Te **llevo** al centro a las dos.	*I'll take you downtown at two o'clock.*

3. **Llevarse** is used to add intensity to the idea expressed and may be translated *to take away* or *to carry away.* It may also imply the notion of making a purchase or stealing.

Víctor **se llevó** mis llaves y ahora no puedo entrar.	*Victor took away (left with) my keys and now I can't get in.*
Me **llevo** la blusa roja, señorita.	*I'll take (buy) the red blouse, Miss.*

B. *Other verbs that express* to take

Many different Spanish verbs are used to express actions commonly stated in English by *to take* + a preposition or by a set phrase such as *to take a trip* or *to take place.* You will have to learn such verbs and phrases as you encounter them. The following list gives some of the common verbs and phrases that express *to take.*

sacar	*to take out*	**Saca** la basura, por favor.
quitar	*to take away*	Deben **quitar** las sillas de allí.
subir	*to take up*	¿**Subes** el paquete al cuarto piso?
bajar	*to take down*	María **baja** la revista a su padre.
hacer un viaje	*to take a trip*	**Hace un viaje** todos los inviernos.
tardar (en)	*to take a long time*	¿Vas a **tardar** mucho **en** volver?
dar un paseo	*to take a walk*	¿Quieres **dar un paseo** por el mar?
sacar fotos	*to take photographs*	¿Quién **sacó esas fotos** tan buenas?
tener lugar	*to take place*	La reunión **tiene lugar** en su despacho.

Ejercicios

A. Conteste las preguntas que le hace un(a) compañero(a) de clase.

MODELO: *E1:* ¿Tomas un refresco o una cerveza cuando hace calor?
E2: Normalmente tomo una limonada.

1. ¿Tomas el autobús o el metro cuando vas al centro?
2. ¿Cuánto tardas en llegar a tu primera clase desde tu casa?
3. ¿Qué tal si damos un paseo este fin de semana?
4. ¿Me puedes llevar a casa esta noche?
5. ¿Llevas suficiente dinero para prestarme cinco dólares hasta mañana?
6. ¿Haces algún viaje todos los años? ¿Adónde?

B. Complete las frases de los siguientes diálogos con la forma correcta de **tomar, llevar,** o **llevarse.**

1. —Hola, Diana. ¿Me puedes _____ a la biblioteca?
   —¿Por qué no _____ el metro? A estas horas hay demasiado tráfico en el centro.
2. —¿Qué _____ allí, Marcos? ¿No es mi informe para la clase de historia?
   —Pero, ¡me _____ por idiota! No tengo por qué _____ tu informe.

Actividades para la comunicación

A. ¿Dónde está...? Uno de sus amigos está de visita en su pueblo y está un poco desorientado. Déle instrucciones para ir del hotel a los lugares que él quiere visitar. Usando el mapa de la siguiente página, emplee algunas de las siguientes frases en sus direcciones.

caminar una cuadra (dos cuadras)
caminar hasta la próxima esquina
doblar a la izquierda (derecha)
pasar enfrente de...

seguir derecho hasta...
cruzar la calle (avenida)...
andar hasta...

MODELO: parque
E1: Por favor, ¿cómo llego al parque?
E2: Para llegar allí, caminas una cuadra hasta la Avenida de las Flores, doblas a la izquierda y andas hasta la Calle Mayor. Allí está la entrada al parque.

1. restaurante
2. museo de arte
3. hospital
4. cine

5. teatro
6. iglesia
7. mercado
8. estadio de fútbol

B. Entrevistas. La ciudad ofrece muchos atractivos para ciertas personas. Entreviste a algunos(as) compañeros(as) de clase sobre las actividades que hacen en su ciudad o, si no viven en una ciudad, cuando van a una ciudad grande. Use algunas de las frases sugeridas u otras.

MODELO: asistir a: (conciertos, conferencias, obras de teatro)
        E1:   *¿Asistes a muchos conciertos en la ciudad?*
        E2:   *A veces asisto a un concierto de rock, particularmente si tocan en el estadio.*

1. visitar: (museos, galerías de arte, a amigos o parientes)
2. comer en un restaurante: (chino, italiano, mexicano)
3. comprar su ropa: (en tiendas elegantes, en grandes centros comerciales, en boutiques)
4. participar en: (un club social, un maratón, un grupo coral)
5. asistir a: (conciertos, espectáculos especiales, el ballet)
6. pasear por: (los parques, el centro, las avenidas principales)

C. Opiniones. Exprese su punto de vista sobre los siguientes temas relacionados con la vida urbana. Puede usar las frases sugeridas u otras originales. Luego, pregunte a un(a) compañero(a) qué opina sobre el mismo tema.

MODELO: ciudades grandes / (no) ofrecer una vida sana
     E1:   *Las ciudades grandes no ofrecen una vida sana generalmente.*
       (Luis), ¿qué opinas tú sobre la vida en las ciudades grandes?
     E2:   *Pues, me parece que hay muchas ciudades muy atractivas y limpias, pero también hay otras horribles.*

1. transporte público / funcionar muy bien (mal)
2. apartamentos / (no) necesitar muchas reparaciones
3. sueldos / (no) subir rápidamente en la ciudad
4. oportunidades para empleo / (no) existir en gran abundancia
5. exhibiciones culturales / (no) ocurrir con frecuencia

D. Mi punto de vista. Imagínese que Ud. visita una ciudad como Nueva York, Los Ángeles o alguna otra que Ud. conoce. Dé un comentario sobre algunas de las cosas o algunos de los lugares de esa ciudad. Puede usar las frases sugeridas u otras originales.

estación de metro	policía	parque	hotel
autobús	taxista	agua	centro comercial
calle	museo	clima	drama

MODELO   1:   *Los hoteles del centro parecen muy caros.*

MODELO   2:   *La policía pasa por las calles continuamente.*

E. Situaciones. Desarrolle (*Develop*) con otras personas de la clase diálogos de por lo menos tres comentarios por persona. Base los diálogos en las siguientes situaciones típicas de la vida urbana.

1. Un(a) turista habla con un(a) policía sobre la mejor manera de llegar al Museo de Arte Contemporáneo.
2. Un hombre pierde su paciencia en medio de un enorme atasco de tráfico y habla con su esposa sobre los problemas que ve.
3. Un(a) joven no puede usar su coche porque no funciona bien la transmisión automática. Habla con un(a) amigo(a) sobre los medios de transporte que puede usar para llegar a su trabajo. Al final toma una decisión sobre cuál va a usar.
4. Dos personas discuten las ventajas y las desventajas de vivir en el campo o en la ciudad. No están de acuerdo.

CAPÍTULO 2

•

A divertirse

Estas parejas se divierten en el parque de atracciones del monte Tibidabo, Barcelona, España.

Conversación

1. ¿Qué hacen la mayoría de los jóvenes durante sus horas libres? Y en su caso, ¿cuáles son sus diversiones favoritas?
2. ¿Hay discotecas y otros clubes para los jóvenes donde Ud. vive? ¿Qué tipo de música tocan? ¿Van allí los jóvenes con mucha frecuencia? ¿Y Ud.?
3. ¿Prefiere Ud. divertirse de noche o de día? ¿Cómo se divierte durante el día? ¿Y por la noche?
4. ¿Qué deportes practica Ud.? ¿Es experto(a) en algún deporte? ¿En cuál(es)?
5. ¿Le gusta coleccionar alguna cosa? ¿Discos? ¿Carteles? ¿Otra cosa?
6. ¿Qué juegos de mesa prefiere jugar en su tiempo libre?
7. ¿Toca Ud. algún instrumento musical? ¿Cuál? ¿Desde cuándo lo toca?
8. Mire la fotografía de la página anterior. ¿Cómo cree Ud. que se sienten las personas montadas en el látigo (whip)?

Vocabulario temático

actuación, la performance; behavior
afición, la liking; hobby
ajedrez, el chess
anfitrión(ona), el(la) host (hostess)
aperitivo, el appetizer; aperitif
barbacoa, la barbecue
boite, la nightclub
butaca, la theater seat; armchair
cantimplora, la canteen (for liquids)
cartel, el poster, sign, billboard
cinta, la tape; ribbon
compañerismo, el companionship
compás, el compass; rhythm, beat
conjunto, el musical group
crucigrama, el crossword puzzle
chiste, el joke
desfile, el parade
disfraz, el disguise, mask
ensayo, el rehearsal; essay
espectáculo, el entertainment; show
estampilla, la stamp
función, la function, operation; show
maquillaje, el cosmetic make-up, act of putting on make-up

mochila, la backpack, knapsack
palomitas, las popcorn
pasatiempo, el pastime, hobby
patinaje, el skating
rompecabezas, el puzzle
torneo, el tournament
tuna, la student music group of guitarists and singers

apetecer to have an appetite for, to desire
ensayar to practice, to rehearse
entretener to entertain, to pass the time
merendar (ie) to snack

gratis free of charge

al aire libre outdoors
ciencia ficción, la science fiction
en vivo live (performance)
fuegos artificiales, los fireworks
ir de excursión to go on a tour or trip
jugar a las damas to play checkers
novela policíaca, la mystery novel
parque de atracciones, el amusement park

I. Present indicative of stem-changing verbs

Martín: Oye, Evita, ¿**recuerdas** a qué hora abre la discoteca "Punqui"?
Eva: A las diez, me parece. Pero no **quiero** ir allí esta noche; **prefiero** ir a la
          nueva boite de la calle Príncipe.
Martín: ¿Ah sí? ¿Y cómo es? ¿Sabes algo del sitio?
Eva: La **recomienda** Julia. Dice que el ambiente es fenomenal, que **sirven** unas
          bebidas exóticas y que no **cierran** hasta las cuatro de la mañana.

A. *Verbs with a stem change e > ie and o > ue*

	recomendar e > ie	preferir e > ie	volver o > ue
yo	recomiendo	prefiero	vuelvo
tú	recomiendas	prefieres	vuelves
Ud., él, ella	recomienda	prefiere	vuelve
nosotros/as	recomendamos	preferimos	volvemos
vosotros/as	recomendáis	preferís	volvéis
Uds., ellos, ellas	recomiendan	prefieren	vuelven

1. Some verbs have a stem change from **e** to **ie** and from **o** to **ue** when the last vowel of the stem is stressed. In the present indicative this change occurs in all forms except the first and second person plural.

2. The following verbs have a stem change from **e** to **ie** and are conjugated like **recomendar** and **preferir**.

-ar verbs	**-er verbs**	**-ir verbs**
cerrar	atender	advertir
comenzar	defender	arrepentirse
despertar(se)	descender	convertir
empezar	encender	divertirse
encerrar	entender	invertir
merendar	perder	mentir
pensar	querer	sentir(se)
sentar(se)		sugerir

3. The verb **adquirir** (*to acquire*) follows the pattern of verbs with a stem change **e** to **ie**. The stem vowel **i** changes to **ie: adquiero, adquieres, adquiere, adquirimos, adquirís, adquieren.**

4. The following verbs have a stem change from **o** to **ue** and are conjugated like **volver.**

-ar verbs		-er verbs		-ir verbs
almorzar	probar	devolver	poder	dormir
aprobar	recordar	doler	resolver	morir
contar	sonar	llover	soler	
costar	soñar	mover		
encontrar	volar			
mostrar				

5. The verb **jugar** (*to play*) has a stem change from **u** to **ue** in all persons of the present indicative except in the first and second person plural. The verb **oler** (*to smell*) adds **h-** before **ue** in all persons except in the first and second person plural.

jugar (u > ue):   ju**e**go, ju**e**gas, ju**e**ga, jugamos, jugáis, ju**e**gan
oler (o > hue):   **hue**lo, **hue**les, **hue**le, olemos, oléis, **hue**len

B. *Verbs with a stem change e > i*

pedir	servir
pido	sirvo
pides	sirves
pide	sirve
pedimos	servimos
pedís	servís
piden	sirven

1. Some verbs ending in **-ir** have a change in the last vowel of the stem from **e** to **i** in all persons except in the first and second person plural.

2. The following verbs have a stem change from **e** to **i** and are conjugated like **pedir** and **servir.**

conseguir	elegir	seguir
corregir	medir	sonreír
despedirse	reír	vestir(se)

3. Verbs ending in **-guir,** such as **seguir,** have a spelling change in the first person singular to keep the same pronunciation of the **g** in the stem: **sigo.**

4. Verbs ending in **-gir,** such as **elegir,** also have a spelling change in the first person singular to keep the regular pronunciation of the **g** in the stem: **elijo.**

In the vocabulary sections of this text, stem changes are indicated in parentheses after the infinitive; for example, **recomendar (ie), volver (ue), preferir (ie, i), dormir (ue),** and **pedir (i).**

Comprehension questions

1. How many stems does the verb **contar (ue)** have in the present indicative? Explain why.

2. In the present indicative of the verb **defender (ie),** does the stem change in the verb form corresponding to **nosotros**? And in the verb form corresponding to **tú**? Give the **nosotros** and **tú** forms.

3. In the present indicative of the verb **devolver (ue),** does the stem change in the verb form corresponding to **ellas**? And in the verb form corresponding to **usted**? Give the **ellas** and **usted** forms.

4. In the present indicative of the verb **reír (i),** does the stem change in the verb form corresponding to **vosotros**? And in the verb form corresponding to **ustedes**? Give the **vosotros** and **ustedes** forms.

Ejercicios

A. Haga las siguientes preguntas a un(a) compañero(a) de clase, quien le contesta. Luego, dé su propia reacción a la respuesta.

MODELO: *E1:*   Cuando estás en un restaurante elegante, ¿pides primero un aperitivo o la comida?
   E2:   *Normalmente pido un aperitivo.*
   E1:   *Yo no; yo siempre pido una bebida y luego la comida.*

1. Después de clase, ¿prefieres dar un paseo o descansar?
2. ¿Almuerzas en casa, en un restaurante o en la universidad?
3. ¿Quieres ver una película, una obra teatral o escuchar discos?
4. Cuando tienes un día libre, ¿sueles descansar o prefieres practicar un deporte?

5. ¿Qué recomiendas a los visitantes a esta ciudad, una excursión organizada o una salida informal?
6. ¿Juegas en algunos torneos este año?
7. ¿Encuentras que te concentras mejor por la mañana o por la tarde?
8. ¿Entiendes perfectamente todas las reglas del juego de damas?

B. Explíquele a un(a) compañero(a) de clase por qué las personas indicadas no pueden asistir a un ensayo de una obra teatral que van a presentar. Use las frases siguientes.

no volver hasta el domingo
no querer ver a su ex-novio(a) allí
seguir enfermo(a)
despedirse de sus abuelos
pensar estudiar para un examen

dolerle una muela
empezar su nuevo trabajo
soler ensayar con su banda
no poder hasta las tres
no querer ensayar tanto

MODELO: Juan
E1: *¿Puede venir Juan el sábado?*
E2: *No; lo siente mucho, pero sigue enfermo.*

1. Sara
2. tú
3. Javier y Mercedes
4. los Alonso
5. tú y tu esposa
6. Claudia
7. Ramón
8. tú y tu hermano

C. Todo le sale bastante mal esta semana, y Ud. se lamenta de varias cosas. Exprese sus sentimientos usando expresiones como **qué lata (fastidio)**, **qué pena (lástima)**, **cuánto lo lamento (siento)**, y **qué mala suerte.**

MODELO: Pedro / no almorzar conmigo hoy
¡Cuánto lo siento! Pedro no almuerza conmigo hoy.

1. (yo) / no encontrar tiempo para ver la exposición de fotos
2. (yo) / no poder jugar al ajedrez contigo mañana
3. mi novio(a) / no conseguir boletos para ver "Evita"
4. (yo) / perder el último recital del guitarrista Paco de Lucía
5. la compañía teatral / no repetir esa comedia otro día
6. llover demasiado de modo que se cancela el desfile
7. (tú) / no querer usar un disfraz para la fiesta mañana
8. mis amistades / nunca entender mis chistes

D. Acaban de operar a un(a) amigo(a) suyo(a). Como Ud. lo(la) encuentra sin ganas de hacer nada, trata de animarlo(la) y le sugiere algunos pasatiempos o distracciones, usando las frases siguientes. Luego, su amigo(a) le contesta por qué no quiere hacer esas actividades.

probar este juego de cartas
volver a pintar como antes
pedir un televisor para la habitación
conseguir papel para escribir cartas
  a tus amigos

empezar a leer *Don Quijote*
elegir tú un juego para jugar
contarme la historia que escribiste
jugar a las damas

MODELO: E1:   *¿Por qué no pruebas este juego de cartas?*
          E2:   *No pruebo el juego porque no me gustan los juegos de cartas (estoy aburrido[a] de todo, estoy cansado[a], etc.).*

II. Indefinite articles

Enriqueta: ¡Tengo **un** hambre increíble! Me apetece comer **unos** tacos de aperitivo, y luego **una** ensalada, **un** plato de carne, fruta...

Susana: Basta, pues. Cierta chica que conozco siempre habla de adelgazar. Si comes así, vas a subir medio kilo de **un** tirón.

Enriqueta: Ya lo sé, pero... ¡me muero de hambre! Empiezo la dieta otro día. Por ahora, vamos a **un** restaurante de autoservicio; así podemos escoger **un** poco de todo.

A. *Forms of the indefinite article*

1. The indefinite article agrees in gender and number with the noun it modifies. It is never contracted.

2. Masculine nouns may be preceded by **un** or **unos.** Feminine nouns may be preceded by **una** or **unas.**

	Singular	Plural
Masculine	**un** refresco **un** éxito	**unos** refrescos **unos** éxitos
Feminine	**una** bebida **una** feria	**unas** bebidas **unas** ferias

3. When the indefinite article immediately precedes a singular feminine noun beginning with a stressed **a-** or **ha-,** the masculine form **(un)** of the article is used.
Observe the following examples and note that the feminine article **unas** is used in
the plural and that adjectives follow the normal rules of agreement. (See *Capítulo
1.5* for a similar rule with definite articles.)

Alguien está tocando **un** arpa.	*Someone is playing a harp.*
Tengo **unas ansias** locas de escuchar a Plácido Domingo cantar **unas arias.**	*I have a mad desire to listen to Plácido Domingo sing a few arias.*
—Estoy a dieta y tengo **un hambre** terrible.	*I'm on a diet and am terribly hungry.*
—Yo también tengo **una terrible hambre.**	*I'm terribly hungry, too.*

B. *Uses of the indefinite article*

1. In both Spanish and English, the indefinite article is used before a noun whose
specific identity is unknown to the listener.

Fuimos a **una** discoteca estupenda.	*We went to a fabulous discotheque.*
Conocimos allí a **unos** jóvenes muy simpáticos.	*We met some very nice young men there.*

2. The plural indefinite article forms **unos** and **unas** may be used before a plural
noun to express *some* or *several*. Use of the article is optional, as is *some* in
English.

¿Puedes conseguir **(unos)** boletos para ver el circo?	*Can you get (some) tickets to see the circus?*
Quiero **(unas)** flores en la sala para la fiesta.	*I want (some) flowers in the living room for the party.*

3. The plural forms **unos** and **unas** are also used to express *about* (*approximately,
more or less*) before a numerical expression.

Esa cantante ha grabado **unos** diez discos.	*That singer has recorded about ten records.*
Pues, yo creo que tiene **unos** quince, por lo menos.	*Well, I think that she has about fifteen, at least.*

4. No article is used in either Spanish or English before a noun referring to an
unspecified measure or amount.

No tengo muchos pasatiempos, pero
colecciono discos y me gusta resolver crucigramas.

*I don't have many hobbies, but I do
collect records and I like to solve
crossword puzzles.*

Necesitamos cerveza y refrescos para
la barbacoa.

*We need beer and soft drinks for the
barbecue.*

5. In contrast to English usage, the indefinite article is generally not used in Spanish after the verbs **buscar, encontrar, tener, llevar** (*to wear*), and **haber,** and after the prepositions **sin** and **con.**

—¿**Buscas músico** o cantante para el
conjunto?

*Are you looking for a musician or a
singer for the group?*

—Ya **tenemos cantante,** pero no **encontramos guitarrista.** El conjunto
no puede estar **sin guitarrista.**

*We already have a singer, but we can't
find a guitar player. The group can't
be without a guitar player.*

6. The indefinite article is usually not used after **ser** when followed by a noun or a noun phrase expressing nationality, profession, or religious or political affiliation. The indefinite article *is* used, however, when the noun is modified and expresses subjective information or an impression or opinion about someone. Note in the following examples that the article is always used in English.

—¿Sabías que Pedro Roca es actor de
cine?

*Did you know that Pedro Roca is a
movie actor?* (**actor de cine** =
profession)

—Claro que sí. Es argentino como yo.
Es **un** actor de gran talento.

*Of course. He's an Argentinian like
me. He's a very talented actor.* (**un
actor de gran talento** = opinion)

7. The indefinite article is not used with the following adjectives and numbers in Spanish.

cien(to) *a (one) hundred*	mil *a (one) thousand*
cierto *a certain*	otro *another*
medio *half a*	tal *such a*

Hay **otra** película de Buñuel en
cartelera.

There's another Buñuel film showing.

No puedo ir al cine. Tengo **mil** cosas
que hacer.

*I can't go to the movies. I have a
thousand things to do.*

La película empieza en **media** hora.

The film begins in half an hour.

8. In contrast to English usage, the indefinite article is not used in Spanish after **qué** (*what*) in exclamations.

¿Fuiste al concierto de Arrau? ¡Qué
pianista! ¡Qué gran pianista!

*Did you go to the Arrau concert?
What a pianist! What a great pianist!*

Summary of the uses of the indefinite article

Uses	Examples
To refer to a noun unknown to the listener	**Un** joven quiere hablar contigo.
To express *some* or *several* before a plural noun	Traje **unos** discos para tu hermana.
To express *approximately* before a number	El disco tiene **unas** doce canciones.
With a modified noun that refers to someone's profession, nationality, or ideological affiliation in a subjective way	Julio Iglesias es **un** cantante español muy conocido. Eres **un** socialista fanático.

No article	Examples
With a noun or noun phrase that refers to someone's profession, nationality, or ideological affiliation	Es **cantante**. Es **cantante** de tangos. Es **argentino**. Es **nacionalista**.
To refer to a nonspecific measure or amount	Canta **canciones** folklóricas sudamericanas.
After verbs like **buscar, encontrar, tener, llevar** (*to wear*), **haber**	¿**Llevas** traje oscuro esta noche? ¿**Hay** pianista para el concierto?
With **cierto, cien(to), medio, otro, mil, tal**	Vamos a **otro** club.
After **qué** in exclamations	¡**Qué** crucigrama más difícil!

Comprehension questions

1. Is **un** or **una** used before the feminine noun **arpa**? Explain why.

2. What is the meaning of **unas** in each of the following sentences? **Hacemos unas excursiones estupendas. Paseamos por unas tres horas.**

3. Which of the following sentences requires an indefinite article? **Es _____ bailarina. Es _____ bailarina con mucha experiencia.**

4. In which of the following sentences can the indefinite article be omitted? **¿Busca Ud. una casa? ¿La fiesta es en una casa o en un apartamento?** Explain why.

5. Which one of the following sentences requires an indefinite article? **Su colección de sellos vale _____ millón de dólares. Su colección de sellos vale _____ mil dólares.**

6. Review the dialogue at the beginning of this section. Why are **un, una** and not **el, la** used in the phrases **una ensalada** and **un restaurante de autoservicio?**

Ejercicios

A. Complete las conversaciones y comentarios con la forma correcta del artículo indefinido si es necesario.

1. —¿Qué tienes ahí, Clara? ¿_____ bandera?
   —Sí, es _____ bandera mexicana. La compré cuando fui a ver _____ desfile en la capital.
2. —¿Qué te pasa? ¿Por qué te ríes?
   —Recordaba lo que me pasó ayer con _____ amigo. Fuimos al cine y, al traernos él _____ refresco, _____ palomitas, _____ dulces y _____ otras cosas, perdió el equilibrio y lo dejó caer todo encima de _____ pobre señor que estaba delante de él. ¡Fue _____ desastre!
3. —Pero, Cristi, ¡qué _____ paquete tan grande!
   —Sí, me compré _____ blusa sin _____ botones y _____ otra que tiene _____ cierto parecido con la que llevaste al baile anoche.
   —Hablando de ropa, ¿vas a llevar _____ falda o _____ pantalones esta noche?
   —Fíjate, ¡qué _____ coincidencia! Te iba a hacer la misma pregunta.

B. Imagínese que no le alcanza el dinero este mes para unas compras que quiere hacer. Pida la cantidad aproximada que necesita a un(a) amigo(a), según el modelo.

MODELO: discos
         E1:   *¿Me puedes prestar dinero para unos discos?*
         E2:   *¿Cuánto necesitas?*
         E1:   *Unos quince dólares.*

1. entradas para el cine
2. nueva raqueta de tenis
3. zapatos para correr
4. regalo para mi hermano(a)
5. cintas de vídeo
6. nuevo libro de rompecabezas

C. Dé su propia definición de las siguientes personas y cosas. Use palabras que ya conoce. Lo importante es comunicar la idea para que otra persona comprenda de qué habla.

MODELO: payaso
Un payaso trabaja en un circo y hace reír a otras personas.

1. pasatiempo
2. crucigrama
3. aperitivo
4. jardín botánico

5. ajedrecista
6. barbacoa
7. feria
8. desfile

D. Usted está pasando un mes con una familia española. La señora de la casa le pregunta sobre sus hábitos de comida. Responda dando ejemplos de su dieta.

MODELO: Señora: *Y usted, ¿qué toma por las mañanas?*
Usted: *Yo por las mañanas tengo un hambre tremenda.*
Como unos huevos, tocino, unas tostadas, un jugo de naranja y un café con leche.

1. a media mañana
2. para cenar

3. a media tarde
4. de almuerzo

III. Formation of questions

José: ¿Qué hacemos este fin de semana?
Rosa: No sé... siempre hacemos lo mismo. ¿Hay algo de interés en el periódico?
José: Pues, la exposición del libro ha comenzado, el circo está en la ciudad todavía,... Ah, hay un espectáculo de patinaje. ¿Qué te parece?
Rosa: Estupendo. ¿Por qué no invitas a tus amigos los Caballero y vamos con ellos?

A. *Questions that can be answered with sí or no*

1. Word order is flexible in questions that can be answered with **sí** or **no**. In sentences with an explicit subject, the subject may immediately follow the main verb or the verb and its complements.

¿Tiene **Julio** ganas de ver el circo?
¿Compró los boletos **Ana**?
¿Vio **usted** la exposición?
¿Quieren ir al parque de atracciones **ustedes**?

Does Julio want to see the circus?
Did Ana buy the tickets?
Did you see the exposition?
Do you want to go to the amusement park?

2. In informal language, a question may have the same word order as a declarative sentence but is pronounced with rising intonation.

¿Ana compró los boletos?	*Did Ana buy the tickets?*
¿Julio tiene ganas de ver el circo?	*Does Julio want to see the circus?*

B. *Questions with interrogative words and phrases*

1. In questions with an interrogative word, the interrogative word generally begins the sentence. If there is an explicit subject, it usually follows the verb or the complement of the verb.

¿**Quién** quiere ir al cine?	*Who wants to go to the movies?*
¿**Qué** película quieres ver tú?	*What film do you want to see?*
¿**Cuándo** quiere ver esa película Elena?	*When does Elena want to see that film?*

2. The interrogative adjectives **cuánto(a), cuántos(as)** must agree with the noun they modify in both gender and number.

¿**Cuánto tiempo** dura el espectáculo?	*How long does the show last?*
¿**Cuántas entradas** necesitamos?	*How many tickets do we need?*

3. Interrogative words always have a written accent. Observe in the following examples that the interrogative words also have a written accent when they are used in an interrogative sense in declarative sentences.

¿**Qué** hacemos el sábado?	*What shall we do on Saturday?*
No sabe **qué** hacer el sábado.	*He doesn't know what to do on Saturday.*

4. The following words are the most frequently used interrogative words.

cómo *how*	cuántos(as) *how many*
cuál(es) *which (one, ones), what*	dónde *where*
cuándo *when*	qué *what*
cuánto(a) *how much*	quién(es) *who, whom*

5. In Spanish as well as in English, many verbs are used with a preposition to convey a specific meaning. In Spanish, the preposition must precede the interrogative word at the beginning of a question.

¿**Adónde** van el domingo?	*Where are you going (to) on Sunday?*
¿**Con quién** vas a salir?	*Who are you going to go out with?*
¿**De quién** son esos boletos?	*Whose tickets are those?*

6. Interrogative words that are frequently preceded by a preposition include **adónde, de dónde, a quién, con quién, de quién, para quién, para qué,** and **por qué**.

—¿**Con quién** va Rosa al partido?　　*Who's Rosa going to the game with?*
—Va con Paco.　　*She's going with Paco.*

—¿**Para qué** llamas a Carlos?　　*What are you calling Carlos for?*
—Para invitarlo a la fiesta.　　*To invite him to the party.*

C. *Qué versus cuál(es)*

1. **Qué** followed by the verb **ser** usually asks for a definition, but may also ask for identification, classification, or information of a general sort. **Cuál(es)** followed by the verb **ser** asks for some specific information.

—¿**Cuál es** tu pasatiempo favorito?　　*What's your favorite pastime?*
—Es la filatelia.　　*It's philately.*
—¿**Qué es** la filatelia?　　*What's philately?*
—Es la colección de sellos.　　*It's stamp collecting.*

—¿**Qué es** ese saco?　　*What's that bag?*
—Es mi mochila.　　*It's my backpack.*

2. **Qué** followed by any verb other than **ser** asks a more general question and is normally used to ask about something that has not been specified or mentioned. **Cuál(es)** followed by any verb other than **ser** asks about a specific choice that is clear to the speaker.

—¿**Qué** haces este fin de semana?　　*What are you doing this weekend?*
　¿**Qué** planes tienes?　　*What plans do you have?*
—Pues, quiero ir al teatro. Hay tres　　*Well, I want to go to the theater. There*
　obras buenísimas, pero no sé **cuál**　　*are three excellent plays, but I don't*
　ver primero.　　*know which one to see first.*
—¿**Cuál** de ellas has leído? Yo vería　　*Which one of them have you read? I*
　ésa primero.　　*would see that one first.*

Comprehension questions

1. To change the declarative sentence **Los muchachos juegan al tenis** into a question, can the subject **los muchachos** be placed both after the main verb **juegan** and after the verb complement **al tenis**? Explain your answer.

2. **Voy con Carlos** is the answer to which of the following questions? ¿**Quién va al parque de atracciones?** ¿**Con quién va al parque de atracciones?** ¿**Quién va al parque de atracciones con usted?**

3. Should **qué** or **cuál** be used in each of the following questions? ¿____ **es su pasatiempo favorito?** ¿____ **es la pintura abstracta?**

4. To ask someone a general question about what sports they practice, should you use **qué** or **cuáles** in the following sentence? ¿____ **deportes practicas?** How would you ask someone to tell you which specific sports they prefer? **De todos los deportes, ¿ ____ prefieres?**

Ejercicios

A. Haga las siguientes preguntas sobre pasatiempos y diversiones a sus compañeros(as) de clase usando **¿cuál?, ¿cuáles? o ¿qué?**

MODELO: ¿____ es un documental?
          ¿Qué es un documental?

1. ¿____ es tu pasatiempo favorito?
2. ¿____ significa la palabra *desfile*?
3. ¿____ de estos tres vídeos quieres ver?
4. ¿____ día vas al concierto de jazz?
5. ¿____ son los deportes que más te gustan?
6. ¿A ____ de los clubes quieres ir esta noche?
7. ¿Con ____ amigos vas a hacer camping el próximo fin de semana?
8. ¿En ____ de esas dos bolsas tienes las entradas?

B. Entreviste a un(a) compañero(a) de clase sobre su vida social y sus actividades personales usando los temas que se dan a continuación u otros de su propia invención. Se pueden hacer varias preguntas diferentes con cada tema.

MODELO: invitar a salir
          E1:   *¿A cuántas chicas diferentes invitas a salir cada semana?*
          E2:   *Pues, normalmente invito a tres o cuatro.*

          E1:   *¿Te invita a salir Julio todas las semanas?*
          E2:   *Sí, hasta ahora me invita todos los sábados.*

1. practicar deportes
2. pasar el fin de semana
3. asistir a conciertos
4. ir de excursión
5. trabajar en su colección de monedas
6. llamar por teléfono
7. preferir juegos de cartas o el ajedrez
8. manejar el coche

C. Ud. piensa ir a un concierto que da una tuna de España, pero primero quiere saber todos los detalles. Pregúntele a un(a) amigo(a) el día, la hora, el sitio, la forma de llegar allí, el precio, etc. Pregunte también sobre la tuna y el tipo de música que van a presentar. Su amigo(a) contestará en parte según el siguiente anuncio.

¡LA TUNA CANTA!

Directamente de la Universidad de Salamanca. ¡Concierto único! ¡En vivo! Música folklórica española. Vestidos e instrumentos tradicionales.

Sábado, 15 de octubre. 8 de la noche. Teatro de la Universidad. Entrada, 10 dólares. Butacas reservadas. Recepción sigue.

¡No pierda este concierto!

MODELO: E1:   *¿Qué día canta la tuna?*
E2:   *Canta el sábado, 15 de octubre.*

D. Después de escuchar lo que un(a) compañero(a) le cuenta sobre unos amigos suyos, Ud. hace dos preguntas para obtener más información y su compañero(a) contesta sus preguntas.

MODELO: *E1:*   Mario empieza lecciones de piano hoy.
E2:   *¿Y cuánto cuestan las lecciones?*
E1:   *Creo que a $15 la hora.*
E2:   *¿Quién es su maestro?*
E1:   *El señor Alvelo.*

1. Tomás piensa invitar a salir a la hermana de Benjamín.
2. Jaime y Hugo se quedan en casa esta noche; no nos acompañan a la discoteca.
3. Voy a ir con Elena al parque de atracciones este fin de semana.
4. Cecilia tiene que tocar en un recital mañana por la tarde.

IV. Demonstrative adjectives and pronouns

Carla: **Esta** tienda de música tiene una maravillosa selección de instrumentos.
Leonardo: ¿Te gusta **aquella** guitarra, la que está en la pared de al fondo?
Carla: Pues... prefiero **ésta** que está aquí y **ésas** que están detrás de ti. Es que **aquélla** del fondo es eléctrica y no me interesa una guitarra eléctrica.
Leonardo: Bueno, tú eres la guitarrista. Para mí, todo **esto** es nuevo.

A. *Forms and uses of demonstrative adjectives*

1. Demonstrative adjectives generally precede the noun they modify, and agree in gender and number with the noun modified.

	Singular		Plural
Masculine	**Feminine**	**Masculine**	**Feminine**
este conjunto	**esta** función	**estos** conjuntos	**estas** funciones
ese piano	**esa** guitarra	**esos** pianos	**esas** guitarras
aquel ritmo	**aquella** melodía	**aquellos** ritmos	**aquellas** melodías

2. Demonstrative adjectives are used to locate nouns in space and to indicate their relative distance from the speaker: **este** is used to pinpoint persons or objects near the speaker; **ese** points out persons or objects away from the speaker (often near the listener) while **aquel** refers to persons and objects far away from both speaker and listener. In practice, **ese** and **aquel** are frequently used interchangeably to indicate something that is far away from the speaker. **Aquel** always refers to the most distant object when more than one distant object is mentioned.

—¿Te gusta **esta** flauta? — *Do you like this flute?*
—No, prefiero **esa** flauta de al lado. — *No, I prefer that flute right next to it.*
—¿Y qué piensas de **aquella** flauta que está allá? — *And what do you think of that flute that's way over there?*

3. Demonstrative adjectives are also used to locate nouns in time: **este** is used to refer to the present and immediate future; **ese** refers to the near past or to the near or remote future; **aquel** points to the remote past or, for some speakers, to the remote future.

—¿No vienes a la fiesta **esta** noche? — *Aren't you coming to the party tonight?*

—No, hay muchas fiestas **este** mes. Hay una fiesta la semana que viene y me viene mejor **esa** semana. — *No, there are many parties this month. There's a party next week and that week is better for me.*
—¿Recuerdas cuando íbamos a fiestas todas las semanas? ¡Qué tiempos **aquellos**! — *Do you remember when we went to parties every week? Those were the days!*

—¿Qué diversiones tendrán en el siglo XXV?

What amusements will they have in the 25th century?

—No me puedo imaginar cómo serán **esos (aquellos)** tiempos.

I don't have any idea what those times will be like.

B. *Forms and uses of demonstrative pronouns*

1. The demonstrative pronouns are the same in form as the demonstrative adjectives except that they are often written with an accent on the stressed vowel. In modern usage, the written accent is not required unless the meaning of the pronoun would otherwise be ambiguous. In this text, written accents are always used on demonstrative pronouns.

   —¿Es **éste** el disco que quieres?

   Is this the record you want?

   —No, **ése** no me gusta. Pásame **aquél,** el que está en el sobre azul.

   No, I don't like that one. Hand me that one over there, the one in the blue jacket.

2. The demonstrative pronouns agree in number and gender with the noun to which they refer.

   —Estos fuegos artificiales son mejores que los del año pasado.

   These fireworks are better than last year's.

   —Sí, **éstos** son los mejores que hemos visto.

   Yes, these are the best we've seen.

3. The neuter pronoun forms **esto, eso,** and **aquello** are invariable and never carry a written accent. They are used to refer to nonspecific, unnamed objects or to ideas, actions, and situations in a general, abstract sense.

   —¿Qué es **eso**?

   What's that?

   —¿**Esto**? Es un recuerdo del carnaval.

   This? It's a souvenir of the carnival.

   —¿Fuiste al carnaval sin invitarme? ¡**Eso** sí que me molesta!

   You went to the carnival without inviting me? That does bother me!

   —Oh, **aquello** no fue tan divertido.

   Oh, that wasn't so amusing.

4. The demonstrative pronouns **aquél** and **éste** are used to express *the former* and *the latter*. **Éste** refers to the nearest noun (the one said or written last) and **aquél** refers to the more distant noun.

   No sé por qué discutí los planes para la excursión con mi novia y mis padres. ¡**Éstos** dicen que no debemos ir y **aquélla** dice que ahora no quiere ir!

   I don't know why I discussed the plans for the excursion with my girlfriend and my parents. The latter say that we shouldn't go and the former says that she doesn't want to go now!

Comprehension questions

1. Review the dialogue at the beginning of this section. Point out the three demonstrative pronouns that are used to refer to **guitarra.** Explain the relative distance implied by each pronoun in terms of *near to, farther from,* and *far from.*

2. Would you use **estos** or **esos** in the following sentence? **No tenemos vacaciones en** _____ **momentos.** And in the following sentence? **El próximo verano vamos a Europa; nos vamos a divertir mucho en** _____ **meses.** Explain your choices.

3. Would you use **ese, ése,** or **eso** in each of the following sentences? **Me gusta jugar al básquetbol;** _____ **me entretiene. Me gusta jugar al básquetbol;** _____ **deporte me entretiene.**

4. Would you use **esta, ésta,** or **esto** in each of the following sentences? _____ **obra de teatro es interesante. Unos críticos dicen que la obra es buena y otros que es mala. Todo** _____ **da más publicidad a la obra.**

5. Complete the following sentence with **éstas** and **aquéllas** to state that the speaker prefers detective stories to science fiction. **Las historias de ciencia ficción no me gustan; prefiero las novelas policíacas porque encuentro que** _____ **siempre son más imaginativas que** _____ **.**

Ejercicios

A. Con otros compañeros de clase, exprese sus preferencias según el modelo.

MODELO: Para la playa este verano, quiero comprar este traje de baño. (camisetas bonitas, toalla de muchos colores)
  E1: *Yo, no. Yo quiero comprar estas camisetas bonitas.*
  E2: *Pues, yo, por mi parte, quiero comprar esta toalla de muchos colores.*

1. En vez de salir, hoy prefiero leer estos libros de chistes. (novela de aventuras, librito sobre ajedrez, crítica musical, cuentos satíricos)
2. Cuando estamos en el centro, a veces visitamos aquel museo. (jardines botánicos, exposición de arte contemporáneo, colección de antigüedades, edificio muy alto)
3. ¡Qué tienda más estupenda! Quiero comprar ese juego de ajedrez. (juego de damas, discos antiguos, cajas de música, botella de perfume)

B. Usted va a dar una fiesta y habla con la persona de servicio para darle algunas indicaciones. Imagínese que ustedes están frente a la mesa del dibujo, al lado de los platos. Use los adjetivos demostrativos apropiados de acuerdo con la distancia a la que se encuentran los objetos.

MODELO: platos / no son suficientes
Estos platos no son suficientes.

1. queso / hay que cortarlo
2. tazas / están sucias
3. cafetera / hay que llenarla
4. torta / necesita un utensilio para cortarla

5. vino / está caliente
6. mantequilla / es muy poco
7. tenedor / no es suficiente
8. pollo / está demasiado crudo

C. Otra persona viene a ayudarle con la fiesta. Él/Ella pregunta qué platos hay que servir, y Ud. le indica. Imagine que Ud. está junto a los platos del dibujo anterior y la otra persona está al lado de la cafetera. Use adjetivos demostrativos e indique la posición relativa del objeto usando expresiones como **allí, allí al fondo, ahí a tu lado, aquí, aquí a mi lado, aquí cerca,** etc.

MODELO: queso / ensalada
Ayudante: *¿Servimos ahora aquel queso?*
Anfitrión(ona): *No, ahora servimos esta ensalada aquí a mi lado.*

1. fruta / ensalada
2. pollo / pan
3. café / vino
4. torta / pollo y arroz

5. pan / queso
6. pastel / fruta
7. queso / torta y pastel
8. vino / café con crema y azúcar

D. Exprese su preferencia entre las siguientes opciones y explique la razón.

MODELO: una obra de teatro y un museo
Entre una obra de teatro y un museo, prefiero éste porque aquélla es demasiado cara.

1. la natación y el patinaje
2. una discoteca y un cabaret
3. el bridge y la canasta
4. las cartas y el ajedrez

5. un parque de atracciones y una obra musical
6. la música clásica y la música popular

V. Possessive adjectives and pronouns

Queridísima Chabela:

¿Cómo estás hoy, **mi** querido angelito? Todo marcha igual por aquí, muy pocas novedades. ¿Van bien **tus** clases? Las **mías** acaban el día 22 y después nos veremos...

Un amigo **mío**... ¿te acuerdas de Jaime?... quiere hacer una excursión a **su** casa de verano cerca de un lago este fin de semana. Tiene un barco de vela estupendo. Pero, la verdad: no sé si voy. Tú sabes, **mi** amor, que no me divierto mucho en estas excursiones sin ti. Creo que me quedaré en casa contemplando **tu** foto, repitiendo **tu** nombre, recordando **nuestros** momentos juntos y deseando de todo corazón que estés pensando en...

Tu Pedro

A. *Forms of possessive adjectives*

Short form		Long form	
Singular	**Plural**	**Singular**	**Plural**
mi	mis	mío/a	míos/as
tu	tus	tuyo/a	tuyos/as
su	sus	suyo/a	suyos/as
nuestro/a	nuestros/as	nuestro/a	nuestros/as
vuestro/a	vuestros/as	vuestro/a	vuestros/as
su	sus	suyo/a	suyos/as

1. The short forms of the possessive adjectives precede the noun they modify, and agree with the noun in gender and number. Possessive adjectives always agree with the object or person that is possessed, not with the possessor.

La fiesta es en **mi** casa.	*The party is in my house.*
Puedes invitar a **tus** amigos.	*You can invite your friends.*
Paco, **tu** vecino, viene con **su** novia.	*Paco, your neighbor, is coming with his girlfriend.*

2. The long forms of the possessive adjectives follow the noun they modify, and agree with that noun in gender and number. The long forms also always agree with the object or person that is possessed, not with the possessor.

Un amigo **mío** tiene una fiesta a fin de mes.	*A friend of mine is having a party at the end of the month.*
Te diré que las fiestas **suyas** son excelentes.	*I'll tell you that his parties are excellent.*

B. *Uses of possessive adjectives*

1. The short form possessive adjectives are more frequently used than the long form possessive adjectives. The long forms are often used for emphasis or contrast, or in constructions equivalent to *a friend of mine* (**un amigo mío**).

—¿**Tu** amigo Rubén juega al básquetbol?	*Does your friend Rubén play basketball?*
—Sí, está en el equipo de Antonio Véliz, un amigo **mío.**	*Yes, he's on the team of Antonio Véliz, a friend of mine.*
—Pues, **su** equipo no es muy bueno; el equipo **nuestro** es mucho mejor.	*Well, his team is not very good: our team is much better.*

2. In Spanish, the definite article is generally used instead of a possessive form when referring to parts of the body and articles of clothing.

¡Qué bueno que terminó el partido de básquetbol! Voy a quitarme **el** uniforme. ¡Me duele todo **el** cuerpo!	*I'm so happy the basketball game is over! I'm going to take off my uniform. My whole body aches!*

C. *Possessive pronouns*

1. The possessive pronouns are the same in form as the long form possessive adjectives.

—Mañana juega mi equipo de béisbol contra el **tuyo.**	*Tomorrow my baseball team plays against yours.*
—Pues, tu equipo va a perder: el **nuestro** es mejor.	*Well, your team is going to lose: ours is better.*

2. Possessive pronouns are used to replace a possessive adjective + a noun: **mi equipo** > **el mío.** They are generally used with a definite article and agree in gender and number with the noun they replace. After the verb **ser,** the article may be omitted. (See *Capítulo 10.3* for use of the neuter forms **lo mío, lo tuyo, lo suyo,** etc.)

—¿Es **tuyo** este balón de fútbol?   *Is this soccer ball yours?*
—No, no es **mío.** Dejé **el mío** en casa.   *No, it's not mine. I left mine home.*

D. *Clarification of third person possessive forms*

1. Third person possessive adjectives and pronouns **(su, sus, suyo/a, suyos/as)** may be ambiguous since they can refer to any of six possible possessors: **él, ella, usted, ellos, ellas, ustedes.**

Voy a **su** fiesta.   *I'm going to his/her/your/their party.*

2. In most cases, the context determines which meaning is intended. To clarify the intended meaning of a possessive adjective or pronoun, possessive phrases such as **de él, de ella, de usted,** etc. may be used after the noun.

Voy a la fiesta suya.   *I'm going to his/her/your/their party.*
Voy a la fiesta **de ella.**   *I'm going to her party.*
Voy a la suya.   *I'm going to his/hers/yours/theirs.*
Voy a la **de ustedes.**   *I'm going to yours.*

Comprehension questions

1. Which one of the following two sentences would you use to emphasize that only one of several invitations, yours (the speaker's), is lost? **No encuentro la invitación mía. No encuentro mi invitación.**

2. You stop to greet a friend on the street and ask about his/her family. Which of the following two questions is more commonly used to ask about your friend's family? **¿Cómo está tu familia? ¿Cómo está la familia tuya?**

3. You are at the theater with a friend and notice that she has a new dress. To talk about her dress, would you use the definite article **el** or the possessive adjective **tu** in each of the following sentences? **¡_____ vestido es muy elegante! Vas a tener que darme el nombre de la modista que te hizo _____ vestido.**

4. Several friends are talking about the number of posters in their collections. Which of the following two sentences would the last person who speaks be more likely to say? **La colección mía tiene cincuenta carteles. La mía tiene cincuenta carteles.** Explain your choice.

5. The following two sentences can be used to indicate that the speaker does not remember a female acquaintance's name: **No recuerdo el nombre de ella. No recuerdo su nombre.** Which one should be used in each of the following contexts?

—¿**Conoces a esa pareja?**   —¿**Conoces a esa joven?**
—**Él se llama Andrés, pero** _____ .   —**Sí, pero** _____ .

6. Review Pedro's letter at the beginning of this section. Indicate a pronoun that appears as a possessive adjective and as a possessive pronoun. How can you distinguish between the two uses?

Ejercicios

A. Complete el siguiente párrafo escrito por Pablo, el compañero de cuarto de Tomás y también el siguiente diálogo entre Pablo y Tomás con el equivalente en español de las palabras entre paréntesis.

Tomás me ha invitado al recital de canto de (*his*) _____ hermana Lupe. Lupe es una famosa cantante y (*her*) _____ actuaciones son siempre un gran acontecimiento en (*our*) _____ ciudad. (*Their*) _____ padres también eran cantantes famosos. (*My*) _____ afición por la música nunca ha sido grande, pero Lupe me ha cautivado con (*her*) _____ dinamismo y sensibilidad.

—Tomás, ¿tienes (*my*) _____ entradas para el concierto de esta noche? No encuentro (*mine*) _____ por ninguna parte.
—Claro que no tengo (*yours*) _____ ; pero (*mine*) _____ están aquí, encima de la cómoda.
—Mira, chico, que aquí hay cuatro; dos de éstas son (*mine*) _____ . Y ¿qué dices ahora?
—Digo que como siempre (*my*) _____ cosas están donde deben estar y (*yours*) _____ están donde no deben estar. ¡Qué chico más desorganizado!

B. Las siguientes personas van a pasar unas horas en la tertulia (*get-together*) de Emilio esta noche. Diga con quiénes piensan venir.

MODELO: Claudio / compañeros
          Claudio piensa venir con unos compañeros suyos.

1. Marta / socio   4. Guillermo y Juanita / pariente
2. nosotros / amigas   5. Francisco / tío
3. yo / colegas   6. Patricio y yo / prima

C. Después de una representación de una obra teatral, los actores tratan de identificar a los dueños de algunas cosas que se han dejado en los vestuarios (*dressing rooms*). Conteste las siguientes preguntas de ellos afirmativamente, según el modelo.

MODELO: ¿Es de Ud. este programa?
Sí, es mío.

1. ¿Es tuya aquella cámara?
2. ¿Son de los López estos boletos?
3. ¿Son de nosotros estos carteles?
4. Este disfraz de oso es de Julio, ¿verdad?
5. ¿De quién es toda esta ropa, de Emilia?
6. ¿Es de Berta este maquillaje?
7. ¿Es mía esta peluca?
8. Aquí hay una chaqueta y una camisa. ¿Son de Alberto?

D. Imagínese que está con un(a) amigo(a) en una fiesta. Están a punto de marcharse cuando su anfitrión(ona) les pregunta si tienen todo lo que trajeron. Con un(a) compañero(a) de clase, represente la situación, según el modelo.

MODELO: discos
E1:   *¿Tienes tus discos?*
E2:   *Sí, tengo los míos, pero mi novio(a) no tiene los suyos.*

1. guitarra	3. disfraz	5. platos
2. cintas de música	4. juegos	6. abrigo

E. Represente con otro(a) estudiante un diálogo similar al siguiente en que le pide prestado a su amigo(a) algo que necesita para hacer una excursión de camping. Use el nombre de otro(a) estudiante de la clase en la respuesta.

MODELO: una mochila
E1:   *¿Me puedes prestar una mochila?*
E2:   *Lo siento. Necesito la mía, pero a lo mejor (Carlos) puede prestarte la suya.*

1. un compás	3. unas botas	5. una linterna
2. un saco de dormir	4. una cantimplora	6. una tienda

VI. **Preguntar** versus **pedir**

1. The verb **preguntar**, *to ask*, is used to request information from someone.

Vamos a **preguntar** cuáles son las especialidades de la casa.	*Let's ask what the house specialties are.*
¿**Preguntaste** si aceptan tarjetas de crédito aquí?	*Did you ask if they accept credit cards here?*

2. The expression **hacer una pregunta** means *to ask a question.*

¿Me quieren **hacer alguna pregunta**   *Do you want to ask me any questions*
   sobre el menú?   *about the menu?*

3. **Preguntar por** means to *inquire about someone or something,* and the reflexive form **preguntarse** expresses *to ask oneself* and *to wonder.*

¿**Preguntamos por** Juan Miguel? Es   *Shall we ask (inquire) about Juan Mi-*
   camarero aquí, ¿verdad?   *guel? He's a waiter here, isn't he?*
¡A buena hora **te preguntas** si tienes   *A fine time to wonder if you have any*
   dinero!   *money!*

4. **Pedir (i)** expresses the English meanings *to ask for, to request someone to do something,* and *to order* (in a restaurant, etc.). Observe in the following examples that **pedir** means *to ask for* and does not require the preposition **por** or **para** to complete its meaning.

—¿**Pediste** un café para mí?   *Did you ask for (order) a coffee for*
                                  me?

—No, **pedí** la cuenta.   *No, I asked for the bill.*

¿Quieres **pedir** postre?   *Do you want to order dessert?*
¡**Piden** $10.00 por una botella de vino   *They're asking $10.00 for (in ex-*
   corriente!   *change for) a bottle of ordinary*
                                            wine!

Ejercicios

A. Indique qué verbo o expresión verbal se usa en español para comunicar la expresión indicada en inglés.

1. Your friends Pilar and Ramón *asked about you* at the banquet.
2. Julio *asked me for* the money for the tickets, but I'm broke.
3. First, Mario *asked* me a lot of questions, then he *asked* me to give him Sara's telephone number.
4. I *wonder* if he plans to invite her to the dance.
5. Some friends dropped by so we *ordered* a pizza and played some poker.
6. Did Carol *ask* you to take her home?

B. Unos amigos van por primera vez al restaurante "Los Gauchos". Complete los siguientes comentarios suyos con **preguntar, preguntarse, hacer preguntas** o **pedir** para saber cómo les fue allí.

1. Bueno, ya estamos en el famoso restaurante Los Gauchos. Elena, ¿ya sabes qué vas a _____ ?
2. Si no entiendes el menú, puedes _____ al camarero.

3. Por mi parte, no hay dudas; siempre _____ el arroz con pollo y una ensalada mixta.

4. Tardan mucho con la comida, ¿no les parece? ¿Quieres _____ si recuerdan que estamos aquí?

5. Debemos _____ a nuestros amigos si conocen otro restaurante mejor.

6. ¿Por qué no _____ la cuenta para pagar estas bebidas y luego salir? Podemos comer en otra parte.

7. ¡Qué lástima! A veces yo _____ cómo ganan dinero los negocios que tratan así a sus clientes.

8. Antes de salir para otro restaurante, quiero hablar con el gerente y _____ si este tipo de servicio es normal o si algunos camareros no pudieron trabajar esta noche.

Actividades para la comunicación

A. Diversiones y pasatiempos. Pase por la sala de clase y averigüe los pasatiempos de por lo menos tres estudiantes. Luego, dé una presentación a la clase según el modelo.

MODELO: *Encuentro que estas tres personas tienen los siguientes pasatiempos. Esta chica aquí juega al tenis, ese chico que está a su lado lee y aquél va a algún club para bailar.*

B. Entrevista. Imagínese que Ud. tiene la oportunidad de hacer dos preguntas a las siguientes personas famosas o a otras de su propia selección. ¿Qué preguntas haría Ud.?

MODELO: Julio Iglesias
E1: *Sr. Iglesias, ¿cuál es su canción favorita?*
E2: *Después de un concierto, ¿está Ud. muy cansado o quiere divertirse un poco?*

1. Cantinflas
2. Luis Buñuel
3. José Ferrer
4. El Rey Juan Carlos Borbón de España

5. Sofía Loren
6. Plácido Domingo
7. Fidel Castro
8. El Presidente de México

C. Situaciones. Con un(a) compañero(a) de clase, desarrolle un diálogo de por lo menos tres comentarios por persona, basado en las siguientes situaciones de la vida social.

1. Dos jóvenes piensan organizar una fiesta en dos semanas. Se hacen preguntas sobre la lista de los invitados y la comida.

2. Un(a) estudiante invita a un(a) joven a ir a un espectáculo de patinaje. El(La) joven no puede aceptar la invitación y se lo explica muy cortésmente.

3. Un(a) estudiante está en un café entre clases y pide algo para comer y para beber a un(a) camarero(a).

4. Hay dos fiestas muy interesantes este fin de semana y dos jóvenes hablan de la situación y tratan de decidir a qué fiesta asistir.

D. Una invitación. Acepte o rechace la invitación que le hace otro(a) estudiante de la clase. Si la rechaza, dé una razón. Puede utilizar algunas de las expresiones que aparecen a continuación para hacer la invitación.

¿Quieres...?   ¿Puedes...?   ¿Te apetece...?
¿Te gustaría...?   ¿Tienes ganas de...?   ¿Qué tal si...?

MODELO: una exposición de fotografía
           E1:   *¿Tienes ganas de ver la exposición de fotografía?*
           E2:   *Sí, con mucho gusto, gracias. (No, no puedo ir porque estoy muy ocupado[a] esta noche.)*

1. un torneo de tenis   4. un parque de atracciones
2. una comedia muy divertida   5. un espectáculo de variedades
3. una película de aventuras   6. un desfile de modas

E. Basándose en el siguiente dibujo y en el modelo, represente con otro(a) estudiante un diálogo de por lo menos tres comentarios por persona en que conversen sobre este conjunto musical, el tipo de música que toca, algo de lo que saben sobre la vida de uno de los músicos o cualquier otro aspecto del concierto que quieran mencionar.

MODELO: E1:   *¿Qué te parecen los Rockers? Son fantásticos, ¿verdad?*
           E2:   *Me gustan un poco, pero en mi opinión tocan canciones muy aburridas.*
           E1:   *¿Aburridas? Estoy seguro(a) de que ninguna otra persona piensa como tú.*
           E2:   ...

CAPÍTULO 3

◆

Viajes y turismo

Como el gobierno mexicano reconoce la importancia del turismo para su economía
nacional, estimula el desarrollo de complejos turísticos y la modernización de su sistema
de transporte.

Conversación

1. ¿Qué medio de transporte prefiere usar durante los viajes cortos? ¿Y en los largos? ¿Por qué?
2. Cuando está Ud. en una ciudad desconocida, ¿tiene problemas de orientación o le es fácil encontrar los sitios que busca? ¿Por qué?
3. ¿Prefiere Ud. comprar su pasaje de avión de un(a) agente de viajes o directamente de la aerolínea? ¿Por qué?
4. ¿Prefiere Ud. ir en una excursión organizada (*package tour*) o planear su propio itinerario? ¿Por qué?
5. ¿Saca Ud. muchas fotografías cuando viaja? ¿Manda postales a casa? ¿A quiénes?
6. Cuente alguna experiencia agradable de un viaje y otra desagradable.
7. En la foto de la página anterior, ¿le parece a Ud. que hay turistas entre los pasajeros que bajan del avión? ¿Qué le hace pensar que se trata de turistas?
8. ¿Conoce Ud. algunas atracciones turísticas en México? ¿Cuáles?

Vocabulario temático

acogida, la welcome, reception
aduana, la customs; customs house
arena, la sand
azafata, la stewardess, air hostess
demora, la delay
descuento, el discount
ducha, la shower (in bathroom)
equipaje, el luggage
escaparate, el store window
extranjero, el foreign country
formulario, el form, blank
gira, la tour
habitación, la room
horario, el schedule, timetable
huésped(a), el(la) guest
letrero, el sign
maleta, la suitcase
maravilla, la something wonderful
paisaje, el scenery, landscape
parada, la stop
pasaje, el ticket; passageway
pasajero(a), el(la) passenger
recorrido, el run, distance traveled
recuerdo, el souvenir; memory

reserva, la reservation
viajero(a), el(la) traveler
vuelo, el flight

despegar to take off (airplane)
facturar to check (luggage)
hospedar to lodge, to receive as a guest
parar to stop
recoger to pick up, to get

acogedor(a) welcoming, friendly
lujoso(a) luxurious
pintoresco(a) picturesque
playero(a) pertaining to the beach
vencido(a) expired; defeated

camino de (a) on the road (way) to
hacer escala to make a stopover
hacer las maletas to pack (luggage)
prestar declaración to make a formal declaration
tarjeta de seguro, la insurance card
tomar el sol to sunbathe

I. Verbs with irregular forms and spelling changes in the present indicative

Arturo:	¿Qué haces, Javier?
Javier:	Como ves, **hago** las maletas.
Arturo:	Ah, sí, **tienes** un viaje de negocios, ¿verdad?
Javier:	Sí, **salgo** mañana por la mañana, muy temprano. Por eso **tengo** que tener todo listo hoy.
Arturo:	¿Y quién te lleva al aeropuerto?
Javier:	¿Cómo? ¡**Eres** bastante olvidadizo, hombre! Me **dices** que me llevas y ahora no te acuerdas.
Arturo:	Perdona,... **estoy** en las nubes. No te preocupes; **conduzco** yo.

A. *Irregular first person singular*

Verbs ending in a vowel + -cer / -cir

> **conocer:** conozco, conoces, conoce, conocemos, conocéis, conocen
> **conducir:** conduzco, conduces, conduce, conducimos, conducís, conducen

1. Verbs that end in a vowel + **-cer** or **-cir** are irregular in the first person singular, which ends in **-zco**. All other forms are regular.

—No **conozco** muy bien el camino al aeropuerto.	*I don't know the road to the airport very well.*
—No te preocupes. **Conduzco** yo.	*Don't worry. I'll drive.*

2. Other verbs like **conocer** and **conducir** include:

agradecer	desconocer	ofrecer	producir
aparecer	establecer	parecer	reconocer
crecer	nacer	permanecer	traducir
desaparecer	obedecer	pertenecer	

First person singular ending in -go

hacer:	**hago,** haces, hace, hacemos, hacéis, hacen
poner:	**pongo**
salir:	**salgo**
traer:	**traigo**
valer:	**valgo**

1. Some verbs are irregular in the first person singular of the present indicative, which ends in **-go**. All other forms are regular, as shown by the verb **hacer** in the chart on the preceding page.

—¿Qué haces?	*What are you doing?*
—¿Yo? Pues, **hago** las maletas.	*Me? Well, I'm packing the suitcases.*
—¿Cuándo sales de viaje?	*When are you leaving on your trip?*
—**Salgo** a las tres.	*I'm leaving at three o'clock.*
¿Dónde **pongo** los boletos para no perderlos?	*Where do I put the tickets so as not to lose them?*

2. Note that the verb **traer** adds **i** before the **-go** ending. Other verbs like **traer** include **atraer, caer(se),** and **distraer(se)**.

Traigo muchos recuerdos de mi último viaje.	*I've got many souvenirs from my last trip.*
Nunca **caigo** en el error de llevar demasiado equipaje.	*I never make the mistake of carrying too much luggage.*

3. The verb **oír** is irregular in the first person singular, which ends in **-igo**. In addition, **oír** adds a **y** before the ending in all forms except in the first and second persons plural: **oigo, oyes, oye, oímos, oís, oyen.**

—¿**Oyes** el ruido de los motores?	*Do you hear the noise of the engines?*
—¿Qué dices? No **oigo** nada.	*What are you saying? I don't hear anything.*

First person singular ending in -go and stem change

tener	venir	decir
ten**go**	ven**go**	di**go**
tienes	vienes	dices
tiene	viene	dice
tenemos	venimos	decimos
tenéis	venís	decís
tienen	vienen	dicen

1. **Tener, venir,** and **decir** have two irregular features in the present indicative: the first person singular ends in **-go** and all other persons except the first and second persons plural have a stem change. The stems of **tener** and **venir** have a change from **e** to **ie;** the stem of **decir** has a change from **e** to **i**.

Vengo de la agencia de viajes. Me **dicen** que la excursión que **tienen** programada es formidable.

I'm coming from the travel agency. They tell me that the excursion they've planned is excellent.

2. Other verbs like **tener, venir,** and **decir** include **entretener, mantener, obtener, prevenir,** and **contradecir.**

Other verbs with irregular first person singular forms

caber	dar	saber	ver
quepo	**doy**	**sé**	**veo**
cabes	das	sabes	ves
cabe	da	sabe	ve
cabemos	damos	sabemos	vemos
cabéis	dais	sabéis	veis
caben	dan	saben	ven

Caber, dar, saber, and **ver** are regular in the present indicative with the exception of the first person singular. Note that the written accent is not retained for the **vosotros** form of **dar** and **ver.**

Mis maletas caben en el coche, pero yo ya no **quepo.**

My suitcases fit in the car, but I don't fit anymore.

Yo no **sé** dónde pones tú todas tus cosas.

I don't know where you put all your things.

B. *Irregular verbs*

estar	ser	ir
estoy	soy	voy
estás	eres	vas
está	es	va
estamos	somos	vamos
estáis	sois	vais
están	son	van

Estar, ser, and ir are irregular in the present indicative.

—¿**Estás** de vacaciones?	*Are you on vacation?*
—Sí, **estoy** de vacaciones por un mes.	*Yes, I'm on vacation for a month.*
—¿**Vas** a algún sitio?	*Are you going anywhere?*
—Sí, **voy** a la playa por dos semanas.	*Yes, I'm going to the beach for two weeks.*
—¡Qué afortunado **eres**!	*How lucky you are!*

C. *Spelling changes*

Verbs ending in a consonant + -cer

1. Verbs ending in a consonant + **-cer** have a spelling change from **c** to **z** in the first person singular in order to preserve the **s** sound in the stem: **convencer** > **convenzo.**

—Tenemos que convencer al guía que debemos salir temprano mañana.	*We have to convince the guide that we should leave early tomorrow.*
—Está bien, yo lo **convenzo.** No te preocupes.	*All right, I'll convince him. Don't worry.*

2. Other verbs like **convencer** include **ejercer** and **vencer.**

Verbs ending in -ger and -gir

1. Verbs that end in **-ger** and **-gir** have a spelling change from **g** to **j** before **-o** in the first person singular in order to preserve the **jota** sound in the stem: **recojo, dirijo.**

—¿A qué hora me recoges?	*What time will you pick me up?*
—Te **recojo** a las siete.	*I'll pick you up at seven.*

2. Other verbs in this group are **coger, corregir, exigir,** and **proteger.**

Verbs ending in -uir

1. Verbs ending in **-uir** have a spelling change from **i** to **y** before the ending in all forms except in the first and second person plural: **incluyo, incluyes, incluye, incluimos, incluís, incluyen.**

—¿Por qué tiene tanto éxito esa agencia de viajes?	*Why is that travel agency so successful?*
—Son muy responsables y siempre **incluyen** lugares interesantes en sus giras.	*They're very responsible and they always include interesting places in their tours.*

2. Other verbs in this group include **atribuir, concluir, constituir, contribuir, destruir, distribuir, excluir, influir, obstruir,** and **sustituir.**

Verbs ending in -iar and -uar

1. Some verbs that end in **-iar** and **-uar** require a written accent in all forms of the present indicative except the first person plural. Note that the accent in the **vosotros** form is part of the regular ending: **envío, envías, envía, enviamos, enviáis, envían; continúo, continúas, continúa, continuamos, continuáis, continúan.**

Siempre **envío** una postal a los abuelos cuando viajo.	*I always send my grandparents a post-card when I travel.*
Ellos **continúan** con nosotros hasta Santiago.	*They're continuing with us to Santiago.*

2. Other verbs like **enviar** include **ampliar, confiar, enfriar,** and **guiar.**

3. Other verbs like **continuar** include **acentuar, efectuar, graduar(se),** and **situar.**

4. Note that some common verbs like **apreciar, copiar,** and **estudiar** are regular.

Comprehension questions

1. The infinitive that corresponds to the form **tengo** is **tener.** Give the infinitives that correspond to the following verb forms: **caigo, quepo, pertenezco,** and **valgo.**

2. Which form of **merecer** is irregular: **mereces** or **merezco**?

3. Which form of **ver** is irregular: **ven** or **veo**? Explain the irregularity.

4. Is a verb ending in **-ger** like **recoger** subject to a stem change or a spelling change? Explain.

5. What are the two main irregularities in the present indicative of verbs like **tener, venir,** and **decir**?

Ejercicios

A. Ud. le cuenta a un(a) amigo(a) una experiencia que tuvo camino del aeropuerto. Complete el siguiente párrafo usando el presente de indicativo "histórico".

(Ser) _____ las ocho de la mañana. Yo (estar) _____ en un taxi que me (conducir) _____ al aeropuerto. El conductor (ir) _____ despacio porque detrás (venir) _____ dos coches de policía. Yo (tener) _____ que estar en el aeropuerto a las 8:15. El taxista (conocer) _____ bien la carretera pero yo (desconocer) _____ la distancia al

aeropuerto. (Estar) _____ muy nervioso(a) y le (decir) _____ al taxista que (ir) _____ a perder mi avión. Él me asegura que (ser) _____ un experto en crisis como ésta y me sonríe por el espejo retrovisor. De repente yo (oír) _____ la sirena de la policía. Eso me (convencer) _____ de que voy a perder el avión.

B. Imagínese que Ud. prepara la sección turística de su periódico local y tiene que viajar mucho. Diga lo que suele hacer cuando está de visita en las siguientes ciudades.

MODELO: Ciudad de México / dar una vuelta por el Zócalo
Cuando estoy en la Ciudad de México, siempre doy una vuelta por el Zócalo.

1. San Francisco / ver el Puente de *Golden Gate*
2. Santiago de Chile / tener tiempo para visitar el Cerro Santa Lucía
3. Lima, Perú / hacer compras en el Barrio Miraflores
4. Granada, España / ir a la Alhambra
5. Panamá / salir a dar un paseo cerca del Canal
6. Guadalajara, México / enviar una postal de la Plaza de los Mariachis
7. la región andina / incluir una visita a las ruinas en mi itinerario
8. Buenos Aires / permanecer allí unos días extras para visitar a unos amigos

C. Un(a) amigo(a) se pone muy nervioso(a) cuando se prepara para un viaje. Tranquílícelo(la) ofreciéndole su ayuda, según las indicaciones.

MODELO: ¡Todavía necesito una maleta! (prestarte una maleta)
No te preocupes. Yo te presto una maleta.

1. ¡Ay, qué cabeza la mía! Mi pasaporte está en mi oficina. (recogerte el pasaporte)
2. ¡Qué confusión! Necesito reservas de hotel todavía. (hacerte las reservas)
3. ¡Se me olvidó recoger mi pasaje de avión! (traerte el pasaje de la agencia)
4. ¡Estas maletas no llevan mi nombre! (ponerte el nombre en el equipaje)
5. ¡Nunca he pasado por la aduana! (decirte qué hacer en la aduana)
6. ¡No puedo dejar mi coche por tanto tiempo en el aeropuerto! ¿Quién lo conduce desde el aeropuerto a mi casa? (conducirlo a tu casa)

D. Usted acaba de comprar un pasaje de avión para ir de vacaciones a México. Conteste las siguientes preguntas que le hace un(a) amigo(a) quien también quiere ir de vacaciones. Use los verbos indicados en sus respuestas.

1. ¡Hola! ¿Cómo **estás**?
2. Veo que tienes un pasaje de avión; ¿**sales** pronto de viaje?
3. ¿**Confías** en que va a hacer buen tiempo entonces?
4. Bueno, yo creo que **merezco** unas vacaciones también, ¿y tú?
5. A propósito, ¿**sabes** cuándo abre la Agencia Meliá?
6. ¿**Conoces** a alguien en esa agencia?
7. Voy a conseguir un pasaje... ¿me **haces** un favor?
8. ¿Me **puedes** prestar una maleta? No tengo una maleta buena.

II. Uses of the verbs **ser, estar,** and **haber**

Víctor: (*Bostezando*) No entiendo nada. Llevamos una semana de vacaciones y **estoy** cansadísimo.

Sonia: Ah, lo que ocurre **es** que **eres** un caso excepcional. ¿**Hay** un museo interesante? Pues, allí tienes que **estar** tú. ¿**Hay** una exposición de arte, un concierto, una obra de teatro? Allí **estás** tempranito.

Víctor: Tenemos que aprovechar el tiempo. Las vacaciones **son** breves.

Sonia: Pero cuando regreses, ¡vas a tener que tomar vacaciones para descansar de tus vacaciones!

A. *Some uses of ser*

1. The verb **ser** is used before a noun or noun phrase to describe or define a subject, and often indicates equivalence between two noun phrases: **Avianca = aerolínea colombiana; mis dos hermanas = azafatas.**

Avianca **es** una aerolínea colombiana.	*Avianca is a Colombian airline.*
Mis dos hermanas **son** azafatas de Avianca.	*My two sisters are stewardesses for Avianca.*

2. **Ser** is used before prepositional phrases introduced by **de** to indicate origin, ownership, or the material of which something is made.

Ese piloto **es** de Colombia.	*That pilot is from Colombia.*
Este equipaje **es** del piloto.	*This luggage belongs to the pilot.*
Sus maletas **son** de cuero colombiano.	*His suitcases are (made) of Colombian leather.*

B. *Ser and estar + adjective*

1. The verb **ser** is used with adjectives describing characteristic and inherent qualities that can be verified objectively. Such adjectives include those of nationality, color, size, and shape.

El turismo **es** importante para la economía mexicana.	*Tourism is important for the Mexican economy.*
Esos turistas **son** mexicanos.	*Those tourists are Mexican.*
Sus maletas **son** grandísimas.	*Their suitcases are very big.*

2. **Estar** is used with adjectives to describe states and conditions, including unexpected or unusual qualities, or a change in the usual characteristics of a noun.

Después de varias horas, el avión **está** listo para despegar.	*After several hours, the plane is ready to take off.*
Los viajeros **están** nerviosos por la demora.	*The travelers are nervous due to the delay.*
Hasta el piloto **está** inquieto por el retraso en el horario.	*Even the pilot is anxious about the delay in the schedule.*

3. **Estar** frequently conveys the speaker's subjective perceptions regarding how someone or something *looks, feels,* or *tastes.* Compare the different meanings conveyed by **ser** and **estar** in the following sentences.

La comida en esta aerolínea **es** buena, pero hoy **está** terrible. La sopa **está** desabrida; el café **está** frío.	*The food in this airline is good, but today it's terrible. The soup is tasteless; the coffee is cold.*

4. Some adjectives convey different meanings depending on whether they are used with **ser** or **estar**.

Ese guía **es** aburrido; siempre repite lo mismo.	*That guide is boring; he's always repeating the same things.*
Los turistas **están** aburridos con su conferencia.	*The tourists are bored by his lecture.*
Es interesado; sólo **está** interesado en las propinas.	*He's selfish; he's only interested in tips.*

5. The following list shows the meanings conveyed by some common adjectives when they are used with **ser** and **estar**.

ser	estar
aburrido *boring*	aburrido *bored*
bueno *good*	bueno *healthy, good*
callado *reserved, quiet*	callado *silent*
interesado *selfish*	interesado *interested*
limpio *tidy*	limpio *clean* (now)
listo *smart, clever*	listo *ready*
loco *insane*	loco *crazy, frantic*
malo *evil*	malo *sick*
verde *green* (color)	verde *green* (not ripe)
vivo *alert, lively*	vivo *alive*

6. **Estar vivo** (*to be alive*) and **estar muerto** (*to be dead*) are viewed as conditions and are always expressed by **estar**.

—¿**Están vivos** los pasajeros?	*Are the passengers alive?*
—Sí, pero el piloto **está muerto**.	*Yes, but the pilot is dead.*

C. *Ser, estar, and haber for location*

1. The verb **ser** is used to locate definite events in space or time. In this construction, **ser** is a synonym for **tener lugar** (*to take place*).

La charla sobre un viaje por el Amazonas **es** a las siete de la tarde.	The talk about a trip along the Amazon River is at seven o'clock in the evening.
La charla **es** en el auditorio principal.	The talk is in the main auditorium.

2. The verb **estar** is used to locate definite persons or things in space or time.

El conferenciante va a **estar** en el auditorio a las dos.	The lecturer will be in the auditorium at two o'clock.
El auditorio **está** en la primera planta.	The auditorium is on the first floor.

3. The verb **haber** is used to locate indefinite events, people, or things in space or time. It asserts the existence of events and conditions.

Hay muchas personas en el auditorio.	There are many people in the auditorium.
Hay charlas todos los viernes aquí.	There are talks every Friday here.

D. *Estar and ser + past participle*

1. **Estar** is used with a past participle to express a condition or state that is often the result of an action. The past participle functions as an adjective and agrees in gender and number with the noun it modifies.

Nuestras reservaciones **están confirmadas.**	Our reservations are confirmed.
El itinerario ya **está decidido.**	The itinerary is already decided.

2. **Ser** is used with a past participle in a passive voice construction to refer to an action being performed. The person who performs the action, if stated, is expressed by a phrase with **por**. The past participle agrees in number and gender with the noun it modifies. Note that the passive voice construction with **ser** is not used as frequently in Spanish as in English (see *Capítulo 8.5*).

La excursión **es organizada** por la agencia de viajes La Continental.	The excursion is organized by the Continental Travel Agency.
Nuestras reservaciones **han sido confirmadas** por nuestra agente.	Our reservations have been confirmed by our agent.
El itinerario detallado **fue anunciado** hace unos días.	The detailed itinerary was announced a few days ago.

3. Compare the following sentences and observe that, when **estar** is used with a past participle, the focus is on the condition or state of being of the subject; when **ser** is used, the focus is on the action.

Nuestro viaje ya **está programado** y las reservaciones **están confirmadas.**	*Our trip is already planned and the reservations are confirmed.*
Nuestros viajes **son programados** por nuestro agente de viajes.	*Our trips are planned by our travel agent.*
Las reservaciones **son confirmadas** por la agencia de viajes.	*The reservations are confirmed by the travel agency.*

For other uses of **ser** and **estar,** consult the following sections of the text: **ser** with impersonal expressions, *Capítulo 9.3;* **estar** with progressive tenses, *Capítulo 6.2;* **ser** and **estar** with past participles, *Capítulo 8.1.*

Summary of the uses of ser, estar, and haber

Uses of ser

To describe or define a subject
To indicate origin, ownership, or material
To describe inherent, verifiable characteristics
To locate definite events
To express an action in the passive voice

Examples

Mi prima **es** directora de hotel.
Ese auxiliar de vuelo **es** de Perú.

¿**Es** de madera el yate?
La azafata **es** muy eficiente.
La celebración **es** allí.
El avión **fue asaltado** por terroristas.

Uses of estar

To describe states and conditions and for subjective appraisals
To locate definite persons and things
Followed by a past participle, to express a condition or state, often the result of an action

Examples

¿Quién **está** enfermo?
¿Por qué **estás** tan enfadada hoy?
Los huéspedes **están** allí.
Varios pasajeros **están** mareados; no **están** dormidos.
El asiento **está** ocupado.

Uses of haber

To locate an indefinite event, person, or thing; to assert the existence of events or conditions

Examples

Hay algunos alpinistas en el monte.
Dicen que **hay** mucha nieve allí.
Hay dos campamentos en ese lago.

Comprehension questions

1. Which of the equivalents of *to be,* **ser, estar,** or **haber,** are appropriate in the following sentences? **El vuelo _____ a las siete. A las siete _____ un vuelo.** Explain the reasons for your choices.

2. Which of the following sentences expresses surprise at how elegant a friend looks today? **¡Qué elegante estás! ¡Qué elegante eres!**

3. How would you describe a guide who is not a very entertaining person? **El guía es aburrido. El guía está aburrido.**

4. Does **¡Está vivo!** describe someone who is quite lively or someone found alive?

5. Is the verb *are* in the following sentences translated into Spanish by the same word? *They are from Venezuela. They are in Venezuela.* Explain.

6. In the following sentence, how would you indicate that all seats are taken? **Los asientos _____ ocupados.**

Ejercicios

A. La persona que viaja enfrenta muchas situaciones diversas. Explique cómo se siente Ud. en las siguientes situaciones. Termine las frases usando el verbo **estar** y adjetivos como **alegre, ansioso(a), cansado(a), confuso(a), emocionado(a), nervioso(a), satisfecho(a), triste,** etc.

MODELO: Cuando sueño con hacer un viaje,...
Cuando sueño con hacer un viaje, estoy muy contento(a).

1. Al planear mi itinerario,...
2. Cuando trato de decidir cuánto dinero me va a costar el viaje,...
3. El día antes de la salida,...
4. En el momento de partir,...
5. Precisamente cuando el avión despega,...
6. Al llegar a mi destino,...
7. Si no sé el idioma del país adonde voy,...
8. Cuando tengo que concluir el viaje,...

B. Diga dónde están los siguientes lugares en la ciudad donde Ud. vive y qué hay cerca de ellos.

MODELO: los campos de tenis
Los campos de tenis están en el parque deportivo. Hay dos gasolineras en la esquina.

1. la casa de su mejor amigo(a)
2. su tienda de ropa favorita
3. el estadio de fútbol
4. los dormitorios universitarios
5. la piscina
6. su banco
7. un buen restaurante
8. la alcaldía

C. Con un(a) compañero(a) de clase, represente un diálogo que ocurre en una tienda para turistas en un puerto libre. Siga el modelo.

MODELO: flores: Japón / seda
E1: *¿De dónde son estas flores?*
E2: *Creo que son de Japón.*
E1: *¿Y de qué material son?*
E2: *Pues, son de seda.*

1. blusa: Chile / poliéster
2. figuras: La República Dominicana / cerámica
3. poncho: Bolivia / lana
4. gorro: País Vasco / algodón
5. zapatillas: Perú / piel de llama
6. utensilios: México / madera

D. Ud. acaba de volver de un viaje que no salió muy bien. Use la forma correcta de **estar** o **ser** y exprese su disgusto a otro(a) estudiante. Incluya expresiones como los siguientes:

¡Qué desastre!   ¡No lo vas a creer!
¡Un problema tras otro!   ¡Ay, qué viaje!

MODELO: los hoteles: caro / incómodo
¡Qué desastre! ¡Los hoteles allí son muy caros y también son incómodos!

1. las habitaciones: pequeño / mal arreglado
2. el transporte público: lento / irregular
3. el metro: lleno / viejo
4. el agua de las playas: frío / sucio
5. el cambio del dólar: bajo / difícil de obtener en muchos lugares
6. los museos: mal cuidado / cerrado al mediodía

E. Con otro(a) estudiante, complete los siguientes diálogos con la forma correcta de **ser, estar** o **haber**, según el caso.

1. —José _____ muy listo; siempre _____ capaz de resolver todos sus problemas durante un viaje.
—Sí, pero también _____ muy interesado; no ayuda a nadie.

2. —Mi pasaporte _____ vencido. ¿Dónde puedo renovarlo?
—_____ varios lugares en el centro, pero a estas horas _____ cerradas las oficinas.

3. —¿_____ algún viaje a México para el mes próximo?
—Sí, señora, _____ salidas todas las semanas, y también _____ algunas excursiones que _____ bastante baratas. ¿_____ Ud. interesada en algún lugar especial?
—Sí, en el Yucatán. Todo el mundo dice que _____ una zona muy bella.
—Tiene razón. Las ruinas y las playas _____ fabulosas.

4. —Por fin tengo algunos planes firmes. Yo _____ interesado en partir el próximo sábado. ¿_____ algún vuelo muy temprano?
—Tiene suerte; _____ uno que sale a las siete y media. ¿_____ bien?
—Magnífico. Y ¿_____ éste un vuelo sin paradas o hace escala en alguna
parte?
—Hace una sola parada, pero _____ directo. No _____ necesidad de cambiar
de avión.

III. Descriptive adjectives

Mario: Bueno, ya hemos visto muchos hoteles y tenemos que decidirnos. ¿En cuál
nos hospedamos? ¿En ese hotel **lujoso** de la calle del Sol?

Elisa: No sé; los hoteles **lujosos** son siempre caros. ¿Te acuerdas de aquel **pequeño** y **simpático** hotel de la calle Miramar? ¿Qué te parece?

Mario: Muy bien. Tiene habitaciones **espaciosas, limpias** y muy **acogedoras.**

Elisa: Y además tiene una **estupenda** vista de la ciudad. Allí nos hospedamos, ¿de
acuerdo?

Mario: Perfecto.

A. *Forms of descriptive adjectives*

1. In general, adjectives that end in unstressed -o in the masculine singular have four
forms: masculine and feminine, and singular and plural. Adjectives that end in
any other vowel or a consonant generally have two forms: singular and plural.

	Singular	Plural
Four-form adjective ending		
Unstressed vowel **-o** in the masculine singular	apurado, apurada	apurados, apuradas
Consonant in masculine singular and refers to nationality or ends in **-án, -ín, -ón,** or **-or**	español, española juguetón, juguetona hablador, habladora holgazán, holgazana pequeñín, pequeñina	españoles, españolas juguetones, juguetonas habladores, habladoras holgazanes, holgazanas pequeñines, pequeñinas
Two-form adjective ending		
Vowel other than **-o** in the masculine singular	triste deportista	tristes deportistas
Consonant other than previously mentioned in the masculine singular	real fácil cortés feliz	reales fáciles corteses felices

2. The following antonym pairs of adjectives ending in **-or** have only two forms:

mejor(es)	peor(es)	interior(es)	exterior(es)
menor(es)	mayor(es)	anterior(es)	posterior(es)
superior(es)	inferior(es)		

—¿Cuáles son los **mejores** hoteles y pensiones de la ciudad?

—Bueno, el **mejor** hotel es el Cervantes y la **mejor** pensión es la Pensión Palenque.

Which are the best hotels and boarding houses in town?

Well, the best hotel is the Cervantes and the best boarding house is the Palenque.

3. A few adjectives have two masculine singular forms: a shortened form is used when the adjective precedes a masculine singular noun. Common adjectives in this group include the following.

bueno	buen	santo	san
malo	mal	tercero	tercer
primero	primer		

Te deseo un **buen** viaje.
No es un **mal** día para viajar.
Es mi **primer** vuelo.
Estoy en el **tercer** asiento.

I wish you a happy trip.
It's not a bad day to travel.
It's my first flight.
I'm in the third seat.

4. The adjective **grande** (*big, large*) also has a shortened form, **gran,** that is used before either a masculine or a feminine singular noun. Note that **gran (grandes)** means *great* when it precedes the noun it modifies.

¡Qué **gran** idea la de venir!
Son **grandes** amigos.
No tengo maletas **grandes.**

What a great idea to come!
They are close (great) friends.
I don't have big suitcases.

5. The shortened form of **santo, san,** is used before a masculine singular noun, except when the noun begins with **To** or **Do: Santo Tomás** and **Santo Domingo,** but **San Pedro.**

B. *Agreement of descriptive adjectives*

1. Descriptive adjectives agree in gender and number with the noun they modify.

Nos hospedaremos en un hotel **moderno** en el centro.
Tiene habitaciones **espaciosas** y **limpias.**

We'll stay at a modern hotel downtown.
It has spacious and clean rooms.

2. If a single adjective follows and modifies two or more nouns, one of which is masculine, the masculine plural form of the adjective is used.

Aquel turista lleva una corbata y un sombrero **negros.**	*That tourist is wearing a black tie and a black hat.*
La guía distribuye unos folletos y unas revistas **peruanos.**	*The guide is distributing Peruvian brochures and magazines.*

3. If a single adjective precedes and modifies two or more nouns, it agrees with the first noun.

Vimos **maravillosas** ruinas y monumentos por todo el país.	*We saw wonderful ruins and monuments throughout the country.*

C. *Position of adjectives*

General usage

1. A descriptive adjective usually follows the noun it modifies. When the descriptive adjective follows the noun, it specifies or restricts the noun; that is, it sets the noun apart from other nouns in the same category.

Los hoteles **lujosos** son caros.	*Luxury hotels are expensive.*
¿Son las ruinas **aztecas** las más antiguas?	*Are the Aztec ruins the oldest?*

2. When the descriptive adjective precedes the noun it modifies, no contrast with other nouns in the same category is implied. The focus is on the noun itself, and the adjective stresses an important or inherent quality of the noun.

Los **lujosos** hoteles del norte me encantan.	*I love the luxury hotels in the north.*
¿Te acuerdas de aquel **lindo** hotel donde estuvimos en San Sebastián?	*Do you remember that pretty hotel where we stayed in San Sebastián?*

3. Use of an adjective before a noun occurs more frequently in written Spanish as a rhetorical device in fiction, poetry, or essays. It is also common in oratory.

Debemos revitalizar nuestra **debilitada** economía. Tenemos que explotar la **extraordinaria** belleza de nuestra **privilegiada** región con una **vigorosa** campaña para promover el turismo.	*We must revitalize our weakened economy. We have to exploit the extraordinary beauty of our privileged region with a vigorous campaign to promote tourism.*

Adjectives that usually follow the noun

1. Adjectives that refer to color, shape, or nationality, and adjectives related to disciplines, technology, and the sciences usually follow the noun they modify because they distinguish the noun from others in the same category.

El turismo es importante para la economía **mexicana.**

Tourism is important for the Mexican economy.

La economía es diversificada: industria **petrolera,** producción **automotriz,** etc.

The economy is diversified: oil industry, automobile production, etc.

2. For purposes of emphasis, adjectives of color or shape may precede the adjective, especially to achieve a poetic effect.

Usted puede contemplar **rojos** atardeceres desde esas playas de **claras** aguas.

You can contemplate red sunsets from those beaches of clear water.

Adjectives that usually precede the noun

Proper nouns refer to a unique person or thing. Since the name distinguishes the noun, a descriptive adjective precedes a proper noun and is used to emphasize a characteristic of the noun.

¿Conoces al **intrépido** Andrés? Pues, va a escalar el **imponente** Popocatépetl.

Do you know that intrepid Andrés? Well, he's going to climb the imposing Popocatépetl (a volcano).

Adjectives with a change in meaning

1. There are a number of adjectives that have a change in meaning depending upon whether they are used before or after the noun. When the adjective precedes the noun, it often has a figurative, abstract meaning: **viejo amigo** emphasizes a friend of long standing. When the adjective follows the noun, it often has a more concrete, objective meaning: **amigo viejo** emphasizes a friend who is old in age.

Antonio no es un hombre **viejo.** Somos **viejos** amigos y sé de lo que hablo.

Antonio is not an old man. We're old friends and I know what I'm talking about.

La Trinidad, iglesia **grande** e imponente, es un **gran** atractivo turístico.

The Trinidad, a large and imposing church, is a great tourist attraction.

2. The following chart shows the different meanings of some adjectives, depending on their position in relation to the noun.

	Before the noun	After the noun
cierto	*some, certain*	*sure, certain*
gran/grande	*great, excellent*	*big, tall*
medio	*half*	*middle*
mismo	*same*	*(the thing) itself*
nuevo	*another, different*	*brand new*
pobre	*pitiful, poor*	*destitute, poor*
propio	*own*	*proper*
puro	*sheer*	*pure, unadulterated*
viejo	*of old standing, former*	*aged, old*

Shading meaning with adjective position

1. An adjective that evaluates the noun it modifies by referring to subjective qualities (**importante, impresionante, increíble, urgente, complicado**) may precede or follow the noun, depending on the intent of the speaker. The adjective follows the noun if the speaker wants to contrast one noun with another. Adjectives that follow the noun give the impression of conveying more objective or factual information.

Tengo una noticia **importante.**	*I have an important piece of news.*
Necesito resolver unos asuntos **urgentes** antes del viaje.	*I need to settle some urgent matters before the trip.*
La aduana tiene una lista de reglamentos **complicados.**	*Customs has a list of complicated regulations.*

2. The adjective precedes the noun if the speaker wishes to stress the quality of the noun itself, regardless of possible contrasts; the contrasts either do not exist or are ignored by the speaker. Adjectives that precede the noun give the impression of conveying more emotional or exaggerated information.

Las **imponentes** alturas de Machu Picchu nos impresionaron a todos.	*The imposing heights of Machu Picchu impressed us all.*
Fue una **inolvidable** experiencia.	*It was an unforgettable experience.*

3. Compare the position and meaning of the descriptive adjectives in the following examples.

El piloto recibió una llamada **urgente** de la torre de control.	*The pilot received an urgent call from the control tower.*
El piloto respondió rápidamente a la **urgente** llamada de la azafata.	*The pilot quickly responded to the urgent call from the stewardess.*
Pasamos unas horas **aburridas** en el aeropuerto en espera del vuelo.	*We spent a few boring hours at the airport waiting for our flight.*
Carlos nos dio una **aburrida** explicación de cada foto de su último viaje.	*Carlos gave us a boring explanation about each picture of his last trip.*

Noun modified by two or more adjectives

1. The same principles governing the position of single adjectives apply when several adjectives modify a noun. Adjectives precede the noun to stress the qualities themselves, and follow the noun to establish an implicit contrast with other nouns.

Me escribe mi **estimado** y **recordado amigo** Claudio.	*My dear and well-remembered friend Claudio writes to me.*
Quiere visitar **ruinas mayas, aztecas o incas.**	*He wants to visit Mayan, Aztec, or Incan ruins.*

2. If a sentence combines subjective and objective adjectives, the subjective adjective usually precedes the noun, and the objective adjective usually follows the noun.

Piensa escribir una **interesante novela épica moderna.**	*He intends to write an interesting modern epic novel.*

Comprehension questions

1. Which of the following sentences would you use to talk about a trip you are taking in your brand new car? **Voy de viaje en mi nuevo coche. Voy de viaje en mi coche nuevo.** What does the other sentence mean?

2. Would you use **San** or **Santo** in each of the following sentences? _____ **Domingo es la capital de la República Dominicana. Voy a ir a la fiesta de** _____ **Carlos.**

3. Which of the following two phrases implies that all ruins are impressive? **las ruinas impresionantes, las impresionantes ruinas**

4. You are writing an article on tourism for a newspaper. Which of the following two sentences would you write to give a more factual tone? **Creemos que nuestra investigación presenta datos importantes para apreciar el impacto del turismo. Creemos que nuestra investigación presenta importantes datos para apreciar el impacto del turismo.**

5. Review the dialogue at the beginning of this section. Explain the special meaning given by Mario and Elisa to **hotel** by using the adjective **lujoso** after the noun. Why does Elisa use **pequeño** and **simpático** before the noun?

Ejercicios

A. Describa a los personajes y el escenario del dibujo usando tantos adjetivos de la lista como sea posible.

bien vestido	elegante	intrépido	misterioso
calvo	espacioso	joven	oscuro
cobarde	estrecho	limpio	pequeño
cortés	fuerte	mal vestido	sucio
delgado	gordo	miedoso	viejo

MODELO: *La mujer es delgada. Ella no es cobarde.*

1. la mujer
2. el hombre
3. los dos juntos
4. el sótano
5. las escaleras

B. El director de Aerolíneas Cóndor expresa su satisfacción con algunos nuevos empleados. Lea la descripción que hace de Rodolfo y luego cambie la descripción para que se aplique primero a Josefina y después a Florencia y a Ramón juntos.

Rodolfo es un buen empleado porque es puntual, trabajador y cooperativo. Es un joven bastante bajo, delgado y fuerte y todos creen que es extraordinariamente simpático. Es el primer empleado portugués que tenemos en la aerolínea.

C. Ud. quiere hacer un viaje a Yucatán pero no quiere ir solo(a). Por eso trata de convencer a su amigo(a) que lo(la) acompañe describiéndole algunos de los atractivos de la región. Use las frases que se dan a continuación y hable con mucha exageración.

MODELO: playas (magnífico), arena (blanco), aguas (cristalino)
Yucatán tiene unas magníficas playas de blanca arena y cristalinas aguas.

1. hoteles (maravilloso), habitaciones (lujoso), ruinas (famoso)
2. clima (fantástico), días (caluroso), noches (templado)
3. tienda (fabuloso), objetos (precioso), vendedores (amable)
4. estilo de vida (encantador), costumbres (pintoresco), cultura (variado)

D. Traduzca al español las siguientes oraciones.

MODELO: The first flight to Caracas is at 6 A.M.
El primer vuelo a Caracas es a las seis de la mañana.

1. I need a new (different) passport.
2. The trip itself is not a bad idea, but we made the same trip last year.
3. The travel agent is the woman with the large suitcase.
4. Venezuela has a certain quality that I like very much.
5. That monument to Bolívar is a great work of art.

IV. The personal a

Rosario: Sonríe, sonríe. ¿Ves **a aquel señor** en la otra acera?
Diana: (*Perpleja*) No, no veo **a ningún señor.** Sólo veo una cámara fotográfica inmensa y muchos otros aparatos.
Rosario: Pues mira bien. Detrás de todos esos aparatos, vas a ver **a un señor** que nos saca una foto.
Diana: Ah, sí, ahora lo veo. El turismo, qué bendición, ¿no? Ya ni podemos comprar frutas tranquilamente en la plaza del mercado.

A. *Before a direct object referring to a person*

1. A direct object that refers to a specific person or persons is normally preceded by the preposition **a.** This usage is sometimes referred to as the *personal a.*

¿**A quién** buscamos? Buscamos **a nuestra guía.**
Quiero conocer **a mis parientes chilenos.**

Who(m) are we looking for? We're looking for our guide.
I want to meet my Chilean relatives.

2. When the direct object does not refer to anyone specific, the preposition **a** is generally not used.

Necesitan turistas ingleses para promover el turismo.	*They need English tourists to promote tourism.*

3. After the verbs **tener** and **haber** the preposition **a** is normally not used before a direct object referring to a person. When **tener** is equivalent to *to hold* or *to be,* the personal **a** is used.

No tengo hijos varones.	*I don't have sons.*
Tengo dos hijas; sólo hay una hija aquí conmigo.	*I have two daughters; there is only one daughter here with me.*
Tengo **a mi hija** aquí conmigo.	*I have my daughter here with me. (My daughter is here with me.)*
Tengo **a mi otra hija** enferma.	*I have my other daughter sick. (My other daughter is sick.)*

B. *Before indefinite expressions*

1. The preposition **a** is always used before **alguien** (*someone*) and **nadie** (*no one*) when they are used as direct objects.

—¿Esperas **a alguien**?	*Are you waiting for someone?*
—No, no espero **a nadie**.	*No, I'm not waiting for anyone.*

2. The preposition **a** is also used before **todo, alguno,** and **ninguno** when they refer to people and are used as direct objects.

Debo hacer unas llamadas para invitar **a algunos amigos.**	*I have to make a few calls to invite a few friends.*
Quiero invitar **a todos mis vecinos** también.	*I want to invite all my neighbors too.*

C. *With actions usually associated with humans*

The preposition **a** is used before a nonhuman direct object in order to give that object human qualities. This personification is frequently used to stress the importance of the object or concept to an individual.

El poeta saluda **a las flores** en sus versos.	*The poet greets the flowers in his verses.*
No encuentro **a mi gatito.**	*I can't find my kitten.*
Conoce íntimamente **a Madrid.**	*He knows Madrid well.*

For further information on the personal **a,** consult *Capítulo 6.3;* for indefinite expressions, see *Capítulo 6.4.*

Comprehension questions

1. In which of the following two sentences would you use the personal **a** before the direct object? **¡Por fin encuentro _____ los pasaportes! ¡Por fin encuentro _____ mi padre!**

2. Which of the following two sentences better expresses the fact that you do not have a specific person in mind, that is, that any tall stewardess will do? **Necesitamos a una azafata alta. Necesitamos una azafata alta.**

3. In which of the following two sentences would you use the preposition **a** before the direct object? **No reconozco _____ ninguna maleta. No reconozco _____ ningún pasajero.**

Ejercicios

A. Complete las siguientes oraciones con la preposición **a** si es necesaria. Preste atención a la contracción **al.**

1. ¿Vas a acompañar _____ tu esposo en su viaje?
2. ¿Cuándo vas a facturar _____ las maletas?
3. Quiero reservar _____ nuestros asientos.
4. Me interesa conocer _____ el piloto del avión.
5. La azafata cuenta _____ los pasajeros antes de despegar.
6. Busco _____ una azafata; quiero tomar café.
7. Veo _____ la azafata al fondo del avión.
8. ¿Buscas _____ tu mamá? ¿No? Entonces, ¿_____ quién buscas?

B. Ud. es un(a) turista muy curioso(a). Mira con mucho interés todo lo que encuentra a su alrededor y saca muchas fotografías. Diga a su compañero(a) de viaje lo que va a fotografiar.

MODELO: la estatua de Pancho Villa
          Voy a fotografiar la estatua de Pancho Villa.

1. aquel palacio
2. aquellos jóvenes cerca de la playa
3. el hombre del traje marrón
4. ese letrero tan curioso
5. los futbolistas que juegan en aquel campo
6. aquellos rascacielos nuevos
7. toda la gente que hace cola allí
8. los turistas de aquel grupo

V. Direct and indirect object pronouns

Carlos:	¡Oye, Manolo, faltan solamente tres días para la excursión de esquí!
Manolo:	Sí, hombre, ¡y espero pasar**lo** muy bien!
Carlos:	A propósito, ¿tenemos boletos para el tren del sábado?
Manolo:	No, pero **los** puedo comprar esta tarde porque voy a pasar por la agencia.
Carlos:	Entonces, ¿**te** doy el dinero ahora o más tarde?
Manolo:	**Me lo** puedes dar más tarde, cuando **te** dé los boletos. No me gusta andar con mucho dinero encima.

A. *Direct object pronoun forms*

Singular		Plural	
me	*me*	nos	*us*
te	*you* (familiar)	os	*you* (familiar)
lo	*him, you* (formal, m.)	los	*them* (m.), *you* (formal, m.)
la	*her, you* (formal, f.)	las	*them* (f.), *you* (formal, f.)

1. A direct object pronoun is used to replace a direct object phrase when the context is clear.

—¿Qué ves?	*What do you see?*
—Veo un anuncio.	*I see an announcement.*
—Yo también **lo** veo.	*I see it too.*

—¿A quién ves?	*Who(m) do you see?*
—Veo a mis amigos.	*I see my friends.*
—Yo también **los** veo.	*I see them too.*

2. A direct object pronoun generally precedes a conjugated verb. See pages 86 and 87 for more on the position of object pronouns.

Compro los boletos y luego **los** pongo en un lugar seguro.	*I'll buy the tickets and then put them in a safe place.*

3. Note that in some regions of Spain and Hispanic America, **le** is often used as a direct object pronoun instead of **lo** when referring to people.

Vi a Andrés y **le** invité a salir con nosotros el próximo fin de semana.	*I saw Andrés and I invited him to go out with us next weekend.*

4. The invariable pronoun **lo** is used to refer to previously mentioned ideas or qualities. In this usage, **lo** refers back to a direct object clause or to the complement of linking verbs such as **ser, estar,** and **parecer.** In English, this use of **lo** either has no equivalent or is translated as *so* or *it.*

—Alicia, ¿crees que podemos ver el Museo Antropológico esta tarde?	*Alicia, do you think we can see the Anthropological Museum this afternoon?*
—No **lo** creo. ¿**Lo** dejamos para mañana?	*I don't think so. Can we leave it for tomorrow?*
—Está bien. Pareces cansada y probablemente **lo** estás.	*It's all right. You seem tired and you probably are.*

B. *Indirect object pronoun forms*

Singular		Plural	
me	*(to) me*	nos	*(to) us*
te	*(to) you* (familiar)	os	*(to) you* (familiar)
le (se)	*(to) him, her, you* (formal, m./f.)	les (se)	*(to) them, you* (formal, m./f.)

1. Indirect object pronouns have the same forms as direct object pronouns in the first and second persons: **me, nos; te, os.**

2. Third person indirect object pronouns vary in number only: **le** (singular), **les** (plural).

3. In Spanish, indirect object pronouns usually precede a conjugated verb. In English, a prepositional phrase, such as *to her, for me, from us,* is frequently used instead of an indirect object pronoun. This construction is not used in Spanish. Compare the following Spanish and English sentences.

Me vende los boletos.	*He sells the tickets to (for) me.*
Le compro los boletos.	*I buy the tickets from (for) him/her/ you.*
Nos da los boletos.	*He/She gives us the tickets (gives the tickets to us).*

4. In Spanish, the indirect object in the third person singular and plural is generally expressed twice in the same sentence: with the indirect object pronoun **le** or **les** and with a phrase beginning with **a.** There is no English equivalent for the redundant indirect object pronoun.

Le pido información **al agente de viajes.**	*I ask the travel agent for information.*
Les prepara un viaje **a sus clientes.**	*He's preparing a trip for his customers.*
Les promete mandar los boletos **a los viajeros** en seguida.	*He promises to send the tickets promptly to the travelers.*

5. The indirect object pronouns **me, te, nos,** and **os** can be emphasized by adding the phrases **a mí, a ti, a nosotros/as,** and **a vosotros/as,** respectively.

Te traigo los boletos.	*I'm bringing the tickets for (to) you.*
A ti te traigo los boletos.	*I'm bringing the tickets for* ***you*** *(just for you).*

6. The indirect object pronouns **le** and **les** can refer to six different persons: **a él, a ella, a Ud., a ellos, a ellas,** and **a Uds.** When context does not clearly indicate the correct interpretation of **le** and **les,** a phrase beginning with **a** may be added for clarification as well as for emphasis.

Carlos **le** factura el equipaje.	*Carlos is checking the luggage for him (her, you).*
Carlos **le** factura el equipaje **a ella.**	*Carlos is checking the luggage for her.*

C. *Uses of the indirect object pronoun*

In Spanish, indirect objects are frequently used in the following contexts:

Verbs and expressions	Examples
Verbs of communication: **hablar, contar, decir, explicar**	**Le explico** mi plan de viaje a Rosa.
Verbs of giving: **dar, entregar, pasar**	**Le doy** todos los detalles.
Verbs of taking: **arrancar, quitar, robar**	**Le quito** todas sus dudas.
Verbs indicating state of mind: **alegrar, gustar, indignar, molestar, ofender, sorprender**	**Me sorprende** su falta de comprensión.
Verbs indicating the person affected in impersonal expressions: **costar, faltar, ser difícil/importante/urgente,** etc.	**A mi compañero de viaje le es difícil** entender los problemas de Rosa.
	Me falta la reserva de hotel todavía.
Verbs used with reference to parts of the body, clothing, and personal belongings: **doler, quebrar(se), fracturar(se), romper(se), lavar(se), poner(se), quitar(se), planchar, coser, arreglar**	**A Rosa le duele la cabeza** de tanto viajar hoy.
	Le lavo la ropa para su viaje.

D. *Position of object pronouns*

1. The indirect object pronoun precedes the direct object pronoun when the two are used together.

¿El pasaporte? El agente **me lo** revisa.	*The passport? The agent is inspecting it for me.*
¿Dónde está mi visado? El agente **me lo** pide.	*Where is my visa? The agent is asking me for it.*

2. The indirect object pronouns **le** and **les** are changed to **se** when used with the direct object pronouns **lo, la, los,** and **las.** The meaning of **se** can be clarified by a prepositional phrase with **a.**

—¿Me da usted sus boletos, señor?	*Will you give me your tickets, sir?*
—Sí, **se los** doy ahora mismo.	*Yes, I'll give them to you right now.*
—¿Me pasa usted su pasaporte?	*Will you give me your passport?*
—Cómo no, **se lo** paso de inmediato.	*Of course, I'll give it to you right away.*
—¿Tienes mi pasaporte?	*Do you have my passport?*
—Todavía no. **Se lo** di al agente.	*Not yet. I gave it to the agent.*

3. The object pronouns immediately precede a conjugated verb in all the simple and perfect tenses and in negative commands.

La explicamos.	*We explain it.*
Te la explico.	*I explain it to you.*
Te la hemos explicado.	*We have explained it to you.*
¡No **me la** expliques!	*Don't explain it to me!*

4. The object pronouns used with a verb form that includes an infinitive or a present participle may precede the conjugated verb or may be attached to the infinitive or the present participle. When pronouns are attached to an infinitive or present participle, a written accent is frequently needed to maintain the proper stress of the verb.

Lo queremos consultar. (Queremos consultar**lo**.)	*We want to consult him.*
Te la estoy explicando. (Estoy explicándo**tela**.)	*I am explaining it to you.*

5. Object pronouns are always attached to affirmative commands, thus forming a single word. A written accent is frequently needed to maintain the proper stress of the verb.

¡Contéstame, háblame!	*Answer me, speak to me!*

6. First person affirmative plural commands drop the final **s** of the ending before the object pronoun **se** or **nos.**

Saqué**monos** las fotos para el pasaporte.	*Let's get our pictures taken for our passports.*
¿Los boletos? Envié**mose**los a Amanda.	*The tickets? Let's send them to Amanda.*

Summary of direct and indirect object pronouns

Sequence:	(se)	me	lo(s)
		te	la(s)
		nos	le(s)
		os	

Position:	Object pronoun(s) + verb	Verb + object pronoun(s)
Infinitive:	**Me** va a hablar.	Va a hablar**me.**
Present participle:	**Me** está hablando.	Está hablándo**me.**
Simple tense:	**Me** habla.	
Perfect tense:	**Me** ha hablado.	
Affirmative command:		¡Háblame!
Negative command:	¡No **me** hables!	

Comprehension questions

1. What pronoun(s), **las** or **les,** would you use in the following sentence to talk about some female friends of yours? _____ **llevamos al aeropuerto y** _____ **facturamos el equipaje.**

2. **Me duele el brazo** means *My arm hurts.* How can you stress in Spanish that *my* (and not someone else's) arm hurts?

3. Would you use **se** or **le** in each of the following sentences? **El turista** _____ **escribe una tarjeta postal a su esposa. El turista** _____ **la escribe.** Explain your choices.

4. The pronoun **se** in a sentence such as **Se la doy** can refer to six different people receiving something. Give four possible meanings of this sentence in English.

5. The sentence **Voy a visitar las ruinas** has two versions when **las ruinas** is replaced by a direct object pronoun. **Voy a visitarlas** is one version. What is the other one?

Ejercicios

A. Su compañero(a) de cuarto quiere saber a quiénes desea invitar Ud. a una pequeña fiesta para ver fotos de su último viaje a Sudamérica.

MODELO: Emilia
      E1: *¿Piensas invitar a Emilia?*
      E2: *¿A Emilia? Claro que la invito.*

1. Leonardo
2. Marcos y Luis
3. Chabela
4. Dorotea y Rosalía
5. tus amigos de la universidad
6. las chicas del trabajo
7. el estudiante de Chile
8. la amiga de Roberto

B. Un(a) amigo(a) le ayuda a hacer las maletas para su próximo viaje a Costa Rica y también le pregunta sobre las cosas que va a llevar. Dígale si las necesita o no y explique por qué.

MODELO: la maleta nueva
      E1: *¿Vas a llevar la maleta nueva?*
      E2: *Sí, la necesito porque mi maleta vieja ya no sirve.*

1. la máquina de afeitar
2. el papel para la correspondencia
3. los sobres de correo aéreo
4. las zapatillas
5. los mapas de la América Central
6. la calculadora
7. el diccionario de español
8. las vitaminas

C. Ud. forma parte de un grupo de estudiantes que visita Santander, España. Van a un parque para comer y hablan de las cosas que tienen para comer y beber. Haga un breve diálogo, según el modelo.

MODELO: una botella de soda
      E1: *Aquí tengo una botella de soda. ¿Quién la quiere?*
      E2: *A ver, Tomás y yo la queremos, gracias.*

1. un poco de queso
2. unas manzanas
3. unos huevos cocidos
4. una barra de chocolate
5. un bocadillo de chorizo
6. unos botes de Coca Cola
7. unas galletas sabrosas
8. una tortilla de patata

D. Bárbara acaba de regresar de un viaje a Puerto Rico y les entrega a sus amigos unos regalos. Describa lo que le da a cada uno.

MODELO: unos escudos puertorriqueños / a Fernando
Bárbara le da unos escudos puertorriqueños a Fernando.

1. unas sandalias de cuero / a Claudio
2. una novela de aventuras / a Rita
3. un mapa de la isla / a Paula y a Esteban
4. unos libros de cocina / a ti
5. unos artefactos típicos / a los señores Moreno
6. un disco muy popular / a su profesor de español
7. una camisa de deportes / a mí
8. unas tarjetas postales / a nosotras

E. Haga preguntas a otro(a) estudiante de la clase sobre los siguientes temas, según el modelo. El primer estudiante repite la respuesta para toda la clase. Atención: algunas frases no tienen complemento directo (*direct object*).

MODELO: prestar dinero a tus amigos para un viaje
E1:   *¿Les prestas dinero a tus amigos para un viaje?*
E2:   *Sí, se lo presto.*
E1:   *Dice que se lo presta.*

1. molestar (a ti) los preparativos para un viaje
2. contar (a mí) lo que haces cuando estás en Sudamérica
3. mandar tarjetas postales a tu novio(a) cuando estás de viaje
4. escribir muchas cartas a tus familiares sobre las maravillas que ves
5. gustar (a ti) los atractivos turísticos en general
6. ser molesto (a ti) cuando no sabes el idioma del país donde viajas
7. traer regalos a tus amigos después de un viaje
8. enseñar tus fotografías a tus colegas de trabajo

VI. **Saber** versus **conocer**

1. The verbs **saber** and **conocer** both express *to know* in Spanish. **Saber** is used to express *to be aware of, to understand, to know because of study or memorization,* or *to find out something for the first time.*

El guía **sabe** que es una ruta muy difícil.	*The guide knows that it is a very difficult route.*
¿**Saben** todos lo que deben llevar en el viaje?	*Does everyone know what they should wear on the trip?*

| Luisa puede ayudarnos en Barcelona porque **sabe** hablar catalán. | *Luisa can help us in Barcelona because she knows how to speak Catalan.* |
| Anoche **supimos** que íbamos a llegar a Barcelona durante la feria. | *Last night we found out that we were going to arrive in Barcelona during the city celebration.* |

2. **Conocer** is used to express *to know a person, to meet a person for the first time, to be familiar with a particular place or object*, and usually refers to knowledge that can be acquired firsthand.

Nosotros no **conocemos** a ningún catalán.	*We don't know any Catalonians.*
¡Cuántas ganas tengo de **conocer** a algunos hablantes de catalán!	*I'm so anxious to meet some native speakers of Catalan!*
—¿**Conoces** la ciudad de Barcelona?	*Are you familiar with (Do you know) the city of Barcelona?*
—Yo, no, pero Toni **conoce** bien las calles del centro.	*I don't, but Toni knows the downtown streets firsthand.*

Ejercicios

A. Pídale más información a un(a) compañero(a) de clase sobre las siguientes personas, cosas o lugares. Use los verbos **saber** o **conocer,** según el caso.

MODELO: ¿_____ bien las calles del centro?
E1: *¿Conoces bien las calles del centro?*
E2: *Sí, las conozco muy bien.*

1. ¿_____ cuándo partimos para la región catalana?
2. ¿Qué idiomas _____ hablar? ¿Hablas catalán?
3. ¿Qué restaurantes buenos _____ en Barcelona?
4. ¿_____ dónde se encuentran las Ramblas?
5. ¿_____ tus amigos que yo te acompaño en el viaje?
6. ¿Cuándo voy a _____ a algunos de tus amigos?
7. ¿_____ lo que me cuenta mi mamá de Cataluña?
8. Hay unas playas estupendas en la Costa Dorada. ¿_____ nadar bien?
9. ¿_____ los museos más importantes de Barcelona?
10. ¿_____ cómo se llega al museo de pintura de Picasso?

B. Imagínese que un(a) compañero(a) de clase prepara un viaje a España. Hágale preguntas usando **saber** o **conocer.**

MODELO: qué aerolínea vas a usar
E1: *¿Sabes qué aerolínea vas a usar?*
E2: *Sí, voy a usar Iberia.*

1. las costumbres de los españoles
2. qué documentos necesitas para el viaje
3. a alguien en Gerona
4. cuál es el itinerario de tu recorrido por España
5. cambiar tu dinero a pesetas
6. la comida española
7. algo sobre la política española

Actividades para la comunicación

A. ¡Decisiones, siempre hay que tomar decisiones! Ud. ha pasado dos semanas maravillosas en México, pero mañana tiene que volver a casa. Está pensando en los regalos y recuerdos que quiere comprar para sus amigos y parientes. Piense en una o varias personas y exprese su decisión según el modelo, mencionando también cuándo se lo va a dar.

MODELO   1:   *A Susana le compro un anillo de cobre. Se lo doy pasado mañana si puedo.*

MODELO   2:   *A mis tíos les llevo suéteres de muchos colores. Se los entrego la próxima semana.*

B. Adivinanzas. Con los adjetivos de la lista u otros, haga una descripción de una ciudad, monumento, museo u otro sitio que Ud. ha conocido en un viaje. Pare después de cada oración para que sus compañeros puedan adivinar lo que es.

alto(a)	cercano(a)	enorme	lejano(a)
antiguo(a)	cómodo(a)	frío(a)	nuevo(a)
caluroso(a)	divertido(a)	interesante	pintoresco(a)

MODELO: E1:   *Pienso en una ciudad antigua y muy alta.*
E2:   *Creo que es Denver.*
E1:   *No, Denver no es antigua. Ésta es una ciudad sudamericana.*
E3:   *¿Es La Paz, Bolivia?*
E1:   *Sí, tienes razón.*

C. Consejos. Con un(a) compañero(a) de clase, desarrolle un diálogo de cuatro comentarios por persona en el cual uno(a) de Uds. describe lo que quiere hacer durante sus vacaciones y el(la) otro(a) le da consejos. Trate de incluir los verbos **ser, estar, haber, saber** y **conocer.**

MODELO: E1:   *Quiero conocer un lugar nuevo. ¿Sabes dónde hay unas playas estupendas y unos hoteles excelentes pero no muy caros?*
E2:   *¿Conoces la playa de Manzanillo? Es grande, el agua no es muy fría y los hoteles son bien razonables.*
E1:   *¿Hay mucha gente joven allí? (Continúe)*

D. Conversaciones. Desarrolle con un(a) compañero(a) de clase diálogos de por lo menos tres comentarios por persona, basándose en las siguientes situaciones relacionadas con el turismo.

1. Ud. pasa por la aduana y contesta las preguntas del(de la) aduanero(a) sobre dónde ha viajado, por cuánto tiempo y las cosas que trae del extranjero.
2. Ud. quiere ir con Carlos y Manolo a una excursión de esquí. Haga una reserva de hotel e incluya la siguiente información en su diálogo: tipo de habitación que quiere (individual, doble o triple), por cuánto tiempo, si quiere ducha o baño completo, el precio y si incluye el desayuno.
3. Ud. se encuentra por primera vez en Santo Domingo, capital de la República Dominicana, y necesita pedir direcciones a varios sitios a uno de los empleados de su hotel (el Teatro Nacional, la Plaza de la Cultura, el Mercado Modelo, la Catedral Santa María la Menor, el Museo del Hombre Dominicano, el Alcázar [*Fortress*] de Colón).

E. ¡Por fin las vacaciones! Ud. es uno(a) de los pasajeros en el autobús del dibujo. Estudie la escena, y luego explique oralmente o por escrito por qué hace Ud. la excursión, con quiénes la hace, y cómo es el sitio donde va a tomar unas vacaciones. Describa cómo es alguna persona del grupo.

CAPÍTULO 4

•

Los medios de comunicación

El personal técnico de un estudio de televisión de San Juan, la capital de Puerto Rico, sigue el desarrollo de un programa.

Conversación

1. ¿Lee Ud. el periódico todos los días? ¿A menudo? ¿Poco? ¿Qué sección del periódico prefiere Ud. leer? ¿Por qué?
2. ¿Qué tipo de programas prefiere Ud. ver en la televisión? ¿Y en la radio?
3. ¿Cree Ud. que en general la prensa informa imparcialmente al público? Diga por qué tiene esa opinión.
4. Se dice que una sola imagen vale más que mil palabras. Piense en el anuncio de televisión que más le llama la atención. ¿Por qué le gusta tanto?
5. Semanalmente se publican 1.383 revistas en este país. ¿Compra Ud. revistas con frecuencia? ¿Está Ud. suscrito(a) a alguna revista? ¿Cuál?
6. Si pudiera Ud. crear un periódico, ¿qué secciones nuevas propondría Ud.?
7. Mire la fotografía de la página anterior. ¿Qué tipo de programa, cree Ud., están mirando los técnicos?
8. En su opinión, ¿qué medio de comunicación influye más a la gente? Dé razones.

Vocabulario temático

aviso, el piece of information; advice; warning
cadena, la network; chain
caricatura, la caricature, cartoon
censura, la censorship, censoring
cita, la quote; appointment; date
corresponsal, el(la) correspondent
crónica, la column, feature story
diseño, el design; sketch, drawing
documental, el documentary
edición, la edition; publication
ejemplar, el copy, issue
guionista, el(la) scriptwriter
imagen, la image, picture
imprenta, la printing house
locutor(a), el(la) announcer
mensaje, el message
noticiero, el newscast
periodismo, el journalism
portavoz, el(la) spokesperson
propaganda, la advertising; propaganda
publicidad, la advertising
radioemisora, la radio station
reportaje, el news report
televidente, el(la) television viewer
titular, el headline

averiguar to find out, to inquire
censurar to censor, to censure
desmentir (ie, i) to deny
dibujar to design; to draw
entrevistar to interview
imprimir to print
redactar to write; to edit
verificar to verify

controvertido(a) controversial
enfático(a) emphatic
escandaloso(a) shocking
fiable reliable
llamativo(a) attractive, eye-catching
televisivo(a) television-related

artículo de fondo, el in-depth report, editorial
en primera plana on the first page
medios de comunicación, los mass media
noticias meteorológicas, las weather report
rueda de prensa, la press conference
testigo ocular, el(la) eyewitness
tiras cómicas, las comic strips

I. The preterit

Lima, 6 de noviembre.

Esta mañana **ocurrió** un atraco en el Banco Continental. Según declaraciones de la policía, un hombre joven, delgado, de más o menos 1,75 de estatura, con el rostro cubierto por una máscara, **entró** en las oficinas centrales del Banco Continental alrededor de las once de la mañana. **Amenazó** a un cajero con un revólver, **pidió** una cantidad indeterminada de dinero y **huyó**. **Subió** en un automóvil que esperaba frente al banco. La policía **hizo** preguntas a varios testigos, pero no **obtuvo** ninguna pista importante.

A. *Regular forms*

-ar verbs	-er verbs	-ir verbs
trabajar	**comer**	**vivir**
trabaj**é**	com**í**	viv**í**
trabaj**aste**	com**iste**	viv**iste**
trabaj**ó**	com**ió**	viv**ió**
trabaj**amos**	com**imos**	viv**imos**
trabaj**asteis**	com**isteis**	viv**isteis**
trabaj**aron**	com**ieron**	viv**ieron**

1. The preterit endings of regular **-er** and **-ir** verbs are the same.

   Anoche Miguel **trabajó** en la radioemisora hasta las nueve.
   Last night Miguel worked at the radio station until 9 o'clock.
   Luego **comió** y **decidió** dar un paseo antes de acostarse.
   He then ate and decided to take a stroll before going to bed.

2. Regular **-ar** and **-ir** verbs have the same form in the first person plural of the preterit and present indicative. Context usually clarifies which is intended.

   No **entrevistamos** al Presidente hoy porque lo **entrevistamos** ayer.
   We're not interviewing the President today because we interviewed him yesterday.

B. *Stem-changing -ir verbs*

e > ie/i	o > ue/u	e > i/i
preferir	**dormir**	**pedir**
preferí	dormí	pedí
preferiste	dormiste	pediste
prefirió	durmió	pidió
preferimos	dormimos	pedimos
preferisteis	dormisteis	pedisteis
prefirieron	durmieron	pidieron

1. Stem-changing verbs ending in **-ir** have an irregular stem in the third person singular and plural of the preterit: **e > ie** verbs change **e** to **i**; **o > ue** verbs change **o** to **u**; **e > i** verbs change **e** to **i**. All other forms of **-ir** stem-changing verbs are regular in the preterit.

Yo le **pedí** una explicación del accidente al policía, pero en lugar de darme una explicación me **pidió** identificación.	*I asked the policeman for an explanation concerning the accident, but instead of giving me an explanation he asked me for identification.*
Yo **preferí** escribir los titulares, pero los otros reporteros **prefirieron** redactar el artículo.	*I preferred to write the headlines, but the other reporters preferred to write the article.*
El pobre reportero **durmió** mal después de presenciar el accidente.	*The poor reporter slept badly after witnessing the accident.*

2. Stem-changing verbs ending in **-ar** and **-er** are regular in the preterit. (See *Capítulo 2.1* for stem-changing verbs in the present.)

El reportero **se despertó, encendió** la radio y **comenzó** a escuchar las noticias. **Hablaron** del atraco al Banco Continental.	*The reporter woke up, turned the radio on, and began to listen to the news. They talked about the holdup at the Banco Continental.*

C. *Irregular verbs*

1. The verbs **andar, caber, estar, poder, poner, saber,** and **tener** have an irregular stem containing the stem vowel **u** in the preterit. There is no written accent on the first and third person singular endings since stress is on the next-to-last syllable.

	Stems of other irregular verbs like **tener**
Model: tener	
tuve	andar: **anduve**
tuv**iste**	caber: **cupe**
tuv**o**	estar: **estuve**
tuv**imos**	poder: **pude**
tuv**isteis**	poner: **puse**
tuv**ieron**	saber: **supe**

—Los bomberos **pusieron** una escalera bajo las ventanas.

The firefighters put a ladder under the windows.

—¿**Pudiste** obtener informaciones de la tragedia?

Were you able to get information about the tragedy?

—**Tuve** una entrevista con el comandante de los bomberos, pero nunca **supe** la causa de la tragedia.

I had an interview with the commander of the firefighters, but I never found out the cause of the tragedy.

2. The preterit form of the impersonal expression **hay** (*there is/there are*) is **hubo** (*there was/there were*).

Hubo un incendio a las primeras horas de la madrugada.

There was a fire at the crack of dawn.

3. The verbs **hacer, querer,** and **venir** have an irregular stem in the preterit containing the stem vowel **i**. (Note that there is a spelling change in the third person singular of **hacer: c** changes to **z** to maintain the pronunciation of the stem.)

hacer	**querer**	**venir**
hice	quise	vine
hic**iste**	quis**iste**	vin**iste**
hizo	quiso	vino
hic**imos**	quis**imos**	vin**imos**
hic**isteis**	quis**isteis**	vin**isteis**
hic**ieron**	quis**ieron**	vin**ieron**

El candidato **vino** a la ciudad, pero no **quiso** hablar con los reporteros.

The candidate came to town, but he refused to talk to the reporters.

Un portavoz **hizo** declaraciones más tarde.

A spokesman made some statements later.

4. The verbs **decir, traer,** and **traducir** have an irregular stem ending in **-j** in the preterit. The ending of the third person plural is **-eron,** not **-ieron.**

decir	traer	traducir
dij**e**	traj**e**	traduj**e**
dij**iste**	traj**iste**	traduj**iste**
dij**o**	traj**o**	traduj**o**
dij**imos**	traj**imos**	traduj**imos**
dij**isteis**	traj**isteis**	traduj**isteis**
dij**eron**	traj**eron**	traduj**eron**

El Ministro de Asuntos Exteriores no **dijo** mucho durante la entrevista.
Los intérpretes **tradujeron** sus palabras.
Todos piensan que **trajo** un mensaje de paz.

The Minister of Foreign Affairs did not say much during the interview.
The interpreters translated his words.
Everybody thinks he brought a message of peace.

5. Verbs such as **conducir, deducir, introducir, producir,** and **reducir** follow the pattern of **traducir.**

El último discurso del Presidente **produjo** confusión. Algunas declaraciones **introdujeron** malentendidos entre los periodistas que lo entrevistaban.

The President's last speech caused some confusion. Some statements created misunderstandings among the journalists who were interviewing him.

6. The verbs **ir** and **ser** have identical forms in the preterit. Context determines which verb is intended. Note that there is no written accent on monosyllabic forms.

---

ir and **ser: fui, fuiste, fue, fuimos, fuisteis, fueron**

El debate entre los candidatos **fue** ayer.
Muchos periodistas **fueron** a la rueda de prensa que hubo después.

The debate among the candidates was yesterday.
Many journalists went to the press conference that took place afterwards.

7. The verb **dar** has the same endings as regular **-er** and **-ir** verbs in the preterit, except it has no written accent: **di, diste, dio, dimos, disteis, dieron.**

En sus anuncios televisados, los candidatos **dieron** sus opiniones sobre los acontecimientos recientes.

In their TV spots, the candidates gave their opinions on recent events.

D. *Verbs with spelling changes*

1. When the stem of an **-er** or **-ir** verb ends in a vowel, the regular preterit endings of the third person singular and plural change to **-yó** and **-yeron.** All other forms of the verb are regular.

—**Leí** el informe. Ud. también lo **leyó,** ¿verdad?
—Sí, todos lo **leyeron.**

I read the report. You read it too, didn't you?
Yes, everybody read it.

2. Some verbs that undergo this spelling change include **caer, creer, huir, influir, leer,** and **oír.**

—¿**Oyeron** ustedes lo que dijo el locutor?
—Sí, según él los sospechosos **huyeron** en un Fiat blanco.

Did you hear what the radio announcer said?
Yes, according to him the suspects fled in a white Fiat.

3. Verbs ending in **-car, -gar,** and **-zar** have a spelling change in the first person singular of the preterit in order to preserve the pronunciation of the last consonant of the stem: **c** becomes **qu; g** becomes **gu;** and **z** becomes **c.** All other forms of the preterit are regular.

Busqué el micrófono de mi grabadora.
Almorcé con un corresponsal de *La Nación.*
Entregué la cinta antes de las cinco a la radioemisora.

I looked for the microphone to my tape recorder.
I had lunch with a correspondent of La Nación.
I delivered the tape before five o'clock to the radio station.

4. Some common verbs that have these spelling changes include the following:

c > qu: buscar, indicar, sacar, and **tocar**
g > gu: entregar, jugar, llegar, and **pagar**
z > c: alcanzar, almorzar, comenzar, and **empezar**

5. Verbs ending in **-guar** have a change from **u** to **ü** in the first person singular of the preterit in order to preserve the pronunciation of the vowel **u**. All other forms of the verb are regular. Verbs of this type include **apaciguar, atestiguar,** and **averiguar.**

Averigüé más detalles sobre el accidente aéreo.	*I found out more details about the plane wreck.*
Las declaraciones de los ejecutivos de la aerolínea **apaciguaron** los ánimos.	*The statements by the executives of the airline calmed people down.*

Comprehension questions

1. Give the infinitives that correspond to the following preterit forms: **traduje, puse, me entretuve, supe.**

2. Give the infinitives that correspond to the following preterit forms: **fui, di, bebí.** Which of these three forms is regular? Explain how you can tell.

3. Explain the spelling changes of the following preterit forms: **apagué, influyó, averigüé.**

4. Identify which of the following verb forms in the preterit is also a form of the present indicative: **salimos, bebimos, vendimos, perdimos.**

5. The sentence **Fue por la mañana** could be the answer to the following two questions: **¿Cuándo fue el accidente?; ¿Cuándo fue el periodista al lugar del accidente?** Give the two meanings of the answer in English.

6. Give the two preterit forms of the verb **corregir** that have a stem change.

Ejercicios

A. Cambie Ud. el presente de indicativo por el pretérito para así describir un día en la vida de Máximo, reportero del periódico *Las Últimas Noticias*.

MODELO: Por la mañana, Máximo se dirige a su escritorio, deja allí su cuaderno y va por una taza de café.
Por la mañana, Máximo se dirigió a su escritorio, dejó allí su cuaderno y fue por una taza de café.

1. Frente a la cafetera, se encuentra con el director de programación, quien le felicita por su último reportaje.
2. Los dos hombres se dan la mano y luego charlan sobre la próxima reunión del Concejo Municipal.

3. Máximo vuelve a su mesa de trabajo y hace una serie de llamadas telefónicas.
4. Se informa de la agenda de la reunión y arregla una entrevista con dos miembros del Concejo Municipal.
5. Luego Máximo busca un taxi y se reúne con los dos políticos en un café.
6. Los políticos le expresan su punto de vista y piden su cooperación.
7. Después de una hora, termina la entrevista y los tres van a la reunión del Concejo Municipal.
8. Al concluir la reunión, el reportero corre al teléfono, se conecta con una colega y le lee su reportaje.

B. La película "Obsesión" se estrenó con un rotundo fracaso. El presidente de MGM habla con el director de la película. Haga el papel del director y use verbos apropiados en el pretérito al responder.

MODELO: *Presidente:*   Pero, ¿no estudiaron ustedes el mercado?
               Director: *Sí, ¡claro que lo estudiamos! Nunca esperamos una re-*
                             cepción tan mala a la película.

1. ¿Escogieron Uds. a los actores?
2. ¿Por qué no reescribieron las partes más flojas?
3. ¿Tuvieron alguna idea de este fracaso durante la filmación?
4. ¿Redactaron los periodistas de *El Diario* su crítica?
5. ¿Por qué no corrigieron los errores al editar la película?
6. ¿Entrevistaron a los actores en televisión?
7. ¿Averiguaron cuántos cines quitaron ya la película de su programación?
8. ¿Saben Uds. que destruyeron mi reputación?

C. Explique a un(a) amigo(a) las siguientes circunstancias relacionadas con su trabajo de redactor(a) en la revista *Imágenes*. Termine la frase de una manera lógica.

MODELO: Hoy no pienso trabajar tarde porque anoche...
            Hoy no pienso trabajar tarde porque anoche trabajé hasta las ocho y
            media.

1. Muchas veces llego a la oficina temprano, pero esta mañana...
2. Normalmente empiezo a trabajar a las siete y media, pero esta mañana...
3. Típicamente los reporteros están aquí hasta las cinco, pero ayer...
4. No vamos a publicar más artículos sobre el alcalde porque en el número pasado ya...
5. Generalmente el fotógrafo va con Elena, pero esta mañana...
6. De ahora en adelante no publico ningún artículo sin verificar los datos porque en el número pasado...

D. Ud. conversa con un(a) amigo(a) sobre unos sucesos recientes. Conteste las preguntas de su amigo(a) y añada alguna observación personal.

MODELO: mirar el debate televisado entre los dos candidatos
E1: *¿Miraste el debate televisado entre los dos candidatos?*
E2: *Sí, lo miré y me pareció pura propaganda.*

1. leer la noticia sobre la sobrepoblación en el último número de *El País*
2. ver el artículo sobre Panamá
3. informarse de los últimos datos sobre la inflación
4. enterarse de la crítica sobre la telenovela "Rosita"
5. escuchar el reportaje sobre el próximo viaje del presidente
6. oír el último rumor sobre el reciente concierto de rock

II. Uses of the preterit

(*Noticiero radial*)
En una rueda de prensa esta tarde, el señor Antonio Briceño, portavoz del Ministerio de Hacienda, **explicó** la reciente devaluación de la moneda nacional. El señor Briceño se **puso** muy incómodo cuando le **pidieron** su opinión sobre las declaraciones del Diputado Zúñiga, miembro del partido de oposición. **Calificó** de irresponsables las declaraciones de este parlamentario. En una entrevista que **concedió** hace dos días, el señor Zúñiga **declaró** que el país está entrando en un nuevo ciclo inflacionario. El señor Briceño **desmintió** esa aseveración y **enfatizó** que la mayoría de los indicadores económicos muestran que el nivel de los precios al consumidor no ha subido.

A. *Concept of the simple past tense*

In Spanish the simple past tense has two sets of verb forms: the preterit and the imperfect. These tenses express different aspects or perceptions of the past and are not interchangeable. In general terms, the preterit describes completed past actions or events; the imperfect describes habitual or repeated actions in the past or a past action or event viewed as it was in progress. (*See Capítulo 5.2* for a discussion of the imperfect versus the preterit.)

Fui a la rueda de prensa, pero no **aprendí** nada nuevo.	*I went to the press conference, but I didn't find out anything new.*
Había muchos reporteros allí que **hacían** preguntas ajenas al tema discutido.	*There were many reporters there who were asking questions irrelevant to the topic being discussed.*

Los reportajes en directo (live) *atraen la atención del público que observa a un ciudadano hacer declaraciones para un canal de televisión en Barcelona, España.*

B. *Completed action*

1. The preterit is used to express a past action or series of actions that are viewed as completed.

Recibí una noticia estupenda: me **aceptaron** en el programa radial "Nuevas Voces". Por eso **llamé** a todos mis amigos, les **conté** la noticia y luego **tuvimos** una fiesta.	*I received a wonderful piece of news: they accepted me at the radio program "Nuevas Voces." So I called all my friends, told them the news, and we then had a party.*

2. The preterit may focus on the beginning or the end of a past action, state, or event, or it may view the action in its entirety from beginning to end. The use of time references establishes whether the beginning, the end, or the whole duration of an action is expressed: **a las cinco** (beginning); **hasta las seis** (end); **de las cinco a (hasta) las seis, entre las cinco y las seis** (from beginning to end).

El Presidente **comenzó** a hablar a las cinco por la televisión. **Habló** hasta las seis.	*The President began to talk at five o'clock on television. He spoke until six o'clock.*
Ese día yo **escribí** a máquina entre la una y las cinco de la tarde y luego **escuché** el discurso presidencial.	*That day I typed between one and five in the afternoon and then listened to the presidential speech.*

3. The preterit, with or without an explicit time boundary, conveys the idea of completed action. Speakers tend to use a time boundary when the time reference is not obvious or has not been previously mentioned: **dos veces por semana, el viernes pasado, (durante) doce horas.**

El mes pasado el Presidente **habló** dos veces por la televisión.

Last month the President spoke twice on television.

El viernes pasado no **ocurrió** nada de interés periodístico durante las primeras horas de la mañana.

Last Friday nothing newsworthy happened during the early morning hours.

Trabajé doce horas y me **acosté** totalmente agotado.

I worked for twelve hours and went to bed completely exhausted.

C. *Changes in state or condition*

Sudden or abrupt changes in mental or physical states or conditions in the past are expressed in the preterit.

Al oír la noticia por la radio, no **supe** qué pensar.

Upon hearing the news on the radio, I didn't know what to think.

Primero me **sentí** triste. Pero después **pensé** que debía reaccionar.

First I felt sad. But then I thought that I should react.

Por eso me **senté** a redactar una carta al director de la radioemisora.

That's why I sat down to write a letter to the director of the radio station.

D. *Hace + a time expression with the preterit*

Hace and a time expression used with a verb in the preterit corresponds to English *ago*. Observe, in the following examples, the two basic preterit constructions with **hace**: preterit verb + **hace** + time expression and **hace** + time expression + **que** + preterit verb.

Filmé el documental **hace tres semanas.**

I filmed the documentary three weeks ago.

Hace dos días que se estrenó en los cines.

It premiered in the movie houses two days ago.

For other uses of **hace** with time expressions, consult *Capítulo 1.2* and *Capítulo 9.4.*

Comprehension questions

1. Which of the following sentences indicates a change in emotional condition and would therefore require the preterit in Spanish? *I was sad. I became sad.*

2. Why is the preterit used in the following sentence? **Anoche escuché la radio hasta las once de la noche.** And in the following sentence? **Me contó la historia de su vida.**

3. How would you express the following sentence in Spanish? *Two months ago there was an interesting debate on TV.* In what other way could you express this same sentence?

4. Review the news report that appears at the beginning of this section. Point out a preterit verb form that focuses on the beginning of a past action and one that signals an abrupt change in state or condition.

Ejercicios

A. Lea la siguiente carta de la sección ''Cartas al director'' de un periódico. Complete la carta con los verbos indicados en el pretérito.

Sr. Editor:

Hace una semana Uds. (publicar) _____ en su sección de ''Nuevas ideas'' un artículo que yo (escribir) _____ sobre el tema del uso del vídeo en el aula. Para ese artículo (conseguir) _____ hacerles una entrevista a varios profesores. También (entregar) _____ una encuesta a 100 estudiantes para averiguar sus opiniones. El resultado fue que muchas personas (llamar) _____ a mi casa y (pedir) _____ más información sobre el uso del vídeo en el aula. En mi artículo (decir) _____ que el interés del público no era muy grande, opinión que todas las llamadas (corregir) _____. Es obvio que en mi artículo (cometer) _____ un error y agradezco a sus lectores su generosidad porque me (ayudar) _____ a cambiar de opinión: hay mucho interés en el uso del vídeo en el aula.

B. Pregunte a un(a) amigo(a), fotógrafo(a) de una revista de turismo, sobre su último viaje.

MODELO: llegar de tu último viaje: ¿cuándo?
E1: *¿Cuándo llegaste de tu último viaje?*
E2: *Pues, llegué el viernes por la tarde.*

1. alojarte esta vez: ¿dónde?
2. recorrer ciudades: ¿qué?
3. usar medios de transporte: ¿qué?
4. hacer el viaje: ¿por qué?
5. acompañarte: ¿quién?
6. sacar fotos interesantes: ¿cuántas?

C. Imagínese que Ud. es el(la) nuevo(a) concejal municipal de la ciudad. Conteste las preguntas que le hacen en una entrevista.

MODELO: E1: ¿Por qué quiso ser concejal municipal?
E2: *Quise ser concejal porque decidí que tenía que hacer algo para resolver los problemas de esta ciudad.*

1. ¿Qué educación formal tuvo Ud. antes de entrar en la política?
2. ¿Cuándo decidió ser candidato(a)?
3. ¿Por cuántos votos ganó Ud. la elección?
4. ¿Cómo se sintieron su esposo(a) y Ud. cuando la oposición habló mal de Ud.?
5. ¿Qué le dijo Ud. a su oponente después de las elecciones?
6. ¿Qué personas o compañías le ayudaron a financiar su campaña política?
7. ¿Por qué no entregó a tiempo su declaración de contribuciones?
8. ¿Por qué votó en contra del último proyecto de construcción municipal?

D. Exprese la reacción de sorpresa de las siguientes personas respecto a un gran desastre aéreo. Use los siguientes verbos u otros de su propia selección: **no saber, sentirse, enojarse, confundirse, desmayarse, callarse, comenzar a, sentarse, acostarse.**

MODELO: un testigo ocular
«*No pude creerlo; me sentí confuso y luego muy triste*».

1. una amiga de uno de los pasajeros
2. un pariente de una de las víctimas
3. un sobreviviente
4. un empleado en la torre de control
5. usted
6. la presidenta de la aerolínea
7. el primer periodista en la escena
8. un miembro de la Cruz Roja

III. Constructions with **gustar** and verbs like **gustar**

Teresa: ¡Qué curioso! Miras la página editorial y te echas a reír. ¿Qué **te parece** tan divertido?

Benito: ¡Oh! Es que **me encanta** la caricatura que trae hoy. ¡Mírala, qué graciosa!

Teresa: No la entiendo; ¿no **te parece** que **le falta** algo?

Benito: Pero, chica, **me sorprende** que no la entiendas. Con una sola mirada se entiende el chiste. Ahora **a mí me molesta** tener que explicarte algo tan obvio.

Teresa: Pero anda, hombre; **nos sobra** tiempo antes de salir para que me la expliques. ¡Y a mí también **me gustan** los chistes!

A. *Constructions with gustar*

1. The verb **gustar** corresponds in meaning, but not in grammatical structure, to the English verb *to like*. In English, the person who likes is the subject of the verb, while the person or thing liked is the direct object. In Spanish, however, the person who likes is the indirect object of the verb **gustar,** while the person or thing liked is the subject.

   Me **gustan** las caricaturas. (*indirect object* + **gustar** + *subject*)   *I like cartoons.* (subject + *like* + direct object)

2. **Gustar** is closer in structure to the English expression *to be pleasing* than *to like*.

   Le **gusta** el trabajo de editor.   *Editorial work is pleasing to him.* (literally)

3. **Gustar** is generally used with third person subjects. If the subject is plural, the plural form of **gustar** must be used. The subject usually follows the verb in sentences with **gustar.**

   No me **gusta** mucho esa radioemisora, pero me **gustan** mucho los concursos que ofrece.   *I don't like that radio station very much, but I like the contests it offers.*

4. When the subject of **gustar** is an infinitive or an infinitive phrase, the verb is always singular.

   No nos **gusta** oír siempre de catástrofes.   *We don't like to hear about catastrophes all the time.*

   Le **gusta** escribir e informar al público sobre los sucesos en el extranjero.   *He likes to write and inform the public about foreign events.*

5. Since Spanish does not have a subject pronoun for inanimate objects, *it* can never be expressed as the subject of the verb **gustar.**

   —¿Te **gustó** el artículo sobre la manifestación antinuclear?   *Did you like the article about the antinuclear demonstration?*

   —Sí, me **gustó** mucho.   *Yes, I liked it a lot.*

6. An indirect object phrase may be used in addition to the indirect object pronoun for emphasis, contrast, or for clarification.

   A mí me **gusta** la sección deportiva del periódico, pero **a Julio** le **gusta** más la sección cultural.   *I like the sports section in the newspaper, but Julio likes the cultural section better.*

B. *Verbs similar to gustar*

1. Verbs that are similar to **gustar** describe how a person reacts to something, to someone, or to an event. Observe the construction used in the following sentences: indirect object + verb + subject.

Me **encantan** las revistas de cine.	*I love movie magazines.*
A ellos les **fascinan** las entrevistas con actores.	*They are fascinated by interviews with actors.*
Nos **sorprendió** la noticia sobre el matrimonio de la actriz.	*We were surprised by the news story about the actress's marriage.*
A ella le **molestan** las noticias escandalosas.	*She is bothered by scandalous news stories.*
A él no le **agradó** nuestro comentario.	*He was not pleased with our comment.*

2. The following list shows some common verbs that are used like **gustar.** Some of these verbs may also be used, although with a different meaning, with reflexive pronouns. (Consult *Capítulo 5.4* for further discussion.)

agradar	doler	fascinar	ofender
asombrar	encantar	indignar	preocupar
disgustar	enojar	molestar	sorprender

C. *Some verbs used with or without an indirect object*

1. Verbs such as **faltar** and **quedar** are used in constructions like **gustar.** They also may be used without an indirect object to form impersonal statements. Use of the indirect object personalizes the statement or emphasizes the person affected by the action.

Me faltan titulares para esta noticia.	*I need headlines for this news story.*
Faltan titulares para esta noticia.	*Headlines are missing for this news story.*
Nos quedan sólo dos entrevistas para mañana.	*We have only two interviews left (to do) for tomorrow.*
Quedan sólo dos entrevistas para mañana.	*There are only two interviews left for tomorrow.*

2. Other verbs and expressions like **faltar** and **quedar** include **bastar, convenir, hacer daño, importar, interesar, parecer,** and **sobrar.**

A la gente no le **interesan** tantas noticias de desastres.	*People are not interested in so many news stories of disasters.*
No nos **importan** en absoluto esas noticias.	*Those news stories don't concern us in the least.*

Comprehension questions

1. Would you use **Él, Lo,** or **Le** in the sentence _____ **gusta este periódico?** Explain why.

2. Would you use **gusta** or **gustan** in each of the following sentences? **A ellos no les** _____ **el editorial del periódico. A ella le** _____ **los titulares.**

3. Would a simple **te** or a more emphatic **a ti te** be more appropriate in the second sentence that follows? **A nosotros nos sorprendió mucho esa noticia.** _____ **sorprendió también, ¿verdad?** Explain your choice.

4. Would you use **Falta** or **Te falta** to state that the listener does not have enough time to read the newspaper? _____ **tiempo para leer el periódico.** And to state that there is not enough time to read the newspaper? _____ **tiempo para leer el periódico.**

5. How would you express in Spanish *Yes, I like it* in answer to the question, **¿Te gusta esa revista?** Explain your answer.

Ejercicios

A. Ud. trabaja en las oficinas de una radioemisora. Conteste las siguientes preguntas relacionadas con su trabajo y el de sus compañeros, usando las frases entre paréntesis.

MODELO: ¿Qué le pasa a la jefa hoy? (preocupar el nuevo empleado)
Es que le preocupa el nuevo empleado.

1. ¿Por qué está tan contenta Luisa? (gustar sus nuevas responsabilidades)
2. ¡Qué mala cara traes! ¿Qué te pasa? (doler la cabeza de tanto mirar el procesador de textos)
3. ¿Qué le pasa a Javier? (ofender la evaluación que le hizo su jefe)
4. ¿Por qué no vienen a comer Benjamín y Ernesto? (quedar demasiado trabajo)
5. ¡Parece que perdiste a tu mejor amigo! ¿Qué pasa? (molestar compartir una mesa de trabajo)
6. ¿Viste que Jorge cerró la puerta muy fuerte cuando salió? (indignar las exigencias del nuevo jefe)

B. Imagínese que Ud. participa en un programa llamado "El público habla". Exprese su punto de vista sobre temas relacionados con los medios de comunicación, usando verbos como **gustar, molestar, convenir, importar, hacer daño, ofender, fascinar,** etc.

MODELO: los actores de Hollywood
E1: *¿Le gustan los actores de Hollywood?*
E2: *Sí, (No, no) me agradan (interesan, gustan, etc.) los actores de Hollywood.*

1. los actores temperamentales
2. las referencias sexuales en el cine
3. las películas viejas
4. la música popular actual
5. la popularidad de los vídeos
6. los noticieros de la televisión
7. el poder de la prensa
8. los programas cómicos

C. Pregúntele a un(a) compañero(a) de clase su opinión sobre diversos aspectos de la televisión.

MODELO: parecer superficiales las noticias
E1: *¿Te parecen superficiales las noticias?*
E2: *No, a mí me parecen adecuadas y a veces estupendas. (Sí, a mí me parecen muy superficiales y a veces tontas.)*

1. interesar las telenovelas nocturnas
2. disgustar los avisos comerciales
3. encantar los programas para niños
4. asombrar la cantidad de violencia que hay
5. fascinar los nuevos programas de este año
6. preocupar las muchas horas que miran la televisión los niños

IV. Comparatives and superlatives

Carmen: Oye, quiero anunciar mi consultorio para bodas modernas. ¿Qué les parece **mejor,** anunciar en el periódico, en la radio o en la televisión?

Silvia: Yo creo que el periódico es **el** modo **más directo** de informar al público. Y recuerda que es **tan** popular **como** la televisión.

Marisol: Hmm, yo pondría un anuncio en la radio. No es **el** medio de comunicación **más económico,** pero **más** gente **de lo que** uno cree escucha la radio.

Ernesto: Bueno, la televisión es **mejor;** claro,... si uno tiene dinero. Es **el menos** económico de todos los medios, pero es **el más eficaz.** Una sola imagen, como dicen, vale **más que** mil palabras.

A. *Comparisons of inequality*

1. The word **más** is used in comparisons of inequality to express superiority in quantity, quality, or frequency. **Menos** is used to express inferiority under similar circumstances. The word **que** (*than*) is invariable and relates the two terms of the comparison. Observe the structure of comparisons with nouns, adjectives, and adverbs in the following sentences.

Esta revista tiene **más** entrevistas **que** opiniones editoriales.	*This magazine has more interviews than editorial opinions.*
Las entrevistas son **más** entretenidas **que** los reportajes.	*Interviews are more entertaining than news reports.*
Los editoriales se leen **menos** fácilmente **que** los reportajes.	*Editorials are read less easily than news reports.*
La gente lee **menos** ahora **que** antes.	*People read less now than before.*

2. The phrases **más que** and **menos que** are used after a verb to express *more than* and *less than*.

Los reporteros trabajan **más que** los editores.	*Reporters work more than editors.*
Los editoriales me agradan **menos que** las entrevistas.	*Editorials are less pleasing to me than interviews.*

3. The phrase **no...más que** is used to express *only* when an exact number or amount is mentioned. **No...más de** is used with amounts to express *no more than*.

No puedo redactar **más que** dos artículos esta tarde.	*I can write only two articles this afternoon.*
No hay espacio en la página para **más de** tres anuncios.	*There isn't room for more than three ads on the page.*

4. The word **de** is used instead of **que** before a number in a scale of measurement or an expression of quantity. **Más de** and **menos de** are equivalent to *over, a greater number than* and *under, a lesser number than*, respectively. If the meaning is not that of over or under a specific number, then **que** is used, as in the last of the following examples.

El periódico local tiene **más de** cien empleados.	*The local newspaper has more than (over) one hundred employees.*
Imprime un poco **menos de** setenta mil ejemplares cada día.	*It prints a little less than (under) seventy thousand copies every day.*
Una imagen vale **más que** mil palabras.	*A picture is better (is more effective, more valuable) than a thousand words.*

5. In comparisons of nouns in which the second term of the comparison is a clause with a conjugated verb, the pattern **de** + definite article + **que** is used before the clause. The article agrees with the noun to which it refers.

Las radioemisoras tienen **más** empleados **de los que** uno imagina.

Radio stations have more employees than one imagines.

La radio disfruta de **menos** popularidad **de la que** tenía antes.

Radio enjoys less popularity than it used to have before.

6. In comparisons with adjectives, adverbs, or general ideas in which the second term of the comparison is a clause with a conjugated verb, **de lo que** is used before the clause. (For other uses of the neuter article **lo,** consult *Capítulo 10.3.*)

El periódico local es **más** grande **de lo que** la gente piensa. Influye la opinión pública **más de lo que** la gente cree.

The local newspaper is greater than people think. It influences public opinion more than people believe.

B. *Comparisons of equality*

1. The adverb **tan** is used to express a comparison of equality with adjectives and adverbs. The word **como** is invariable and is used to relate the terms of the comparison: **tan** + adjective/adverb + **como.**

Muchos piensan que la prensa es **tan** poderosa **como** el gobierno.

Many think that the press is as powerful as the government.

La prensa informa **tan** imparcialmente **como** puede.

The press informs as impartially as it can.

2. The adjective **tanto** is used to express a comparison of equality with nouns. **Tanto** agrees with the noun it modifies. The invariable word **como** relates the terms of the comparison: **tanto(a/os/as)** + noun + **como.**

En este periódico hay **tantos** reporteros **como** reporteras.

In this newspaper there are as many male reporters as there are female reporters.

Dedican **tantas** páginas a la sección de deportes **como** a la sección de negocios.

They devote as many pages to the sports section as they do to the business section.

3. The invariable adverb **tanto** is used to express a comparison of equality when actions are being compared. The word **como** relates the terms of the comparison: verb + **tanto** + **como.**

Leemos **tanto como** podemos.

We read as much as we can.

Leemos **tanto** periódicos **como** revistas.

We read newspapers as well as magazines.

C. *Superlatives*

1. The superlative expresses the highest or lowest degree of a quality when comparing people or things to a group. The superlative is formed by the definite article (+ noun) + **más/menos** + adjective. Note that **de** is used to introduce the group from which the superlative is selected.

Radio El Mundo es **la radioemisora más popular de** la ciudad.	*El Mundo is the most popular radio station in town.*
¿Quién es **el locutor más popular de** la radioemisora?	*Who is the most popular announcer in the radio station?*

2. The noun in a superlative construction can be omitted when the referent is clear.

Muchos dicen que la locutora Ana Torrealba es una de **las más dinámicas de** nuestra radioemisora.	*Many say that radio announcer Ana Torrealba is one of the most dynamic in our radio station.*
Otros dicen que Pilar Gatica es **la más dinámica.**	*Others say that Pilar Gatica is the most dynamic.*
¿Sabe usted cuál es **la menos dinámica?**	*Do you know which is the least dynamic?*

3. To indicate the highest degree of a quality without a specific comparison, an adverb such as **muy, sumamente,** or **extremadamente** can be used before the adjective, or the suffix **-ísimo/a/os/as** can be attached to the adjective.

Esta noticia es **sumamente interesante.**	*This piece of news is extremely interesting.*
Esta noticia es **interesantísima.**	*This piece of news is most interesting.*

4. The chart that follows shows the most common spelling changes that occur when the suffix **-ísimo** is added to an adjective.

final vowel is dropped	bello, bellísimo
-ble becomes **-bil**	amable, amabilísimo
c becomes **qu**	rico, riquísimo
g becomes **gu**	largo, larguísimo
z becomes **c**	feliz, felicísimo
written accent is dropped	fácil, facilísimo

—Es un documental **larguísimo,** ¿verdad?	*It's a very long documentary, isn't it?*
—Sí, pero **interesantísimo.** Fue **dificilísimo** filmarlo, pero salió bien.	*Yes, but most interesting. It was very difficult to film, but it turned out well.*

D. *Irregular comparatives and superlatives*

1. A few adjectives have, in addition to their regular forms, irregular comparative and superlative forms.

Adjective	Comparative	Superlative
bueno	más bueno, mejor	(el) más bueno, (el) mejor
malo	más malo, peor	(el) más malo, (el) peor
grande	más grande, mayor	(el) más grande, (el) mayor
pequeño	más pequeño, menor	(el) más pequeño, (el) menor

Radio Universo es **la mejor** radioemisora de la ciudad.

Los medios de comunicación ofrecen **los mayores** servicios a nuestro país.

Radio Universo is the best radio station in town.

Mass media offer the most important services to our country.

2. The irregular forms of adjectives are much more frequently used than the regular forms, which often have limited, specialized meanings. **Mejor** and **peor** indicate the degree of a quality: **más bueno** and **más malo** frequently have a moral connotation.

El nuevo director es **mejor** que el último.

Sabe transformar **las peores** ideas en **los mejores** documentales.

Es, además, una de las personas **más buenas** que he conocido.

The new director is better than the last one.

He knows how to turn the worst ideas into the best documentaries.

He is also one of the kindest persons I have met.

3. The irregular forms **mayor** and **menor** refer to age, importance, or size; **más grande** and **más pequeño** are used more often to refer to physical size.

Mi hermano **menor** trabaja para la radio El Mundo, que es una de las **mayores** radioemisoras de la ciudad.

Sin embargo, el edificio donde está la planta es uno de **los más pequeños** del centro de la ciudad.

My younger brother works for the radio station El Mundo, which is one of the largest (most important) radio stations in town.

However, the building where the plant is located is one of the smallest in the downtown area.

4. The following adverbs have irregular comparative forms: **bien/mejor; mal/peor; mucho/más; poco/menos.**

Escucho mucho la radio. Escucho diferentes radioemisoras, pero escucho **más** la radio El Mundo. Se escucha **mejor** que las otras radioemisoras.

I listen to the radio a lot. I listen to different radio stations, but I listen more to radio El Mundo. It has a better sound than the other stations.

Summary of comparatives and superlatives

Comparisons of inequality

más/menos + noun/adjective/adverb + **que**

verb + **más/menos que**

no...más que + amount

no...más de + amount

más/menos de + amount

más/menos + noun + **de** + **el/la/los/las** + **que** + clause

más/menos + **de lo que** + clause

Examples

Este periódico es **más imparcial que** ése.

Leo menos que ella.

No leo **más que dos** periódicos cada día.

No puedo leer **más de cuatro** periódicos por falta de tiempo.

Leo **menos de cinco** páginas diarias.

Leo **más páginas de las que tú crees.**

Leo **más de lo que tú crees.**

Comparisons of equality

tan + adjective/adverb + **como**

tanto/a/os/as + noun + **como**

verb + **tanto como**

Esta locutora es **tan responsable como** aquélla.

Los reporteros trabajan **tantas horas como** los locutores.

Los reporteros **trabajan tanto como** los locutores.

Superlatives

el (+ noun) + **más/menos** + adjective

muy + adjective

adjective + **-ísimo/a/os/as**

Es **el periódico más importante** de la ciudad. Y es **el más imparcial** también.

Es un periódico **muy responsable.**

Es un periódico **importantísimo.**

Comprehension questions

1. Which one of the following sentences would you use to indicate that an interview is not going to last more than three hours? **La entrevista no va a durar más de tres horas. La entrevista no va a durar más que tres horas.**

2. Would you use **que** or **de lo que** in each of the following sentences? **Las revistas tienen menos artículos de actualidad _____ los periódicos. Los periódicos son más importantes _____ piensa la gente.** Explain the meaning of each sentence.

3. Would you use **de lo que** or **de los que** in each of the following sentences? **Gastamos más _____ ganamos. Gastamos más dólares _____ ganamos.**

4. Would you use **tan** or **tanto** in each of the following sentences? **No escribo _____ como un reportero. No estoy _____ ocupado como un reportero.**

5. Would you use **más grandes** or **mayores** or both in each of the following sentences? **La inflación es uno de los _____ problemas económicos que tenemos. Esta fábrica de automóviles es una de las _____ del país.** Explain the meaning of each sentence.

6. Review the dialogue that appears at the beginning of this section. Could the regular comparative **más bueno** be used instead of **mejor**? Explain.

7. Why was Ernesto in the dialogue able to omit the noun **medio** from his expressions **el menos económico** and **el más efectivo**?

Ejercicios

A. El profesor de una clase de periodismo pide a los estudiantes de la clase que comparen el trabajo de Andrés con el de Manuel. Con otro(a) compañero(a) de clase, represente esta situación.

   MODELO: el artículo / informativo
   >   E1:   *Yo creo que el artículo de Andrés es más informativo que el de Manuel.*
   >   E2:   *Pues, en mi opinión es menos informativo.*

   1. las fotos / originales
   2. el editorial / profundo
   3. los titulares / llamativos
   4. la investigación / completa
   5. los testigos oculares / convincentes
   6. la entrevista / reveladora

B. Usted es corresponsal de la revista *Viajar es vivir*. Está pasando el invierno en Ciudad de México para escribir un artículo sobre lo divertido que puede ser viajar durante esa época del año. Use los adjetivos de la siguiente lista para ayudarle a escribir una oración sobre cada tema.

barato(a)	cómodo(a)	inolvidable	pintoresco(a)
bonito(a)	divertido(a)	moderno(a)	sabroso(a)

MODELO: los pasajes
Creo que los pasajes son tan baratos en invierno como en verano.

1. la comida   3. el paisaje   5. las vacaciones
2. la ropa   4. los trenes   6. los hoteles

C. Dos supervisores de una estación de televisión evalúan a varios empleados y llegan a conclusiones completamente contrarias. Con otro(a) compañero(a) de clase, represente su conversación.

MODELO: mensajero diligente / la oficina
       E1:   *Es el mensajero más diligente de la oficina.*
       E2:   *Al contrario; es el menos diligente de todos.*

1. guionista inspirado / la sección
2. entrevistadora aburrida / el noticiero de las 6:00
3. reporteros hábiles / nuestra estación
4. secretarias eficientes / la oficina
5. meteorólogo preparado / la ciudad
6. camarógrafos creativos / el estado

D. Lorenzo y Juana acaban de ver en vivo su programa televisado favorito, una telenovela llamada "Por este mundo pasé yo". Los dos están encantados con su experiencia. Con otro(a) compañero(a) de clase, exprese su alto grado de satisfacción de dos maneras: con un adjetivo terminado en **-ísimo(a)** y con **muy, sumamente** o **extremadamente**.

MODELO: una intriga complicada
       Lorenzo: *¡Fue una intriga complicadísima!*
       Juana: *Es verdad, ¡una intriga sumamente complicada!*

1. un comienzo original
2. un conflicto intenso
3. un protagonista amable
4. unos antagonistas fuertes
5. unos papeles secundarios maravillosos
6. una conclusión feliz

E. Un(a) compañero(a) empieza a expresar su opinión sobre los medios de comunicación, pero Ud. lo interrumpe y termina la frase con una comparación más enfática.

MODELO: la radio / ser buena (la televisión)
       E1:   *La radio es buena...*
       E2:   *Sí, pero la televisión es mucho mejor.*

1. Charles Schulz / dibujar bien (Gary Trudeau)
2. el teletipo / costar poco (el teléfono)

3. *El Día* / ser un periódico malo (*La Prensa*)
4. John Chancellor / parecer ser un hombre bueno (Walter Cronkite)
5. el nuevo reportero / escribir mal (el viejo)
6. la cantidad de publicidad en la radio / ser grande (la televisión)

F. Una reportera le explica a otro reportero la información que tiene sobre un político de la ciudad. Complete las frases para terminar sus ideas.

MODELO: El Sr. Goldsmith es _____ interesante como dijo Ud.
El Sr. Goldsmith es tan interesante como dijo Ud.

1. A él le parece que necesita más secretarias _____ tiene.
2. Sus secretarias son _____ buenas como las nuestras.
3. Nadie tiene _____ paciencia como su secretaria administrativa.
4. Él gasta _____ dinero que todos los demás concejales juntos.
5. El Sr. Goldsmith trabaja menos _____ la gente cree.
6. Este concejal viaja _____ frecuentemente como su antecesor.
7. Esta tarea fue menos difícil _____ dijo el jefe.
8. Yo tengo más datos _____ puedo usar.

V. Question words used in exclamations

Eduardo: **¡Qué** noticia más increíble!
Yolanda: **¿De qué** hablas?
Eduardo: **¡Cómo!** ¿En qué mundo vives tú? Escuché por la radio que se han puesto en contacto con una civilización extraterrestre. **¡Quién** se hubiera imaginado tal cosa!
Yolanda: **¡Cuánto** admiro tu ingenuidad! **¡Qué** bobo eres! ¿No sabes que hoy es el Día de los Inocentes?

A. *Cómo and cuánto in exclamations*

1. **Cómo** and **cuánto** can be used interchangeably, as in the second sentence that follows, when they directly modify a verb. However, **cómo** expresses *how* in the sense of *in what way;* **cuánto** expresses *how* or *how much* in the sense of *to what extent.*

¡Cómo puedes creer esa noticia!   *How can you believe that piece of news!*

¡Cómo (cuánto) odio al reportero que escribió eso!   *How (How much) I hate the reporter who wrote that!*

2. **Cuánto/a** + a noun expresses *how much* or *how many* in exclamations; **cuánto** agrees with the noun it modifies.

¡**Cuánto** dinero cuesta un anuncio en la televisión!	*How much money an ad on television costs!*
¡**Cuántas** veces hay que corregir las pruebas de imprenta!	*How many times one has to correct the galley proofs!*

B. *Quién in exclamations*

Exclamations with **quién** + a verb are often used to talk about wishes that probably will never be fulfilled. The verb is in the past subjunctive for wishes referring to the present and in the past perfect subjunctive for wishes referring to the past.

¡**Quién** pudiera escribir editoriales tan bien como ella!	*I wish I were able to write editorials as well as she does!*
¡**Quién** hubiera podido asistir a la última rueda de prensa en el palacio presidencial!	*I wish I had been able to attend the last press conference at the presidential palace!*

C. *Qué in exclamations*

1. **Qué** + a verb corresponds to English *what.*

¡**Qué** importa una entrevista más!	*What does another interview matter!*
¡**Qué** sabes tú de ese tema!	*What do you know about that topic!*

2. **Qué** + an adjective corresponds to English *how.*

¡**Qué** increíble!	*How unbelievable!*
¡**Qué** increíble es este reportaje!	*How unbelievable this news report is!*

3. **Qué** + a singular noun corresponds to English *what a;* with a plural noun, **qué** is equivalent to *what.* Note that no indefinite article appears in the Spanish sentences.

¡**Qué** noticiero vimos!	*What a newscast we saw!*
¡**Qué** reporteros tienen!	*What reporters they have!*

4. If the noun in an exclamation with **qué** is modified by an adjective, the construction **qué** + noun + **más/tan** + adjective is used.

¡**Qué** noticiero **más (tan)** interesante!	*What an interesting newscast!*
¡Que reporteros **más (tan)** preparados!	*What well-prepared reporters!*

5. **Qué** + an adverb in exclamations expresses *how* something is done.

¡Qué fácilmente se imprimen las revistas!	*How easily magazines are printed!*
¡Qué rápido lees el periódico!	*How quickly you read the newspaper!*

Comprehension questions

1. Would you use **cómo** or a form of **cuánto** in each of the following exclamations? **¡_____ noticias leemos cada día! ¡_____ puedes leer tantas noticias!** What does each mean?

2. To indicate that you wished you had written a certain editorial, would you use **escribiera** or **hubiera escrito? ¡Quién _____ ese editorial!**

3. Would you use **qué** or **cómo** to exclaim how modern a piece of teletype equipment is? **¡ _____ moderno es ese teletipo!**

4. In the exclamation **¡Qué terrible tragedia!,** the adjective **terrible** precedes the noun **tragedia.** If the adjective were placed after the noun, what would the resulting exclamation be?

5. Review the dialogue that appears at the beginning of this section. Give two alternate ways of expressing Eduardo's first exclamation. What other exclamation word could Yolanda have used instead of **cuánto** in the first sentence of her final utterance?

Ejercicios

A. Complete Ud. las frases siguientes con una palabra exclamativa apropiada.

MODELO: ¡_____ escribe ese cronista!
¡Cómo escribe ese cronista!

1. ¡_____ locutor más aburrido!
2. ¡_____ pudiera escribir como ella!
3. ¡_____ escribe a máquina él!
4. ¡_____ personas se ofendieron con ese aviso comercial!
5. ¡_____ titular tan engañoso!
6. ¡_____ le gusta ser el primero con una noticia!
7. ¡_____ no quisiera entrevistar al Ministro de Hacienda!
8. ¡_____ artículos malos se redactan todos los días!

B. Hoy el(la) editor(a) del periódico *Informemos* está de mal humor y expresa sus pensamientos siempre con una frase exclamativa. Exprese sus pensamientos, usando la palabra exclamativa más apropiada.

MODELO: Esta página tiene mucha propaganda.
          ¡Cuánta propaganda tiene esta página!

1. Este artículo de fondo es muy aburrido.
2. Los reportajes están muy flojos hoy.
3. Es un diseño feo.
4. El corrector de pruebas trabaja mal.
5. Siento mucho la renuncia de ese reportero.
6. Saqué muchas fotos que no sirven.

VI. Ways of expressing *to realize*

1. In Spanish, several verbs are used to express the range of meanings of *to realize*. **Darse cuenta (de)** means *to realize* in the sense of being or becoming aware of something. **Comprender** is synonymous with **darse cuenta (de)** when it expresses understanding or realizing something that was not understood before.

No **se dio cuenta de** la hora.

She didn't realize (wasn't aware of) what time it was.

Gregorio **se da cuenta** de las ventajas de ser periodista.

Gregorio realizes (is aware of) the advantages of being a journalist.

En ese momento Gregorio **se dio cuenta de (comprendió)** las ventajas de ser periodista.

At that very moment Gregorio realized (became aware of) the advantages of being a journalist.

¿Ahora **comprendes (te das cuenta de)** tu error?

Now do you understand (are you aware of) your error?

Cuando me lo explicó, **comprendí (me di cuenta de)** mi error.

When she explained it to me, I understood (became aware of) my error.

Comprendió (Se dio cuenta) en seguida **(de)** que era mejor no contradecir al guionista.

He understood (became aware) at once that it was better not to contradict the scriptwriter.

2. **Realizar** means *to realize* in the sense of accomplishing or achieving a goal or fulfilling a desire. **Llevar a cabo** also expresses realizing or accomplishing in the sense of carrying out or completing a goal or project.

Dudo que pueda **realizar (llevar a cabo)** el trabajo en el plazo fijado.

I doubt that I can accomplish (carry out) the work in the indicated time.

¿Para cuándo piensa **llevar a cabo (realizar)** el proyecto?

By when do you intend to complete (to accomplish) the project?

Soñaba con ser locutora, pero no **realizó (llevó a cabo)** su sueño.

She used to dream about becoming an announcer, but she didn't fulfill (accomplish) her dream.

Ejercicios

A. Diga qué verbo o expresión verbal se usa en español para expresar las palabras indicadas. Si hay más de una respuesta posible, dé todas las posibilidades.

1. Now do you *realize* that you should have checked your facts first?
2. I always wanted to work in public relations; I have now *realized* that goal.
3. Don't you *realize* that you cannot have a byline for every story?
4. You must *realize* that being a good photographer is very difficult.
5. Did you *carry out* the assignment as we discussed?
6. After interviewing the President, I *realized* that I *had fulfilled* a lifelong dream.

B. El director del periódico *La Opinión* le hace algunas preguntas a uno de sus reporteros más jóvenes sobre una tarea que le acaba de dar. Con un(a) compañero(a) de clase, represente su conversación usando uno de los verbos presentados en esta sección.

MODELO: ¿_____ los diversos aspectos de esta tarea?
        E1: ¿*Te das cuenta de los diversos aspectos de esta tarea?*
        E2: *Sí, creo que lo comprendo todo.*

1. ¿_____ que necesito este artículo para la edición de las cinco?
2. ¿Necesitas ayuda para _____ todo esto antes de las tres?
3. ¿_____ que sin muchos datos este artículo no sale bien?
4. ¿Ahora _____ la diferencia entre un artículo de fondo y uno para la primera plana?
5. ¿Crees que este tipo de artículo nos ayuda a _____ nuestra meta de informar bien al público?

Actividades para la comunicación

A. Ahora le toca a Ud. Dé su opinión sobre distintos temas que se tratan con frecuencia en la prensa y en la televisión. Use verbos como **gustar, encantar, fascinar, faltar, enojar, sorprender, preocupar, interesar, molestar** e **indignar** para expresar su opinión. Puede opinar sobre los temas sugeridos u otros que le interesen.

MODELO: los derechos humanos
        Me preocupa oír que hay tantos casos de abuso de los derechos humanos.

1. las armas nucleares
2. los descubrimientos arqueológicos
3. los acuerdos internacionales para los intercambios culturales

4. la política económica del país
5. la ayuda financiera a los estudiantes universitarios
6. los avances en la medicina

B. Dígame lo que piensa. Averigüe lo que opina un(a) compañero(a) de clase sobre los medios de comunicación de este país o de su propia ciudad.

MODELO: cadena de televisión / informativo
   E1:   *¿Cuál te parece que es la cadena de televisión más informativa de este país?*
   E2:   *Creo que la cadena más informativa es la PBS.*
   E1:   *¿Y no es tan informativa la NBC?*
   E2:   *Quizás, pero me molestan las interrupciones de los anuncios comerciales en la NBC.*

1. periódico / leído
2. revista / divertido
3. radioemisora / popular

4. noticiero / fiable
5. canal de televisión / comercializado
6. tiras cómicas / gracioso

C. Al día en las noticias. Ud. conversa con dos amigos sobre sucesos recientes de interés general. Pregúnteles si conocen el tema, usando verbos como **ver, oír, leer, mirar** o **escuchar** y luego añada su propia opinión. Después, sus amigos darán otra opinión.

MODELO: los programas anoche en el Canal 4
   E1:   *¿Viste los programas anoche en el Canal 4? ¡Qué aburridos fueron!*
   E2:   *¿Tú crees? Pues, encontré que el nuevo programa de misterio en el Canal 4 fue muy divertido.*
   E3:   *Yo también vi ese mismo programa; fue interesantísimo.*

1. las tiras cómicas del periódico del domingo pasado
2. el último episodio de la telenovela
3. el reportaje en el periódico sobre el último partido de fútbol
4. el nuevo programa radial de música rock
5. las noticias meteorológicas en la radio esta mañana
6. los titulares en primera plana del periódico de hoy

D. Situaciones. Desarrolle con otro(a) compañero(a) de clase diálogos de por lo menos tres comentarios cada uno, basándose en las siguientes situaciones. Use el pretérito lo más posible.

1. Ud. llegó tarde a su trabajo en las oficinas de la revista *Ahora*. Explíquele a su jefa el por qué e infórmele sobre el progreso de los artículos que tiene entre manos.

2. Ud. entrevista a un actor o a una actriz de fama nacional. Le hace preguntas sobre su trabajo y le pide que compare los papeles y las películas que ha realizado, como, por ejemplo, cuáles fueron los peores, los mejores, los más difíciles o más fáciles de todos y cuáles fueron los papeles que más le gustaron o que no le gustaron.

3. Ud. conversa con dos amigos sobre los diferentes programas de televisión que vio anoche y los comparan, hablando de cuál fue el más cómico, el más sentimental, el más dramático, el mejor escrito, etc.

E. Discusión. Lea el siguiente comentario editorial y hable de los temas indicados. Después, dé una terminación lógica al comentario, según las indicaciones que siguen.

Nuestra Ciudad

Una de las cosas que me encanta hacer los domingos es salir con la familia a hacer un recorrido por nuestro gran Parque Chapultepec. A mis hijos les gusta hacer volar sus cometas y a mi esposa siempre le fascina observar a los extranjeros y turistas que visitan el parque. El domingo pasado, sin embargo, descubrí algo que me molestó enormemente. Me parece que los habitantes de nuestra ciudad no se preocupan por conservar el parque en un estado de limpieza. Vi con asombro que una familia tiró los desechos de su almuerzo a la laguna del parque...

1. ¿Hay problemas como éste en la ciudad donde Ud. vive? ¿Cuáles son?
2. ¿Le parece bueno el titular o puede sugerir otro mejor?
3. Dé una conclusión al artículo, usando verbos como **sorprender, ofender, agradar** e **importar** e incluya también alguna comparación.
4. Comente sobre algo que le ha molestado a Ud. y que ha pensado discutir en un comentario editorial.

CAPÍTULO 5

◆

Estar en forma

A muchos niveles de la sociedad hispana se puede apreciar una preocupación por estar en forma. Unas estudiantes de la Universidad Nacional Autónoma de México, fundada en 1551, trotan (jog) por el recinto universitario.

Conversación

1. ¿Se considera Ud. una persona activa o inactiva? ¿Qué hace Ud. para mantenerse en forma? ¿Levanta pesas? ¿Hace ejercicios aeróbicos? ¿Corre o camina?
2. ¿Participa Ud. en algún deporte? ¿En cuáles? ¿O es que prefiere Ud. ver los deportes? ¿Cuáles?
3. ¿Qué sabe Ud. de los deportes en Hispanoamérica? ¿Cuáles son los más populares? ¿Ha visto alguna vez un partido de fútbol según se juega en Europa e Hispanoamérica?
4. ¿Es Ud. miembro de algún salón de ejercicios o de algún gimnasio? ¿Recomienda Ud. esto para todas las personas?
5. ¿Sube y baja Ud. de peso con frecuencia o se mantiene a un nivel adecuado para su altura? ¿Por qué aumenta uno de peso? ¿Cuál es el mejor modo de rebajar?
6. Escoja una de las personas en la foto anterior. Imagínese cómo es su vida y explique por qué esa persona quiere mantenerse en forma.

Vocabulario temático

alimento, el food; nourishment
calentamiento, el warm-up; heating
camaradería, la team spirit
caminata, la walk, stroll
carrera, la race; career
competencia, la competition; rivalry; competence
deportista, el(la) sportsperson
entrenamiento, el training, coaching
gimnasta, el(la) gymnast
higiene, la hygiene, cleanliness
maratón, el marathon
nadador(a), el(la) swimmer
Olimpiadas, las Olympic games
saltador(a), el(la) jumper
salud, la health
vestuario, el locker room; clothes

agacharse to crouch
calentarse (ie) to warm up
ducharse to take a shower
entrenarse to work out, to train
esforzarse (ue) to make an effort
fatigarse to tire out
fortalecerse to build up one's strength; to get strong

fumar to smoke
lanzar to throw
refrescarse to cool off
relajarse to relax
saltar to jump
sudar to sweat

animado(a) lively; encouraged
débil weak
enérgico(a) energetic
pálido(a) pale
sobresaliente outstanding

en plena forma in top shape
estirar los músculos to stretch
guardar la línea to watch one's figure
hacer ejercicio to exercise
levantador(a) de pesas, el(la) weight lifter
levantar pesas to lift weights
marcar un gol to score a goal
ponerse a dieta to go on a diet
subir (bajar) de peso to gain (lose) weight

I. The imperfect

Mi queridísima Celia:

...¡Qué vieja me siento! Ayer, después de correr un poco, **estaba** cansadísima y me **costaba** respirar. Debe ser la inactividad, mi trabajo sedentario, mi pereza, ¡nada más!

Te acuerdas que antes **llevaba** una vida bastante activa. **Iba** al gimnasio dos o tres veces por semana y **caminaba** al trabajo. En el verano, **hacía** largas caminatas por la playa casi todos los fines de semana; en el invierno, **iba** a esquiar cuando **podía.**

Tengo que volver a hacer ejercicio para recuperar mi energía. Todo esto va a cambiar y vas a ver pronto a una nueva persona...

Un fuerte abrazo de

Susana

The imperfect is one of the two sets of simple past tense forms in Spanish. It is used to describe past states or conditions, customary or habitual actions in the past, or past actions that are viewed in progress. (See *Capítulo 4.1* and *2* for a discussion of the preterit.)

A. *Forms of the imperfect*

1. Regular verbs

-ar verbs trabajar	-er verbs correr	-ir verbs vivir
trabaj**aba**	corr**ía**	viv**ía**
trabaj**abas**	corr**ías**	viv**ías**
trabaj**aba**	corr**ía**	viv**ía**
trabaj**ábamos**	corr**íamos**	viv**íamos**
trabaj**abais**	corr**íais**	viv**íais**
trabaj**aban**	corr**ían**	viv**ían**

The imperfect forms of all **-ar** verbs contain a characteristic **-aba** in the ending. The first person plural has a written accent on the stressed **a: -ábamos.** The imperfect endings of **-er** and **-ir** verbs are identical and contain **-ía** in all forms.

Cuando **vivíamos** en San Francisco **trabajábamos** mucho, pero siempre **teníamos** tiempo para hacer ejercicio.

When we lived in San Francisco we worked a lot, but we always had time to exercise.

Corríamos por la mañana y durante los fines de semana **jugábamos** al tenis.

We would run in the morning and play tennis on weekends.

2. Irregular verbs: **ir, ser, ver**

ir	ser	ver
iba	era	veía
ibas	eras	veías
iba	era	veía
íbamos	éramos	veíamos
ibais	erais	veíais
iban	eran	veían

The only verbs that are irregular in the imperfect are **ir, ser,** and **ver. Ver** is considered irregular because an **e** is added to its stem in the imperfect.

Cuando **eras** más joven, te **veía** a menudo en el gimnasio.
Ibas allí a practicar judo.

When you were younger, I often saw you in the gymnasium.
You used to go there to practice judo.

B. *Uses of the imperfect*

1. The imperfect is used to talk about habitual or customary actions in the past. In English, this use of the imperfect is expressed with *used to, would,* or with a simple past tense form. In English, context makes clear that a simple past tense form refers to a habitual or customary action. Observe the English equivalents of the imperfect in the following examples.

Antes yo **iba** al gimnasio todos los sábados. El gimnasio **cerraba** **tarde. Hacía** ejercicios aeróbicos y luego **levantaba** pesas.

Before, I used to go to the gym every Saturday. The gym closed late. I would do aerobic exercises and then lift weights.

2. The imperfect is used to focus on an action in progress at a certain point in the past. Two simultaneous actions in progress are also expressed using the imperfect. In English, a past progressive tense is used to express this meaning.

—¿Qué **hacías** a las siete?
—**Practicaba** mis ejercicios de calentamiento. Y tú, ¿qué **hacías**?
—Pues, mientras tú te **preparabas** para correr, yo **jugaba** al básquetbol con unos amigos.

What were you doing at 7:00?
I was practicing my warm-up exercises. And what were you doing?
Well, while you were getting ready to run, I was playing basketball with some friends.

3. The imperfect is used to provide the background information or setting of an action or actions in the past. The time of day at which a past action occurred is considered background information and always is expressed in the imperfect.

Eran las ocho de la tarde. El gimnasio **estaba** lleno de gente. Todos **estábamos** listos para comenzar los ejercicios. La profesora **estaba** en el centro del gimnasio. **Llevaba** una malla negra.

It was eight o'clock in the evening. The gym was full of people. We were all ready to start exercising. The instructor was in the center of the gym. She was wearing a black leotard.

4. The imperfect is generally used with verbs that express a mental, emotional, or physical condition or state in the past.

—**Pensaba** que te **gustaba** el deporte, pero ayer no fuiste al estadio.

I thought you liked sports, but yesterday you didn't go to the stadium.

—No me **sentía** bien. Me **dolía** la cabeza y **estaba** cansada.

I wasn't feeling well. My head hurt and I was tired.

5. The imperfect is used to report speech that was originally uttered using the present indicative. Compare the use of the present in a direct quote with the use of the imperfect in reported speech in the following examples.

El médico me dijo: «Ud. **está** en buenas condiciones físicas. Ud. **puede** practicar alpinismo».

The doctor told me: "You are in good physical condition. You can practice mountain climbing."

El médico me dijo que **estaba** en buenas condiciones físicas y que **podía** practicar alpinismo.

The doctor told me that I was in good physical condition and that I could practice mountain climbing.

Summary of the uses of the imperfect

Habitual and customary action in the past	Antes yo **practicaba** el béisbol todos los veranos.
Ongoing action in the past	Ayer, a las cuatro, yo me **entrenaba** para el próximo maratón.
Description in the past	El campo de fútbol **estaba** lleno de espectadores. Los jugadores del equipo de casa **llevaban** camisetas rojas, los visitantes **vestían** uniforme verde.
Telling time in the past	**Eran** las nueve.
Mental, emotional, physical conditions in the past	Antes me **gustaba** hacer alpinismo. **Subía** montañas altísimas y no me **cansaba.**
Reporting what was said in the present	El entrenador de nuestro equipo nos dijo que **teníamos** que descansar bien antes del próximo partido.

Comprehension questions

1. Which of the following two sentences contains an imperfect form that refers to an action viewed as it was occurring at a certain point in the past? **Antes levantaba pesas a menudo. Levantaba pesas cuando tú entraste en el gimnasio.** What kind of action does the other imperfect form express?

2. Why is the imperfect form **eran** used in the following sentence? **Miré mi reloj y vi que eran las tres y diez.**

3. Which of the following sentences would be expressed with the imperfect of *jumped* and *called* in Spanish? *I don't know why, but I jumped when they called my name. I don't know why, but I jumped whenever they called my name.* Explain why.

4. Review the letter that appears at the beginning of this section. Which of the five principal uses of the imperfect is demonstrated in the second paragraph of the letter? And in the first paragraph?

Ejercicios

A. Exprese los párrafos siguientes en el imperfecto.

1. Cuando **vamos** al gimnasio, siempre **hacemos** una serie de ejercicios de calentamiento antes de comenzar. **Estiramos** los músculos primero porque **es** muy importante calentarse al principio. Nos **divertimos** mucho en el gimnasio porque siempre **hay** muchos amigos allí y porque nos **sentimos** mejor después de hacer un poco de ejercicio.

2. Yo **tengo** un buen puesto en un salón de ejercicios. **Soy** la persona encargada de tocar la música. Como me **gusta** mucho la música rock, siempre lo **paso** bien escuchando las canciones y mirando a los clientes. Ellos **saltan** y **bailan** al ritmo de la música que yo **decido** tocar.

B. Ud. intenta convencer a un(a) amigo(a) de los beneficios del ejercicio. Cuéntele los casos de algunas personas y cómo el hacer o el no hacer ejercicio ha cambiado su vida. Dé una conclusión original.

MODELO 1: Susana / vida activa: ir al gimnasio, caminar al trabajo, jugar al tenis
Antes Susana llevaba una vida activa. Iba al gimnasio, caminaba al trabajo y jugaba al tenis. Ahora no hace ejercicio, toma el autobús al trabajo y se siente mal.

MODELO 2: yo / vida inactiva: fumar mucho, comer mal, no poder correr
Antes yo llevaba una vida inactiva. Fumaba mucho, comía mal y no podía correr. Ahora no fumo, hago ejercicio y estoy mejor.

1. Martín y Beatriz / vida activa: hacer caminatas, ir a esquiar, mantenerse en forma
2. tú y yo / vida inactiva: siempre usar el coche, subir a la oficina en ascensor, no practicar ningún deporte
3. yo / vida activa: participar en varios deportes, leer libros sobre la higiene, pasar mucho tiempo al aire libre
4. tú / vida inactiva: tener malas costumbres, ser muy perezoso(a), no seguir una buena dieta
5. Elena / vida activa: nadar mucho, levantar pesas, correr por la pista municipal
6. Samuel y Jorge / vida inactiva: dormir demasiado, salir muy poco de la casa, no cuidarse bien

C. Ud. es miembro de la famosa familia López, ganadores de varias medallas en atletismo durante las Olimpiadas. En este momento Ud. participa en un programa televisado. Conteste las preguntas que le hace la locutora acerca de su familia.

MODELO: *E1:*   ¿Qué hacían Uds. para mantenerse en buena forma?
          E2:   *Nosotros practicábamos varios deportes, especialmente el básquetbol y, claro, el atletismo.*

1. ¿Dónde se entrenaban Uds., al aire libre o en un gimnasio?
2. ¿Qué rutina seguían Uds. al principio de una sesión?
3. ¿Qué actividades eran las mejores para calentarse antes de una sesión?
4. ¿Cuántas veces a la semana levantaban Uds. pesas?
5. ¿Qué miembro de la familia era el más entusiasta?
6. ¿Quién tenía menos ganas de entrenarse regularmente?
7. ¿Creían Uds. que llegarían a ser campeones del mundo?

D. Averigüe las condiciones físicas, los intereses y los deportes que practicaba un(a) compañero(a) de clase cuando tenía quince años. En la respuesta se pueden usar las siguientes frases u otras de su propia selección.

jugar al (tenis, básquetbol)	bajar de peso
tomar lecciones de ballet	no hacer nada
montar en bicicleta	no gustarme los deportes
ser miembro de un equipo de béisbol	preferir leer libros de aventuras

MODELO: estar en buenas condiciones físicas cuando tenía 15 años
          E1:   *¿Estabas en buenas condiciones físicas cuando tenías 15 años?*
          E2:   *Sí, porque montaba en bicicleta todos los días.*

1. practicar algún deporte
2. entrenarse a menudo
3. tener problemas de peso
4. hacer ejercicio con regularidad
5. participar en algún deporte
6. interesarle el baile clásico
7. ser un(a) chico(a) activo(a)
8. correr con los compañeros

II. The preterit versus the imperfect

"Nuestra salud"

De nuestro corresponsal en Barranquitas, Heriberto Martínez.

Visitamos ayer el Gimnasio Hércules para apreciar personalmente el método de ejercicios aeróbicos. **Llegamos** alrededor de las diez de la mañana y **observamos** la sesión de trabajo que **duró** un poco menos de una hora. **Era** contagioso ver a un grupo de hombres y mujeres que **saltaban** y **bailaban** al ritmo de una música muy movida. Al término de la sesión, **entrevistamos** a un señor con sus buenos kilos de más, quien **sudaba** copiosamente y **respiraba** con alguna dificultad. Nos **expresó**: «Vi el anuncio en el periódico y **decidí** probar este sistema. Al principio no me **convencía** mucho, pero ahora debo decirle que me encanta. Antes me **sentía** siempre cansado, pero ahora me siento en plena forma».

A. *General contrast*

1. The preterit and the imperfect express two different ways of viewing specific actions or conditions in the past. The preterit is used to describe an action, event, or condition seen as completed, and may focus on the beginning, the end, or on the entire action from beginning to end.

La actriz **demostró** su método de hacer ejercicio anoche.	*The actress demonstrated her exercise method last night.*
La actriz **demostró** (**empezó** a demostrar) su método a las ocho.	*The actress demonstrated (began to demonstrate) her method at eight o'clock.*
La actriz **demostró** su método hasta las nueve.	*The actress demonstrated her method until nine o'clock.*
Demostró su método desde las ocho hasta las nueve.	*She demonstrated her method from eight to nine o'clock.*

2. The imperfect is used to focus on an action or condition as it was in progress at a point in time in the past.

La actriz **demostraba** su método cuando entré al gimnasio.	*The actress was demonstrating her method when I entered the gymnasium.*
Todos **se concentraban** en lo que ella **hacía.**	*Everybody was concentrating on what she was doing.*

3. Actions or conditions that are expressed in the preterit are viewed as completed at the precise point in time being evoked in the past. Actions or conditions that are expressed in the imperfect are viewed in progress at the time in the past being

evoked; that is, the speaker focuses on the middle of an action and the beginning or end are not of concern. Observe the difference in perspective as shown in the following diagram.

Completed action

Practicaron los ejercicios entre las ocho y las nueve. (Preterit)

Beginning (completed)	*Middle* (in progress)	*End* (completed)
Abrieron la sesión a las ocho. (Preterit)	Cuando entré a las ocho y media **tocaban** una música muy movida. (Imperfect)	**Hicieron** ejercicios hasta las nueve. (Preterit)

4. In narration, the preterit keeps the plot moving by reporting what happened, by recording changes in conditions, and by specifying the beginning or end of actions. The imperfect fills in the background against which the actions or events took place and gives descriptions of the setting and the physical condition or mental states of the characters involved.

Anoche **llovía,** pero **fui** al gimnasio de todos modos. **Había** mucha gente allí y **noté** que muchos **parecían** cansados. Yo también **estaba** cansado, pero cuando **terminamos** la sesión de ejercicios, todos nos **veíamos** más animados.

It was raining last night, but I went to the gym anyway. There were lots of people there and I noticed that many seemed tired. I was tired too, but when we finished our exercise session, we all looked more lively.

5. Some expressions are more usually associated with the preterit and others with the imperfect, as is shown in the following list. However, the viewpoint or intent of the speaker is what ultimately determines which verb form is used.

Preterit	**Imperfect**
anoche *last night*	siempre *always*
ayer *yesterday*	a menudo *often*
el (verano) pasado *last (summer)*	frecuentemente *frequently*
la (semana) pasada *last (week)*	todos los días *every day*
hace (un mes) *a (month) ago*	generalmente *generally*

Anoche **soñaba** que **hacía** ejercicios aeróbicos cuando de repente me **caí** de la cama. No **dormí** muy bien anoche.

Last night I dreamt that I was doing aerobic exercises when all of a sudden I fell out of my bed. I didn't sleep well last night.

B. *Recurrence of events or conditions*

When referring to recurrent actions or events, the preterit is used to report that the actions or conditions have taken place and are viewed as completed. The imperfect emphasizes the habitual repetition of the actions or conditions.

Fui al gimnasio muchas veces durante mis últimas vacaciones.	*I went to the gym many times during my last vacation.*
El verano pasado **fui** a menudo al salón de ejercicios.	*Last summer I often went to the exercise room.*
El verano pasado **iba** a menudo al salón de ejercicios.	*Last summer I would go to the exercise room frequently.*

C. *Simultaneous or overlapping events and conditions*

1. When two or more past events or conditions are viewed together, the imperfect sets the scene for the main action, which is in the preterit. The imperfect presents the setting in which the main action took place, the physical condition or emotional states of the people involved, or the actions that were in progress when the main action occurred. Observe in the following examples that in English the past progressive tense (*I was jumping*) is generally used to refer to an action in progress in the past and the simple past tense (*the phone rang*) is used to refer to the main action.

Cuando **sonó** el teléfono, yo **hacía** mis ejercicios aeróbicos.	*When the phone rang, I was doing my aerobic exercises.*
Saltaba y **bailaba** cuando alguien **tocó** a la puerta.	*I was jumping and dancing when someone knocked at the door.*
Relajaba los músculos cuando el reloj **marcó** las siete.	*I was relaxing my muscles when the clock struck seven.*

2. When a cause-and-effect relationship exists between two or more actions in the past, that is, when one action caused the other to happen, the preterit is used. The order of presentation—cause/effect or effect/cause—does not matter.

Cuando **escuché** la música, **salté**.	*When I heard the music, I jumped.*
Salté cuando **escuché** la música.	*I jumped when I heard the music.*
Todos **dejamos** de bailar cuando el instructor **dio** la orden.	*We all stopped dancing when the instructor gave the order.*

3. Simultaneous actions in progress in the past are expressed in the imperfect. (See Section I of this chapter.)

Mientras Uds. **nadaban** nosotros **jugábamos** al voleibol.	*While you were swimming we were playing volleyball.*

D. *Physical conditions and emotional states*

1. Physical conditions and emotional states in the past are usually expressed in the imperfect. The focus is on the description of the condition or state, and the speaker has little interest in when the condition began or ended.

Hombre, ¡qué mala cara **tenías** ayer! **Estabas** pálido. **Parecías** cansado.

You looked awful yesterday, pal! You were very pale. You seemed to be tired.

2. Occasionally, a speaker may wish to emphasize a sudden change in physical condition or emotional state, or to report that a past condition existed only during a specific time frame. This is conveyed by use of the preterit.

Me **sentí** mal después de mis ejercicios.

I felt bad after my exercises. (change in condition)

Por diez minutos **tuve** dificultad para respirar.

For ten minutes I had difficulty in breathing. (condition with time boundaries)

Estuve preocupado todo el resto del día.

I was worried the rest of the day. (condition with time boundaries)

E. *Verbs that differ in meaning*

The English equivalents of **conocer, saber, poder,** and **querer** vary, depending on whether they are used in the preterit or the imperfect. Observe the differences in meaning as shown in the following lists and examples.

Preterit	**Imperfect**
Conocí *I met (became acquainted with)*	Conocía *I was acquainted with, knew (over a period of time)*
Supe *I found out, I learned (beginning of knowing)*	Sabía *I knew, I had the knowledge*
Pude *I succeeded in, I managed, I could*	Podía *I was able to (capability)*
No pude *I failed at, I couldn't*	No podía *I wasn't able to (due to circumstances)*
Quise *I tried*	Quería *I wanted*
No quise *I refused*	No quería *I didn't want*

Hace una semana **conocí** a un amigo tuyo en la piscina. Yo **conocía** a su hermano, pero no a él.

A week ago I met a friend of yours at the swimming pool. I knew his brother, but not him.

No **sabía** que practicaba la natación. Lo **supe** ayer por casualidad.

I didn't know he went in for swimming. I found that out yesterday by chance.

Me dijo que antes él **podía** nadar una milla, pero la semana pasada apenas **pudo** completar media milla.

He told me that before, he was able to swim a mile. But last week he barely succeeded in completing half a mile.

Le pregunté si **quería** practicar conmigo, pero no **quiso** ese día por tener otro compromiso.

I asked him if he wanted to practice with me but he refused to that day because he had another commitment.

Summary of main differences between preterit and imperfect

Preterit

General contrast

Completed action viewed as whole, at beginning, end, or from beginning to end; keeps plot moving

Ayer **llovió** y por eso **se suspendió** la competencia.

Empecé a correr maratones a los 20 años.

Ayer nos **entrenamos** hasta las siete.

Imperfect

Action in progress in the past or existing condition (middle); gives background, setting

Como **llovía** a cántaros, decidieron suspender la competencia.

Los atletas **estaban** completamente mojados.

A las seis, todavía **estábamos** en el campo donde nos **entrenábamos.**

Recurring events or conditions

Set of events or conditions viewed as completed

La primavera pasada **participé** en tres carreras de cien metros.

Repeated or habitual action or condition

La primavera pasada me **entrenaba** casi todos los días para las carreras de cien metros.

Preterit	Imperfect
Simultaneous, overlapping actions, events, conditions	
What happened during or what interrupted an action or existing condition in progress	Action in progress in the past, existing condition or state (setting)
Cuando tú **entraste** al gimnasio, yo jugaba al básquetbol.	**Nadábamos** cuando tú apareciste en la piscina.
Cause-and-effect relationship	Simultaneous actions in progress
Marcamos el gol de la victoria y el partido **terminó**.	Yo **corría** por el parque mientras tú **asistías** a tu clase de baile.
Physical conditions and emotional states	
Change in condition or state	Condition or state at a given point, without concern for when it occurred
Me **sentí** débil después de mi entrenamiento de fútbol.	¡Qué día ayer! No sé qué me **pasaba**. No **tenía** energía, me **sentía** débil, **estaba** deprimido.

Comprehension questions

1. Do you use **tenía** or **tuve** in each of the following sentences? **Cuando todavía no _____ dieciséis años, comencé a interesarme en el levantamiento de pesas. Ayer _____ una sesión de levantamiento de pesas bastante intensa.**

2. Would you use **entendió** or **entendía** in each of the following sentences? **Leyó las instrucciones varias veces y finalmente las _____. Siempre leía las instrucciones varias veces y finalmente las _____.** Explain your choices.

3. Would you use **corrí** or **corría** in each of the following sentences? **El verano pasado por lo general _____ casi diez kilómetros cada día. Durante un mes completo _____ casi quince kilómetros cada día.** Explain your choices.

4. What form of **conocer** would you use in each of the following sentences? **La semana pasada yo _____ a tu instructor de tenis. En esa fecha yo no _____ a tu instructor de tenis todavía.** What do the sentences mean in English?

5. Review the article that appears at the beginning of this section. Locate a verb in the imperfect that emphasizes customary past actions, one that expresses a physical condition in the past, and one that refers to an action in progress at a certain point in time. Give two examples that show the use of the preterit to keep the plot moving.

Ejercicios

A. Complete los siguientes párrafos, usando el imperfecto o el pretérito de los verbos entre paréntesis, según el contexto.

El verano pasado mi hermano y yo (decidir) ＿＿＿ un día que (ir) ＿＿＿ a empezar un programa de ejercicios físicos. Me (gustar) ＿＿＿ mucho la idea porque (saber) ＿＿＿ que (ser) ＿＿＿ muy importante hacer ejercicio con regularidad.

 Nosotros (asistir) ＿＿＿ a un excelente salón de ejercicios, el Gimnasio Hércules, tres veces por semana durante todo el verano. ¡No (faltar) ＿＿＿ nunca! ¡Qué buen programa (ser) ＿＿＿! Los instructores (tener) ＿＿＿ mucha paciencia y todos los días nos (estimular) ＿＿＿ a progresar. Al terminar una sesión, nosotros siempre (estar) ＿＿＿ bastante cansados. Sin embargo, nos (sentir) ＿＿＿ satisfechos.

 A finales de julio por fin (poder) ＿＿＿ tomar unas vacaciones. Nosotros (hacer) ＿＿＿ un viaje de dos semanas al Parque Yellowstone y nos (divertir) ＿＿＿ mucho. Pero cuando (volver) ＿＿＿ a casa ya no (tener) ＿＿＿ deseos de volver a la disciplina del programa. Por desgracia, desde ese momento en adelante nosotros (dejar) ＿＿＿ de participar en el programa y como resultado (comenzar) ＿＿＿ de nuevo a subir de peso.

B. Muy pocas personas de su equipo de tenis asistieron ayer a una sesión optativa de práctica. Explíquele a su entrenador(a) lo que hicieron las siguientes personas y por qué lo hicieron, en vez de asistir a la práctica. Use expresiones como **querer, tener que, desear, interesarle, tener ganas** u otras similares.

MODELO: Teresa (dar un paseo)
  Entrenador(a): *¿Qué hizo Teresa ayer durante la práctica?*
  Usted: *Dio un paseo porque quería descansar un poco.*

1. los hermanos Ramírez (estudiar en la biblioteca)
2. tú (entrenarse en la piscina de la universidad)
3. tu amiga Virginia (acompañarme a la piscina)

4. Chabela (ir al médico)
5. Máximo (salir a una entrevista)
6. Miguel (pasar media hora en la sauna)

C. Describa cómo pasaron Elena y su amiga Marta el sábado pasado, basándose en los siguientes dibujos. Haga el papel de Elena y hable de lo que hicieron, cómo era el día y cómo se sentían, usando el pretérito y el imperfecto.

MODELO: *1.* ser sábado: llamar a mi amiga Marta
Era sábado y quería ir a la playa. Llamé a mi amiga Marta y decidimos vernos allí.

2. salir de casa: sentirme feliz
3. montarme en el coche: irme a la playa
4. ponerme el traje de baño: reunirme con Marta
5. nadar en el mar: temperatura del agua ser agradable
6. tomar el sol: escuchar la radio
7. cambiarnos de ropa: irnos en el carro
8. tomar algo en un café: ser un día maravilloso

D. Cambie el siguiente cuento al pasado usando el pretérito o el imperfecto, según el contexto. También imagínese una conclusión para este episodio. ¿Qué descubrió Arturo en la oficina? ¿Cómo resolvió la situación?

"Terror en el Gimnasio Hércules"

Al entrar al Gimnasio Hércules, Arturo, el dueño, se da cuenta de que las luces están encendidas. Se sorprende, pues al salir siempre las apaga. Entra a la sala

principal cuando de repente escucha un ruido en la oficina. Entonces piensa con terror que hay un ladrón en su gimnasio. En voz alta pregunta quién está allí. Siente más ruidos y luego un largo silencio. Entra cuidadosamente a su oficina. Allí descubre que la puerta está abierta y todos los papeles están en el piso. No ve a nadie, pero siente terror y todo su cuerpo tiembla. Vuelve a escuchar ruidos en el vestuario. No sabe qué hacer.

E. Explíquele a otra persona qué edad tenía y en qué condiciones estaba cuando hizo Ud. las siguientes cosas por primera vez.

MODELO: seguir una dieta
Yo tenía catorce años y estaba un poco gordo(a) cuando seguí una dieta por primera vez.

1. empezar a guardar la línea
2. tomar la decisión de comer más frutas y vegetales
3. montar en bicicleta
4. practicar un deporte seriamente
5. comenzar a levantar pesas
6. hacerme miembro de un equipo deportivo
7. invitar a mi mejor amigo(a) a mi gimnasio
8. ir a esquiar

III. Some idioms with **tener** and **hacer**

Ramiro: ¿Aló? ¿Claudia?

Claudia: (*Con sueño*) Sí, con ella. ¿Quién habla?

Ramiro: Soy yo, Ramiro, tu fiel compañero de ejercicios. Mira, no **hace** muy **buen tiempo** esta mañana. ¿Qué te parece, salimos a correr esta mañana o no?

Claudia: ¡Cuánto te gusta madrugar! Pues, no **tengo** muchas **ganas** de correr ahora. **Hace frío** incluso dentro de la casa.

Ramiro: **Tienes razón;** afuera la temperatura es de cinco grados centígrados. ¿Qué tal si corremos esta tarde entonces, como a las tres? Según el pronóstico del tiempo, **hará** menos **frío** y no va a estar tan nublado.

Claudia: Me parece bien; es sábado y no **tenemos prisa.** Nos vemos a las tres. ¡Chau!

A. *Idioms with tener*

1. In Spanish, the verb **tener** + a noun is used to express some common physical and mental conditions. The equivalent English construction is *to be* + an adjective.

   —¿Cuántos **años tiene** ese ciclista?   *How old is that cyclist?*
   —**Tiene** unos veintidós **años.**   *He's about twenty-two years old.*
   —Parece que **tiene prisa;** hace los ejercicios de calentamiento muy rápidamente.   *It seems that he's in a hurry; he's doing his warm-up exercises very fast.*
   —**Tienes razón.**   *You're right.*

2. Nouns used in idioms with **tener** are modified by adjectives (**mucho, tanto, poco**), not by adverbs (**muy, tan, poco**).

   —¿Por qué tienes **tanta** prisa?   *Why are you in such a hurry?*
   —Tengo **mucho** frío.   *I'm very cold.*

3. The following is a list of common idioms with **tener.**

tener (veinte) años *to be (twenty) years old*	tener gracia *to be funny*
tener calor *to be hot*	tener hambre *to be hungry*
tener celos *to be jealous*	tener miedo *to be afraid*
tener cuidado *to be careful*	tener prisa *to be in a hurry*
tener la culpa *to be the one at fault*	tener razón *to be right*
	no tener razón *to be wrong*
tener éxito *to be successful, to succeed*	tener sed *to be thirsty*
	tener sueño *to be sleepy*
tener frío *to be cold*	tener suerte *to be lucky*
tener ganas (de) *to be desirous of, to feel like*	tener vergüenza *to be shy; to be ashamed*
	no tener vergüenza *to be shameless*

B. *Idioms with hacer*

1. The verb **hacer** + a noun is used in many Spanish expressions concerning the weather. In English the verb *to be* + an adjective expresses the same meaning.

   Hace calor, no **hace frío.**   *It's hot, it isn't cold.*
   Hace buen tiempo últimamente.   *The weather has been nice lately.*
   Hacía fresco ayer.   *It was cool yesterday.*
   Ayer **hizo viento,** pero al menos **hizo sol.**   *Yesterday it was windy, but at least it was sunny.*

2. Nouns that follow **hacer** are modified by adjectives (**mucho, tanto, poco**), not by adverbs (**muy, tan, poco**).

Hizo **mucho** frío el día de la carrera.　　*It was very cold the day of the race.*

3. The following list shows common idioms with **hacer.**

hacer buen tiempo *to be nice (weather)*	hacer mal tiempo *to be unpleasant (weather)*
hacer calor *to be hot*	hacer sol *to be sunny*
hacer fresco *to be cool*	hacer viento *to be windy*
hacer frío *to be cold*	

4. **Estar** + an adjective is also used in certain weather expressions. Two of the most common are **estar nublado** (*to be cloudy*) and its opposite **estar despejado** (*to be clear*).

Comprehension questions

1. Would a person describing his/her body temperature say: **Hace calor** or **Tengo calor?**

2. How would you complete the following sentence to say that you're not very cold? **No tengo ＿＿＿ frío.**

3. To indicate that Pablo is very careful, would you use **tiene** or **es** in the following context? **Pablo ＿＿＿ mucho cuidado.**

Ejercicios

A. Explique por qué las personas indicadas hicieron las siguientes cosas, usando una expresión con **tener.**

MODELO:　Julia: no ir al salón de ejercicios ayer
　　　　　Julia no fue al salón de ejercicios ayer porque tenía sueño.

1. yo: traer una chaqueta a la práctica
2. nosotros: no poder terminar todos los ejercicios
3. tú: comer un bocado en medio de la práctica
4. Catalina: rebajar veinticinco kilos
5. Hugo y Diego: llevar sólo una camiseta y pantalones cortos
6. Enrique y yo: decidir no hacer los ejercicios más difíciles

B. Ud. es entrenador(a) de un equipo juvenil de fútbol y va con su equipo a la playa para tomar el sol y descansar. Conteste las muchas preguntas que le hacen los jóvenes con una expresión apropiada con **tener.**

MODELO: *E1:*   ¿Cómo es que decidiste acompañarnos a la playa hoy?
　　　　　　E2:   *Vine hoy porque tengo ganas de descansar al sol.*

1. ¿Por qué no nadas ya que estás en la playa?
2. ¿Por qué trajiste toda esta comida?
3. ¿Cuatro refrescos? ¿Por qué tomas tantos?
4. ¡Encontré un billete de $10.00! ¿Qué te parece?
5. ¿Por qué miras tanto tu reloj?
6. Pasaste toda la tarde acostado(a) en la toalla de playa. ¿Por qué?

C. Imagínese que Ud. es un(a) entusiasta del entrenamiento físico y que trata de mantenerse activo(a) todo el año. Diga en qué actividad participa durante diferentes meses del año y por qué.

MODELO 1:   *En enero yo hago ejercicio en el gimnasio porque hace mal tiempo afuera.*

MODELO 2:   *En julio yo nado mucho porque hace bastante calor. Así me siento refrescado(a).*

IV. Reflexive, reciprocal, and impersonal constructions

Sonia Méndez, periodista de El Sol, *entrevista al boxeador Antonio Ruiz, campeón de los pesos livianos.*

Srta. Méndez:	**Se dice** que Ud. lleva una vida muy disciplinada. Quizá demasiado disciplinada.
Sr. Ruiz:	Sí, es verdad. **Me levanto** a las seis todas las mañanas; **me entreno** por la mañana y por la tarde y nunca **me acuesto** después de las diez.
Srta. Méndez:	¿Y Ud. no **se aburre** con ese ritmo de vida tan riguroso y tan rutinario?
Sr. Ruiz:	Vea Ud.; al principio, **me quejaba** de todo, pero muy pronto noté que no **me fatigaba** ni tampoco **me enfermaba**. Ahora pienso que todo el mundo debe **cuidarse** y hacer mucho ejercicio. El ejercicio nos ayuda a **sentirnos** mejor y hasta a **entendernos** mejor.

A. *Forms and position of reflexive pronouns*

Reflexive pronouns	Nonreflexive pronouns	
Direct/indirect object	Direct object	Indirect object
me	me	me
te	te	te
se	**lo, la**	**le (se)**
nos	nos	nos
os	os	os
se	**los, las**	**les (se)**

1. Reflexive pronouns are the same in form as object pronouns in the first and second persons singular and plural: **me, te, nos, os.** The reflexive pronoun **se** is used for both the third person singular and plural forms.

   Yo **me entreno** por la mañana, Carlos **se entrena** a las dos de la tarde y sus primos **se entrenan** a las siete.

   I train in the morning, Carlos trains at two in the afternoon, and his cousins train at seven o'clock.

2. Remember that the pronoun **se** replaces the indirect object pronouns **le** or **les** when they are used before the direct object pronouns **lo, la, los,** or **las.** In such cases, **se** is not a reflexive pronoun. (See *Capítulo 3.5.*)

   —¿Quién puede explicarle a Roberto el nuevo programa de ejercicios?
   —Pues, yo **se** lo explico.

   Who can explain the new exercise program to Roberto?
   Well, I'll explain it to him.

3. Reflexive pronouns are used in the same position as direct and indirect object pronouns. In sentences with a conjugated verb and in negative commands, they precede the verb. They follow and are attached to the verb in affirmative commands. In verb phrases consisting of a conjugated verb and an infinitive or present participle, they may be attached to and follow the infinitive and present participle or precede the conjugated verb. (See *Capítulo 3.5.*)

   —¡Cuidado! ¡Quéde**se** donde está! ¡No **se** mueva!

   Watch out! Stay where you are! Don't move!

   —¿**Se** hizo daño el gimnasta?
   —No sé. No **me** explico cómo pudo accidentar**se** (**se** pudo accidentar). Estaba entrenándo**se** (**Se** estaba entrenando) como lo hace siempre.

   Did the gymnast hurt himself?
   I don't know. I can't understand how he could have an accident. He was training the same way he usually does.

B. *General usage*

1. Reflexive pronouns are used to indicate that the direct or indirect object in a sentence is the same as the subject. In the absence of an object, reflexive pronouns simply show that the action of the verb is reflected back to the subject. Compare the following pairs of reflexive and nonreflexive constructions.

El levantador de pesas **se observa** en el espejo.	*The weight lifter observes himself in the mirror.*
Cada vez que pasa la gimnasta, el levantador de pesas **la observa.**	*Every time the gymnast goes by, the weight lifter observes her.*
Ese atleta tiene unos kilos de más; tiene que **cuidarse.**	*That athlete has a few extra pounds; he has to take care of himself.*
Él dice que el médico del equipo no piensa **cuidarlo** más si no baja de peso.	*He says that the team doctor doesn't intend to take care of him any more if he doesn't lose weight.*

2. Reflexive constructions are used more frequently in Spanish than they are in English, and many verbs that are reflexive in Spanish are nonreflexive in English. The pronouns *myself, yourself, himself, herself,* and so forth, often signal a reflexive construction in English.

El gimnasta **se mira** en el espejo.	*The gymnast looks at himself in the mirror.*
Después de hacer sus ejercicios, **se afeita** y **se ducha.**	*After doing his exercises, he shaves (himself) and takes a shower.*
Dice que **se siente** bien todo el día.	*He says he feels great all day.*

3. Most verbs that can take a direct object can be used in a reflexive construction also. In such instances, the reflexive pronoun functions as a direct object, showing that the subject both performs and receives the action. Observe the difference in meaning of the following nonreflexive and reflexive constructions.

Entrena a los atletas.	*He coaches (trains) the athletes.*
Los atletas **se entrenan.**	*The athletes train.*
Los atletas **levantan** pesas.	*The athletes lift weights.*
Los atletas **se levantan.**	*The athletes get up.*
Los ejercicios **cansan** a los atletas.	*Exercises tire the athletes.*
Los atletas **se cansan.**	*The athletes get tired.*

4. Some Spanish verbs have a change in meaning when they are used in reflexive constructions. Compare the meaning of the nonreflexive and reflexive verbs in the following list.

acercar *to bring near*	acercarse *to approach*
acordar *to agree on*	acordarse *to remember*
comportar *to entail; to endure*	comportarse *to behave*
enterar *to inform*	enterarse *to find out*
equivocar *to mistake (A for B)*	equivocarse *to be mistaken*
ir *to go*	irse *to leave*
llamar *to call*	llamarse *to be called (named)*
morir *to die*	morirse *to die (nonviolently)*
parecer *to seem*	parecerse *to resemble*
preguntar *to ask (a question)*	preguntarse *to wonder*

5. Note that **morirse,** and not **morir,** is used figuratively as shown in the following examples.

Hemos corrido muchas millas. **Me muero** de hambre.	*We have run many miles. I'm dying of hunger.*
Y nosotros **nos morimos** de sed.	*And we're dying of thirst.*

C. *Verbs that are always reflexive*

1. Some verbs in Spanish are always used in the reflexive form.

Mi vecino **se queja** de su salud, pero no **se abstiene** de comer alimentos grasos y no **se atreve** a ir al médico.	*My neighbor complains about his health, but he doesn't abstain from eating fatty foods and he doesn't dare go to the doctor.*

2. The following list shows some common verbs in this category.

abstenerse *to abstain*	dignarse *to deign*
arrepentirse *to repent*	jactarse *to boast*
atreverse *to dare*	quejarse *to complain*
ausentarse *to be absent*	

D. *Reflexive verbs that indicate change*

1. Some verbs that are used to indicate a change in body position or in how a person feels mentally or physically are reflexive in Spanish and nonreflexive in English.

El entrenador **se arrodilló** para examinar a un jugador caído.

The coach kneeled down to examine a fallen player.

Se alegró al ver que no estaba lesionado.

He became happy upon seeing that he wasn't injured.

2. The following list includes some main categories of verbs that are reflexive in Spanish but nonreflexive in English. Note that the English equivalent is often expressed by *to become* or *to get* + an adjective. (See also Section V of this chapter.)

Body movements

acostarse *to go to bed*	inclinarse *to bow, to lean*
agacharse *to crouch*	levantarse *to get up, to rise*
arrodillarse *to kneel down*	pararse *to stand up*
hincarse *to kneel down*	sentarse *to sit down*

Mental states

aburrirse *to get bored*	entristecerse *to become sad*
alegrarse *to become happy*	indignarse *to become indignant*
avergonzarse *to be ashamed*	ofenderse *to feel offended*
enojarse *to get mad, angry*	preocuparse *to worry*
enorgullecerse *to be proud*	sorprenderse *to become surprised*

Physical states

cansarse *to get tired*	enrojecer(se) *to blush*
debilitarse *to weaken, to grow weaker*	fatigarse *to tire out*
	fortalecerse *to get strong, to build up one's strength*
desmayarse *to faint*	
enfermar(se) *to get sick*	resfriarse *to get a cold*

3. Verbs that express mental states or emotional reactions can frequently be used with either a direct or indirect object pronoun or with a reflexive pronoun. Observe in the following examples that the construction with the direct or indirect object pronoun places emphasis on the inanimate object or event that provokes the response; the reflexive construction emphasizes the person who responds or reacts to the object or event.

A ella la eligieron entrenadora del año. **La alegró** mucho tal honor.

She was elected coach of the year. Such an honor made her very happy.

A ella la eligieron entrenadora del año. **Se alegró** mucho con tal honor.

She was elected coach of the year. She became very happy with such an honor.

Al corredor **le preocupa** su salud.
El corredor **se preocupa** por su salud.

His health worries the runner.
The runner is worried about his health.

E. *The reflexive construction with parts of the body and clothing*

1. A reflexive construction is used with parts of the body and articles of clothing when the subject and the person receiving the action are the same. In such instances, the reflexive pronoun functions as an indirect object.

Como los dos equipos tenían uniforme similar, los jugadores del equipo de casa **se quitaron** la camisa roja y **se pusieron** una amarilla.	*Since both teams had similar uniforms, the home-team players took off their red shirts and put on yellow ones.*

2. The indirect object pronoun is used with parts of the body and clothing when the person receiving the action is different from the subject.

El entrenador **le puso** una chaqueta al jugador lesionado.	*The coach put a jacket on the injured player.*
El doctor **le examinó** la rodilla.	*The doctor examined his knee.*

3. The following list shows some common verbs used with the reflexive pronoun and parts of the body and clothing.

afeitarse *to shave (oneself)*	ponerse *to put on (clothing)*
fracturarse *to fracture (bone)*	probarse *to try on*
lavarse *to wash*	quebrarse *to break*
limpiarse *to clean*	quitarse *to take off (clothing)*
peinarse *to comb*	

F. *The reflexive se with accidental or unintentional events*

1. Spanish has a special construction that is used to describe events that are the result of chance rather than of conscious decision. Observe the form of the verbs in the following sentences.

¡Qué día! **Se me olvidó** mi clase de baile, **se me rompieron** los anteojos y **se me averió** el coche.	*What a day! I forgot my dance class, my glasses broke, and my car broke down on me.*

2. Contrast **Rompí los anteojos** (could be intentionally) with **Se me rompieron los anteojos** (by accident). The latter statement implies that, although the person involved might have caused the mishap through negligence or carelessness, he/she did not deliberately plan it.

3. In sentences that describe unplanned occurrences, the inanimate object is the grammatical subject of the action. The reflexive pronoun **se** is used to show that the receiver of the action is the same as the grammatical subject. The person involved in the action or who inadvertently caused it to happen is viewed as the indirect object (the person to whom something happens). The verb is always in the third person singular or plural.

reflexive pronoun	+	indirect object	+	verb	+	subject
Se		me		rompieron		los anteojos.
Se		nos		perdió		el balón.

4. Verbs that are frequently used to express accidental or unplanned events include **caer, ocurrir, olvidar, perder, quebrar,** and **romper.**

Fui a jugar al tenis y **se me quebró** la raqueta.

I went to play tennis and my racket broke.

Pedí prestada una y luego **se me rompió**.

I borrowed one and then it broke on me.

G. *Reciprocal constructions*

1. In Spanish the plural reflexive pronouns **nos, os,** and **se** are used to indicate that an action is reciprocal. Note in the following examples that *each other* or *one another* is used in English to express reciprocal action.

Los dos boxeadores **se saludaron, se desearon** suerte y luego comenzaron a **darse** golpes.

The two boxers greeted each other, wished each other luck, and then began to hit one another.

2. Some common verbs used in reciprocal constructions include **abrazarse, amarse, ayudarse, besarse, casarse, comprometerse, darse la mano, despedirse, escribirse, felicitarse, saludarse,** and **telefonearse.**

Los tenistas **se dieron la mano** y **se felicitaron** después del partido.

The tennis players shook hands and congratulated each other after the game.

3. Although a reciprocal construction is identical to a reflexive construction with a plural subject, in actual communication the specific context or the meaning of the verb generally indicates which meaning is intended.

Los ciclistas **se saludaron.**

The cyclists greeted each other.

Los atletas **se miraron.**

The athletes looked at themselves/at each other.

Los bailarines **se miraron** en el espejo durante la práctica de postura.

The dancers looked at themselves in the mirror during their posing practice.

Los miembros del equipo **se miraron** con asombro cuando llegó el nuevo dueño. ¡Era una mujer!

The team members looked at each other with astonishment when the new owner arrived. It was a woman!

4. Prepositional complements or adverbs may be added to clarify that a sentence has a reciprocal meaning.

No podíamos creer que habíamos derrotado a los campeones. **Nos mirábamos unos a otros** totalmente asombrados.

We couldn't believe that we had defeated the champions. We looked at each other totally amazed.

5. The following phrases can be added to clarify a reciprocal construction.

entre sí
entre nosotros/as (mismos/as)
(el) uno a(l) otro

(la) una a (la) otra
(los) unos a (los) otros
(las) unas a (las) otras

H. *Impersonal se*

1. The pronoun **se** with a singular verb can be used to indicate that a sentence has an indefinite subject or that no individual in particular performs an action.

Se juega mucho al básquetbol aquí.
Se dice que en esta ciudad **se vive** bien.

Here people play basketball a lot.
They say that one lives well in this city.

2. There are several English equivalents of the impersonal construction with **se.**

Se vive bien en la ciudad.

People live well in the city.
One lives well in the city.
You (indeterminate) live well in the city.
They (indeterminate) live well in the city.

3. The word **uno** is used to express an impersonal statement with reflexive verbs in order to differentiate between a personal subject (*he, she, you*) and the indefinite use of **se** (*one, people,* etc.).

Se siente bien después de nadar.   *He/She feels good after swimming.*
Ella se siente bien después de hacer   *She feels good after exercising.*
ejercicio.
Uno se siente bien después de correr.   *One feels good after running.*

Summary of the uses of reflexive, reciprocal, and impersonal constructions

Obligatory reflexive constructions with some verbs

Él **se queja** de su salud.

Reflexive construction when subject and direct/indirect object are identical

La gimnasta **se levanta** temprano para correr.
¿Siempre **te hablas** cuando participas en una competencia?

Reflexive verbs that indicate change

Me aburro y **me deprimo** cuando no hago ejercicio.

Reflexive construction with parts of body and clothing when subject and receiver (indirect object) are identical

El ciclista **se quita** el casco.
Ella **se lava** las manos.

Se for accidental or unplanned events
Se, nos, os for reciprocal actions
Se for impersonal statements

Se me olvidaron los zapatos de tenis.
Paco y Sara **se hablan** por teléfono.
Se come bien en ese restaurante.

Comprehension questions

1. Which of the following phrases is not reflexive? **me entrené, se entrenó, te entrenaste, nos entrenaron**

2. Which of the following sentences is used to indicate that the speaker accidentally lost his or her keys? **Se me perdieron las llaves. Perdí las llaves.**

3. In which of the following sentences does **se** signal an impersonal statement? **Creo que se trabaja mucho aquí. Creo que Ud. se preocupa mucho.**

4. Review the interview that appears at the beginning of this section. In Mr. Ruiz's last statement, he uses two verbs that could be either reciprocal or reflexive. How could you clarify his statement to avoid possible confusion?

Ejercicios

A. Ud. trabajó en los preparativos de unas competencias especiales para personas con impedimentos físicos. Explique lo que hicieron Ud. y algunos de los espectadores y participantes el día de las competencias.

MODELO: Julia: vestirse / vestir a su hija
Julia se vistió y luego vistió a su hija.

1. Elena: arreglarse / arreglar su sillón de ruedas para la carrera
2. (yo): mirarse en el espejo / mirar a los demás atletas
3. mis tíos: sentar a un grupo del hospital / sentarse ellos
4. (tú): presentarse a los jueces / presentar al equipo de natación
5. Gonzalo: informarse de la hora del comienzo / informar a los atletas
6. (nosotros): prepararse / preparar a los saltadores

B. Ud. juega al béisbol en el equipo universitario. Conteste las siguientes preguntas de otro miembro del equipo, explicándole lo que ocurrió por casualidad antes del partido de esta tarde.

MODELO: ¿Ya no tiene su camisa de béisbol Luis? (perder)
No, se le perdió la camisa anoche.

1. ¿No trajiste mi toalla? (olvidar)
2. ¿Rompieron los nuevos jugadores los dos mejores bates? (quebrar)
3. ¿Dejaste caer en el lodo el guante que te presté? (caer)
4. ¿No nos trajeron más jabón para la ducha? (acabar)
5. ¿Acabas de pensar en una buena estrategia para ganar el partido mañana? (ocurrir)
6. ¿No encuentras tu uniforme? (perder)

C. Ud. pertenece a un equipo de esgrima (*fencing*). Conteste las preguntas de un(a) compañero(a) de clase sobre el espíritu de camaradería que existe entre los miembros del equipo.

MODELO: Uds., los deportistas: entenderse muy bien
E1:   *Uds., los deportistas, ¿se entienden muy bien?*
E2:   *Sí, nos entendemos muy bien entre nosotros.*

1. los atletas de ambos equipos: saludarse al entrar en el gimnasio
2. María y Claudia: darse consejos para mejorar su técnica
3. Raúl y Elisa: animarse después de perder una competencia
4. Margarita y Ud.: apoyarse en los momentos difíciles
5. los equipos: darse la mano después de un partido

D. Cuéntele a un(a) compañero(a) cómo se siente Ud. en las siguientes circunstancias. Puede usar una de las expresiones que se dan a continuación u otras de su propia selección.

aburrirse	deprimirse	entristecerse	ponerse furioso(a)
alegrarse	divertirse	frustrarse	preocuparse
avergonzarse	enojarse	irritarse	sorprenderse

MODELO: Cuando no puedo terminar mis ejercicios...

E1: *Cuando no puedo terminar mis ejercicios, me irrito y también me preocupo un poco por mi salud.*

E2: *Pues, yo me deprimo y me pongo a dieta inmediatamente.*

1. Cuando llego tarde a la sesión de...
2. Cuando noto que estoy cansado(a)...
3. Cuando no tengo nada que hacer...
4. Cuando hago ejercicio regularmente, noto que...
5. Cuando mis compañeros(as) de equipo me felicitan...
6. Cuando no puedo hacer algo que antes podía hacer...
7. Cuando no puedo correr porque hace mal tiempo...
8. Cuando el entrenador me grita...

E. Prepare una breve explicación de cómo vive un(a) atleta sobresaliente. Seleccione el deporte que más le interesa y siga la forma que se presenta en el modelo.

MODELO: *Un(a) campeón(ona) de tenis se levanta antes de amanecer, se entrena más de una hora antes de desayunar, se esfuerza por seguir una dieta balanceada...*

V. Spanish equivalents of *to become*

Spanish has several specific verbs and verbal expressions that are used to express the meaning of the English verb *to become* in the sense of *to come to be.* In some cases only one verb or expression is appropriate; in others, there is a choice depending on what specific meaning of *to become* is intended.

A. *Change of state: hacerse*

1. **Hacerse,** the most widely used equivalent of *to become,* can be followed by a noun or an adjective and indicates transition from one state or condition to another.

Él **se hizo** gran corredor en distancias cortas.

He became a great short-distance runner.

Y tú **te hiciste** famoso en la carrera de diez mil metros.

And you became famous in the ten-thousand-meter race.

2. When referring to people, **hacerse** stresses the fact that the change of state depends on the voluntary effort of the person or persons involved.

Se hizo levantador de pesas.	*He became a weight lifter.*
Se hizo famoso por el mucho peso que levantaba.	*He became famous for the great amount of weight he lifted.*

3. Some reflexive verbs are equivalent to **hacerse** + a related adjective. (See Section IV of this chapter for reflexive verbs that indicate change.)

fortalecerse = hacerse fuerte	*to get strong(er)*
suavizarse = hacerse suave	*to soften, to become softer*

B. *Change in physical or emotional state: ponerse*

1. **Ponerse** is followed by an adjective to indicate a sudden and temporary change in physical appearance, condition, or emotional state.

¡Qué partido más reñido! ¿Viste qué roja **me puse**?	*What a competitive game! Did you see how red I became?*
Después, en el vestuario, **me puse** bastante pálida.	*Later, in the locker room, I became quite pale.*
Mis compañeras **se pusieron** bastante nerviosas.	*My teammates became quite nervous.*

2. Some reflexive verbs are equivalent to **ponerse** + a related adjective. (See Section IV of this chapter for reflexive verbs that indicate change.)

alegrarse = ponerse alegre	*to become happy*
entristecerse = ponerse triste	*to become sad*

C. *Change through gradual process: llegar a ser*

Llegar a ser can be followed by either nouns or adjectives, and is used to indicate acquisition of a new state through a gradual, lengthy process.

Llegó a ser una de las mejores escritoras sobre la nutrición.	*She became one of the best writers on nutrition.*
Llegó a ser jefa de redacción de una revista en ese campo.	*She became editor in chief of a magazine in that field.*
También **llegó a ser** conocida como un personaje político.	*She also became well known as a political personage.*

D. *Radical change: volverse*

Volverse is used to indicate a radical change of state or condition, and is followed by an adjective.

Antonia **se volvió** muy desconfiada después del accidente.	*Antonia became very wary after the accident.*
A partir de entonces ya no fue la misma persona; **se volvió** pesimista.	*From then on she was not the same person; she became a pessimist.*

E. *To assume a new condition: convertirse, transformarse*

Convertirse en or **transformarse en** are used to indicate that someone or something has assumed a new state.

¡Qué extraño! **Se ha convertido** en un fanático por el esquí.	*How strange! He has become a fanatic about skiing.*
Está muy cambiado. **Se ha transformado** en un gran deportista.	*He's very different. He's become a great athlete.*

F. *To be left in a state or condition: quedarse*

Quedarse is used to indicate that someone, having acquired or been left in a new state, has remained in it either permanently or for a certain period of time. **Quedarse** frequently implies loss or deprivation.

Se quedó cojo.	*He became lame.*
Me quedé atónito.	*I was astonished.*
Mi amigo **se quedó** ciego después de un accidente de alpinismo.	*My friend was left blind after a mountain-climbing accident.*

Ejercicios

A. Indique qué verbo o expresión verbal se usa en español en lugar de la expresión indicada en inglés. A veces hay más de una respuesta posible.

1. If I don't have a daily workout, I *become* an impossible monster.
2. Her skin always *gets* red in the middle of her aerobics class.

3. What a shame that the trainer *has become* such an ogre!

4. It *became* impossible to remain in that class after the instructor insulted me about my physique.

5. Jumping *becomes* boring after several minutes.

6. Our captain *became* (*was left*) lame after taking a bad fall.

7. That clumsy oaf *has* actually *become* a graceful athlete.

8. We want *to become* famous authors of exercise manuals.

B. Conteste las siguientes preguntas que un(a) compañero(a) de clase le hace con el fin de conocer un poco mejor sus ideas, actitudes y costumbres.

1. ¿No te pones triste cuando subes de peso sin quererlo? ¿Se te hace difícil bajar de peso? ¿Te pones de mal humor con facilidad cuando estás a dieta? ¿Te enfermas? ¿En qué circunstancias te irritas?

2. ¿Cuál es tu opinión de esta generación de jóvenes? ¿Se hacen cada vez más conservadores? ¿Menos enérgicos? ¿Te parece que todos quieren llegar a ser ricos y famosos? ¿No te indignas nunca con la nueva generación?

3. ¿Por qué quiere todo el mundo ponerse delgado y fuerte hoy día? ¿Te vuelve loco(a) este fanatismo por la perfección del cuerpo? ¿Cómo te sientes cuando ves a una persona más atractiva que tú? ¿Te pones triste? ¿Celoso(a)?

4. En el futuro, ¿qué quieres llegar a ser? ¿Piensas hacerte rico(a) y famoso(a)? Algunas personas se transforman en fanáticos por realizar sus ambiciones. ¿Lo haces tú? ¿Cómo te pones cuando deseas algo intensamente? ¿Te vuelves imposible?

Actividades para la comunicación

A. **Una historia verdadera.** Imagínese que Ud. decidió hace poco tiempo hacerse miembro de un club deportivo y ponerse a dieta. Explíquele a un(a) amigo(a) las razones por su decisión e incluya los siguientes datos: (1) descripción de su condición física y su estado de ánimo; (2) por qué se sentía y estaba así; y (3) qué resultado inmediato tuvo su acción.

MODELO: *Durante los seis últimos meses yo me levantaba todas las mañanas con poca energía y sin ganas de hacer nada. No quería comer ni hablar con nadie. Estaba aburrido(a)... Por fin, el mes pasado, me hice miembro de un club deportivo y empecé a participar en varias actividades... De pronto me sentí mucho mejor.*

B. ¡Qué desastre! ¿Verdad que a veces nada marcha bien? Con un(a) compañero(a), desarrolle un breve diálogo, diciendo qué les ha pasado recientemente que les ha demostrado que algunos días es mejor no tratar nada nuevo sino quedarse en casa.

MODELO: E1:   *¡Qué cabeza tengo! Se me olvidaron los zapatos de tenis para mi clase de gimnasia.*

E2:   *Pues, a todos nos pasan esas cosas. A mí se me quedó el traje de baño en casa ayer y no pude nadar.*

C. Cadena de comentarios. En cadena, mencione una actividad que hace recíprocamente con un(a) amigo(a). Trate de mantener la cadena sin repetir ninguna actividad.

MODELO: E1:   *Miguel y yo nos llamamos por teléfono antes de ir a entrenarnos para ver quién va a manejar.*

E2:   *Pues, Elena y yo nos animamos mucho la una a la otra durante los ejercicios de calentamiento.*

D. Curiosidad. Paula, una nueva estudiante de Colombia, es una joven que tiene mucho interés en los deportes y también en otros aspectos de la cultura norteamericana. Conteste su pregunta inicial, y luego otra pregunta que ella le hace sobre el mismo tema.

MODELO: *Paula:*   *¿Se practica mucho aquí el ciclismo?*
Usted: *Sí, bastante, pero creo que en Colombia se practica más que en Estados Unidos.*
Paula: *¿Tienes ganas de practicar ese deporte?*
Usted: *Pues, me interesa mucho, pero ya hace tiempo que me dedico a la natación.*

1. Si uno tiene ganas de nadar, ¿dónde hay una buena piscina cerca de la universidad?
2. ¿Qué hacen para divertirse aquí en el invierno?
3. ¿Qué deportes se practican cuando hace mal tiempo? ¿Y cuando hace buen tiempo?
4. Si uno tiene deseos de conocer gente, ¿adónde se puede ir?
5. ¿Tienes miedo de salir solo(a) por la noche aquí?
6. Durante el invierno, ¿qué tiempo hace aquí?
7. ¿Se preocupan los jóvenes de aquí por comer vegetales y frutas?
8. ¿Por qué tienen tanta prisa todos los americanos?

E. En mis tiempos de atleta... Antes Ud. era más activo(a). Escoja dos o tres escenas de las que aparecen a continuación y describa lo que hacía para mantenerse en forma, con quiénes practicaba, cómo era el tiempo cuando se entrenaba, en qué condiciones físicas estaba en aquellos días, cómo se sentía cuando podía participar en deportes y otras cosas similares.

CAPÍTULO 6

•

En la política

El nuevo presidente de Colombia, Virgilio Barco Vargas, y sus partidarios celebran en Bogotá el triunfo en las elecciones presidenciales.

Conversación

1. ¿Qué aspectos de la vida política le son atractivos a Ud.? ¿Y qué aspectos le disgustan? ¿Por qué?
2. Cuando Ud. oye la palabra «política», ¿en qué piensa y por qué?
3. ¿Le gusta discutir de política con sus amigos y familiares? ¿Por qué?
4. ¿Son útiles los debates entre los candidatos presidenciales? En su opinión, ¿cuál es la mejor forma de informarse sobre los puntos de vista de cada candidato?
5. ¿Qué asunto político le interesa o le preocupa más en estos días? Explique.
6. ¿Se considera Ud. un(a) activista político(a)? Si no es activista, ¿piensa serlo algún día? ¿Por qué sí, o por qué no?
7. Imagínese que Ud. es una de las personas en la fotografía anterior. ¿Qué va a hacer ahora para celebrar la victoria de su candidato?

Vocabulario temático

acuerdo, el   agreement, accord
aliado(a), el(la)   ally
apoyo, el   support
ayuntamiento, el   city hall; municipal government
campaña, la   campaign
concejal(a), el(la)   council member
conciudadano(a), el(la)   fellow citizen
deuda, la   debt
dirigente, el(la)   leader
electorado, el   electorate
embajada, la   embassy
gabinete, el   cabinet
mandato, el   mandate, command
manifestación, la   demonstration
mejora, la   improvement
oyente, el(la)   listener
panfleto, el   pamphlet, brochure
partidario(a), el(la)   follower, party member
partido, el   party; game, match
pleito, el   lawsuit, case; dispute
refugiado(a), el(la)   refugee
rehén, el   hostage
senado, el   senate
sindicato, el   trade union
tasa, la   rate

arriesgar   to take a chance, to run a risk
encarcelar   to imprison
forjar   to forge, to make
inscribir   to register, to enroll
mediar   to mediate
reclutar   to recruit
secuestrar   to kidnap, to hijack

aterrador(a)   terrifying
centrista   centrist
derechista   rightist
izquierdista   leftist

caricatura política, la   political cartoon
congelar los precios   to freeze prices
cumplir una promesa   to keep a promise
derechos humanos, los   human rights
golpe de estado, el   coup d'état
hacer una declaración   to make a statement
perder terreno   to lose ground
potencia mundial, la   world power
pronunciar un discurso   to give a speech

I. The present participle: Forms and uses

Teresa: Vas a escuchar el debate entre los candidatos presidenciales esta noche, ¿verdad?

Ernesto: Los debates son una pérdida de tiempo. Además, estoy **leyendo** una novela interesantísima.

Teresa: Oye, Ernesto, tú vas a votar por primera vez este año. **Informándote** de lo que dicen los candidatos, estarás mejor preparado para dar tu voto.

Ernesto: ¿Ah, sí? ¿Y cómo me voy a informar **viendo** a cinco candidatos **insultándose** los unos a los otros, como pasó en el debate de la semana pasada? En mi opinión, me informo mejor **leyendo** el periódico y **hablando** con la gente.

A. *Forms of the present participle*

-ar verbs	-er verbs	-ir verbs
vot**ando**	ofrec**iendo**	debat**iendo**
recomend**ando**	defend**iendo**	

1. To form the present participle of regular verbs, the infinitive ending **-ar** is replaced by **-ando,** and the infinitive endings **-er** and **-ir** are replaced by **-iendo.** Verbs ending in **-ar** and **-er** that have a stem change in the present indicative have regular past participles.

2. Observe the irregularities in the present participles of the following categories of verbs.

-ir stem changes (e > i; o > u)	Irregular verbs	-yendo ending of -ir and -er verbs (stem ends in vowel)
sugerir > sugiriendo	decir > diciendo	ir > **yendo**
pedir > pidiendo	poder > pudiendo	caer > ca**yendo**
dormir > durmiendo	venir > viniendo	construir > constru**yendo**
		creer > cre**yendo**
		destruir > destru**yendo**
		leer > le**yendo**
		oír > o**yendo**

3. The present participle of the few **-er** and **-ir** verbs whose stem ends in **ll** or in **ñ** is **-endo,** not **-iendo: bullir > bullendo; reñir > riñendo.**

B. *Uses of the present participle*

1. The present participle is used with the verb **estar** to form the progressive tenses. The progressive tenses are used to emphasize that an action is in progress. (See Section II of this chapter on progressive tenses.)

Estamos viviendo momentos emocionantes en estas elecciones.	*We are living thrilling moments in these elections.*
El partido del gobierno **está perdiendo** terreno.	*The government party is losing ground.*
Los candidatos **estaban discutiendo** las reformas que anunció el presidente.	*The candidates were discussing the reforms that the president announced.*

2. The present participle is used as an adverbial complement to describe the manner in which an action is carried out. Observe the similarity to English in the following sentence, except for the use of *by.*

El candidato presidencial comenzó el debate **hablando** muy lentamente.	*The presidential candidate began the debate by talking very slowly.*
Usando gestos y pausas de modo muy dramático, captó la atención de sus oyentes.	*Using gestures and pauses in a very dramatic way, he captured the attention of his listeners.*

3. The present participle is also used as an adverbial complement to explain the cause, reason, or time of an action, or the condition under which an action is carried out.

El senador Contreras dijo que, **viajando** por Europa, un día recibió una amenaza por teléfono.	*Senator Contreras said that, while traveling in Europe, he received a threat over the phone one day.*
Sabiendo que estaba vigilado, se cuidaba mucho.	*Knowing that he was being watched, he was very cautious.*
Siendo extranjero, no sabía si ir a su embajada o a la policía.	*Being a foreigner, he didn't know whether to go to his embassy or to the police.*

4. The present participle used as an adverbial complement may include subject and object pronouns, including reflexive pronouns. A subject pronoun is placed after the present participle. Object pronouns are attached to the participle, forming one word, and a written accent is required on the **a** or **e** of the participle ending to retain the original stress.

Siendo él extranjero, se sentía inseguro.	*Being a foreigner, he felt insecure.*
Viéndose en peligro, llamó a la embajada de su país.	*Seeing himself in danger, he called the embassy of his country.*

5. The present participle can be used with verbs of perception (**ver, oír, escuchar, sentir**) to report direct perception of an action or event. Although an infinitive construction may also be used with verbs of perception, use of the present participle stresses that the action is being viewed in progress. (See *Capítulo 8.4* for use of the infinitive with verbs of perception.)

Oí a alguien **dando** (dar) un portazo.	*I heard someone slamming (slam) the door.*
Luego vi a uno de los candidatos **abandonando** (abandonar) el salón de conferencias.	*Then I saw one of the candidates leaving (leave) the conference room.*

C. *Differences in usage between Spanish and English*

1. In Spanish, an infinitive, and not a present participle, is used after a preposition. (Consult *Capítulo 8.4* and Section III of this chapter on use of an infinitive after a preposition.)

Antes de empezar el debate, el moderador consultó a los candidatos.	*Before beginning the debate, the moderator consulted the candidates.*
Insistió **en hablar** en privado con los candidatos.	*He insisted on speaking in private with the candidates.*

2. The present participle cannot be used as a noun in Spanish as it can in English. In Spanish, a noun or an infinitive that functions as a noun is used instead. When an infinitive is used as a noun, it may be preceded by the definite article **el.**

(El) secuestrar a un candidato es un delito grave.	*Kidnapping a candidate is a serious offense.*
Planearon **el secuestro** del senador Ramírez.	*They planned the kidnapping of Senator Ramírez.*

3. In Spanish, with rare exceptions, a present participle cannot directly modify a noun, as it can in English. An adjective, **de** + a noun, or a clause fulfilling the function of an adjective is used in Spanish to modify a noun.

Hablé con el refugiado político brevemente en la sala **de espera.**	*I talked briefly with the political refugee in the waiting room.*
Me dijo que llevaba una vida **aterradora.**	*He told me that he led a terrifying life.*
Recibía mensajes **amenazantes.**	*He received threatening messages.*
Dos hombres **que llevaban trajes negros** lo seguían a todas partes.	*Two men wearing (who were wearing) black suits followed him everywhere.*

Comprehension questions

1. Would you use **entendiendo** or **entender** in each of the following sentences? **Para _____ la situación política, hay que prestar atención a las declaraciones del Presidente. _____ las declaraciones del Presidente, uno comprende la situación política.** Explain why.

2. Is a present participle (**pronunciando**) or a clause (**que pronuncia**) used in each of the following sentences? **Conozco a una persona _____ discursos a favor del candidato izquierdista. Una persona está _____ un discurso a favor del candidato izquierdista.**

3. What form of **decir** would you use in each of the following sentences? **El dirigente salió sin _____ una palabra a nadie. El dirigente salió _____ «hasta luego» a todo el mundo.** Explain why.

4. Is an infinitive (**hacer**) or a present participle (**haciendo**) used in each of the following sentences? **_____ demasiadas promesas es peligroso. No va a salir elegido _____ tantas promesas.**

Ejercicios

A. Un(a) amigo(a) suyo(a) es candidato(a) al senado estudiantil de su universidad. Haga el papel de uno(a) de sus voluntarios y dé sugerencias para su campaña.

MODELO: (tú) poder influir a más gente / poner carteles en las residencias estudiantiles
Puedes influir a más gente poniendo carteles en las residencias estudiantiles.

1. (tú) poder informar al estudiantado / distribuir panfletos que explican tu plataforma
2. (tú) no conseguir nada / arriesgarse a una confrontación con tus oponentes
3. (tú) no crearse problemas con la prensa / decir la verdad en todo momento
4. (tú) darse a conocer sin gastar mucho dinero / hacer discursos frente a la cafetería
5. (tú) ahorrar dinero y tiempo / pedir ayuda a todos tus amigos
6. (tú) obtener el apoyo de los que van en su propio coche a la universidad / referirse a los problemas de estacionamiento

B. Conteste las siguientes preguntas sobre las actividades políticas con relación a la visita reciente del presidente a su ciudad. Responda afirmativamente y utilice el verbo de percepción indicado y el participio presente en su descripción de las actividades.

MODELO: ¿Llegó el presidente a la ciudad? (ver)
Sí, lo vi llegando a su hotel.

1. ¿Gritaron sus partidarios su apoyo a su política doméstica? (sentir)
2. ¿Participó Arturo en la protesta sobre la reciente subida de precios? (ver)
3. ¿Ya manifestaron los partidarios del grupo de oposición? (oír)
4. ¿Arrestaron los policías a los manifestantes violentos? (ver)
5. ¿Distribuyeron mucha propaganda por la calle? (ver)

C. Dentro de una semana habrá un referéndum en su ciudad para regular el precio de los alquileres. Complete las siguientes oraciones con el equivalente en español de las palabras que aparecen entre paréntesis. Atención: a veces no se usa el participio presente sino otras formas gramaticales.

MODELO: La mujer (*distributing*) ____ los panfletos pro regulación de los alquileres es la bibliotecaria de ciencias políticas.
*La mujer que distribuye los panfletos pro regulación de los alquileres
es la bibliotecaria de ciencias políticas.*

1. El panfleto (*explaining*) ____ la posición del alcalde llegó a la biblioteca ayer.
2. Vi a muchos estudiantes de ciencias políticas (*reading it*) ____ en la biblioteca
esta mañana.
3. Anoche muchos estudiantes fuimos a la manifestación pro regulación de los
alquileres; apenas llegamos cuando vimos a una manifestante (*painting*)
____ un letrero incitador.
4. (*By offering*) ____ su respaldo a favor de la regulación, el alcalde quiere
ganar los votos estudiantiles.
5. Sin (*committing herself*) ____ a defender ninguna causa en particular, otra
candidata dice que estudiará todos los asuntos de interés para los votantes.
6. (*Beginning*) ____ con el próximo discurso, los candidatos sólo van a hablar
de los problemas económicos municipales.
7. (*Voting*) ____ es muy importante en una democracia.
8. Antes de (*deciding*) ____ cómo vamos a votar, debemos conocer a fondo a
los candidatos y los problemas del día.

D. Con otro(a) compañero(a) de clase, discuta la posibilidad de llevar a cabo los
objetivos que aparecen a continuación. Ofrezca una o dos soluciones posibles.

MODELO: bajar la tasa de interés
E1:   *¿Cómo se puede bajar la tasa de interés?*
E2:   *Creo que se puede bajar la tasa de interés disminuyendo la
cantidad de dinero que hay y reduciendo la deuda nacional.*

1. hacer votar a más personas
2. disminuir los armamentos nucleares
3. reducir la inflación
4. ayudar a los que tienen hambre en África
5. limitar el crimen en las grandes ciudades
6. cuidar mejor a los ancianos

II. Progressive tenses

Alberto: ¿Por qué te ríes tanto? ¿Qué hay de divertido en el periódico hoy? Dime, ¿qué **estás leyendo**?

Nicolás: **Estoy mirando** las caricaturas políticas. Ven, mira ésta. **Siguen burlándose** del Ministro de Hacienda y de sus intentos de controlar la inflación.

Alberto: Pues, te diré que no le encuentro mucha gracia. La situación económica **va empeorando** y no debemos **estar riéndonos.**

Nicolás: Tú siempre tan serio, Alberto. Ese caricaturista sólo **está tratando** de alegrarnos un poco la vida.

A. *Forms of progressive tenses*

1. The verb **estar** + a present participle is used to form the progressive tenses. Observe the forms of the present, the imperfect, and the preterit progressive.

Present progressive	Imperfect progressive	Preterit progressive
estoy votando	estaba perdiendo	estuve discutiendo
estás votando	estabas perdiendo	estuviste discutiendo
está votando	estaba perdiendo	estuvo discutiendo
estamos votando	estábamos perdiendo	estuvimos discutiendo
estáis votando	estabais perdiendo	estuvisteis discutiendo
están votando	estaban perdiendo	estuvieron discutiendo

2. The present participle is invariable, but the verb **estar** may be conjugated in any tense.

Están presentando la segunda parte de un programa excelente sobre los derechos humanos.

They're presenting the second part of an excellent program about human rights.

Anoche **estuvieron hablando** de la situación en América Latina.

Last night they were talking about the situation in Latin America.

No voy a poder ver el programa final porque mañana a esa hora **estaré viajando** hacia California.

I'm not going to be able to see the final program because at that time tomorrow I'll be traveling to California.

B. *Use of the progressive tenses*

1. The progressive tenses are used to describe an action or event in progress or while being performed. They are less frequently used in Spanish than in English. Use of the progressive tenses stresses an action that is, was, or will be in progress. If no such emphasis is intended, the simple tenses are preferred.

En estos momentos miles de personas **están aplaudiendo** el discurso del candidato derechista. **Están escuchando** el discurso con mucha atención.	*Right now thousands of people are applauding the speech by the right-wing candidate. They're listening to the speech with a great deal of attention.*
Los miembros de la oposición **finalizan** una marcha de protesta. **Protestaban** por el desempleo y la alta tasa de inflación.	*The members of the opposition are concluding a protest march. They were protesting unemployment and the high rate of inflation.*

2. The progressive tenses refer to actions and events and are generally not used if the verb refers to a condition or state. A simple tense is preferred to describe a condition or state.

Me siento triste por los resultados de la elección.	*I'm feeling sad because of the results of the election.*
Me sentía contento antes de las elecciones.	*I was feeling happy before the elections.*

3. In contrast to English, the present progressive is never used in Spanish for anticipated future action. Either the simple present, the **ir** + **a** + infinitive construction, or the future is used to convey anticipated future action in Spanish.

Voto en las próximas elecciones.	*I'm voting in the next elections.*
Voy a votar/Votaré en las próximas elecciones.	*I'm going to vote/I'll vote in the next elections.*

C. *Alternatives to estar in the progressive construction*

1. **Estar** + a present participle is the construction most commonly used to emphasize action in progress; however, the verbs **andar, ir,** and **venir** may also be used with the present participle to refer to actions in progress. Use of **andar** emphasizes a continuous action that occurs repeatedly for an indefinite period of time; **ir**

stresses the early stages of a long-lasting action; and **venir** stresses the fact that an action that began in the past has continued for some time.

Mucha gente **anda buscando** trabajo.	*Many people are going around looking for work.*
Ahora la situación económica **va empeorando.** Hace meses que los precios **vienen subiendo.**	*Now the economic situation is growing worse. Prices have been going up for months.*

2. The present participle is also used in Spanish after the verbs **seguir** and **continuar** to indicate continuation of an action in progress.

La situación económica **sigue empeorando.**	*The economic situation keeps on growing worse.*
Los precios **continúan subiendo.**	*Prices continue rising. (Prices continue to rise.)*

D. *Position of object pronouns*

The two parts of the compound verb in the progressive tenses cannot be separated. Pronouns either precede the conjugated verb or are attached to the end of the present participle, forming one word. When a pronoun is attached, a written accent is required on the participle ending to retain the original stress.

Presta atención. El candidato **está explicándonos** su programa económico.	*Pay attention. The candidate is explaining his economic platform to us.*
Para mí, **nos sigue haciendo** promesas difíciles de cumplir.	*In my opinion, he keeps on making us promises that are difficult to keep.*

Comprehension questions

1. How could you express the following sentence to stress that the action is in progress? **Pronuncia un discurso en estos momentos.**

2. Would you use **escucho** or **estoy escuchando** in each of the following sentences? **¡Silencio; no te das cuenta de que _____ a mi candidato! _____ a mi candidato esta noche.**

3. Which of the following sentences is more appropriate to stress the repeated efforts made by the police? **La policía está buscando a los secuestradores. La policía anda buscando a los secuestradores.**

4. Review the dialogue that appears at the beginning of this section. Which of the progressive constructions might have been formed in the simple present tense? Explain.

Ejercicios

A. Haga el papel de un(a) jefe(a) político(a) y pregunte a varios ayudantes si están haciendo las siguientes cosas ahora mismo. En la respuesta se puede usar los pronombres objetos en cualquiera de las dos posiciones posibles.

MODELO: redactar la carta de protesta al gobernador
  Jefe(a): *¿Estás redactando la carta de protesta al gobernador ahora mismo?*
  Ayudante: *Sí, estoy redactándola en este momento. (Sí, la estoy redactando en este momento.)*

1. reunir estadísticas sobre el desempleo en esta ciudad
2. ocuparse de la próxima entrevista con la prensa
3. prepararme una lista de las posibles preguntas de los reporteros
4. buscarme los datos de la última encuesta sobre el servicio de seguridad pública
5. leer el informe sobre la demora en terminar las reparaciones a las calles
6. efectuar los cambios de organización que discutimos
7. conseguir información sobre las demandas de los sindicalistas
8. organizar una reunión de reconciliación con los dirigentes de la oposición

B. En la narración siguiente, dé la forma correcta de **andar, ir, venir, seguir** o **continuar,** según el contexto. A veces hay más de una respuesta correcta.

Mi amigo Alberto es un fanático por la política. Cada vez que le pregunto si _____ leyendo algo sobre este tema en los periódicos y las revistas, me contesta que sí, que siempre _____ buscando materia que le informe de la teoría o de la práctica de la política. Dice que hace años que _____ informándose de esa carrera. Pero la semana pasada me dijo algo nuevo: que desde hacía varios días ya _____ pensando seriamente en cómo entrar en la política. Yo le dije que debía _____ estudiando eso por mucho tiempo porque iba a ser una de las decisiones más importantes de su vida.

C. Explique lo que las siguientes personas están haciendo en este momento y lo que estaban haciendo antes, según el modelo.

MODELO: yo: mirar la manifestación / charlar con mi vecino
  En este momento estoy mirando la manifestación, pero antes estaba charlando sobre política con mi vecino.

1. los candidatos: participar en el debate / preparar sus discursos
2. (nosotros): hacer llamadas a los dirigentes del partido / reunir fondos para la acción política
3. (yo): escribir mi discurso para esta noche / leer algunos panfletos de la oposición

4. (nosotros): divulgar las nuevas decisiones a la prensa / debatir estas ideas con la jefa
5. el candidato opositor y sus camaradas: escoger a su candidato para el senado / discutir su estrategia para las elecciones
6. (nosotras): elaborar nuestra posición acerca de los derechos humanos / entrevistarnos con un reportero

D. Haga el papel del(de la) alcalde(sa) de su ciudad y conteste las siguientes preguntas de algunos reporteros del periódico local. En la respuesta, use un verbo apropiado en el tiempo progresivo apropiado.

MODELO 1:　¿Cree Ud. que el concejal Martínez decía la verdad durante la discusión de hoy?
Claro que no. Estaba escondiendo algo.

MODELO 2:　¿Trata Ud. de reconciliar su punto de vista con el de Martínez?
Sí, efectivamente. Estoy negociando un acuerdo con él.

1. ¿Sus partidarios le comunican a Ud. su punto de vista con frecuencia?
2. ¿Se ocupa Ud. mucho en estos días de la situación de viviendas para los pobres?
3. ¿Solamente trataba de vigilar su imagen con los votantes cuando les prometió controlar la violencia?
4. ¿Hace su administración algo para bajar los costos médicos?
5. ¿Ocultaba Ud. sus verdaderos motivos cuando pidió más dinero para la policía?
6. ¿Piensa Ud. subir los sueldos de los empleados municipales?

III. Prepositions and prepositional pronouns

*(Parte **de** un discurso **de** un político **de** oposición **al** saber los resultados **de** una elección.)*

Conciudadanos: **en** las elecciones **de** hoy, el pueblo ha demostrado claramente que se siente decepcionado **con** el gobierno. Consideremos los resultados **de** las elecciones **de** hace tres años: **sobre** el setenta y cinco por ciento **de** los candidatos elegidos fueron **del** gobierno. Esta vez, **en** cambio, **según** los últimos cómputos oficiales, el gobierno apenas logró una mayoría precaria **de** un cincuenta y dos por ciento. **Sin** duda, el pueblo no confía **en** todos sus gobernantes. El pueblo quiere que sigamos investigando y denunciando la corrupción **dentro del** gobierno. ¡**A mí, a ti, a** todos **nosotros** nos corresponde ahora insistir **en** un gobierno honesto, justo y verdaderamente representativo!

A. *Common prepositions*

Common simple prepositions

a *at, to*	durante *during*	para *for*
ante *before, in the presence of*	en *in, on*	por *for, by, through*
	entre *between, among*	según *according to*
bajo *under*		sin *without*
con *with*	excepto *except*	sobre *upon, on, above, around (approximately)*
contra *against*	hacia *toward*	
de *of, from*	hasta *until, up to*	
desde *from, since*		

Common compound prepositions

a través de *across*	debajo de *under*	frente a *opposite to, facing*
acerca de *about, concerning*	delante de *in front of*	
	dentro de *inside*	fuera de *outside; except*
además de *besides*	después de *after*	
al lado de *next to*	detrás de *behind*	junto a *next to, near*
alrededor de *around*	encima de *on top of*	lejos de *far from*
antes de *before*	enfrente de *in front of, facing*	
cerca de *near*		

See *Capítulo 7.3* for use of **para** and **por**. Consult *Capítulo 8.4* for use of **a, con, de,** and **en** after certain verbs.

B. *The preposition a*

1. The preposition **a** is used before direct objects that refer to people. This use of the preposition **a** is called the personal **a.**

Pienso ver **a Luisa** esta tarde para recoger los panfletos.	*I intend to see Luisa this afternoon to pick up the pamphlets.*

2. **A** is also used before indirect object phrases and may be used with a prepositional pronoun to emphasize or clarify an indirect object pronoun.

—¿Le doy el panfleto **a Luisa**?	*Do I give the pamphlet to Luisa?*
—No, por favor, démelo **a mí**.	*No, give it to me, please.*

3. The preposition **a** is used with verbs of motion to indicate direction or destination.

El dirigente socialista va **a Lima**.	*The socialist leader is going to Lima.*
Viaja **a la capital** regularmente.	*He travels to the capital regularly.*
Llega **al centro** por la mañana.	*He arrives downtown in the morning.*

4. The preposition **a** is used to indicate location when the meaning intended is *at* in the sense of *beside, next to.*

El periodista está **a la puerta.**   *The journalist is at the door.*
El candidato lo hace pasar y ambos se   *The candidate shows him in and they*
    sientan **a la mesa.**   *both sit down at the table.*

5. The preposition **a** is used to indicate a point in time.

El atentado tuvo lugar **a las siete.**   *The attack took place at seven o'clock.*
Al principio, nadie tenía miedo.   *At first, no one was frightened.*
A las dos horas, supimos que habían   *After two hours, we found out that*
    secuestrado al Ministro de Asuntos   *they had kidnapped the minister of*
    Exteriores.   *foreign affairs.*

6. The preposition **a** is used in certain expressions that indicate the manner in which something is done or the means by which it is done.

Los secuestradores huían **a gatas** por   *The kidnappers were fleeing on all*
    un estrecho túnel.   *fours through a narrow tunnel.*
Fueron tomados **a la fuerza.**   *They were captured by force.*

7. The preposition **a** introduces prices and rates.

—¿**A cuánto** están las insignias del   *How much are the party insignias?*
    partido?
—**A veinticinco pesos** la docena.   *Twenty-five pesos a dozen.*

—¿**A qué velocidad** conduce ella?   *How fast does she drive?*
—**A ciento diez kilómetros** por hora.   *At one hundred ten kilometers per*
    hour.

8. **Al,** the contraction of **a** + **el,** is used with an infinitive to express simultaneity. The English equivalent of **al** + an infinitive is *on/upon* + a present participle, or a phrase beginning with *when* followed by a conjugated verb.

Al saber los primeros resultados de la   *Upon learning the first results of the*
    encuesta electoral, me asusté   *electoral survey, I was very*
    mucho.   *frightened.*
Pero **al leer** la encuesta con más   *But when I read the survey more care-*
    cuidado, me di cuenta de que todo   *fully, I realized everything was going*
    iba bien.   *well.*

9. The following list includes some common idiomatic expressions with the preposition **a.**

a causa de   *because of*

al comienzo de   *at the beginning of*

al contrario   *on the contrary*

a eso de   *around, about, approximately*

a fin de   *so that*

a fondo   *thoroughly*

a fuerza de   *by dint of, by force of*

a gusto   *at will*

a mano   *by hand*

a lo mejor   *probably, maybe*

al menos   *at least*

a menudo   *often*

a oscuras   *in the dark*

a pesar de   *in spite of*

a pie   *on foot*

a principios de   *at the beginning of*

a tiempo   *on (in) time*

a veces   *sometimes, at times*

a la vez   *at the same time*

poco a poco   *little by little*

Los militantes **a menudo** llegan **a tiempo.** Hoy **a lo mejor** aparecen tarde **a causa del** desfile.

The militants often arrive on time. Today they'll probably show up late because of the march.

C. *The preposition de*

1. The preposition **de** is used to indicate origin and source. With verbs of motion, **de** signals the point of departure.

   Ese refugiado es **de Centroamérica.**
   Salió **de Guatemala** en octubre.

   That refugee is from Central America.
   He left Guatemala in October.

2. The preposition **de** is used to locate an hour in the day and a date in the month.

   Son las tres **de la tarde.**
   Hoy estamos a 4 **de diciembre.**

   It's three in the afternoon.
   Today is the fourth of December.

3. The preposition **de** is used to indicate possession, including close association or relationship between objects. In Spanish, possession or ownership must be indicated by the construction *noun* + **de** + *noun (owner)*. Note that in phrases indicating authorship of a work, the preposition **de** and not **por** is used.

   —Vamos a la manifestación en el coche **de mi padre.** Aquí tengo las llaves **del coche.**
   —Vámonos; llevo esta crítica política **de un autor de la oposición.**

   Let's go to the demonstration in my father's car. Here are the keys to the car.
   Let's go; I'm taking (along) this political critique by an author from the opposition party.

4. The preposition **de** is used to indicate the contents of a receptacle.

   Le dieron al preso político una taza **de café** y un plato **de sopa.** Él pidió un vaso **de agua.**

   They gave the political prisoner a cup of coffee and a bowl of soup. He asked for a glass of water.

5. The preposition **de** is used to link two nouns in order to indicate the material of which something is made. The English equivalent of this construction may be an adjective or a prepositional phrase with *of.*

Estaba en la cárcel, detrás de una reja **de hierro.**	*He was in jail, behind an iron grating.*
Estaba sentado en una caja **de madera.**	*He was sitting on a wooden box.*

6. The preposition **de** is also used to form adjectival phrases that call attention to the distinctive characteristic(s) of a person or object. When **de** introduces a descriptive phrase, it frequently corresponds to the English *with.*

Era un hombre **de ojos vivos,** pero **de aspecto triste.**	*He was a man with lively eyes, but (with) a sad look.*
Aunque hacía frío, llevaba una camisa **de manga corta.**	*Although it was cold, he was wearing a short-sleeved shirt.*

7. The following list shows some common idiomatic expressions that begin with the preposition **de.**

de buen/mal humor *in a good/bad mood*	de pie *standing up*
de buena/mala gana *willingly/ unwillingly*	de prisa *in a hurry*
	de pronto *suddenly*
de esta/esa manera *(in) this/that way*	de repente *suddenly*
de manera/modo *in a manner/way*	de todos modos *anyway, in any case*
de memoria *by heart*	de veras *really, truly*
de nuevo *again*	de vez en cuando *from time to time*

De vez en cuando se publica un reportaje sobre las personas desaparecidas.	*From time to time, a report on missing persons is published.*
De repente todos los periódicos piden explicaciones.	*Suddenly all the newspapers demand an explanation.*

D. *The preposition en*

1. The preposition **en** is used to indicate location when no motion is involved. **En** signals a point in space enclosed within boundaries, corresponding in general to English *in, within,* or *at.*

Los candidatos están **en los estudios de televisión.**	*The candidates are in the TV studios.*
Tienen sus notas **en los maletines.**	*They have their notes in their briefcases.*

2. **En** also means *on* when referring to position. **Encima de** (*on, on top of*) is also used to refer to position, particularly when emphasizing location.

Los maletines de los candidatos están **en la mesa.**

The candidates' briefcases are on the table.

Encima de cada maletín hay un papel con una nota del moderador.

On top of each briefcase is a paper with a note from the moderator.

3. The preposition **en** is also used to indicate the time in which or when something took place.

La última crisis ministerial ocurrió **en 1985. Fue en abril. En aquel momento,** todos estábamos preocupados.

The last cabinet crisis took place in 1985. It was in April. At that time, we were all worried.

4. The preposition **en** is used with a means of transportation. **Por** can also be used with a means of transportation.

Durante la campaña, viajábamos **en (por) automóvil.**

During the campaign, we traveled by car.

Era peligroso ir **en (por) tren.**

It was dangerous to go by train.

5. The preposition **en** is used in certain idiomatic expressions.

en cambio   *on the other hand*
en cuanto a   *as far as . . . is concerned*

en lugar/vez de   *instead of*
en seguida   *right away*

En cuanto al discurso, nos pareció muy dogmático.

As far as the speech was concerned, we thought it was very dogmatic.

A mis amigos, **en cambio,** el discurso les pareció aburrido.

My friends, on the other hand, thought the speech was dull.

E. *The construction verb + (preposition) + noun complement*

No preposition in Spanish versus preposition in English

In contrast to English, the frequently used verbs **buscar, esperar, mirar, pagar,** and **pedir** do not require a preposition before a direct object to complete their meaning. The preposition **a,** or personal **a,** must be used, however, when the direct object is a person. Notice the use of *for* and *at* in some English equivalents.

—¿**Buscas a** alguien?
—No, no **busco a** nadie.

Are you looking for someone?
No, I'm not looking for anybody.

Miro la manifestación.
Miro a los manifestantes.

I'm watching the demonstration.
I'm looking at the demonstrators.

Preposition in Spanish versus no preposition in English

Some verbs require a preposition before a noun complement in Spanish, but not in English. The list that follows shows some common verbs that require a preposition in Spanish.

abusar de *to abuse*	dudar de *to doubt*
acercarse a *to approach*	entrar en/a *to enter*
acordarse de *to remember*	fiarse de *to trust*
asistir a *to attend*	fijarse en *to notice*
cambiar de *to change*	gozar de/con *to enjoy*
carecer de *to lack*	influir en *to influence*
casarse con *to marry*	jugar a *to play (a game)*
confiar en *to trust*	olvidarse de *to forget*
cumplir con *to carry out*	parecerse a *to resemble*
desconfiar de *to mistrust*	renunciar a *to give up*
disfrutar de/con *to enjoy*	salir de *to leave (a place)*

Algunos políticos **abusan de** la confianza del electorado y **carecen de** liderazgo. Los votantes no **confían en** ellos.

Some politicians abuse the confidence of the voters and lack leadership. Voters don't trust them.

Verbs with different prepositions in Spanish and English

Some verbs require a preposition in Spanish that differs from the preposition used in English. Compare the following frequently used Spanish verbs and prepositions with their English equivalents.

admirarse de *to be amazed at*	hablar de *to talk about*
consistir en *to consist of*	inquietarse por/con *to worry about*
contar con *to count on*	pensar en *to think of/about*
decidirse por *to decide on*	preguntar por *to inquire about*
depender de *to depend on*	reírse de *to laugh at*
despedirse de *to say good-by to*	servir de *to serve as*
enamorarse de *to fall in love with*	soñar con *to dream of*
felicitar por *to congratulate on*	

Sueña con las próximas elecciones cada noche. Quiere ganar para **servir de** representante a toda su comunidad. **Cuenta con** la ayuda de muchos votantes.

He dreams of the next elections every night. He wants to win in order to serve as a representative for all of his community. He counts on the help of many voters.

F. *Prepositional pronouns*

Subject pronouns	Prepositional pronouns
yo	mí
tú	ti
usted, él, ella	usted, él, ella; sí (*reflexive*)
nosotros/as	nosotros/as
vosotros/as	vosotros/as
ustedes, ellos, ellas	ustedes, ellos, ellas; sí (*reflexive*)

1. Prepositional pronouns are the same in form as the subject pronouns, except for **mí** and **ti**. **Sí** is the reflexive form of **usted(es)**, **él/ellos**, and **ella(s)** used after a preposition.

La victoria electoral de nuestro partido no depende completamente **de mí**.

Electoral victory for our party isn't completely up to me.

Puedes contar **con nosotros**.

You can count on us.

Vamos a votar **por ella**.

We're going to vote for her.

No vamos al desfile **sin ti**.

We're not going to the parade without you.

Los políticos no deben pensar sólo **en sí**.

Politicians should not think only of themselves.

2. The adjective **mismo/a/os/as** may be used to emphasize a reflexive prepositional pronoun.

Tengo confianza **en mí mismo.** Pero ellos dudan **de sí mismos.**

I have confidence in myself. But they have doubts about themselves.

3. After the preposition **con**, **mí** and **ti** have the special forms **conmigo** and **contigo**, respectively. The third person reflexive pronoun **sí** becomes **consigo** after the preposition **con**.

La candidata habló con Juan y **conmigo**.

The candidate spoke with Juan and me.

Cuenta **contigo** para su campaña.

She's counting on you for her campaign.

Ese orador parece hablar **consigo** y no con la gente.

That speaker seems to be talking to himself and not to the people.

4. The prepositions **entre, hasta, excepto,** and **según** require a subject pronoun, not a prepositional pronoun.

Esto debe quedar **entre tú y yo.**   *This must remain between you and me.*

Según tú, ¿cuál es el problema?   *According to you, what's the problem?*
Todos están de acuerdo, **excepto tú.**   *They all agree, except for you.*

Summary of important uses of *a, de,* and *en*

The preposition a

	Examples
Direct object (personal **a**)	Llamó **a las autoridades.**
Indirect object	Le señalé el error **al encuestador.**
Direction (*toward*)	El refugiado emigró **a Ecuador.**
Location (*beside, next to*)	Llegó **a la urna** y depositó el voto.
Time (point in time)	La reunión comenzó **a las once.**
Means, manner	Procesaron la encuesta **a mano.**
Price, rate	Estos banderines del partido están **a ochenta pesos** la docena.
Simultaneous action	**Al concluir** la ceremonia, me fui.

The preposition de

Origin, point of departure	El embajador es **de La Paz.** Viene ahora **de Buenos Aires.**
Time (of day, dates)	El vuelo llega a las seis **de la mañana.**
Possession, close association, authorship	Ese altoparlante es **del partido.** Me gustó el informe **del delegado.**
Contents	Fue un documento **de ocho páginas.**
Material something is made of	El maletín **de cuero** pertenece al ministro.
Characteristics	Es una persona **de mucha discreción.**

The preposition en

Location (*in, on*)	La urna electoral está **en aquel cuarto.** Mi pasaporte está **en tu escritorio.**
Time when something occurs	Las próximas elecciones se celebran **en 1996.**
Transportation	El presidente va a todas partes **en helicóptero.**

Comprehension questions

1. In one of the following two sentences the preposition **a** should be used. Identify the sentence and explain why it needs a preposition. **No comprendo _____ ese dirigente. No comprendo _____ ese panfleto.**

2. Would you use **a** or **en** in each of the following sentences? **El micrófono está _____ la mesa. Los candidatos se sentaron _____ la mesa.**

3. Would you use **a** or **en** in each of the following sentences? **La casa está _____ aquel parque. Hay dos encuestadores _____ la puerta. Quieren saber si vamos a votar _____ noviembre.**

4. Would you use **de** or **con** in each of the following sentences? **El senador _____ la barba larga quiere vernos. Yo no quiero hablar _____ el senador. Habla _____ modo extraño.**

5. Which of the following two sentences is used to indicate the destination of the presidential train? **El tren presidencial llega de Caracas. El tren presidencial llega a Caracas.** What does the other sentence mean?

6. Would **tú** or **ti** be used in the following sentences? **Para _____, votar es importantísimo. Según _____, votar es importantísimo.** Explain.

Ejercicios

A. Diga Ud. dónde está el ayuntamiento de su ciudad con relación a los siguientes lugares.

MODELO: la biblioteca
   La biblioteca está enfrente del (junto al, detrás del, lejos del, etc.) ayuntamiento.

1. el parque principal
2. la universidad
3. el banco más grande
4. el hospital
5. el restaurante más popular
6. las tiendas más elegantes

B. Use la preposición correcta en las siguientes frases sobre el estudio de las ciencias políticas. A veces no se necesita usar ninguna preposición y otras veces hay varias posibilidades.

1. Aquel hombre alto, el _____ los pantalones azules que lleva el maletín _____ cuero, es el doctor Ramírez, profesor _____ ciencias políticas.
2. Dicen que ha escrito varios libros _____ la política hispanoamericana _____ el siglo XX.
3. Sus libros han influido mucho _____ la opinión pública _____ las dos últimas décadas.
4. Si vas _____ la biblioteca, ¿me traes, por favor, el libro que necesitamos _____ la política _____ la Argentina?

5. También busco _____ un libro _____ el profesor Navarro _____ la situación económica _____ los países andinos.

6. El profesor nos dijo ayer que _____ el 30% _____ los países hispanoamericanos tienen gobiernos militares.

7. Normalmente comprendo _____ las conferencias _____ ese profesor, pero ayer no comprendí _____ nada; sólo pude comprender _____ su asistente después de la clase _____ el período _____ discusión.

8. Estoy pensando _____ escribir un trabajo _____ los problemas _____ transición cuando un país cambia _____ un gobierno militar _____ un gobierno democrático.

C. Las siguientes frases se refieren a un incidente que ocurrió durante una sesión de un congreso político. Dé la preposición o expresión que comunique el equivalente de las expresiones en inglés entre paréntesis. A veces hay más de una respuesta correcta.

(After) _____ defender su opinión (about) _____ la necesidad de congelar los precios, el ministro salió (in a rush) _____ de la reunión; parecía estar (in a bad mood) _____. (According to) _____ algunos testigos, tiró su portafolio (on top of) _____ la mesa (near to) _____ el jefe del comité selecto. (Besides) _____ eso, (upon) _____ llegar (next to) _____ un camarógrafo, le arrancó la cámara (from) _____ sus manos (without) _____ decir palabra. (At) _____ ese momento, hubo mucha confusión; (before) _____ volver a la agenda del día, los miembros del comité se consultaron unos a otros por varios minutos. (Suddenly) _____, el jefe se puso (in front of) _____ el grupo y les dijo (in a way) _____ muy formal que (because of) _____ la hora, iban a descansar un rato.

D. Use las preposiciones compuestas de la lista para completar las siguientes frases tomadas de un boletín noticiero sobre un golpe de estado. Sólo puede utilizar cada preposición una vez.

| a causa de | a eso de | dentro de | junto a |
| acerca de | a través de | después de | |

Y ahora un boletín _____ los últimos sucesos en el palacio nacional. Aparentemente hubo un intento de golpe de estado _____ las tres de la tarde. Corre el rumor de que la guardia presidencial quedó encerrada _____ el cuartel. El cuartel está situado _____ la casa donde vive la familia del presidente. _____ media hora llegaron a la escena nuestros reporteros y fotógrafos. Ellos pudieron observar los sucesos desde la calle y _____ las rejas de hierro que rodean el terreno del palacio. _____ los sucesos ocurridos esta tarde, nosotros vamos a interrumpir toda nuestra programación para traerles las últimas noticias.

E. Usted trabaja para Luisa Rosales, candidata al senado y miembro del partido centrista. Conteste las siguientes preguntas que le hace a Ud. una periodista, sustituyendo las frases indicadas con un pronombre preposicional apropiado.

MODELO: ¿Consultó la Sra. Rosales a **su encargado de relaciones de prensa?**
No, me consultó a mí. (Sí, lo consultó a él.)

1. ¿Viene un sindicalista mañana para hablar con **la Sra. Rosales**?
2. La candidata está bastante fastidiada con **los periodistas de esta ciudad,** ¿verdad?
3. ¿Ya leyó la Sra. Rosales la propuesta escrita por **los oficiales del presidente**?
4. ¿Ya se fue el ministro? ¿Se despidió de **la Sra. Rosales y de Ud.**?
5. ¿Cree Ud. que su candidata da la impresión de que se ha olvidado de **sus partidarios**?

IV. Indefinite expressions and their negatives

Yolanda: ¿Qué te pareció el discurso del líder de la oposición?

Irene: Pues, me parece que **no** dijo **nada.**

Yolanda: ¿Cómo puedes decir eso? **Cualquiera** que haya escuchado bien ese discurso se da cuenta de que el hombre es un gran patriota.

Irene: Pues, lo único que le interesa es salir reelegido. **Ni** él **ni** los otros políticos de su partido han hecho **nada** por el país.

Yolanda: Exageras; él está realmente interesado en resolver los problemas del país.

Irene: ¡Qué ingenua eres! **Ningún** miembro de la oposición puede resolver **nada.**

Yolanda: Tú no cambias; **siempre** fiel al partido en el poder.

Miembros del Partido Revolucionario Institucional de México tratan de inscribir a nuevos miembros, futuros votantes.

A. *Comparison chart of indefinite expressions and their negatives*

Negative	Affirmative [some]	Affirmative [all]
Pronouns		
nada *nothing, not . . . anything*	algo *something, anything*	todo *everything*
nadie *no one, nobody, not . . . anybody/anyone*	alguien *someone, somebody, any-one, anybody*	todos/as *everyone, everybody, all*
Pronouns / Adjectives		
ningún, ninguno/a *no (+ noun), no one, none, not . . . any/anybody*	algún, alguno/a/os/as *some (+ noun), any, someone*	todo/a *every, all* todos/as los/las *all, every, everyone*
[nadie]	cualquier(a) *any, anyone (at all)*	[todo/a/os/as]
Adverbs		
nunca, jamás *never, not . . . ever*	alguna(s) vez/veces *sometime(s), ever*	siempre *always*
tampoco *neither, not . . . either*		también *also, too*
Conjunctions		
ni *nor, not . . . or*	o *or*	y *and*
ni ... ni *neither . . . nor, not either . . . or*	o ... o *either . . . or*	[y]

B. *No with other negative words*

Negative sentences in Spanish contain one or more negative words. The negation **no** is used only if no other negative word precedes the verb.

—**No** propuso **nadie** un aumento de los impuestos.

No one proposed a tax increase.

—**Nadie** quiere proponer esa medida. En **ningún** distrito, **nunca ningún** candidato ha propuesto un aumento de los impuestos y ha ganado.

Nobody wants to propose that measure. In no district has a candidate ever proposed a tax increase and won.

C. *Indefinite pronouns and adjectives and their negatives*

1. The indefinite pronouns **alguien** and **nadie** refer only to people. When used as direct objects, they are preceded by the preposition **a**.

Alguien amenazó al presidente.	*Somebody threatened the president.*
Nadie amenazó al vicepresidente.	*Nobody threatened the vice president.*
La policía no encarceló **a nadie.**	*The police did not imprison anybody.*

2. **Algo** and **nada** refer only to objects and events.

—¿Hay **algo** sobre las elecciones municipales en el periódico?	*Is there anything on the municipal elections in the newspaper?*
—Sí, hay **algo,** pero no dicen **nada** de nuestro candidato.	*Yes, there's something, but they don't say anything about our candidate.*

3. The adjectives **algún, alguno/a/algunos/as** and **ningún, ninguno/a** can refer to people, objects, and events. When they modify direct object nouns referring to people, they are preceded by the preposition **a**.

Vi **a algunos** policías cerca del centro electoral. No esperan **ningún** incidente violento, ¿verdad?	*I saw some policemen near the polls. They don't expect any violent incident, do they?*

4. **Alguno/a/os/as** and **ninguno/a** are pronouns that replace nouns referring to people or objects. They may be used by themselves or followed by a prepositional phrase beginning with **de**. When **alguno** or **ninguno** replaces a direct object referring to a person or persons, the preposition **a** precedes the indefinite word.

—¿Leíste los programas electorales?	*Did you read the electoral platforms?*
—Leí **algunos. Ninguno** era muy profundo, me parece.	*I read some. None was very profound, it seems to me.*
—¿Conoces **a algunos de** estos dirigentes?	*Do you know any of these leaders?*
—No, no conozco **a ninguno (de ellos).**	*No, I don't know any (of them).*

5. The negative adjective **ningún/ninguna** and the pronoun **ninguno/a** are almost always used in the singular. They are used in the plural only to modify or replace a noun that is always plural: **No hay ningunos pantalones azules; La agencia de viajes no ofrece ningunas vacaciones en Tibet.**

6. The indefinite word **cualquiera** may be used as an adjective or a pronoun. When used as an adjective before a masculine or feminine noun, **cualquiera** is shortened to **cualquier.**

—**Cualquiera** puede votar en estas elecciones, ¿verdad?	*Anyone can vote in these elections, right?*
—Bueno, **cualquier** elector que esté debidamente inscrito.	*Well, any voter who is duly registered.*

D. *Indefinite adverbs*

1. **Nunca** and **jamás** both mean *never.* **Nunca** is more frequently used in everyday speech. In questions, **jamás** or **alguna vez** may be used to mean *ever;* **jamás** is preferred when a negative answer is expected.

—¿Has escuchado **jamás** un discurso más demagógico?	*Have you ever listened to a more demagogic speech?*
—No, **nunca.** (No, **jamás.**)	*No, never.*
—¿Ha hecho campaña **alguna vez** antes este candidato?	*Has this candidate ever campaigned before?*
—Sí, ésta es la tercera vez que intenta salir elegido.	*Yes, this is the third time that he's trying to get elected.*

2. For emphasis, **nunca** and **jamás** may be used together, in that order.

Nunca jamás voy a votar por ese candidato otra vez.	*I will never ever again vote for that candidate.*

3. **Tampoco,** the negative counterpart of **también,** may be used alone in a phrase or preceded by **no** or **ni.**

—Hoy no puedo asistir a la reunión de nuestro partido.	*I can't attend the meeting of our party today.*
—Yo **tampoco. (Ni** yo **tampoco.)** ¿Y tú, puedes ir?	*Me neither. And you, can you go?*
—Yo **tampoco** puedo asistir. (Yo **no** puedo asistir **tampoco.**)	*I can't attend either.*
—Yo podría asistir mañana.	*I could attend tomorrow.*
—Yo **también.**	*Me too.*

E. *The conjunctions o and ni*

1. The conjunction **o** is used to mention alternatives; the conjunction **ni** to negate alternatives.

¿Es republicano **o** demócrata tu hermano José?

Is your brother José a Republican or a Democrat?

José no es republicano **ni** demócrata; es apolítico. **Ni** vota **ni** se interesa en las elecciones.

José is neither a Republican nor a Democrat; he's apolitical. He neither votes nor is interested in elections.

2. In contrast to English, when **o** and **ni** are used to offer or negate the choices between the subjects of a sentence, the verb is in the plural.

—**(O)** El plebiscito **o** el referéndum **van** a tener lugar la próxima semana.

Either the plebiscite or the referendum is taking place next week.

—Estás equivocado. **Ni** el plebiscito **ni** el referéndum se **van** a llevar a cabo pronto.

You're wrong. Neither the plebiscite nor the referendum is going to take place soon.

3. When **o** and **ni** offer or negate the choices between the objects of a verb, the conjunction is required before the last object and is optional before previously mentioned objects. **No** precedes the verb when **ni** is used.

—Aquí van a hacer (**o**) una rebelión **o** una revolución.

They're going to have a rebellion or a revolution here.

—Falta mucho para eso; **no** hacen (**ni**) manifestaciones **ni** marchas de protesta.

There's a long way to go before that; they're not having demonstrations nor protest marches.

4. **Ni** before a noun phrase is equivalent to *not even*.

Ni los legisladores entienden las muchas leyes que nos gobiernan.

Not even the legislators understand the many laws that govern us.

Comprehension questions

1. Should you use **alguna** or **cualquier** in each of the following sentences? **Puedes ir a votar a _____ hora. ¿O prefieres _____ hora en particular?**

2. Should **algo** or **nada** be used in each part of the following conversational exchange? —**¿Entiendes _____ de ese programa electoral? —No, no entiendo _____ .**

3. What present indicative form of **hablar** should be used in the following sentence? **Mis padres son políticos, pero ni mi padre ni mi madre _____ de política en casa.**

4. The word **nunca** in the sentence **Nunca leo los sondeos de opinión** can also follow the verb. What would be the resulting sentence if **nunca** followed the verb?

Ejercicios

A. Imagínese que Ud. es miembro del gabinete del gobierno y que dentro de pocos minutos va a participar en un debate televisado. Ud. contempla la escena por detrás del telón del sitio del debate y comenta con un(a) ayudante lo que ve y luego lo que no ve.

MODELO: representantes / senador
Veo a algunos representantes, pero no veo a ningún senador.

1. gente joven / gente mayor
2. altavoces / micrófono
3. miembros del partido / jefe
4. carteles de protesta / cartel de apoyo
5. periodistas / comentarista de televisión
6. desconocidos / cara simpática

B. Domingo acaba de llegar a Madrid donde va a pasar un semestre estudiando el sistema político español. Pero, nadie del programa fue al aeropuerto a recogerlo y se siente perdido. Haga el papel de Domingo y conteste con frases negativas las preguntas que le hace un empleado de la oficina de información.

MODELO: *Empleado:* ¿Conoce Ud. a alguien en Madrid?
Domingo: *No, no conozco a nadie.*

1. ¿Llegó alguna de sus maletas?
2. ¿Tiene Ud. alguna dirección o teléfono?
3. ¿Habló Ud. con alguien del programa de Madrid?
4. ¿Tiene Ud. moneda española?
5. ¿Ha estado Ud. antes alguna vez en España?
6. ¿Ha comido Ud. algo hoy?

C. A Ud. le gusta incitar discusiones y por eso a veces contradice a todo el mundo. Responda a los siguientes comentarios de forma contradictoria, y comience cada frase con expresiones como **¡Qué tontería!, ¡Imposible!, ¡Qué barbaridad!** y **¡Qué va!**

MODELO: Después de la próxima reunión del liderato mundial, vamos a comprendernos todos a la perfección.
¡Qué tontería! Nunca vamos a comprendernos totalmente.

1. Las conferencias internacionales siempre nos conducen hacia la paz.
2. Algunos de los diplomáticos de este país saben hablar varios idiomas.
3. En esta nueva generación de líderes internacionales, seguramente hay algunos candidatos con ideas nuevas.
4. Alguien del gobierno va a dimitir (*resign*) pronto; ya verás.
5. El Ministro de Asuntos Exteriores va a hablar mañana sobre los problemas del Medio Oriente o los de Hispanoamérica.
6. Los políticos de la derecha en Europa van a hacer algo diferente en su estrategia electoral este año.

D. Ud. suele ver algo positivo en todo. Responda a los comentarios siguientes con frases afirmativas. Empiece cada oración con **No es cierto.**

MODELO: No aprendimos nada en la conferencia sobre los impuestos estatales.
No es cierto. Aprendimos algo; de hecho, aprendimos mucho.

1. La gente joven no asiste nunca a las conferencias políticas.
2. Ninguna agencia gubernamental quiere contratar a estudiantes en el verano.
3. ¿Sabes que los graduados de este año no admiran a ningún político?
4. Nadie entiende el proceso democrático como la gente que tiene una educación universitaria.
5. Tú tampoco ves nada positivo en el uso de la energía nuclear.
6. Ningún político presta atención a las necesidades económicas de los estudiantes universitarios.

V. Spanish equivalents of *to miss*

The Spanish verbs and expressions **perder(se), faltar, hacer falta, echar de menos,** and **extrañar** can each express English *to miss* or *to be missing,* even though they may also have other meanings. Which verb is used depends upon the context. Note that although these five expressions are those most frequently used to express *to miss,* other verbs are also possible.

1. **Perder** is used to refer to missing a means of transportation or an opportunity. Some sense of responsibility for the loss is expressed or implied.

El alcalde salió tarde y **perdió** el avión. *The mayor left late and missed the plane.*

Parece que **perdió** la oportunidad de asistir a un congreso importante. *It appears he missed the chance to attend an important conference.*

2. **Perderse** is used in the sense of missing an event, activity, or moment, especially something agreeable or exciting, or of special interest to the person(s) affected. **Perderse** expresses an emotional involvement or intensity that is lacking with **perder**.

Me perdí el desfile del ejército.	*I missed my chance to see the army's parade.*
¡**Te perdiste** un banquete excepcional después del desfile!	*You missed out on an exceptional banquet after the parade!*

3. **Faltar (a)** signifies *to miss* in the sense of simply not attending a class, an appointment, or other event; no sense of responsibility is implied. **Faltar** is used to indicate that someone or something is not present.

¿Por qué **faltó** el presidente **a** la reunión ayer?	*Why did the president miss the meeting yesterday?*
Faltaron los micrófonos hasta el comienzo de la reunión.	*The microphones were missing until the beginning of the meeting.*

4. **Hacer falta** is used to indicate that someone or something is not present, although desired or needed. **Hacer falta,** used in the sense of *to miss* or *to be missing*, implies a certain degree of need for the absent person or thing.

Me **hiciste falta** en la reunión; necesitábamos un voto más para aprobar el proyecto.	*I needed you at the meeting; we needed one more vote to approve the project.*
Hace falta más participación directa en el proceso político.	*More direct participation is needed (missing) in the political process.*

5. To miss someone or something in an emotional way is most often expressed with **echar de menos** or **extrañar**. Both suggest regret for the absence. Although **hacer falta** can also be used with this meaning, it occurs much less frequently.

Echo mucho **de menos** las revistas políticas de mi país.	*I very much miss the political magazines of my country.*
También **extraño** mi anterior actividad política.	*I also miss my previous political activity.*
Parece que me **hace falta** el ambiente político.	*It appears that I miss the political arena.*

Ejercicios

A. Hace un mes que Ud. empezó a trabajar en la campaña electoral de un candidato presidencial. Responda a las siguientes preguntas de un(a) compañero(a) de clase de una manera personal, inventando una respuesta imaginaria, si quiere. Utilice **perder(se), faltar, hacer falta, echar de menos** o **extrañar**.

MODELO: Te ves triste; ¿echas de menos a alguien?
Claro, echo mucho de menos a mi novio(a), porque no lo(la) veo con mucha frecuencia ahora.

1. ¿Por qué faltaste a la rueda de prensa?
2. ¿Qué te faltan, tus notas para la reunión?
3. ¿Te hace falta más tiempo para practicar tu discurso?
4. ¿Te perdiste el último discurso televisado del presidente o lo escuchaste?
5. ¿Qué cosas echas de menos cuando viajas durante las campañas políticas?
6. Te ves confuso(a) en este momento; ¿te hace falta algo?
7. ¿Has perdido alguna vez un vuelo en esta campaña?
8. ¿A quién extrañas más cuando estás fuera de casa? ¿Por qué?

B. Complete el siguiente diálogo con la forma correcta de **perder(se), faltar, hacer falta** o **echar de menos,** según el contexto.

Camilo: ¿Qué pasó anoche, Paula? ¿Por qué _____ a la reunión sobre las próximas elecciones?

Paula: _____ porque _____ el autobús de las siete. No hay otro autobús después de esa hora.

Camilo: ¡Qué mala suerte! _____ una reunión estupenda y todos nosotros te _____.

Paula: Gracias, Camilo. ¿Tomaste apuntes? ¿Me los prestas? Me _____ para preparar un informe.

Actividades para la comunicación

A. Sugerencias para los políticos. En forma de cadena, exprese algunos modos de solucionar los siguientes problemas políticos o cívicos.

MODELO: ¿Cómo se puede resolver el problema del déficit nacional?
E1:   *Se puede resolver ese problema gastando menos dinero del presupuesto nacional.*
E2:   *Subiendo los impuestos. (Etc.)*

1. ¿Cómo consiguen dinero para sus campañas los candidatos?
2. ¿De qué manera podemos entendernos mejor con otros países?
3. ¿Cómo se pueden mejorar las carreteras y las autopistas de este país?
4. ¿En qué forma podemos aumentar el número de votantes en las elecciones?
5. ¿De qué modo podemos mejorar el sistema educativo de este país?

B. Especulaciones. Converse con otro(a) estudiante sobre los posibles resultados, buenos o malos, si las personas indicadas continúan haciendo las siguientes u otras acciones imaginarias.

MODELO: el presidente / insistir en tener más armamentos
E1: *¿Qué va a pasar si el presidente sigue (continúa) insistiendo en tener más armamentos?*
E2: *Si eso sigue (continúa) así, algunos senadores nunca van a apoyar el presupuesto.*

1. los terroristas / secuestrar aviones
2. las potencias mundiales / discutir sin llegar a un acuerdo sobre el armamento nuclear
3. algunos países / abusar de los derechos humanos
4. nuestros diplomáticos / dialogar con los líderes comunistas
5. los gobernadores / subir los impuestos
6. los militares / pedir cada vez más armamentos costosos

C. Ayer y hoy. Dígale a otro(a) estudiante de la clase lo que estaban haciendo las siguientes personas u otras de su elección hace unos años en comparación con lo que están haciendo ahora. Se permite un poco de exageración.

MODELO: los fabricantes de computadoras
Hace cinco años todos los fabricantes de computadoras estaban ganando mucho dinero, pero ahora algunos están perdiendo dinero y están cayendo en la bancarrota.

1. mi familia
2. los locutores de radio
3. yo
4. mi mejor amigo(a)
5. el gobernador de este estado
6. mi político(a) favorito(a)

D. Al ataque. Imagínese que Ud. es candidato(a) para una posición política muy importante y en este momento está hablando con un reportero sobre su adversario(a). Enumere algunas cosas que su adversario(a) hace mal o condiciones que están peores hoy que antes.

MODELO: *Mi adversario(a) no hace nada por los pobres ni por los ancianos. Nadie puede creer lo que dice. Algunas personas piensan que él (ella) no puede mejorar la economía de este estado.*

E. Puntos de vista. Describa algún aspecto de la vida política o social de su universidad, ciudad, estado, país u otro país que esté cambiando o que sea especialmente interesante en estos momentos. ¿Qué están haciendo Ud., sus amigos, o los líderes políticos para llevar a cabo los cambios? Puede describir una situación verdadera o una imaginaria.

MODELO: *Pues, en este momento la vida social de mi universidad está cambiando. En realidad se está haciendo muy interesante con bailes, fiestas y conciertos. No sé quién está organizando eso...*

CAPÍTULO 7

◆

La vida universitaria

Varios alumnos charlan por los pasillos de la Pontífica Universidad Católica de Chile en Santiago. El año académico en Chile se extiende desde marzo hasta diciembre.

Conversación

1. ¿Por qué estudia Ud. una carrera universitaria? ¿Por qué estudia Ud. en esta universidad?
2. ¿Cómo se imaginaba Ud. que iba a ser su vida universitaria antes de asistir a esta universidad? ¿Y cómo ha resultado ser?
3. ¿Cuáles son los problemas más grandes que ha tenido que enfrentar en esta universidad? ¿Cómo los resolvió Ud.?
4. ¿Ha solicitado alguna vez una beca o un préstamo estudiantiles? Explique.
5. ¿Estudia Ud. solamente la noche antes de un examen o con regularidad? ¿Por qué?
6. ¿Cuál cree Ud. que es el verdadero valor de tener un diploma universitario, ganar más dinero o tener una mejor preparación para la vida? Explique su respuesta.
7. ¿Le gustaría a Ud. tener sus clases en una universidad de arquitectura colonial como la de la foto en la página anterior? Explique.
8. ¿De qué hablarán los alumnos de la foto? ¿De qué hablan Ud. y sus amigos entre clases?

Vocabulario temático

alumnado, el student body
apuntes, los notes
auditorio, el auditorium; audience
beca, la scholarship
conferencia, la lecture
conocimiento, el knowledge
consejero(a), el(la) advisor
consulta, la consultation
charla, la chat, discussion
dato, el fact
decano(a), el/la dean
doctorado, el doctorate
especialidad, la major
horario, el schedule
informe, el report; information
internado, el internship
materia, la subject matter, subject
matrícula, la enrollment; registration
préstamo, el loan
profesorado, el professoriate
promedio, el average
rector(a), el(la) university president
requisito, el requirement

tablón, el bulletin board
tarifa, la price, cost, charge

abarcar to deal with; to include
aclarar to clarify
aconsejar to advise
aprobar (ue) to pass; to approve
atrasar to fall behind; to delay
matricular(se) to enroll; to register
patrocinar to sponsor
postular to apply for
repasar to review
suspender to fail (academically); to suspend
trasladar(se) to change residence; to move to a new job

escolar scholastic

cambiar de especialidad to change one's major
curso obligatorio, el required course
residencia de estudiantes, la dormitory, student housing

I. The future tense

Profesor:	Antes de terminar la clase, quiero comunicarles que el Departamento de Español **patrocinará** una charla sobre los problemas del desarrollo en la América Latina. **Tendrá** lugar el jueves próximo a las siete en el auditorio. **Hablará** el Dr. Salcedo, profesor visitante de Colombia. **Habrá** luego una sesión de preguntas y comentarios en la cual **participarán** varios alumnos hispanoamericanos. Espero verlos a todos allí.
Susana:	(*En voz baja*) Paco, ¿qué tal si vamos? **Será** interesante, ¿no crees?
Paco:	No sé si **podré** ir. Tengo examen el viernes y estoy muy atrasado en mis estudios.
Susana:	Como siempre. Bueno,... **iré** y luego te **contaré**.

A. *Regular forms*

estudiar	aprender	escribir
estudiar**é**	aprender**é**	escribir**é**
estudiar**ás**	aprender**ás**	escribir**ás**
estudiar**á**	aprender**á**	escribir**á**
estudiar**emos**	aprender**emos**	escribir**emos**
estudiar**éis**	aprender**éis**	escribir**éis**
estudiar**án**	aprender**án**	escribir**án**

The future stem of most Spanish verbs is the infinitive: **estudiar-, aprender-, escribir-.** The future endings are the same for all Spanish verbs: **-é, -ás, -á, -emos, -éis,** and **-án.**

B. *Irregular stems*

1. Twelve verbs have an irregular stem in the future.

Infinitive	Stem	First person sing.
The **-e-** from the infinitive ending **-er** is dropped		
caber	**cabr-**	yo cabré
haber	**habr-**	yo habré
poder	**podr-**	yo podré
querer	**querr-**	yo querré
saber	**sabr-**	yo sabré

Infinitive	Stem	First person sing.
The vowel of the infinitive ending is replaced with **-d-**		
poner	**pondr-**	yo pondré
salir	**saldr-**	yo saldré
tener	**tendr-**	yo tendré
valer	**valdr-**	yo valdré
venir	**vendr-**	yo vendré
Short irregular stem		
decir	**dir-**	yo diré
hacer	**har-**	yo haré

2. Verbs whose stems contain **-hacer, -poner, -tener,** or **-venir** also have the same irregularities in the stem of the future. Note that in forming the future stem, the verb **satisfacer** follows the pattern of verbs ending in **-hacer,** except that it changes **-facer** to **-far-: satisfacer** > **satisfar-.**

-hacer > **-har-**
deshacer   *to undo*
rehacer   *to do again*

-tener > **-tendr-**
contener   *to contain*
detener   *to detain; to arrest*
mantener   *to maintain; to support*
retener   *to retain*

-poner > **-pondr-**
componer   *to compose; to repair*
imponer   *to impose*
proponer   *to propose*
suponer   *to suppose*

-venir > **-vendr-**
convenir   *to be convenient*
intervenir   *to intervene*
prevenir   *to prevent; to warn*

C. *Uses of the future*

1. The future tense is primarily used to refer to events or conditions that will take place after the moment of speaking.

La vida **será** más fácil después de obtener mi diploma. **Trabajaré** para una empresa importante y **tendré** un puesto interesante.

Life will be easier after I get my diploma. I'll work for an important company and I'll have an interesting job.

2. The future is also used in a clause to express what will most likely occur under certain conditions.

Si termino mis tareas antes de las cinco, **iré** a la charla del profesor Salcedo.	*If I finish my homework before five o'clock, I'll go to Professor Salcedo's lecture.*
Si tengo un examen mañana, no **podré** acompañarte al festival de cine.	*If I have an exam tomorrow, I won't be able to go with you to the movie festival.*

3. The future tense may be used to speculate about activities or states that are in progress in the present. Observe the use of the future to express probability or conjecture in the following examples. (See Section V in this chapter for use of **deber** to express probability.)

—¿Cuántos años **tendrá** el profesor Cardona?	*I wonder how old Professor Cardona is?*
—**Tendrá** unos veinticinco años a lo más.	*He must be twenty-five years old at the most.*
—No está en su oficina. ¿Dónde **estará** ahora?	*He's not in his office. Where do you suppose he is now?*
—**Estará** en clase.	*He's probably in class.*
—¿**Estará** enseñando en este edificio?	*I wonder if he's teaching in this building?*
—Probablemente.	*Probably.*

4. Compare the meanings conveyed by use of the present and the future in the following sentences.

Es la una.	*It's one o'clock.* (The speaker is certain of the time.)
Será la una.	*It must be one o'clock.* (The speaker is guessing.)

5. In contrast to Spanish, the future is not used in English to express probability. Note the various ways of expressing probability in English.

¿Qué hora **será**?	*What time can it be?* *I wonder what time it is?*
Serán las tres.	*It's probably three o'clock.* *I guess it's three o'clock.* *I suppose it's three o'clock.* *It must be three o'clock.*

6. The future tense may also be used to order someone to do something and to promise to do something.

—Susana, **llevarás** este ensayo al profesor Díaz, como me lo prometiste ayer.
—Cómo no, se lo **llevaré** ahora mismo.

Susana, take this essay to Professor Díaz, as you promised me yesterday.
Fine, I'll take it to him right away.

D. *Other ways of expressing future time*

1. A present indicative form of **ir** + **a** + an infinitive may be used to refer to events in the future in Spanish. The English equivalent is *to be going to* + an infinitive. In informal Spanish the **ir** + **a** + infinitive construction is used more frequently than is the future tense.

Voy a matricularme para el segundo semestre.
Vamos a esforzarnos por salir mejor esta vez, ¿verdad?

I'm going to enroll for the second semester.
We're going to make an effort to do better this time, right?

2. The simple present indicative may be used in Spanish to indicate scheduled events in the future. The English equivalent is often expressed by the present progressive tense. (See *Capítulo 1.2* for use of the present indicative with future meaning.)

Mañana **salimos** para la universidad a primera hora.
Tenemos un examen a las nueve.

Tomorrow we're leaving for the university first thing in the morning.
We're having an exam at nine o'clock.

Comprehension questions

1. In which of the following sentences can the present indicative form **dan** be replaced by the future form **darán**? **Esta tarde dan una charla sobre las carreras médicas. Generalmente los viernes dan una charla sobre las carreras médicas.**

2. What is the English equivalent of the future form **será** in the following dialogue? **—¿Quién es ese señor? —No sé; será el nuevo profesor de historia del arte.**

3. Give two other ways in Spanish of expressing the future form **me quedaré** in the following sentence. **Esta tarde me quedaré en la biblioteca.**

Ejercicios

A. Ud. está encargado(a) de una fiesta en su residencia de estudiantes. Dígales a las varias personas mencionadas exactamente cuáles son sus responsabilidades.

MODELO: Ricardo / poner una invitación en el tablero de la cafetería
Ricardo, tú pondrás una invitación en el tablero de la cafetería.

1. Ana y yo / conseguir los permisos que necesitamos
2. Margarita / comprar las bebidas
3. Juan y Antonio / encargarse de la comida
4. Paulina / contratar un conjunto de música
5. Cecilia y Edmundo / arreglar las decoraciones
6. Bárbara y yo / cobrar el dinero a la puerta de entrada
7. Ramón / mantener el orden durante la fiesta
8. Eugenio y Leonardo / hacer la limpieza después

B. Ud. trata de obtener el permiso de sus padres para estudiar español un semestre en el extranjero con un grupo de estudiantes de su universidad. Conteste sus preguntas, informándoles de los detalles del programa.

MODELO: ¿cómo pagar (tú) los gastos? (con el dinero de mi trabajo de verano)
Padres: *¿Cómo pagarás los gastos?*
Usted: *Pagaré los gastos con el dinero de mi trabajo de verano.*

1. ¿cómo viajar (Uds.) allí? (juntos en avión)
2. ¿dónde vivir (tú)? (con una familia seleccionada por la universidad)
3. ¿acompañarles algún profesor? (la profesora Morales)
4. ¿dónde tener (Uds.) las clases? (en un edificio alquilado por la universidad)
5. ¿recibir (tú) suficientes créditos allí? (quince créditos)
6. ¿poder (Uds.) viajar a otros sitios durante el programa? (a tres países diferentes)
7. ¿volver (tú) a casa al terminar el semestre o quedarse allí algunas semanas? (quedarse diez días)
8. ¿estar con un(a) amigo(a) (tú) durante ese último período? (con todo el grupo)

C. Explique en frases completas la siguiente agenda de un(a) amigo(a) para la próxima semana. Después haga Ud. su propia agenda para la próxima semana diciendo algunas cosas que hará Ud. cada día.

MODELO: lunes / terminar de pintar la mesa
El lunes (José) terminará de pintar la mesa.
El lunes yo iré con mi hermana de compras.

1. martes / conseguir boletos para el concierto
2. miércoles / trasladarse a otro dormitorio
3. jueves / devolverle los discos a Lupe

4. viernes / venir pronto a casa para preparar el examen
5. sábado / tener a José y a Ana como invitados
6. domingo / saber si los padres de (José) vienen al partido de béisbol

D. Por fin ha llegado el viernes y Ud. especula con un(a) amigo(a) acerca de algunos planes que tienen para divertirse más tarde y durante el fin de semana.

MODELO: Si termino esta tarea antes de las tres,...
           E1:   *Si termino esta tarea antes de las tres, iré al café con los demás. ¿Y tú?*
           E2:   *Pues, yo me quedaré aquí porque tengo que planchar la ropa para mi cita de esta noche.*

1. Si saco una buena nota en el examen, esta noche...
2. Si no hace frío mañana,...
3. Si Roberto está en la discoteca esta noche,...
4. Si tenemos tiempo el domingo,...
5. Si mis amigos(as) insisten en estudiar esta noche,...
6. Si todos deciden comer pizza después del cine,...

E. Sus compañeros de clase se sienten nerviosos el día antes de un examen importante de Historia de Europa. Trate de calmarlos con respecto a las siguientes situaciones.

MODELO: ¡Ay! No encuentro mis apuntes de este semestre.
           No te preocupes; estarán en tu casa.

1. ¡Qué horrible! Se me perdió el libro de texto.
2. ¡No faltaba más! Necesito hablar con la profesora, pero no está en su oficina.
3. ¿Sabes qué pasó? Alguien ha tomado prestada de la biblioteca la monografía que tenemos que leer.
4. No voy a poder acordarme de nada en el examen; hay que aprender de memoria muchas cosas.
5. Nunca entiendo bien las preguntas que hace la profesora. ¡No sé qué voy a hacer!

II. The conditional

Victoria: (*Con indecisión*) Buenas tardes, ¿**podría** decirme dónde queda la oficina donde dan información sobre las becas?
Sr. Parra: Pues, aquí es. ¿Qué información necesita?
Victoria: Es sobre la beca "Liberty". Me dijeron que aquí me **darían** los formularios que hay que llenar.
Sr. Parra: Sí, cómo no. No va a postular este semestre, ¿no?
Victoria: Pues sí, señor. Un amigo me dijo que todavía tengo tiempo.

Sr. Parra: Lo siento, pero su amigo no **leería** nuestro último boletín. El plazo para presentar las solicitudes para este semestre se cumplió hace dos semanas.

Victoria: ¿Y cuándo **podría** solicitar la beca para el próximo semestre, entonces?

Sr. Parra: Vuelva a vernos antes del fin de este semestre. **Deberíamos** tener todos los documentos preparados para aquel entonces.

A. *Forms of the conditional*

aconsejar	prometer	escribir
aconsejar**ía**	prometer**ía**	escribir**ía**
aconsejar**ías**	prometer**ías**	escribir**ías**
aconsejar**ía**	prometer**ía**	escribir**ía**
aconsejar**íamos**	prometer**íamos**	escribir**íamos**
aconsejar**íais**	prometer**íais**	escribir**íais**
aconsejar**ían**	prometer**ían**	escribir**ían**

1. The stem used to form the conditional is the infinitive, the same stem used to form the future. The endings of the conditional are always regular and are the same for all Spanish verbs; they are the same as the imperfect endings of **-er** and **-ir** verbs: **-ía, -ías, -ía, -íamos, -íais,** and **ían.**

2. All verbs that have an irregular stem in the future, also have the same irregular stem in the conditional: yo **vendría, saldría, diría.** (Consult Section I of this chapter for a list of verbs with irregular stems in the future.)

B. *Uses of the conditional*

1. The conditional is used to express what would or could occur, but possibly may not occur due to circumstances.

—¿En qué cursos te vas a matricular este semestre?

What courses are you going to take this semester?

—No sé todavía porque no he hablado con la consejera; **querría** seguir un curso sobre teorías económicas.

I don't know yet because I haven't talked to the advisor; I'd like to take a course on economic theories.

Con una beca, no **tendría** que trabajar y **podría** dedicarme de lleno al estudio.

With a scholarship, I wouldn't have to work and I could devote myself to studying full-time.

2. The conditional is also used to refer to and to report future events or conditions as viewed from a point in the past.

Mi consejero me dijo que la ingeniería **sería** un buen campo en los próximos años. Me explicó que **habría** muchas oportunidades nuevas en ese campo.

My advisor told me that engineering would be a good field in the next few years. He explained to me that there would be many new opportunities in that field.

3. Just as the future tense can be used to express probability or conjecture about activities or states in progress in the present, the conditional may be used to imply probability or conjecture about activities or states in progress in the past.

—Un amigo me dijo que la reunión sería en esta sala.
—Lo siento, pero no **estaría** bien informado.

A friend told me that the meeting would be in this room.
I'm sorry, but he was probably not well informed.

—¿Qué le pasó a Julia? No vino a nuestra reunión del club de fotografía.
—**Tendría** un examen al día siguiente.

What happened to Julia? She didn't come to our meeting of the photography club.
She probably had an exam the following day.

4. The conditional is used to convey politeness or to soften suggestions with verbs such as **deber, poder, querer, preferir, desear,** and **gustar.** Use of the simple present indicative is more matter-of-fact and usually more informal. (See *Capítulo 11.4* for use of the imperfect subjunctive to express politeness.)

Querría saber si estoy matriculado como oyente en la clase de antropología. ¿**Podría** usted verificar esa información?

I'd like to know if I'm registered as an auditor in the anthropology class. Could you check that information?

5. Just as the future is used to express that something is more or less likely to occur under certain conditions, the conditional is used to indicate highly unlikely or contrary-to-fact situations. (This use of the conditional is treated in *Capítulo 12.2.*)

Si tuviera más tiempo, **participaría** en más actividades sociales en esta universidad.

If I had more time, I would participate in more social activities at this university.

Comprehension questions

1. Pedro says: **«Me graduaré en mayo».** Would a person reporting Pedro's statement use the future form **se graduará** or the conditional form **se graduaría** in the following sentence? **Pedro me dijo que _____ en mayo.**

2. What is the meaning of the phrase **estaría enferma** in the following dialogue? **—Ella no vino a clase ayer. ¿Sabe usted por qué? —No, no sé; estaría enferma.**

3. How would you politely ask a friend to lend you one of his/her textbooks? **¿Me puedes prestar el texto de sociología? ¿Me podrías prestar el texto de sociología?**

Ejercicios

A. Dé una excusa por qué Ud. no puede hacer los siguientes favores que algunos compañeros le piden.

MODELO: ¿Me puedes ayudar con este problema? (no tener tiempo)
Te ayudaría, pero no tengo tiempo en este momento.

1. ¿Me prestas tu calculadora? (necesitarla hoy)
2. ¿Me escribes este trabajo a máquina? (estar descompuesta la máquina)
3. ¿Me corriges la ortografía de este informe? (tener que trabajar ahora)
4. ¿Me pasas tu diccionario de español por unos momentos? (no tenerlo conmigo)
5. ¿Me dejas tu cuaderno de apuntes para la clase de geografía? (tener que estudiar geografía esta noche)
6. ¿Repasas conmigo la materia para el examen de historia del arte? (tener otro compromiso en este momento)

B. Un(a) compañero(a) de clase comenta varias cosas que ocurrieron ayer. Explíquele lo que probablemente pasó.

MODELO: el profesor de física / faltar a clase (estar enfermo)
Compañero(a):   *Ayer el profesor de física faltó a clase.*
Usted: *Estaría enfermo.*

1. varios estudiantes / no terminar la tarea de estadística (estar descompuestas las computadoras)
2. la profesora de química / suspender a Raúl (faltar mucho a clase y no hacer los problemas de laboratorio)
3. Tomás / dormirse en la clase de geología (acostarse tarde después de la fiesta)

4. (yo) / sacar una nota sobresaliente en contabilidad (ser un genio por un día)
5. Pablo / terminar el examen muy rápido (querer juntarse con sus amigos en el café)
6. ningún profesor / darnos tareas para el fin de semana (no gustarles perder su popularidad con los estudiantes)

C. Ud. sale por primera vez con un(a) chico(a) a quien no conoce muy bien. Para causarle una buena impresión, Ud. expresa sus deseos y gustos con más cortesía de lo normal.

MODELO: *Amigo(a):   ¿Dónde quieres cenar?*
          Usted: *Querría cenar en un restaurante cerca del mar.*

1. ¿Debemos esperar el autobús o tomar un taxi?
2. ¿Dónde prefieres sentarte?
3. ¿Qué quieres comer esta noche?
4. ¿Deseas algo para tomar?
5. ¿Qué te gusta comer para el postre, fruta o algo dulce?
6. ¿Prefieres volver a la residencia o escuchar música?

D. Pregúnteles a sus compañeros de clase si les gustaría hacer las siguientes cosas y otras relacionadas con la vida universitaria. La persona interrogada contesta y explica el por qué.

MODELO: estudiar algo sólo por placer
          E1:   *¿Te gustaría estudiar algo sólo por placer?*
          E2:   *Sí, me gustaría mucho; tomaría una clase de astronomía.*

1. tener más oportunidades para conocer a otras personas
2. cambiar de residencia
3. conversar con el profesor sobre tu nota en el último examen
4. ser presidente del alumnado
5. seguir estudiando todo el verano
6. ser profesor(a) en una universidad como ésta

III. The prepositions **para** and **por**

(En el tablón de anuncios, frente al centro estudiantil)

Salgo **para** Chicago a fines de mayo. Tengo espacio **para** un pasajero. Interesados llamar **por** teléfono al 343-6578.

¿Saldrá de vacaciones este verano **por** unas semanas, **por** unos meses? ¿Necesita que le cuiden su casa? Llame **por** favor al 561-0962. Estudiante responsable, excelentes referencias.

Vendo coche económico, en buen estado. Treinta millas **por** galón. Verlo frente a la panadería La Estrella (desde la esquina de Constitución y América, camine **por** América dos cuadras hacia el norte). Consideraría cambio **por** motocicleta. Llame al 652-7685. Pregunte **por** Oscar.

¿Vas a las máquinas **por** refrescos y dulces todas las noches? ¿Pagas un precio ridículo **por** cada lata? **Por** un precio módico, cómprate un minirefrigerador en excelentes condiciones. **Para** antes de fin de año, ya habrás recuperado tu inversión. **Para** comenzar a ahorrar dinero, llama a Ernesto, 343-8721.

> The prepositions **para** and **por** are both equivalent to *for* in some contexts; however, each has numerous other meanings as well. In general, **para** is used to express purpose, direction toward or destination to a point in space or time; in contrast, **por** is used to express the cause of an action, exchange or substitution of one item for another, and movement through or along space or time.

Dos compañeros disfrutan de un descanso en una residencia universitaria española.

A. *The preposition para*

1. The preposition **para** is used to introduce phrases that indicate movement or direction toward a destination or goal, or that designate a recipient.

Salgo **para** Chicago a fines de mayo.
I'm leaving for Chicago at the end of May.

Ese autobús va **para** la universidad.
That bus is going to the university.

¿Hay algún mensaje **para** mí?
Is there a message for me?

Trabajo **para** la clínica de la universidad.
I work for the university clinic.

2. The idea of destination with **para** also includes phrases that express purpose and the use for which something is intended.

En la biblioteca hay estantes especiales **para** las revistas.
In the library there are special shelves for journals.

Necesito una cinta **para** la máquina de escribir.
I need a ribbon for the typewriter.

Tengo que ir a clase **para** entregar mi ensayo.
I have to go to class (in order) to hand in my essay.

Hablaré con la profesora **para** aclarar la tarea.
I'll talk with the professor (in order) to clarify the assignment.

3. The preposition **para** is used in phrases that refer to a specific time limit or a fixed point in time, not to the duration of a period of time.

—Voy a dejar la tarea **para** mañana. Estoy seguro de que la terminaré **para** el jueves.
I'm going to leave the assignment for tomorrow. I'm sure (that) I'll finish it by Thursday.

—No debes dejarla **para** el último momento.
You shouldn't leave it for the last minute.

4. When a member or small group is singled out as different from other members of the group, **para** is used to express an implied comparison of inequality.

Esa profesora ha tenido un éxito insólito **para** ser una persona tan joven. Sus estudiantes son muy listos **para** su edad.
That professor has had unusual success for (considering that she is) such a young person. Her students are very bright for their ages.

5. The preposition **para** introduces the person holding an opinion or making a judgment.

Para mí, la educación es lo más importante. **Para** mi primo Alfredo, lo más importante es el dinero.
For me (In my opinion), education is the most important thing. For my cousin Alfredo, money is the most important thing.

B. *Uses of* por

1. The preposition **por** is used to express the cause, reason, or motive of an action.

No fui a clase **por** estar (porque estaba) enferma.	*I didn't go to class because I was ill.*
No asistí a la conferencia **por** una emergencia en casa.	*I didn't attend the lecture because of an emergency at home.*
No escribí el ensayo **por** sentirme poco inspirado ayer.	*I didn't write the essay because I wasn't very inspired yesterday.*

2. In passive sentences, **por** is used to express the agent of an action. (*See Capítulo 8.5* for a discussion of passive constructions.)

Ese cuento no fue escrito **por** Borges sino **por** Cortázar.	*That short story was not written by Borges but by Cortázar.*

3. **Por** is frequently used to express motion along or through a place; **por** is also used to indicate an indefinite location.

Ayer andábamos **por** el centro en busca de una librería. Caminamos **por** muchas calles antes de encontrar una.	*Yesterday we were walking around downtown looking for a bookstore. We walked along many streets before finding one.*
La mejor librería de la ciudad queda **por** el edificio La Mundial.	*The best bookstore in the city is located around the La Mundial building.*

4. The preposition **por** is also used to express a means of transportation or communication.

Carlos te llamó **por** teléfono. Dice que te va a mandar los libros **por** correo. Sale para Málaga **por** avión mañana.	*Carlos called you on the phone. He says he's going to send you the books by mail. He's leaving for Málaga by plane tomorrow.*

5. With expressions of time, **por** indicates the duration or the amount of time something lasts. **Durante** may also be used with the same meaning, or no preposition at all need be used.

Hablé con el profesor **por** dos horas.	*I spoke with the professor for two hours.*
Tendré que faltar a clase (**por, durante**) una semana.	*I'll have to miss classes for a week.*

6. The preposition **por** is used to express the exchange or substitution of one thing for another.

Cambié mi motocicleta **por** una computadora.	*I exchanged my motorcycle for a computer.*
Me ofrecieron poco dinero **por** la moto.	*They offered me little money for the motorcycle.*

7. A price rate or a rate or unit of measure is expressed with **por.**

Este semestre gasté unos veinte dólares **por** libro.	*This semester I spent about twenty dollars per book.*
En mi clase de literatura tengo que leer tres novelas **por** mes y escribir un ensayo **por** novela.	*In my literature class I have to read three novels a month and write one essay per novel.*

8. **Por** indicates the person(s) or object(s) *instead of, on behalf of, for the sake of,* or *in favor of* whom or what something is done.

El ayudante dio la clase **por** la profesora.	*The teaching assistant taught the class for (instead of) the professor.*
Ese líder estudiantil lucha **por** mejores programas en la universidad.	*That student leader fights for (on behalf of) better university programs.*
Trabaja **por** el bienestar de todos los estudiantes. Voy a votar **por** él.	*He works for (the sake of) the welfare of all students. I'm going to vote for (in favor of) him.*

9. The preposition **por** introduces the object of an errand after a verb of movement such as **ir, venir, mandar, regresar, salir,** and **volver.**

El decano **mandó por** la documentación sobre el nuevo estudiante. El secretario **fue por** los papeles a la oficina. Luego **volvió por** más información.	*The dean sent for the files on the new student. The secretary went to the office for the papers. Later he returned for more information.*

10. Common expressions with **por** include the following.

por ahora *for the time being*	por más (mucho) que *however much*
por cierto *of course, by the way*	
por consiguiente *consequently*	por otra parte *on the other hand*
por eso *that's why*	por poco *almost*
por fin *finally, at last*	por supuesto *of course, naturally*
por lo menos *at least*	por último *finally, lastly*
por lo tanto *therefore*	

C. *Para versus por*

1. The preposition **para** is used to focus on the purpose or goal of an action. In contrast, **por** is used to focus on the motive or cause of an action.

   Casi todos los estudiantes cumplieron los requisitos **para** graduarse.

   Almost all the students fulfilled the requirements for graduation.

   Unos pocos no se graduaron **por** no cumplir los requisitos.

   A few did not graduate because they didn't fulfill the requirements.

2. In cases in which motion is involved, **para** indicates movement toward a place or destination; **por** indicates movement along or through a place.

   Iba **para** el laboratorio cuando noté un olor horrible.

   Iba para – – – → el laboratorio

   Iba **por** el laboratorio cuando noté un olor horrible.

   Iba por – – – – – – → el laboratorio

3. With expressions of time, **para** refers to a specific point or limit in time; **por** refers to the duration of a period of time.

   Le pedí hora a mi consejera **para** el viernes. Hablaremos **por** unos treinta minutos.

   I made an appointment with my advisor for Friday. We'll talk for about thirty minutes.

4. Compare the use of **para** and **por** in the following examples and observe that **para** expresses the recipient of an action; **por** expresses the person for whom or instead of whom the action is performed.

   Trabajo **para** la biblioteca.

   I work for the library (my employer).

   Trabajo **por** el bibliotecario.

   I'm working for (in place of, instead of, on behalf of) the librarian.

Comprehension questions

1. Would you use **por** or **para** in each of the following sentences? _____ **mí, esa calculadora no vale mucho. ¿Cuánto darías tú _____ esa calculadora?**

2. Give at least two meanings of **por** in this sentence. **La estudiante va por la profesora Menéndez.**

3. Should **por** or **para** be used in each of the following sentences? **Sabe mucho _____ un estudiante de primer año. No quiero cambiar de especialización ni _____ un millón de dólares.**

4. Complete the following sentences with **para** and **por. Estudiaré** _____ **doce horas** _____ **aprobar mi examen final.** _____ **tener éxito, debes trabajar mucho; debes hacerlo** _____ **ti y** _____ **tu familia.** Explain your choices.

5. Review the advertisements that appear at the beginning of this section. Point out and explain three different uses of **para** and five uses of **por**.

Ejercicios

A. Conteste las siguientes preguntas de un(a) compañero(a), usando **por** o **para** en su respuesta.

MODELO: E1:   ¿Para qué viniste a una universidad tan lejos de tu casa?
          E2:   *Vine aquí para tener la oportunidad de vivir por mi cuenta.*

1. ¿Quién toma apuntes por ti cuando faltas a clase?
2. ¿Cuántos años más piensas estudiar?
3. ¿Cuál es tu campo de especialización? ¿Por qué decidiste especializarte en ese campo?
4. ¿Adónde vas para estudiar durante los fines de semana?
5. ¿Para qué asignatura estudias más? ¿Por qué?
6. Para ti, ¿cuál es el problema más serio de la educación hoy?

B. Imagínese que se va a México entre semestres. Cuéntele a un(a) amigo(a) sobre los preparativos para su viaje, usando **para** o **por,** según el contexto.

MODELO: Mañana iré _____ México _____ avión _____ pasar allí las vacaciones de primavera.
          Mañana iré para México por avión para pasar allí las vacaciones de primavera.

1. Julia no viene conmigo a México _____ estar enferma.
2. Estaré en aquel país _____ una semana.
3. Voy a dejar el hacer las maletas _____ el jueves.
4. _____ lo que cuesta la excursión, los hoteles son muy buenos.
5. Decidí ir a México porque es un sitio ideal _____ pasar las vacaciones.
6. Fui _____ mis billetes, pero la agencia todavía no los tenía.
7. Caminé _____ toda la ciudad buscando un regalo para mis amigos mexicanos y por fin encontré algo bonito.
8. Estoy leyendo un libro sobre México escrito _____ un célebre historiador mexicano.

C. Dé una excusa distinta—real o imaginaria—para cada situación. Compare su excusa con las de dos compañeros más y decidan cuál es la más eficaz, cómica, original, etc.

MODELO: Ud. no terminó un trabajo de investigación.
   E1: *No lo terminé por no sentirme bien.*
   E2: *No lo terminé por estar ocupado(a) anoche.*
   E3: *No lo terminé por un problema personal.*

1. A Ud. lo(la) suspendieron en un examen de su especialización.
2. Ud. faltó a clase tres veces la semana pasada.
3. Ud. tuvo que pedir prestados veinte dólares a su compañero(a) de cuarto.
4. Ud. no tomó los apuntes que le había prometido a un(a) amigo(a).
5. Ud. no fue al trabajo durante el fin de semana.
6. Ud. no compró el libro de química.

D. Rosita acaba de llegar a una nueva ciudad para estudiar en la universidad. Necesita comprarse algunas cosas y en este momento responde a los anuncios que ha encontrado en el tablón de anuncios. Complete su diálogo con **por** o **para,** según el contexto.

Rosita: Necesito un minirefrigerador _____ mi apartamento. ¿Todavía está de venta el que Ud. anunció en el tablón de anuncios?
Ernesto: Sí, pero salgo ahora _____ una clase. ¿Puede pasar _____ aquí _____ la tarde?
Rosita: _____ supuesto. No hay ningún problema.
Ernesto: Muchas gracias _____ su llamada. Nos veremos pronto.

Rosita: Bueno, si su coche da treinta millas _____ galón, entonces deseo verlo.
Oscar: _____ eso le digo que _____ obtener otro coche igual, tendría que pagar _____ lo menos quinientos dólares más.
Rosita: ¿_____ dónde quedan las calles Constitución y América?
Oscar: Si viene _____ autobús, baje frente al Banco Continental y camine _____ la calle América hasta llegar a la calle Constitución. Pregunte _____ mí en la panadería. Si no estoy aquí, pregunte _____ mi hermano Nicolás.

Rosita: ¿Me puede dar más información sobre los esquís que Ud. vende? _____ ejemplo, ¿cuánto pide _____ ellos?
Martín: Sólo $60.00. _____ esquís de segunda mano, están en excelente estado. Además, ofrezco unas botas casi nuevas _____ $30.00.

IV. The conjunctions **pero, mas,** and **sino (que)**

Manuel: Te veo ir a clases, **pero** nunca te veo estudiar. Sabes que el examen no es el jueves **sino** mañana martes, ¿no?

Alberto: No pensaba decirte mi secreto sobre cómo estudiar, **pero** como tú eres mi compañero de cuarto, haré una excepción.

Manuel: No sé exactamente cuál es tu secreto, **pero** me lo puedo imaginar.

Alberto: Bueno, no te compras un libro nuevo **sino que** te consigues uno usado. Como ya trae marcadas todas las partes esenciales, no necesitas estudiar día tras día **sino que** ¡basta con unas horas la noche antes del examen!

Manuel: ¡Qué memoria tan mala tienes! ¡Hiciste exactamente eso, **pero** no aprobaste el último examen!

A. *Pero and mas*

The conjunction **pero** establishes a contrast between two sentences; it corresponds to English *but* in the sense of *however*. **Mas,** written without an accent, is a synonym of **pero** used mainly in written Spanish.

Esta universidad no es grande, **pero** es una de las mejores en mi campo de especialización.	*This university isn't big, but it's one of the best in my field.*
Pedí una beca, **pero** no sé todavía si me la darán.	*I asked for a scholarship, but I don't know yet if they'll give it to me.*
Se puede seguir este curso el primer año, **mas** se requiere una preparación académica en historia del arte moderno.	*This course can be taken the first year, but it requires academic preparation in the history of modern art.*

B. *Sino and sino que*

1. The conjunctions **sino** and **sino que** are used to correct or clarify information. They are used when the first part of a sentence is negative and the second part contradicts or is in opposition to the first part. Both **sino** and **sino que** correspond to English *but,* in the sense of *but rather* or *but on the contrary.*

—¿Vas a especializarte en ciencias políticas?	*Are you going to specialize in political science?*
—No, no me voy a especializar en ciencias políticas **sino** en economía. No es que la política no sea importante, **sino que** la economía me dará mejores oportunidades de empleo.	*No, I'm not going to major in political science but in economics. It's not that politics is not important but rather that economics will give me better job opportunities.*

2. **Sino que,** not **sino,** must be used before a clause with a conjugated verb.

No me voy a graduar este semestre, **sino que** esperaré hasta el próximo.

I won't graduate this semester, but will wait until the next one.

No me voy a graduar este semestre **sino** el próximo.

I won't graduate this semester but the next one.

Comprehension questions

1. Would you use **pero** or **sino** in the following sentences? **Ese joven vive en un apartamento, _____ le gustaría vivir en una residencia de estudiantes. A ese joven no le agrada vivir lejos del recinto universitario _____ cerca.** Explain your choices.

2. Would you use **sino** or **sino que** in the following sentences? **No se interesa por las humanidades _____ quiere especializarse en administración de empresas. No quiere estudiar _____ charlar con sus amigos.**

3. Would you use **pero, sino,** or **sino que** in the following sentences? **No voy a asistir a otra universidad, _____ voy a pasar un año en el extranjero. No quedaron plazas en el curso sobre computadoras, _____ pude inscribirme en el curso sobre estadística avanzada. No me gustan las ciencias naturales _____ las ciencias sociales.** Explain your choices.

Ejercicios

A. Complete los dos editoriales siguientes de un periódico universitario con **pero, sino** o **sino que.**

1. El año pasado la administración universitaria declaró que estudiaría la posibilidad de no invertir más dinero en los países que no respetan los derechos humanos, _____ hasta la fecha no solamente no ha vuelto a tratar el tema _____ se ha negado categóricamente a comentarlo. Entendemos muy bien que es un dilema a nivel nacional, _____ no creemos que la situación deba continuar así. Las acciones de la universidad no contribuyen nada con respecto a los derechos humanos _____ empeoran la situación no solamente en este país _____ en todos los países donde hay una historia de injusticia hacia las minorías.

2. Un portavoz de la administración universitaria anunció ayer que la universidad no podría continuar operando con los actuales precios de la enseñanza. Dijo que habría un aumento general en todas las categorías, _____ que no se efectuaría este año _____ el siguiente. Le advertimos al estudiantado que esta subida no es solamente excesiva _____ es absurda. Si la administración quiere

mantener buenas relaciones con el estudiantado, no subirá los precios _____ buscará medios para controlar los gastos universitarios y para aumentar el nivel de donaciones privadas.

B. Es la época del año cuando todo estudiante tiene que escoger una residencia para el próximo año académico. Ud. va a varias residencias para informarse de sus características y servicios. Converse con un(a) compañero(a) de clase, *según el modelo.*

MODELO: los cuartos: grande, regular, incómodo, cómodo
E1:   *¿Son grandes los cuartos?*
E2:   *No, no son grandes sino regulares.*
E1:   *¿Son incómodos entonces?*
E2:   *No, no son incómodos, pero tampoco son muy cómodos.*

1. los estudiantes en los pasillos: tranquilo, un poco ruidoso, molesto, silencioso
2. las actividades sociales: interesante, típico, monótono, variado
3. los baños: moderno, regular, viejo, nuevo
4. los roperos: espacioso, pequeño, inservible, bueno
5. las camas: blando, duro, terrible, lujoso

C. Complete las oraciones siguientes con una conclusión original. Emplee **sino que** si es necesario.

MODELO: Mi beca no cubre todos mis gastos, pero...
Mi beca no cubre todos mis gastos, pero me ayuda mucho.

1. No quiero hacer el doctorado sino...
2. Voy a comprar una computadora, pero...
3. Juan no va a comprar una computadora sino...
4. Rafael no es antropólogo sino...
5. La sociología no es una ciencia exacta, pero...
6. Me gustaría especializarme en humanidades, pero...
7. Mis hermanos no asisten a esta universidad sino...
8. Debería tomar algo práctico como contabilidad, pero...

V. Expressions of obligation and probability

1. The constructions **tener que** + infinitive, **deber** + infinitive, and **haber que** + infinitive are used to express obligation.

Tengo que terminar el ensayo para mañana. Por eso, **debo levantarme** a las seis.	*I have to finish the essay by tomorrow. That's why I ought to get up at 6 o'clock.*
Hay que tomar un autobús para ir a la universidad desde aquí.	*One must take a bus to go to the university from here.*

2. **Tener que** + infinitive is used to express a strong personal or individual obligation. **Deber** + infinitive is the most common way of communicating duty or moral obligation. The sense of obligation can be softened by using **deber** in the conditional or past subjunctive.

Tenemos que redactar un informe sobre nuestros experimentos en el laboratorio.	*We have to write a report on our laboratory experiments.*
Debo quedarme en casa esta noche para comenzar mi ensayo.	*I must stay at home tonight in order to start my essay.*
Tú también **debieras comenzar** lo antes posible.	*You also really ought to start as soon as possible.*

3. **Haber que** + infinitive is used in the third person singular to express a strong impersonal necessity or obligation. English equivalents are often *one must (has to), you must, people must,* or *it is necessary to.*

Para sacar una buena nota en biología, **hay que asistir** a todas las sesiones de laboratorio.	*In order to get a good grade in biology, one must attend all of the lab sessions.*
El semestre pasado, **había que entregar** dos informes sobre los experimentos.	*Last semester, it was necessary to turn in two reports on the experiments.*

4. **Deber (de)** + infinitive is often used to express probability. As explained in Sections I and II of this chapter, the future tense and the conditional tense also commonly fulfill this expressive function. The addition of **de** to **deber** is usually restricted to written language, although some Spanish speakers use **deber de** for probability in oral language.

El profesor **debe (de) estar** enfermo.	*The professor must be (is probably) sick.*
Debió volver a casa para recuperarse.	*He probably returned home to get well.*

Ejercicios

A. Diga qué verbo o expresión verbal se usa en español para expresar la palabra o expresión indicada en inglés. A veces hay más de una respuesta posible.

1. The students *should arrive* here at four o'clock.
2. Because of her illness, she *had to stay* home from class.
3. You *really ought to think* twice before agreeing to give two reports in one week.

4. *It's necessary* to consult with one's advisor about course changes.
5. What *must one do* to satisfy that instructor?
6. They *are probably* in class at this hour.
7. Do you *have to go* to class tonight or can you stay home?
8. If you have an assignment, you *ought to finish* it now.

B. Un(a) nuevo(a) compañero(a) de clase acaba de trasladarse a su universidad y le pide consejo a Ud. Responda a sus preguntas sobre la vida universitaria, utilizando alguna expresión de obligación en cada respuesta.

MODELO: ¿Cuántas clases por día tiene cada estudiante?
Normalmente hay que asistir a cinco clases por día y a alguna sesión de laboratorio.

1. ¿Hay mucho que leer en esta clase?
2. ¿Qué hago para sacar un libro de la biblioteca?
3. ¿En qué clases hay muchas presentaciones orales?
4. ¿Es necesario tomar una clase de matemáticas para graduarse?
5. ¿Con quién hablo para cambiar mi campo de especialización?
6. ¿Cómo se puede conseguir un préstamo estudiantil aquí?
7. ¿Cómo son las multas que cobra la biblioteca cuando los libros se entregan tarde?
8. ¿Qué puedo hacer para tener acceso a una computadora sin tener que pagar mucho dinero?

Actividades para la comunicación

A. Predicciones. ¿Cómo será la educación en las universidades de los Estados Unidos al terminar este siglo? Haga una predicción sobre la situación educacional en este país hacia fines del siglo veinte, basándose en los siguientes temas u otros que se le ocurran.

MODELO: duración de los estudios
Para el fin de este siglo, las carreras universitarias durarán cinco años porque necesitaremos más conocimientos.

1. costo de la educación
2. método de pagar la educación
3. tipo de estudiante promedio
4. carrera(s) más popular(es)
5. carrera(s) menos popular(es)
6. nuevas especializaciones

B. Decisiones difíciles. Roberto y Juanita son amigos desde hace muchos años. Han estudiado juntos en la universidad y ahora conversan sobre lo que piensan hacer para su graduación en la primavera y después que se gradúen. Juanita tiene planes bien definidos, pero Roberto aún no sabe lo que quiere hacer. Invente su conversación.

MODELO:　¿seguir estudiando?
　　　　　Roberto:　*¿Vas a seguir estudiando después de la graduación?*
　　　　　Juanita:　*No, no lo creo; empezaré a trabajar para mi tío en la farmacia. ¿Y tú?*
　　　　　Roberto:　*No sé; me gustaría conseguir una maestría, pero no sé qué estudiar. También podría trabajar un año o más hasta saber qué quiero hacer.*
　　　　　Juanita:　*En tu lugar, creo que trabajaría un poco antes de decidir.*

1. ¿seguir estudiando mucho durante el último semestre?
2. ¿pedir cartas de recomendación a los profesores ahora?
3. ¿asistir a la "Feria de Trabajos" de la universidad?
4. ¿enviar todas tus cosas a casa antes de graduarte?
5. ¿participar en la ceremonia de graduación?
6. ¿empezar a trabajar de inmediato o tomar unas vacaciones largas?

C. Entrevista de trabajo. Cada primavera vienen a su universidad representantes de varias compañías para ofrecerles a los estudiantes trabajo de verano en sus programas de internado. A Ud. le interesaría trabajar para una agencia de viajes. Con otro(a) estudiante desarrolle la entrevista que Ud. tiene con el(la) representante de una agencia de viajes, usando **por** o **para** en su entrevista.

MODELO:　¿propósito de su visita?
　　　　　E1:　*¿Por qué vino Ud. a hablar con nosotros?*
　　　　　E2:　*Para informarme mejor sobre su programa de internado.*

1. ¿experiencias de viaje?
2. ¿duración de viajes?
3. ¿razón para viajar?
4. ¿experiencias de trabajo?
5. ¿años de trabajo?
6. ¿horas de trabajo semanales?
7. ¿sueldo recibido?
8. ¿razón de querer trabajar en esta compañía?

D. ¿Qué haría Ud.? Informe a sus compañeros de clase qué haría Ud., cómo se sentiría o cómo cambiarían su vida las siguientes cosas.

MODELO:　con una beca
　　　　　Con una beca, yo no tendría que trabajar y sacaría buenas notas.

1. con un excelente trabajo
2. con un apartamento más cerca de la universidad
3. con 20.000 dólares

4. con una computadora
5. con un auto deportivo
6. con una máquina de escribir eléctrica
7. con unas notas más altas
8. con un cuarto individual en la residencia

E. **Explicaciones.** Explíquele a un(a) compañero(a) dos o tres cosas que tiene Ud. que hacer en la próxima semana. Para cada cosa, dé detalles como para qué o quién la hace, por cuánto tiempo, para cuándo debe tenerla terminada y cómo piensa hacerla.

MODELO: *Tengo que hacer un informe para la clase de español para el miércoles. Iré a la biblioteca por unos libros. Me quedaré allí por varias horas para leer algunos artículos...*

CAPÍTULO 8

◆

El mundo del trabajo

Estudiantes de arqueología trabajan en las excavaciones cerca del Zócalo, en el centro de la Ciudad de México.

Conversación

1. ¿Qué trabajos ha tenido o ha realizado Ud.? ¿Eran trabajos que le gustaban? ¿Aprendió algo haciéndolos?
2. ¿Prefiere un puesto en que trabaja con las manos, con la mente o con las dos? ¿Por qué?
3. ¿Qué le importa más a Ud. en el trabajo: el ambiente agradable, los buenos compañeros, el sueldo alto, la posibilidad de tomar muchas decisiones importantes? Explique.
4. ¿Qué tipo de preguntas haría Ud. en una entrevista de trabajo? ¿Qué tipo de preguntas no haría?
5. ¿Para qué está Ud. preparándose en la universidad? ¿Qué metas tiene con respecto a su trabajo futuro?
6. ¿Por qué, cree Ud., es importante el trabajo de los estudiantes que se ven en la fotografía de la página anterior?

Vocabulario temático

anuncio, el advertisement; announcement
ascenso, el promotion
asesor(a), el(la) consultant, advisor
asesoramiento, el professional advice
aspirante, el(la) applicant
bolsa, la stock market
cita, la appointment; date
compañía, la company
contador(a), el(la) accountant
empresa, la company, enterprise
fábrica, la factory
gerente, el(la) manager
inversión, la investment
mecanógrafo(a), el(la) typist
mercado, el market
meta, la goal
obrero(a), el(la) worker, laborer
planilla, la sheet of paper, form
plaza, la position, job
puesto, el job, position
solicitud, la application
sucursal, la branch office
traslado, el transfer
vacante, la vacancy, opening (job)

contratar to hire
despedir (i) to fire, to lay off
entrenar to train
evaluar to evaluate
jubilarse to retire
renunciar to quit (a job)

capacitado(a) qualified, prepared
prometedor(a) promising
ventajoso(a) advantageous

aumento de sueldo, el salary increase, raise
cámara de comercio, la chamber of commerce
convenio colectivo, el labor agreement
de jornada completa full-time
de media jornada part-time
escala de salarios, la wage scale
garantía de trabajo, la job guarantee
jefe(a) de ventas, el(la) sales manager
junta directiva, la board of directors
sala de espera, la waiting room
seguridad de trabajo, la job security

I. Past participle: Forms and uses

(Mónica Avilar, reportera para la Cadena Nacional de Televisión, informa sobre el progreso en las negociaciones para solucionar la huelga en la industria textil.)

Esta mañana, según fuentes óficiales dentro de la directiva de la industria textil, **ha habido** muestras de progreso en las negociaciones para solucionar la huelga. En las palabras de un portavoz: «Una propuesta muy justa y ventajosa para los trabajadores **fue entregada** anoche a los líderes del sindicato. Creo que la puerta **está abierta** para una resolución». A pesar de ese aire de optimismo, un líder del sindicato nos **ha informado** que todavía queda sin satisfacer la demanda sindicalista de protección **garantizada** de los empleos durante períodos de depresión económica. «Resolver ese problema será esencial», nos dijo el líder sindicalista; «los obreros de esta industria nunca aceptarán un contrato sin garantías de trabajo».

A. *Forms of the past participle*

-ar verbs	**-er** verbs	**-ir** verbs
acept**ado**	establec**ido**	decid**ido**
busc**ado**	ofrec**ido**	ped**ido**
encontr**ado**	ten**ido**	recib**ido**

1. To form the past participle of regular verbs, the infinitive ending **-ar** is replaced by **-ado,** and the infinitive endings **-er** and **-ir** are replaced by **-ido.**

2. When the infinitive stem of an **-er** or **-ir** verb ends in **a, e,** or **o,** a written accent is required on the **i** of the past participle ending **-ido: traer** > **traído, leer** > **leído, oír** > **oído.**

3. Common verbs that have an irregular past participle include the following.

Infinitive	Past participle	Infinitive	Past participle
abrir	**abierto**	poner	**puesto**
cubrir	**cubierto**	resolver	**resuelto**
decir	**dicho**	romper	**roto**
escribir	**escrito**	ver	**visto**
hacer	**hecho**	volver	**vuelto**
morir	**muerto**		

4. Most verbs whose stems are similar to the ones in the preceding list also have an irregular past participle.

Model verb	Related verb	Irregular past participle
abrir	reabrir	reabierto *reopened*
cubrir	descubrir	descubierto *discovered*
(e)scribir	describir	descrito *described*
	inscribir	inscrito *inscribed, registered*
	transcribir	transcrito *transcribed*
(h)acer	deshacer	deshecho *undone*
	rehacer	rehecho *redone*
	satisfacer	satisfecho *satisfied*
poner	componer	compuesto *composed*
	imponer	impuesto *imposed*
	suponer	supuesto *supposed*
volver	devolver	devuelto *returned, given back*
	revolver	revuelto *stirred*

B. *Uses of the past participle*

1. The past participle is most frequently used with the auxiliary verb **haber** to form the perfect tenses. **Haber** agrees with the subject in person and number, but the past participle is invariable. (Consult Sections II and III of this chapter for the perfect tenses.)

El aspirante no **ha encontrado** trabajo todavía, pero **ha tenido** varias entrevistas.

The applicant hasn't found a job yet, but he has had several interviews.

He **recibido** la solicitud, pero todavía no la **he llenado.**

I've received the application, but I haven't filled it out yet.

2. The construction **ser** + a past participle is used to form the passive voice. The past participle agrees in gender and number with the subject of the sentence. (Consult Section V of this chapter for the passive construction.)

En nuestra compañía los candidatos **son entrevistados** por el jefe de personal.

In our company candidates are interviewed by the personnel manager.

Ayer más de veinte candidatos **fueron entrevistados,** pero sólo tres **fueron seleccionados** como finalistas.

Yesterday over twenty candidates were interviewed, but only three were selected as finalists.

3. **Estar** + a past participle is used to refer to a condition or state that is generally the result of a previous action. The past participle agrees in gender and number with the subject. (Consult *Capítulo 3.2* on **ser** and **estar** + a past participle.)

Nuestra compañía **está situada** en un pequeño pueblo.	*Our company is located in a small village.*
La Junta Directiva **está decidida** a encontrar un nuevo jefe de ventas.	*The board of directors is determined to find a new sales manager.*
Los tres finalistas para el puesto **están seleccionados.** Fueron seleccionados ayer.	*The three finalists for the position have been selected. They were selected yesterday.*
Ayer antes de las tres, todas las entrevistas **estaban terminadas.**	*Yesterday before three o'clock, all interviews were finished.*

4. The past participle can be used as an adjective to modify a noun. The past participle agrees in gender and number with the noun modified.

Los obreros **despedidos** protestaron al gerente de la fábrica.	*The workers that were fired complained to the manager of the factory.*
Le dijeron que la decisión **tomada** por él era injusta.	*They said that the decision made by him was unfair.*

5. The past participle can also be used to introduce an adverbial clause that expresses ideas such as time or reason. If the adverbial clause has a subject, it is placed after the past participle.

Terminadas las negociaciones, los obreros quedaron contentos.	*Once the negotiations were over, the workers were happy.* (time)
Resueltos los problemas, los empleados volvieron al trabajo.	*The problems having been solved, the employees returned to work.* (reason)

6. Sentences with adverbial clauses headed by past participles, such as **Terminadas las negociaciones,** belong to the written rather than the spoken language. In the spoken language, the adverbial clause is generally preceded by phrases such as **una vez que** (*once*) or **luego que** (*as soon as*). The same idea may also be expressed by using two sentences joined by the conjunction **y.**

Una vez (Luego) que las negociaciones terminaron, los empleados volvieron al trabajo.	*Once the negotiations were over, the employees returned to work.*
Terminaron las negociaciones y los empleados volvieron al trabajo.	*The negotiations ended and the employees returned to work.*

Comprehension questions

1. Would you use **escrito, escrita,** or **escritas** in the following sentences? **Mi secretaria ha _____ una descripción del puesto vacante. La última carta ya está _____. Las solicitudes ya fueron _____ por los aspirantes.** Explain each of your choices.

2. Would you use a form of **ser (fue)** or **estar (estaba)** in the following sentences? **Cuando llegó la supervisora, el problema ya _____ solucionado. El problema _____ solucionado por los empleados antes de la llegada de la supervisora a su sección.**

3. Frequently the past participle is used with another verb such as **haber, ser,** or **estar.** In the news report that appears at the beginning of this section, why is **garantizada** not used with a verb?

Ejercicios

A. Ud. regresa entusiasmado(a) de una entrevista para un trabajo de verano en una agencia de turismo internacional. Cuéntele a un(a) amigo(a) sus impresiones de la entrevista.

MODELO: Hay sólo dos vacantes _____ y se presentaron diez candidatos. (abrir)
Hay sólo dos vacantes abiertas y se presentaron diez candidatos.

1. La oficina está bien _____: está muy cerca del metro y de una parada de autobús. (situar)
2. Yo tenía varias preguntas _____ antes de ir y estaba bien _____ sobre la compañía. (preparar, informar)
3. Es una compañía bien _____ en el turismo; es _____ mundialmente. (establecer, reconocer)
4. El sueldo _____ para este puesto es alto para la industria en general. (ofrecer)
5. Todos los beneficios de la compañía están _____ en este folleto. (resumir)
6. Estoy _____ con las condiciones de trabajo según me las explicaron. (satisfacer)

B. Cuente las gestiones hechas por un(a) joven para encontrar trabajo, cambiando las siguientes oraciones según el modelo.

MODELO: Abrí la carta y luego vi una invitación a una entrevista de empleo para una compañía de seguros de vida.
Abierta la carta, vi una invitación a una entrevista de empleo para una compañía de seguros de vida.

1. Leí la carta y luego llamé a la secretaria para confirmar la cita.
2. Preparé mi resumen y luego lo reescribí a máquina.
3. Hice todos los preparativos y luego salí para la entrevista.
4. Encontré la oficina indicada y luego me presenté a la recepcionista.
5. Completé las planillas necesarias y luego las dejé con la recepcionista.
6. Terminé la entrevista y luego supe que sólo buscaban un ayudante voluntario. ¡Qué vida!

C. Imagínese que Ud. está bastante cansado(a) de su trabajo y que se queja de él con un(a) amigo(a). Utilice **estar** + el participio pasado del verbo sugerido.

MODELO: la comida en la cafetería de la empresa / siempre / recocer / y es muy cara
La comida en la cafetería de la empresa siempre está recocida y es muy cara.

1. la puerta de mi oficina / siempre / abrir / y mi supervisor nunca deja de observarme
2. las mesas de trabajo / normalmente / cubrir de papeles / y el piso de la oficina está sucio
3. las copiadoras / descomponer / casi todos los días
4. el aire acondicionado / normalmente / apagar / cuando hace calor
5. el jefe / siempre / irritar / por algo insignificante
6. ¡yo / no / disponer / a seguir trabajando bajo esas condiciones!

D. Conteste las siguientes preguntas que le hará un(a) compañero(a) de clase de una forma personal y con una oración completa.

MODELO: *E1:*   ¿Estás interesado(a) en tu trabajo actual o estás aburrido(a)? ¿Por qué?
E2:   *Pues, estoy algo aburrido(a) porque no participo en las decisiones tomadas por los jefes.*

1. ¿Estás satisfecho(a) con tu sueldo actual? ¿Cuánto te pagan por hora?
2. ¿En qué parte de la ciudad está situado el lugar de tu trabajo? ¿Es un lugar conveniente o no? ¿Por qué?
3. ¿Hay empleados allí matriculados en la universidad? ¿La empresa les paga sus estudios universitarios?
4. ¿Hay algunas plazas desocupadas en tu sección? ¿Cuándo las van a llenar?
5. ¿Tienes un contrato firmado con la compañía o trabajas sin contrato? Si no tienes contrato, ¿qué garantías de trabajo tienes?
6. ¿Cómo son las evaluaciones de trabajo allí? ¿Son evaluaciones escritas u orales?

II. Perfect tenses in the present and the past

(En una entrevista)

Sr. Regalado: Bueno... ¿Me podría Ud. decir por qué **ha solicitado** este puesto?

Claudio: Hace tiempo que deseo volver al campo de mi especialización—la ley y los contratos.

Sr. Regalado: Sí... Pero veo en su resumen que no **ha tenido** mucha experiencia con contratos.

Claudio: Es cierto. Sin embargo siempre me **ha interesado** ese aspecto de la ley y nunca **he dejado** de aspirar a una carrera en ese campo.

Sr. Regalado: Hmm... Como Ud. sabe, **hemos hecho** fuertes inversiones en el mercado sudamericano. ¿Presentaría inconvenientes para Ud. el tener que viajar a menudo?

Claudio: Ninguno. De hecho, siempre **había soñado** con la posibilidad de ir a Sudamérica, pero nunca **había pensado** que llegaría a realizar mi sueño tan pronto.

A. *Forms of the perfect tenses*

Present perfect	Past perfect
he trabajado	**había** trabajado
has trabajado	**habías** trabajado
ha trabajado	**había** trabajado
hemos trabajado	**habíamos** trabajado
habéis trabajado	**habíais** trabajado
han trabajado	**habían** trabajado

1. The perfect tenses consist of a form of the auxiliary verb **haber** followed by a past participle, which is invariable in form. To form the present perfect, the auxiliary verb **haber** is conjugated in the present tense; to form the past perfect, **haber** is conjugated in the imperfect.

2. Object pronouns precede the auxiliary verb in the perfect tenses. The negation **no** precedes object pronouns.

La máquina copiadora **se ha** descompuesto.   *The copy machine has broken down.*

El técnico todavía **no la ha** arreglado.   *The technician hasn't fixed it yet.*

B. *Uses of the present perfect*

1. The present perfect is used to refer to past events that continue or are expected to continue into the present, or that have some bearing on the present. (Consult *Capítulo 9.4* for use of **hacer** in ongoing events.)

Le **hemos enviado** los contratos que pidió.	*We have sent you the contracts you requested.*
¿Los **ha recibido** ya?	*Have you received them yet?*

2. The present perfect is also used with time references, such as **hoy, esta semana, este mes, este año,** when the time reference is to a present time that has not yet ended. However, the simple preterit is used when the speaker views the action as completely finished and therefore detached from the current moment.

No la **hemos visto** esta mañana.	*We haven't seen her this morning.*
Llegué muy temprano esta mañana a la oficina.	*I arrived at the office very early this morning.*
Usted no **ha recibido** ninguna carta hoy.	*You haven't received any letter today.* (Mail delivery not over)
No **recibió** usted ninguna carta hoy.	*You didn't receive any letter today.* (Mail delivery over)

3. Since both the present perfect and the preterit refer to past events, the distinction between these two tenses tends to blur and they are often used interchangeably. Regional preferences also exist and in general, the present perfect is more widely used in Spain than in Latin America.

¿**Ha llegado (Llegó)** el jefe ya?	*Has the boss arrived yet?*
¿**Seguiste (Has seguido)** un curso para aprender a escribir a máquina?	*Did you take a course to learn how to type?*

C. *Uses of the past perfect*

1. As in English, the past perfect tense is used in Spanish to refer to a past event that took place prior to another past event, whether stated or implied. It distinguishes the relationship in time between two past events. (Consult *Capítulo 9.4* for use of **hacer** in ongoing events.)

Me sentí cansado ayer porque el día anterior **había tenido** muchas entrevistas.	*I felt tired yesterday because the day before I had had many interviews.*
En varios lugares, ya **habían contratado** a alguien para el puesto que yo solicitaba.	*In several places, they had already hired someone for the position that I was applying for.*

2. In reported speech, the past perfect is used to report a quote that was made using the preterit or the present perfect.

Mi jefe dijo: «Nuestras ventas aumentaron el mes pasado, pero este mes han declinado un poco».

My boss said: "Our sales increased last month; this month they've declined a bit."

Mi jefe dijo que nuestras ventas **habían aumentado** el mes pasado, pero que este mes **habían declinado** un poco.

My boss said that our sales had increased last month but had declined a bit this month.

D. *The preterit perfect*

1. The preterit perfect is formed with the preterit of **haber** + a past participle: **hube, hubiste, hubo, hubimos, hubisteis, hubieron** + (trabaj**ado**).

2. The preterit perfect is used to refer to the first of two or more past events that follow each other closely in time.

Apenas **hube llegado** a casa, comuniqué a mis padres la noticia de mi ascenso.

No sooner had I arrived home when I communicated to my parents the news about my promotion.

3. The preterit perfect is used almost exclusively in written Spanish. In spoken Spanish, two sentences in the preterit joined by **y** are used.

Llegué a casa **y** les **conté** a mis padres la noticia de mi ascenso.

I arrived home and told my parents the news about my promotion.

Comprehension questions

1. Would the present perfect **han despedido** or the preterit **despidieron** more likely be used in the following sentences? _____ **a muchos obreros el mes pasado. No _____ a muchos obreros este mes.** Explain.

2. Should the present perfect **he conseguido** or the past perfect **había conseguido** be used in the following sentences? **He estado preocupado porque hasta ayer todavía no _____ trabajo. No me gusta ninguno de los trabajos que _____ hasta ahora.**

3. Should the past perfect **habían negociado** or the imperfect **negociaban** be used in the following sentences? **La supervisora me dijo que los empleados siempre _____ sus contratos individualmente. La secretaria me dijo que hasta ahora no _____ ningún contrato.**

Ejercicios

A. Imagínese que Ud. trabaja en un gran almacén de ropa. Responda a las preguntas o a las órdenes de algunos compañeros de trabajo. Use un pronombre en la respuesta si es necesario.

MODELO 1:   ¿A qué hora vuelve la supervisora?
Ya ha vuelto.

MODELO 2:   ¿Puedes sacar las camisas de las cajas?
Ya las he sacado.

1. ¿Cuándo traerán una caja de suéteres de la otra sucursal?
2. ¿Terminarás pronto con los cambios de precios?
3. ¿Vas a pedir tu cambio de horario pronto?
4. ¿Crees que puedes resolver tu conflicto con el jefe?
5. ¿Puede el mensajero enviar el pedido inmediatamente?
6. Lleve los recibos a la directora, por favor.
7. ¿A qué hora vas a avisarle al supervisor que no puedes trabajar mañana?
8. Antes de almorzar, tú y Josefa deben poner las medias nuevas en su lugar.

B. Imagínese que Ud. trabaja como coordinador(a) en la radioemisora de la universidad. En este momento corre de un lugar a otro averiguando si varias personas y cosas están preparadas o no para transmitir el próximo programa. Con otro(a) estudiante, represente las situaciones que se dan a continuación.

MODELO: llegar el locutor de la tarde / no llegar hace cinco minutos
E1:   *¿Ha llegado el locutor de la tarde?*
E2:   *No había llegado todavía hace cinco minutos.*

1. escoger los discos el asistente / no prepararlos hace media hora
2. redactar las noticias la editora / no redactarlas hace un rato
3. traer el nuevo micrófono el técnico / no traerlo hace un cuarto de hora
4. encontrar Héctor la cinta de efectos especiales / no encontrarla hace poco
5. volver el ingeniero de su descanso / no volver hace diez minutos
6. transcribir Gustavo el anuncio a otra cinta / no hacerlo hace una hora

C. Basándose en los siguientes dibujos, cuéntele a un(a) compañero(a) lo que les ha pasado hoy a unos amigos en la oficina donde usted trabaja. Use las siguientes indicaciones y añada uno o dos comentarios más.

MODELO: Juanita y Felipe: ir a hablar con el jefe esta mañana
Juanita y Felipe han ido a hablar con el jefe esta mañana.
Les ha sido una experiencia bastante desagradable.

1. el jefe: enfadarse mucho porque hicieron mal un trabajo importante, no despedirlos, pedirles otro trabajo para el viernes
2. Jorge: volver hoy de las vacaciones, encontrar su mesa llena de papeles, sentirse agobiado por tanto trabajo

D. Las siguientes personas tienen que trabajar veinte horas por semana mientras estudian en la universidad. Como resultado, han tenido que hacer algunas cosas que nunca habían hecho antes. Exprese la situación de estas personas usando las indicaciones dadas y una terminación original.

MODELO: Mario: reducir sus gastos personales
Mario ha reducido sus gastos personales; nunca había economizado antes.

1. mis sobrinos: recibir un préstamo de mi hermana
2. Julia y Laura: mudarse de apartamento
3. (yo): cambiarme de especialización académica
4. (nosotros): cancelar nuestros planes para unas vacaciones en la playa
5. Mónica: buscar ayuda para su clase de estadística
6. (tú): dejar de jugar al golf durante el verano

III. Future and conditional perfect

Ricardo: Vaya, vaya; por fin te veo contenta. ¿Te **habrás ganado** unos millones en la lotería?

Enriqueta: No, Ricardo, no es eso. ¿Te acuerdas de ese puesto al que me presenté la semana pasada?

Ricardo: Sí, cómo no; la entrevista duró muy poco y tú pensabas que te **habrían eliminado**.

Enriqueta: Bueno, ¡felicítame! ¡Acaban de ofrecerme el puesto!

A. *Forms of the future and conditional perfect*

Future perfect	Conditional perfect
habré terminado	**habría** terminado
habrás terminado	**habrías** terminado
habrá terminado	**habría** terminado
habremos terminado	**habríamos** terminado
habréis terminado	**habríais** terminado
habrán terminado	**habrían** terminado

The future perfect is formed with the future of the auxiliary verb **haber** + a past participle. The conditional perfect is formed with the conditional of **haber** + a past participle. As with other perfect tenses, the past participle is invariable.

B. *Use of the future perfect*

As in English, the future perfect is used to refer to a future event that will have been completed prior to another future event or prior to a specific time in the future. It distinguishes the relationship in time between two future events.

El viernes a más tardar ya **habrán terminado** de entrevistar a los candidatos.

Next Friday at the latest they will have finished interviewing the applicants.

Dentro de diez días **habrán llenado** la plaza vacante.

In ten days they will have filled the vacant position.

C. *Uses of the conditional perfect*

1. The conditional perfect may be used when recounting past events in order to express the expectation that one event will be completed before a specific point in time. It distinguishes the relationship in time between two past events.

El supervisor estaba seguro de que **habría llenado** la vacante para esa tarde.

The supervisor was certain that he would have filled the vacancy by that afternoon.

Para entonces **habría seleccionado** al candidato más capacitado.

By then he would have selected the best-qualified candidate.

2. The conditional perfect is used to report what someone said in the future perfect. In this usage, it functions as the past of the future perfect.

El jefe dijo: «Para las tres de la tarde ya habremos entrevistado a todos los candidatos».

The boss said: "By three o'clock in the afternoon we will have interviewed all the candidates."

El jefe dijo que para las tres de la tarde ya **habríamos entrevistado** a todos los candidatos.

The boss said that by three o'clock in the afternoon we would have interviewed all the candidates.

3. The conditional perfect is also used to express what would have happened in the past under certain conditions. Use of the conditional perfect implies that the event never actually took place. (Consult *Capítulo 12.2* for use of the conditional perfect with **si**-clauses.)

No pudimos llenar la plaza vacante; sólo se presentó un candidato. Con más tiempo, **habríamos anunciado** la vacante en varios periódicos locales y seguramente **se habrían presentado** más candidatos.

We were unable to fill the vacant position; only one candidate applied. With more time, we would have announced the vacancy in several local newspapers and surely more applicants would have applied.

D. *Future and conditional perfect to indicate probability*

1. The future perfect is used to express probability regarding an action in the past, viewed from the perspective of the present.

—¿**Habrá tenido** algún accidente el jefe? Son las nueve y todavía no ha llegado.

Could the boss have had an accident? It's nine o'clock and he hasn't arrived yet.

—No, tenía que reunirse con el presidente del Banco Continental. La reunión **habrá durado** más de media hora.

No, he had to meet with the president of the Continental Bank. The meeting must have lasted over half an hour.

2. The conditional perfect is used to express probability in the past, viewed from a point of reference that is also in the past. (See *Capítulo 7.1* and *7.2* on probability.)

Al salir de mi entrevista, pensé que quizá **habría dicho** algo inapropiado. Imaginé que me **habrían eliminado** como candidato. ¡Qué sorpresa a los tres días cuando me ofrecieron el puesto!

When I left my interview, I thought that I probably had said something inappropriate. I imagined that they had probably eliminated me as a candidate. What a surprise three days later when they offered me the job!

Comprehension questions

1. Should the future perfect **habrá escrito** or the conditional perfect **habría escrito** be used in the following sentence? **El jefe todavía no ha escrito una carta de recomendación para mí; yo pensaba que para esta fecha ya la _____**. Explain.

2. Would you use the future perfect (**habrá encontrado**) or the conditional perfect (**habría encontrado**) to express the probability that Ramiro found a job? **Ramiro no ha venido a la entrevista; _____ otro puesto. Ramiro no nos había contestado si trabajaría o no con nosotros; _____ otro puesto.**

3. Should the conditional perfect **habría conseguido** or the conditional **conseguiría** be used in the following sentences? **Me prometió que, el lunes próximo, iría al banco y _____ el dinero que me debía. Me prometió que, antes del lunes próximo, _____ el dinero que me debía.**

Ejercicios

A. Algunos amigos especulan sobre lo que habrán hecho ellos mismos y otros amigos al final de un período de diez años. Utilizando el futuro perfecto, diga qué habrán logrado las siguientes personas.

MODELO: Carolina: hacerse ejecutiva de un banco internacional
Creo que Carolina se habrá hecho ejecutiva de un banco internacional.

1. Silvia: tener la oportunidad de trabajar en un país de habla española
2. Josefina: llegar a ser presidenta de alguna empresa grande
3. (yo): triunfar en el campo de la administración de negocios
4. (tú): lograr dirigir algún periódico rural
5. Gloria y Carlos: renunciar a su trabajo para dar la vuelta al mundo
6. todos nosotros: hacernos muy ricos

B. Es bastante común mirar al pasado y arrepentirse de haber tomado cierta decisión o de haber hecho cierta cosa. Diga lo que habrían hecho las siguientes personas en otras circunstancias. Use expresiones como **con más dinero, con más tiempo, con más educación, con mejores oportunidades,** o **con mejor suerte** y el condicional perfecto (*conditional perfect*).

MODELO: Enrique: terminar su programa de estudios en administración comercial
Con más dinero Enrique habría terminado su programa de estudios en administración comercial.

1. (tú): ganar un sueldo mucho mejor
2. Carmen y yo: abrir un buen negocio independiente

3. Gilberto y Pablo: ser ingenieros famosos
4. Lucía: establecer una empresa de asesores profesionales
5. (yo): dejar el negocio de mi padre
6. Sara y Teresa: utilizar más su preparación académica

C. Ud. especula sobre la explicación de ciertas acciones de diversas personas que trabajan en su oficina. Luego, un(a) compañero(a) comenta lo que dijo otra persona acerca del mismo asunto.

MODELO: *Usted:* Creo que el mecanógrafo habrá llegado tarde hoy por el atasco. (su jefa: pura vagancia)

Colega: ¿Tú crees? Pues su jefa creía que habría llegado tarde por pura vagancia.

1. Pienso que se habrán reunido los directores para firmar el nuevo convenio colectivo. (supervisores: rechazarlo)
2. Creo que Elena habrá presentado su renuncia por cuestiones de sueldo. (otros empleados: razones de salud)
3. Es mi opinión que Rodolfo habrá sido trasladado a otra sección por su propia preferencia. (Martín: problemas personales)
4. Pienso que los nuevos empleados habrán organizado la protesta por sus sueldos muy bajos. (otros de la oficina: tareas aburridas)
5. Creo que Beatriz habrá cambiado su fecha de vacaciones por la enfermedad de un pariente. (Josefina: para complacer a su jefa)

IV. The infinitive

Supervisora:	Mauricio, ¿**has empezado a redactar** el informe mensual de estadísticas de productividad?
Mauricio:	Lo **iba a hacer** esta tarde. **Terminar** esa tarea siempre me da satisfacción porque es lo más aburrido de mi puesto.
Supervisora:	(*Se pone seria*) Pues, ¿**necesito recordarte** el lema de esta oficina: «**Poner** buena cara a todo y **no quejarse** nunca»?
Mauricio:	(*Arrepentido*) **No me quejo de tener que hacerlo.** Solamente fue una broma.
Supervisora:	Entonces, **cuento con tener** el informe encima de mi escritorio mañana a primera hora. Y esta vez **sin hacer** errores de cálculo, ¿eh?
Mauricio:	Claro que sí, sin falta. (*Susurrando*) ¡Qué lío! ¡Otro regaño de mi jefa! **De poder trasladarme** a otra sección, lo haría sin demora.

A. *Forms of the infinitive*

	-ar verbs	**-er** verbs	**-ir** verbs
Simple infinitive	trabaj**ar**	comer	consegu**ir**
Perfect infinitive	**haber** trabaj**ado**	**haber** comido	**haber** consegu**ido**

1. A simple infinitive ends in **-ar, -er,** or **-ir**. Verbs ending in **-ar** form the largest group. A perfect infinitive consists of the infinitive of the auxiliary verb **haber** followed by the past participle of a verb.

2. Object pronouns are attached to the infinitive, forming one word. If the infinitive is preceded by a verb or verb phrase such as **deber, ir a, necesitar, poder, querer, tener que,** which functions like an auxiliary or modal verb, the object pronouns may also be placed before this verb.

¿Yo? ¿**Pedirle** un aumento de sueldo al jefe? No me atrevo.

Me? Request a raise from the boss? I don't dare.

No entregues las estadísticas sin **revi-sarlas** bien.

Don't turn the statistics in without reviewing them well.

Quieren (Van a/Pueden) trasla-darme a otra sección.

They want to (They are going to/They may) transfer me to a different section.

Me quieren (van a/pueden) trasladar a otra sección.

They want to (They are going to/They may) transfer me to a different section.

B. *The infinitive as a subject*

1. The infinitive can be used to introduce phrases that function as the subject of a sentence. The subject normally follows the main verb or the verbal expression. The definite article **el** may precede an infinitive subject: **El** demostrar entusiasmo es importante.

Es importante **demostrar entusiasmo en una entrevista. (Demostrar entusiasmo en una entrevista** es importante.)

It's important to show enthusiasm during an interview. (Showing enthusiasm during an interview is important.)

A los jefes les molesta **ver a aspirantes poco entusiastas. (Ver a aspirantes poco entusiastas** les molesta a los jefes.)	*It bothers bosses to see unenthusiastic applicants. (Seeing unenthusiastic applicants bothers bosses.)*
El vestirse adecuadamente para una entrevista es esencial.	*Dressing properly for an interview is essential.*

2. Impersonal expressions **(ser importante)** and verbs that describe states of mind **(enojar)** are the two most common constructions that accept infinitives as subjects.

Nos es necesario **terminar el informe para mañana.**	*It's necessary for us to finish the report by tomorrow.*
Le aburre mucho **hacer trabajos repetitivos.**	*It bores him to do repetitive tasks.*
A mí me enoja **apurarme sin necesidad en la oficina.**	*It makes me mad to hurry needlessly at the office.*

3. The following list shows some common verbs referring to states of mind. (Consult *Capítulo 9.3* for a list of impersonal expressions.)

aburrir	*to bore*	gustar	*to be pleasing, to like*
agradar	*to please*	indignar	*to irritate*
alegrar	*to make happy*	molestar	*to bother*
asustar	*to scare*	sorprender	*to surprise*
enojar	*to make angry*		

C. *The infinitive as a verbal complement*

The construction verb + (preposition) + infinitive

1. The infinitive may be used as a direct object to complement the idea expressed by a verb if the person performing the action expressed by the infinitive is the same as the subject of the main verb.

Necesito hablar con la recepcionista.	*I need to talk to the receptionist.*
Deseo ver al gerente.	*I wish to see the manager.*

2. With some verbs, especially verbs of influencing such as **sugerir, desear, recomendar,** the person performing the action expressed by an infinitive is the same as the direct or indirect object pronoun of the main verb. (Consult *Capítulo 9.2* for a list of verbs of influencing.)

Te sugiero **completar** esta planilla lo antes posible. Si deseas, yo **te** ayudo a **llenarla.**	*I suggest that you fill out this form as soon as possible. If you wish, I'll help you to fill it out.*

3. Here is a list of frequently used verbs that may be directly followed by an infinitive.

deber *to have to*	parecer *to seem*
decidir *to decide*	pensar *to think, to plan*
dejar *to let, to allow*	poder *to be able*
desear *to desire*	preferir *to prefer*
esperar *to hope, to expect*	querer *to want*
necesitar *to need*	saber *to know how*

4. Some verbs are immediately followed by an infinitive; others require a preposition such as **a, de, en,** or **con** before the infinitive. The following list shows some common verbs that are followed by a preposition before an infinitive.

Verb + a

aprender a   *to learn*
ayudar a   *to help*
comenzar a   *to begin*
decidirse a   *to decide*
empezar a   *to begin*
enseñar a   *to teach*
prepararse a   *to prepare*
volver a   *to do something again*

Verb + de

acabar de   *to have just*
acordarse de   *to remember*
cansarse de   *to tire*
dejar de   *to fail to*
pensar de   *to think of* (opinion)
quejarse de   *to complain about*
tratar de   *to try*
tratarse de   *to be a question of*

Verb + en

consistir en   *to consist of*
insistir en   *to insist on*
pensar en   *to think of*

Verb + con

contar con   *to count on*
soñar con   *to dream of*

The infinitive and verbs of perception

1. Verbs of perception such as **ver, oír, escuchar,** and **sentir** can be followed by an infinitive complement even though the subject of the conjugated verb and the person or thing performing the action expressed by the infinitive are different. The infinitive immediately follows the verb of perception and object pronouns precede the verb of perception.

No **siento funcionar** la máquina copiadora. No **la siento funcionar.**	*I don't hear the copy machine function(ing). I don't hear it function(ing).*
Oigo sonar el teléfono. **Lo oigo sonar.**	*I hear the phone ring(ing). I hear it ring(ing).*

2. If a direct object of the verb of perception refers to a person, it is preceded by the preposition **a** (personal **a**). (See *Capítulo 6.1* on verbs of perception + a present participle.)

Vi pasar **al cartero.** Lo vi pasar.	*I saw the mailman go(ing) by. I saw him go(ing) by.*
No he visto entrar **a la jefa.** No la he visto entrar.	*I haven't seen the boss enter(ing). I haven't seen her enter(ing).*

D. *The infinitive as an adverbial complement*

1. An infinitive may be used after a preposition or a prepositional phrase when there is no change in subject. The prepositional phrase functions as an adverbial complement, expressing ideas of time, manner, purpose, and condition. Notice in the following examples that a present participle may be used in English after a preposition, but not in Spanish.

Al llegar al centro, compró el periódico.	*On arriving downtown, he bought the newspaper.*
Buscó la sección "Oferta de Empleos" **sin leer** las otras secciones.	*He looked for the Help Wanted section without reading the other sections.*
Estudió cada aviso **para ver** si encontraba un puesto interesante.	*He studied each ad to see if he could find an interesting job.*
De encontrar algo interesante, presentaría su solicitud de inmediato.	*If he found something interesting, he'd apply right away.*

2. The adverbial construction **al** + infinitive expresses an action that happens at the same time as that of the main clause. English equivalents include *upon/on* + a present participle; *when/as* + a conjugated verb.

Al entrar en su oficina, notó un montón de papeles sobre el escritorio que necesitaban su firma. **Al terminar** de firmarlos, casi no sentía su mano.	*Upon entering his office, he noticed a pile of papers on his desk that needed his signature. When he finished signing them, he could hardly feel his hand.*

3. The adverbial construction **de** + infinitive is equivalent to a conditional **si**-clause. (See *Capítulo 12.2* on conditional **si**-clauses.)

De tener la oportunidad, me trasladaría a otra sección. Y **de encontrar** un puesto interesante, presentaría mi solicitud de inmediato.	*If I had the opportunity, I'd transfer to another section. And if I found an interesting position, I'd present my application right away.*

E. *The infinitive modifying an adjective or a noun*

As a modifier of an adjective or a noun, the infinitive is preceded by a preposition, usually **de**.

El problema del desempleo es **fácil de explicar.**	*The unemployment problem is easy to explain.*
Puede ser **difícil de resolver.**	*It may be hard to solve.*
Hay varios **aspectos por analizar.**	*There are several aspects yet to analyze.*

F. *The infinitive as a command*

1. The infinitive may be used by itself or modified by complements to express a command. This construction is frequently used to give impersonal instructions.

Completar la planilla.	*Fill out the form.*
Escribir en letras mayúsculas.	*Write in capital letters.*
No **doblar.**	*Do not fold.*

2. The infinitive as a command may be preceded by the preposition **a,** especially in colloquial language.

Y ahora, **a callar** todos y **a trabajar.** **A terminar** ese informe pronto.	*And now, everybody be quiet and work. Finish that report soon.*

Summary of the uses of the infinitive

Usage	Example
Subject	Es importante **vestirse** apropiadamente para una entrevista.
Verbal complement	Espero **encontrar** un puesto interesante. Cuento con **tener** una entrevista pronto.
Object of a verb of perception	Sentí **entrar** a alguien en la oficina.
Adverbial complement	**Al abrir** la puerta, vi a un joven. **Sin esperar** mi saludo, me preguntó si yo era el jefe de personal.
Modifier of an adjective or noun	Estaba cansado **de subir** los cinco pisos.
Command	**Cumplir** con las obligaciones del trabajo. No **llegar** nunca al trabajo atrasado.

Comprehension questions

1. In which of the following two sentences can the infinitive be preceded by the definite article **el**? **Es fatigoso presentarse a muchos empleos. Necesito presentarme a muchos empleos.** Explain why.

2. Should the infinitive **telefonear** or the present participle **telefoneando** be used in the following sentence? **Insistimos en _____ al gerente.**

3. Do you use **llenar, el llenar,** or **de llenar** to indicate that a position is hard to fill? **Este puesto es difícil _____.**

4. Two of the following three sentences request an applicant to fill out a form using capital letters. Identify these two sentences. **Escriba con letras mayúsculas. Escribo con letras mayúsculas. Escribir con letras mayúsculas.** What does the other sentence mean?

Ejercicios

A. Imagínese que Ud. es un(a) consejero(a) en una oficina de empleos y que ayuda a una persona que solicita trabajo por primera vez. Déle consejos usando **deber** o **poder** y uno de los siguientes verbos con la preposición apropiada: **aprender, empezar, pensar, tratar,** o **dejar.**

MODELO 1: decidir qué tipo de trabajo quiere
Debe tratar de decidir qué tipo de trabajo quiere.

MODELO 2: leer los avisos clasificados
Puede empezar a leer los avisos clasificados.

1. preparar un resumen profesional
2. decidir qué sueldo necesita
3. enterarse de las oportunidades de empleo
4. pensar negativamente
5. llenar con mucho cuidado las solicitudes de empleo
6. investigar bien las compañías que lo(la) van a entrevistar

B. Un(a) compañero(a) de trabajo le pregunta a Ud. si se ha enterado de lo que pasa con Ana, una compañera suya que se quejó a su supervisor de las condiciones de trabajo. Exprese lo que pasó usando los verbos **ver** y **oír,** un infinitivo y el complemento pronominal correcto, según las indicaciones.

MODELO: Ana: entrar en la oficina del supervisor
E1: *¿Viste a Ana entrar en la oficina del supervisor?*
E2: *Sí, la vi entrar. (No, no la vi entrar.)*

1. los dos: discutir en voz alta
2. Ana: salir de la oficina del supervisor abruptamente

3. el supervisor: decir que ella no tenía razón
4. Ana: telefonear al departamento de personal

C. Imagínese que a Ud. lo(la) están entrevistando para un trabajo y que Ud. expresa sus deseos y opiniones a un(a) jefe(a) de personal. Termine las siguientes frases usando un infinitivo como complemento verbal e insertando una preposición si es necesaria.

MODELO: Estoy tratando...
          Estoy tratando de encontrar un trabajo con más responsabilidades.

1. Espero poder...
2. A mí me gustaría...
3. Estoy seguro(a) de que puedo...
4. Para poder vivir bien, yo necesito...
5. Si me dan el puesto, yo voy...
6. Antes de concluir la entrevista, debo...

D. Exprese sus actitudes, ideas y sueños con respecto al trabajo, explicándole a un(a) compañero(a) qué cosas le gustan y qué cosas no le gustan. Use algunas de las frases siguientes u otras similares de su invención. Luego, pídale a su compañero(a) que hable de sí mismo(a).

Me molesta (molestaría)...   Me aburre (aburriría)...
Me es importante...   Me enoja...
Sueño...   Insisto...
Me gusta (gustaría)...   Quiero un trabajo que consista...
Tengo ganas...   Me fascina (fascinaría)...

MODELO: E1:   *Me aburre hacer siempre lo mismo en el trabajo. Y a ti, ¿qué te aburre?*
          E2:   *A mí me aburre estar sentado(a) todo el día en una oficina.*

V. The passive voice and alternative constructions

(Josefina, vicepresidenta de una agencia de publicidad, conversa con su asistenta administrativa sobre el trabajo de un nuevo empleado.)

Josefina: Rosalía, ¿sabes quién dirige la campaña publicitaria para la nueva línea de zapatos deportivos Jaguar?

Rosalía: La versión final del vídeo publicitario **fue escrita por** Guillermo Seco, quien dirigió también toda la producción.

Josefina: Ha sido un gran éxito, ¿verdad? **Me dicen** que **se hizo** con un presupuesto mínimo y que **ha sido recibido** muy favorablemente.

Rosalía: Es cierto. El Sr. Seco es una persona sumamente capacitada. **Se le han dado** varios proyectos importantes y los ha hecho muy bien.

Josefina: Sí, **se nota** que es muy capaz.

A. *Active versus passive constructions*

1. The *active voice* is used in sentences in which the subject performs, carries out, or causes the action expressed by the verb. The direct object is the person or thing acted upon. Observe the pattern *subject* + *verb (action)* + *direct object* in the following sentences.

El contratista despidió a los obreros. | *The contractor fired the workers.*

La empresa aprobó el presupuesto anual. | *The company approved the annual budget.*

2. The *passive voice* is used in sentences in which the person or thing acted upon is the grammatical subject of the sentence. The verb is expressed by a form of **ser** + a past participle. The person or thing that performs the action (agent), if mentioned, is expressed by a prepositional phrase introduced by **por.** Observe in the following sentences that the action is viewed from the perspective of the person or thing acted upon.

Los obreros fueron despedidos por el contratista. | *The workers were fired by the contractor.*

El presupuesto anual fue aprobado por la empresa. | *The annual budget was approved by the company.*

3. Compare the construction of the active voice to the passive voice in the following chart.

Active voice	**Subject**	**Action**	**Person/thing acted upon**
	El contratista	**despidió**	a los obreros.
Passive voice	**Person/thing acted upon**	**Action**	**Agent**
	Los obreros	**fueron despedidos**	por el contratista.

4. The passive voice construction focuses attention on the recipient of an action, not on the agent. If the agent is unknown or considered to be unimportant, it may not be mentioned in the sentence at all.

Los obreros **fueron despedidos.** | *The workers were fired.*

El presupuesto anual **fue aprobado.** | *The annual budget was approved.*

5. The verb **ser** + a past participle expresses an action in the passive voice. The verb **estar** + a past participle refers to a condition; frequently such a condition has resulted from a previous action. (Consult Section I in this chapter and *Capítulo 3.2* on **ser** and **estar** + a past participle.)

El presupuesto **fue aprobado** ayer por la empresa.	*The budget was approved by the company yesterday.*
El presupuesto **está aprobado;** la empresa lo aprobó ayer.	*The budget has been approved; the company approved it yesterday.*

B. *Agreement of the past participle in passive constructions*

The past participle in a passive voice construction functions as an adjective and therefore must agree in gender and number with the subject of the sentence.

El contador fue autoriza**do** por el gerente para firmar cheques.	*The accountant was authorized by the manager to sign checks.*
La contadora fue autoriza**da** por el gerente para firmar cheques.	*The accountant was authorized by the manager to sign checks.*
Los cajeros fueron entrena**dos** por el supervisor.	*The cashiers were trained by the supervisor.*
Las cajeras fueron entrena**das** por el supervisor.	*The cashiers were trained by the supervisor.*

C. *Alternatives to the passive voice*

In Spanish, the passive voice is used much less frequently than in English, especially in the spoken language. A **se** construction, a verb in the third person plural, or reversal of the order of the subject and the direct object can also be used in Spanish to deemphasize the performer of an action.

Se construction

1. The pronoun **se** is frequently used with a third person form of the verb in sentences in which the performer of the action is irrelevant or unknown and therefore not mentioned. There are several English equivalents of the passive **se** construction.

Se publican anuncios en el periódico.	*Ads are published in the newspaper.* *They/You (impersonal) publish ads in the newspaper.* *People/One publish(es) ads in the newspaper.*

2. The **se** construction is formed by the pronoun **se** and a verb in the third person singular or plural. The subject follows the verb, and the verb agrees with the subject.

Se publicó un anuncio en el periódico.	*An ad was published in the newspaper.*
Se describieron todos los puestos vacantes en la empresa.	*All the available positions in the company were described.*
Se recibieron muchas solicitudes.	*Many applications were received.*

3. If the verb in the **se** construction is followed by a noun that refers to an anonymous or unknown person or persons, the noun functions as the grammatical subject and the verb agrees with it in number.

Se busca una secretaria ejecutiva.	*They are looking for an executive secretary.*
Se necesitan buenos mecanógrafos.	*They need good typists.*

4. If the verb in the **se** construction is followed by a noun that refers to a specific person or persons, the noun functions as a direct object and is preceded by the preposition **a** (personal **a**). The verb is always conjugated in the third person singular in this situation.

Se entrevista a un candidato para el puesto vacante.	*They are interviewing a candidate for the vacant position. (A candidate for the vacant position is being interviewed.)*
Ayer **se entrevistó a** cinco candidatos.	*Yesterday five candidates were interviewed.*

5. A direct object noun that refers to a specific person or persons in a passive **se** construction can be replaced by a direct object pronoun. Female direct objects are replaced by the feminine direct object pronouns **la** and **las**. However, male direct objects or, in the plural, a combination of male and female direct objects, are replaced by **le** and **les**.

Se respeta mucho a la administradora. **Se la** respeta mucho.	*The administrator is much respected. She is much respected.*
Se respeta mucho a las administradoras. **Se las** respeta mucho.	*The administrators are much respected. They are much respected.*
Se contrató a un nuevo gerente. **Se le** contrató.	*They hired a new manager. They hired him.*
Se contrató a tres nuevos gerentes. **Se les** contrató.	*They hired three new managers. They hired them.*

6. An indirect object pronoun may be used after the pronoun **se**.

Se les explicó el trabajo a los aspirantes.	*The job was explained to the applicants.*

A mí **se me** explicaron mis nuevas responsabilidades.	*My new responsibilities were explained to me.*
Se le dio un aumento de sueldo al nuevo empleado.	*The new employee was given a raise.*

Verb in the third person plural

A construction in the active voice, using the third person plural form of the verb, is also frequently used when the performer of an action is not mentioned or is irrelevant.

Entrevistaron a los aspirantes.	*They interviewed the applicants.*
Grabaron las entrevistas.	*They recorded the interviews.*
Seleccionarán a los finalistas pronto.	*They'll select the finalists soon.*

Reversal of subject–direct object order

1. An active sentence in which normal word order (subject + verb + direct object) is reversed (direct object + verb + subject) is sometimes used rather than the passive voice. When normal word order is reversed, a redundant direct object pronoun must be used before the verb.

El horario de trabajo **lo** estableció la presidenta.	*The work schedule was established by the president.*
El horario de trabajo **lo** modificó la supervisora.	*The work schedule was modified by the supervisor.*

2. Use of the direct object in the normal subject position emphasizes the person or thing acted upon. If no emphasis is desired, normal word order is used.

La huelga **la** declararon los obreros.	*The strike was declared by the workers.*
Los obreros declararon la huelga.	*The workers declared the strike.*

D. *Restrictions on the passive construction in Spanish*

1. In Spanish, a **se** construction is often used in sentences that express general truths or that refer to or describe situations, conditions, or states that prevail at a certain point in time. In contrast to English, the passive voice is not used in such cases.

Nuestra empresa **se compone** de tres departamentos: el de producción, el de administración y el de publicidad.	*Our company is composed of three departments: production, administration, and publicity.*
Normalmente, las decisiones sobre los tres departamentos **se toman** en juntas especiales.	*Normally, decisions concerning the three departments are made at special meetings.*

2. In Spanish, an indirect object cannot become the subject of a passive sentence. A sentence in the active voice or a construction with **se** must be used. This restriction does not apply to English.

El sindicato le dio un ultimátum a la empresa.	*The union gave the company an ultimatum.*
[The indirect object **a la empresa** cannot become the subject of a passive sentence.]	*The company was given an ultimatum by the union.*

3. The active voice is preferred in Spanish when using the progressive tenses.

Entrevistan (Están entrevistando) a los aspirantes.	*They're interviewing the applicants.*
[Passive equivalent avoided.]	*The applicants are being interviewed.*

4. Verbs indicating necessity or requirement are expressed in the active voice or by a **se** construction in Spanish.

Se necesitan (Necesitan) nuevos líderes en nuestra compañía.	*New leaders are needed in our company.*
Se requiere mucha energía para el puesto de presidente.	*Much energy is required for the position of president.*

Summary of the passive voice and alternative constructions

Passive voice

Person/thing acted upon + **ser** + a past participle	Las peticiones de los obreros **fueron aceptadas** por la empresa.
	El conflicto entre la empresa y los obreros **fue resuelto** ayer.

Alternatives to the passive

Se construction	**Se** ha producido un conflicto entre los obreros y su sindicato.
	Se estudian diversos modos de resolver el conflicto.
Verb in third person plural	**Eliminan** empleos a causa de la automatización de las empresas.
Reversed order of subject and direct object	**Las reglas** de nuestra compañía las crearon **los obreros.**

Comprehension questions

1. In which of the following sentences must **presentados** be used? **No han sido ____ muchos productos todavía. No han ____ muchos productos a esos distribuidores todavía.** Explain why.

2. Should **fue** or **estuvo** be used in the following sentences? **Esa oficina ____ cerrada a las seis de la tarde ayer. Esa oficina ____ cerrada todo el día ayer.** How do you know?

3. Should **resolvió** or **lo resolvió** be used in the sentence **El problema ____ la supervisora?** And in **La supervisora ____ el problema?** Explain why.

4. The following three sentences all mean that the responsible employee was identified. Which one is used less frequently? **Se identificó al empleado responsable. El empleado responsable fue identificado. Identificaron al empleado responsable.**

5. Would you complete the following sentences with **consideró** or **consideraron?** **Se ____ muchos problemas en la junta especial. Se ____ un solo problema en la junta especial.**

Ejercicios

A. Cambie las siguientes noticias laborales de la sección «Comercio y comerciantes» a la voz pasiva. Utilice el mismo tiempo verbal que aparece en la frase original.

MODELO: La fábrica de automóviles F.E.A. despidió a unos 500 obreros.
   Unos 500 obreros fueron despedidos por la fábrica de automóviles F.E.A.

1. El Ministro de Trabajo firmará el nuevo convenio colectivo mañana con el sindicato de mineros.
2. El Banco Nacional va a adquirir el Banco Comercial.
3. Un portavoz del gobierno ha anunciado nuevas medidas antiinflacionarias a la prensa.
4. Los directores de la Compañía Sandoval aprobaron la nueva escala de salarios ayer.
5. Los dirigentes de la industria pesquera pronostican una rápida mejora económica.
6. El presidente de la Asociación de Agentes de Turismo pidió mayor estabilidad en las tarifas aéreas.

B. Ud. contesta las preguntas de un(a) compañero(a) de trabajo para ponerle al día de lo que ha pasado en el departamento mientras él/ella estaba fuera en un viaje de negocios.

MODELO 1:   anunciar tu promoción
    E1:   *¿Anunciaron tu promoción?*
    E2:   *Sí, ya se ha anunciado. (No, todavía no se ha anunciado.)*

MODELO 2:   entrenar al nuevo mensajero
    E1:   *¿Entrenaron al nuevo mensajero?*
    E2:   *Sí, ya se le entrenó. (No, todavía no se le ha entrenado.)*

1. contratar a una nueva secretaria
2. implementar la reestructuración del departamento
3. celebrar la reunión sobre beneficios de salud
4. pedir nuevos muebles para la oficina
5. establecer las nuevas metas de productividad
6. resolver el desacuerdo entre nuestro departamento y el de publicidad

C. Ya hace dos semanas que Tomás Rivera trabaja para la compañía telefónica. Tomás toma un café con un grupo de amigos y contesta sus preguntas sobre su nuevo trabajo. Utilice la construcción con **se** como en el modelo.

MODELO: ¿Cómo es el horario? (empezar a las 8:30 y salir a las 4:30)
    Amigo(a):   ¿Cómo es el horario?
    Tomás: *Se empieza a las 8:30 y se sale a las 4:30.*

1. ¿Hay algunos descansos? (tomar un sólo descanso)
2. ¿Ganan un buen sueldo en tu departamento? (ganar un sueldo bajo al principio)
3. ¿Cuántas semanas de vacaciones dan? (dar dos semanas de vacaciones el primer año)
4. ¿Con qué frecuencia reciben un aumento de sueldo? (recibir un aumento de sueldo después de seis meses)
5. ¿Hay un cuarto especial para los que fuman? (usar los cuartos de descanso en el primer piso)
6. ¿Pagan por el uso del teléfono para llamadas personales? (no pagar por llamadas personales locales)

D. Conteste de dos maneras las preguntas basadas en la siguiente invitación a los empleados de la compañía Instrumentación Científica. Un(a) estudiante contesta usando la voz pasiva y otro(a) contesta cambiando el lugar del verbo y del objeto directo.

Instrumentación Científica
Avenida Nogales, 816
Col. Juárez, CP. 06598
México, D.F.

Reunión anual:	16 de junio
Hora:	10:00 de la mañana
Lugar:	Sala de los Fundadores
Discurso principal:	Sra. Francisca Blanes, Directora, Agencia Federal de Comercio
Patrocinadores:	Cámara de Comercio, Col. Juárez
Música:	Los Mariachis Guitarras de Oro

MODELO: ¿Qué compañía organizó la reunión?
   E1:   *La reunión fue organizada por la compañía Instrumentación Científica.*
   E2:   *La reunión la organizó la compañía Instrumentación Científica.*

1. ¿Dónde se celebró la reunión?
2. ¿Quién pronunció el discurso principal?
3. ¿Qué grupo patrocinó el evento?
4. ¿Para qué fecha fijaron la reunión?
5. ¿A qué hora se abrió la primera sesión?

VI. Trabajar, funcionar, and similar verbs

1. **Trabajar** is used to express *to work* in the general sense of doing physical labor or fulfilling the requirements of a job.

Ella **trabaja** para mantener a sus hijos.	*She works in order to support her children.*
Pasé toda la mañana **trabajando** en el jardín.	*I spent all morning working in the garden.*

2. Several verbs in Spanish may be used to express putting into motion or operating a machine or device. **Manejar** is used more frequently with means of land transportation (motorcycle, car, bus, etc.). **Operar** and **hacer funcionar** are used more frequently with other types of machines and devices.

¿Qué tipo de automóvil **maneja** Carlos?	*What kind of car does Carlos drive (operate)?*

¿Tú sabes **hacer funcionar** esta máquina?	*Do you know how to run (work) this machine?*
Lo siento, pero no sé **operar** una computadora.	*I'm sorry, but I don't know how to operate (work) a computer.*

3. The verbs most frequently used to refer to the functioning of a machine or device are **funcionar** and **andar. Caminar** and **marchar** are used to a lesser degree to express this meaning.

—La fotocopiadora está descompuesta; no **funciona** bien.	*The photocopier is broken; it's not working well.*
—No sé por qué no la reparan; esa máquina nunca **anda** bien.	*I don't know why they don't repair it; that machine never runs (works) well.*

4. **Hacer trabajar** is used to express the idea of making someone else work.

—En este trabajo, ¿te **hacen trabajar** mucho?	*Do they make you work a lot on this job?*
—Sí, chico; me **hacen trabajar** como un burro.	*Yes, man; they make me work like a mule.*

Ejercicios

A. Indique qué verbo o expresión verbal se usa en español en lugar de la palabra o expresión indicada.

1. When did you begin *to work* for that agency?
2. If your typewriter doesn't *work,* take it to the shop.
3. Do you know how *to work* that new coffee machine?
4. They told me they *worked* there for five years before coming here.
5. My watch must not be *working* well; I thought it was time to go home.
6. The boss shouldn't *work* us so hard when the air conditioner is broken.

B. Conteste las siguientes preguntas de un(a) amigo(a), según su propia experiencia.

MODELO: ¿Sabes operar una computadora?
     Sí, aprendí a operar computadoras en la escuela.

1. ¿Por qué trabajas tanto?
2. ¿Crees tú que el sistema educativo funciona bien?
3. ¿Adónde se puede llevar una máquina de escribir cuando no funciona bien?
4. ¿Qué haces para llegar a tiempo a una cita si tu reloj no anda bien?
5. ¿Quién te hacía trabajar más, tu madre o tu padre?
6. ¿Cuánto tiempo hacía que sabías operar una computadora?

Actividades para la comunicación

A. ¿Qué dirá el futuro? Entreviste a un(a) compañero(a) sobre lo que cree que habrá logrado profesionalmente de aquí a 5 o 6 años. Prepárese para hablar de sí mismo(a) también. Use los temas siguientes y otros de su propia invención.

encontrar un puesto en tu espe-
    cialización
probar varios trabajos

ahorrar suficiente dinero
recibir varias promociones
llegar a ocupar un puesto importante

MODELO: E1:   *¿Habrás encontrado un puesto en tu especialización?*
              E2:   *Creo que sí. Espero haber encontrado un puesto interesante. Y tú, ¿crees que te habrás metido en la política?*
              E1:   *Pues, no estoy seguro(a), pero espero poder utilizar mi preparación universitaria.*

B. Anuncios de empleo. Lea los siguientes anuncios y después descríbale a un(a) amigo(a) cada trabajo y sus requisitos. Use verbos como **necesitar, solicitar, buscar, ofrecer, pedir, anunciar, requerir** y **llamar.** Luego prepare un anuncio de empleo similar para otro trabajo distinto.

MODELO: *(Anuncio 1) Se anuncia un trabajo de secretaria para una empresa internacional. Se necesita (busca) una secretaria bilingüe con conocimientos de...*

C. Soñar no cuesta nada. Cada estudiante toma turno para describir su trabajo ideal. ¿Cómo se lo imagina Ud.? Piense en el sueldo, los compañeros, las condiciones de trabajo, el horario, los supervisores, etc.

MODELO: E1:   *En el trabajo ideal, se trabaja sólo tres días a la semana.*
              E2:   *Y también (se) dan dos meses de vacaciones.*
              E3:   *Y solamente se evalúa a los jefes, no a los trabajadores.*

D. En una entrevista. Con un(a) compañero(a) desarrolle una entrevista para un puesto que a usted le gustaría tener. Durante la entrevista el(la) entrevistador(a) pide que le explique dónde ha trabajado antes, qué responsabilidades ha tenido, por qué ha cambiado de empleo varias veces, por qué está interesado(a) en el puesto y otras preguntas similares. Ud. debe preguntar sobre el sueldo, el horario y cuándo le informarán de una decisión.

MODELO: Entrevistador(a): *Veo en su resumen que ha trabajado en varios sitios.*

Usted: *Sí, hasta ahora, he tenido cinco puestos diferentes. Primero, he trabajado de cajero(a) en un restaurante...*

E. Diálogos. Con un(a) compañero(a) de clase, desarrolle un diálogo con respecto a las situaciones presentadas a continuación. Incluya entre tres a cinco comentarios por persona.

1. Ud. le pide un aumento de sueldo a su jefe(a) y le explica por qué cree que lo merece. Pídale también que le diga cuándo le comunicará su decisión. Puede decirle también qué hará si no le dan el aumento (marcharse del trabajo, hablar con la directora de personal, etc.), pero ¡tenga cuidado! ¡A lo mejor lo(la) despide!

2. Su jefe(a) pide una entrevista privada con Ud. porque ha llegado tarde al trabajo tres días seguidos y ha hecho mal varias tareas. También menciona que ha presentado varios informes tarde. Explíquele las razones y conteste sus preguntas.

CAPÍTULO 9

◆

Arte y literatura

Las librerías hispanas ofrecen una variedad de libros de texto y libros de interés general. También sirven como centros de difusión de nuevas ideas con tertulias y otras actividades culturales. (Miami, Florida)

Conversación

1. ¿Es importante el estudio del arte y de la literatura en una carrera universitaria? ¿Por qué sí o por qué no?
2. ¿Qué pintores o escuela de pintores le gustan más? ¿Conoce la obra de algún pintor español o hispanoamericano? Explique.
3. En su opinión, ¿cuáles son las ventajas (o desventajas) de que los estudiantes de arte pasen un semestre en un país extranjero como parte de sus estudios?
4. ¿Qué tipo de literatura le gusta leer? ¿Quién es su autor(a) favorito(a)? ¿Por qué prefiere a ese(esa) autor(a)?
5. ¿Qué obras de autores hispanos ha leído Ud.? ¿Ha leído en inglés alguna novela de Gabriel García Márquez? ¿De Isabel Allende?
6. Cuando visita Ud. un museo, ¿le gusta ir con guía o por su propia cuenta? ¿Por qué?
7. Cuando Ud. va a una librería, ¿le gusta ojear (*browse*) muchos libros o hace su compra rápidamente sin detenerse? ¿Por qué?
8. Describa el ambiente de la librería en la fotografía de la página anterior. ¿Cómo se compara con el ambiente en la(s) librería(s) cerca de su universidad?

Vocabulario temático

acuarela, la watercolor
anécdota, la anecdote
argumento, el plot; argument
concurso, el contest
conferencia, la lecture
crítica, la criticism
cuadro, el painting, picture
cuento, el story, short story
diapositiva, la slide
dramaturgo(a), el(la) dramatist, playwright
esbozo, el outline, sketch
escultura, la sculpture
estilo, el style
exposición, la exposition, exhibit
juez, el(la) judge
juicio, el judgment
jurado, el jury, panel of judges
lectura, la reading, reading assignment
lienzo, el canvas
óleo, el oil painting
pincel, el artist's brush, paintbrush
pintor(a), el(la) painter

pintura, la painting
poesía, la poetry
premio, el prize, award
reconocimiento, el recognition
reseña, la review
tejido, el weaving

captar to secure, to get; to captivate
conmover (ue) to move (emotionally)
dibujar to draw, to sketch
exhibir to exhibit
influir to influence

ficticio(a) fictitious
realista realistic
técnico(a) technical
valioso(a) valuable

bellas artes, las fine arts
cuento de hadas, el fairy tale
trabajo de investigación, el research paper

I. Present subjunctive: Forms

(En un museo de arte contemporáneo)

Guía: ¿Tienen más preguntas? Bueno... Les pido que **pasen** al siguiente salón y que **formen** un círculo...

Susana: Perdón, señor; ¿no podemos quedarnos un ratito más aquí? Es necesario que **tomemos** notas y que **dibujemos** un poco para nuestra clase.

Guía: Lo siento, señorita; hay otros grupos que vienen detrás de nosotros. Lamento que no **tengamos** tiempo esta vez. Espero que **comprendan** nuestra situación.

A. *Concept of the subjunctive mood*

The subjunctive mood is much more frequently used in Spanish than in English. In general, it is used after verbs and expressions that reflect doubt, disbelief, emotion, desires, and suggestions made to influence another person's actions. It is also used to describe persons or situations that are unknown to the speaker or situations that haven't occurred or been experienced by the speaker.

—Dudo que **lleguemos** a tiempo al concierto. No creo que con**sigamos** buenos asientos.

—Siempre recomiendan que uno **compre** los boletos con anticipación. Pero no tú. No hay nadie que **sea** más desorganizado que tú.

—Me molesta que **pidas** todo con anticipación.

I doubt we'll arrive at the concert on time. I don't think we'll get good seats.

They always recommend that one buy tickets ahead of time. But not you. There's nobody who's more disorganized than you.

It bothers me that you ask for everything ahead of time.

B. *Present subjunctive of regular verbs*

	-ar verbs **pasar**	**-er verbs** **aprender**	**-ir verbs** **escribir**
Stem:	**yo pasó**	**yo aprendó**	**yo escribó**
	pas**e**	aprend**a**	escrib**a**
	pas**es**	aprend**as**	escrib**as**
	pas**e**	aprend**a**	escrib**a**
	pas**emos**	aprend**amos**	escrib**amos**
	pas**éis**	aprend**áis**	escrib**áis**
	pas**en**	aprend**an**	escrib**an**

The present subjunctive stem of most verbs is formed by dropping the **-o** ending of the first person singular present indicative: **-ar** verbs add endings containing the vowel **-e; -er** and **-ir** verbs add endings containing the vowel **-a.** Note that the subjunctive forms of the first and third person singular are identical.

El guía pide que **pasemos** al siguiente salón. Recomienda que **aprendamos** más sobre el arte moderno.	*The guide asks us to go on to the next room. He recommends that we learn more about modern art.*
¿Es esencial que **escribas** un informe después de visitar el museo?	*Is it essential that you write a report after visiting the museum?*
—¿Es preciso que Ud. **tome** notas sobre cada cuadro?	*Is it necessary that you take notes on each painting?*
—Sí, el profesor quiere que yo **tome** notas para mi informe.	*Yes, the professor wants me to take notes for my report.*

C. *Irregular first person singular form*

Present indicative	Stem	Present subjunctive
yo estóý	est-	yo **esté**
yo dóý	d-	yo **dé**
yo conozcó	conozc-	yo **conozca**
yo hagó	hag-	yo **haga**
yo oigó	oig-	yo **oiga**
yo salgó	salg-	yo **salga**
yo traduzcó	traduzc-	yo **traduzca**

1. The present subjunctive of verbs with an irregular first person singular form ending in **-o** or **-oy** in the present indicative is formed by dropping the **-o** or **-oy** and adding the subjunctive endings. (See *Capítulo 3.1* for verbs with an irregular first person singular form.)

Es urgente que me **des** el libro sobre Picasso que te presté; lo necesito.	*It's urgent that you give me the book on Picasso that I loaned you; I need it.*
La profesora de arte quiere que **hagamos** un informe sobre Picasso y Dalí.	*The art professor wants us to do a report on Picasso and Dalí.*

2. The present subjunctive forms of **estar** have a written accent on all forms except the first person plural. Although one-syllable words do not generally require a

written accent, the first and third person singular of **dar (dé)** have an accent to distinguish them from the preposition **de.**

---

estar: esté, estés, esté, estemos, estéis, estén
dar: dé, des, dé, demos, deis, den

D. *Present subjunctive of stem-changing verbs*

pensar e > ie	volver o > ue	preferir e > ie/i	dormir o > ue/u	pedir e > i
piense	vuelva	prefiera	duerma	pida
pienses	vuelvas	prefieras	duermas	pidas
piense	vuelva	prefiera	duerma	pida
pensemos	volvamos	prefiramos	durmamos	pidamos
penséis	volváis	prefiráis	durmáis	pidáis
piensen	vuelvan	prefieran	duerman	pidan

1. Stem-changing **-ar** and **-er** verbs conjugated like **pensar** and **volver** have a stem change **e** to **ie** and **o** to **ue,** respectively, in all persons except the first and second person plural, just as they do in the present indicative. Note that the verb **jugar** follows the pattern of **o** to **ue** stem changes in the present subjunctive, except that it changes **u** to **ue** (just as in the present indicative).

Siento que Uds. **piensen** que no me interesa el arte abstracto. ¡Es que no lo entiendo!	*I'm sorry that you think abstract art doesn't interest me. It's that I don't understand it!*
Quiero que **vuelvas** al museo mañana con nosotros; dan una charla muy interesante.	*I want you to return to the museum with us tomorrow; they're giving a very interesting lecture.*
Es preciso que tu niñito no **juegue** junto a las esculturas.	*It's necessary that your little boy not play by the sculptures.*

2. Stem-changing **-ir** verbs conjugated like **preferir** and **dormir** have stem changes in all persons of the present subjunctive. Verbs with a stem change **e** to **ie** and **o** to **ue** in the present indicative have the same change in the present subjunctive. They have an additional change **e** to **i** and **o** to **u** in the first and second persons plural.

Me alegro que te **diviertan** tanto los cuadros de Dalí. ¡Pero es una vergüenza que te **duermas** en las conferencias sobre su arte!	*I'm glad Dalí's paintings amuse you so much. But it's a shame you fall asleep in the lectures about his art!*

El guía se sorprende que nosotros **prefiramos** no acercarnos a la exhibición.	*The guide is surprised that we prefer not to get close to the exhibition.*

3. Stem-changing **-ir** verbs conjugated like **pedir** have a stem change **e** to **i** in all persons of the present subjunctive.

¿Cómo es posible que **pidan** tanto por ver la exposición de Goya?	*How is it possible that they charge so much to see the Goya exhibit?*

E. *Irregular forms of the present subjunctive*

haber:	**hay**a,	**hay**as,	**hay**a,	**hay**amos,	**hay**áis,	**hay**an
ir:	**vay**a,	**vay**as,	**vay**a,	**vay**amos,	**vay**áis,	**vay**an
saber:	**sep**a,	**sep**as,	**sep**a,	**sep**amos,	**sep**áis,	**sep**an
ser:	**se**a,	**se**as,	**se**a,	**se**amos,	**se**áis,	**se**an

The verbs **haber, ir, saber,** and **ser** have an irregular stem in the present subjunctive: **hay-, vay-, sep-,** and **se-.**

—Me dijiste que irías a la conferencia sobre Goya esta tarde. ¿Quieres que **vaya** contigo?	*You told me that you'd go to the lecture on Goya this afternoon. Do you want me to go with you?*
—Con mucho gusto, pero dudo que la conferencia **sea** esta tarde. Que yo **sepa,** no creo que **haya** conferencias esta semana.	*Gladly, but I doubt the lecture is this afternoon. As far as I know, I don't think there are lectures this week.*

F. *Spelling changes in the present subjunctive*

buscar c > qu	pagar g > gu	alcanzar z > c	averiguar u > ü
bus**que**	pa**gue**	alcan**ce**	averi**güe**
bus**ques**	pa**gues**	alcan**ces**	averi**gües**
bus**que**	pa**gue**	alcan**ce**	averi**güe**
bus**quemos**	pa**guemos**	alcan**cemos**	averi**güemos**
bus**quéis**	pa**guéis**	alcan**céis**	averi**güéis**
bus**quen**	pa**guen**	alcan**cen**	averi**güen**

1. The present subjunctive forms of all verbs ending in **-car, -gar, -zar,** and **-guar** undergo the following spelling changes in order to preserve the pronunciation of the final stem consonant: **c > qu; g > gu; z > c; u > ü**. These verbs also have the same spelling changes in some forms of the preterit. (See *Capítulo 4.1* for other verbs with these spelling changes.)

—No sé qué hacer. Es urgente que **empiece** mi informe sobre los muralistas mexicanos.	*I don't know what to do. It's urgent that I begin my report on the Mexican muralists.*
—¿Quieres que te **busque** alguna información? Voy a la biblioteca hoy.	*Do you want me to look for some information for you? I'm going to the library today.*
—Muchas gracias. Yo voy también, pero sé que es imposible que **averigüe** todo hoy.	*Thanks. I'm going too, but I know it's impossible to (that I) find out everything today.*

2. Verbs ending in a consonant + **cer** or **cir** have a spelling change from **c** to **z** in all persons of the present subjunctive to preserve the pronunciation of the final stem consonant. Common verbs in this group include **convencer, ejercer, esparcir,** and **vencer.**

convencer (c > z):	convenza, convenzas, convenza, convenzamos, convenzáis, convenzan
esparcir (c > z):	esparza, esparzas, esparza, esparzamos, esparzáis, esparzan

Dices que Dalí es un genio. No creo que me **convenzas** sin buenas razones.	*You say Dalí is a genius. I don't think you'll convince me without good reasons.*

3. Verbs ending in **-guir** have a spelling change **gu** to **g** and verbs ending in **-ger** and **-gir** have a change **g** to **j** in all forms of the present subjunctive in order to preserve the pronunciation of the final stem consonant.

distinguir (gu > g)	escoger (g > j)	exigir (g > j)
distinga	escoja	exija
distingas	escojas	exijas
distinga	escoja	exija
distingamos	escojamos	exijamos
distingáis	escojáis	exijáis
distingan	escojan	exijan

Es posible que el profesor de arte **exija** un trabajo de investigación bastante largo este semestre.	*It's possible that the art professor will require a rather long research paper this semester.*
Quiere que **escojamos** un tema pronto, aunque todavía no **distingamos** bien las características de las diferentes escuelas de pintura.	*He wants us to choose a topic soon, even though we may not yet distinguish well the characteristics of the various schools of painting.*

4. Some common verbs that undergo these spelling changes include the following.

gu > g	**-ger/-gir > j**
conseguir (i) *to obtain*	coger *to catch*
extinguir *to extinguish*	elegir (i) *to choose*
perseguir (i) *to persecute; to pursue*	emerger *to emerge*
seguir (i) *to continue; to follow*	exigir *to require*
	recoger *to pick up*
	surgir *to come up, to arise*

5. Verbs ending in **-uir** add **y** before all endings of the present subjunctive. Common verbs in this group include **construir, contribuir, destruir, huir,** and **influir.**

---

influir (u > uy):	influya, influyas, influya, influyamos, influyáis, influyan

---

Es posible que las experiencias de mi niñez **influyan** en los temas que escojo para mis acuarelas.	*It's possible that my childhood experiences influence the topics I choose for my watercolors.*

Comprehension questions

1. What are the infinitives of the following present subjunctive forms? **traiga, haya, quepa, conduzca**

2. In the present subjunctive of the verb **conseguir (i),** does the stem change in the verb form corresponding to **vosotros**? What changes does **conseguir** undergo in the present subjunctive?

3. In the present subjunctive of the verb **acostarse (ue),** does the stem change in the verb form corresponding to **nosotros**? And in the verb form corresponding to **tú**?

4. In the present subjunctive of the verb **sentir (ie/i),** which stem is used in the verb form corresponding to **yo**? And in the verb form corresponding to **nosotros**?

5. Does the present indicative or the present subjunctive of the verb **dialogar** undergo a spelling change in the verb form corresponding to **nosotros**? Explain.

Ejercicios

A. Imagínese que Ud. es profesor(a) de arte y explica a un grupo de estudiantes lo que espera de ellos. Expréseles los requisitos empleando la expresión **Es muy importante que Uds....**

MODELO: llegar a la hora a las clases
          Es muy importante que Uds. lleguen a la hora a las clases.

1. poder trabajar sin interrupciones
2. leer con cuidado el programa de la clase
3. establecer una rutina de trabajo eficaz
4. aprender los nombres y la obra de muchos artistas
5. hacer un informe mensual sobre un(a) artista
6. escribir los informes a máquina
7. ir a visitar los museos de arte
8. conseguir reproducciones de obras maestras

B. Ud. es guía en el Museo de Arte Contemporáneo, y hoy pasa el día pidiendo disculpas al público por distintas situaciones. Use **Siento que** o **Lamento que** para dar excusas.

MODELO: No tenemos espacio para más personas.
          Lamento que no tengamos espacio para más personas.

1. No se permite sacar fotos.
2. El salón de Velázquez está cerrado por obras.
3. No podemos entrar allí ahora.
4. El salón de Beruete sigue cerrado.
5. No sabemos la respuesta a su pregunta.
6. Su niño no puede sentarse en aquella silla.

C. Ud. piensa ir de viaje por España para ver sus museos y monumentos artísticos. En este momento comenta a un(a) amigo(a) lo que espera de su viaje.

MODELO: (nosotros) / ir al Museo Picasso en Barcelona
          Espero que vayamos al Museo Picasso en Barcelona.

1. los guías / llevarnos a Toledo para ver las pinturas de El Greco
2. el grupo / tener bastante tiempo libre en el Museo del Prado
3. el Museo del Prado / estar abierto hasta muy tarde
4. (nosotros) / ver las pinturas negras de Goya
5. (tú) / poder ver *Guernica* también un día
6. las visitas / incluir un viaje a El Escorial
7. mi prima / venir también
8. (tú) / finalmente decidir acompañarnos

II. The subjunctive versus the indicative in noun clauses

Cruz María: ¿Qué te pasa, Elena? Noto que **estás** un poco preocupada.
Elena: Sí. Es a causa del proyecto que tenemos para la clase de literatura. Lo he ido dejando y ya es urgente que lo **empiece.** ¡La profesora quiere que se lo **entregue** a fines de esta semana!
Cruz María: Pues, pídele que te **dé** una semana más si no crees que lo **puedas** terminar a tiempo. Me sorprende que te **preocupes** tanto.
Elena: Pues, dudo que la profesora me **dé** otra semana. ¡Ya me lo ha postergado una vez!

A. *Dependent clauses*

1. A dependent clause consists of a subject and a verb, but cannot stand alone as a sentence; it is linked to the main verb of a sentence by a conjunction or linking word. In Spanish, **que** is the most frequently used linking word to introduce a dependent clause. Note in the following examples that, in English, *that* may be omitted; **que** is seldom omitted in Spanish, however.

Creo **que** voy a escribir sobre Gabriel García Márquez para mi proyecto de literatura.

I think (that) I'm going to write about Gabriel García Márquez for my literature project.

Algunos críticos dicen **que** en sus obras este escritor capta la esencia de la sociedad hispanoamericana.

Some critics say (that) this writer captures the essence of Hispanic American society in his works.

2. In a sentence containing a dependent clause, the main verb is conjugated in the indicative or it is a command form; the verb in the dependent clause may be conjugated in the indicative or the subjunctive depending upon what the main verb expresses.

García Márquez piensa que **hay** muchos pueblos en Hispanoamérica como Macondo, su pueblo ficticio.

García Márquez thinks that there are many villages in Hispanic America like Macondo, his fictitious village.

Muchos lectores dudan que Macondo **sea** un pueblo imaginario. ¡Les parece tan real!

Many readers doubt Macondo is an imaginary village. It seems so real to them!

3. Dependent clauses can function as noun phrases, adjectives, or adverbs, as shown in the sentences that follow. This chapter deals with the use of the subjunctive in noun clauses; see *Capítulo 10.4* for the use of the subjunctive in adjective clauses, and *Capítulo 11.3* for the subjunctive in adverbial clauses.

Es importante **que Uds. conozcan la poesía de Pablo Neruda.** (*noun clause functioning as a subject*)

It's important that you become familiar with the poetry of Pablo Neruda.

Recomiendo **que Uds. lean *España en el corazón.*** (*noun clause functioning as a direct object*)

I recommend that you read España en el corazón.

Es un libro **que les va a conmover.** (*adjective clause*)

It's a book that will move you.

Traten de leerlo **tan pronto como puedan.** (*adverbial clause*)

Try to read it as soon as you can.

B. *Influencing in noun clauses*

1. The subjunctive is used in a dependent clause after a verb or expression that refers to an attempt to influence someone's behavior or attitude. Verbs and expressions of influencing may be as strong as commands or demands, or as mild as recommendations and suggestions. Expressions of desire or hope may also be means of influencing. In each case, the subject of the main verb expresses the desire or preference that someone do something or that something take place.

La profesora exige que **hagamos** un trabajo de veinte páginas.

The professor requires us to (that we) write a twenty-page paper.

Es esencial que **termine** de leer 300 páginas esta noche.

It's essential that I finish reading 300 pages tonight.

Mi compañero de cuarto sugiere que **cambie** mis hábitos de estudio.

My roommate suggests that I change my study habits.

Pedro quiere que **vaya** con él a una conferencia sobre la novela hispanoamericana actual.

Pedro wants me to go with him to a lecture on the current Hispanic American novel.

2. Influencing is expressed with verbs and expressions such as the following.

aconsejar *to advise*
decir *to say, to tell*
dejar *to let, to allow*
desear *to wish, to desire*
esperar *to hope*
exigir *to require*
hacer *to have (someone do something)*
insistir *to insist*

mandar *to order*
pedir *to ask, to request*
permitir *to allow*
preferir *to prefer*
prohibir *to prohibit, to forbid*
querer *to want*
recomendar *to recommend*
rogar *to beg*
sugerir *to suggest*

ser esencial *to be essential*
ser importante *to be important*
ser mejor *to be better*

ser necesario *to be necessary*
ser preciso *to be necessary*
ser urgente *to be urgent*

3. Compare the following sentences and notice that the indicative is used in the dependent clause to report a fact or to express awareness; there is no attempt to influence the behavior or attitude of another person.

Carolina dice que la conferencia **em-pieza** a las siete. (*reports a fact*)
Carolina says the conference begins at seven o'clock.

Juan dice que **vayamos** sin él porque tiene que pasar por la biblioteca primero. (*influencing*)
Juan says we should go without him because he has to go by the library first.

El profesor insiste que la librería **tiene** los libros que necesitamos. (*reports a fact*)
The professor insists the bookstore has the books we need.

El profesor insiste que **hagamos** un informe sobre algún escritor que hemos estudiado. (*influencing*)
The professor insists that we should do a report on a writer that we have studied.

C. *Emotional response and subjective viewpoint in noun clauses*

1. The subjunctive is used in a dependent clause after verbs or expressions that convey an emotional response or subjective viewpoint.

—Es una lástima que no **conozcas** ningún cuento de Cortázar.
It's a pity you don't know any short story by Cortázar.

—¿Sientes que yo no **comparta** tu interés en la literatura?
Are you sorry I don't share your interest in literature?

2. Some common verbs used to express emotional reaction include the following.

alegrar(se) *to be happy*	molestar *to bother*
deplorar *to deplore*	quejarse *to complain*
gustar *to please*	sentir *to be sorry*
lamentar *to regret*	sorprender *to surprise*

3. Impersonal expressions that may indicate emotion, subjectivity, coloring facts with one's own view, opinions, and prejudices also are followed by the subjunctive in a dependent clause. Some common impersonal expressions that require the subjunctive include the following.

ser agradable *to be nice*	ser lamentable *to be a pity*
ser bueno *to be good*	ser malo *to be bad*
ser curioso *to be odd, unusual*	ser natural *to be natural*
ser deplorable *to be deplorable*	ser normal *to be normal*
ser estupendo *to be great*	ser raro *to be strange*
ser extraño *to be strange*	ser una lástima *to be a pity*
ser increíble *to be unbelievable*	ser vergonzoso *to be shameful*

4. When a main verb or expression, such as **saber, ser obvio,** and **ver,** is used to report what a speaker perceives as factual information or when the intention of the speaker is to acknowledge or recognize a fact, the indicative is used in the dependent clause.

Sé que García Márquez **recibió** el Premio Nobel en 1982.	*I know that García Márquez received the Nobel Prize in 1982.*
Es obvio que **merecía** ese reconocimiento.	*It's obvious that he deserved that recognition.*
Veo que te **entusiasma** ese escritor.	*I see that you are enthusiastic about that writer.*

D. *Doubt, disbelief, and denial versus certainty and belief in noun clauses*

1. The subjunctive is used in a dependent clause after verbs or expressions of doubt, uncertainty, disbelief, or denial. The speaker doubts, questions, denies, or regards as untrue the existence of something, or that an event or action will occur.

Dudo que un hispano **obtenga** el Premio Nóbel el año próximo.	*I doubt a Hispanic will receive the Nobel Prize next year.*
No es seguro que Carlos Fuentes **reciba** el premio. Sin embargo, **no creo** que no lo **merezca.**	*It's not certain Carlos Fuentes will receive the prize. However, I don't think he doesn't deserve it.*
Muchos **niegan** que el Premio Nóbel **sea** un premio exclusivamente literario; dicen que la política también influye.	*Many deny the Nobel Prize is an exclusively literary prize; they say that politics also has an influence.*

2. Compare the following examples and note that the indicative is used in a dependent clause after verbs and expressions of certainty or belief.

Estoy segura de que **llegarás** a ser una escritora excelente.	*I'm sure you'll become an excellent writer.*
Creo que **vas** a soportar bien los sacrificios que eso supone.	*I believe you're going to endure well the sacrifices this entails.*
No niego que **es** difícil a veces ser una persona célebre.	*I don't deny it's hard sometimes to be a celebrity.*
Es evidente que las celebridades no **tienen** vida privada.	*It's evident that celebrities don't have privacy.*

3. The following list shows verbs and impersonal expressions of certainty and belief that are normally followed by the indicative, and verbs of doubt and disbelief that are followed by the subjunctive.

Indicative: belief/certainty	Subjunctive: disbelief/doubt
creer *to believe*	·no creer
no dudar *to not doubt*	dudar
estar seguro *to be sure*	no estar seguro
no negar *to not deny*	negar
pensar *to think*	no pensar
ser claro *to be clear*	no ser claro
ser cierto *to be certain*	no ser cierto
ser evidente *to be evident*	no ser evidente
ser indudable *to be doubtless*	no ser indudable
ser seguro *to be sure, certain*	no ser seguro
ser verdad *to be true*	no ser verdad

4. In interrogative sentences, the speaker's intent, viewpoint, or attitude determines whether the subjunctive or indicative is used in a dependent clause after expressions of certainty and belief. The subjunctive is used when the speaker wishes to convey some degree of doubt or disbelief or when he/she is asking about something unknown; otherwise, the indicative is used.

¿Estás seguro de que te **interese** leer a Borges? (*doubt*)	*Are you sure that you're interested in reading Borges?*
¿Es cierto que **vas** a leer tres novelas cortas este fin de semana? (*speaker sees no doubt*)	*Is it certain that you're going to read three short stories this weekend?*
¿Crees que estos cuentos de Borges **sean** interesantes? (*asks about unknown*)	*Do you believe these short stories by Borges are interesting?*

E. *The subjunctive in independent clauses*

1. The subjunctive is occasionally found in independent clauses, that is, clauses containing a subject and a verb and that can stand alone as a sentence. The subjunctive is also used in set exclamations such as **¡Viva(n)!** and **¡Muera(n)!** to express an emotion, or in sentences that express a desire or hope, in which a main verb such as **espero** is implied: **Que te mejores. Que te diviertas.**

2. The subjunctive is also used to express wishes after **ojalá** (*May God—Allah—grant*); in modern usage, **ojalá** is equivalent to *I hope*.

Ojalá (que) **termine** mi cuento este fin de semana.

I hope I'll finish my short story this weekend.

Ojalá (que) alguna revista **publique** mi cuento pronto.

I hope a magazine will publish my short story soon.

3. The subjunctive may be used to emphasize doubt or uncertainty in independent clauses after **probablemente** (*probably*) and **a lo mejor, acaso, quizá(s),** and **tal vez** (*maybe, perhaps*). Use of the indicative after these words and phrases implies a greater likelihood that what follows will take place.

—**Probablemente escriba** sobre Isabel Allende. **Tal vez pueda** completar el trabajo a tiempo esta semana.

I'll probably write about Isabel Allende. Maybe I'll be able to finish my work on time this week.

—**A lo mejor** no **tendrás** que pedir una postergación esta vez.

Maybe you won't have to ask for an extension this time.

4. The subjunctive is also used in independent clauses to express indirect commands intended for a third person or persons. (See *Capítulo 10.1* for indirect commands.)

—Sara quiere que le pases su trabajo a máquina.

Sara wants you to type her paper.

—Que lo **haga** ella. Yo no tengo tiempo.

Let her do it. I don't have the time.

F. *Infinitive versus conjugated verb in the subjunctive*

1. In Spanish, the subject of an impersonal expression may be either a dependent clause introduced by **que** or an infinitive or infinitive phrase. The subjunctive is used in a dependent clause to refer to a specific person or persons; an infinitive is used when the impersonal expression applies to everyone in general. (See Section III of this chapter on impersonal expressions.)

Es preciso que estudiemos la cultura y civilización de Hispanoamérica para entender mejor su literatura.

It's necessary that we study the culture and civilization of Latin America in order to better understand its literature.

Es preciso estudiar la cultura y civilización de Hispanoamérica para entender mejor su literatura.

It's necessary to study the culture and civilization of Latin America in order to better understand its literature.

266 ◆ Capítulo 9 Arte y literatura

2. With verbs that express wishes and emotions **(querer, temer, alegrarse),** the subjunctive is used in the dependent clause when the subject of the main verb and that of the dependent clause are different. When there is no change in subject, the infinitive is used.

—**Quiero que leas** este informe sobre Carlos Fuentes. Y no **temas dar**me tu sincera opinión.

—**Me alegro de que tengas** confianza en mi juicio. **Quiero tomar**me todo el fin de semana para leer tu trabajo.

I want you to read this report on Carlos Fuentes. And don't be afraid to give me your candid opinion.

I'm glad you trust my judgment. I want to take all weekend to read your work.

3. The subjunctive is also used in dependent clauses after some adverbial conjunctions, such as **antes de que, para que, sin que,** and **con tal de que,** when the subject of the main verb and that of the dependent clause are different. If there is no change in subject, the prepositional form of the conjunctions (without **que**) is used before an infinitive. (See *Capítulo 11.3* on the subjunctive in adverbial clauses.)

Quiero leer esa novela **antes de que** la **estudiemos** en clase.

Quiero comprarla **antes de ir** a clase.

I want to read that novel before we study it in class.

I want to buy it before going to class.

4. Verbs of influencing **(mandar, recomendar, aconsejar),** normally used with an indirect object, can be used either with a dependent clause containing a conjugated verb in the subjunctive or with an infinitive. The infinitive is more frequent with the verbs **mandar, hacer,** and **dejar,** whereas the subjunctive is more frequent with other verbs of influencing.

El profesor **nos hace leer** dos libros cada semana y no **nos deja consultar** traducciones.

Nos sugiere que tomemos notas a medida que leamos. Y **nos aconseja que consultemos** otros libros para obtener más información.

The professor has us read two books each week and he doesn't let us consult translations.

He suggests that we take notes as we read. And he advises us to consult other books to obtain more information.

Summary of the subjunctive in noun clauses

In dependent clauses

Attempt to influence	Te **sugiero** que **leas** las obras de Octavio Paz.
Emotional reaction to facts	**¡Qué lástima** que no **puedas** asistir a la charla sobre García Márquez!
Subjective viewpoints, opinions	**Es extraño** que todavía no **termines** de escribir tu cuento.
Doubt, disbelief, and denial	**Dudo** que **escribas** obras de teatro. **No creo** que **tengas** mucho talento.

In independent clauses

Set exclamations and expressions	**¡Viva** la literatura fantástica! **¡Que desaparezca** la literatura realista!
After **ojalá**	**Ojalá** (que) **publiquen** tu novela pronto.
After **quizá(s), tal vez, acaso, a lo mejor, probablemente**	**Quizá escriba** sobre el escritor chileno José Donoso.
In indirect commands	Yo no pienso regalarte esa novela; **que** te la **regale** tu compañero de cuarto.

Comprehension questions

1. Why is the subjunctive required in the following two sentences? **Dudo que él escriba un cuento de ciencia ficción. Es estupendo que él escriba un cuento de ciencia ficción.**

2. Should you use **leen** or **lean** in the following sentences? **Es verdad que los jóvenes _____ poco hoy en día. No es bueno que los jóvenes _____ tan poco.** Explain.

3. Which of the following two questions would you ask to imply that the selection of a poem for a prize in a literary contest is not fair? **¿Piensan Uds. que la selección de ese poema es justa? ¿Piensan Uds. que la selección de ese poema sea justa?**

4. Would the infinitive **asistir** or a clause beginning with **que asista** be used to indicate that the editor wants to go to the conference? **El editor quiere _____ al congreso.** And to indicate that the editor wants someone else to go? **El editor quiere _____ al congreso.**

5. Review the dialogue that appears at the beginning of this section. Point out examples of the use of the subjunctive after a verb expressing (1) an attempt to influence; (2) a subjective viewpoint; and (3) doubt, disbelief, or denial.

Ejercicios

A. Imagínese que Ud. es miembro del comité que organiza una feria del libro. Exprese las sugerencias, preguntas y comentarios de los miembros durante la primera reunión. Atención: a veces se usa el indicativo y no el subjuntivo.

MODELO: ¿es posible / yo encargarme de la publicidad?
¿Es posible que yo me encargue de la publicidad?

1. es probable / los participantes pedir más medidas de seguridad este año
2. es importante / la prensa tener la publicidad un mes antes
3. es obvio / hacer falta una variedad de actividades suplementarias
4. ¿creen / el público interesarse en una rifa (*raffle*)?
5. dudo / exhibir muchos autores nuevos
6. recomiendo / (nosotros) buscar un lugar más espacioso este año

B. Se ha encontrado, bajo circunstancias algo misteriosas, un manuscrito original en la biblioteca de su universidad. Según los primeros estudios, parece tener un gran valor literario. Exprese los comentarios de diferentes personas sobre esta novedad, usando el indicativo o el subjuntivo, según el contexto.

MODELO: Es extraño que _____ tal cosa en esta ciudad, ¿verdad? (ocurrir)
Es extraño que ocurra tal cosa en esta ciudad, ¿verdad?

1. Estoy seguro(a) de que alguien _____ hacer una broma. (querer)
2. El presidente se alegra de la publicidad que esto le _____ a la universidad. (traer)
3. ¿Crees que _____ haber otros manuscritos valiosos en la biblioteca? (poder)
4. Es evidente que lo _____ que estudiar cuidadosamente otros expertos más. (tener)
5. Es de esperar que _____ ser un extraordinario descubrimiento literario. (resultar)
6. No hay duda de que esto _____ el acontecimiento literario más significativo en la historia de nuestra biblioteca. (representar)

C. Conteste las siguientes preguntas sobre la literatura para niños y para adolescentes, dando su opinión o reacción. Use verbos y expresiones como **es bueno, es malo, es curioso, es estupendo, es horrible, me sorprende, me alegro, creo, es cierto, es verdad,** etc.

MODELO: *E1:*   Hay mucha variedad en los libros para jóvenes, ¿verdad?
            E2:   *Sí, es maravilloso que haya una selección tan buena.*

1. Aparece mucha violencia en los libros para niños, ¿no crees?
2. Los cuentos de hadas son muy populares todavía, ¿no?
3. ¿Verdad que los libros enseñan muy poco sobre las costumbres de otras culturas?
4. Los padres examinan cuidadosamente la lectura de sus hijos hoy en día, ¿verdad?
5. Los argumentos de muchos libros para jóvenes son poco reales, ¿no?
6. Casi todos los nuevos libros para niños tratan un aspecto de la nueva tecnología, ¿no es verdad?

D. Carmelo Mendoza Zurinaga es un escritor muy exigente (*demanding*) cuando se trata de la publicación de un libro suyo. Vuelve loca a la gente de la editorial con sus exigencias y quejas. Haga el papel de Carmelo y exprese sus deseos para su última novela.

MODELO: Insisto en que mi foto _____ cada anuncio. (acompañar)
            Insisto en que mi foto acompañe cada anuncio.

1. Es esencial que yo _____ el diseño para la cubierta. (aprobar)
2. Me parece ridículo que Uds. _____ comentarios sobre mi estilo. (hacer)
3. Me molesta muchísimo que los editores _____ a cambiar lo que escribo. (atreverse)
4. Señores, el gran público quiere que mis obras _____ de mi pluma, no de la suya. (salir)
5. Si estos problemas vuelven a ocurrir, tal vez yo _____ mis obras a otra editorial en el futuro. (enviar)

E. Reaccione de una manera personal a los comentarios de un(a) amigo(a), mostrando su acuerdo o desacuerdo con lo que dice. Use un infinitivo en su respuesta.

MODELO: Amigo(a):   ¡No quiero que vayas un año entero a España para estudiar literatura!
           Usted: *Pues, yo tampoco quiero ir un año entero... un semestre quizá.*

1. Me molesta que pases tanto tiempo leyendo para tu clase sobre Galdós.
2. Me parece innecesario que escribas un informe de veinte páginas para esta clase.

3. No es buena idea que dediques todo tu tiempo a la clase de arte; tienes otras clases.
4. Temo que pierdas la película sobre José Donoso si no te apuras.
5. Siento que no puedas acompañarnos al Museo de Arte Contemporáneo.
6. Es una lástima que tengas que trabajar esta tarde.

III. Impersonal expressions

Felicia:	En mi opinión, **es preciso participar** en el concurso de arte. Y tú, Jorge, ¿vas a participar?
Jorge:	Supongo que sí. **Es mejor exhibir** algo, por si acaso, ¿no? Siempre **es posible que yo gane** algo.
Felicia:	(*Con ironía*) ¡Qué optimista! **Es evidente que no tienes** muchas ganas de participar. A ti **te es difícil aceptar** las críticas de los jueces, ¿verdad?
Jorge:	Me conoces demasiado bien; pero también **es verdad que hay** que seguir un sinnúmero de instrucciones para esos concursos y para eso, ¡no tengo paciencia!

A. *Constructions with impersonal expressions*

1. Impersonal expressions such as **es bueno, es cierto, es una lástima,** etc. are followed by an infinitive or infinitive phrase or by a dependent clause introduced by the conjunction **que.** The infinitive or dependent clause functions as the subject of the impersonal expression. Observe in the following examples that *it* functions as the subject of the impersonal expression in English.

Es esencial participar en concursos de arte.	*It's essential to participate in art contests.*
Me es imposible presentar algo para el concurso de arte.	*It's impossible for me to present something for the art contest.*
¿Es cierto que has recibido un premio de $2.500?	*Is it true that you've received a prize of $2,500?*
Es una lástima que no puedas presentar una obra esta vez.	*It's a pity that you're unable to present a work this time.*

2. The third person singular of **ser** in an impersonal expression can be conjugated in any tense. (See *Capítulo 12.3* for sequence of tenses.)

¿Te **fue** difícil preparar una selección representativa de tus cuadros?	*Was it hard for you to prepare a representative selection of your paintings?*
Era evidente que les sorprendió la selección del jurado.	*It was evident that the jury's decision surprised you.*
¡**Sería** estupendo obtener el primer premio en el concurso de arte!	*It would be great to get first prize in the art contest!*

B. *Impersonal expression* + *infinitive*

1. An infinitive or infinitive phrase is used as the subject of an impersonal expression to make generalizations that apply to *everyone.*

—**Es posible apreciar** la pintura sin tener conocimientos técnicos profundos, ¿verdad?	*It's possible to appreciate painting without having a thorough technical knowledge, isn't it?*
—Sí, pero en mi opinión, **es mejor tener** alguna formación teórica.	*Yes, but in my opinion, it's better to have some theoretical training.*

2. Some impersonal expressions followed by an infinitive can be used to apply to a specific person or persons. In such cases, an indirect object pronoun representing the specific person to whom the impersonal expression applies precedes the verb.

Me es difícil decidir qué pintar para el concurso.	*It's hard for me to decide what to paint for the contest.*
Nos es urgente escoger un tema pronto.	*It's urgent for us to choose a topic soon.*

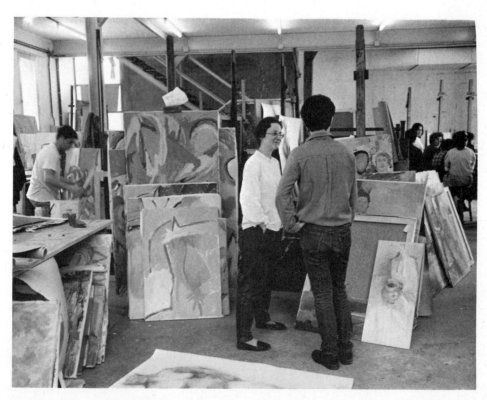

Estos jóvenes de un taller de arte en Barcelona, España, se preparan para una carrera artística.

3. An indirect object phrase, such as **a él, al artista,** may be used for emphasis or clarification. (See *Capítulo 3.5* for the use of indirect object phrases.)

Al artista le es imposible aguantar una vida muy regimentada.	*It's impossible for an artist to stand a very regimented life.*
Y por eso **a ti te** es preciso tener un horario flexible, ¿verdad?	*And that's why it's necessary for you to have a flexible schedule, right?*

4. Impersonal expressions that may take an indirect object include the following.

ser difícil *to be difficult*	ser necesario *to be necessary*
ser esencial *to be essential*	ser posible *to be possible*
ser fácil *to be easy; to be likely*	ser preciso *to be necessary*
ser importante *to be important*	ser urgente *to be urgent*

C. *Impersonal expression + dependent clause*

1. An impersonal expression followed by a dependent clause is used to make a statement concerning a specific person or persons. When the impersonal expression reports facts or makes a statement about something that is considered certain, the verb in the dependent clause is conjugated in the indicative.

Es verdad que algunos artistas **son** felices llevando una vida bohemia.	*It's true that some artists are happy leading a bohemian life.*
Es obvio que te atrae la idea de una vida bohemia.	*It's obvious that the idea of a bohemian life attracts you.*

2. Impersonal expressions that are followed by the indicative in the dependent clause include the following.

ser cierto *to be certain*	ser obvio *to be obvious*
ser claro *to be clear*	ser seguro *to be sure*
ser evidente *to be evident*	ser verdad *to be true*

3. When the impersonal expression introduces an emotional response, an opinion, or a statement of doubt, disbelief, or possibility, the verb in the dependent clause is in the subjunctive.

Es curioso que nunca **pintes** rostros humanos en tus cuadros.	*It's curious that you never paint human faces in your paintings.*
Es estupendo que el departamento de arte **exhiba** las obras de los estudiantes.	*It's great that the art department exhibits works by the students.*
Es natural que te **pongas** nerviosa con el concurso.	*It's natural that you get nervous because of the contest.*

Comprehension questions

1. Which of the following two sentences would you use to inform someone that you won't be able to arrive on time? **Me es imposible llegar a la hora. Es imposible llegar a la hora.** What is the meaning of the other sentence?

2. Restate the sentence **Te es difícil aceptar críticas** so that it applies to everyone.

3. Would you use **recibe el premio** or **reciba el premio** in the following sentences? **Es seguro que Manolo _____. No es seguro que Manolo_____.**

4. Would you use **tienes ganas** or **tengas ganas** in the following sentences? **Es evidente que no _____ de participar en el concurso de arte. Es una lástima que no _____ de participar en el concurso de arte.**

Ejercicios

A. Ud. le pide su opinión a un(a) compañero(a) que es artista sobre las cualidades, aptitudes y aprendizaje que exije la carrera de artista. Use expresiones como **es esencial, es importante, es bueno/malo** y los temas sugeridos.

MODELO:　tener buen ojo para el color
　　　　　E1:　*¿Es importante tener buen ojo para el color?*
　　　　　E2:　*En mi opinión, sí, es importante.*

1. entender las varias escuelas de arte
2. tener ideas creativas y originales
3. crear esbozos de lo que uno va a pintar
4. haber vivido profundas experiencias emocionales
5. dominar la técnica artística

B. Resuma algunas de las reglas y requisitos que hay que seguir para el concurso de arte y que tanto le molestan a Jorge en el diálogo al comienzo de esta sección. Use expresiones como **es necesario, es esencial, es importante** y las siguientes indicaciones.

MODELO:　(Ud.) / acompañar el cuadro con varios documentos
　　　　　Es preciso que acompañe el cuadro con varios documentos.

1. (Ud.) / limitarse a las categorías establecidas
2. las dimensiones de los cuadros / no pasar ciertas medidas
3. (Ud.) / escribir un informe sobre su obra
4. el cuadro / llegar por correo certificado antes del día 30
5. (Ud.) / dejar su obra en manos de los jueces por un mes

C. Ud. toma una clase de pintura impresionista y posimpresionista. Hable de sí mismo(a) y de sus compañeros de clase, explicando qué cosas son fáciles, difíciles, necesarias, importantes, etc. para distintas personas.

MODELO: distinguir entre las obras de Manet y Monet (yo)
         A mí me es difícil distinguir entre las obras de Manet y Monet.

1. reconocer las obras de Renoir (Julio)
2. pasar horas viendo diapositivas (nosotros)
3. aprender de memoria los títulos de las obras de van Gogh (tú)
4. pronunciar las palabras francesas (yo)
5. decidir qué obras tienen más valor artístico (Ud.)

D. Ud. tiene un(a) amigo(a) que es autor(a) de libros de ciencia ficción. En estos momentos se siente un poco deprimido(a) y tiene una opinión pesimista de su futuro. Reaccione a sus comentarios, tratando de animarlo(la) y de ofrecerle sugerencias prácticas, usando expresiones como **es preciso, es mejor, es posible, es urgente, es obvio, es importante, es necesario** y **es claro.**

MODELO: *Amigo(a):*   Las dos casas editoras que tenían mi último libro me lo han rechazado.
         Usted: *Pues, es preciso que lo envíes a varias casas más.*

1. Tengo un agente literario con poca imaginación.
2. El público no compra mis libros.
3. Creo que la gente está cansada de la ciencia ficción.
4. Las librerías no exhiben bien mis novelas.
5. Los vendedores ponen precios exorbitantes a todos los libros hoy en día.
6. Últimamente, no puedo concentrarme en mi trabajo.

IV. **Hacer** in time expressions

Carlos: Me dicen que **has estado escribiendo** una novela.
Marcos: Es más bien una colección de cuentos. ¿Cómo te enteraste?
Carlos: Me lo dijo Susana **hace unos días.** ¿Y cómo va esa colección?
Marcos: Pues, en pocas palabras: ¡sudor, frustración, nada! Trabajaba productivamente **desde hacía un mes,** pero de momento se me ha quedado la mente en blanco.
Carlos: No te desanimes, hombre. Ven a casa a cenar. **Hace tiempo que** no vienes. ¡A ver si te inspira una comida sabrosa!

A. *Past event ongoing in the present or past*

1. The simple present tense is used in two synonymous constructions with **hace** + a time expression to refer to events, actions, or states that began in the past but continue at the moment of speaking. Note that the present perfect progressive is used in English.

Present + **desde hace** + duration

Miro ese cuadro **desde hace media hora.**

Hace + duration + **que** + present

Hace media hora que miro ese cuadro.

—¿Desde cuándo escribes una novela?

—Bueno, **escribo desde hace** dos meses.

—¿Y cuánto tiempo hace que trabajas en este capítulo?

—Ya **hace** una semana **que trabajo** en éste y ¡sólo es el tercero!

For how long have you been writing a novel?

Well, I've been writing for two months.

And for how long have you been working on this chapter?

I've been working on this one for a week now and it's only the third one!

2. To talk about events, actions, or states that began in the past and continued to a later point in the past, the imperfect is used with **hacía** + a time expression. The past perfect progressive is used in the English equivalent.

Imperfect + **desde hacía** + duration

Miraba ese cuadro **desde hacía media hora.**

Hacía + duration + **que** + imperfect

Hacía media hora que miraba ese cuadro.

Le informé a la editora que **trabajaba desde hacía** dos semanas en el capítulo. Y fíjate, ella me dijo que **hacía** una semana **que lo esperaba.**

I informed the publisher that I had been working on the chapter for two weeks. And just imagine, she told me that she'd been waiting for it for a week.

3. The present perfect progressive can also be used to express past actions ongoing in the present, and the past perfect progressive can be used to refer to actions that began in the past and continued to a later point in the past. These constructions more closely parallel the English equivalents; however, a construction with **hace** or **hacía** is preferred.

He estado trabajando (por) unas cuatro horas diarias en mi novela.	*I've been working on my novel for about four hours a day.*
Había estado pensando en el argumento por dos semanas cuando hice un cambio fundamental.	*I had been thinking about the plot for two weeks when I made a fundamental change.*

B. *Hace to express* ago

The patterns **hace** + duration and **hace** + duration + **que** are used with the preterit to express *ago.*

Mandé uno de mis cuentos a tres revistas literarias **hace un mes.**	*I sent one of my short stories to three literary magazines a month ago.*
Hace una semana que una me **contestó,** diciéndome que desgraciadamente no podían publicarlo.	*A week ago one of them answered me, telling me that unfortunately they were not able to publish it.*

Comprehension questions

1. Identify which two of the following sentences indicate that the speaker has been looking at a painting for twenty minutes. **He mirado este cuadro por veinte minutos. He estado mirando este cuadro por veinte minutos. Miro este cuadro desde hace veinte minutos.**

2. Which of the following sentences indicates that the speaker is no longer working on an anthology? **Hace un año que trabajo en esta antología. Hace un año que trabajé en esta antología.**

3. Would you use **hace** or **desde hace** in the following sentences? **Mi esposo escucha una ópera _____ dos horas. Mi esposo escuchó una ópera _____ dos horas.**

4. Would you use **hace** or **hacía** in the following sentences? **_____ dos semanas que por fin escribió su trabajo sobre El Greco. _____ dos semanas que escribía su trabajo sobre El Greco.**

Ejercicios

A. Cuéntele a un(a) compañero(a) algunos sucesos del mundo artístico y literario, indicando cuándo tuvieron lugar.

MODELO: haber una subasta (*auction*) de obras impresionistas
Hubo una subasta de obras impresionistas hace unos días.

1. inaugurarse una exhibición de Renoir
2. haber un robo de artefactos precolombinos en el Museo de Antropología
3. ganar el Premio Nóbel un escritor hispano
4. anunciarse la construcción de una segunda biblioteca nacional en la capital
5. iniciarse una serie de conferencias por distinguidos novelistas extranjeros

B. Pregúntele a un(a) compañero(a) de clase cuánto tiempo hace que participa o no participa en las siguientes actividades.

MODELO: no leer una novela buena
E1: *¿Cuánto tiempo hace que no lees una novela buena?*
E2: *Pues, creo que hace dos meses.*

1. no aprender de memoria un poema
2. dibujar o pintar un cuadro
3. ir a un museo
4. asistir a un ballet clásico
5. ver una representación teatral
6. tomar una clase de música

C. Hubo un robo en el museo de su ciudad, y ahora la policía interroga al director del museo acerca del personal del museo, las medidas de seguridad y otras cosas relacionadas. Haga el papel del director y conteste las preguntas mencionando un período de tiempo lógico.

MODELO: E1: ¿Cuánto tiempo hacía que trabajaba en el museo el guardia que se marchó la semana pasada?
E2: *Hacía seis meses que trabajaba aquí.*

1. ¿Y cuánto tiempo hacía que preguntaba ese guardia sobre las medidas de seguridad?
2. ¿Hace cuánto tiempo que tienen Uds. este mismo personal de seguridad?
3. ¿Cuánto tiempo hace que tienen Uds. este sistema de alarmas?
4. ¿Cuánto tiempo hacía que intentaba Ud. obtener otra póliza de seguros para las obras?
5. Dígame, ¿desde cuándo tienen aquí esta valiosa colección de pinturas españolas?

V. Ahorrar(se), guardar, and salvar

1. **Ahorrar** refers to *saving money or time*, and often conveys the idea of storing up something or preventing waste. In a reflexive construction, it is used in the sense of sparing oneself something or saving time or work.

Queremos **ahorrar** dinero ·para un viaje a Europa.	*We want to save money for a trip to Europe.*
(Me) ahorro un montón de tiempo ¡y papel! con un procesador de textos.	*I save (myself) a great deal of time— and paper—with a word processor.*
Uno se ahorra mucho esfuerzo cuando discute sus ideas con otra persona antes de escribir.	*A person saves himself a lot of effort when he discusses his ideas with another person before writing.*

2. **Guardar** expresses *to save* in the sense of putting aside or keeping something for someone.

Guardé el programa de la exposición de arte.	*I saved the program from the art exhibition.*
Vuelvo pronto; ¿me **guardas** un asiento?	*I'll be right back; will you save me a seat?*

3. **Salvar** means *to save* in the sense of rescuing someone or something from danger, harm, or destruction.

—¿Te enteraste de que hubo un incendio en el museo?	*Did you know that there was a fire in the museum?*
—Sí, pero afortunadamente **salvaron** todas las obras de arte.	*Yes, but fortunately they saved all the works of art.*
No quería ir a la conferencia; ¡me **salvaste** con tu llamada!	*I didn't want to go to the lecture; you saved me with your call!*

Ejercicios

A. Diga qué verbo se usa en español para expresar la palabra o expresión indicada.

1. *Save yourself* problems; apply early for the European art tour.
2. Why do you *save* all your rough drafts and sketches?
3. Thank you for *saving* me from that horrible art critic.

4. *Save* me a place in line while I find out what time the gallery opens.
5. To *save* time, we request that you ask your questions at the end of the session.
6. Thanks for the warning; you *saved* me from bumping into that statue.

B. Complete los siguientes diálogos con la forma correcta de uno de los verbos estudiados en esta sección.

1. —¿Pudieron _____ las pinturas del incendio?
   —Casi todas. Si quieres, te _____ el periódico para que puedas leer todos los detalles.
2. —¿Cómo logras _____ dinero con tantos gastos en pinturas, lienzos, pinceles y demás?
   —Pero, chica, no _____ nada. ¡Mi presupuesto está hecho un desastre!
3. —Escucha, Juanito, no aguanto una palabra más de este conferenciante. Salgo por un momento, pero regreso. ¿Me _____ el asiento?
   —Claro, como siempre; tú te _____ un mal rato y yo me quedo aquí como un bobo.

Actividades para la comunicación

A. Cadena. En cadena, dé su opinión sobre las características personales y hábitos de trabajo que necesita desarrollar un(a) escritor(a). También comente las cosas que son importantes, interesantes, buenas o malas, etc. Use algunas de las ideas de la lista u otras que se le ocurran.

buen sentido del humor   mucha experiencia   ser individualista
buen(a) observador(a)   mucha disciplina   estilo expresivo

MODELO: E1: *Le es esencial al escritor tener un buen sentido del humor.*
          E2: *Es importante que un escritor se conozca muy bien.*

B. Una entrevista. En grupo, entreviste a un(a) compañero(a) que hará el papel de un(a) escritor(a) conocido(a). Averigüe información tal como cuánto tiempo hace que se dedica a escribir, qué opina de su profesión y qué recomendaciones tiene para futuros escritores.

MODELO: E1: *¿Cree que es fundamental saber mucha gramática para escribir bien?*
          E2: *No, no es absolutamente necesario.*
          E3: *Pues, ¿es importante que un(a) escritor(a)...*

C. **La cultura hispana en EE.UU.** Para satisfacer la demanda de la comunidad hispana de su ciudad, la biblioteca pública quiere dedicar un salón a libros en español, pero también quiere ofrecer charlas, películas, exhibiciones, etc., para que todos puedan conocer mejor la cultura hispánica. Con toda la clase, haga sugerencias, dé opiniones y exprese sus esperanzas sobre lo que debe o puede hacer la biblioteca. Use algunas de las siguientes ideas y piense en otras también.

mapas y fotografías	exhibiciones de esculturas
un mural representativo de la	biografías de artistas importantes
cultura hispana en EE.UU.	programas de música hispánica
charlas por escritores hispanos	

MODELO: E1: *Espero que ofrezcan charlas sobre la literatura hispánica.*
E2: *Es preciso pedir la colaboración de los hispanos de la ciudad.*
E3: *Es posible que se pueda hacer un mural...*

D. **Mesa redonda.** En grupo de cinco o seis personas, dé sus opiniones y recomendaciones sobre los hábitos de lectura de la juventud. Hable de lo poco que lee la gente y por qué y lo que se puede hacer para estimular mejores hábitos de lectura. Escoja un(a) moderador(a) para dirigir la discusión y hacer preguntas para animarla.

MODELO: E1: *¿Es verdad que leen poco los jóvenes hoy en día?*
E2: *Sí, no hay duda que leen poco. Pero, en realidad, no creo que la televisión influya mucho...*

E. **Narración.** Prepare una breve descripción de una actividad literaria o artística en que está Ud. participando. Puede ser real o imaginaria, un éxito o un fracaso, seria o cómica. Luego, cuéntela a la clase.

MODELO: *Hace tres semanas que estoy inscrito(a) en una clase de cerámica. Como no sé nada de eso, he empezado con objetos sencillos: platos, floreros, ceniceros. Más que nada, me importa aprender lo suficiente para hacer algunos regalos para mi familia. Ojalá que termine este proyecto con éxito porque siempre me ha sido muy difícil crear obras de artesanía.*

CAPÍTULO 10

♦

De compras

Mucha gente aprecia la conveniencia de los grandes centros comerciales para hacer sus compras. Aquí se ve una vista parcial de la Casa de Hierro en la Ciudad de México.

Conversación

1. ¿Le gustan las compras? ¿Qué cosas le gusta comprar? ¿Por qué?
2. ¿Qué opina de los centros comerciales como lugares de reunión y diversión para ir a cines, restaurantes o sencillamente para ir de tienda a tienda? ¿Va Ud. a estos sitios solo(a) o con amigos?
3. ¿Cuáles son las características de un buen dependiente? ¿Qué cosas le molestan más de los dependientes?
4. Cuando Ud. va de compras, ¿en qué se fija más: en los precios, la calidad, la marca, la apariencia, etc.? Explique.
5. ¿Tiene Ud. una tarjeta de crédito? Si tiene una o varias, ¿la(s) usa con frecuencia? ¿Por qué sí o por qué no? Si no tiene ninguna, explique por qué no.
6. ¿Prefiere hacer compras en los centros comerciales, como el de la fotografía de la página anterior, o en las pequeñas tiendas locales? ¿Cuáles son las ventajas y las desventajas de cada uno?

Vocabulario temático

almacén, el   department store; warehouse
caja, la   cash register; box
cajero(a), el(la)   cashier
calidad, la   quality
cartel, el   sign, poster
dependiente(a), el(la)   store clerk
descuento, el   discount
diseño, el   design
equipo, el   equipment
escaparate, el   store window
etiqueta, la   tag; label; slip of paper
factura, la   invoice, bill
ganga, la   bargain
garantía, la   guarantee, warranty
joya, la   jewel
liquidación, la   close-out sale
marca, la   brand
pendiente, el   earring
propietario(a), el(la)   owner
rebaja, la   discount, mark-down, sale
recibo, el   receipt
regalo, el   gift
saco, el   coat
sortija, la   ring

surtido, el   stock; selection, assortment
talla, la   size
venta, la   sale

atender (ie)   to wait on, to help
cobrar   to charge; to cash
probarse (ue)   to try on

barato(a)   inexpensive
caro(a)   expensive

de moda   in fashion, in style
en oferta   on sale
hacer cola   to stand in line
hacer un pedido   to order
hacer juego   to match, to go well
juego de platos, el   set of dishes
lucir bien   to look nice
oso de peluche, el   teddy bear
por consignación   on consignment
ropa para damas, la   women's clothing
sección de caballeros, la   men's department
tarjeta de crédito, la   credit card

I. Commands with **usted** and **ustedes, nosotros,** and indirect commands

Max: Oye, Laura, no **sigamos.** ¡Estoy muerto! **Busquemos** el regalo para tus padres otro día.

Laura: Una tienda más. **Entremos** aquí al Salón Mar del Plata. ¿Ves el cartel del escaparate? Tienen rebajas.

¡GRANDES REBAJAS!

Vea nuestra fabulosa colección de ropa de invierno.
Aproveche descuentos de hasta el 50% en artículos de regalo.
Todo lo que necesita para el hogar. Selección estupenda.
Compare nuestros precios y **recuerde...**
¡GRAN CALIDAD A PRECIOS INCOMPARABLES!

Max: Bueno, bueno, **vamos.** Pero **sentémonos** a tomar algo primero. No tengo tanta energía como tú para las compras.

A. *Commands with* usted *and* ustedes

Ud. and Uds. command forms		
comprar	**vender**	**subir**
compre (Ud.)	venda (Ud.)	suba (Ud.)
compren (Uds.)	vendan (Uds.)	suban (Uds.)

1. **Usted** and **ustedes** affirmative and negative command forms are exactly the same as the corresponding present subjunctive forms of the verb.

Es necesario que usted **venda** su moto pronto. Es urgente que no **espere** demasiado. (*present subjunctive*)

It's necessary that you sell your motorcycle soon. It's urgent that you not wait too long.

Venda su moto. No **espere** demasiado. (**usted** command)

Sell your motorcycle. Don't wait too long.

2. Irregular verbs and verbs with stem and spelling changes in the present subjunctive show the same changes in **usted** and **ustedes** command forms.

Infinitive	Present sub- junctive (Ud.)	Ud. command
alcanzar	alcance	**alcance**
buscar	busque	**busque**
dar	dé	**dé**
distinguir	distinga	**distinga**
estar	esté	**esté**
hacer	haga	**haga**
ir	vaya	**vaya**
pagar	pague	**pague**
pedir (i)	pida	**pida**
pensar (ie)	piense	**piense**
salir	salga	**salga**
sugerir (ie)	sugiera	**sugiera**
volver (ue)	vuelva	**vuelva**

3. Use of the subject pronoun is optional with all Spanish commands. When used, the subject pronoun follows the verb. The subject pronoun is used for emphasis, for contrast, or as a matter of courtesy.

Espere (usted) por favor; lo atiendo de inmediato.

Please wait; I'll help you right away.

Vayan ustedes a la sección de sombreros; nosotros iremos a mirar los zapatos.

Go to the hat department; we'll go look at the shoes.

—¿Dónde debo firmar esta solicitud de crédito?

Where should I sign the credit application?

—**Firme usted** aquí, por favor.

Sign here, please.

4. When enumerating a series of commands, the subject pronoun may be used with the first command, but is omitted thereafter.

Vaya (usted) al tercer piso, **busque** la sección de caballeros y **hable** con el señor Gómez.

Go to the third floor, find the men's department, and speak to Mr. Gómez.

5. In affirmative commands, reflexive and object pronouns are attached to the verb, forming a single word. When pronouns are attached to a command form, a written accent is required when the stressed syllable is the third or fourth from the end. Note that a command form such as **dé** retains the written accent whether or not pronouns are attached.

Pruébese ese saco, por favor.
Pruébeselo. Déme su saco; yo se lo guardo.
No nos gusta este modelo; **búsquennos** otro, por favor.

Try on that coat, please. Try it on.
Give me your coat; I'll keep it for you.
We don't like this model; look for another one for us, please.

6. In negative commands, reflexive and object pronouns precede the verb.

Si quiere comprar un televisor, **no lo compre** en esta tienda; no tienen buenos precios.
Si no le gusta ese saco, **no se lo pruebe.**

If you want to buy a TV set, don't buy it in this store; they don't have good prices.
If you don't like that coat, don't try it on.

B. *Nosotros commands*

1. In a command with **nosotros,** the speaker invites another person or a group to participate in an activity or type of behavior. A **nosotros** command corresponds to English *let's* + a verb. An affirmative **nosotros** command can be expressed with **vamos a** + an infinitive or by using the **nosotros** form of the present subjunctive.

Vamos a comprar pan francés.
(**Compremos** pan francés.)
Caminemos hasta la panadería.

Let's buy French bread.

Let's walk to the bakery.

2. Reflexive and object pronouns follow and are attached to the end of the present subjunctive **nosotros** form in affirmative commands. As with **Ud.** and **Uds.** commands, a written accent is required when the stressed syllable is the third or fourth from the end. Note in the following examples that when the pronoun **se** or the reflexive pronoun **nos** is attached to a **nosotros** command, the final **s** of the verb is dropped.

Miguel no ha visto este anuncio sobre cámaras fotográficas; **mostrémoselo.**
Hay una liquidación en La Primavera. **Apurémonos.**

Miguel hasn't seen this ad about cameras; let's show it to him.

There's a sale at La Primavera. Let's hurry.

3. The present indicative, not the present subjunctive, is used to express an affirmative **nosotros** command with **ir** (*to go*) and **irse** (*to leave*).

—**Vamos** de compras al centro.
—Sí, **vámonos** ya.

Let's go shopping downtown.
Yes, let's leave now.

4. A negative **nosotros** command is formed only with **no** + a present subjunctive verb form. Object pronouns precede the verb in negative **nosotros** commands.

No salgamos de compras todavía.   *Let's not go out shopping yet.*
No regresemos muy tarde.   *Let's not return too late.*
No nos apresuremos mucho.   *Let's not hurry too much.*
No vayamos a una tienda de zapatos.   *Let's not go to a shoe store.*

C. *Indirect commands*

1. Direct commands are addressed directly to a particular person or persons. Indirect commands are intended to be conveyed to a third person or persons and are formed by **que** + a third person singular or plural verb form in the present subjunctive. (See *Capítulo 9.2* on use of the subjunctive in independent clauses.)

—Atienda a ese cliente.   *Help that customer.*
—Ahora no puedo; estoy atendiendo   *I can't now; I'm helping that lady. Let*
a esa señora. **Que lo atienda**   *Paco help him; he's not busy.*
Paco, que no está ocupado.

2. Object pronouns precede the verb in indirect commands. The subject (that is, the person or persons supposed to carry out the indirect command) follows the verb or verb phrase.

—¿Quién puede preparar estas   *Who can prepare these invoices?*
facturas?
—**Que las escriba Inés;** ella tiene   *Let Inés write them; she has a lot of*
mucha experiencia. Por favor,   *experience. Please don't let Benito*
que no se ocupe Benito de ellas; la   *take care of them; last time he made*
última vez hizo muchos errores.   *many mistakes.*

Comprehension questions

1. How could you express the following command in another way? **¡Compremos el regalo para tus padres en el Salón Mar del Plata!**

2. Would you use **Vayan ustedes** or **Vayan** to stress contrast in the following sentence? _____ **de compras ahora; nosotros descansaremos.**

3. What are the affirmative commands that correspond to the following negative commands? **¡No nos sentemos a tomar algo! ¡No lo compre!** What change does the verb form undergo?

4. Identify which two of the following three sentences are **nosotros** commands. **Compramos un estéreo. Vamos a comprar un estéreo. Compremos un estéreo.**

5. Would you use **él nos atienda** or **nos atienda él** in the following indirect command? **Que _____ la próxima vez.**

Ejercicios

A. Es su primer día de trabajo como dependiente(a) en el Salón Mar del Plata y hace muchas preguntas a su supervisor(a). Con un(a) compañero(a), represente la situación, contestando las preguntas con mandatos afirmativos o negativos.

MODELO: *E1:*   ¿Quiere Ud. que abra estas cajas ahora?
          E2:   *Sí, ábralas ahora, por favor. (No, no las abra hasta la tarde.)*

1. ¿Puedo tomar un descanso ahora?
2. ¿Quiere que haga el pedido esta mañana?
3. ¿Guardo estas cajas vacías o las pongo en la basura?
4. ¿Cambio todos los precios o solamente los de esta sección?
5. ¿Quiere que yo lea algún manual de reglas de trabajo?
6. ¿Es posible que yo salga un poco temprano hoy?

B. Ud. y unos amigos venden muebles, ropa y libros de segunda mano por consignación para los estudiantes de su universidad y luego se quedan con un porcentaje de lo que ganan. Conteste las preguntas de los socios (*partners*) que le ayudan a organizar el negocio. Use mandatos afirmativos o negativos.

MODELO: *E1:*   ¿Ponemos los radios y los estéreos juntos?
          E2:   *Sí, pónganlos juntos. (No, no los pongan juntos.)*

1. ¿Organizamos los libros por asignatura?
2. ¿Colgamos toda esta ropa ahora o más tarde?
3. ¿Movemos ese sofá al otro extremo del cuarto?
4. ¿Colocamos los libros en los estantes o los dejamos sobre la mesa?
5. ¿Traemos más etiquetas para poner precios?
6. ¿Ponemos una etiqueta especial en los objetos ya vendidos?

C. Ud. ha decidido descansar este sábado: no quiere hacer nada. Por desgracia los diferentes miembros de su familia quieren que haga varias cosas. Conteste sus preguntas, empleando un mandato indirecto.

MODELO: ¿Me ayudas a hacer las compras?
          Yo no, que te ayude (Gustavo).

1. ¿Me acompañas al almacén esta tarde?
2. ¿Quieres recoger el televisor? Ya está reparado.

3. ¿Quieres ir al centro con nosotros?
4. ¿Nos llevas en tu coche a la droguería?
5. ¿Quieres buscar un regalo de cumpleaños para papá?

D. Ud. está de compras en el centro con un(a) amigo(a). Ud. sugiere que los dos hagan varias cosas y su amigo(a) acepta o rechaza las ideas. Si la rechaza, debe proponer otra actividad.

MODELO: ver unas máquinas fotográficas
           E1: *Veamos unas máquinas fotográficas.*
           E2: *De acuerdo. Veamos algunas. (No, no veamos esas cosas hoy.*
                Vamos al cine.)

1. entrar en este almacén
2. escuchar algunos discos nuevos
3. buscar ropa en oferta
4. tomar un café
5. probarnos unos zapatos
6. ir a la joyería
7. gastar el aumento de sueldo
8. quedarnos en el centro para cenar

E. ¿Qué consejo les daría Ud. a los consumidores que tienen las siguientes quejas? Proponga soluciones, usando mandatos afirmativos y negativos.

MODELO: Siempre gasto demasiado dinero.
         Pues, no salga de compras con tanta frecuencia. (Lleve poco dinero y deje en casa sus tarjetas de crédito.)

1. No me gustan las tiendas cerca de donde vivo.
2. Compro muchas cosas inútiles.
3. No hay donde aparcar en el centro.
4. Los precios son demasiado caros; todo cuesta una barbaridad.
5. Las colas para pagar son interminables.
6. Los cajeros del supermercado son lentísimos.

II. Relative pronouns

Beatriz: Bueno, mujer, gracias por traerme a la tienda... (*En voz baja*) Oye, ¿ves a aquel chico **que** ahora se acerca a la señora de la chaqueta verde?
Mónica: ¿**El que** tiene el saco azul?
Beatriz: Exacto. Bueno, ese chico es **el que** trabaja para la hermana de mi vecino, **la cual** es dueña de una cadena de joyerías. El vecino dice que él tiene un gran porvenir.
Mónica: ¡Ah, sí, el joven **de quien** me hablaste ayer y **que** te vuelve loca! Pero no me parece tan atractivo como me lo pintaste. No sé **lo que** ves en él.
Beatriz: ¡Estás ciega! ¡No digo más!

A. *Relative pronouns and restrictive and nonrestrictive relative clauses*

1. A relative pronoun, such as **que, quien, el cual,** introduces a dependent clause that refers to a person, thing, or idea, which is the antecedent. The relative pronoun follows the antecedent and, in contrast to English, cannot be omitted in Spanish.

Entre los regalos **que** traigo, hay uno para ti. Ah, este chico, **quien** me ha ayudado con los paquetes, es hermano de Benito.	*Among the presents (that) I'm bringing, there's one for you. Ah, this boy, who has helped me with the packages, is Benito's brother.*

2. As in English, a dependent clause introduced by a relative pronoun can be either nonrestrictive or restrictive. A nonrestrictive clause gives parenthetical, nonessential information about a specific antecedent and is set off by commas.

Los cajeros, **que no tienen experiencia,** tienen un cursillo esta tarde.	*The cashiers, who don't have experience, have a short course this afternoon.* (All cashiers will take the course.)

3. A restrictive clause gives information necessary to identify an antecedent and is essential to the meaning of the sentence.

Los cajeros **que no tienen experiencia** tienen un cursillo esta tarde.	*The cashiers who don't have experience have a short course this afternoon.* (Only those cashiers without experience take the course.)

B. *The relative pronoun* ***que***

1. The relative pronoun **que** (*that, which, who, whom*) refers to people and things, and is the most frequently used relative pronoun.

La dependienta **que** me atendió era poco simpática.	*The saleswoman who helped me was not very nice.*
Los vestidos **que** compré el año pasado ya no están de moda.	*The dresses I bought last year aren't in style anymore.*

2. **Que** is used in nonrestrictive and restrictive relative clauses. In restrictive clauses, it can function as the subject or direct object of the clause.

El dueño de la tienda, **que** me pareció muy dinámico, me dio su tarjeta. (*subject*)	*The store owner, who seemed to me to be very dynamic, gave me his card.*

El almacén **que** está cerca de mi casa vende aparatos electrodomésticos. (*subject*)	*The store that is near my house sells electric appliances for the home.*
El chico **que** me presentaste ayer trabaja en la heladería. ¡Qué guapo es! (*object*)	*The boy you introduced me to yesterday works in the ice-cream parlor. He's so handsome!*

3. **Que** is the most frequently used relative pronoun after the prepositions **a, de, con,** and **en.** In contrast to English, the preposition always precedes the relative pronoun in Spanish.

—¿Te gustó la joyería **en que** entramos ayer?	*Did you like the jewelry store that we went into yesterday?*
—Sí, me encantó el diseño **con que** adornaron los escaparates.	*Yes, I loved the design that they trimmed the store windows with.*

C. *The relative pronoun* **quien(es)**

1. The relative pronoun **quien(es)** (*who, whom*) refers only to people and agrees in number with its antecedent. **Quien(es)** is used interchangeably with **que** in nonrestrictive clauses.

El señor Barrios, **quien (que)** lleva tres años en la tienda, piensa marcharse.	*Mr. Barrios, who's been with our store three years, intends to leave.*
Las dos dependientas, **quienes (que)** son muy amigas, entraron en la tienda el mismo año.	*The two saleswomen, who are very close friends, started working in the store the same year.*

2. **Quien(es)** cannot be used in restrictive clauses as the equivalent of *who;* **que** is used instead.

—Ese es el cajero **que** me cobró demasiado dinero.	*That's the cashier who charged me too much money.*
—¡Qué extraño! Es el empleado **que** tiene más experiencia en esta tienda.	*How strange! He's the employee who has the most experience in this store.*

3. In restrictive clauses, **a quien** or **a quienes** functions as the direct object of the dependent clause when the relative pronoun refers to people. Note that **que** may also be used.

No vi bien al señor **a quien (que)** saludaste. ¿Era tu jefe?	*I didn't see well the gentleman you greeted. Was he your boss?*
Acaban de entrar los dos clientes **a quienes (que)** atendiste ayer.	*The two customers you waited on yesterday just came in.*

4. **Quien(es)** is also used after simple prepositions in restrictive clauses when referring to a person or persons.

Vi a la farmacéutica **a quien (con quien, de quien)** hablaste ayer.

I saw the pharmacist to whom (with whom, about whom) you spoke yesterday.

Es la señora **para quien** trabajé el año pasado.

It's the woman for whom I worked last year.

D. *The relative pronouns el cual and el que*

1. **El cual** (*which, who, whom*) and **el que** (*which, who, whom*) may be used to refer to persons or things and agree in gender and number with the antecedent.

Robaron el carro de la señora Herrera, **la cual** no tiene dinero para comprarse otro.

They stole the car of Mrs. Herrera, who doesn't have money to buy herself another.

Vamos a ver los escaparates en **los cuales (los que)** hay muchas joyas de diseño oriental.

Let's go see the store windows in which there's a lot of oriental design jewelry.

2. Both **el cual** and **el que** are used after simple and compound prepositions when referring to people or things. A form of **el cual** is more common, especially after compound prepositions. **Que** and **quien(es)** are not used after compound prepositions.

Conozco desde hace muchos meses a las dependientas **con las cuales (las que)** conversaba.

I've known for many months the saleswomen I was talking with.

¿Puedes leer la etiqueta **al lado de la cual (la que)** están las sortijas de oro?

Can you read the tag next to which the gold rings are?

3. A form of **el cual** can be used instead of **que** or **quien** in nonrestrictive relative clauses, although it is less common. However, when more than one noun, each with a different gender or number, precedes the relative pronoun, a form of **el cual** is preferred to **que** or **quien** in order to avoid ambiguity.

Voy a comprar unos pendientes para mi hermana, **la cual** se entusiasma por esas cosas.

I'm going to buy some earrings for my sister, who loves those things.

Mi cuñado, **el cual** se encuentra en Europa, dice que nos ha comprado muchos regalos.

My brother-in-law, who is in Europe, says that he has bought many presents for us.

La novia de mi hermano, **la cual** se encuentra en Europa, dice que ha comprado muchos regalos.

My brother's fiancee, who (referring to the fiancee) is in Europe, says that she has bought many presents.

4. A form of **el que** may also be used in nonrestrictive clauses, usually with the meaning of *the one(s) who* or *that*. It is not generally interchangeable with **el cual.** Notice the difference in emphasis in the following examples.

Mi hermana, **la que** se interesa en los negocios, es ahora la propietaria de la mueblería La Mundial. (There may be more than one sister.)	*My sister, the one that's interested in business, is now owner of the La Mundial furniture store.*
Mi hermana, **la cual** se interesa en los negocios, es ahora la propietaria de la mueblería La Mundial. (There is only one sister.)	*My sister, who is interested in business, is now owner of the La Mundial furniture store.*

5. A form of **el que** is often used to refer to an implied or understood noun when the noun has been previously mentioned or when context is clear.

Me encanta tu vestido. ¿Es **el que** te compraste en el almacén La Campana?	*I love your dress. Is it the one you bought at La Campana (store)?*
—¿Conoces a esa chica?	*Do you know that girl?*
—¿**La que** me vendió los discos?	*The one who sold me the records?*

6. **Quien** or **quienes** may replace a form of **el que** when the understood noun is a person or persons.

El que (Quien) compra siempre lo más barato no siempre ahorra dinero.	*He who always buys the cheapest things doesn't always save money.*
Los que (Quienes) sólo compran en las rebajas necesitan mucha paciencia, ¿no crees?	*Those who buy only during sales need lots of patience, don't you think?*

See Section III of this chapter for use of **lo cual** and **lo que.**

E. *The relative pronoun cuyo*

1. The relative pronoun **cuyo** means *whose, of which*. **Cuyo** precedes the noun that is possessed and agrees in gender and number with that noun.

La librería de la calle Quinta, **cuyo propietario** es el Sr. Méndez, es la mejor de la ciudad.	*The bookstore on Fifth Street, whose owner is Mr. Méndez, is the best in town.*
Allí compré unos libros **cuyas fotografías** eran excelentes.	*I bought some books there whose photographs were excellent.*

2. Note that in Spanish **de quién** corresponds to English *whose* in a question.

—¿**De quién** son todos estos   *Whose are all these packages?*
paquetes?
—Son de tu tía Amparo; anduvo de   *They're your aunt Amparo's; she*
compras.   *went shopping.*

F. *The relative pronoun cuanto*

1. The relative pronoun **cuanto** (*everything, all that*) is used to express quantity.

¡No necesitas comprar **cuanto** ves en   *You don't need to buy all that you see*
la tienda!   *in the store!*

2. The phrase **todo lo que** (*all that*) is a synonym of **cuanto,** and is more frequently used in spoken Spanish.

¡Siempre quieres comprar **todo lo que**   *You always want to buy all that you*
ves!   *see!*
Mi amigo compra **todo lo que** ve en   *My friend buys all he sees on sale.*
liquidación.

Summary of the uses of the relative pronouns

In nonrestrictive relative clause

que   el cual   Diego, **que (quien, el cual)** me regaló
quien   el que   este libro, vende artículos deportivos.
                               Este vestido, **que (el cual, el que)** com-
                               pré hace dos años, siempre luce bien.

In restrictive relative clause

As subject: que   La dependienta **que** trabaja en nuestra
                               tienda es muy eficaz.
                               El supermercado **que** está en la esquina
                               vende más barato.

As direct object: que, a quien   La chica **a quien (que)** conocí ayer
                                    trabaja en una farmacia.
                                    El traje **que** me probé ayer me quedó
                                    muy bien.

In restrictive relative clause

After a, de, con, en: que, quien, el cual, el que	Regálale unos pendientes a la muchacha **con quien (con la cual, con la que)** sales.
	Debes comprarte la cámara **de que (de la cual, de la que)** te hablé.
After other simple prepositions: el cual, el que, quien	Ese es el jefe **para el cual (para el que, para quien)** trabajo.
After compound prepositions: el cual, el que	Vamos a la tienda **frente a la cual (frente a la que)** dejamos el auto.
Possessive relative pronoun: cuyo	Esa relojería, **cuyo dueño** es el señor Méndez, cierra a las seis.
Relative pronoun to express quantity: cuanto	No necesitas comprar **cuanto** ves en una tienda.

Comprehension questions

1. In one of the following sentences, the relative clause **que me vendió el televisor** is a nonrestrictive relative clause. Identify this sentence. **Tú conoces al empleado que me vendió el televisor. Aquel empleado, que me vendió el televisor, fue amonestado por su jefe. El empleado que me vendió el televisor recibió un aumento de sueldo.**

2. Would you use **el cual, la cual,** or **quien** to indicate that the neighbor's son, and not the neighbor, works at a bakery? **Hablé con el hijo de la vecina, _____ trabaja en una panadería.**

3. In the dialogue at the beginning of this section Beatriz asks: ¿**«Ves a aquel chico que ahora se acerca a la señora de la chaqueta verde**»? Can **quien** be used instead of **que** in this sentence? Explain why or why not.

4. Which relative pronouns can be used in the following sentence? **Ayer compré el automóvil de _____ te había hablado la semana pasada.**

5. Would you use **cuyo** or **cuya** in the following sentence? **Ahí va la señora _____ hijo trabaja en la carnicería.** Explain why.

Ejercicios

A. Complete las siguientes oraciones con **que** o **quien(es)** de acuerdo con el contexto. En algunos casos ambas formas pueden usarse.

1. ¿Por qué no te pones el suéter _____ te compré?
2. La factura de los muebles, _____ llegó hace tres semanas, todavía está sin pagar.
3. ¿Qué te parece el cuadro _____ pienso darles a mis padres?
4. Mi hermana, _____ fue a la tienda conmigo, lo escogió.
5. Mi novio es la persona _____ mejores regalos me hace.
6. Compré aperitivos para _____ quieran comer algo más tarde.

B. Describa brevemente a un(a) amigo(a) algunas cosas y personas que Ud. vio durante una visita a una tienda de música. Use un pronombre relativo apropiado en su descripción.

MODELO: En la tienda de música compré una revista...
En la tienda de música compré una revista que incluye una lista de los discos más populares.

1. En esa tienda vi una flauta...
2. También encontré unos discos...
3. La dependienta,...
4. Había una chica allí...
5. La selección de instrumentos,...
6. Me fijé mucho en una guitarra...

C. Dos amigos que están de compras conversan mientras caminan por el centro hacia una tienda donde les espera una amiga. Complete sus oraciones con el pronombre relativo más apropiado.

1. —Hay una buena librería cerca de aquí, _____ nombre no recuerdo.
   —Ah, sí; tú quieres decir la librería _____ se especializa en libros de ciencia ficción. Allí está...
2. —Oye, ¿te fijaste en el nombre de la mueblería delante de _____ dejé el coche?
   —¿No fue la misma mueblería contra _____ tu papá puso un pleito?
3. —Dicen que la policía llegó muy pronto a esa zapatería allí dentro de _____ se cometió un robo ayer.
   —Sí, pero ¡qué terrible fue ese robo! El propietario, _____ tiene un hijo en nuestra universidad, también fue asaltado hace seis meses.
4. —No sé nada más del robo; te he dicho absolutamente _____ averigüé.
   —Está bien. Voy a hablar con Jaime, _____ madre estaba cerca de aquí cuando sucedió.
5. —Ricardo compró un pasaje en esa agencia de viajes; va a visitar a sus hermanos, _____ viven en Los Ángeles.
   —Pues, yo conozco muy bien a una de las agentes _____ trabaja allí. Es vecina mía.
6. —Vámonos; aquélla es la tienda enfrente de _____ María nos va a esperar.
   —De acuerdo. Y luego vamos a los almacenes La Estrella, _____ quedan muy cerca de aquí.

D. Ud. y un(a) amigo(a) visitan una mueblería porque él(ella) necesita algunas cosas para amueblar su apartamento. Su amigo(a) le hace una serie de preguntas basándose en los dos dibujos y Ud. le contesta, expresando otra preferencia. Use expresiones como **¿Qué te parece(n)...?, ¿Qué opinas de...?, ¿Te gusta(n)...?** en las preguntas y utilice pronombres relativos en las respuestas.

MODELO: E1: *¿Te gusta el cuadro que tiene un barco?*
E2: *Francamente, prefiero el que parece ser obra de un bohemio.*

III. Nominalization of adjectives and neuter lo

Ricardo: ¡Héctor, hombre! ¿De dónde salió ese coche deportivo tan fabuloso?
Héctor: (*Entusiasmado*) Es una joya, ¿verdad? Ya sabes **lo que** sufrí con el viejo y **lo molesto** que era.
Ricardo: Claro... pero **lo único** que no entiendo es cómo has podido comprarlo. ¡Con **lo caros** que son esos coches! Parece que has optado por la vida del «jet set».
Héctor: Bueno, deja **lo del «jet set»** y súbete. Demos una vuelta y te lo cuento todo.

A. *Nominalization of adjectives*

1. When context is clear, a noun that is modified by an adjective or adjective phrase may be eliminated to avoid repetitiveness. When this happens, the adjective is said to be nominalized, that is, it functions as a noun. Observe in the following

examples that the nominalized adjective, as well as the accompanying article, demonstrative adjective, or possessive adjective, agree in gender and number with the understood noun.

—¿Prefieres los pantalones grises o **los azules?**

Do you prefer the gray pants or the blue ones?

—Me gustan **los azules,** pero **estos grises** me quedan mejor.

I like the blue ones, but these gray ones fit me better.

—Srta., ¿está en liquidación este sofá blanco?

Miss, is this white sofa on sale?

—No, **el blanco** está a precio regular. Pero **este azul** tiene un precio muy ventajoso.

No, the white one is our usual price. But this blue one has a very attractive price.

2. The indefinite article **un** becomes **uno** before a nominalized adjective.

—¿Tienen Uds. un sillón verde en este estilo colonial?

Do you have a green armchair in this colonial style?

—No, sólo queda **uno** blanco.

No, there's only a white one left.

3. A **de** phrase or **que** clause that functions as an adjective may also be nominalized.

Encontré la sección de los relojes, pero no encuentro **la de las carteras.**

I found the watch department, but I can't find the one for purses.

—¿Es ésta la lámpara que compraste la semana pasada?

Is this the lamp you bought last week?

—No, **la que compré** es ésa otra.

No, the one I bought is that other one.

B. *Lo before masculine singular adjectives*

Lo is the neuter form of the definite article. It is invariable and is used with a masculine singular adjective to refer to an abstract idea or quality. Observe in the following examples the various English equivalents of **lo** + an adjective.

Lo importante es llegar temprano a los almacenes.

What is important is to get to the shops early.

Lo difícil será encontrar vestidos a buen precio.

The difficult thing will be to find dresses at a good price.

Todos los vendedores piensan solamente en **lo suyo.**

All the salespeople think only about their own interests.

Una vez que decidamos comprar algo, debemos seguir **lo acordado** en cuanto a dividir los gastos.

Once we decide to buy something, we should stick to what we agreed upon as far as sharing expenses.

C. **Lo** + **de** + *phrase*

1. **Lo** + **de** is used to nominalize an adjective phrase that refers to a situation or fact in a general way; that is, there is no specific noun modified.

¿Cómo va **lo de** la venta de tu casa?	*How's (the matter about) the sale of your house going?*
Lo del incendio en los almacenes García fue muy sospechoso, ¿verdad?	*The (thing about the) fire in the García store was very suspicious, wasn't it?*

2. **Lo** + **de** may correspond to phrases such as the following.

el asunto de *the matter of*	el problema de *the problem of*
la parte de *the part of*	la cuestión de *the issue of*

—¿Y en qué quedó el asunto de la venta del coche?	*And how was the matter of the car sale resolved?*
—**Lo del coche** quedó bien. Ya se vendió.	*The car-sale thing went well. We already sold it.*
—¿Te afecta el problema de la inflación?	*Does the inflation problem upset you?*
—No, **lo de la inflación** me tiene sin cuidado.	*No, I'm not worried about inflation matters in the least.*

D. *Lo* + *variable adjective or lo* + *adverb*

Lo followed by a variable adjective or an adverb expresses the degree or extent of a quality. A variable adjective agrees in gender and number with the noun to which it refers. In this usage **lo** corresponds to English *how*.

Siempre me ha sorprendido **lo caros** que son esos productos.	*I've always been surprised at how expensive those products are.*
Todos se quejan de **lo mal** que se venden.	*Everyone complains about how badly they sell.*

E. *Lo que* and *lo cual*

1. The neuter relative pronoun **lo que** is used in restrictive relative clauses to refer to an indefinite antecedent. This usage of **lo que** corresponds to English *what,* in the sense of *that which.*

—No me has dicho **lo que** quieres que te regale para tu cumpleaños.	*You haven't told me what you want me to give you as a birthday present.*
—**Lo que** quiero es que me des una sorpresa.	*What I want is for you to surprise me.*

2. The neuter relative pronouns **lo cual** and **lo que** may be used in nonrestrictive relative clauses to refer to an antecedent that is an entire clause. In this usage they correspond to the English pronoun *which*.

—No me has pedido mi opinión acerca de esa venta, **lo cual (lo que)** me ha molestado mucho.

You haven't asked for my opinion concerning that sale, which has bothered me a lot.

—He estado fuera de la ciudad, **lo que (lo cual)** me ha impedido hablar contigo.

I've been out of town, which has prevented me from talking to you.

F. *The neuter pronoun lo*

1. The neuter pronoun **lo** is used to replace a previously expressed situation or occurrence in its entirety.

—Los padres de Ricardo le han dado dinero para comprar un coche. ¿**Lo** sabías?

Ricardo's parents have given him money to buy a car. Did you know it?

—No, pero **lo** esperaba. Ricardo me **lo** había mencionado.

No, but I was expecting it. Ricardo had mentioned it to me.

2. **Lo** is also used to replace a predicate noun or adjective after linking verbs such as **estar, parecer,** and **ser.**

—¿Están contentos tus padres con su nueva casa?

Are your parents happy with their new home?

—Sí, **lo** están. En realidad, todos **lo** estamos. Ha sido una excelente compra.

Yes, they are. In fact, we all are. It's been an excellent purchase.

Comprehension questions

1. Explain why **los** and not **lo** is used before the adjective **domésticos** in the following sentence. **Entre los productos electrónicos japoneses y los domésticos, ¿cuáles prefieres?**

2. Would you use **económico** or **económicos** in the following sentence? **Nadie se imagina lo _____ que son esos automóviles.** Explain why.

3. Are the following two uses of **lo** + adjective that appear in the dialogue at the beginning of this section the same or different? **Ya sabes lo molesto que era (el coche viejo). Lo único que no entiendo es cómo has podido comprarlo.** Explain.

4. In which of the following sentences can **lo que** be replaced by **lo cual**? **Compro lo que me agrada. Voy de compras los sábados, lo que me agrada mucho. Lo que me agrada a mí no le agrada a todo el mundo.**

5. To inquire about matters pertaining to bargains at a department store, would you use **lo que** or **lo de**? **¿Supiste ＿＿＿ las gangas del almacén El Gallo?**

Ejercicios

A. Ud. y un(a) amigo(a) están en una tienda de ropa y hablan de sus preferencias, según el modelo.

MODELO: los calcetines de algodón / los calcetines de lana
　　　　E1:   *¿Prefieres comprar los calcetines de algodón o los de lana?*
　　　　E2:   *Prefiero los de algodón porque se lavan mejor.*

1. las sandalias de cuero / las sandalias de corcho (*cork*)
2. la corbata ancha / la corbata delgada
3. las camisas a cuadros / las camisas a rayas
4. los zapatos negros / los zapatos grises
5. el cinturón de cuero / el cinturón elástico

B. Conteste las siguientes preguntas, dando una opinión personal sobre las compras. Use **lo** + un adjetivo apropiado en su respuesta.

MODELO: ¿Qué es lo peor de hacer compras?
　　　　Para mí, lo peor es no encontrar lo que quiero.

1. ¿Crees que lo barato es siempre lo mejor?
2. ¿Qué es lo más importante para ti al escoger un regalo para alguien?
3. ¿Qué es lo peligroso de las tarjetas de crédito?
4. ¿Te enoja lo indiferentes que son algunos dependientes en las tiendas? ¿Y lo insistentes que son otros? ¿Por qué?
5. ¿Qué es lo más molesto de tener que devolver algo a una tienda?
6. ¿Qué es lo mejor de los grandes centros comerciales modernos? ¿Y lo peor?

C. Ud. participa en una encuesta sobre varios asuntos que afectan a muchos consumidores. Conteste las siguientes preguntas empleando siempre la estructura **lo de,** según el modelo.

MODELO: ¿Qué opina Ud. de las continuas subidas de los precios?
　　　　Lo de los precios es un desastre. (Como no compro mucho, lo de los precios no me afecta.)

1. ¿Qué opina Ud. de las modas contemporáneas?
2. ¿Qué le parece la calidad de la ropa hoy día?
3. ¿Qué opina Ud. de las leyes para la protección del consumidor?

4. ¿Cuál es su reacción con respecto al problema de la seguridad de los productos farmacéuticos?
5. ¿Qué le parecen los anuncios de los carros en la televisión?
6. ¿Cuál es su opinión sobre las garantías para los carros nuevos? ¿Y los de segunda mano?

D. En grupos de tres o cuatro personas, dé su opinión sobre las siguientes cuestiones u otras similares relacionadas con la moda. Use algunas de las frases sugeridas u otras de su invención para expresar sus opiniones.

lo que me encanta...	lo bueno...	lo que me molesta...
lo que me enoja...	lo malo...	lo sorprendente...
lo que me agrada...	lo curioso...	lo maravilloso...

MODELO: los cambios frecuentes
    E1: *Me gusta vestirme a la moda, pero lo que me molesta son los cambios frecuentes.*
    E2: *Para mí, lo bueno de los cambios es que no me aburro. Siempre hay cosas nuevas.*

1. los colores   3. los diseños   5. las marcas
2. el surtido   4. los precios   6. las telas

IV. Use of the indicative versus the subjunctive in adjective clauses

Felipe: ¿Te ayudo a buscar un regalo para tu novia?
Paco: Bueno, pero no tengo una idea clara de qué comprar. Busco algo **que sea diferente, que sea único, que le haga saber lo mucho que la quiero.**
Felipe: ¡Pues, me alegro de que no pidas mucho! ¿Qué tal un sombrero **que haga juego con su abrigo nuevo?**
Paco: Ya tiene uno **que lo acompaña perfectamente.**
Felipe: ¡Ay, los enamorados! Mira, Paco, te sugiero un collar de perlas—claro, escoje perlas **que no sean muy caras.** Y así le puedes decir que representan las lágrimas **que derramas cuando no estás con ella.**

A. *The indicative in adjective clauses*

The indicative is used in a dependent adjective clause when the noun or pronoun modified refers to a specific person or thing that is known to exist. (See *Capítulo 9.2* for an explanation of dependent clauses.)

Hay buenas rebajas en algunos aparatos electrodomésticos que **vi** anunciados en el periódico.

There are good bargains on some electric home appliances that I saw advertised in the newspaper.

Busco la lavadora Lux que **se anuncia** en la televisión.

I'm looking for the Lux washing machine that is advertised on TV.

Conozco varias tiendas que **tienen** el modelo que buscas.

I know several stores that have the model you're looking for.

Tengo un hermano que **gasta** todo su dinero en equipo de esquí.

I have a brother who spends all his money on ski equipment.

B. *The subjunctive in adjective clauses*

1. The subjunctive is used in a dependent adjective clause when the person or thing modified is unknown to the speaker and may or may not exist. Observe in the following examples that the person or thing modified is indefinite.

—¿Hay alguna tienda cerca que **venda** lámparas?

Is there a store nearby that sells lamps?

—No, no conozco ninguna tienda cerca que las **venda.**

No, I don't know any store nearby that sells them.

—¿Conoces a alguien con experiencia que también **sepa** hablar español?

Do you know anybody with experience who also knows how to speak Spanish?

—Es imposible encontrar a alguien que **tenga** esa preparación.

It's impossible to find someone who has that background.

2. The personal **a** is often not used before a direct object that is an indefinite person or whose existence is unknown. The personal **a** is used however before indefinite expressions such as **alguien, alguno, nadie,** and **ninguno.**

Busco dependientes que tengan experiencia.

I'm looking for salespersons who have experience.

Busco **a** alguien que me reemplace durante mis vacaciones.

I'm looking for someone who can replace me during my vacation.

3. The subjunctive is always used in dependent adjective clauses after negative expressions such as **nadie, nada,** and **ningún.** The person or thing modified is nonexistent or at least unknown within the speaker's realm of experience.

No conocemos a nadie que **quiera** trabajar en esta joyería.

We don't know anyone who wants to work at this jewelry store.

No encuentro ninguna sortija que me **guste.**

I don't find any ring that I like.

No hay nada que me **interese** comprar en esta tienda.

There's nothing that I'm interested in buying in this store.

4. Use of the subjunctive or the indicative in a dependent clause may depend upon context.

El vendedor pide un aumento del 10%. No me importa lo que **tengo** que pagarle.	*The salesman is asking for a 10% raise. It doesn't matter what I (do) have to pay him.* (**Lo** refers to a known amount; use of the indicative implies that the speaker is willing to pay the amount.)
Necesitamos otro vendedor urgentemente. No me importa lo que **tenga** que pagarle.	*We need another salesperson urgently. It doesn't matter what I (may) have to pay him.* (**Lo** refers to an unknown amount.)
Compra lo que **necesitas**.	*Buy what you need.* (I do know what you need to buy.)
Compra lo que **necesites**.	*Buy what(ever) you (may) need.* (I don't know what you may need to buy.)

Comprehension questions

1. Would you use the indicative **vende** or the subjunctive **venda** to talk about a store that is well known for its bargains? **La ropa que se _____ en esa tienda es buena y barata.**

2. In the dialogue at the beginning of this section, Felipe advises Paco to choose pearls that are not very expensive: **Escoje perlas que no *sean* muy caras.** Explain why **son** cannot be used in this sentence.

3. Would you use the indicative **quieres** or the subjunctive **quieras** to tell a friend that he or she can buy anything whatever? **Compra lo que _____.**

4. Would you use the indicative **regala** or the subjunctive **regale** in the following sentence? **No hay nadie que _____ tantos discos a sus amigos como mi hermano.**

5. Would you use the indicative **produce** or the subjunctive **produzca** to indicate that there is no country that produces more cars than Japan? **No hay país que _____ más coches que Japón.** And to indicate that Japan is the country that produces the most cars? **Japón es el país que _____ más coches.**

Ejercicios

A. Ud. trabaja en un supermercado y se encuentra bastante molesto(a) porque le parece que falta gente para distintos trabajos. Exprese su frustración contradiciendo a un(a) compañero(a) que no ve la situación de la misma manera.

MODELO: *E1:*   Creo que hay una persona que puede sustituirte el sábado.
  E2:   ¡Qué va! No habrá nadie que pueda sustituirme.

1. Creo que hay un cajero que te dará cambio.
2. Estoy seguro(a) de que hay alguien desocupado que te ayudará a abrir las cajas de frutas.
3. Yo sé de un empleado que tomará tu turno en la caja esta tarde.
4. Me parece que uno de los jóvenes te podrá ayudar a poner los precios en las latas.
5. No cabe duda que alguien te ayudará a desempacar el camión que viene pronto.

B. Haga el papel de Paco, quien todavía medita sobre lo que va a regalar a su novia, y exprese sus pensamientos. Use el presente del subjuntivo o del indicativo, según el contexto.

MODELO: Quiero algo que (ser) _____ único y que le (hacer) _____ saber lo mucho que la quiero.
  Quiero algo que sea único y que le haga saber lo mucho que la quiero.

1. Ya tiene un sombrero que (hacer) _____ juego con su abrigo nuevo.
2. Quizá pueda encontrar unas perlas que no (costar) _____ demasiado.
3. Se me olvidó que ya tiene unos pendientes de plata que (llevar) _____ a menudo.
4. Sé que quiere una blusa de seda que (ir) _____ con su traje azul, pero las blusas son muy caras y no encuentro una que me (gustar) _____.
5. Menciona con frecuencia que quiere unas figuras de cristal que (ser) _____ muy delicadas y que (tener) _____ aspecto oriental.
6. Creo que voy a comprarle este oso de peluche que (parecerse) _____ al otro que ya tiene.

C. Imagínese que Ud. está de compras en un gran almacén. Una dependienta lo(la) acaba de atender. Descríbale los objetos siguientes que Ud. busca.

MODELO: una chaqueta
  Busco una chaqueta que sea de lana pero que no cueste más de cincuenta dólares.

1. una camisa	3. un reloj digital	5. un abrigo
2. un traje	4. una cartera	6. un frasco de perfume

D. Describa su fantasía con respecto a los siguientes temas. Sea imaginativo(a) y trate de incluir tres frases descriptivas con tres verbos distintos.

MODELO: encontrar una tienda de ropa
Yo quiero encontrar una tienda de ropa que tenga un surtido excelente, que no cobre mucho y que ofrezca crédito sin interés.

1. conocer un(a) vendedor(a)
2. comprar un automóvil
3. trabajar en una tienda

4. descubrir una computadora
5. tener un jefe
6. regalarles a mis padres algo

V. Some Spanish equivalents of *to move*

1. **Mover (ue)** is the most common verb used in Spanish to express *to move*. The reflexive form **moverse** refers to bodily movement or the physical motion of something such as a vehicle.

   ¿Quieres **mover** la mesa un poco?
   Si la **movemos** hasta aquí, parece abrir un poco la sala.

   Will you move the table a bit?
   If we move it over to here, it seems to open up the room a bit.

   Si Ud. **se mueve,** no lo puedo medir.
   Las hojas **se movían** con el viento.
   El camión **se movió** lentamente.

   If you move, I can't measure you.
   The leaves moved in the wind.
   The truck moved slowly.

2. The verb **trasladar(se)** may be used as a synonym of **mover(se),** but it most commonly refers to *moving, transferring,* or *being transferred* from one place to another, as for business reasons.

   Y ahora, ¿cómo vamos a **trasladar** todos estos muebles a casa?
   Me trasladaron a Filadelfia.

   And now, how are we going to move all these pieces of furniture home?
   They moved (transferred) me to Philadelphia.

   Me traslado a otra universidad el semestre que viene.

   I'm going to move (transfer) to another university next semester.

3. **Transportar** refers to *moving things from one place to another,* usually for a fee.

   ¿Qué compañía **transportará** tus efectos personales?

   Which company will move (transport) your belongings?

4. A simple change of residence is most often expressed by **mudarse.**

   ¿Cuántas veces **te has mudado** este año?

   How many times have you moved this year?

5. *To move,* in the sense of taking a turn in a game such as chess or cards, is expressed by **jugar** or **hacer una jugada.**

Te toca **jugar (hacer una jugada).**   *It's your turn to move.*

6. *To move someone emotionally* is expressed with **impresionar** or **conmover (ue).**

La ceremonia me **impresionó** mucho.   *The ceremony moved me a great deal.*

Parece que a él no le **conmueve** nada.   *It seems as though nothing moves him.*

Ejercicios

A. Indique qué verbo o expresión verbal se usa en español en lugar de la palabra o expresión indicada.

1. I've had *to move* to three different dorms since I've been here.
2. Her interpretation of that piano concerto always *moves* me very much.
3. Don't *move* until I finish pinning this hem.
4. I'm being *moved* to the head office; I hope the company will arrange *to move* my belongings.
5. I want to see if Cristóbal *moves* his car.
6. Help me *move* this bed.
7. It *moved* them deeply to see so many volunteers give blood for their daughter.
8. Are you going *to move* or look at the chessboard all night?

B. Reaccione a las siguientes situaciones con una pregunta o un comentario. Use **mover(se), trasladar(se), transportar, mudarse, jugar, hacer una jugada, impresionar** o **conmover,** según el caso.

MODELO: Sus padres están hablando de vivir en otra ciudad.
   No tengo ganas de mudarme de aquí.

1. Ud. juega al «Scrabble» y hace diez minutos que su oponente mira sus letras.
2. Su mejor amigo le dice que se va a otra universidad.
3. Ud. acaba de comprar un piano, pero vive en el tercer piso de un edificio que no tiene ascensor.
4. Su compañero(a) de cuarto acaba de decirle que no le gusta cómo están dispuestos los muebles de la sala.
5. Su modista se queja de su abundante energía mientras trata de ajustar su nuevo traje.
6. Ud. acaba de asistir con un(a) amigo(a) a uno de los mejores conciertos que jamás ha escuchado.

Actividades para la comunicación

A. ¡Qué trabajo más difícil! Ud. trabaja en un gran almacén y atiende las quejas de los clientes. Dé instrucciones, consejos o sugerencias, según el caso, a las personas con los siguientes problemas.

MODELO: un hombre se queja de un juguete eléctrico defectuoso
E1: *Este juguete eléctrico que compré ayer salió defectuoso.*
E2: *Lleve su recibo de compra al jefe de reparaciones y haga los arreglos necesarios con él.*

1. dos jóvenes no encuentran la sección de deportes
2. una persona se queja de lo cara que es la ropa
3. un hombre no sabe qué regalar a su esposa
4. dos muchachos están perdidos y buscan la salida de la tienda
5. un niño llora porque no encuentra a su mamá
6. un cliente quiere cambiar unos pantalones porque necesita una talla más grande

B. De compras. Ud. está de compras en la sección de deportes de un gran almacén. Busca algunos regalos y también unas cosas para hacer camping. Describa al (a la) dependiente(a) lo que necesita.

MODELO: Quiero un saco de dormir que...
E1: *Quiero un saco de dormir que sirva en un clima muy frío.*
E2: *Muy bien. Éste es un modelo que es muy liviano pero que abriga muchísimo.*

1. Necesito una raqueta que...
2. Esta raqueta tiene un precio que...
3. Quiero ver unas pelotas de tenis que...
4. Yo he visto antes una mochila que...
5. ¿Sabe Ud. de otra marca de compás que...?
6. Tráigame el modelo de cantimplora que...

C. ¿Qué le regalo? Ud. busca un regalo importante. Entra en una joyería y le explica a un(a) dependiente(a) que Ud. no tiene mucho dinero, pero que quiere el mejor regalo posible. Descríbale también algo sobre lo que había pensado regalar. Represente la situación con un(a) compañero(a).

MODELO: E1: *¿En qué puedo servirle?*
E2: *Busco un regalo bonito. Quiero algo de oro, pero que no sea muy caro.*
E1: *Dígame, ¿cuánto piensa gastar?*
E2: *Lo malo es...*

D. Una compra desastrosa. Cuéntele a un(a) compañero(a) de clase una compra equivocada, real o imaginaria, que Ud. ha hecho en el pasado. Diga lo que compró y por qué fue una selección mala, y dé detalles tales como qué hizo con el artículo, qué dijo la persona a la cual se lo regaló, etc. ¿Intentó devolverlo? ¿No lo usó nadie? ¿Lo tiró a la basura o se lo dio a alguien?

MODELO: *Una vez le compré un oso de peluche a mi novia, pero ¡qué desastre lo del oso! Cuando lo vio, ella se quedó callada y yo creí que iba a llorar. Luego me explicó que su novio anterior, quien siempre le mentía, le había regalado otro oso igual y que sencillamente no podía aceptar éste. Cuando traté de devolverlo a la tienda, me dijeron que no lo podían recibir a causa de una pequeña mancha que había en la cara. Al final se lo regalé a mi hermanita, a quien le gustó mucho. Todo quedó bien con mi novia cuando le regalé un anillo muy bonito.*

E. Mi reacción. Comente uno de los siguientes anuncios con un(a) amigo(a). Compare lo que se pide y se ofrece con sus propias capacidades y experiencia y también con lo que Ud. busca en un trabajo.

IMPORTANTE EMPRESA
NECESITA
VENDEDORES
AMBOS SEXOS
Solicitar entrevista
262 32 00 y 262 32 09
AUVISA AUDIOVISUALES, S. A.
Príncipe de Vergara, 55, 2º C
28006 MADRID

EMPRESA DE COSMÉTICA
PROFESIONAL NECESITA
VENDEDORES/AS
para Madrid y zona centro

Se requiere: experiencia en ventas, preferible conozcan el sector, tener vehículo propio.

Se ofrece: fuertes ingresos, a convenir. Se garantiza absoluta discreción.

Llamar al teléfono 413 86 46

VENDEDOR
DECORADOR
PARA TIENDA DE MUEBLES

Imprescindible experiencia en puesto similar y en Estudios de decoración. Edad máxima, 35 años. Buena presencia.

Interesados, escribir enviando foto e historial profesional al Apartado de Correos 46347 de Madrid.
(Ref. Goya 28350094. M004)

MODELO: E1:   *Tengo experiencia, pero lo malo es que no tengo carro.*
                   E2:   *Lo de la buena presencia es fácil. ¡Soy guapísimo y siempre me visto a la última moda!*
                   E1:   *Me parece que lo bueno es que garantizan un sueldo mínimo.*

CAPÍTULO 11

◆

Las máquinas en nuestras vidas

Los empleados de una compañía de telecomunicaciones y de distribución de computadoras en New Jersey prueban y reparan aparatos en el taller de la compañía.

Conversación

1. ¿Le es fácil o difícil aprender a usar una máquina? ¿Por qué?
2. ¿Por qué cree Ud. que algunas personas temen la tecnología? ¿La teme Ud.? ¿Por qué?
3. ¿Qué aparatos electrodomésticos considera Ud. necesarios en su casa? ¿Cuáles no le son esenciales? Explique.
4. ¿Cuál es su actitud hacia las computadoras? Explique. ¿Sabe Ud. usar una?
5. ¿Cuáles son cinco actividades humanas que una computadora puede hacer? Mencione otras cinco en las que una computadora es de poca o ninguna utilidad.
6. Compare la vida suya con la de sus padres. ¿Qué máquinas han causado los mayores cambios? ¿Es mejor ahora la vida? Explique.
7. ¿Encuentra Ud. que el taller de la compañía en la fotografía de la página anterior es un lugar agradable para trabajar? ¿Tiene muchas comodidades? Explique.
8. ¿Le gustaría trabajar en un ambiente como el del taller? ¿Por qué sí o no?

Vocabulario temático

abrelatas, el   can opener
aparato, el   apparatus, device, machine
aspiradora, la   vacuum cleaner
batidora, la   mixer
botón, el   button
cámara (fotográfica), la   camera
computadora, la   computer
equipo, el   equipment; set
grabadora, la   tape recorder
impresora, la   printer
lavadora, la   washing machine
lavaplatos, el   dishwasher
mantenimiento, el   maintenance
máquina, la   machine
marca, la   brand name
nevera, la   refrigerator
reparación, la   repair
repuesto, el   spare part
surtido, el   stock, selection
tecla, la   key (on typewriter, etc.)
tostadora, la   toaster
utilidad, la   usefulness

ajustar   to adjust
archivar   to file

armar   to put together
automatizar   to automate
computarizar   to computerize
dañarse   to become damaged
vaciar   to empty

técnico(a)   technical

aparato electrodoméstico, el   home electrical appliance
carro de cambios manuales, el   car with manual transmission
contestador automático, el   answering machine
energía nuclear, la   nuclear energy
horno de microondas, el   microwave oven
máquina de coser, la   sewing machine
procesador de textos (palabras), el   word processor
secador de pelo, el   hair dryer
sistema de alta fidelidad, el   high fidelity system
tabla de microcircuitos, la   circuit board

I. Familiar commands: **tú** and **vosotros**

Por las mañanas un reloj automático me despierta con melodías programadas la noche anterior. Me canta electrónicamente: «**Levántate** perezosa y **prepárate** para enfrentar otro día».

Para el desayuno una tostadora eléctrica me tuesta el pan exactamente como me gusta. Me dice: «**No te apures; cómetelo** todo».

Antes de salir de la casa, la radio me informa del estado del tiempo. Me susurra: «**No olvides** tu paraguas y **ten** cuidado con el tráfico».

A veces me pregunto si podría vivir sin las máquinas. La verdad: me veo obligada a confesar que no. ¿Y qué dice Ud.?

A. *Affirmative tú commands*

1. The affirmative **tú** command form of most Spanish verbs is identical to the third person singular of the present indicative: **él toma, toma (tú).** If a subject pronoun is used, it follows the verb.

   Mira (tú) este folleto.   *Look at this brochure.*
   Sigue las instrucciones.   *Follow the instructions.*
   Trae la grabadora y **enciéndela.** *Bring the tape recorder and turn it on.*

2. The following verbs have irregular affirmative **tú** command forms.

decir: **di**	poner: **pon**	tener: **ten**
hacer: **haz**	salir: **sal**	venir: **ven**
ir: **ve**	ser: **sé**	

3. Observe in the following examples that **sé** has a written accent to distinguish it from the pronoun **se.** The **tú** command form of **ir** and **ver** is identical: **ve;** context usually makes the meaning clear.

   Sé más cuidadoso con ese cuchillo eléctrico. **Ve** las instrucciones en el manual.   *Be more careful with that electric knife. See the instructions in the manual.*
   Pon ese aparato sobre la mesa. **Ve** al almacén por un repuesto.   *Put that device on the table. Go to the warehouse for a replacement.*

4. Reflexive and object pronouns follow and are attached to affirmative commands. When object pronouns are attached, a written accent is added if the stress falls on the third or fourth syllable from the end.

   Dime cómo funciona este radiorreloj, pero **explícamelo** lentamente. **Acuérdate** de que no soy una persona con inclinaciones técnicas.   *Tell me how this clock radio works, but explain it to me slowly. Remember that I'm not a person with technical inclinations.*

B. *Negative tú commands*

1. The negative **tú** command form is identical to the second person singular of the present subjunctive. (See *Capítulo 9.1* for present subjunctive forms.)

   No repares ese secador de pelo.   *Don't repair that hair dryer.*
   No pierdas tiempo.   *Don't waste time.*
   No repitas nuestro error.   *Don't repeat our mistake.*

2. Reflexive and object pronouns precede the verb in negative commands.

   No te olvides de encender la cafetera eléctrica por la mañana.   *Don't forget to turn on the electric coffeepot in the morning.*
   No me digas que tienes cosas más importantes que hacer.   *Don't tell me you have more important things to do.*

C. *Vosotros commands*

1. To form the affirmative **vosotros** command, the **-r** of the infinitive is replaced by **-d: arreglar, arreglad.** Remember that **vosotros** is primarily used in Spain, whereas in Hispanic America **ustedes** forms are used for familiar plural commands. (See *Capítulo 10.1* for **ustedes** command forms.)

   Ahorrad tiempo en la cocina; **comprad** un horno de microondas.   *Save time in the kitchen; buy a microwave oven.*
   Vivid cómodamente con la ayuda de los aparatos electrodomésticos Láser.   *Live comfortably with the help of Láser home electrical appliances.*

2. The negative **vosotros** command is identical to the second person plural of the present subjunctive.

   No uséis esos aparatos sin leer las instrucciones.   *Don't use those appliances without reading the instructions.*
   No toquéis esos botones.   *Don't touch those buttons.*

3. As with other command forms, reflexive and object pronouns follow and are attached to affirmative **vosotros** commands; they precede the verb in negative commands. When pronouns are attached to an affirmative command, a written accent may be required on the stressed syllable of the stem to reflect proper stress.

La grabadora se descompuso. **Man-dadla** a reparar. **No la reparéis** vosotros mismos. **No os desaniméis.**

The tape recorder broke. Send it for repairs. Don't repair it yourselves. Don't get discouraged.

4. When the reflexive pronoun **os** is attached to an affirmative **vosotros** command, the final **-d** of the verb is dropped and a written accent is added to the **i** of **-ir** verbs: **limpiad, limpiaos; poned, poneos; vestid, vestíos.** Exception: **id, idos.**

Comprehension questions

1. Which of the following command forms are affirmative **tú** commands? **explique, arregle, entiende, pague, ve**

2. Indicate which of the following command forms is not identical to a present subjunctive form: **no juguéis, duerme, no sigas, tráigalo.**

3. Would you use **enciende, enciendes,** or **enciendas** in the following command given to a roommate? _____ **ese estéreo; el sonido te encantará.**

4. In the narration at the beginning of this section, the toaster addresses one person in the familiar command: «**No te apures; cómetelo todo**». What familiar command forms would this machine use to address two or more people in Spain?

Ejercicios

A. Déle instrucciones a una persona que aprende el uso de un procesador de textos. Use mandatos con **tú** y después repita el ejercicio dirigiéndose a un grupo usando mandatos con **vosotros.**

MODELO: encender el procesador de textos
Enciende el procesador de textos.
Encended el procesador de textos.

1. abrir el manual de instrucciones
2. no comenzar todavía el primer ejercicio
3. hacer las correcciones indicadas
4. tocar esta tecla para borrar la letra anterior
5. poner números a las páginas
6. no apagar la máquina sin archivar el documento en el disco
7. no poner el disco al sol ni al calor
8. tener cuidado de no doblar el disco

B. Ud. es muy particular y le molesta cuando ve que su compañero(a) de apartamento maltrata varios aparatos electrodomésticos o no hace las cosas como Ud. cree que deben hacerse. Déle instrucciones al respecto y use pronombres cuando sea posible.

MODELO: no poner tanto detergente en la lavadora / usar menos o dañas la máquina
No pongas tanto detergente en la lavadora; usa menos o dañas la máquina.

1. no dejar agua en la plancha / vaciarla cuando termines de usarla
2. no meter un cuchillo en la tostadora / sacar el pan con los dedos
3. no hacer las cuentas mentalmente / hacerlas con la calculadora
4. no encender tantos aparatos a la vez / ahorrar electricidad
5. no dar golpes al televisor / ajustarlo usando los botones
6. no subir tanto el volumen del equipo estereofónico / bajarlo un poco para no molestar a los vecinos

C. Ud. dirige la reparación de aparatos eléctricos y electrónicos. Responda a los comentarios y preguntas de los técnicos, dándoles instrucciones sobre el trabajo y las prioridades. Use mandatos afirmativos y negativos e incluya pronombres cuando sea apropiado.

MODELO: ¿Avisamos al cliente que esta máquina de coser está lista?
Sí, avisadle esta mañana. (No, no le aviséis todavía; hay que probarla primero.)

1. ¿Pedimos los repuestos que necesitamos para esta máquina de escribir?
2. Tenemos que reparar este radiorreloj para mañana, pero no han llegado las piezas todavía. ¿Qué hacemos?
3. ¿Debemos intentar arreglar esta tostadora otra vez?
4. Creemos que el problema con este amplificador está en esta tabla de microcircuitos. ¿Debemos reemplazarla?
5. ¿Llamamos ahora al dueño de este lavaplatos para explicarle el problema?
6. Pensamos probar esta lavadora tan pronto como yo termine con la instalación del nuevo motor. ¿Está bien?

D. Ud. es jefe(a) de una compañía de equipo electrónico en California. Ahora conversa con uno de sus vendedores sobre un viaje de negocios que él hará muy pronto. Conteste sus preguntas, usando mandatos familiares y pronombres cuando sean apropiados y luego dé un mandato que aclare la situación.

MODELO: *Vendedor:*   ¿Quieres que yo lleve conmigo la nueva calculadora programable?
          Usted: *Sí, llévala. Úsala para impresionar a los nuevos clientes. (No, déjala aquí. Ponla allí encima de mi escritorio).*

1. ¿Debo llamarte antes de salir mañana?
2. ¿Será prudente hablar con Máximo, el comprador de la Compañía Cruz?
3. ¿Será mejor pasar la primera noche en Fresno o en Oakland?
4. ¿Quieres que te traiga las quejas del distribuidor de Santa Bárbara?
5. ¿Debo ir a la feria tecnológica de San Diego?
6. ¿Puedo enviar los pedidos directamente al almacén?

II. Adverbs of manner

Jaime Digital, "joven" de muy pocos meses, se ofrece para trabajos manuales y rutinarios. Funciona **automáticamente.** Trabaja 24 horas al día sin descansos, y no pide ni sueldo, ni beneficios, ni facilidades especiales. Trabaja **intensa, metódica** y **silenciosamente** y siempre procede **con toda calma. Solamente** exige un mínimo de mantenimiento. Para mayor información, póngase en comunicación de inmediato con la amiga de Jaime, Nora Duarte, Compañía Robots Computarizados, calle Esquivel 543, teléfono 7-34-87.

A. *Types of adverbs*

Adverbs modify verbs, adjectives, and other adverbs, to specify such things as place, degree, time, and manner. Adverbs are usually placed after the verb or before the adjective modified.

¿Ves **allí** a aquel señor?	*Do you see that man over there?* (place)
Es un inventor **muy** famoso.	*He's a very famous inventor.* (degree)
Todavía trabaja en su último invento, un robot que puede preparar la cena.	*He's still working on his latest invention, a robot capable of preparing supper.* (time)
Trabaja **intensamente** para acabarlo **pronto.**	*He's working very hard to finish it soon.* (manner, time)

B. Adverbs ending in **-mente**

1. Adverbs ending in **-mente** are generally adverbs of manner that tell *how* something is done. They are formed by adding the suffix **-mente** (usually equivalent to English *-ly*) to the feminine form of the adjective: **ruidosa, ruidosamente; difícil, difícilmente; amable, amablemente.** A written accent is retained when **-mente** is added.

Yo dormía **plácidamente** cuando el reloj despertador sonó **ruidosamente.**	*I was sleeping peacefully when the alarm clock went off noisily.*

Me levanté **rápidamente.**

I got up quickly.

Llamé a un técnico con quien tenía una cita y me saludó **amablemente** un contestador automático.

I called a technician with whom I had an appointment and an answering machine greeted me pleasantly.

2. When two or more adverbs ending in **-mente** modify the same word, only the last adverb in the series takes the ending **-mente.** All preceding adverbs have the feminine singular form of the corresponding adjective.

Ese inventor habla **rápida** y **atropelladamente.**

That inventor speaks quickly and in a rushed way.

Pero siempre procede **lenta, tranquila** y **metódicamente** cuando trabaja en sus inventos.

But he always proceeds slowly, calmly, and methodically when he works on his inventions.

C. *Adverbial phrases*

1. Two common alternatives to adverbs of manner ending in **-mente** are the constructions **con** + noun, and **de manera (modo)** + adjective.

Mi sobrinito recibió **con alegría** un coche para armar.

My little nephew joyfully received a car to put together.

Se puso a armar las piezas **con entusiasmo.**

He started putting the parts together enthusiastically.

Pero después de unos momentos, trabajaba **de modo** más **lento** y su madre tuvo que terminar de armarlo.

But after a few minutes, he was working more slowly and his mother had to finish putting it together.

2. Compare the following alternative phrases to some adverbs ending in **-mente:**

con + noun	Adverb in **-mente**
con cuidado	cuidadosamente
con claridad	claramente
con calma	calmadamente
con cariño	cariñosamente

de modo/manera + adjective	Adverb in **-mente**
de modo rápido	rápidamente
de manera completa	completamente
de modo cortés	cortésmente
de manera gradual	gradualmente
de modo prudente	prudentemente

D. *Adjectives functioning as adverbs*

An adjective can function as an adverb of manner when used with an intransitive verb (one that cannot take a direct object) or with a verb that expresses a state or condition. The adjective modifies both the subject and the verb simultaneously and agrees with the subject.

Entraron muy **contentos** a la tienda de aparatos electrónicos.	*They went into the electronics shop in a happy mood.*
Salieron bien **enfadados.**	*They left quite annoyed.*
Se quedaron **decepcionados** con el vendedor.	*They were disappointed with the salesman.*

Comprehension questions

1. Give the sentence obtained by combining the following sentences: **Funciona lentamente. Funciona ruidosamente.**

2. Which of the following sentences indicate that someone writes clearly? **Escribe de la claridad. Escribe claramente. Escribe con claridad.**

3. To indicate that someone was sad when he or she arrived home, would you use **triste** or **tristemente? Llegó ＿＿＿ a casa.**

Ejercicios

A. Describa cómo funciona una oficina después de modernizarla con los últimos modelos de computadoras, procesadores de texto, máquinas de escribir electrónicas, copiadoras, etc., usando adverbios en **-mente.**

MODELO: Las secretarias trabajan con tranquilidad y precisión.
Las secretarias trabajan tranquila y precisamente.

1. Las computadoras se utilizan con regularidad.
2. Las llamadas de teléfono se transfieren de manera instantánea.
3. Las cartas y los documentos se escriben con facilidad y de modo perfecto.
4. Todos trabajan de manera productiva y eficiente.
5. Las copias se producen con claridad y rapidez.
6. Los cálculos se hacen con precisión y de forma casi automática.

318 ◆ Capítulo 11 Las máquinas en nuestras vidas

B. El departamento de lenguas extranjeras de su universidad acaba de abrir un nuevo laboratorio de lenguas equipado con varias máquinas computarizadas, grabadoras muy modernas y mucho equipo de vídeo. Exprese las reacciones de algunas personas que vieron el nuevo laboratorio.

MODELO: la jefa del laboratorio / quedar / contento con todo
La jefa del laboratorio quedó contenta con todo.

1. algunos nuevos ayudantes / mirar / asombrado el equipo
2. una de las estudiantes / decir que / los programas de la computadora / resultar / aburrido
3. la recepcionista / quedar / indiferente ante todo
4. la mayoría de los estudiantes / salir / ilusionado / pero un poco inseguro
5. dos de los ayudantes graduados / mostrarse / muy entusiasmado

C. Ud. sigue un cursillo de filmación. Conteste lógicamente las preguntas de un(a) amigo(a) que se interesa en seguirlo también, explicándole cómo le va y usando un adverbio en **-mente.**

MODELO: ¿Se da atención individual a cada estudiante? (cuidadoso)
Sí, los instructores supervisan cuidadosamente el trabajo de cada estudiante.

1. ¿Es difícil aprender a usar las cámaras, los monitores, los micrófonos y demás? (fácil)
2. ¿Y se aprende a ponerle música al sonido? (rápido)
3. ¿Los estudiantes tienen bastante tiempo para crear sus propios guiones? (apresurado)
4. ¿Usan vídeo para dar ejemplos de lo que es bueno y malo? (eficaz)
5. ¿Explica el instructor de forma que un novato pueda entender? (paciente y amable)
6. ¿Estás satisfecho(a) con el cursillo? (completo)

D. Cada estudiante pensará en una máquina de oficina o en un aparato electrodoméstico que utiliza. Luego, en forma de cadena, expresará exactamente cómo esa máquina lo(la) ayuda a trabajar de una manera más satisfactoria. Use adverbios en **-mente** o frases que incluyan **de modo/manera** y **con.**

MODELO: *Con el procesador de textos hago mis tareas más rápidamente y con mayor precisión que antes.*

III. Use of the indicative versus the subjunctive in adverbial clauses

Ana María: ¿Ud. quiere noventa dólares por esta máquina de escribir eléctrica, **a pesar de que es un modelo bien antiguo**?

Vendedora:	Así es. **Como Ud. ve,** está en perfectas condiciones. Y **aunque los modelos nuevos tengan ciertos adelantos,** se paga mucho **cuando hay que repararlos.**
Ana María:	Bueno, a esta máquina hay que repararle una tecla que está suelta. No se la puedo comprar, **a menos que me haga una rebaja.** ¿Me la vende por cincuenta dólares?
Vendedora:	Mire, **para que las dos quedemos contentas,** déme sesenta dólares y la máquina es suya.
Ana María:	Pues, me parece bien.

A. *Adverbial clauses*

1. An adverbial clause modifies the main verb of a sentence and is introduced by conjunctions such as **cuando, como, aunque,** and **porque.** An adverbial clause conveys information about aspects such as the time, place, manner, condition, cause, purpose, or result of the main action. An adverbial clause may also express a supposition or uncertainty about the main action.

Arregla esa grabadora **cuando puedas.**	*Fix that tape recorder whenever you can.* (time)
Arregla la lavadora **para que podamos usarla pronto.**	*Fix the washing machine so that we can use it soon.* (purpose)
Arregla el radiorreloj **porque necesito usarlo pronto.**	*Fix the clock radio because I need to use it soon.* (reason)
Arregla la aspiradora **en caso de que la necesitemos mañana.**	*Fix the vacuum cleaner in case we need it tomorrow.* (supposition)

2. Both the indicative and the subjunctive are used in adverbial clauses. The indicative is used to express an action, event, or situation that does happen, has happened, or is certain to happen. The subjunctive is used if an adverbial clause conveys doubt, uncertainty, or possibility, or if the adverbial clause refers to an action that has not yet taken place or come about. Compare the use of the indicative and subjunctive in the following adverbial clauses.

Camilo viene a verme **porque va** a reparar el televisor.	*Camilo is coming to see me because he's going to fix the TV.*
Tengo todo preparado **puesto que llegará** pronto.	*I have everything prepared since he'll arrive soon.*
Le explicaré el problema **en cuanto llegue.**	*I'll explain the problem to him as soon as he arrives.*
Habrá terminado **antes de que empiece** el partido de béisbol que queremos ver.	*He'll have finished before the baseball game (that) we want to watch starts.*

B. *Conjunctions followed by a verb in the indicative*

1. The indicative is used in an adverbial clause that gives the reason for a situation or for the occurrence of an action or event.

Reparan la lavadora **porque está** descompuesta.

They're fixing the washing machine because it's broken.

Tendré que ir a la lavandería automática, **ya que** la lavadora no **estará** lista hasta el lunes.

I'll have to go to the laundromat since the washing machine will not be ready until next Monday.

2. Conjunctions that indicate reason or cause include the following.

como	*since*	puesto que	*since, because*
porque	*because*	ya que	*since, because*

C. *Conjunctions followed by a verb in the subjunctive*

1. The subjunctive is used in an adverbial clause to refer to an event that has not yet taken place at the time indicated by the tense of the main verb.

Vengo a hablar contigo **a fin de que** me **expliques** cómo funciona este vídeo.

I'm coming to speak with you so that you can explain to me how this video works.

Aquí están las instrucciones, **en caso de que** las **necesites.**

Here are the directions in case you need them.

Explícame cómo se usa **antes de que** yo lo **haga** funcionar.

Explain to me how it's used before I start it.

No quiero usar el vídeo **sin que** alguien me **muestre** primero cómo funciona.

I don't want to use the video without having someone show me first how it works.

2. The subjunctive is always used after the following conjunctions.

a fin de que	*in order that*	en caso (de) que	*in case that*
a menos (de) que	*unless*	para que	*so that*
antes (de) que	*before*	sin que	*without*
con tal (de) que	*provided that*		

3. If the subject of a dependent clause is the same as that of the main verb, an infinitive, not an adverbial clause, is used. The prepositional form of the conjunction (without **que**) is used. (See *Capítulo 9.2* on use of the infinitive versus a conjugated verb.)

Llevaré el carro al mecánico **antes de regresar** a casa.

I'll take the car to the mechanic before returning home.

Llevaré el carro al mecánico **antes de que regreses** a casa.

I'll take the car to the mechanic before you return home.

D. *Conjunctions followed by a verb in the indicative or the subjunctive*

Conjunctions of time

1. Conjunctions that introduce adverbial clauses referring to time are followed by the indicative to refer to events that habitually occur or take place in the present, or that have occurred in the past.

Cuando hago cálculos complicados, uso una computadora. (habitual action: indicative)	*When I do complicated calculations, I use a computer.*
Cuando calculé mis impuestos sobre la renta, usé una computadora. (past event: indicative)	*When I computed my income tax, I used a computer.*

2. The subjunctive is used after conjunctions of time to refer to future or anticipated events that have not yet taken place.

Cuando haga cálculos complicados, voy a usar una computadora. (anticipated event: subjunctive)	*When I do complicated calculations, I'm going to use a computer.*
Cuando los cálculos **sean** más simples, usaré mi calculadora. (anticipated event: subjunctive)	*When the calculations are simpler, I'll use my calculator.*

3. The following conjunctions of time may be followed by the indicative or the subjunctive.

cuando *when*	hasta que *until*
después (de) que *after*	mientras (que) *while; as long as*
en cuanto *as soon as*	tan pronto como *as soon as*

De modo que, de manera que

The conjunctions **de modo que** (*so that*) and **de manera que** (*so that*) may convey two different meanings: the result of an action or the purpose of an action. They are followed by the indicative to imply result and by the subjunctive to imply purpose. When used to imply purpose, **de modo (manera) que** is synonymous with **para que.**

Me apuré **de modo que terminé** pronto. (result: indicative)	*I hurried up so that I finished soon.*
Apúrate **de modo que termines** pronto. (purpose: subjunctive)	*Hurry up so that you may finish soon.*

Aunque, a pesar (de) que

1. The conjunctions **aunque** (*although, even though, even if*) and **a pesar (de) que** (*in spite of*) are followed by the indicative to introduce facts or situations viewed as factual.

Aunque necesito una nevera, no compraré una todavía.	*Even though I need a refrigerator, I won't buy one yet.*
A pesar de que tenía dinero, decidí no comprar una cámara fotográfica.	*In spite of the fact that I had money, I decided not to buy a camera.*

2. When **aunque** or **a pesar de que** introduce a clause that expresses a supposition or a conjecture, they are followed by the subjunctive.

Aunque los cuchillos eléctricos **faciliten** las tareas de la cocina, no voy a comprar uno porque creo que son peligrosos.	*Even though electric knives may simplify chores in the kitchen, I'm not going to buy one because I think they're dangerous.*
No uso los contestadores automáticos, **a pesar de que puedan** aumentar la productividad de mi pequeño negocio.	*I don't use answering machines, in spite of the fact that they may increase the productivity of my small business.*

3. The verb in the clause introduced by **aunque** may be conjugated in the subjunctive if it refers to a fact that the speaker considers irrelevant to the main point being made in the sentence.

Aunque un horno de microondas **ahorre** tiempo, lo cual no niego, nunca usaré uno porque las tortas no quedan bien.	*Even though a microwave oven saves time, which I don't deny, I'll never use one because cakes don't turn out well.*

Como, donde, según

The conjunctions **como** (*as, in any way*), **donde** (*where, wherever*), and **según** (*according to*) are used in adverbial clauses referring to place and manner. The indicative is used in clauses that refer to a specific, known place or manner; the subjunctive is used to refer to a nonspecific or unknown place or manner.

—¿Coloco el paquete **donde** tú me **pediste**?	*Do I place the package where you asked me to?* (a specific place)
—Colócalo **donde haya** lugar.	*Place it wherever there's room.* (any place)
—¿Lo coloco **como** me **dijiste**, de costado?	*Do I place it the way you told me, on its side?* (a specific way)
—Colócalo **como quieras**; no importa.	*Place it any way you want; it doesn't matter.* (any way)

Summary of the indicative versus the subjunctive in adverbial clauses

Conjunction	Followed by:	*Examples*
como (*reason*) porque puesto que ya que	*Indicative:* reason	Tendré que ir a la lavandería automática **ya que** mi lavadora **está** descompuesta.
a fin de que a menos (de) que antes (de) que con tal (de) que en caso (de) que para que sin que	*Subjunctive:* not yet realized	Avísame **en caso de que sepas** de una nevera usada en venta. Compra esa batidora **antes de que** se **termine** la liquidación.
como (*time*) cuando después (de) que en cuanto hasta que mientras (que) tan pronto como	*Indicative:* occurs or occurred *Subjunctive:* anticipated (not realized)	**Cuando** la grabadora se **descompone,** la llevo al técnico. **Cuando** la grabadora se **descomponga** la próxima vez, trataré de arreglarla yo misma.
a pesar de que aunque	*Indicative:* fact *Subjunctive:* fact is irrelevant	Compré un cuchillo eléctrico **aunque** no lo **necesito** realmente. Cómprate un cuchillo eléctrico **aunque** no lo **necesites** realmente; están baratos.
de manera que de modo que	*Indicative:* result *Subjunctive:* purpose	Tenemos un televisor portátil **de modo que** nunca **perdemos** nuestros programas favoritos. Vamos a comprarnos un televisor portátil **de modo que** nunca **perdamos** nuestros programas favoritos.
como (*manner*) donde según	*Indicative:* specific, known *Subjunctive:* non-specific, unknown	Ve a la tienda **donde tienen** aparatos electrodomésticos. Ve a una tienda **donde tengan** aparatos electrodomésticos.

Comprehension questions

1. Would you use the present indicative **ofrecen** or the present subjunctive **ofrezcan** in the following sentences? **Voy a comprarte este horno de microondas porque me _____ un buen precio. Voy a comprarte este horno de microondas, con tal de que me _____ un buen precio.** Explain why.

2. Would you use the present indicative **vendo** or the present subjunctive **venda** in the following sentences? **Tan pronto como _____ una computadora, siempre me compro otra. Tan pronto como _____ esta computadora, me compraré otra.** Explain the meaning of each.

3. In one of the following sentences **de modo que** expresses the purpose of the action; in the other, it expresses the result obtained. Identify each usage. **Ella explica todo claramente de modo que todos entienden. Ella explica todo claramente de modo que todos entiendan.**

4. Which one of the following sentences indicates that the speaker leaves his electric shaver where he is always able to find it? **Dejo la máquina de afeitar eléctrica donde la pueda encontrar. Dejo la máquina de afeitar eléctrica donde la puedo encontrar.** What does the other sentence mean?

5. In the dialogue at the beginning of this section, the salesperson says in her last utterance **«... para que las dos quedemos contentas».** Could the indicative form **quedamos** be used in this context? Explain.

Ejercicios

A. Ud. es una persona de necesidades sencillas y es bastante escéptico(a) con respecto a las novedades tecnológicas. Exprese sus ideas, combinando las siguientes frases con la conjunción indicada y usando el indicativo o el subjuntivo, según el contexto.

MODELO: No tengo necesidad de máquinas. Prefiero no complicarme la vida. (porque)
No tengo necesidad de máquinas porque prefiero no complicarme la vida.

1. No uso ni batidora ni abrelatas eléctricos. Los métodos antiguos sirven perfectamente. (puesto que)
2. Antes teníamos varios aparatos en casa. Me cansé de arreglarlos continuamente. (hasta que)
3. Mi familia insiste en que yo use un horno de microondas. Yo puedo ahorrar mucho tiempo. (para que)

4. Es posible que cambie de opinión. Los aparatos duran más tiempo. (cuando)
5. Pero supongo que hay muy poca posibilidad de que yo me convenza. Soy una persona de ideas bien definidas. (ya que)

B. Ud. va a dejar la universidad un semestre para viajar a Hispanoamérica y quiere vender casi todo lo que tiene. Explique a un(a) amigo(a) por qué o para qué lo hace y bajo qué condiciones venderá algunas cosas. Use algunas de las siguientes conjunciones: **porque, para que, con tal (de) que, hasta (que), a menos que, tan pronto como,** o **antes (de) que.**

MODELO: Tengo que vender todas estas cosas...
Tengo que vender todas estas cosas para que mi amigo(a) y yo tengamos suficiente dinero para vivir en Hispanoamérica tres meses.

1. No bajaré el precio del estéreo...
2. Trataré de guardar mi radiorreloj...
3. Creo que será fácil vender esta nevera...
4. Es preciso encontrar una persona que compre este escritorio...
5. No voy a poner un anuncio en el periódico...
6. Les dije a mis padres que necesito hacer esto...

C. Varios amigos le piden favores a Ud. y también le hacen algunas invitaciones, pero Ud. está muy ocupado(a) en estos días así que les explica cuándo y bajo qué circunstancias podrá hacer lo que quieren. Conteste sus preguntas y use algunas de las siguientes conjunciones: **cuando, tan pronto como, después (de) que, en cuanto, con tal (de) que, a menos (de) que.**

MODELO: *E1:* ¿Me dejas usar tu procesador de textos?
  E2: *Sí, claro. Puedes usarlo con tal de que no tenga que enseñarte a usarlo.*

1. ¿Puedes venir conmigo a comprar un televisor?
2. ¿Me ayudas a descifrar las instrucciones para mi nuevo proyector?
3. ¿Puedes ver qué pasa con mi carro?
4. ¿Cuándo vienes a ver las diapositivas de mi viaje?
5. ¿Vienes con nosotros esta noche al club Azul 99?
6. ¿Quieres acompañarme a un seminario sobre la tecnología y las humanidades?

D. Imagínese que Ud. tiene un robot capaz de hacer cualquier cosa. Sueñe un poco y diga cómo lo usaría. Dé dos o tres posibilidades, y use **para que,** según el modelo.

MODELO: *El robot lavará mi ropa para que yo pueda dedicar más tiempo a los deportes y para que tenga más tiempo libre.*

E. Haga el papel de un(a) vendedor(a) que trata de vender uno de los aparatos que aparecen en el siguiente dibujo a un(a) cliente. Trate de persuadirlo(la) que el modelo es una ganga, usando una variedad de conjunciones adverbiales y el indicativo o el subjuntivo, según el contexto.

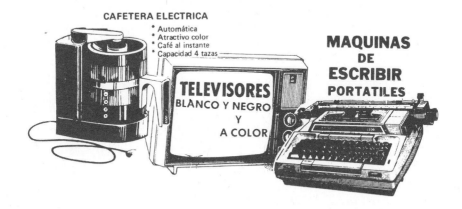

MODELO: *Esta cafetera eléctrica es una compra magnífica puesto que está en oferta durante esta semana. Y, en caso de que no pueda pagar la cantidad completa, le ofrecemos facilidades de pago. Estoy seguro(a) de que le gustará porque hace un café instantáneo delicioso y Ud. nunca tendrá que repararla a menos que no siga las instrucciones.*

IV. Imperfect subjunctive

Arturo: ¿Y cómo le va a tu compañero de cuarto en su lucha con las máquinas?

Víctor: No muy bien, te diré. Si **pudiera,** me mudaría hoy mismo.

Arturo: ¿Problemas de nuevo con la lavadora automática?

Víctor: ¿Cómo adivinaste? Al entrar hoy en el apartamento, vi espuma por todas partes. ¡Fue una suerte que no **pasara** nada grave!

Arturo: ¿Pero no te pidió hace unos días que le **explicaras** cómo funciona ese aparato?

Víctor: Sí, sí, pero creo que aunque se lo **explicara** mil veces no lo entendería. Hemos redistribuido el trabajo y ahora él promete no tocar ningún aparato. Ojalá resulte.

A. *Forms of the imperfect subjunctive*

	-ar verbs	-er verbs	-ir verbs
	comprar	entender	vivir
Stem:	ellos compraron	ellos entendieron	ellos vivieron

-ra endings

comprara	entendiera	viviera
compraras	entendieras	vivieras
comprara	entendiera	viviera
compráramos	entendiéramos	viviéramos
comprarais	entendierais	vivierais
compraran	entendieran	vivieran

-se endings

comprase	entendiese	viviese
comprases	entendieses	vivieses
comprase	entendiese	viviese
comprásemos	entendiésemos	viviésemos
compraseis	entendieseis	vivieseis
comprasen	entendiesen	viviesen

1. The stem of the imperfect subjunctive is formed by dropping **-ron** from the third person plural form of the preterit.

2. The imperfect subjunctive has two sets of endings. The **-ra** endings are used more frequently both in Spain and in Hispanic America; the **-se** endings are used primarily in Spain and are more common in the written than in the spoken language. Notice that first and third person singular forms are identical and that first person plural forms have a written accent.

3. All verbs that have an irregular stem in the third person plural form of the preterit maintain the irregular stem in the imperfect subjunctive.

4. The verbs **ir** and **ser** have identical forms in the imperfect subjunctive, and context determines which verb is meant. The following list summarizes regular and irregular imperfect subjunctive forms.

Infinitive	Third person plural preterit	Stem	+ Endings	= Imperfect Subjunctive
comprar	compraron	**compra-**	ra/se	yo comprara
pensar (ie)	pensaron	**pensa-**	ra/se	yo pensara
sentir (ie, i)	sintieron	**sintie-**	ra/se	yo sintiera
dormir (ue, u)	durmieron	**durmie-**	ra/se	yo durmiera
pedir (i, i)	pidieron	**pidie-**	ra/se	yo pidiera
estar	estuvieron	**estuvie-**	ra/se	yo estuviera
dar	dieron	**die-**	ra/se	yo diera
ir / ser	fueron	**fue-**	ra/se	yo fuera
hacer	hicieron	**hicie-**	ra/se	yo hiciera
decir	dijeron	**dije-**	ra/se	yo dijera

B. *Uses of the imperfect subjunctive*

1. The imperfect subjunctive is used in the same types of independent and dependent clauses and under the same circumstances as the present subjunctive. (Consult *Capítulo 9.2* for use of the present subjunctive in independent clauses, *Capítulo 9.2* for use of the present subjunctive in noun clauses, *Capítulo 10.4* for use of the present subjunctive in adjective clauses, and Section III of this chapter for use of the subjunctive in adverbial clauses.)

Ojalá todo el mundo se convenciera pronto de la importancia de las máquinas.	*I wish everyone could be convinced soon of the importance of machines.* (independent clause)
Les pedí a los secretarios **que aprendieran a usar un procesador de textos.**	*I asked the secretaries to learn how to use a word processor.* (noun clause)
No hubo ningún empleado **que encontrara difícil trabajar con el nuevo equipo.**	*There was no employee who found it hard to work with the new equipment.* (adjective clause)
Instalé varias computadoras **para que se facilitara el trabajo de la oficina.**	*I installed several computers so as to facilitate office work.* (adverbial clause)

2. The imperfect subjunctive is used in a dependent clause when the main verb is in the past or in the conditional. In this sense, the imperfect subjunctive is the past of the present subjunctive.

Main verb	Dependent clause
preterit	
imperfect	
past perfect	imperfect subjunctive
conditional	
conditional perfect	

Fue necesario que **compráramos** una computadora.	*It was necessary for us to buy a computer.*
Dudábamos que una máquina nos **ayudara** mucho con el trabajo de la oficina.	*We doubted that a machine could help us much with the work in the office.*
Ahora sabemos que las máquinas simplifican nuestras tareas, pero no **querríamos** que nuestro negocio **dependiera** exclusivamente de ellas.	*We now know that machines simplify our tasks, but we wouldn't like our business to depend exclusively on them.*
Habríamos querido que los empleados se **acostumbraran** gradualmente a los cambios.	*We would have liked for the employees to get used to changes slowly.*

3. The imperfect subjunctive can be used after a verb in the present indicative if the action reported in the dependent clause occurred before the main action.

Es una lástima que no **tuviera** una máquina fotográfica antes de mi viaje.	*It's a pity that I didn't have a camera before my trip.*

4. The imperfect subjunctive, with **-ra** endings only, is used with **deber, poder,** and **querer** to phrase a statement or a question in an especially polite way. The conditional tense can also be used for this purpose. (See *Capítulo 7.2* for use of the conditional to express politeness.)

Quisiera (Querría) tener una actitud más positiva hacia las máquinas.	*I would like to have a more positive attitude toward machines.*
¿**Pudiera (Podría)** Ud. indicarme qué beneficios obtendré si uso máquinas en mi negocio?	*Could you tell me what benefits I will obtain if I use machines in my business?*

5. The imperfect subjunctive is used in conditional sentences and in **como si** clauses (see *Capítulo 12.2*).

Si alguien me **pidiera** consejos sobre un buen oficio, le recomendaría la reparación de computadoras.	*If someone asked me for advice about a good trade, I would recommend computer repairs.*
Mi jefe actúa **como si** las máquinas, y no las personas, **fueran** el fundamento de su negocio.	*My boss acts as if machines, and not people, were the foundation of his business.*

Comprehension questions

1. Would you use **Espero** or **Esperaba** in the following sentences? _____ **que el teléfono sonara pronto.** _____ **que el teléfono suene pronto.**

2. Would you use **contestes** or **contestaras** in the dependent clause of the following sentences? **Es bueno que** _____ **mis llamadas telefónicas. Sería bueno que** _____ **mis llamadas telefónicas.**

3. What form of **repetir (repetí** or **repitiera)** would you use in the following sentences? **Era necesario que yo** _____ **la información. Era verdad que yo** _____ **la información.**

4. Would you use **usaba** or **usara** in the following sentences? **Me preguntó si yo** _____ **computadoras. Me pidió que yo** _____ **computadoras.**

5. In the dialogue at the beginning of this section, Víctor says: **«Fue una suerte que no pasara nada grave».** Would he use **pasara** or **pasó** if he said that it was a fact that nothing serious happened? **«Fue un hecho que no** _____ **nada grave».**

Ejercicios

A. Ud. le prestó una grabadora a un(a) amigo(a) que luego se la devolvió en mal estado, cosa que Ud. no descubrió hasta unos días después. Cuando le habló por teléfono a su amigo(a), él(ella) negó que fuera responsable. Conteste las preguntas de un(a) compañero(a) de clase que escuchó su conversación telefónica, usando las siguientes indicaciones.

MODELO: ¿Por qué hablaste tanto por teléfono? (querer / darme alguna explicación)
Pues, quería que él(ella) me diera alguna explicación.

1. ¿Qué fue eso de reparar algo? (pedir / llevarla a arreglar)
2. Te oí decir, «Eso no es cierto». ¿Qué pasó? (dudar / decirme la verdad)
3. ¿Por qué hablaste en voz tan alta? (sorprenderme / comportarse de esa manera)
4. Al final hablaron de dinero, ¿verdad? (querer / pagar la reparación)
5. ¿Qué le dijiste al final de la conversación? (decirle / no volver a pedirme prestado nada)
6. ¿Cómo te sentiste después de colgar el aparato? (sentir mal / hacer una cosa así)

B. Imagínese que le han sucedido a Ud. las siguientes cosas. Diga cómo se sintió Ud. y luego cuente la reacción de otros, usando un verbo o expresión de la lista.

sorprenderle	alegrarle	molestarle
asustarle	enojarle	parecerle estupendo
decepcionarle	avergonzarle	preocuparle

MODELO: Un amigo fue a la exhibición de vídeo sin invitarme. (mis otros amigos)
Me molestó que fuera a la exhibición de vídeo sin invitarme. A mis otros amigos les sorprendió que él hiciera tal cosa.

1. Una tía me regaló una grabadora. (mis primos)
2. Mis padres me dieron dinero para un carro. (mi novio/a)
3. No se pudo arreglar la máquina de escribir. (las secretarias)
4. Tú no me devolviste mi calculadora. (mis padres)
5. Un pariente ofreció darme una orientación sobre los sistemas de alta fidelidad. (mi compañero[a] de cuarto)

C. Ud. y dos amigos(as) buscan un apartamento, pero tienen diferencias de opinión sobre lo que quieren, el precio y las comodidades que desean tener. Han visto varios apartamentos y ahora Ud. expresa sus preferencias. Use algunas de las siguientes ideas y otras originales y empiece cada oración con **me gustaría, preferiría, recomendaría, querría, sería mejor,** etc.

MODELO: buscar un apartamento más barato
Preferiría que buscáramos un apartamento más barato.

1. seguir buscando hasta obtener algo más económico
2. visitar algunos lugares un poco más modestos
3. conseguir un apartamento cerca de la universidad
4. encontrar un sitio cerca de una lavandería automática
5. alquilar un apartamento con aire acondicionado
6. tener un apartamento con un buen sistema de seguridad

D. Exprese de forma muy cortés lo que diría Ud. a un(a) dependiente(a) en las siguientes circunstancias. Dé dos o tres oraciones para cada situación, usando **deber, querer** y **poder.**

MODELO: (*Situación*) Ud. regaló una máquina de afeitar a su padre, pero no le gusta la marca. Quiere cambiarla por otra. No tiene el recibo.
Perdone, señora. ¿Pudiera Ud. cambiarme esta máquina de afeitar por otra de diferente marca? Yo quisiera una de la marca Internacional, si es posible. Sé que yo debiera tener el recibo, pero desgraciadamente lo perdí.

1. Ud. acaba de enterarse de que ofrecen a un fabuloso descuento un estéreo que Ud. quiere desde hace mucho tiempo. Por desgracia, el precio descontado se venció ayer. Ud. trata de convencer al vendedor que le venda el aparato por el precio especial.
2. Ud. tiene problemas con un horno de microondas que compró; es que la puerta no cierra bien. Antes de hacer un viaje a la tienda, Ud. llama por teléfono para preguntar cuál podría ser el problema y lo que debería hacer.
3. Ud. compró hace poco una grabadora para su carro, pero cuando trató de hacer la instalación descubrió que el manual estaba escrito en japonés. Como Ud. no entiende japonés, le pide instrucciones al dependiente.

V. Dejar, salir, and other equivalents of *to leave*

1. The verbs **dejar** and **salir** are the two most common verbs used to express the different meanings of *to leave*.

La vendedora **dejó** unas líneas del contrato en blanco.	*The salesperson left a few lines of the contract blank.*
Al **salir** de la oficina, **dejó** algunos de sus papeles allí.	*Upon leaving the office, she left some of her papers there.*

2. **Dejar** often refers to leaving someone or something, including the idea of postponing an action. Either **dejar** or **abandonar** is used to express the notion of leaving a person, thing, or place quite abruptly or relatively permanently.

Déjame en la tienda donde compré la tostadora, por favor. Voy a **dejarla** allí para que la reparen.	*Leave me off at the store where I bought the toaster, please. I'm going to leave it there so that they can repair it.*
Decidí **dejar** el resto de mi trabajo para mañana.	*I decided to leave the rest of my work for tomorrow.*
¿Sabías que el ladrón **dejó (abandonó)** su coche allí?	*Did you know that the thief left (abandoned) his car right there?*

3. **Salir** refers to *leaving* from or toward a place, often with the meaning *to go out* or *to go away from/toward*.

¿**Saliste** de la oficina temprano?	*Did you leave the office early?*
Alberto **sale** para El Paso pronto.	*Alberto leaves for El Paso soon.*

4. When no particular place is mentioned, the verb **irse**, *to leave* or *to go away*, is preferred. The lack of focus upon a particular place is the most important distinction between **irse** and **salir. Marcharse** is a synonym of **irse.**

Si te apuras, **nos vamos** pronto.	*If you hurry up, we'll leave soon.*
Cecilia **se marchó** ayer.	*Cecilia left yesterday.*

Ejercicios

A. Indique qué verbo se usa en español en lugar de la palabra o expresión indicada. A veces hay más de una respuesta correcta.

1. Please *leave* that machine there for me.
2. He says he is sorry for *leaving* his job at the computer store.
3. The equipment repairmen *left* this morning without advising me.
4. Can you *leave* me in front of the Holmes Building?

5. We're going *to leave* for San Francisco on business about the 18th of June.
6. *Leave* the windows and doors locked, please.
7. Can you *leave* your house earlier so we can meet before work?
8. We're *leaving* everything in your hands; good luck.

B. Complete las oraciones con la forma apropiada de **dejar, salir** o **irse,** según el contexto.

1. —Estoy cansadísima; ¿puedo _____ estos cálculos para otro momento?
   —Está bien esta vez, pero no me gusta que _____ todo para mañana.
2. —Tomás dijo que iba a _____ a las once para pasar por nosotros.
   —Espero que él _____ temprano, así llegaremos a la hora de comer.
3. —¿Puedo _____ mi estéreo contigo por unos días?
   —Cómo no. Ahora tengo un favor que pedirte: necesito ir a la calle Princesa. ¿Me puedes _____ allí?
4. —Bernardo no dijo nada; se enojó y _____ abruptamente.
   —¡Qué raro! ¿Será que le molesta que no decidimos qué día vamos a _____?

Actividades para la comunicación

A. Consejos gratis. Sugiérale una o varias soluciones a un(a) compañero(a) que le cuenta algún problema, real o imaginario. Después cuéntele a su compañero(a) un problema suyo para que le aconseje a Ud.

MODELO: E1: *Se me rompió la cámara que me dejó una amiga. Y no tengo dinero para pagar la reparación.*

E2: *Sé sincero(a) y promételе que le pagarás tan pronto como puedas.*

E2: *Mi novio(a) se enojó porque no salí con él(ella) el sábado pasado. ¡No parece entender que tengo exámenes!*

E1: *Regálale algo, y dile cariñosamente lo mucho que lo(la) quieres y también que saldrás con él(ella) en cuanto terminen los exámenes.*

B. ¡A aprender! Describa a los compañeros de clase una experiencia que ha tenido al aprender el funcionamiento de alguna máquina o al familiarizarse con un nuevo trabajo. Explique si fue fácil o difícil, cómo se sentía antes, durante y después de aprenderlo y cómo lo(la) trató la persona que le enseñó.

MODELO: *Jamás olvidaré cómo aprendí a manejar un carro. Me enseñó mi padre en un carro de cambios manuales. Yo creo que aprendí bastante rápida y fácilmente. A veces mi padre se enfadaba a pesar de que trataba de enseñarme pacientemente. ¡Probablemente tenía miedo de que le hiciera algo al carro!*

C. No dude; ¡compre Ud.! Hable con un(a) posible comprador(a) de las ventajas de algo que Ud. vende de segunda mano. Explíquele la condición de lo que vende, cómo cuidarlo y conteste las preguntas que le haga. Puede hablar de las máquinas y los aparatos que se dan a continuación u otros de su invención.

una bicicleta	un amplificador	una calculadora
una nevera	un televisor	una lavadora
una máquina de escribir	una impresora	un ventilador

MODELO: E1: *Esta bicicleta está casi nueva aunque tiene tres años. Los cambios funcionan perfectamente.*
E2: *¿Necesita cuidados especiales?*
E1: *No, con tal de que la trate bien, no tendrá ningún problema.*

D. En cadena. Hay quienes opinan que todos tendremos que saber usar una computadora. ¿Sabe Ud. usar una? Si contesta que sí, diga por qué o para qué decidió aprender su manejo. Si contesta que no, diga por qué no, o bajo qué condiciones aprendería.

MODELO: E1: *Yo aprendí a usar una computadora porque mis padres insistieron en que lo hiciera.*
E2: *Yo no sé usar una computadora, y sólo voy a aprender cuando no me quede más remedio.*

E. Pidiendo ayuda. Imagínese que Ud. compró un equipo estereofónico, pero ha tenido que volver a la tienda a causa de algunas dificultades. Con un(a) compañero(a) de clase, desarrolle un breve diálogo utilizando las ideas siguientes u otras de su invención. Explique su problema, cómo intentó resolverlo y pida ayuda al(a la) dependiente(a).

el amplificador *amplifier*	el cartucho *cartridge*
el plato giratorio *turntable*	la grabadora *tape recorder*
el sintonizador *tuner*	el altavoz *speaker*

MODELO: Ud. tuvo problemas con la instalación del cartucho.
Dependiente(a): *¿En qué puedo servirle?*
Usted: *Tuve problemas al instalar este cartucho. Aunque leí las instrucciones con cuidado, no pude hacerlo correctamente. Yo quisiera devolvérselo a menos que me pueda ayudar.*
Dependiente(a): *Bueno, en primer lugar, debiera...*

1. El amplificador no se enciende.
2. El plato giratorio no da vueltas.
3. El sintonizador no mantiene la correcta sintonización después de varios minutos.
4. Los altavoces no suenan tan bien en casa como en la tienda.
5. La grabadora destruye la cinta que Ud. usa.
6. Ud. revisó la cuenta y cree que le cobraron demasiado dinero.

CAPÍTULO 12

◆

¿Cómo será el futuro?

Visión de una colonia espacial del siglo XXI, según ingenieros aeronáuticos de la NASA.

Conversación

1. En su opinión, ¿qué problemas deberemos resolver para tener un futuro mejor? ¿Cree Ud. que se resolverán problemas como la contaminación, la paz mundial, la sobrepoblación? ¿Por qué sí o por qué no?
2. ¿Qué avances cree que veremos en la medicina? ¿Habrá una cura para todas las enfermedades? ¿Subirá el promedio de años de vida? Explique.
3. ¿Es importante la exploración del espacio? ¿Por qué? ¿Qué beneficios no relacionados con el espacio nos ha traído hasta ahora?
4. ¿Le gusta pensar en cómo será la vida en el futuro? ¿Lee novelas de ciencia ficción? ¿Cuál es su fantasía más grande con respecto a su propia vida en el futuro?
5. Mire la fotografía de la página anterior. ¿Qué aspectos de la colonia espacial diseñada por los ingenieros le atraen? ¿Qué aspectos le disgustan?
6. Si Ud. tuviera la oportunidad, ¿viviría en una colonia espacial? Dé razones.

Vocabulario temático

aparición, la appearance
astronauta, el(la) astronaut
avance, el advance
cohete, el rocket
colonia, la colony, community
contaminación, la pollution
cura, la cure
desarme, el disarmament
desperdicio, el waste, refuse
ecología, la ecology
espacio, el space
especie, la species
fase, la phase
futurología, la futurology
índice, el index
invento, el invention
mantenimiento, el maintenance
meta, la goal
promedio, el average
sobrepoblación, la overpopulation
superpotencia, la superpower
tratado, el treaty, agreement
videoteléfono, el video telephone

agotar to use up, to exhaust
apoyar to support, to be in favor of

colonizar to colonize
contaminar to pollute
descubrir to discover
inquietar to worry, to upset
maximizar to maximize

extraterrestre extraterrestrial
factible feasible
humanizante humanizing
imprevisto(a) unforeseen
interplanetario(a) interplanetary
subterráneo(a) underground

desarme nuclear, el nuclear disarmament
energía solar, la solar energy
estación de mando, la command center
estar a punto de to be about to
fuente de energía, la energy source
medidas de seguridad, las security measures
nave espacial, la spaceship
preservación del ambiente, la environmental protection
recurso natural, el natural resource

I. Perfect tenses of the subjunctive

(Gilberto y Carolina son un matrimonio que vive en el año 2030. Gilberto, un científico, está a punto de comenzar un turno de seis meses en una colonia experimental submarina.)

Carolina: No te preocupes, mi amor. Es natural que **hayas estado** un poco nervioso en estos últimos días.

Gilberto: Sí, sé que ando muy nervioso. Siento mucho que **hayas tenido** que soportar mi mal humor.

Carolina: Recuerdo que estabas igual de nervioso la primera vez. Te gustó que te **hubieran seleccionado,** pero estabas muy preocupado.

Gilberto: He estado en esa colonia muchas veces, pero no creo que me **haya acostumbrado** totalmente a vivir bajo el agua. ¡Ojalá me **hubieran mandado** a una colonia espacial!

Carolina: No digas eso; las colonias submarinas son más seguras. No conozco a nadie que **haya ido** al espacio y le **haya gustado** vivir allí.

A. *Forms of the perfect tenses of the subjunctive*

Present perfect	Past perfect (-ra)	Past perfect (-se)
haya terminado	hubiera terminado	hubiese terminado
hayas terminado	hubieras terminado	hubieses terminado
haya terminado	hubiera terminado	hubiese terminado
hayamos terminado	hubiéramos terminado	hubiésemos terminado
hayáis terminado	hubierais terminado	hubieseis terminado
hayan terminado	hubieran terminado	hubiesen terminado

1. The present perfect subjunctive is formed with a present subjunctive form of the auxiliary verb **haber** + a past participle. (See *Capítulo 8.1* for regular and irregular past participles.)

Es una lástima que no te **haya interesado** mucho el libro sobre futurología que te pasé. Siento que todavía no lo **hayas terminado** de leer, pero tendré que devolverlo a la biblioteca hoy.

It's a pity the book on futurology I gave you hasn't interested you much. I'm sorry you haven't finished reading it yet, but I'll have to return it to the library today.

2. The past perfect subjunctive is formed with the imperfect subjunctive of **haber** + a past participle. Either the **-ra** or **-se** endings of the imperfect subjunctive of **haber** may be used; however, the **-ra** endings are more common, especially in the spoken language.

Muchos esperaban que para ahora ya **hubieran colonizado** el espacio y **hubieran fundado** pequeñas ciudades allí.

Many were hoping that by now they would have colonized space and founded small cities there.

B. *Use of the present perfect subjunctive*

1. The present perfect subjunctive may be used in a dependent clause that requires the subjunctive. The main verb may be in the present, present perfect, future, future perfect, or in a command form.

Ha sido una gran sorpresa que **hayan dejado** de construir casas subterráneas en el desierto. En el futuro, la gente exigirá viviendas que **hayan sido** equipadas para soportar el calor del desierto.

No esperes que dentro de poco **hayan revolucionado** la arquitectura.

It's been a great surprise that they've stopped building underground homes in the desert. In the future, people will demand houses that have been equipped to stand desert heat.

Don't expect that they will have revolutionized architecture in a short while.

2. When the present perfect subjunctive refers to a recent past event, it corresponds chronologically to the present perfect indicative. The action occurs prior to that of the time expressed by the main verb.

—Mi hermano dice que **ha comprado** varios libros sobre exploración submarina en la Librería Don Quijote.

—Pues, dudo que los **haya comprado** allí, porque esa librería se especializa en literatura clásica.

My brother says he's bought several books on underwater exploration at the Don Quijote bookstore.

Well, I doubt he bought them there because that bookstore specializes in classical literature.

3. When the present perfect subjunctive refers to an event that may or will have happened before a point of reference in the future, it corresponds chronologically to the future perfect indicative.

—¿Crees que **habrán resuelto** el problema de la contaminación del ambiente dentro de cincuenta años?

—No, me parece dudoso que lo **hayan resuelto** para entonces.

Do you think they'll have solved the problem of environmental pollution within fifty years?

No, it seems doubtful to me that they'll have solved it by then.

4. The present perfect subjunctive is used in independent clauses after **ojalá (que),** **tal vez,** and **quizá(s)** to express a conjecture or wish about a future or past action.

—Ojalá (que) la energía nuclear **haya resuelto** muchas de nuestras necesidades para el año 2000.	*I hope nuclear energy will have solved many of our needs by the year 2000.*
—Y ojalá (que) **hayan tomado** medidas de seguridad con las plantas que ya han construido.	*And I hope they will have taken safety measures with the plants they have already built.*

C. *Use of the past perfect subjunctive*

1. The past perfect subjunctive may be used in dependent clauses that require the subjunctive; the main verb may be in the past (preterit, imperfect, past perfect) or in the conditional or conditional perfect.

Cuando visitamos las ruinas de Machu Picchu, mucha gente dudó que seres extraterrestres nos **hubieran visitado** y **hubieran construido** esa ciudad. Otros, sin embargo, dijeron que no les habría sorprendido que seres de otros planetas **hubieran vivido** entre nosotros.	*When we visited the ruins of Machu Picchu, many people doubted that beings from outer space had visited us and had built that city. Others, however, said that it wouldn't have surprised them if (that) beings from other planets had lived among us.*

2. When the past perfect subjunctive refers to an event that may have or has happened prior to the time expressed by the main verb, it corresponds chronologically to the past perfect indicative.

No sabía que te **habías interesado** en la ecología.	*I didn't know you had become interested in ecology.*
Me sorprendió que te **hubieras interesado** en la ecología.	*It surprised me that you had become interested in ecology.*

3. When the past perfect subjunctive refers to an event that may or will occur before a point of reference in the future, it corresponds chronologically to the conditional perfect of the indicative.

—¿Pensabas que **habríamos visto** grandes avances en la medicina para fines de los años 80?	*Did you think we would have seen many advances in medicine by the end of the '80s?*
—No, nunca creí que **hubiéramos visto** mucho para entonces.	*No, I never thought we would have seen much by then.*

4. The past perfect subjunctive is used in independent clauses after **ojalá (que), tal vez,** and **quizá(s)** to express a wish about a past action that is contrary to what actually happened.

Con más tiempo, quizá **hubiéramos hecho** más para proteger a los animales y tal vez **hubiéramos salvado** algunas especies.

With more time, maybe we could have done more to protect animals, and perhaps we would have saved some species.

See Section II of this chapter for use of the past perfect subjunctive in contrary-to-fact statements.

Comprehension questions

1. Would you use the present perfect indicative **ha visto** or the present perfect subjunctive **haya visto** in the following sentences? **Dice que todavía no _____ la nueva película sobre los extraterrestres. Es extraño que todavía no _____ la nueva película sobre los extraterrestres.**

2. Is the present perfect subjunctive **haya asistido** or the past perfect subjunctive **hubiera asistido** used in the following sentences? **Me alegro de que mi hermana _____ a la conferencia sobre la sobrepoblación la semana pasada. Me alegré de que mi hermana _____ a la conferencia sobre la sobrepoblación la semana pasada.**

3. Would you use the present perfect subjunctive **hayan instalado** or the past perfect subjunctive **hubieran instalado** in the following sentences? **¡Ojalá (que) dentro de poco _____ vídeos en nuestras salas de clase! ¡Ojalá (que) el año pasado _____ vídeos en nuestras salas de clase!**

4. In the dialogue at the beginning of this section, Carolina says: **«Te gustó que te hubieran seleccionado...».** Can the present perfect subjunctive **hayan seleccionado** be used in this same context? Explain.

Ejercicios

A. Imagínese que vive en el siglo XXI y que su esposo(a) trabaja desde hace un mes en una colonia experimental submarina. Ha pasado una semana sin que lo(la) llame a Ud. Especule sobre las posibles razones de su silencio, comenzando sus frases con **Es posible, Es probable** o **Puede ser.**

MODELO: estar más ocupado de lo que pensaba
          Es posible que haya estado más ocupado(a) de lo que pensaba.

1. tener problemas imprevistos
2. enfermarse de repente
3. no poder conectar con la tierra
4. salir a fotografiar la zona
5. llamar cuando (yo) estaba fuera
6. asumir nuevas responsabilidades

B. Por fin lo(la) ha llamado su esposo(a) desde la colonia submarina. Exprese sus sentimientos frente a los comentarios que le hace a Ud., usando **Me sorprende, Me molesta, Siento, Qué bueno/bien, Me alegra,** según el modelo.

MODELO: Terminé la primera fase de pruebas.
¡Qué bien que la hayas terminado!

1. Últimamente me he sentido mal por la falta de movimiento.
2. Decidí hacer ejercicio en el gimnasio todos los días.
3. Descubrí unas extrañas plantas desconocidas.
4. No conseguí la ayuda que quería para terminar los análisis.
5. No tuve ni un día libre durante la última semana y media.
6. Ayer encontré a un colega que puede ayudarme en el laboratorio.

C. Ud. asistió a un congreso sobre problemas de ecología porque le interesa ese tema. Cuéntele a un(a) compañero(a) las cosas que le parecieron bien y las que no, usando **Me alegró, Me pareció estupendo, No me gustó** o **Me molestó** y añadiendo una razón que apoye su opinión.

MODELO: Se habían propuesto varias soluciones concretas para eliminar la contaminación del agua.
Me alegró que se hubieran propuesto varias soluciones para eliminar la contaminación del agua. Ya era tiempo de que se resolviera ese problema.

1. El director no había dado mucho tiempo para preguntas.
2. Habían decidido dedicar más fondos al estudio de la sobrepoblación.
3. Los delegados no habían apoyado restricciones más estrictas sobre los automóviles.
4. No se había dicho nada nuevo sobre la preservación de las zonas forestales.
5. Los participantes habían insistido en volver a reunirse dentro de seis meses.
6. El comité ejecutivo había anunciado otra reunión a nivel nacional.

D. Converse con un(a) compañero(a) de clase sobre la posibilidad de que dentro de cien años hayamos hecho las siguientes cosas. Empiece la respuesta con **no creo, dudo, es posible, es probable, ojalá** y termine dando una razón para su opinión.

MODELO: agotar los recursos naturales
E1:   *¿Crees que habremos agotado los recursos naturales dentro de cien años?*
E2:   *Francamente, yo dudo que para entonces los hayamos agotado. Los científicos siempre descubren nuevas soluciones a nuestros problemas.*

1. eliminar el hambre
2. lograr el desarme nuclear
3. conseguir la paz mundial
4. instituir una semana de trabajo de tres días
5. salvar las especies en peligro de extinción
6. establecer colonias en algunos de los planetas

II. Si-clauses

(Una estudiante de arquitectura habla de su visión del futuro.)

A menudo dibujo en mi mente planos de lo que serán las ciudades futuras. En primer lugar, no veo centros urbanos inmensos. Muchos creen que **si** no **se hubiera producido** este desarrollo incontrolable de las grandes ciudades, nunca **habríamos tenido** los graves problemas socioeconómicos que ahora nos inquietan tanto. Veo ciudades humanas, con proporciones humanas y humanizantes. Áreas verdes armoniosamente distribuidas, viviendas en que se maximiza el empleo de la luz y de la energía solar. Ah, **si** Ud. sólo **pudiera** ver mis ciudades imaginarias, **querría,** como yo, poder vivir hasta ese tiempo futuro.

A. *Conditional sentences*

A conditional sentence consists of a main clause and a dependent clause introduced by **si.** A conditional sentence may express a situation that is factual or that is likely to occur, or may express a situation that is contrary to fact or unlikely to happen. A **si**-clause may be used before or after the main clause with no change in meaning.

Si ha habido logros en la lucha contra el cáncer, también ha habido decepciones.	*If there have been successes in the fight against cancer, there have also been disappointments.* (fact)
Si recibimos suficientes fondos, podremos continuar con nuestra investigación sobre las causas del cáncer.	*If we receive enough funds, we will be able to continue our investigation on the causes of cancer.* (likely to happen)
Habríamos avanzado más con nuestra investigación si hubiéramos tenido más dinero.	*We would have made more progress in our research if we had had more money.* (contrary to fact)

B. *Si-clauses in the indicative*

1. The indicative is used in the **si**-clause and in the main clause to express *facts.* Various combinations of tenses are possible, and usage is similar to English.

Antes **solía** correr por las tardes **si hacía** buen tiempo. Ahora sólo **corro si** el índice de contaminación **es** bajo.	*Before, I used to run in the afternoons if the weather was nice. Now I run only if the pollution index is low.*

Si ahora **hay** más conciencia con respecto a la preservación del ambiente, **se debe** a las muchas campañas publicitarias.

If there is more awareness now about environmental protection, it is due to the many publicity campaigns.

2. To refer to an event that is probable or likely to occur in the future, the verb in the **si**-clause is in the present indicative, and the verb of the main clause is in the present or future tense or is a command form. The verb in a **si**-clause is never in the present subjunctive.

Si **termino** el trabajo esta tarde, **voy** a la conferencia sobre la arquitectura del futuro.

If I finish my work this afternoon, I'm going to the lecture on the architecture of the future.

Si tú también **vas** a esa conferencia, **llámame** antes de salir e iré contigo.

If you're also going to that lecture, call me before leaving and I'll go with you.

Si no **podemos** ir esta noche, **iremos** a la conferencia de la semana próxima.

If we can't go tonight, we'll go to next week's lecture.

C. *Contrary-to-fact statements*

1. To refer to a situation that is contrary to fact or highly unlikely to happen in the present or in the future, the verb of the **si**-clause is in the imperfect subjunctive and that of the main clause is generally in the conditional.

Si **existieran** vehículos interplanetarios, **iría** a Marte ahora mismo.

If there were interplanetary vehicles, I would go to Mars right now.

Si **pudiera** recorrer ese planeta, **exploraría** sus canales.

If I could travel around that planet, I would explore its canals.

2. To refer to a past situation that never took place and therefore is contrary to fact, the **si**-clause is in the past perfect subjunctive and the main clause is usually in the conditional perfect.

Si **hubieran existido** los vehículos interplanetarios cuando yo era niño, **habría sido** astronauta.

If there had been interplanetary vehicles when I was a child, I would have been an astronaut.

Habría viajado por todo el sistema solar **si hubiera sido** posible.

I would have traveled all around the solar system if it had been possible.

D. *Como si clauses*

The conjunction **como si** (*as if*) can also be used in a dependent clause to express a contrary-to-fact situation. **Como si** + the imperfect subjunctive refers to a contrary-to-fact situation in the present. **Como si** + the past perfect subjunctive refers to a contrary-to-fact situation in the past.

¿Por qué me miras así, **como si** yo **fuera** un ser extraterrestre?

Why are you looking at me that way, as if I were an extraterrestrial?

¿No me reconoces? Actúas **como si** nunca antes me **hubieras visto.**

Don't you recognize me? You're acting as if you had never seen me before.

Summary of si-clauses

Usage	Si-clause	Main clause	Examples
Facts: present and past	Indicative	Indicative	**Si** no **hemos colonizado** el espacio, **es** porque tenemos miedo.
Likely future events	Present indicative	Future, present indicative, command	**Si** no **queremos** destruir la especie humana, **limitemos** las armas nucleares.
Contrary to fact: present	Imperfect subjunctive	Conditional	**Si hubiera** menos restricciones, más industrias **contaminarían** el ambiente.
Contrary to fact: past	Past perfect subjunctive	Conditional perfect	**Si** la gente **hubiera mostrado** más interés, **se habría utilizado** más la energía solar.

Usage	Como si clause	Examples
Contrary to fact: present	Imperfect subjunctive	Algunos países usan petróleo **como si** esta fuente de energía **fuera** inagotable.
Contrary to fact: past	Past perfect subjunctive	Hablas de la colonización del espacio **como si** ya **hubieran fundado** ciudades espaciales.

Comprehension questions

1. Which of the following two sentences expresses a factual situation in the past? **Si no había contaminación, salíamos a pasear. Si no hubiera contaminación, saldríamos a pasear.** What does the other sentence express?

2. Is the future **necesitaremos** or the conditional **necesitaríamos** used in the following sentences? **Si quisiéramos viajar a otros planetas, _____ vehículos interplanetarios. Si queremos conocer otros planetas, _____ vehículos interplanetarios.**

3. Would you use the present indicative **si controlamos** or the imperfect subjunctive **si controláramos** to replace the phrase **siempre que controlemos** in the following sentence? **No tendremos contaminación, siempre que controlemos el desarrollo de las industrias.**

4. In the last sentence of the narration at the beginning of this section, the architecture student uses the verb forms **pudiera** and **querría**. Explain why she does not use the verb forms **puede** and **querrá**.

La idea de que se logre crear un robot que simplifique nuestras vidas intriga tanto a niños como a adultos. (Los Ángeles, California)

Ejercicios

A. Comente a un(a) amigo(a) lo que Ud. hará durante la semana si tiene tiempo. Después, repita el ejercicio diciendo lo que haría si tuviera tiempo.

MODELO: leer la novela de ciencia ficción que me recomendaste ayer
Si tengo tiempo esta semana, leeré (voy a leer) la novela de ciencia ficción que me recomendaste ayer. (Si tuviera tiempo esta semana, leería la novela de ciencia ficción que me recomendaste ayer.)

1. asistir a la reunión del nuevo club de futurología
2. escuchar la conferencia del experto en problemas ecológicos
3. escribir una carta al periódico sobre la gente que echa desperdicios al río
4. informarme mejor de la actual posición del gobierno sobre el control de armamentos
5. hacer algunos dibujos de ciudades futurísticas para la clase de arquitectura
6. recorrer la exhibición sobre vehículos interplanetarios

B. Exprese de una manera apropiada los resultados de las siguientes especulaciones sobre la vida del siglo XXI.

MODELO 1: Si no tenemos mucho espacio para casas nuevas,...
Si no tenemos mucho espacio para casas nuevas, construiremos edificios más altos.

MODELO 2: Si se desarrollaran otras fuentes de energía,...
Si se desarrollaran otras fuentes de energía, no tendríamos que depender tanto del petróleo.

1. Si resolvemos todos los problemas de la contaminación del ambiente,...
2. Si los científicos se dedicaran a resolver los problemas médicos más serios,...
3. Si el gobierno logra crear oportunidades de empleo para todos,...
4. Si ya no hubiera ni cáncer ni artritis,...
5. Si alguien pudiera descubrir la causa del crimen,...
6. Si ningún país usa la bomba atómica otra vez,...
7. Si elimináramos del mundo la pobreza y el hambre,...

C. Hace diez años que Ud. terminó su carrera universitaria. En un momento de nostalgia, Ud. recuerda cómo eran las condiciones de sus años universitarios. Represente la situación con un(a) compañero(a) de clase, según el modelo.

MODELO: tener sueño durante una clase
E1: *Dime, ¿qué hacías si tenías sueño durante una clase?*
E2: *Si yo tenía sueño durante una clase, hacía muchas preguntas al profesor para despertarme.*

1. faltarte dinero para tus necesidades
2. no sentirte muy bien
3. estar aburrido(a)
4. tener un examen casi imposible
5. no haber suficiente tiempo para estudiar y llevar una vida social
6. sacar una nota mediocre

D. Imagínese que Ud. vive en la primera ciudad espacial y llama a un(a) amigo(a) que vive en la tierra. Cuéntele algo de su vida, usando las siguientes indicaciones.

MODELO: El aire es muy puro; respiro como si... (vivir en una isla desierta; haber desaparecido las enfermedades respiratorias)
El aire es muy puro; respiro como si viviera en una isla desierta y hubieran desaparecido las enfermedades respiratorias.

1. Hay de todo: tiendas, diversiones, campo, parques; es como si... (ser una ciudad terrestre; nosotros vivir en Chicago; nunca haber dejado mi casa)
2. Los robots hacen gran parte del trabajo de mantenimiento como si... (tener mentes propias; ser seres humanos; siempre haber hecho este tipo de trabajo)
3. Yo vivo como si... (ser un rey/una reina; no tener ningún problema; casi nada haber cambiado en mi vida)

III. Sequence of tenses

(Julia Vergara, autora de famosas novelas de ciencia ficción, es entrevistada por Nicolás Ocaño, reportero para un periódico universitario.)

Nicolás: Bueno, si **fuera** posible, **quisiera** que me **explicara** cómo y cuándo se **interesó** en la ciencia ficción.

Julia: ¡Qué interesante que me lo haya preguntado! Cuando **era** niñita, mis padres siempre me **llevaban** a museos y a exhibiciones científicas. Si yo **tenía** preguntas, siempre me **daban** una respuesta aunque **fuera** difícil.

Nicolás: **Es** evidente que sus padres **se preocuparon** de cultivar su mente.

Julia: Desde luego que sí. Y quizá lo más importante **fue** que me **animaron** a imaginarme las diferentes formas que **podría** tomar el mundo del futuro.

Nicolás: En sus libros, Ud. **pinta** una civilización futura que **vive** más en armonía con el medio ambiente que la de ahora. En su opinión, ¿qué **deberían** hacer los jóvenes de ahora para que se **realizara** algo así?

Julia: Exactamente lo que muchos de Uds. hacen ahora: estudiar mucho sin dejar de soñar con algo mejor. Todo es posible.

A. *Main verb and dependent clause in the indicative*

Tenses of the indicative

Present, present perfect	**exploro, he explorado**
Future, future perfect	**exploraré, habré explorado**
Imperfect, past perfect	**exploraba, había explorado**
Preterit, preterit perfect	**exploré, hube explorado**
Conditional, conditional perfect	**exploraría, habría explorado**

1. When both the main verb of a sentence and that of the dependent clause are in the indicative, the tenses combine freely, provided that the combination is logical.

Parece que las conferencias sobre el control de armamentos no **producen** resultados concretos.

It seems that conferences on arms control don't produce concrete results.

Pensamos que las superpotencias no **llegarán** a ningún acuerdo. El año pasado, todos **observaron** que ningún lado **hizo** concesiones.

We think the superpowers won't reach any agreement. Last year, everyone noticed that neither side made any concessions.

Con más concesiones de las superpotencias, todos **creerían** que un desarme total **es** una meta factible.

With more concessions from the superpowers, everyone would believe that a total disarmament is a feasible goal.

2. Command forms combine with the tenses of the present, the future, the past, or the conditional.

Dime qué **haces/harás/hiciste/ hacías/harías.**

Tell me what you are doing/will do/ did/were doing/would do.

B. *Main verb in the indicative, dependent clause in the subjunctive*

Main verb	Dependent clause
Present indicative	Present subjunctive
Present perfect indicative	Present perfect subjunctive
	Imperfect subjunctive

1. If the main verb in the sentence is in the present or present perfect indicative, the verb in the dependent clause is usually in the present or present perfect subjunctive.

Es bueno que **creen** nuevas áreas verdes en la ciudad.

It's good that they create new green areas in the city.

Es una lástima que no **hayan construido** más parques en la ciudad.

It's a pity that they haven't built more parks in the city.

Me **ha sorprendido** que el índice de contaminación no **aumente.**

It has surprised me that the pollution index doesn't increase.

2. A main verb in the present or present perfect may also be followed by a dependent verb in the imperfect subjunctive; in this case, the event expressed by the dependent clause occurred prior to that of the main verb.

Lamento que el año pasado nuestra compañía no nos **permitiera** trabajar en la computadora desde casa.

I regret that last year our company didn't allow us to work on a computer from home.

Main verb	Dependent clause
Future indicative	Present subjunctive
Future perfect indicative	Present perfect subjunctive
Command	

3. If the main verb is in the future or future perfect, the verb of the dependent clause is in the present or present perfect subjunctive.

Será necesario que **resolvamos** pronto el problema de la sobrepoblación.

It'll be necessary for us to (that we) soon solve the overpopulation problem.

Será necesario que antes de diez años **hayamos resuelto** el problema de la sobrepoblación.

Before ten years it'll be necessary to have solved (that we've solved) the overpopulation problem.

Habrán pasado muchos años sin que **resolvamos** nada.

Many years will have elapsed without us solving anything.

4. When the main verb is a command, sequencing usually follows the pattern of verbs in the future: the verb in the dependent clause is in the present or present perfect subjunctive.

No **esperes** que las superpotencias **lleguen** a un acuerdo sobre el control de armamentos.

Don't expect the superpowers to reach an agreement on arms control.

No **esperes** que las superpotencias **hayan llegado** a algún acuerdo en su última reunión.

Don't expect the superpowers to have reached an agreement at their last meeting.

Main verb	Dependent clause
Imperfect indicative	Imperfect subjunctive
Preterit indicative	Past perfect subjunctive
Past perfect indicative	
Preterit perfect indicative	

5. If the main verb is in the past, the verb of the dependent clause is in the imperfect or past perfect subjunctive.

Necesitábamos una compañía que se **especializara** en energía nuclear.

We needed a company that specialized in nuclear energy.

Queríamos una compañía que **hu-biera hecho** avances en ese campo.

We wanted a company that had made progress in that field.

No **encontramos** ninguna compañía que **ofreciera** medidas de seguridad adecuadas.

We didn't find any company that offered appropriate security measures.

Main verb	Dependent clause
Conditional	Imperfect subjunctive
Conditional perfect	Past perfect subjunctive

6. If the main verb is in the conditional or conditional perfect, the verb in the dependent clause is in the imperfect or past perfect subjunctive.

Nos **gustaría** que la energía nuclear no **creara** peligro.

We would like nuclear energy not to create any danger.

Según algunos, **habría sido** mejor que nunca **hubieran descubierto** el secreto del átomo.

According to some, it would have been better that they had never discovered the secret of the atom.

C. Simple versus compound tenses of the subjunctive

1. The simple tenses of the subjunctive (present and imperfect subjunctive) refer to a time that coincides with or comes after that of the main verb.

Dudo que el índice de contaminación **sea** alto hoy.

I doubt that the pollution index will be (is) high today.

Dudo que el índice de contaminación **sea** alto mañana.

I doubt that the pollution index will be high tomorrow.

Era posible que en ese entonces nadie **notara** los efectos de la erosión.

It was possible that at that time nobody noticed the effects of erosion.

Era necesario que en el futuro **controlaran** los efectos de la erosión.

It was necessary to control (that they control) the effects of erosion in the future.

2. The imperfect subjunctive may also refer to a time that is prior to that of the main verb.

Me alegré de que mi robot **decidiera** tomarse un día libre esa semana. **Es** posible que el pobre **estuviera** cansado.

I was glad my robot decided to take a day off that week. It's possible that the poor thing was tired.

3. The compound tenses of the subjunctive (present perfect and past perfect subjunctive) usually refer to a time prior to that of the main verb.

Dudo que **hayan puesto** a la venta los videoteléfonos ayer.

I doubt video telephones went on sale yesterday.

Dudaba que **hubieran puesto** a la venta los videoteléfonos el día anterior.

I doubted video telephones had gone on sale the day before.

4. The compound tenses of the subjunctive may also refer to a future event that will have been completed prior to another future event or prior to a specific time in the future.

Me **parece** dudoso que para el año que viene todo el mundo **haya aceptado** los videoteléfonos.

It seems doubtful to me that by next year everybody will have accepted video telephones.

Me **parecía** dudoso que en un futuro próximo todo el mundo **hubiera aceptado** los videoteléfonos.

It seemed doubtful to me that in a near future everybody would have accepted video telephones.

Comprehension questions

1. Would you use **desarrollen, desarrollarán** or **desarrollaran** in the following sentence? Explain why. **Tendrán que inventar mejores naves espaciales antes de que se _____ los viajes interplanetarios.**

2. Which form, **tengamos** or **hayamos tenido,** is used in the sentence **No creo que _____ mucha contaminación el mes pasado?** And in **No creo que _____ mucha contaminación mañana?**

3. Would you use **se pusieran** or **se hubieran puesto** in the following sentence? **Habría sido estupendo que las superpotencias _____ de acuerdo en la última conferencia sobre el control de armamentos.** Explain why.

4. What form of **poder** is required in each of the following sentences? **Dudaban que la agencia del gobierno les _____ dar una respuesta pronto. Dudaban que la agencia del gobierno les _____ dar una respuesta la semana anterior.**

5. In the dialogue at the beginning of this section, Nicolás asks: **«... ¿qué deberían hacer los jóvenes de ahora para que se realizara algo así»?** If Nicolás had used **deben** instead of **deberían,** what form of **realizar** would he have used?

Ejercicios

A. Exprese opiniones variadas sobre el control de armamentos, cambiando el verbo indicado por las expresiones entre paréntesis. Haga los cambios necesarios en las cláusulas subordinadas usando el subjuntivo o el indicativo, según el contexto.

MODELO: **Parece** que las conferencias sobre el control de armamentos producen resultados concretos. (Esperaba, Parecía, Es maravilloso)
Esperaba que las conferencias sobre el control de armamentos produjeran resultados concretos.
Parecía que las conferencias sobre el control de armamentos producían resultados concretos.
Es maravilloso que las conferencias sobre el control de armamentos produzcan resultados concretos.

1. **Es triste** que las superpotencias no lleguen a acuerdos realmente significativos. (Era una lástima, Queda claro, Sería desafortunado, Fue horrible, Creo)
2. Nos **gustaría** que se resolviera la situación. (gusta, alegró, informaron, agradará, dirán, encantaba)
3. El senado **quiere** que haya más progreso este año. (exigió, no duda, deseaba, sabe, recomendaría, va a insistir)

B. Imagínese que Ud. le cuenta a un(a) amigo(a) su opinión de la película futurística *Mundos que chocan* que vio hace varios días. Complete las oraciones de un modo apropiado.

Pues, yo había decidido no ver esa película, pero Daniel e Inés insistieron en que los (acompañar) _____, de manera que (ir) _____. Pero te digo que si yo (haber) _____ sabido cómo (ir) _____ a resultar, nunca (haber) _____ asistido. Primero salió un grupo de científicos totalmente locos que (querer) _____ hacer experimentos sobre la trayectoria de las órbitas de varios planetas. A pesar de que uno de ellos, Antonio Cuerdo, les aconsejó que no lo (hacer) _____, siguieron adelante y (establecer) _____ estaciones con inmensos cohetes en seis planetas y tres lunas diferentes. Fue imposible que el pobre Antonio los (convencer) _____ del peligro de lo que hacían. Claro, como siempre, (haber) _____ una hermosa mujer, la novia de Antonio, que (estar) _____ en gran peligro. Al final, Antonio y su novia (lograr) _____ destruir la estación de mando de los villanos antes de que éstos (poder) _____ causar daños importantes. Entiéndeme, no es que no me (gustar) _____ las películas futurísticas; lo que pasa es que *Mundos que chocan* no (ser) _____ más que un melodrama de los más insípidos. La próxima vez, cuando Daniel e Inés me (pedir) _____ que los (acompañar) _____ al cine, voy a leer lo que dicen los críticos primero.

C. Reaccione de una manera personal a las siguientes opiniones. Trate de emplear frases como **Yo sé (sabía), No creo (creía), Dudo (Dudaba) mucho, Es (Era) cierto, Qué triste, Es (Era) ridículo,** o **Lamento (Lamentaba) mucho.**

MODELO: No se ha estudiado a fondo el problema de la sobrepoblación.
Lamento mucho que no se haya estudiado a fondo el problema de la
sobrepoblación. Es muy importante que se estudie pronto.

1. El promedio de vida en el año 2100 será 125 años.
2. Desarrollaron comercialmente un videoteléfono hace unos 20 años.
3. En el futuro habrá educación universitaria gratuita para todos.
4. El año pasado varios países más fabricaron armas nucleares.
5. La democracia parece más fuerte ahora en algunos países de Latinoamérica.
6. Dentro de diez años se habrá encontrado una cura para la diabetes.
7. Para el año 2000, muchos países más sacarán petróleo del fondo de los océanos.
8. El año pasado el gobierno permitió la construcción de industrias en varias zonas forestales.

IV. Making requests

(Durante el rodaje de una película de ciencia ficción)

Director: *(Gritando por el megáfono)* ¡No, no, no! ¡Esa escena salió muy lenta! Juanito, ¿**me acercas** un poco más esa máquina de viento? Gracias. Teresa, ¿**podrías poner**le un poco más de sombra a los ojos de Laura?

Julio: Con tantas interrupciones, no terminaremos nunca. Oiga, Manolo, **haga el favor de echar**le más hielo a esta bebida y **de traer**me las zapatillas que dejé en mi habitación.

Director: ¡Les hace falta más brío a los actores! ¡Uds. **deben recordar** que ésta es una guerra cósmica, no un baile de enamorados!

Laura: ¡Qué sarcástico!, ¿verdad Julio? ¿**Podrías decir**le que dejara de usar ese tono con nosotros?

Director: *(Más tarde)* **Acérquense** todos. ¡**Escuchen**! ¡**Escuchen**! Vamos muy retrasados. **Tengan la bondad de llegar** mañana antes de las seis de la mañana. Y tú, Julio, ¿**quieres llegar** a tiempo esta vez? **No** nos **hagas** esperar como lo hiciste esta mañana.

A. *Commands*

1. A command is used to express a direct, straightforward request.

Trae el periódico y **busca** la sección con noticias de cine.

Bring the newspaper and look for the movie section (section with movie news).

Infórmate de lo que dicen sobre los efectos especiales de *La guerra cósmica.*

Find out what they say about special effects in "La guerra cósmica."

2. A command may be softened or made more polite by adding **por favor** anywhere in the sentence, but usually at the end.

Abra el periódico en la página siete, **por favor.**	*Open the newspaper to page seven, please.*
Lea, por favor, el artículo que aparece allí sobre nuevas fuentes de energía.	*Please read the article on new sources of energy that appears there.*

3. A more formal request is made by using the command form of expressions such as **hacer el favor de, tener la bondad de, servirse,** followed by an infinitive.

Tenga la bondad de llegar a tiempo mañana.	*Please be so kind as to arrive on time tomorrow.*
Sírvase firmar este contrato.	*Please sign this contract.*

4. The expression **haga el favor de** can be shortened to **favor de** followed by an infinitive.

Haga el favor de no fumar en este laboratorio.	*Please do not smoke in this lab.*
Favor de no fumar en este laboratorio.	*Please do not smoke in this lab.*

B. *Poder and querer + infinitive*

1. The verbs **poder** and **querer** followed by an infinitive are frequently used to make a direct request. To make a matter-of-fact, straightforward request, the present tense of **poder** or **querer** is used.

¿Puede Ud. **informarme** acerca de las agencias gubernativas que se encargan de la preservación del ambiente? **¿Quiere** Ud. también **darme** el nombre del director de la agencia?	*Can you give me information about the government agencies in charge of environmental protection? Will you also give me the agency director's name?*

2. The conditional or the imperfect subjunctive of **poder** or **querer** is used to make a more formal, polite request.

¿Podría (Pudiera) Ud. indicarme si está a la venta el videocassette de *La guerra cósmica?* **¿Querría (Quisiera)** también darme su catálogo?	*Could you tell me if you have on sale the video cassette "La guerra cósmica"? Would you also give me your catalogue?*

3. In informal language, a question in the present indicative can also be used to make a request.

Julio, ¿me **acercas** la máquina de viento, (por favor)?

Julio, will you (please) bring the wind machine near me?

C. *Deber* + *infinitive*

The verb **deber** followed by an infinitive may be used to make recommendations, suggestions, or implied requests in a more formal and elaborate way than a command. In the present indicative, **deber** generally expresses a forceful recommendation. In the conditional or imperfect subjunctive, **deber** usually expresses a softened, more polite recommendation or implied request.

Debemos preservar el ambiente.
Deberíamos (Debiéramos) hacer marchas de protesta.

We must protect the environment.
We should organize protest demonstrations.

D. *Verb of influencing* + *subjunctive*

A request can also be implied by using a verb or an expression of influencing such as **aconsejar, recomendar, sugerir** followed by a dependent clause in the subjunctive. To make a matter-of-fact request, the main verb is in the present indicative; the dependent verb is in the present subjunctive. To make a more polite request, the verb of influencing is in the conditional; the verb in the dependent clause is in the imperfect subjunctive. (See *Capítulo 9.2* for verbs and expressions of influencing.)

Le **recomiendo** que **conserve** energía.
Le **recomendaría** que **gastara** menos energía.

I recommend that you conserve energy.
I would recommend that you use less energy.

Comprehension questions

1. In the dialogue at the beginning of this section, the director makes the following request: «**Tengan la bondad de llegar mañana antes de las seis de la mañana**». Give a synonym for **Tengan la bondad de.**

2. How would you soften the following request? **¿Pueden Uds. decirnos cuándo llega el director?**

3. Which of the following requests would usually be considered more forceful? **Ud. debiera llamar a la agencia de preservación del ambiente. Ud. debe llamar a la agencia de preservación del ambiente.**

4. How would you rephrase the following command using the verb **sugerir**? **Utilice la energía solar.**

5. Which of these two requests is a more informal way of asking someone to pass the newspaper? **¿Puedes pasarme el periódico? ¿Me pasas el periódico?**

Ejercicios

A. Imagínese que vive en el año 2050 y que acaba de comprar un robot, Centurión, para los quehaceres de casa. Funciona sólo a base de mandatos formales. Explíquele sus deberes alternando entre las expresiones **hacer el favor de, tener la bondad de** y **servirse.**

MODELO: Sáqueme las noticias mundiales de la computadora todas las tardes.
Haga el favor de sacarme las noticias mundiales de la computadora todas las tardes.

1. Sírvanos la cena a las seis.
2. Limpie la casa los sábados.
3. Pague las cuentas usando el teléfono computarizado el 15 y el 30 del mes.
4. Conteste el teléfono cada vez que suena.
5. Haga las compras por las mañanas.
6. Lave la ropa los lunes.

B. Ud. codirige el rodaje de una película de ciencia ficción titulada *La toma del planeta azul* como proyecto para una clase de cinematografía. Conteste las preguntas de distintos miembros del equipo alternando entre las diferentes formas posibles de **deber.**

MODELO: *E1:*   ¿Filmamos este segmento de nuevo?
E2:   *Sí, debemos (debiéramos, deberíamos) filmarlo de nuevo.*

1. ¿Pongo en marcha el robot?
2. ¿Traemos a los androides para la próxima escena?
3. ¿Hacemos la primera escena de la batalla cósmica mañana?
4. ¿Aviso al personal de efectos especiales que necesitamos otras naves espaciales más?
5. ¿Buscamos otro sitio mejor para filmar la escena de reconciliación?
6. ¿Le digo al artista de maquillaje que pinte de nuevo a la heroína?

C. Pida a las siguientes personas las cosas indicadas, usando un pedido con **querer** o **poder,** el presente de indicativo del verbo dado o un mandato. Varíe la forma de hacer los pedidos según requiera la situación.

MODELO: a un(a) amigo(a): dejarle sus notas de una clase; sacarle boletos para el concierto
Déjame tus notas de física. (¿Quieres dejarme tus notas de física?)
¿Me sacas boletos para el concierto del viernes? (¿Quisieras sacarme boletos para el concierto del viernes?)

1. a un(a) compañero(a) de apartamento: lavar los platos; recoger sus cosas de la sala de estar
2. a una profesora: darle a Ud. una extensión para un trabajo escrito; explicarle lo que Ud. tiene que hacer para el próximo proyecto
3. a sus padres: darle más dinero para libros; mandarle de casa su máquina de escribir
4. a un(a) amigo(a): pasarle a Ud. un trabajo a máquina; prestarle a Ud. un diccionario de español
5. a su robot: traerle a Ud. unos refrescos y patatas fritas; prepararle a Ud. un sándwich

V. Spanish equivalents of *short, long,* and *tall*

1. **Corto(a), breve,** and **largo(a)** are used to refer to short and long periods of time.

—No voy a hablar mucho; mi discurso es muy **corto (breve).**
I'm not going to speak a great deal; my speech is very short.
—¡Qué bien! No me gustan las conferencias **largas.**
That's great! I don't like long lectures.

2. The length of something or the relative distance between two points is expressed with **corto(a)** and **largo(a). Breve** is also used to refer to length or extension in the sense of *brief.*

Este brazo mecánico no alcanza; es demasiado **corto.**
This mechanical arm doesn't reach; it's too short.
El cohete es muy **largo.**
The rocket is very long.
Este artículo sobre los robots es muy **breve.**
This article on robots is very short (brief).

3. **Largo(a)** should not be confused with English *large* or *big,* which are expressed by **grande** in Spanish.

¡Qué **grandes** son las nuevas pantallas para los televisores!
How large the new television screens are!

4. **Alto(a)** and **bajo(a)** refer to the height of people and things. Note that **alto(a)** means *tall* when referring to people; it means *tall* or *high* when referring to things. Likewise **bajo(a)** means *short* when referring to people and may mean either *short* or *low* when referring to things.

¡Qué astronauta más **alto**!	*What a tall astronaut!*
Las ciudades del futuro tendrán muchos edificios **altos.**	*Future cities will have many tall (high) buildings.*
Un edificio de cincuenta pisos parecerá **bajo.**	*A fifty-story building will seem low (short).*

5. The expression **de largo** means *in length;* **de alto** means *in height.*

¿Cuántos metros **de largo** tiene esa plataforma espacial?	*How many meters long (in length) is that space platform?*
El cohete tiene doscientos metros **de alto.**	*The rocket is two hundred meters high (in height).*

Ejercicios

A. Indique qué palabra se usa en español para expresar las palabras indicadas.

1. I'm sure the discussion on space travel will be a *long* one.
2. He's too *short* to reach those reports on the highest shelf.
3. We need a *longer* and *higher* table for the buffet; that one is too *short* and *low*.
4. Do you remember how *long* the room was that we reserved for the discussion?
5. Congratulations! That was a *short* but effective presentation.
6. There's a robot with *long* arms and legs in the office? You're nuts!
7. It looks as though this lab coat is too *short* for me.

B. Dé la forma correcta de la palabra más apropiada, según el contexto. A veces hay más de una respuesta posible.

Acabo de leer un cuento de ciencia ficción (*short*) _____, pero buenísimo. Lo más increíble fue la aparición de un animal enorme: muy (*tall*) _____, muy (*long*) _____, en fin, muy, muy grande. Lo mejor de todo fue que el autor se ocupó del animal durante un tiempo muy (*long*) _____, sugiriendo, creo, que ese animal representaba a los seres humanos futuros. En otras palabras, ese animal habría sido el resultado de una serie muy (*long*) _____ de mutaciones causadas por la contaminación del ambiente. A pesar de ser puro cuento, me hizo una impresión muy grande.

Actividades para la comunicación

A. **Favor de...** Imagínese que Ud. va a pasar el próximo año en el extranjero. Está muy ocupado(a) haciendo todos los preparativos. Pida lo que necesita a las siguientes personas, usando una variedad de pedidos formales o informales, según el caso.

MODELO: una agente de viajes
Hágame el favor de reservarme un asiento de turista. ¿Podría ver si hay un vuelo temprano?

1. un taxista
2. un empleado en una tienda de equipaje
3. un empleado de banco donde Ud. quiere comprar cheques de viajero
4. una hermana a quien deja su coche
5. una peluquera
6. un hermano que ha ofrecido ayudarlo(la)
7. un empleado del Departamento de Estado donde Ud. quiere sacar un pasaporte

B. **Soñando.** ¿Qué haría Ud. y cómo cree que sería su vida si ahora mismo las siguientes cosas fueran parte de su vida diaria? Cuénteselo a un(a) compañero(a) de clase y hable también de otras cosas que cree que habrá en el futuro.

robots
educación universitaria por vídeo
computadoras para hacer las tareas
    domésticas

carros que vuelan a gran velocidad
videoteléfonos
viajes extraterrestres

MODELO: *Si tuviera un videoteléfono, lo usaría constantemente para conocer personalmente a las grandes estrellas de cine. También lo usaría para hablar con mis amigos.*

C. **Decisiones.** Piense Ud. en alguna decisión importantísima que tendrá que tomar y que afectará su vida futura. La decisión puede relacionarse con sus estudios, la selección de una carrera, un trabajo, algunas actividades extracurriculares, un matrimonio o cualquier otra cosa significativa. Piense en las ventajas y desventajas de tomar esa decisión y prepare unas líneas que reflejen sus pensamientos.

MODELO: *Si estudio unos años más, puedo graduarme y quizá conseguir un buen puesto, pero si dejara los estudios o si los interrumpiera, podría divertirme y conocer mejor el mundo.*

D. Opine Ud. Con un(a) compañero(a) de clase, haga y conteste las siguientes preguntas.

MODELO: *E1:*   ¿Crees que hay medidas de seguridad adecuadas para garantizar el cumplimiento de los tratados sobre armas nucleares? ¿Por qué opinas así?

　　　　　E2:   *No, yo no creo que haya buenas medidas de seguridad. Me parece casi imposible que las superpotencias descubran las violaciones; dudo mucho que lo puedan hacer en un futuro próximo.*

1. Si pudieras viajar en un vehículo interplanetario, ¿lo harías? ¿Por qué?
2. ¿Crees que algunos seres extraterrestres hayan visitado este planeta? ¿Crees que existan? ¿Se descubrirá vida o la posibilidad de vida en otros planetas?
3. ¿Esperabas que los científicos ya hubieran desarrollado un sistema de energía eficiente y barato? ¿Será importante para el futuro que se haga uso no sólo de la energía solar sino de otras formas de energía nuevas? Explica.
4. ¿Qué tipo de casa tendrías si pudieras elegir entre todos los estilos? ¿Cómo sería la casa de tus sueños?
5. ¿Temes que haya otra guerra mundial? Cuando eras niño(a), ¿temías que hubiera una guerra terrible antes de que fueras adulto(a)? ¿Qué temes acerca del futuro? ¿Qué deseas para el futuro?

E. En cadena. Piense Ud. en lo que quiere de aquí a cinco años y exprese su deseo con sus compañeros de clase en forma de cadena.

MODELO: E1:   *Ojalá que dentro de poco tiempo hayamos visto el fin del terrorismo.*

　　　　　E2:   *Pues, a mí me gustaría que se hicieran más avances en la medicina, especialmente con respecto al cáncer y a las enfermedades cardíacas.*

F. Entrevista a unos expertos. Imagínese que tres miembros de la clase son famosos autores que en sus obras comentan temas futurísticos. Entrevístelos, preguntándoles sobre su visión acerca de varios aspectos del futuro (modos de viajar, guerra o paz, viviendas, comodidades, diversiones), la formación de su punto de vista, los posibles cambios que ven para el futuro próximo y para el lejano también y cualquier otro tema que le interese a Ud.

MODELO: E1:   *¿Será posible que se invente una máquina que produzca energía barata?*

　　　　　E2:   *Dudo mucho que eso sea posible, pero si seguimos invirtiendo mucho dinero en la investigación, estoy seguro(a) de que se encontrarán nuevas fuentes de energía.*

Appendices

Verbs

1. Conjugation of regular verbs

	-ar *verbs*	**-er** *verbs*	**-ir** *verbs*
Infinitive	hablar	comer	vivir
Present participle	hablando	comiendo	viviendo
Past participle	hablado	comido	vivido

Simple tenses: Indicative mood

Present	hablo	como	vivo
	hablas	comes	vives
	habla	come	vive
	hablamos	comemos	vivimos
	habláis	coméis	vivís
	hablan	comen	viven
Imperfect	hablaba	comía	vivía
	hablabas	comías	vivías
	hablaba	comía	vivía
	hablábamos	comíamos	vivíamos
	hablabais	comíais	vivíais
	hablaban	comían	vivían
Preterit	hablé	comí	viví
	hablaste	comiste	viviste
	habló	comió	vivió
	hablamos	comimos	vivimos
	hablasteis	comisteis	vivisteis
	hablaron	comieron	vivieron
Future	hablaré	comeré	viviré
	hablarás	comerás	vivirás
	hablará	comerá	vivirá
	hablaremos	comeremos	viviremos
	hablaréis	comeréis	viviréis
	hablarán	comerán	vivirán
Conditional	hablaría	comería	viviría
	hablarías	comerías	vivirías
	hablaría	comería	viviría
	hablaríamos	comeríamos	viviríamos
	hablaríais	comeríais	viviríais
	hablarían	comerían	vivirían

Simple tenses: Subjunctive mood

Present	hable	coma	viva
	hables	comas	vivas
	hable	coma	viva
	hablemos	comamos	vivamos
	habléis	comáis	viváis
	hablen	coman	vivan

Imperfect (-ra forms)	hablara	comiera	viviera
	hablaras	comieras	vivieras
	hablara	comiera	viviera
	habláramos	comiéramos	viviéramos
	hablarais	comierais	vivierais
	hablaran	comieran	vivieran

Imperfect (-se forms)	hablase	comiese	viviese
	hablases	comieses	vivieses
	hablase	comiese	viviese
	hablásemos	comiésemos	viviésemos
	hablaseis	comieseis	vivieseis
	hablasen	comiesen	viviesen

Affirmative and negative commands

(tú)	habla, no hables	come, no comas	vive, no vivas
(vosotros)	hablad, no habléis	comed, no comáis	vivid, no viváis
(Ud.)	hable, no hable	coma, no coma	viva, no viva
(Uds.)	hablen, no hablen	coman, no coman	vivan, no vivan

Perfect tenses: Indicative mood

Perfect infinitive	haber hablado	haber comido	haber vivido
Perfect participle	habiendo hablado	habiendo comido	habiendo vivido

Present perfect	he hablado	he comido	he vivido
	has hablado	has comido	has vivido
	ha hablado	ha comido	ha vivido
	hemos hablado	hemos comido	hemos vivido
	habéis hablado	habéis comido	habéis vivido
	han hablado	han comido	han vivido

Past perfect	había hablado	había comido	había vivido
	habías hablado	habías comido	habías vivido
	había hablado	había comido	había vivido
	habíamos hablado	habíamos comido	habíamos vivido
	habíais hablado	habíais comido	habíais vivido
	habían hablado	habían comido	habían vivido

Future perfect	habré hablado	habré comido	habré vivido
	habrás hablado	habrás comido	habrás vivido
	habrá hablado	habrá comido	habrá vivido
	habremos hablado	habremos comido	habremos vivido
	habréis hablado	habréis comido	habréis vivido
	habrán hablado	habrán comido	habrán vivido
Conditional perfect	habría hablado	habría comido	habría vivido
	habrías hablado	habrías comido	habrías vivido
	habría hablado	habría comido	habría vivido
	habríamos hablado	habríamos comido	habríamos vivido
	habríais hablado	habríais comido	habríais vivido
	habrían hablado	habrían comido	habrían vivido

Perfect tenses: Subjunctive mood

Present perfect	haya hablado	haya comido	haya vivido
	hayas hablado	hayas comido	hayas vivido
	haya hablado	haya comido	haya vivido
	hayamos hablado	hayamos comido	hayamos vivido
	hayáis hablado	hayáis comido	hayáis vivido
	hayan hablado	hayan comido	hayan vivido
Past perfect (**-ra** *forms*)	hubiera hablado	hubiera comido	hubiera vivido
	hubieras hablado	hubieras comido	hubieras vivido
	hubiera hablado	hubiera comido	hubiera vivido
	hubiéramos hablado	hubiéramos comido	hubiéramos vivido
	hubierais hablado	hubierais comido	hubierais vivido
	hubieran hablado	hubieran comido	hubieran vivido
Past perfect (**-se** *forms*)	hubiese hablado	hubiese comido	hubiese vivido
	hubieses hablado	hubieses comido	hubieses vivido
	hubiese hablado	hubiese comido	hubiese vivido
	hubiésemos hablado	hubiésemos comido	hubiésemos vivido
	hubieseis hablado	hubieseis comido	hubieseis vivido
	hubiesen hablado	hubiesen comido	hubiesen vivido

2. Irregular past participles

abrir	**abierto**	hacer	**hecho**
componer	**compuesto**	morir	**muerto**
cubrir	**cubierto**	poner	**puesto**
decir	**dicho**	resolver	**resuelto**
descubrir	**descubierto**	romper	**roto**
devolver	**devuelto**	ver	**visto**
envolver	**envuelto**	volver	**vuelto**
escribir	**escrito**		

3. Stem-changing verbs

A. Stem-changing verbs ending in -ar and -er

pensar *to think*
(e to ie)

Present indic.	Present subj.
pienso	piense
piensas	pienses
piensa	piense
pensamos	pensemos
pensáis	penséis
piensan	piensen

Commands
piensa, no pienses (**tú**)
pensad, no penséis (**vosotros**)
piense, no piense (**Ud.**)
piensen, no piensen (**Uds.**)

Other verbs (e to ie)
Other verbs (o to ue)

volver *to return, to come back*
(o to ue)

Present indic.	Present subj.
vuelvo	vuelva
vuelves	vuelvas
vuelve	vuelva
volvemos	volvamos
volvéis	volváis
vuelven	vuelvan

Commands
vuelve, no vuelvas (**tú**)
volved, no volváis (**vosotros**)
vuelva, no vuelva (Ud.)
vuelvan, no vuelvan (**Uds.**)

cerrar, comenzar, empezar, entender, perder, sentarse
acordar(se), acostar(se), colgar, costar, demostrar, encontrar, jugar, llover, mover

B. Stem-changing verbs ending in -ir

sentir *to feel*
Present indicative
(e to ie)

siento
sientes
siente
  sentimos
  sentís
sienten

Present subjunctive
(e to ie, i)

sienta
sientas
sienta
  sintamos
  sintáis
sientan

Preterit
(e to i)

sentí
sentiste
  sintió
sentimos
sentisteis
  sintieron

dormir *to sleep*
Present indicative
(o to ue)

duermo
duermes
duerme
  dormimos
  dormís
duermen

Present subjunctive
(o to ue, u)

duerma
duermas
duerma
  durmamos
  durmáis
duerman

Preterit
(o to u)

dormí
dormiste
  durmió
dormimos
dormisteis
  durmieron

servir *to serve*
Present indicative
(e to i)

sirvo
sirves
sirve
  servimos
  servís
sirven

Present subjunctive
(e to i, i)

sirva
sirvas
sirva
sirvamos
sirváis
sirvan

Preterit
(e to i)

serví
serviste
  sirvió
servimos
servisteis
  sirvieron

Imperfect subjunctive (**e** to **i**)	*Imperfect subjunctive* (**o** to **u**)	*Imperfect subjunctive* (**e** to **i**)
sintiera	durmiera	sirviera
sintieras	durmieras	sirvieras
sintiera	durmiera	sirviera
sintiéramos	durmiéramos	sirviéramos
sintierais	durmierais	sirvierais
sintieran	durmieran	sirvieran

Commands	*Commands*	*Commands*
siente, no sientas (**tú**)	duerme, no duermas	sirve, no sirvas
sentid, no sintáis (**vosotros**)	dormid, no durmáis	servid, no sirváis
sienta, no sienta (**Ud.**)	duerma, no duerma	sirva, no sirva
sientan, no sientan (**Uds.**)	duerman, no duerman	sirvan, no sirvan

Other verbs (**e** to **ie, i**)   consentir, convertir, divertir(se), herir, preferir, mentir, sugerir

Other verb (**o** to **ue, u**)   morir

Other verbs (**e** to **i, i**)   concebir, despedir(se), elegir, pedir, repetir, reír, seguir, vestir(se) (**Reír** has an accent on **í** in all forms of the present indicative and in all forms of the present subjunctive except for **riáis**. See also 4G, p. 369.)

4. Orthographic- or spelling-changing verbs

A. Verbs that end in **-ger** or **-gir** change **g** to **j** before **o** or **a**.

escoger   *to choose*

Present indic.	escojo, escoges, escoge, escogemos, escogéis, escogen
Present subj.	escoja, escojas, escoja, escojamos, escojáis, escojan
Commands	escoge, no escojas (**tú**); escoged, no escojáis (**vosotros**); escoja, no escoja (**Ud.**); escojan, no escojan (**Uds.**)

dirigir   *to direct; to conduct; to address*

Present indic.	dirijo, diriges, dirige, dirigimos, dirigís, dirigen
Present subj.	dirija, dirijas, dirija, dirijamos, dirijáis, dirijan
Commands	dirige, no dirijas (**tú**); dirigid, no dirijáis (**vosotros**); dirija, no dirija (**Ud.**); dirijan, no dirijan (**Uds.**)

Other verbs   coger, corregir (i), elegir (i), exigir, proteger, recoger

B. Verbs that end in a vowel + **-cer** or **-cir** change **c** to **zc** before **o** or **a**. (See **conducir** in list of irregular verbs.) Verbs that end in a consonant + **-cer** or **-cir** change **c** to **z** before **o** or **a**.

conocer   *to know, to be acquainted with*

Present indic.	conozco, conoces, conoce, conocemos, conocéis, conocen
Present subj.	conozca, conozcas, conozca, conozcamos, conozcáis, conozcan
Commands	conoce, no conozcas (**tú**); conoced, no conozcáis (**vosotros**); conozca, no conozca (**Ud.**); conozcan, no conozcan (**Uds.**)

convencer *to convince*

Present indic. convenzo, convences, convence, convencemos, convencéis, convencen
Present subj. convenza, convenzas, convenza, convenzamos, convenzáis, convenzan
Commands convence, no convenzas (**tú**); convenced, no convenzáis (**vosotros**); convenza, no convenza (**Ud.**); convenzan, no convenzan (**Uds.**)

Other verbs agradecer, aparecer, crecer, desaparecer, desconocer, ejercer, establecer, nacer, obedecer, ofrecer, parecer, permanecer, pertenecer, producir, reconocer, traducir, vencer

C. Verbs that end in **-car** change **c** to **qu** before **e**. Verbs that end in **-gar** change **g** to **gu** before **e**. Verbs that end in **-zar** change **z** to **c** before **e**.

buscar *to look for*

Preterit busqué, buscaste, buscó, buscamos, buscasteis, buscaron
Present subj. busque, busques, busque, busquemos, busquéis, busquen
Commands busca, no busques (**tú**); buscad, no busquéis (**vosotros**); busque, no busque (**Ud.**); busquen, no busquen (**Uds.**)

pagar *to pay*

Preterit pagué, pagaste, pagó, pagamos, pagasteis, pagaron
Present subj. pague, pagues, pague, paguemos, paguéis, paguen
Commands paga, no pagues (**tú**); pagad, no paguéis (**vosotros**); pague, no pague (**Ud**); paguen, no paguen (**Uds.**)

empezar *to begin*

Preterit empecé, empezaste, empezó, empezamos, empezasteis, empezaron
Present subj. empiece, empieces, empiece, empecemos, empecéis, empiecen
Commands empieza, no empieces (**tú**); empezad, no empecéis (**vosotros**); empiece, no empiece (**Ud.**); empiecen, no empiecen (**Uds.**)

Other verbs acercar, almorzar (ue), comenzar (ie), cruzar, entregar, explicar, indicar, jugar (ue), llegar, obligar, organizar, sacar, tocar

D. Verbs that end in **-guir** drop the **u** before **o** or **a**. Verbs that end in **-guar** change **gu** to **gü** before **e**.

seguir *to follow*

Present indic. sigo, sigues, sigue, seguimos, seguís, siguen
Present subj. siga, sigas, siga, sigamos, sigáis, sigan
Commands sigue, no sigas (**tú**); seguid, no sigáis (**vosotros**); siga, no siga (**Ud.**); sigan, no sigan (**Uds.**)

averiguar *to find out*

Preterit averigüé, averiguaste, averiguó, averiguamos, averiguasteis, averiguaron
Present subj. averigüe, averigües, averigüe, averigüemos, averigüéis, averigüen
Commands averigua, no averigües (**tú**); averiguad, no averigüéis (**vosotros**); averigüe, no averigüe (**Ud.**); averigüen, no averigüen (**Uds.**)

Other verbs apaciguar, atestiguar, conseguir (i), distinguir

E. Verbs ending in **-uir** change unstressed **i** to **y** between vowels. Verbs ending in **-eer** also change unstressed **i** to **y** between vowels.

construir   *to build*

Present indic.	construyo, construyes, construye, construimos, construís, construyen
Present subj.	construya, construyas, construya, construyamos, construyáis, construyan
Preterit	construí, construiste, construyó, construimos, construisteis, construyeron
Imperfect subj.	construyera, construyeras, construyera, construyéramos, construyerais, construyeran
Commands	construye, no construyas (**tú**); construid, no construyáis (**vosotros**); construya, no construya (**Ud.**); construyan, no construyan (**Uds.**)
Present part.	construyendo

creer   *to believe*

Preterit	creí, creíste, creyó, creímos, creísteis, creyeron
Imperfect subj.	creyera, creyeras, creyera, creyéramos, creyerais, creyeran
Present part.	creyendo

Other verbs	concluir, contribuir, destruir, huir, instruir, leer, poseer, sustituir

F. Some verbs ending in **-iar** and **-uar** require a written accent on the **i** and **u** of the stem in some tenses.

enviar   *to send*

Present indic.	envío, envías, envía, enviamos, enviáis, envían
Present subj.	envíe, envíes, envíe, enviemos, enviéis, envíen
Commands	envía, no envíes (**tú**); enviad, no enviéis (**vosotros**); envíe, no envíe (**Ud.**); envíen, no envíen (**Uds.**)

continuar   *to continue*

Present indic.	continúo, continúas, continúa, continuamos, continuáis, continúan
Present subj.	continúe, continúes, continúe, continuemos, continuéis, continúen
Commands	continúa, no continúes (**tú**); continuad, no continuéis (**vosotros**); continúe, no continúe (**Ud.**); continúen, no continúen (**Uds.**)

Other verbs	acentuar, ampliar, confiar, efectuar, enfriar, graduar(se), guiar, situar, variar

G. The verb **reír (i)** drops the **e** of the stem before the ending **-ió** and all endings beginning with **-ie**.

reír(se)   *to laugh*

Preterit	reí, reíste, rió, reímos, reisteis, rieron
Imperfect subj.	riera, rieras, riera, riéramos, rierais, rieran
Present part.	riendo

Other verbs	freír, sonreír(se)

5. Common irregular verbs

Only the tenses with irregular forms are shown.

andar *to walk, to go*

Preterit	anduve, anduviste, anduvo, anduvimos, anduvisteis, anduvieron
Imperfect subj.	anduviera, anduvieras, anduviera, anduviéramos, anduvierais, anduvieran

caber *to fit, to be contained in*

Present indic.	quepo, cabes, cabe, cabemos, cabéis, caben
Preterit	cupe, cupiste, cupo, cupimos, cupisteis, cupieron
Future	cabré, cabrás, cabrá, cabremos, cabréis, cabrán
Conditional	cabría, cabrías, cabría, cabríamos cabríais, cabrían
Present subj.	quepa, quepas, quepa, quepamos, quepáis, quepan
Imperfect subj.	cupiera, cupieras, cupiera, cupiéramos, cupierais, cupieran
Commands	cabe, no quepas (**tú**); cabed, no quepáis (**vosotros**); quepa, no quepa (**Ud.**); quepan, no quepan (**Uds.**)

caer *to fall*

Present indic.	caigo, caes, cae, caemos, caéis, caen
Preterit	caí, caíste, cayó, caímos, caísteis, cayeron
Present subj.	caiga, caigas, caiga, caigamos, caigáis, caigan
Imperfect subj.	cayera, cayeras, cayera, cayéramos, cayerais, cayeran
Commands	cae, no caigas (**tú**); caed, no caigáis (**vosotros**); caiga, no caiga (**Ud.**); caigan, no caigan (**Uds.**)
Past part.	caído

conducir *to conduct, to drive*   (All **-ducir** verbs follow this pattern.)

Present indic.	conduzco, conduces, conduce, conducimos, conducís, conducen
Preterit	conduje, condujiste, condujo, condujimos, condujisteis, condujeron
Present subj.	conduzca, conduzcas, conduzca, conduzcamos, conduzcáis, conduzcan
Imperfect subj.	condujera, condujeras, condujera, condujéramos, condujerais, condujeran

dar *to give*

Present indic.	doy, das, da, damos, dais, dan
Preterit	di, diste, dio, dimos, disteis, dieron
Present subj.	dé, des, dé, demos, deis, den
Imperfect subj.	diera, dieras, diera, diéramos, dierais, dieran
Commands	da, no des (**tú**); dad, no deis (**vosotros**); dé, no dé (**Ud.**); den, no den (**Uds.**)

decir *to say, to tell*

Present indic.	digo, dices, dice, decimos decís, dicen
Preterit	dije, dijiste, dijo, dijimos, dijisteis, dijeron
Future	diré, dirás, dirá, diremos, diréis, dirán
Conditional	diría, dirías, diría, diríamos, diríais, dirían
Present subj.	diga, digas, diga, digamos, digáis, digan
Imperfect subj.	dijera, dijeras, dijera, dijéramos, dijerais, dijeran
Commands	di, no digas (**tú**); decid, no digáis (**vosotros**); diga, no diga (**Ud.**); digan, no digan (**Uds.**)
Present part.	diciendo
Past participle	dicho

estar *to be*

Present indic.	estoy, estás, está, estamos, estáis, están
Preterit	estuve, estuviste, estuvo, estuvimos, estuvisteis, estuvieron
Present subj.	esté, estés, esté, estemos, estéis, estén
Imperfect subj.	estuviera, estuvieras, estuviera, estuviéramos, estuvierais, estuvieran
Commands	está, no estés (**tú**); estad, no estéis (**vosotros**); esté, no esté (**Ud.**); estén, no estén (**Uds.**)

haber *to have*

Present indic.	he, has, ha, hemos, habéis, han
Preterit	hube, hubiste, hubo, hubimos, hubisteis, hubieron
Future	habré, habrás, habrá, habremos, habréis, habrán
Conditional	habría, habrías, habría, habríamos, habríais, habrían
Present subj.	haya, hayas, haya, hayamos, hayáis, hayan
Imperfect subj.	hubiera, hubieras, hubiera, hubiéramos, hubierais, hubieran

hacer *to do, to make*

Present indic.	hago, haces, hace, hacemos, hacéis, hacen
Preterit	hice, hiciste, hizo, hicimos, hicisteis, hicieron
Future	haré, harás, hará, haremos, haréis, harán
Conditional	haría, harías, haría, haríamos, haríais, harían
Present subj.	haga, hagas, haga, hagamos, hagáis, hagan
Imperfect subj.	hiciera, hicieras, hiciera, hiciéramos, hicierais, hicieran
Commands	haz, no hagas (**tú**); haced, no hagáis (**vosotros**); haga, no haga (**Ud.**); hagan, no hagan (**Uds.**)
Past participle	hecho

ir *to go*

Present indic.	voy, vas, va, vamos, vais, van
Imperfect indic.	iba, ibas, iba, íbamos, ibais, iban
Preterit	fui, fuiste, fue, fuimos, fuisteis, fueron
Present subj.	vaya, vayas, vaya, vayamos, vayáis, vayan
Imperfect subj.	fuera, fueras, fuera, fuéramos, fuerais, fueran
Commands	ve, no vayas (**tú**); id, no vayáis (**vosotros**); vaya, no vaya (**Ud.**); vayan, no vayan (**Uds.**)

jugar *to play*

Present indic.	juego, juegas, juega, jugamos, jugáis, juegan
Preterit	jugué, jugaste, jugó, jugamos, jugasteis, jugaron
Present subj.	juegue, juegues, juegue, juguemos, juguéis, jueguen
Commands	juega, no juegues (**tú**); jugad, no juguéis (**vosotros**); juegue, no juegue (**Ud.**); jueguen, no jueguen (**Uds.**)

oír *to hear*

Present indic.	oigo, oyes, oye, oímos, oís, oyen
Preterit	oí, oíste, oyó, oímos, oísteis, oyeron
Present subj.	oiga, oigas, oiga, oigamos, oigáis, oigan
Imperfect subj.	oyera, oyeras, oyera, oyéramos, oyerais, oyeran
Commands	oye, no oigas (**tú**); oíd, no oigáis (**vosotros**); oiga, no oiga (**Ud.**); oigan, no oigan (**Uds.**)
Present part.	oyendo
Past participle	oído

oler   *to smell*

Present indic.	huelo, hueles, huele, olemos, oléis, huelen
Present subj.	huela, huelas, huela, olamos, oláis, huelan
Commands	huele, no huelas (**tú**); oled, no oláis (**vosotros**); huela, no huela (**Ud.**); huelan, no huelan (**Uds.**)

poder   *to be able*

Present indic.	puedo, puedes, puede, podemos, podéis, pueden
Preterit	pude, pudiste, pudo, pudimos, pudisteis, pudieron
Future	podré, podrás, podrá, podremos, podréis, podrán
Conditional	podría, podrías, podría, podríamos, podríais, podrían
Present subj.	pueda, puedas, pueda, podamos, podáis, puedan
Imperfect subj.	pudiera, pudieras, pudiera, pudiéramos, pudierais, pudieran
Present part.	pudiendo

poner   *to put, to place*

Present indic.	pongo, pones, pone, ponemos, ponéis, ponen
Preterit	puse, pusiste, puso, pusimos, pusisteis, pusieron
Future	pondré, pondrás, pondrá, pondremos, pondréis, pondrán
Conditional	pondría, pondrías, pondría, pondríamos, pondríais, pondrían
Present subj.	ponga, pongas, ponga, pongamos, pongáis, pongan
Imperfect subj.	pusiera, pusieras, pusiera, pusiéramos, pusierais, pusieran
Commands	pon, no pongas (**tú**); poned, no pongáis (**vosotros**); ponga, no ponga (**Ud.**); pongan, no pongan (**Uds.**)
Past participle	puesto

querer   *to want, to wish*

Present indic.	quiero, quieres, quiere, queremos, queréis, quieren
Preterit	quise, quisiste, quiso, quisimos, quisisteis, quisieron
Future	querré, querrás, querrá, querremos, querréis, querrán
Conditional	querría, querrías, querría, querríamos, querríais, querrían
Present subj.	quiera, quieras, quiera, queramos, queráis, quieran
Imperfect subj.	quisiera, quisieras, quisiera, quisiéramos, quisierais, quisieran

saber   *to know*

Present indic.	sé, sabes, sabe, sabemos, sabéis, saben
Preterit	supe, supiste, supo, supimos, supisteis, supieron
Future	sabré, sabrás, sabrá, sabremos, sabréis, sabrán
Conditional	sabría, sabrías, sabría, sabríamos, sabríais, sabrían
Present subj.	sepa, sepas, sepa, sepamos, sepáis, sepan
Imperfect subj.	supiera, supieras, supiera, supiéramos, supierais, supieran

salir   *to go out, to leave*

Present indic.	salgo, sales, sale, salimos, salís, salen
Future	saldré, saldrás, saldrá, saldremos, saldréis, saldrán
Conditional	saldría, saldrías, saldría, saldríamos, saldríais, saldrían
Present subj.	salga, salgas, salga, salgamos, salgáis, salgan
Commands	sal, no salgas (**tú**); salid, no salgáis (**vosotros**); salga, no salga (**Ud.**); salgan, no salgan (**Uds.**)

ser   *to be*

Present indic.   soy, eres, es, somos, sois, son
Imperfect indic.   era, eras, era, éramos, erais, eran
Preterit   fui, fuiste, fue, fuimos, fuisteis, fueron
Present subj.   sea, seas, sea, seamos, seáis, sean
Imperfect subj.   fuera, fueras, fuera, fuéramos, fuerais, fueran
Commands   sé, no seas (**tú**); sed, no seáis (**vosotros**); sea, no sea (**Ud.**); sean, no sean (**Uds.**)

tener   *to have*

Present indic.   tengo, tienes, tiene, tenemos, tenéis, tienen
Preterit   tuve, tuviste, tuvo, tuvimos, tuvisteis, tuvieron
Future   tendré, tendrás, tendrá, tendremos, tendréis, tendrán
Conditional   tendría, tendrías, tendría, tendríamos, tendríais, tendrían
Present subj.   tenga, tengas, tenga, tengamos, tengáis, tengan
Imperfect subj.   tuviera, tuvieras, tuviera, tuviéramos, tuvierais, tuvieran
Commands   ten, no tengas (**tú**); tened, no tengáis (**vosotros**); tenga, no tenga (**Ud.**); tengan, no tengan (**Uds.**)

traer   *to bring*

Present indic.   traigo, traes, trae, traemos, traéis, traen
Preterit   traje, trajiste, trajo, trajimos, trajisteis, trajeron
Present subj.   traiga, traigas, traiga, traigamos, traigáis, traigan
Imperfect subj.   trajera, trajeras, trajera, trajéramos, trajerais, trajeran
Commands   trae, no traigas (**tú**); traed, no traigáis (**vosotros**); traiga, no traiga (**Ud.**); traigan, no traigan (**Uds.**)
Present part.   trayendo
Past participle   traído

valer   *to be worth*

Present indic.   valgo, vales, vale, valemos, valéis, valen
Future   valdré, valdrás, valdrá, valdremos, valdréis, valdrán
Conditional   valdría, valdrías, valdría, valdríamos, valdríais, valdrían
Present subj.   valga, valgas, valga, valgamos, valgáis, valgan
Commands   vale, no valgas (**tú**); valed, no valgáis (**vosotros**); valga, no valga (**Ud.**); valgan, no valgan (**Uds.**)

venir   *to come*

Present indic.   vengo, vienes, viene, venimos, venís, vienen
Preterit   vine, viniste, vino, vinimos, vinisteis, vinieron
Future   vendré, vendrás, vendrá, vendremos, vendréis, vendrán
Conditional   vendría, vendrías, vendría, vendríamos, vendríais, vendrían
Present subj.   venga, vengas, venga, vengamos, vengáis, vengan
Imperfect subj.   viniera, vinieras, viniera, viniéramos, vinierais, vinieran
Commands   ven, no vengas (**tú**); venid, no vengáis (**vosotros**); venga, no venga (**Ud.**); vengan, no vengan (**Uds.**)
Present part.   viniendo

ver   *to see*

Present indic.   veo, ves, ve, vemos, veis, ven
Imperfect indic.   veía, veías, veía, veíamos, veíais, veían
Preterit   vi, viste, vio, vimos, visteis, vieron
Present subj.   vea, veas, vea, veamos, veáis, vean
Past participle   visto

Spanish-English Vocabulary

The following Vocabulary contains words and expressions from the text that would not usually be known from first-year study. Most obvious cognates and first-year vocabulary are not included. Occasionally, (*adj.*) is specified beside a word when the definition is not easily recognized as an adjective form. Some expressions are listed following a key cognate or first-year word, for which no definition is given.

abajo down, below, downstairs
abarcar to deal with; to include, to cover
abrazo *m.* embrace, hug
abrelatas *m. sing.* can opener
abstenerse (de) to abstain (from), to refrain (from)
aburrido(a) bored
aburrimiento *m.* boredom
aburrir to bore
abusar (de) to abuse
accidentarse to have an accident
aceite *m.* oil
acentuar to accent; to stress, to emphasize
acera *f.* sidewalk
aclarar to clarify
acogedor(a) welcoming, friendly
acogida *f.* welcome, reception
acomodarse (a) to conform (to); to adapt oneself (to)
acompañar to accompany
aconsejable advisable
aconsejar to advise
acontecimiento *m.* happening, occurrence
acordar (ue) to decide; to agree
acostumbrado(a) accustomed, customary
actuación *f.* performance; behavior
actualidad *f.* present, present time
actuar to act, to perform
acuarela *f.* watercolor
acuerdo *m.* agreement, accord
adecuado(a) adequate
además besides
adivinanza *f.* conjecture; riddle
adivinar to guess; to solve
adorno *m.* adornment, decoration

adquirir (ie, i) to acquire
aduana *f.* customs; custom house
aduanero(a) *m./f.* custom agent
adversario(a) *m./f.* adversary, opponent
advertir (ie, i) to notice; to point out; to advise
afeitarse to shave
afición *f.* liking; hobby
aficionado(a) *m./f.* fan, supporter; (*adj.*) enthusiastic
afortunado(a) fortunate
afueras *f.* outskirts
agacharse to crouch
agotado(a) used up; exhausted; out-of-print
agotar to use up, to exhaust
agradar to please
agradecer to thank
agrado *m.* taste, liking
agregar to add
aguantar to put up with, to tolerate
ahorrar to save (money, time)
aire *m.* **al aire libre** outdoors
aislado(a) isolated
ajedrecista *m./f.* chess player
ajedrez *m.* chess
ajeno(a) somebody else's; outside, alien
ajustar to adjust; to settle
alcalde(sa) *m./f.* mayor
alcaldía *f.* office of mayor
alcanzar to reach; to catch (up with); to understand
alegrar(se) (de) to cheer up, to enliven; to become happy
alentador(a) encouraging
alfombra *f.* carpet, rug
algodón *m.* cotton
aliado(a) *m./f.* ally

alimenticio(a) nourishing, nutritive
alimento *m.* food; nourishment
almacén *m.* department store; warehouse
aló hello
alojamiento *m.* lodging
alpinismo *m.* mountain climbing
alpinista *m./f.* mountain climber
alquilar to rent
altavoz *m.* loudspeaker
altoparlante *m.* loudspeaker
altura *f.* height
alumnado *m.* student body
amanecer *m.* dawn; (*v.*) to dawn
amargo(a) bitter
ambiente *m.* environment; atmosphere
amenaza *f.* threat
amenazante threatening
amenazar to threaten
amistad *f.* friendship
amonestar to warn
amparo *m.* help; protection; shelter
ampliar to enlarge; to amplify
amplificador *m.* amplifier
anciano(a) *m./f.* elderly person; (*adj.*) elderly
anécdota *f.* anecdote
anfitrión(ona) *m./f.* host (hostess)
anillo *m.* ring
animado(a) lively; encouraged
animar to enliven; to encourage
ánimo *m.* nerve; energy; spirit
ansia *f.* anxiety, worry; fear
ansioso(a) anxious, worried
antecesor(a) *m./f.* predecessor; ancestor; (*adj.*) preceding
anteojos *m.* eyeglasses

anterior front; preceding; former
antigüedad *f.* antiquity
antiguo(a) ancient, old
antipático(a) disagreeable, unpleasant
anunciar to advertise; to announce
anuncio *m.* advertisement; announcement
añadir to add; to increase
apaciguar to pacify; to appease
apagar to turn off; to extinguish
aparato *m.* device, machine; **aparato electrodoméstico** home electrical appliance
aparcar to park
aparecer to appear
aparición *f.* appearance
apartado *m.* paragraph, section; heading; (*adj.*) separated; remote; **apartado de correos** post office box
apenas hardly, scarcely
aperitivo *m.* appetizer, aperitif
apetecer to have an appetite for, to desire
aplicar (a) to apply (to)
apoyar to support, to be in favor of
apoyo *m.* support
apreciar to appreciate; to esteem; to assess
aprendizaje *m.* apprenticeship, training period
aprobar (ue) to pass; to approve
aprovechar to make use of; to take advantage of
apuntes *m. pl.* notes; **sacar apuntes** to take notes
apurado(a) hurried; worried; needy
apurarse to hurry up; to worry
archivar to file
archivo *m.* file
arena *f.* sand
arete *m.* earring
argumento *m.* plot; argument
arma *f.* arm, weapon
armamento *m.* armament, arms
armar to put together; to arm
armonía *f.* harmony
armonioso(a) harmonious
arpa *f.* harp

arrabal *m.* suburb; outskirts; slum
arrancar to pull up; to take away from; to start (car, etc.)
arrepentirse (ie, i) to repent, to regret
arriesgar(se) to take a chance, to run a risk
arrodillarse to kneel down
arte *m.* art; **bellas artes** *f.* fine arts
artefacto *m.* artifact; device
artesanía *f.* craftsmanship; handicraft
artículo *m.* **artículo de fondo** in-depth report; editorial
artritis *f.* arthritis
asaltado(a) assaulted
ascenso *m.* promotion
ascensor *m.* elevator
asegurar to assure; to safeguard; to make secure
aseo *m.* cleanliness, neatness
asesor(a) *m./f.* consultant, advisor
asesoramiento *m.* professional advice
aseveración *f.* assertion
asignatura *f.* subject, course
asociar to associate, to relate
asombrar to amaze; to frighten
asombro *m.* amazement; fright
aspiradora *f.* vacuum cleaner
aspirante *m./f.* applicant
astronauta *m./f.* astronaut
asumir to assume; to take on
asunto *m.* matter, subject, topic
asustar to scare
atacar to attack
ataque *m.* attack
atar to tie (up)
atardecer *m.* early evening; (*v.*) to get dark
atasco *m.* traffic jam
ataúd *m.* coffin
atender (ie) to wait on, to help
atentado *m.* illegal act; assault
aterrador(a) terrifying
atestiguar to testify
atletismo *m.* track and field; athletics
atónito(a) amazed, astounded
atormentar to torment; to torture
atraco *m.* holdup, robbery

atraer to attract
atrasar to fall behind; to delay
atreverse (a) to dare (to)
atribuir to attribute
atropellar to run over
auditorio *m.* auditorium; audience
aula *f.* classroom; lecture room
aumentar to increase
aumento *m.* increase; **aumento de sueldo** salary increase, raise
ausencia *f.* absence
ausentarse (de) to absent oneself; to go away
automatizar to automate
automotriz (*adj.*) automotive; self-propelled
autopista *f.* freeway
autoridad *f.* authority
autorizar to authorize
avance *m.* advance
avanzado(a) advanced
aventura *f.* adventure
avergonzar(se) (ue) to shame (to be ashamed)
averiar to damage, to spoil
averiguar to find out, to inquire
aviso *m.* piece of information; advice; warning
ayudante *m./f.* assistant, helper
ayuntamiento *m.* city hall; municipal government
azafata *f.* stewardess, air hostess
azúcar *m.* sugar

balón *m.* (large) ball
bancarrota *f.* bankruptcy
bandera *f.* flag
barato(a) inexpensive
barba *f.* beard
barbacoa *f.* barbecue
barra *f.* bar; railing; rod
barrendero(a) *m./f.* sweeper
barril *m.* barrel; keg
barrio *m.* area (of town), neighborhood
base *f.* base; basis; mounting
bastar to be sufficient
basura *f.* garbage
basurero(a) *m./f.* garbage collector
bate *m.* (baseball) bat
batidora *f.* beater, mixer
beca *f.* scholarship

belleza f. beauty
bello(a) beautiful
bendición f. blessing
beneficio m. benefit, gain; profit
besar to kiss
bienestar m. well-being; welfare
bilingüe bilingual
bimensual bimonthly
biografía f. biography
blando(a) soft; smooth; flabby; mild
bobo(a) m./f. idiot, fool; (adj.) silly; naive
bocacalle f. intersection (street)
bocadillo m. sandwich; snack
bocado m. mouthful; bite; morsel
boda f. wedding
bofetón m. punch (in face); slap
bohemio(a) Bohemian
boite f. nightclub
boletín m. bulletin
boleto m. ticket
bolsa f. bag; handbag; stock market
bomba f. bomb; pump
bombero(a) m./f. firefighter
borrar to erase
bosque m. forest
bostezar to yawn
bota f. boot; leather wine bottle
bote m. can, tin; boat
botella f. bottle
botón m. button, knob
boxeador m. boxer
breve brief
brío m. spirit, verve; determination
broma f. joke; prank
bullir to boil, to bubble up; to swarm
burlarse (de) to mock, to ridicule
bursátil (adj.) stock market
butaca f. armchair

caballero m. gentleman; horseman
cabaña f. cabin
caber to fit
cabo m. end; conclusion; cape; corporal
cadena f. chain; network; **en cadena** in sequence, in series
cafetera f. coffeepot

caja f. box; cash register; safe; cashier's office
cajero(a) m./f. cashier; bank teller
calcular to calculate
calentamiento m. heating; warm-up
calentarse (ie) to become warm; to warm up
calidad f. quality
calificar to qualify; to assess; to grade (an exam)
calmadamente calmly
calmante m. sedative; (adj.) calming, soothing
calmar(se) to calm (down)
calor m. heat, warmth
caluroso(a) hot, warm; enthusiastic
calvo(a) bald
callado(a) quiet, silent
cámara f. camera; chamber; **cámara (fotográfica)** camera; **cámara de comercio** chamber of commerce
camarada m./f. comrade, companion
camaradería f. companionship; team spirit
camello m. camel
caminata f. stroll, walk; hike
camino m. road; path; route; **camino de (al)** on the road (way) to
campamento m. camp
campana f. bell
campaña f. campaign
campeón(ona) m./f. champion
campo m. country; countryside; field; scope, sphere
canal m. **canal de televisión** television channel
canasta f. basket; crate; canasta (card game)
cansar(se) to tire (to become tired)
cántaro m. pitcher, jug
cantidad f. quantity, amount
cantimplora f. canteen (for liquids)
canto m. singing; song
capacidad f. capacity; size; talent, ability

capacitado(a) qualified, prepared
capaz capable, competent
capital m. capital, money; f. capital city
captar to captivate, to get; to secure
cara f. face; appearance
cárcel f. jail
caricatura f. caricature; cartoon; **caricatura política** political cartoon
caricaturista m./f. caricaturist; cartoonist
cariño m. affection, fondness; caress
cariñoso(a) affectionate; tender
carnicería f. butcher shop, meat market
carnicero(a) m./f. butcher
caro(a) expensive
carrera f. career; race
carro m. **carro de cambios manuales** car with manual transmission
cartel m. poster, sign; billboard
cartelera f. billboard; notice board
casarse (con) to get married
casco m. helmet
casualidad f. chance; coincidence; **por casualidad** by chance
cautivar to capture; to charm
célebre famous
celos m. pl. jealousy
celoso(a) jealous; suspicious; zealous
cenicero m. ashtray
censura f. censorship, censoring; criticism
censurar to censor; to censure
centrista (adj.) centrist, center
cercano(a) near, nearby
cerro m. hill
césped m. grass, lawn
cesto m. basket
ciclismo m. cycling
ciclista m./f. cyclist
ciclo m. **ciclo económico bajo** low economic cycle
ciego(a) m./f. blind person; (adj.) blind

cielo *m.* sky; heaven

ciencia *f.* **ciencia ficción** science fiction

cínico(a) cynical

cinta *f.* ribbon; tape

circo *m.* circus

círculo *m.* circle

cita *f.* appointment; (social) date; quote

citar to make an appointment; to date (socially); to quote

ciudadano(a) *m./f.* citizen; (*adj.*) civic, city

claro(a) clear; light; transparent; (*adv.*) clearly

clavel *f.* carnation

cobarde *m./f.* coward; (*adj.*) cowardly

cobrar to cash (a check); to charge; to collect

cobre *m.* copper

cocido *m.* stew; (*adj.*) cooked; boiled

cohete *m.* rocket

cojo(a) *m./f.* crippled person; (*adj.*) crippled, lame

cola *f.* line; last position; tail; **hacer cola** to stand in line

colaborar to collaborate

coleccionar to collect, to save

colega *m./f.* colleague

colgar (ue) to hang (up)

colocación *f.* placing; place; job

colocar to place, to put

colonia *f.* colony; community; suburb

colonizar to colonize; to settle

collar *m.* necklace

comentarista *m./f.* commentator

cometa *m.* comet; *f.* kite

cometer to commit

cómico(a) comical, funny; **tiras cómicas** *f.* comic strips

comisaría *f.* police station

comodidad *f.* comfort; convenience

cómodo(a) comfortable; convenient

compañerismo *m.* companionship; team spirit

compañía *f.* company

compartir to divide (up); to share

compás *m.* beat, rhythm; compass

competencia *f.* competition; rivalry; competence

complemento *m.* complement; accessory

componer(se) (de) to compose (oneself); to put together; to consist of

comportamiento *m.* behavior

comportarse to behave

comprador(a) *m./f.* buyer

compras *f.* purchases; shopping

comprometerse (a) to compromise oneself; to promise to

computación *f.* calculation, computation

computadora *f.* computer

computarizar to computerize

cómputo *m.* calculation, computation

comunicación *f.* **medios de comunicación** means of communication, mass media

concebir (i) to conceive

concejal(a) *m./f.* council member

concejo *m.* council

conciudadano(a) *m./f.* fellow citizen

concluir to conclude

concordancia *f.* agreement; harmony

concurrido(a) busy, crowded

concurso *m.* contest, match, competition

conde(sa) *m./f.* count, countess

conductor(a) *m./f.* driver; conductor

conferencia *f.* lecture; conference

conferenciante *m./f.* lecturer

conferencista *m./f.* lecturer

confianza *f.* confidence; trust; intimacy

confiar (en; a) to entrust; to trust

confuso(a) confused

congelación *f.* freezing; frostbite

congelar to freeze

conjunto *m.* whole; musical group; (*adj.*) joint; united

conmover (ue) to move (emotionally)

conocido(a) *m./f.* acquaintance; (*adj.*) known

conocimiento *m.* knowledge

consejero(a) *m./f.* advisor

consejo *m.* advice

conservador(a) *m./f.* conservative; (*adj.*) conservative

conservar to preserve, to save; to keep up

consignación *f.* **por consignación** on consignment

construir to construct

consuelo *m.* comfort, consolation

consulta *f.* consultation; examination (med.)

consumidor(a) *m./f.* consumer

contabilidad *f.* accounting; bookkeeping

contador(a) *m./f.* accountant; bookkeeper

contaminación *f.* pollution; contamination

contaminar to pollute; to contaminate

contar (ue) to count; **contar con** to count on

contemporáneo(a) contemporary

contenido *m.* content; (*adj.*) restrained, controlled

contestador *m.* answering device; **contestador automático** answering machine

continuo(a) continuous

contradecir to contradict

contratar to contract (for), to hire

contratista *m./f.* contractor

control *m.* control; inspection check

controvertido(a) disputed

convencer to convince

convenio *m.* agreement; covenant; **convenio colectivo** labor agreement

convenir to agree; to suit; to be important

convincente convincing

copia *f.* copy

copiadora *f.* copier

copiar to copy

copioso(a) copious

corazón *m.* heart

corrector(a) *m./f.* proofreader

corredor(a) *m./f.* runner; agent; *m.* corridor

corregir (i) to correct
correspondencia f. correspondence, mail
corresponsal m./f. correspondent
corriente f. current; flow; (adj.) running (water); ordinary
cortar to cut
corte f. (royal) court; law court; m. cut, cutting
cortés courteous
cortesía f. courtesy
cortina f. curtain
coser to sew, to stitch
costa f. coast, coastline; cost, price
costumbre f. custom; habit
crear to create
crecer to grow
crema f. cream
crimen m. crime
cristal m. crystal, glass
crítica f. criticism; critique
criticar to criticize
crítico(a) m./f. critic; (adj.) critical
crónica f. column, feature story; chronicle
cronista m./f. columnist
crucigrama m. crossword puzzle
crudo(a) raw
cruz f. cross
cruzar to cross
cuadra f. city block
cuadro m. picture, painting; description; square; chart
cuartel m. headquarters; barracks
cuchillo m. knife
cuento m. story, short story; **cuento de hadas** fairy tale
cuerdo(a) sane; prudent
cuero m. leather, skin, hide
cuerpo m. body
cuesta f. slope; hill; **cuesta arriba (abajo)** uphill (downhill)
cuestión f. matter, question; dispute
cuestionario m. questionnaire
cuidado m. care; worry, concern; carefulness
cuidar to take care of
culpa f. fault; blame
cumplimiento m. fulfillment; completion

cumplir (con) to carry out, to fulfill; to comply (with)
cura f. cure; m. Catholic priest
cursillo m. short course
cursivo(a) cursive; italic
curso m. course; school year; direction; **curso obligatorio** required course

charla f. chat; discussion
charlar to chat; to gossip
cheque m. check (monetary)
chiste m. joke
chocar to collide, to crash; to shock
chorro m. jet; stream; trickle

dañar(se) to damage (to become damaged); **hacer daño** to do damage, to do harm
daño m. damage; hurt, harm
dato m. fact, datum; piece of information
debido(a) proper, due; right, correct
débil weak
debilitar to weaken
decano(a) m./f. dean
decepcionado(a) disappointed
declaración f. **prestar (hacer una) declaración** to make a formal declaration or statement
declinar to refuse; to deteriorate
decreto m. decree, order
deducir to deduce
defectuoso(a) defective
delantal m. apron
delegado(a) m./f. delegate, representative
delicado(a) delicate; sensitive; touchy
demás (adj.) other, rest; **lo demás** the rest (of it)
demasiado(a) too much/many; (adv.) too; too much
demora f. delay
demostrar (ue) to demonstrate, to show
denunciar to denounce, to accuse
dependiente(a) m./f. store clerk
deportista m./f. athlete, sportsperson

deprimido(a) depressed
derecha f. right wing (pol.); right hand
derechista m./f. rightist (pol.)
derecho m. right, claim, privilege; law, justice; (adj.) right, right-hand; straight; (adv.) straight (ahead); upright; **derechos humanos** human rights
derramar to spill; to pour out
derrotar to defeat
desabrido(a) nasty tasting; embittered
desacuerdo m. disagreement
desafortunado(a) unfortunate
desaparecer to disappear
desarme m. disarmament; **desarme nuclear** nuclear disarmament
desarrollar to develop
desarrollo m. development
desastroso(a) disastrous
descansar to rest
descenso m. descent; decline
descifrar to decipher, to decode; to solve
descompuesto(a) broken
desconfiar (de) to mistrust; to lack confidence in
desconocer to be ignorant of
desconocido(a) m./f. stranger; (adj.) unknown; strange
descortés discourteous
descubrimiento m. discovery
descubrir to discover
descuento m. discount
desempacar to unpack
desempleo m. unemployment
desenlace m. outcome, ending
desfile m. parade; march
desgracia f. misfortune, bad luck; accident
deshacer to undo
designar to designate, to appoint
desigualdad f. inequality
desmayarse to faint
desmentir (ie, i) to deny; to contradict
despacho m. small office
despacio(a) slow; (adv.) slowly
despedir (i) to fire, to lay off
despedirse (i) (de) to take leave (of), to say good-by (to)

despegar to take off (aviation); to unstick
despejado(a) cloudless, clear; open
desperdicio *m.* waste, refuse; wasting
despertador *m.* alarm clock; (*adj.*) awakening
destino *m.* destination; destiny, fate
destruir to destroy
desventaja *f.* disadvantage
detallado(a) detailed
detalle *m.* detail
detener to detain; to stop; to arrest
deuda *f.* debt
devolver (ue) to return, to give back
dialogar to have a dialogue, to converse
diamante *m.* diamond
diapositiva *f.* slide, transparency
diario *m.* newspaper; (*adj.*) daily, everyday
dibujar to draw, to sketch; to design
dictar to dictate; to give (lecture, class)
dieta *f.* **ponerse a dieta** to go on a diet
dignarse to deign to, to condescend to
dimitir to resign
dinamismo *m.* dynamism
diputado(a) *m./f.* delegate, representative; deputy
directiva *f.* board of directors
dirigente *m./f.* leader; (*adj.*) leading
dirigir to direct; to conduct; to address
discoteca *f.* discotheque
disculpa *f.* excuse; apology
discurso *m.* speech; **pronunciar un discurso** to give a speech
discutir to discuss; to argue
diseñador(a) *m./f.* designer
diseño *m.* design; sketch, drawing
disfraz *m.* disguise; mask
disfrutar (de) to enjoy
disminuir to diminish, to lessen
disputa *f.* dispute

distracción *f.* distraction
distribuidor(a) *m./f.* distributor; (*adj.*) distributing
distrito *m.* district
diversión *f.* entertainment; recreation; hobby
divertido(a) entertaining; funny, enjoyable
divertirse (ie, i) to have a good time
divulgar to spread; to publish; to divulge
doblar to double; to fold; to turn (corner); to dub
doble *m.* double; fold
doctorado *m.* doctorate
documental *m.* documentary; (*adj.*) documentary
doler (ue) to hurt, to ache; to grieve
dolor *m.* pain, ache; grief
dorado(a) golden; gilded
dramaturgo(a) *m./f.* dramatist, playwright
droga *f.* drug, medicine
droguería *f.* drugstore
ducha *f.* shower, shower bath
ducharse to take a shower
duda *f.* doubt
dudar to doubt
dueño(a) *m./f.* owner
dulce sweet
durar to last; to endure

ecología *f.* ecology
ecológico(a) ecological
edición *f.* edition; publication; publishing
editorial *m.* editorial, article of opinion; *f.* publishing house; (*adj.*) publishing
efectuar to bring about
eficacia *f.* effectiveness; efficiency
eficaz effective; efficient
ejemplar *m.* issue, copy; example; (*adj.*) exemplary
ejercer to exercise; to exert, to bring to bear
ejercicio *m.* **hacer ejercicio** to exercise; **hacer ejercicios** to do exercises
ejército *m.* army
elector(a) *m./f.* elector, voter

electorado *m.* electorate
electrodoméstico(a) home-electrical
elegir (i) to elect; to choose
embajada *f.* embassy; ambassadorship
embajador(a) *m./f.* ambassador
emigrar to emigrate
emocionado(a) deeply moved
emocionante exciting, thrilling; touching
empeorar to make worse, to worsen
empleado(a) *m./f.* employee
empleo *m.* employment; job
empresa *f.* enterprise; undertaking; company
enamorarse (de) to fall in love (with)
encantado(a) charmed, delighted; bewitched
encantador(a) *m./f.* charmer; (*adj.*) charming, delightful
encarcelar to jail, to imprison
encargado(a) *m./f.* agent, person in charge; (*adj.*) in charge of
encargarse (de) to take charge (of); to look (after)
encender (ie) to turn on; to light
encerrar (ie) to shut in, to enclose; to contain
encima (de) on top (of)
encuentro *m.* meeting, encounter
encuesta *f.* poll; inquiry
encuestador(a) *m./f.* pollster
energía *f.* **energía nuclear (solar)** nuclear (solar) energy
enérgico(a) energetic
enfadado(a) angry, upset
enfado *m.* anger, annoyance
enfático(a) emphatic
enfermarse to get sick
enfrentar to confront
enfriar to cool, to chill
engañoso(a) deceitful; misleading
enorgullecerse to be proud
enrojecer to redden; to blush
ensayar to test; to rehearse, to practice
ensayo *m.* test, trial; rehearsal; essay
ensuciar to soil; to make dirty
enterarse (de) to find out (about)

entrega *f.* delivery
entregar to deliver
entrenador(a) *m./f.* coach; trainer
entrenamiento *m.* coaching; training
entrenar(se) to coach, to train, to work out
entretener(se) to entertain (oneself), to pass the time
entretenimiento *m.* entertainment; training, coaching
entrevista *f.* interview
entrevistador(a) *m./f.* interviewer
entrevistar *f.* to interview
entristecerse to become sad
entusiasmar(se) to fill with enthusiasm (to get excited)
entusiasta *m./f.* enthusiast, fan; (*adj.*) enthusiastic
enumerar to enumerate
enviar to send
envío *m.* sending; shipment
episodio *m.* episode
época *f.* epoch, period of time
equipaje *m.* luggage, baggage
equipar to equip, to furnish
equipo *m.* equipment; team; set
equivocarse to make a mistake
errata *f.* erratum, misprint
esbozo *m.* sketch, outline
escala *f.* stopping place; scale; **escala de salarios** wage scale; **hacer escala** to make a stopover
escalar to climb; to break into; to escalate
escalera *f.* stairs, stairway; ladder
escandaloso(a) shocking
escaparate *m.* store window
escaso(a) scarce; limited
escéptico(a) *m./f.* skeptic, doubter; (*adj.*) skeptical
escoger to choose
escolar scholastic; school
esconder to hide, to conceal
escudo *m.* shield
escultura *f.* sculpture
esforzarse (ue) (por) to make an effort (for)
esfuerzo *m.* effort
espacial (*adj.*) space
espacio *m.* space
esparcir to spread, to scatter; to disseminate

especialidad *f.* specialty; major (school); **cambiar de especialidad** to change one's major
especializarse to specialize; to major (school)
especie *f.* species; kind, sort
espectáculo *m.* entertainment, show; **espectáculo de variedades** variety show
espejo *m.* mirror; **espejo retrovisor** rearview mirror
espionaje *m.* espionage, spying
esquema *m.* diagram; scheme; sketch, outline
esquina *f.* corner
estabilidad *f.* stability
establecimiento *m.* establishment
estación *f.* station; season; **estación de mando** command center
estacionamiento *m.* parking
estadio *m.* stadium
estadísticas *f.* statistics
estampilla *f.* stamp
estante *m.* shelf; rack, stand; bookcase
estatal (*adj.*) state
estatura *f.* stature, height
estereofónico(a) stereophonic
estilo *m.* style
estimado(a) esteemed, respected; Dear
estimular to stimulate
estirar to stretch
estrecho(a) narrow
estrella *f.* star
estreno *m.* debut, first appearance
estudiantado *m.* students, student body
estupendo(a) stupendous, wonderful
etiqueta *f.* etiquette; label, tag; slip of paper
evaluar to evaluate
evitar to avoid
exagerado(a) exaggerated
exagerar to exaggerate
exclamativo(a) exclamatory
excluir to exclude
excursión *f.* **ir de excursión** to go on a tour or trip

exhibir to exhibit, to show
exigencia *f.* requirement
exigente demanding
exigir to demand, to require
éxito *m.* success; hit
explicar to explain
explorador(a) *m./f.* explorer
explotar to exploit; to explode
exponer to exhibit; to expose; to expound
exposición *f.* exposition, showing
extinción *f.* extinction
extinto(a) extinct
extranjero(a) *m./f.* foreigner; *m.* foreign country; (*adj.*) foreign; alien
extrañar to find strange; to miss, to yearn for
extraño(a) strange, odd; extraneous
extraterrestre extraterrestrial
extremado(a) extreme
extremista *m./f.* extremist

fábrica *f.* factory
fabricante *m./f.* manufacturer
facilidad *f.* facility; ease; fluency
factible feasible
factura *f.* bill, invoice
facturar to invoice; to check (luggage)
falta *f.* lack, need; shortage; fault, mistake
faltar to be lacking; to be absent
fama *f.* fame; reputation
fanatismo *m.* fanaticism
farmacéutico(a) *m./f.* pharmacist; (*adj.*) pharmaceutical
farsa *f.* farce
fase *f.* phase
fastidiar to annoy, to bother
fastidio *m.* annoyance, nuisance; boredom
fatigarse to tire out
fatigoso(a) tiring
felicitar to congratulate
fenomenal phenomenal, terrific
fenómeno *m.* phenomenon
feria *f.* fair; celebration; holiday
fiable reliable, trustworthy
fiambre *m.* cold meat, cold food
fiarse (de) to trust; to rely on
ficticio(a) fictitious

fiel faithful, loyal; accurate
figurar to figure (among), to appear
fijarse to notice; to pay attention to
fila *f.* row, line
filatelia *f.* stamp collecting
filmación *f.* filming
financiero(a) financial
firma *f.* signature; firm (company)
firmar to sign
firmeza *f.* firmness
físico *m.* physique; **físico(a)** *m./f.* physicist; (*adj.*) physical
flauta *f.* flute
flojo(a) lazy; weak; loose
flor *f.* flower
florero *m.* vase; **florero(a)** *m./f.* florist
fluir to flow, to run
folklórico(a) (*adj.*) folklore
folleto *m.* pamphlet, brochure
fondo *m.* bottom; far end; background; fund
forestal pertaining to the forest
forjar to forge, to shape; to make
forma *f.* form; shape; **en plena forma** in top shape
formulario *m.* form, blank
fortalecerse to get strong; to build up one's strength
fotocopia *f.* photocopy
fotocopiadora *f.* photocopier
fracaso *m.* failure
franqueza *f.* frankness, openness
frasco *m.* flask, bottle
fregadero *m.* (kitchen) sink
frito(a) fried
fuego *m.* fire; **fuegos artificiales** fireworks
fuente *f.* fountain; source; **fuente de energía** energy source
fuerza *f.* strength
fumar to smoke
función *f.* function, operation; duties; show
funcionamiento *m.* functioning, operation, performance
fundar to found, to institute
futurología *f.* futurology

gabinete *m.* cabinet; study room
galería *f.* gallery

galón *m.* gallon
gallina *f.* hen
gallo *m.* rooster
ganado *m.* stock, livestock; cattle
ganador(a) *m./f.* winner; (*adj.*) winning
ganar to win; to earn
ganas *f.* desires, wishes
ganga *f.* bargain
garantía *f.* guarantee; warranty; **garantía de trabajo** job guarantee
garantizar to guarantee; to warrant
garganta *f.* throat
gasolinera *f.* gasoline station
gastar to spend; to use up; to wear away; to waste
gasto *m.* spending, expenditure; use; wear; waste
gatas: a gatas on all fours
gato(a) *m./f.* cat
gaucho(a) *m./f.* gaucho, cowboy (esp. Argentina)
género *m.* class, kind; gender (grammar)
genio *m.* disposition, character; bad temper; genius
gerente *m./f.* manager
gesto *m.* gesture; grimace; expression on one's face
gimnasta *m./f.* gymnast
gira *f.* tour, trip
giradiscos *m.* turntable
girar to turn, to turn (around); to spin
gobernador(a) *m./f.* governor
gobernante(a) *m./f.* ruler; boss; (*adj.*) governing, ruling
gobernar (ie) to govern
gobierno *m.* government
gol *m.* goal (sports); **marcar un gol** to score a goal
golpe *m.* blow; punch; **golpe de estado** coup d'état
gordo(a) *m./f.* overweight person; (*adj.*) overweight
gota *f.* drop; bead
grabado *m.* engraving, print; (*adj.*) recorded
grabadora *f.* tape recorder
gracia *f.* attractiveness; graciousness; humor

grado *m.* degree; stage; quality
graso *m.* fattiness; greasiness; (*adj.*) fatty; greasy
grasoso(a) fatty; greasy
gratis free of charge
gratuito(a) free (of charge); gratuitous, unjustified
gritar to shout
guardar to keep; to put away; to guard
gubernativo(a) governmental
guerra *f.* war
guía *m./f.* guide, leader; *f.* guidebook; telephone book; guidance
guión *m.* script; subtitle; hyphen, dash
guionista *m./f.* scriptwriter

hábil skillful, proficient; clever
habitación *f.* room; dwelling
habitante *m./f.* inhabitant, resident
hábito *m.* habit; custom
hablador(a) *m./f.* talkative person; (*adj.*) talkative; gossipy
hablante *m./f.* speaker; (*adj.*) speaking
hacienda *f.* large farm, ranch; country estate
hacha *f.* ax, hatchet
hada *f.* fairy
hamaca *f.* hammock
hambre *f.* hunger, famine
heladería *f.* ice-cream parlor
hembra *f.* female
herida *f.* wound
herido(a) *m./f.* injured person; (*adj.*) injured; wounded
hielo *m.* ice; frost
hierro *m.* iron
higiene *f.* hygiene, cleanliness
hincarse to kneel (down)
historiador(a) *m./f.* historian
hogar *m.* home
holgazán(ana) *m./f.* idler, loafer; (*adj.*) idle, lazy
honradez *f.* honesty, integrity
horario *m.* schedule, timetable; (*adj.*) hourly
horno *m.* oven; **horno de microondas** microwave oven
horroroso(a) horrible
hospedar to receive as a guest; to lodge

huelga *f.* strike; walkout
huésped(a) *m./f.* guest; lodger; boarder
huevo *m.* egg
huir to flee, to escape from
humanidad *f.* humanity
humanidades *f. pl.* humanities
humanizante humanizing
humo *m.* smoke

igualdad *f.* equality; sameness, uniformity
ilusionado(a) hopeful; excited, eager
imagen *f.* image; picture
imaginario(a) imaginary
impacientarse to become impatient
impaciente impatient
imponente imposing, impressive
imponer to impose; to enforce
importar to be important; to import
imprenta *f.* printing; press; printing house
impresionante impressive, striking; moving
impresionar to impress; to move
impresionista impressionist(ic)
impresor(a) *m./f.* printer; *f.* (machine) printer
imprevisto(a) unforeseen
imprimir to print; to imprint
impuesto *m.* tax, duty; taxation
inagotable inexhaustible
incendio *m.* fire
inclinarse (a) to incline, to slope; to be inclined (to)
incluir to include
incluso including; even
incómodo(a) uncomfortable
incorporar to incorporate; to help to sit up
increíble unbelievable
indagación *f.* inquiry, investigation
indicador *m.* indicator, gauge, meter, dial
índice *m.* index; ratio, rate; catalogue; table of contents
indicio *m.* indication, sign; piece of evidence
indignar to anger, to make indignant

indudable unquestionable
inesperado(a) unexpected
infección *f.* infection
influir to influence
informe *m.* report, statement; information
ingenuidad *f.* ingenuousness, naiveté
ingenuo(a) ingenuous; simple, unaffected
iniciar to initiate; to begin
inolvidable unforgettable
inquietar(se) to worry, to upset (to become anxious)
inquieto(a) anxious; disturbed
inquilino(a) *m./f.* tenant; renter
inscribir(se) to enroll, to register; to inscribe
inseguro(a) uncertain; insecure; unsafe
inservible useless
insípido(a) insipid; dull
insistente insistent
insólito(a) unusual
inspeccionar to inspect
instantáneo(a): café instantáneo instant coffee
instituir to institute, to begin
intentar to attempt, to try
intento *m.* attempt
intercambio *m.* exchange
interesado(a) interested
internado *m./f.* internee; *m.* internship
interplanetario(a) interplanetary
interrogar to interrogate; to ask
interrumpir to interrupt
intervencionista interventionist
intervenir to intervene; to participate
inútil useless
invento *m.* invention
inversión *f.* investment; inversion, reversal
invertir (ie, i) to invest
invitado(a) *m./f.* guest
ironía *f.* irony
izquierdista *m./f.* leftist (pol.); (*adj.*) leftist

jabón *m.* soap
jactarse (de) to boast (of)
jardín *m.* garden

jefe(a) *m./f.* boss, director; **jefe(a) de ventas** sales manager
jirafa *f.* giraffe
jornada *f.* **de jornada completa** (*adj.*) full-time; **de media jornada** (*adj.*) part-time
joya *f.* jewel, gem
joyería *f.* jewelry store
jubilarse to retire (from employment)
juego *m.* game, sport; play; set, kit; **hacer juego** to match, to go well; **juego de platos** set of dishes
juez *m./f.* judge
jugada *f.* play, move
jugar (ue): jugar a las damas to play checkers
jugo *m.* **jugo de naranja(s)** orange juice
juguetón(ona) playful
juicio *m.* judgment; opinion; sanity
junta *f.* meeting; session; board, committee; **junta directiva** board of directors
juntarse (con) to meet, to assemble; to join
junto(a) joined, united; together; (*adv.*) near, close; together; (*prep.*) near, close to
jurado *m.* jury, panel of judges
justo(a) just, fair; exact, correct; tight; (*adv.*) justly; exactly; tightly
juventud *f.* youth

laboral (*adj.*) labor
lado *m.* side
ladrón(ona) *m./f.* thief
lago *m.* lake
lágrima *f.* tear
lana *f.* wool
lanzar to throw; to launch, to promote
láser *m.* laser; (*adj.*) laser
lata *f.* tin, can; nuisance, bore
látigo *m.* whip
lavadora *f.* washing machine
lavandería *f.* laundry; **lavandería automática** laundromat
lavaplatos *m.* dishwasher
leal loyal, faithful

lector(a) *m./f.* reader
lectura *f.* reading; reading assignment
legislador(a) *m./f.* legislator
lejano(a) distant, remote
lema *m.* motto; slogan
león(ona) *m./f.* lion(ess)
lesionarse to get hurt
letra *f.* letter; bill; draft; learning; lyric
letrero *m.* sign; notice; poster
levantador(a) *m./f.* weight lifter
levantamiento *m.* raising; uprising
levantar: levantar pesas to lift weights
ley *f.* law
libertador(a) *m./f.* liberator; (*adj.*) liberating
libre free
líder *m.* leader
liderato *m.* leadership
lienzo *m.* canvas (art)
limpieza *f.* cleaning; cleanliness; purity; integrity
línea *f.* line; figure; **guardar la línea** to watch one's figure
linterna *f.* lamp, lantern
lío *m.* mess, big problem
liquidación *f.* close-out sale
listo(a) ready; clever
literatura *f.* literature
litro *m.* liter
liviano(a) light; frivolous, trivial
locuaz talkative
locutor(a) *m./f.* announcer, commentator
lodo *m.* mud
lograr to get, to attain; to succeed in
lucir to illuminate; to shine; to show off; **lucir bien** to look nice
lucha *f.* struggle, fight
lujoso(a) luxurious

llama *f.* llama; flame
llamada *f.* call; knock, ring
llamativo(a) attractive, eye-catching
llegada *f.* arrival
llover (ue) to rain
lluvioso(a) rainy

macho *m.* male; (*adj.*) male; masculine; strong, tough
madera *f.* wood
madrugada *f.* dawn, early morning
madrugar to dawn; to arise early in the morning
madurez *f.* maturity
maestría *f.* mastery; expertise; master's degree
malentendido *m.* misunderstanding
maleta *f.* suitcase; **hacer las maletas** to pack (luggage)
maletín *m.* briefcase; small case; satchel
maltratar to treat badly
malla *f.* tights; mesh; net
mancha *f.* spot, mark, smudge
mandado *m.* order; errand
mandato *m.* command; mandate
mando *m.* command; rule; leadership
manejo *m.* handling; running, operation; driving
manga *f.* sleeve
manicomio *m.* mental hospital
manifestación *f.* manifestation; demonstration; riot
manifestante *m./f.* demonstrator; rioter
manifestar (ie) to manifest; to demonstrate; to riot
manta *f.* blanket; shawl
mantenimiento *m.* maintenance
mantequilla *f.* butter
manuscrito *m.* manuscript
maquillaje *m.* cosmetic make-up; act of putting on make-up
máquina *f.* machine; **máquina de coser** sewing machine; **máquina de escribir** typewriter
maquinista *m./f.* machinist; engineer, operator
mar *m./f.* sea
maratón *m.* marathon
maravilla *f.* marvel, something wonderful
maravilloso(a) marvelous, wonderful
marca *f.* brand (name); mark; name tab; record (sports)
mareado(a) seasick; dizzy
marisco *m.* shellfish; seafood

máscara *f.* mask
materia *f.* material; subject; subject matter
matrícula *f.* list; enrollment; registration
matricular(se) to enroll; register
mayoría *f.* majority
mayúscula *f.* capital letter; (*adj.*) capital (letter); big, tremendous
maximizar to maximize
mecanógrafo(a) *m./f.* typist
medalla *f.* medal
mediar to mediate
medición *f.* measurement
medida *f.* measure; measurement; **medidas de seguridad** security measures
medio *m.* middle; means, method; (*adj.*) half; midway; average
medir (i, i) to measure
meditar to meditate
mejora *f.* improvement
mejoramiento *m.* improvement
mejorar to improve
memoria *f.* memory; note, report
menor minor; smaller; less, lesser; younger
mensaje *m.* message
mensajero(a) *m./f.* messenger
mensual monthly
mentir (ie, i) to lie, to tell a falsehood
mercadeo *m.* marketing
mercado *m.* market
mercancía *f.* merchandise
merendar (ie) to snack
mesero(a) *m./f.* waiter (waitress)
meta *f.* goal
método *m.* method
microonda *f.* microwave
miedo *m.* fear
miedoso(a) fearful; timid
miel *f.* honey
milagroso(a) miraculous
mínimo(a) minimum
ministerio *m.* ministry
ministro(a) *m./f.* minister
minoría *f.* minority
misterio *m.* mystery
misterioso(a) mysterious
mixto(a) mixed
mochila *f.* knapsack; backpack

moda *f.* style, fashion; **de moda** in fashion, in style
moderador(a) *m./f.* moderator
moderar to moderate; to restrain
módico(a) reasonable, fair
modo *m.* way, manner, method
mojar to wet, to moisten
molestar to bother, to annoy
molesto(a) annoying; restless; inconvenient
moneda *f.* coin
monetario(a) monetary
monografía *f.* monograph
monótono(a) monotonous
montar to get on; to ride
monte *m.* mountain
montón *m.* heap, pile
morada *f.* dwelling; stay, period of residence
motivar to motivate
motociclista *m./f.* motorcyclist
movimiento *m.* movement
muchedumbre *f.* crowd, great mass, throng
mudarse to move (residence)
mueblería *f.* furniture store or factory
muela *f.* tooth; molar
muerte *f.* death
muerto(a) dead
muestra *f.* sample; sign, indication
multa *f.* fine; penalty
multar to fine; to penalize
mundial worldwide, universal
municipio *m.* municipality; town, township
muñeca *f.* wrist; doll; manikin
muñeco *m.* (boy) doll; puppet, dummy
músculo *m.* muscle; **estirar los músculos** to stretch
músico *m.* musician; (*adj.*) musical
mutación *f.* mutation
mutuo(a) mutual

nacer to be born
nadador(a) *m./f.* swimmer
naranja *f.* orange
narración *f.* narration
natación *f.* swimming

nave *f.* ship, vessel; **nave espacial** spaceship
neblina *f.* mist; fog
negar (ie) to deny; to refuse
negociar to negotiate; to deal
negocio *m.* business; deal, transaction
nervio *m.* nerve
nerviosismo *m.* nervousness; restlessness
neutro(a) neutral; neuter
nevar (ie) to snow
nevera *f.* refrigerator, icebox
nieve *f.* snow
niñero(a) *m./f.* babysitter; (*adj.*) fond of children
niñez *f.* childhood; infancy
nítidamente brightly, cleanly; sharply
nivel *m.* level
nocturno(a) nocturnal, night, evening
nostalgia *f.* nostalgia, homesickness
noticia *f.* news item; **noticias** news, information; **noticias meteorológicas** weather report
noticiero *m.* newscast; news program; newspaper
novato(a) *m./f.* beginner; (*adj.*) raw, green, new
novedad *f.* newness, novelty; strangeness
novedoso(a) novel, new
novela *f.* **novela policíaca** mystery novel
novelista *m./f.* novelist
nube *f.* cloud
nublado(a) cloudy
nublarse to cloud up

obedecer to obey
objetivo *m.* objective, goal; (*adj.*) objective
obra *f.* work; book; play; composition; workmanship
obrero(a) *m./f.* worker, laborer
observador(a) *m./f.* observer; (*adj.*) observant
obstruir to obstruct
ocultar to hide, to conceal
ocupado(a) busy; occupied; taken

ocuparse (de) to occupy oneself (with)
odio *m.* hate
oferta *f.* offer; **en oferta** on sale
óleo *m.* oil painting
oler (ue) to smell
Olimpiadas *f. pl.* Olympic games
olor *m.* smell, odor, scent
olvidadizo(a) forgetful
olvidar to forget
operar to operate (on); to run, to use; to bring about
opinar to give an opinion; to believe
opositor(a) *m./f.* competitor; candidate
optar (por) to opt (for), to choose
optativo(a) optional
oración *f.* sentence; prayer; speech
orador(a) *m./f.* speaker, orator
orden *m.* order, arrangement; *f.* order, warrant, writ; order (religious)
ordenar to put in order; to order, to command; to ordain
organizador(a) *m./f.* organizer
orientarse to orient (oneself); to face
oro *m.* gold
orquesta *f.* orchestra
ortografía *f.* spelling, orthography
oscuro(a) dark, dim
oso *m.* bear; **oso de peluche** teddy bear
oyente *m./f.* listener, hearer; unregistered student, auditor

paciente *m./f.* patient (*adj.*) patient
pago *m.* payment; return, reward
paisaje *m.* landscape, countryside, scenery
pálido(a) pale
palmera *f.* palm, palm tree
palomitas *f.* popcorn
pan *m.* bread
panadería *f.* bakery, baker's shop
panfleto *m.* pamphlet, brochure
pantalla *f.* screen
pantera *f.* panther

paquete *m.* package
parada *f.* stop; stopping place; shutdown; suspension
paraguas *m. sing.* umbrella
paraíso *m.* paradise
parar to stop
parecido *m.* similarity; (*adj.*) similar
pareja *f.* couple, pair
paréntesis *m.* parenthesis
pariente(a) *m./f.* relative, relation
parque *m.* **parque de atracciones** amusement park; **parque deportivo** sports complex
párrafo *m.* paragraph
parte *f.* part, portion
partida *f.* game, match; departure
partidario(a) *m./f.* party member, follower; (*adj.*) partisan
partido *m.* party (pol.); game, match; team, side
pasado *m.* past
pasaje *m.* passage; passageway; fare, ticket
pasajero(a) *m./f.* passenger
pasatiempo *m.* pastime, hobby
paseo *m.* stroll, walk; outing
pasillo *m.* hall, corridor
paso *m.* passing; crossing; step, pace
pastel *m.* cake; pie; pastry
pastelería *f.* pastry, pastry shop
patinaje *m.* skating
patria *f.* native country
patrocinar to sponsor; to support
payaso(a) *m./f.* clown
paz *f.* peace
peatón(ona) *m./f.* pedestrian
pedido *m.* order; request; **hacer el pedido** to order
peligro *m.* danger
peligroso(a) dangerous
pelota *f.* ball
peluca *f.* wig, hairpiece
peluquero(a) *m./f.* hairdresser, barber
pena *f.* grief; sadness; anxiety; regret
pendiente *m.* earring; pendant; (*adj.*) hanging; pending; unsettled

penoso(a) painful, distressing; difficult
pensión *f.* pension; allowance; boarding house; board and lodging
penúltimo(a) penultimate
peor worse
pérdida *f.* loss; waste
pereza *f.* laziness; idleness
perezoso(a) lazy; idle
periodismo *m.* journalism
período *m.* period
perla *f.* pearl
permanecer to remain, to stay
permiso *m.* permission
personaje *m.* personage, character
personal *m.* personnel; (*adj.*) personal, private
personalidad *f.* personality
persuadir to persuade
pertenecer to belong (to)
pesado(a) heavy; boring; difficult, tough
pesar to weigh, to weigh (down); to grieve
pesas *f.* weights; **levantar pesas** to lift weights
pescado *m.* fish
peseta *f.* peseta (monetary unit of Spain)
peso *m.* weight; heaviness; burden; **bajar (subir) de peso** to lose (gain) weight
pesquero(a) (*adj.*) fishing
pico *m.* beak, bill; peak, summit
piel *f.* skin; hide, pelt, fur; leather
pincel *m.* paintbrush, artist's brush
pintar to paint
pintor(a) *m./f.* painter
pintoresco(a) picturesque
pintura *f.* painting; paint; description
piscina *f.* swimming pool
piso *m.* floor, story; flat, apartment
pista *f.* track, trail; clue; course, court
plana *f.* sheet (of paper); page; **en primera plana** on the first page
plancha *f.* iron
planchar to iron

planear to plan
planeta *m.* planet
planilla *f.* form, application form; sheet of paper; list; table
plano(a) flat, level, even, smooth
planta *f.* plant; factory; sole of the foot; floor, story
plata *f.* silver; money
plátano *m.* banana
plato *m.* plate, dish; course (meal)
playero(a) pertaining to the beach
plaza *f.* public square; space; position, job; vacancy
plazo *m.* time limit; period; expiration date; installment payment
plebiscito *m.* plebiscite
pleito *m.* lawsuit; case; dispute
pleno(a) full; complete
población *f.* population; town, city, village
poderoso(a) powerful
poesía *f.* poetry; poem
policía *f.* police, police force; *m./f.* police officer
policíaco(a) (*adj.*) police
poliéster *m.* polyester
polvo *m.* dust; powder
porcentaje *m.* percentage
portafolio *m.* portfolio; briefcase
portátil portable
portavoz *m./f.* spokesperson
portazo *m.* slam (of door)
postal *f.* postcard; (*adj.*) postal
postergar to delay, to postpone; to disregard
postular to postulate; to apply for
potencia *f.* power; potency; **potencia mundial** world power
precario(a) precarious
precio *m.* price; **congelar los precios** to freeze prices
premio *m.* prize, award; reward
prensa *f.* press
preparativo *m.* preparation; (*adj.*) preparatory
presentarse to introduce oneself
preservación *f.* **preservación del ambiente** environmental protection

preservar to preserve, to protect
preso(a) *m./f.* convict, prisoner
préstamo *m.* loan
prestar to lend, to loan; to give (help, etc.)
presupuesto *m.* budget
prevenir to prevent; to warn
previo(a) previous
primario(a) primary
príncipe *m.* prince
principio *m.* principle; beginning, start
prioridad *f.* priority
prisa *f.* hurry
privado(a) private, personal
privilegiar to grant a privilege (to)
probar (ue) to try to; to prove; to test; to taste
probarse (ue) to try on
proceder to proceed
procesador *f.* **procesador de textos (palabras)** word processor
procesamiento *m.* processing
profesorado *m.* teaching profession; teaching staff; professoriate
programación *f.* programming
prohibir to prohibit
promedio *m.* average; middle
promesa *f.* promise; **cumplir una promesa** to keep a promise
prometedor(a) promising
promover (ue) to promote, to advance; to instigate
promulgar to promulgate
pronombre *m.* pronoun
pronosticar to predict
pronóstico *m.* prediction, forecast
propaganda *f.* propaganda; advertising
propietario(a) *m./f.* landlord (landlady); owner
propina *f.* tip, gratuity
propio(a) own, of one's own; characteristic; proper, correct; selfsame, very
proponer to propose
propuesta *f.* proposal
proteger to protect

provocar to provoke; to bring about
proyecto *m.* plan, design; project
prueba *f.* proof; test, trial; testing, sampling; fitting; event (sports)
publicar to publicize
publicidad *f.* publicity, advertising
publicitario(a) (*adj.*) publicity
puesta *f.* setting; stake; **puesta del sol** sunset
puesto *m.* place; position, job; post; stall, stand
punta *f.* end; tip, point
punto *m.* point; item; spot; period; stitch; **estar a punto de** to be about to
puro(a) pure; simple, plain

quebrar(se) (ie) to break, to smash; to go bankrupt
quehacer *m.* job, task, chore
queja *f.* complaint; protest; grumble
quejarse (de) to complain (about)
quemar(se) to burn (up)
queso *m.* cheese
quizá(s) maybe, perhaps

radiación *f.* radiation
radioemisora *f.* radio station
radiorreloj *m.* clock radio
raqueta *f.* racquet
rascacielos *m. sing.* skyscraper
rato *m.* while, short period of time
raya *f.* line; streak; mark; crease; boundary; dash
razón *f.* reason
reaccionar to react
real real; royal
realista realistic
rebaja *f.* reduction; discount, mark-down sale
rebajar to lower, to reduce; to discount
recibo *m.* receipt
reciente recent
recíproco(a) reciprocal, mutual
reclutar to recruit
recoger to pick up, to get, to collect
reconocer to recognize

reconocimiento *m.* recognition
recorrer to go over, to go through; to tour, to travel
recorrido *m.* run, journey; route; distance traveled
recreo *m.* recreation
rector(a) *m./f.* head, chief; principal; university president
recuento *m.* count, recount; inventory
recuerdo *m.* memory, recollection; souvenir; best wishes
recuperar to recuperate
recurso *m.* resource; **recurso natural** natural resource
rechazar to reject, to refuse
red *f.* net; network, system
redacción *f.* writing; editing; newspaper office; editorial staff
redactar to write, to draft; to edit
redactor(a) *m./f.* writer; editor
redondo(a) round
reelegido(a) reelected
reemplazar to replace
reevaluar to reevaluate
reflejar to reflect
refrescar(se) to refresh (oneself), to cool off
refresco *m.* cool drink, soft drink; refreshment
refrigerador *m.* refrigerator
refugiado(a) *m./f.* refugee
regalar to give a gift
regalo *m.* gift
regaño *m.* scolding; scowl; grumble
reglamentario(a) prescribed
reglamento *m.* rules, regulations, code
rehén *m./f.* hostage
reír(se) (i, i) to laugh
reja *f.* grating, grid; bar
relacionar to relate
relajarse to relax
reloj *m.* watch, clock
relojería *f.* watchmaker's shop; watchmaking
renovar (ue) to renew; to renovate
renta *f.* income; rent
renunciar to quit a job, to resign; to surrender
reñir (i) to quarrel; to scold
reparación *f.* repair; repairing

reparar to repair
repartir to distribute; to divide (up)
repasar to review; to check (over)
repentino(a) sudden
repetir (i, i) to repeat
reportaje *m.* report, article, news report
repuesto *m.* spare part; replacement; stock, supply
requisito *m.* prerequisite, requirement
reseña *f.* review; outline, account; critique
reserva *f.* reservation; reserve
reservado(a) reserved
resfrío *m.* cold (illness)
residencia *f.* **residencia de estudiantes** dormitory, student housing
respaldo *m.* support, backing; back (of chair)
respetar to respect
respirar to breathe
restaurante *m.* **restaurante de autoservicio** self-service restaurant
resto *m.* rest, remainder
resultado *m.* result
resumen *m.* summary, résumé
resumir to summarize
retrasar to delay, to postpone; to be slow or late
reunión *f.* meeting, gathering; reunion
reunirse to meet, to gather together
revelador(a) revealing
revelar to reveal
revisar to review; to go over; to revise
rey *m.* king
rifa *f.* raffle
ritmo *m.* rhythm
roble *m.* oak, oak tree
robo *m.* robbery, theft
robot *m.* robot
rodaje *m.* shooting, filming
rodeado(a) surrounded, encircled
rodear to surround, to encircle
rompecabezas *m. sing.* puzzle, riddle; problem

ropa *f.* **ropa para damas** women's clothing
ropero *m.* closet
rosado(a) pink, rosy
rostro *m.* face, countenance
rotundo(a) rotund; forthright
rueda *f.* wheel; roller; circle, ring; **rueda de prensa** press conference
ruido *m.* noise
ruidoso(a) noisy
ruta *f.* route; course
rutina *f.* routine
rutinario(a) routine; ordinary, everyday

sabroso(a) delicious
saco *m.* bag; sack; bagful; sackful; jacket, coat
sacrificio *m.* sacrifice
sala *f.* **sala de espera** waiting room
salado(a) salty
salida *f.* exit, way out; leaving, going out
saliente outstanding; prominent; projecting
saltador(a) *m./f.* jumper
saltar to jump
salud *f.* health
saludar to greet; to salute
saludo *m.* greeting; salute
sandalia *f.* sandal
sano(a) healthy, wholesome
santo(a) *m./f.* saint; (*adj.*) saintly, holy
satírico(a) satiric(al)
satisfacer to satisfy
satisfecho(a) satisfied
secador *m.* dryer; **secador de pelo** hair dryer
sección *f.* section; department; **sección de caballeros** men's department
secuestrador(a) *m./f.* kidnapper; hijacker
secuestrar to kidnap; to hijack; to seize
secundario(a) secondary, minor
seda *f.* silk
sedentario(a) sedentary
seguidor(a) *m./f.* follower, supporter
según according to

seguramente surely; safely, securely
seguridad *f.* safety; security; **seguridad de trabajo** job security
seguro(a) sure; safe; secure
seleccionar to select
sello *m.* stamp; seal
semáforo *m.* traffic light
semanal weekly
semejante similar
seminario *m.* seminar; seminary
senado *m.* senate
sencillez *f.* simplicity; naturalness
sencillo(a) simple; natural
sentimiento *m.* feeling, emotion, sentiment
señal *f.* sign; signal; symptom; indication
señalar to point out
serie *f.* series
serio(a) serious
servidumbre *f.* servitude; servants
siglo *m.* century
significar to signify, to mean
siguiente following; next
silencioso(a) silent
sindical pertaining to a labor union
sindicalista *m./f.* member of a labor union; (*adj.*) pertaining to a labor union
sindicato *m.* trade union; syndicate
sinnúmero *m.* great many, large number
sinónimo *m.* synonym; (*adj.*) synonymous
sintonización *f.* tuning
sintonizador *m.* tuner
sintonizar to tune
sinvergüenza *m./f.* scoundrel; rascal; shameless person
sistema *m.* **sistema de alta fidelidad** high fidelity system
sitio *m.* site, place, spot
situar to place, to put, to set
sobrar to exceed, to surpass; to remain, to be left (over)
sobrepoblación *f.* overpopulation; overcrowding
sobresaliente outstanding

sobreviviente *m./f.* survivor; (*adj.*) surviving

socialdemócrata *m./f.* social democrat

socio(a) *m./f.* associate; member, partner

sol *m.* **tomar el sol** to sunbathe

soldado *m.* soldier

soler (ue) to be accustomed (to)

solicitar to solicit, to ask for

solicitud *f.* request; application; care, concern

solucionar to solve

sombra *f.* shade; shadow; darkness

son *m.* sound; sweet sound

sonar (ue) to ring (bell); to blow (horn); to sound (out); to sound (familiar)

sondeo *m.* poll; **sondeo de mercado** market poll

sonido *m.* sound

sonreír (i) to smile

sonrisa *f.* smile

soñar (ue) to dream

soportar to tolerate; to put up with; to support, to hold up

sorprendente surprising

sorprender to surprise

sorpresa *f.* surprise

sortija *f.* ring

sospechar to suspect, to be suspicious

sospechoso(a) suspicious

sótano *m.* basement

suave soft; gentle; smooth, even

suavizar to soften; to smooth (out); to ease; to make gentler

subasta *f.* auction

subida *f.* rise, increase; ascent; promotion; slope

subjetivo(a) subjective

submarino(a) underwater

subordinado(a) subordinate

subterráneo(a) underground

suceder to happen, to occur; to succeed, to follow

suceso *m.* happening, event; incident

sucio(a) dirty, filthy; vile; bad

sucursal *f.* branch office

sudar to sweat

sudor *m.* perspiration

sueldo *m.* salary; income

suelo *m.* floor; ground; soil, land

sueño *m.* dream; sleep; sleepiness

suerte *f.* luck; fate, destiny

sugerencia *f.* suggestion

sumamente highly, extremely

superpoblación *f.* overpopulation

superpotencia *f.* superpower

suplementario(a) supplementary; extra, additional

surgir to arise, to appear

surtido *m.* stock, merchandise; selection, assortment

suscribir to subscribe

suscriptor(a) *m./f.* subscriber

suspender to fail academically; to suspend; to hang

sustituir to substitute, to replace

susurrar to whisper; to hum; to rustle

tabaco *m.* tobacco

tabla *f.* board; plank; shelf; **tabla de microcircuitos** circuit board

tablero *m.* notice board, bulletin board; board, plank

tablón *m.* notice board, bulletin board; plank; beam

talla *f.* size; height, stature

taller *m.* repair shop

tañer to play (music); to ring (bell)

taquillero(a) *m./f.* ticket clerk

tardar (en) to take (a long) time (to); to be late

tarifa *f.* price, cost, charge; tariff

tarjeta *f.* card; **tarjeta de crédito** credit card; **tarjeta de seguro** insurance card

tasa *f.* rate; measure; estimate

taza *f.* cup; cupful

teatral theatrical

tecla *f.* key (piano, typewriter, etc.)

técnico(a) *m./f.* technician; (*adj.*) technical

tecnológico(a) technological

tejido *m.* woven material; fabric; tissue (anat.)

tela *f.* cloth, material; canvas, painting

telefónico(a) (*adj.*) telephone

telenovela *f.* television soap opera

televidente *m./f.* television viewer

televisivo(a) (*adj.*) television

telón *m.* curtain (theater)

tema *m.* theme, subject matter, topic

temático(a) thematic

temblar (ie) to tremble, to shake; to shiver

temblor *m.* trembling, shivering; earthquake

templado(a) moderate, restrained; lukewarm; mild

temporada *f.* period; season, time of year

temporal *m.* storm; (*adj.*) temporary

tenedor *m.* fork; holder, bearer

tenis *m.* **campo de tenis** tennis court

teoría *f.* theory

teórico *m./f.* theoretician; (*adj.*) theoretic(al)

terciopelo *m.* velvet

terminante final, decisive, definitive

término *m.* end, conclusion; term; boundary

terreno *m.* terrain; soil; ground; land; **perder terreno** to lose ground

terrestre terrestrial, earthly

terrorismo *m.* terrorism

tertulia *f.* social gathering

testigo *m./f.* witness; **testigo ocular** eyewitness

tijeras *f. pl.* scissors

tinieblas *f. pl.* darkness

tiovivo *m.* merry-go-round

tipo *m.* type, sort, kind; character (lit.); build, physique; fellow

tira *f.* strip; band; slip of paper; **tiras cómicas** comic strips

tiro *m.* throw; shot; shooting, firing

tirón *m.* pull, tug, sudden jerk; **de un tirón** all at once, in one jerk

títere *m.* puppet, marionette

titular *m.* headline; (*v.*) to entitle

título *m.* title

tocino *m.* bacon
tono *m.* tone
tontería *f.* silliness, foolish act; stupid remark
torneo *m.* tournament
torre *f.* tower
torta *f.* cake; tart
tostada *f.* toast, piece of toast
tostadora *f.* toaster
tostar (ue) to toast; to tan
trabajador(a) *m./f.* worker; *(adj.)* hard-working, industrious
trabajo *m.* work; **trabajo de investigación** research paper or project; **trabajo de mantenimiento** maintenance work
traducir to translate
traductor(a) *m./f.* translator
trama *f.* plot; scheme, intrigue
transporte *m.* transportation
tranvía *m.* streetcar; tramway
trasladar(se) to move to a new job; to change residence
traslado *m.* move; transfer
tratado *m.* treaty; agreement; treatise, essay
trayectoria *f.* trajectory
tremendo(a) tremendous
tristeza *f.* sadness
triunfar to triumph
trolebús *m.* trolley bus
trotar to jog
tuna *f.* student music group of guitarists and singers
túnel *m.* tunnel
turno *m.* turn; shift (work)

último(a) last (in a series); latest; most remote
unir(se) to join
usuario(a) *m./f.* user
utensilio *m.* utensil
útil useful
utilidad *f.* usefulness

vacante *f.* vacancy, opening (job); *(adj.)* vacant
vaciar to empty (out), to drain
vacío(a) empty; unfilled; superficial; vain
vago(a) *m./f.* tramp, vagrant; lazy person; *(adj.)* vague; wandering
valer to be worth; to be equal (to)
valioso(a) valuable; beneficial
valor *m.* value, worth; courage; bond, security
vaquero(a) *m./f.* cowboy, cowgirl; *(adj.)* cattle; cowboy, cowgirl
variado(a) varied, mixed, assorted
varios(as) several, some; varied; varying
varón *m.* male
vegetal *m.* vegetable; *(adj.)* vegetable
vejez *f.* old age
vela *f.* candle; wakefulness; sail
vencer to defeat; to conquer; to overcome; to expire, to fall due
vencido(a) defeated; losing; due, payable; expired
venta *f.* sale; selling
ventaja *f.* advantage
ventajoso(a) advantageous
ventilador *m.* fan
verdor *m.* greenness; lushness
vergonzoso(a) bashful, shy, timid; modest; shameful, disgraceful
vergüenza *f.* shame; sense of shame; shyness; embarrassment; modesty
verificar to verify
verso *m.* verse
vestido *m.* dress; *(adj.)* dressed; **bien (mal) vestido(a)** well (badly) dressed

vestuario *m.* clothes, wardrobe; costumes; dressing room; locker room
vía *f.* road; route; way; track; passage; system, means
viajero(a) *m./f.* traveler
videoteléfono *m.* video telephone
viento *m.* wind
vigilar to look (after), to watch (over); to be vigilant
villano(a) *m./f.* villain; peasant, rustic person; *(adj.)* coarse, rustic; base, low-down
vino *m.* wine
viña *f.* vineyard
virtud *f.* virtue
vivienda *f.* housing; dwelling place; apartment, flat
vivo(a) living; live, alive; lively, vivid; **en vivo** live (performance)
volar (ue) to fly
voleibol *m.* volleyball
votación *f.* voting; vote
votante *m./f.* voter
votar to vote
voto *m.* vote
voz *f.* voice
vuelo *m.* flight
vuelta *f.* turn; reversal; bend, curve; round, lap; stroll, walk

yate *m.* yacht
yegua *f.* mare
yerno *m.* son-in-law

zapatería *f.* shoe store; shoe factory
zapato *m.* **zapato de tenis** tennis shoe

Answer Key
to Comprehension Questions

Capítulo 1

I. 1. usted; tú; usted   2. **él; ella; ellos;** none   3. contrast; because she refers to herself and Paco, a male   4. **yo;** not necessary to repeat information contained in the question, a pronoun alone suffices   5. vosotros; ustedes

II. 1. toman   2. (he) is going to inaugurate   3. I have been taking   4. lees; leo; hablan, hablamos, aumenta, empeora, sube   5. regresa

III. 1. *m.* **tráfico,** ends in **-o;** terror, ends in **-or;** *f.* **virtud,** ends in **-d; información,** ends in **-ión; sencillez,** abstract noun ending in **-ez**   2. **día,** exception to generalization; **problema, clima,** words of Greek origin ending in **-ma; mano,** exception to generalization; **moto, foto,** abbreviations for **motocicleta, fotografía**   3. peatón (peatona); camarero (camarera)   4. el guía (persona) / la guía (libro); el orden (tidiness) / la orden (command)   5. (el/la) artista   6. by the feminine form of the indefinite article **una**

IV. 1. **locutor (locutores);** ends in a consonant   2. lápiz (lápices)   3. **(el/los) análisis;** ends in an unstressed vowel + **-s**   4. opinión (opiniones)   5. volumen (volúmenes)

V. 1. **el; el** is used before feminine nouns beginning with stressed **(h)a-; la,** because **hamaca** begins with an unstressed **ha-**   2. yes; definite article is used when making a generalization about a noun   3. **la cabeza;** definite article is generally used with parts of the body (the possessor is clear)   4. los sábados   5. **No entiendo (el) italiano;** definite article may be omitted before names of languages after verbs such as **aprender, entender, leer**   6. **en Lima,** article generally not used with city names; **el Perú,** definite article is optional with the names of some countries; **la arquitectura,** definite article used when making a generalization about a noun; **el doctor Quiroga,** definite article used with a title when talking about someone; **el jueves,** article generally used with days of the week; **de lunes a viernes,** article omitted with days of the week in the phrase **de... a...**

Capítulo 2

I. 1. two, **cuent-** and **cont-; contar** has a stem change when the last vowel of the stem is stressed   2. **defendemos,** regular; **defiendes,** stem change   3. **devuelven, devuelve,** stem change in both   4. **reís,** regular; **ríen,** stem change

II. 1. **un; un** is used before feminine nouns beginning with stressed **(h)a-**   2. a few; about   3. **Es una bailarina con mucha experiencia.**   4. **¿Busca Ud. (una) casa?;** any house would do, indefinite article may be omitted after **buscar**   5. **Su colección de sellos vale un millón de dólares**   6. No specific, known **ensalada** or **restaurante de autoservicio** is referred to.

III. 1. yes; position of subject in questions is rather free in Spanish   2. ¿Con quién va al parque de atracciones?   3. cuál; qué   4. qué; cuáles

IV. 1. **aquella guitarra,** far from both speaker and listener; **ésta (guitarra) que está aquí,** near to speaker; **ésas (guitarras) que están detrás de ti,** farther from speaker than from listener   2. **estos, este** forms refer to present; **esos, ese** forms refer to near future   3. eso; ese   4. esta; esto   5. éstas, aquéllas

V. 1. No encuentro la invitación mía. 2. ¿Cómo está tu familia? 3. tu; el 4. **La mía tiene cincuenta carteles;** they are talking about collections and the noun would be understood 5. no recuerdo el nombre de ella; no recuerdo su nombre 6. **un amigo mío,** adjective that modifies the noun **amigo; las mías,** pronoun that replaces the previously mentioned noun **clases**

Capítulo 3

I. 1. caer, caber, pertenecer, valer 2. merezco 3. **veo,** the stem is **ve-,** rather than **v-**
4. spelling change, the last consonant, not the last vowel, of the stem changes (**g** to **j** before **o**)
5. irregular first person, and stem change in the second person singular, and in the third person singular and plural

II. 1. **es,** locates definite event; **hay,** asserts existence of an event 2. ¡Qué elegante estás! 3. El guía es aburrido. 4. someone found alive 5. **Son de Venezuela,** origin; **Están en Venezuela,** location 6. están

III. 1. **Voy de viaje en mi coche nuevo.** The other sentence means *I'm going on a trip in my new (= different) car.* 2. Santo Domingo; San Carlos 3. las impresionantes ruinas 4. Creemos que nuestra investigación presenta datos importantes para apreciar el impacto del turismo. 5. **hotel lujoso,** a category of hotel; **pequeño y simpático hotel,** emphasis on a particular hotel stressing the important qualities and emotional viewpoint of the speaker

IV. 1. ¡Por fin encuentro a mi padre! 2. Necesitamos una azafata alta. 3. No reconozco a ningún pasajero.

V. 1. las, les 2. by using **a mí** for emphasis 3. **le, le** is an indirect object used both for a male or a female; **se, se** replaces **le** when used next to **la** 4. I give it to him, her, you (*formal, singular or plural*), them (*all female, all male, or mixed*). 5. Las voy a visitar.

Capítulo 4

I. 1. traducir, poner, entretenerse, saber 2. **ser** or **ir, dar, beber; beber** is regular because the stem is **beb-** and the ending is **-í,** both regular 3. **apagué, g > gu** before **e; influyó,** unstressed **i** changes to **y** between vowels; **averigüé, u > ü** before **e** 4. salimos 5. (The accident) took place in the morning. (The journalist) went (there) in the morning. 6. corrigió, corrigieron

II. 1. I became sad. (**Me puse triste.**) 2. **Anoche escuché la radio hasta las nueve de la noche,** termination of an action; **Me contó la historia de su vida,** completed past action 3. Hace dos meses hubo un interesante debate en la televisión. Hubo un interesante debate en la televisión hace dos meses. 4. beginning of a past action: **explicó;** abrupt change in state or condition: **se puso incómodo**

III. 1. **Le;** because the person who likes in constructions with **gustar** is expressed by an indirect object pronoun 2. gusta; gustan 3. **A ti te sorprendió;** to emphasize the contrast 4. Te falta; Falta 5. **Sí, me gusta;** understood subject **la revista,** not expressed by a pronoun in Spanish

IV. 1. La entrevista no va a durar más de tres horas. 2. **que; de lo que;** magazines have less articles on current events than newspapers; newspapers are more important than what people think 3. de lo que; de los que 4. tanto; tan 5. **mayores, más grandes;** inflation is one of the greatest (largest) economic problems we have; this car factory is one of the biggest in the country 6. no, no moral connotation 7. noun referred to is clearly understood

V. 1. **cuántas; cómo;** how many news items we read each day! how can you read so many news items! 2. hubiera escrito 3. qué 4. ¡Qué tragedia más (tan) terrible! 5. ¡Qué increíble noticia!; ¡Qué noticia tan increíble!; cómo (¡Cómo admiro tu ingenuidad!)

Capítulo 5

I. 1. **Levantaba pesas cuando tú entraste en el gimnasio;** customary action   2. background information, past time always in imperfect   3. I don't know why, but I jumped whenever they called my name; habitual action   4. habitual and customary action in the past; physical conditions in the past

II. 1. tenía; tuve   2. **entendió,** completed action; **entendía,** habitual action   3. **corría,** customary action; **corrí,** set of events viewed as completed, as a whole   4. **conocí,** Last week I met your tennis instructor; **conocía,** At that time, I was not acquainted with your tennis instructor yet   5. customary past action: **sentía;** physical condition in the past: **sudaba, respiraba;** actions in progress: **saltaban, bailaban**

III. 1. Tengo calor.   2. No tengo mucho frío.   3. Pablo tiene mucho cuidado.

IV. 1. nos entrenaron   2. Se me perdieron las llaves.   3. Creo que se trabaja mucho aquí.
4. cuidarse (a sí mismo); entendernos (mutuamente, unos a otros)

Capítulo 6

I. 1. **Para entender,** infinitive used after a preposition; **entendiendo,** the present participle used as an adverbial complement of manner   2. que pronuncia; pronunciando   3. **decir,** infinitive used after a preposition; **diciendo,** present participle used to express manner   4. hacer; haciendo

II. 1. Está pronunciando un discurso en estos momentos.   2. estoy escuchando; escucho   3. La policía anda buscando a los secuestradores.   4. **qué estás leyendo (qué lees); estoy mirando (miro); está tratando (trata);** present tense is also used for action in progress

III. 1. **No comprendo a ese dirigente;** personal **a** needed before a direct object referring to a person   2. en; a   3. en; a; en   4. de; con; de   5. **El tren presidencial llega a Caracas;** the other sentence means *The presidential train is arriving from Caracas*   6. **ti,** normally used after prepositions; **tú,** used after **según**

IV. 1. cualquier; alguna   2. algo; nada   3. hablan   4. No leo nunca los sondeos de opinión.

Capítulo 7

I. 1. Esta tarde dan (darán) una charla sobre las carreras médicas.   2. he probably is, he must be   3. me voy a quedar, me quedo

II. 1. se graduaría   2. she was probably sick, she must have been sick   3. ¿Me podrías prestar el texto de sociología?

III. 1. para; por   2. the student goes looking for, instead of, on behalf of   3. para; por   4. **estudiaré por doce horas,** period of time; **para aprobar mi examen final,** purpose; **para tener éxito,** purpose; **debes hacerlo por ti y por tu familia,** for the sake of   5. three uses of **para:** destination, **para Chicago;** time limit, **para antes de fin de año;** purpose, **para comenzar a ahorrar dinero;** use for which something is intended, **para un pasajero;** five uses of **por:** period of time, **por unas semanas; por unos meses;** rate, **treinta millas por galón; por cada lata; por un precio módico;** motion along, **camine por América;** exchange, **cambio por motocicleta;** person on behalf of whom something is done, **por Oscar;** object of an errand after a verb of motion, **vas por refrescos;** common expression, **por favor**

IV. 1. **pero,** contrast between two sentences; **sino,** corrects information   2. sino que; sino
3. **sino que,** the second clause, containing a conjugated verb, corrects information; **pero,** the second sentence implies contrast; **sino,** the second phrase corrects information

Capítulo 8

I. 1. **escrito,** the past participle is invariable in the perfect tenses; **escrita,** after **estar** the past participle behaves like an adjective and agrees with the noun it modifies; **escritas,** in the passive voice the past

participle agrees with the subject   2. estaba; fue   3. **garantizada** is an adjective that modifies **protección**

II.   1. **despidieron,** action finished and no relation to present; **han despedido,** present perfect preferred with period of time that isn't over yet   2. había conseguido; he conseguido   3. negociaban; habían negociado

III.   1. **habría escrito,** past event expected to be completed before a specific point in time   2. habrá encontrado; habría encontrado   3. conseguiría; habría conseguido

IV.   1. **Es fatigoso (el) presentarse a muchos empleos,** the article can be used when the infinitive introduces the subject of the sentence   2. telefonear   3. de llenar   4. **Escriba con letras mayúsculas, Escribir con letras mayúsculas;** the other sentence means *I write (I'm writing) using capital letters.*

V.   1. **No han sido presentados muchos productos todavía;** in the passive voice the past participle agrees with the subject   2. **fue,** action took place at six; **estuvo,** condition   3. **lo resolvió,** a redundant direct object pronoun must be used if normal order (subject—direct object) is reversed; **resolvió,** no object pronoun is necessary if normal order (subject—direct object) is used   4. **El empleado responsable fue identificado;** passive voice the least frequent of these three constructions   5. **consideraron; consideró**

Capítulo 9

I.   1. traer, haber, caber, conducir   2. yes; the **u** of the stem is dropped   3. no (**nos acostemos**); yes (**te acuestes**)   4. sient- (sienta); sint- (sintamos)   5. the present subjunctive; **g** > **gu** before **e** to preserve the pronunciation of the final stem consonant

II.   1. The first sentence expresses doubt; the second expresses emotion.   2. **leen,** fact; **lean,** subjective viewpoint   3. ¿Piensan Uds. que la selección de ese poema sea justa?   4. asistir; que asista   5. influencing: **es urgente que lo empiece, quiere que se lo entregue, pídele que te dé una semana más;** subjective viewpoint: **me sorprende que te preocupes;** doubt, disbelief, or denial: **no crees que lo puedas terminar a tiempo, dudo que la profesora me dé otra semana**

III.   1. **Me es imposible llegar a la hora;** the other sentence means *It's impossible (in general) to arrive on time*   2. Es difícil aceptar críticas.   3. recibe el premio; reciba el premio   4. tienes ganas; tengas ganas

IV.   1. He estado mirando este cuadro por veinte minutos; Miro este cuadro desde hace veinte minutos.   2. Hace un año que trabajé en esta antología.   3. desde hace; hace   4. hace; hacía

Capítulo 10

I.   1. ¡Vamos a comprar el regalo para tus padres en el Salón Mar del Plata!   2. vayan Uds.
3. **¡Sentémonos a tomar algo!, sentemos** drops the final **s**; **¡Cómprelo!,** written accent is added
4. Vamos a comprar un estéreo; Compremos un estéreo.   5. nos atienda él

II.   1. Aquel empleado, que me vendió el televisor, fue amonestado por su jefe   2. el cual
3. no, **quien** cannot be used as the equivalent of *who* in a restrictive clause   4. (e)l cual, (e)l que
5. **cuyo;** because **cuyo** modifies the masculine noun **hijo**

III.   1. because **los domésticos** agrees with the understood noun **productos**   2. **económicos;** when **lo** expresses the degree or extent of a quality (*how*), it agrees with the noun it refers to   3. different; **Lo molesto** means *how unpleasant* and shows the use of **lo** + a variable adjective; **lo único** means *the only thing* and shows the use of **lo** + an invariable adjective   4. Voy de compras los sábados, lo que (lo cual) me agrada mucho.   5. lo de

IV.   1. vende   2. The subjunctive, **sean,** is used because the noun modified, *pearls,* may or may not be found.   3. quieras   4. regale   5. produzca; produce

Capítulo 11

I.   1. **entiende, ve** (command form of **ver** and **ir**)   2. duerme   3. enciende   4. No os apuréis; coméoslo todo.

II.   1. Funciona lenta y ruidosamente.   2. Escribe claramente; Escribe con claridad   3. triste

III.   1. **ofrecen,** indicative is used after **porque; ofrezcan,** subjunctive is used after **con tal (de) que**   2. **vendo,** As soon as I sell a computer, I always buy another one; **venda,** As soon as I sell this computer, I'll buy another one   3. **Ella explica todo claramente de modo que todos entienden:** result; **Ella explica todo claramente de modo que todos entiendan:** purpose   4. **Dejo la máquina de afeitar eléctrica donde la puedo encontrar;** the other sentence means *I leave the electric shaver where I (hope I) may find it*   5. no; the clause **para que las dos quedemos contentas** implies purpose and the indicative cannot be used to imply purpose

IV.   1. esperaba; espero   2. contestes; contestaras   3. repitiera; repetí   4. usaba; usara   5. pasó

Capítulo 12

I.   1. ha visto; haya visto   2. haya asistido; hubiera asistido   3. hayan instalado; hubieran instalado   4. No, the present perfect subjunctive cannot be used in a dependent clause after a main verb in the preterit

II.   1. **Si no había contaminación, salíamos a pasear;** the other sentence expresses a hypothetical situation: *If there were no pollution, we would go for a walk.*   2. necesitaríamos; necesitaremos   3. si controlamos   4. It is improbable or impossible that someone can observe the student's mental representations of future cities.

III.   1. **desarrollen;** the main verb is in the future and the subjunctive is required after **antes de que**   2. hayamos tenido; tengamos   3. **se hubieran puesto;** the sentence refers to a past action that would have taken place before another past action   4. pudiera; hubiera podido   5. **realice,** present subjunctive

IV.   1. Hagan el favor de, Sírvanse   2. ¿Podrían (Pudieran) Uds. decirnos cuándo llega el director?   3. Ud. debe llamar a la agencia de preservación del ambiente.   4. Le sugiero que utilice la energía solar.   5. ¿Me pasas el periódico?

INDEX

Credits

Drawings by George M. Ulrich

Black and White Photographs